The edition of *The Complete Works of Frances Ridley Havergal* has five parts:

Volume I *Behold Your King: The Complete Poetical Works of Frances Ridley Havergal*

Volume II *Whose I Am and Whom I Serve: Prose Works of Frances Ridley Havergal*

Volume III *Loving Messages for the Little Ones: Works for Children by Frances Ridley Havergal*

Volume IV *Love for Love: Frances Ridley Havergal: Memorials, Letters and Biographical Works*

Volume V *Songs of Truth and Love: Music by Frances Ridley Havergal and William Henry Havergal*

David L. Chalkley, Editor   Dr. Glen T. Wegge, Music Editor

Frances Ridley Havergal's formal education ended when she was 17, with one term at a young women's school in Düsseldorf, Germany, yet she was a true scholar all her life. Fluent in German and French and nearly so in Italian, she read and loved the Reformers in Latin, German, and French. Knowledge was never an end in itself, only a means to know better her Lord and Saviour and to help to bring others to know Him. The Bible was her only Book, and she studied the Hebrew and Greek texts of Scripture, memorized nearly all the New Testament and large portions of the Old Testament, and loved the Author with all her being.

Frances was brought to a saving knowledge of Christ when she was 14, and the rest of her life was consecrated to her Saviour, the Lord Jesus. Keenly aware of her own sinfulness and inability, her sole desire was to please and glorify Him alone. Very finely gifted, she was truly diligent with her gifts: her poetry is among the finest in the English language, after George Herbert; her prose works are deeply beneficial; a musician to the core, she left behind important compositions. Like her works, her life richly touched the ones near her and countless many who met or heard her. The Lord Jesus Christ was her alone, only beauty, and she glowed Him and His truth. Never wanting attention to herself, Frances' desire of her heart was for herself and for others to know her King, the Lord Jesus Christ. Her works are a gold-mine of help and enrichment. There is life in these pages: her works truly glorify the Lord, truly benefit His people, and powerfully reach those who do not yet know Him.

The Music of Frances Ridley Havergal by Glen T. Wegge, Ph.D.

This Companion Volume to the Havergal edition is a valuable presentation of F.R.H.'s scores, most or nearly all of F.R.H.'s scores very little if any at all seen, or even known of, for nearly a century. What a valuable body of music has been unknown for so long and is now made available to many. Dr. Wegge completed his Ph.D. in Music Theory at Indiana University at Bloomington, and his diligence and thoroughness in this volume are obvious. First an analysis of F.R.H.'s compositions is given, an essay that both addresses the most advanced musicians and also reaches those who are untrained in music; then all the extant scores that have been found are newly typeset, with complete texts for each score and extensive indices at the end of the book. This volume presents F.R.H.'s music in newly typeset scores diligently prepared by Dr. Wegge, and Volume V of the Havergal edition presents the scores in facsimile, the original 19th century scores. (The essay—a dissertation—analysing her scores is given the same both in this Companion Volume and in Volume V of the Havergal edition.)

Dr. Wegge is also preparing all of these scores for publication in performance folio editions.

The Havergal Trust P.O.Box 649 Kirksville, Missouri 63501

An undated phtotgraph of Rev. Charles Busbridge Snepp.

Yours very truly & gratefully
F. R. Havergal

This is a photograph taken by (the prestigious portrait photographers) Elliott and Fry in London on February 1, 1879, one of eight taken of F.R.H. that day by them. In a letter dated February 7, 1879, F.R.H. wrote this: "I have been photographed! Mr. Elliott himself came for me, Saturday, and they tried eight times, and hope one will do! Elliott and Fry both superintended in person; such a fuss! And I forgot to put on tidy frill and cuffs!" (in Division VI of Letters by the Late Frances Ridley Havergal, *page 312; page 232 of Volume IV of the Havergal edition) This would have been Saturday, February 1, 1879, a month and a half after her 42nd birthday and four months before her unexpected early death on June 3.*

Faithfully Yrs
W: H: Havergal.

William Henry Havergal (1793–1870) was the foremost church musician and composer of sacred music in England in his generation. A finely gifted performer and music leader, he composed and published important music, and was a leading reformer of church music practice. He was offered a professorship in music at Oxford University, but he declined that for his first calling, to be a minister and pastor. Though rarely gifted to write music, he preferred to prepare a sermon than to compose a score. Music was a very important part of his ministry, and always a pleasure and rest to him, but he concentrated on music only when his physical health prevented him from his pastoral work. His Sermons, printed in four volumes, are gold. Much or most of the music in this hymnal, Songs of Grace and Glory, *was composed by William Henry Havergal and later adapted by his daughter, Frances Ridley Havergal, for use in this hymnal.*

Songs of Grace and Glory.

New and Enlarged Musical Edition.

Hymnal and Musical Treasures of the Church of Christ
From Many Centuries.

EDITED BY

Charles Busbridge Snepp (words)
and Frances Ridley Havergal (music)

Full Edition of 1100 Hymns with Tunes.

A Facsimile Reprint of
The Definitive "New and Enlarged Musical Edition"
Published by James Nisbet & Co. in 1880

Taken from the New Edition of
The Complete Works of Frances Ridley Havergal

" Knowing her intense desire that Christ should be magnified, whether
by her life or in her death, may it be to His glory
that in these pages she, being dead,
'Yet speaketh!' "

SONGS OF GRACE AND GLORY.
Edited by Charles Busbridge Snepp and Frances Ridley Havergal

ISBN 978-1-937236-56-4 Library of Congress Control Number: 2016919857

Printed in the United States of America *This book is printed on acid-free paper.*

Cover Design by Glen T. Wegge.

Havergal, Frances Ridley
Songs of Grace and Glory: prose, poetry, and music taken from the edition of the complete works of Frances Ridley Havergal / Frances Ridley Havergal. 1. Havergal, Frances Ridley, 1836–1879. 2. Christian Life. 3. Christian Poetry, English. 4. Music. I. Title

This is taken from *The Complete Works of Frances Ridley Havergal.*
David L. Chalkley, General Editor. Dr. Glen T. Wegge, Music Editor.

The purpose of this work is ministry, and any money received by the Havergal Trust from sales of these books is to be applied to continue the work of the Trust, all revenues being applied to cover true costs of production and distribution and then to publish and distribute more books more widely, with very affordable prices, with no financial profit to any involved beyond fair market compensation for time and labor. The purpose of the Trust is to preserve far into the future (if our Lord does not return sooner) works by and about F.R.H., to make available to many these works, and to publish works by other authors similar to Havergal.

While most of the Havergal edition is made of public domain works published before 1923, throughout the edition are numerous items of new work in 2003–2011.

Frances Ridley Havergal used language clearly, specifically, powerfully, precisely, and beautifully, and no alteration of any of her works should be done. At the beginning of the 21st century her words are as simple and fresh as they were when she was here, and they should be left precisely as she wrote them without any change.

Many valuable, important works have been gutted with a pretence of improving or clarifying the language, when the language of Bonar, Spurgeon, Chambers, and others should be left alone in its original clarity, beauty, and power. F.R.H.'s sentences—and very words—have a special power, clarity, beauty, sweetness, and precision which cannot be improved nor even matched—only harmed and distorted—by any changes. Similarly, C. H. Spurgeon, J. C. Ryle, John Owen, John Flavel, Thomas Watson, George Whitefield, Jonathan Edwards, Robert Murray M'Cheyne, and many other similar authors should be left alone in their precise words they originally wrote: any "improvement" of their precise words improves nothing, harms and distorts what they really said, and very often if not always guts what they meant and invites things they never meant. This is far worse than "improving" paintings by Rembrandt, Vermeer, Monet (which would be derided by anyone serious about art), or "improving" scores by Bach, Beethoven, or Rachmaninoff (any true musician cleaves to the original scores with absolute fidelity to the tiniest notated details), and serious people would not accept such against Shakespeare, Nathaniel Hawthorne, Goethe, nor such secular authors. It is a remarkable distortion for an editor to impose "trust me, I know better" rather than the original author.

The photographs and illustrations should also be left just as they are, not "updated," "enhanced," nor changed in any way. ("Improving" Frances does not improve her.)

Many pieces such as "One Hour with Jesus," any of the poems, or other parts of this edition would be very beneficial to print in bulletins, periodicals, and other formats.

The Havergal Trust P.O.Box 649 Kirksville, Missouri 63501

In all that she did, and in all that she wrote, Frances Ridley Havergal's one overriding desire was—as Colossians 1:18 says—"that in all things he [*her Lord*] might have the pre-eminence." She saw herself as an instrument in her Saviour's hand, writing for His sake, His glory alone. Indeed the words of Psalm 45:1 were true of her: "My heart is inditing a good matter: I speak of the things which I have made touching the King: my tongue is the pen of a ready writer."

The truth of Christ, which she so loved, and which He used her to present to others, is what is relevant and important, not Frances herself. Understanding the truth of this, you don't first of all think "what a wonderful, fine lady she was" but "what a Saviour ! she had." Jesus Christ alone was changing her from what she was, to become daily more like Himself. Frances would not want anyone to look solely or primarily at her, but she would want all to see her Lord and Saviour. He was her only beauty, righteousness, wisdom, her all. So as you embark on reading, may you too see the Lord Jesus Christ. To see her King is what she would have wanted, the true conclusion of her works and life, and of any genuine disciple's works and life. The Lamb is all the glory in Emmanuel's land, the kingdom of God.

A NOTE TO THE READER

Serious effort has been made to publish this edition of *The Complete Works of Frances Ridley Havergal* very closely to the original texts of F.R.H. When clear mistakes had been made in the original books, they were corrected without comment, and other, exceptional changes were made only when there was very good reason. Details of spelling and punctuation were preserved as they were found in the original works.

There were many inconsistencies in the original texts. For example, among different books, or even within the same book on occasion, "labour" and "endeavour" might also be spelled "labor" and "endeavor." Even among the original 19th century Havergal books published by James Nisbet & Co. (F.R.H.'s primary publisher), there is much inconsistency in the way quotation marks were done, consistent within the same book but different from one Nisbet book to another. The British way is to place quotations within single quotation marks, and to place quotations in quotations within double quotation marks: 'Jesus says, and says to you, "Come, oh come, to Me."' The American way is the reverse: "Jesus says, and says to you, 'Come, oh come, to Me.'" As this edition was typeset in 2004, the British way of quotation marks was used for the first item, the definitive, remarkably fine Nisbet edition of *The Poetical Works of Frances Ridley Havergal*, because this original volume used the British style of quotation marks. As we proceeded beyond Nisbet's *Poetical Works*, we saw that various original books alternated between the British and American styles, both among different books by the same publisher Nisbet, and also among other contemporary publishers of F.R.H. in the United Kingdom (Home Words Publishing Co. in London, Marcus Ward in Belfast, and others). Even a manuscript in Frances' own handwriting used the American way of quotation marks. Because there was a need for consistency (not an appearance of randomness or chaos), and because comparatively few are likely to see the pages of the original books, all the quotation marks in this edition are given in the American way, except for Nisbet's *Poetical Works*. Besides quotation marks, there were several other details that we would have done differently ourselves now in the 21st century, which we left the same as we found them in the original books.

If, in reading through these volumes, there is an *appearance* of randomness in the way the various works appear printed on the pages, we would ask that the reader please bear in mind that this edition was typeset using the *original* works: numerous volumes of poetry, prose (including biographies, sermons by Frances' father and others, etc.), and music by a number of different authors and publishers. As much as was practicable, considerable effort was made to make these works in this new edition "mirror" the original works—title pages, contents pages, etc.—even though we knew it is unlikely that the vast majority of readers will ever actually *see* these original works.

The desire and earnest effort was that this edition be an "urtext" edition, cleaving very closely to the original text. Exceptions were made when there was good reason, but these were rare. Perhaps the careful reader will also notice that most of the punctuation marks within the text of the Havergal edition have spacing inserted between them and adjacent letters and/or additional punctuation marks, reflecting typesetting practices of the 19th century. Significant effort was expended to accomplish this, the reason being, again, to cleave as closely as possible to the original text, as well as to give the finished version as much of an authentic look as practicable.

The important matter is, that we sought not to "improve" Frances (and her father, her sisters, and the others in this edition) but to present her as she originally wrote.

David Chalkley, Thomas Sadowski, Dr. Glen Wegge

For more than twelve years, Dr. Glen T. Wegge has been involved in the work to complete the Havergal edition. Without payment of money, with remarkable diligence, patience, persistence, and hard work, he has labored to prepare for publication all of the music in the Havergal edition, and also to complete and publish his own book, *The Music of Frances Ridley Havergal*, a Companion Volume to this edition of *The Complete Works of Frances Ridley Havergal.* He has also done so much to bring to completion (in countless hours of work) all of the other books in the Havergal edition. The patience and support of his wife, Denise, are also appreciated. So much thought, diligence, hard work, countless hours, a servant's heart, a labor of love. My estimate or guess is that Glen has worked approximately 1,500 hours on the Havergal edition, without pay. His work is remarkable both in quantity and in quality, first-rate, sterling work. How many times ? (the Lord knows how many times) has he gone back again and again to fix a text or an illustration until it was just right. Most of the details of his work were known only to Glen and me, much now forgotten, but God sees and knows every trace. How compassionately and richly He has blessed us in all of this.

For much or most of the past 100 years, few if any have realized the value of Frances' music, and Glen (who completed his Ph.D. in music theory at Indiana University at Bloomington and is so finely gifted and prepared to do this work) is the first one to analyze and present her music in such a scholarly way. He began his work on this in very difficult circumstances, and his diligence, persistence, and servant's heart are a true example for believers. Glen is worthy of strong gratitude from all those who will be encouraged and enriched by F.R.H.'s poetry, prose, and music.

The Lord reward him as I cannot, as no man can reward.

This is all the Lord's doing. Thanks be to God for His indescribable gift to us in Christ.

David Chalkley

The Complete Works of Frances Ridley Havergal is dedicated to the glory of the Lord Jesus Christ, laying this at His feet and asking Him to bless to others what He has provided,

"for Jesus' sake only"

and is gratefully inscribed to two people:

Miss Janet Grierson,
Mr. Stanley Ward.

Miss Grierson's Biography and her other work on F.R.H. are the most important work on Frances since Maria V. G. Havergal, and she has been invaluably helpful in the preparation of this edition.

Mr. Stanley Ward has been deeply interested in Frances since the 1960's, and his kindness, insights, and help have been truly and profoundly important to this edition.

Thanks be to God for His indescribable gift to us in Christ.

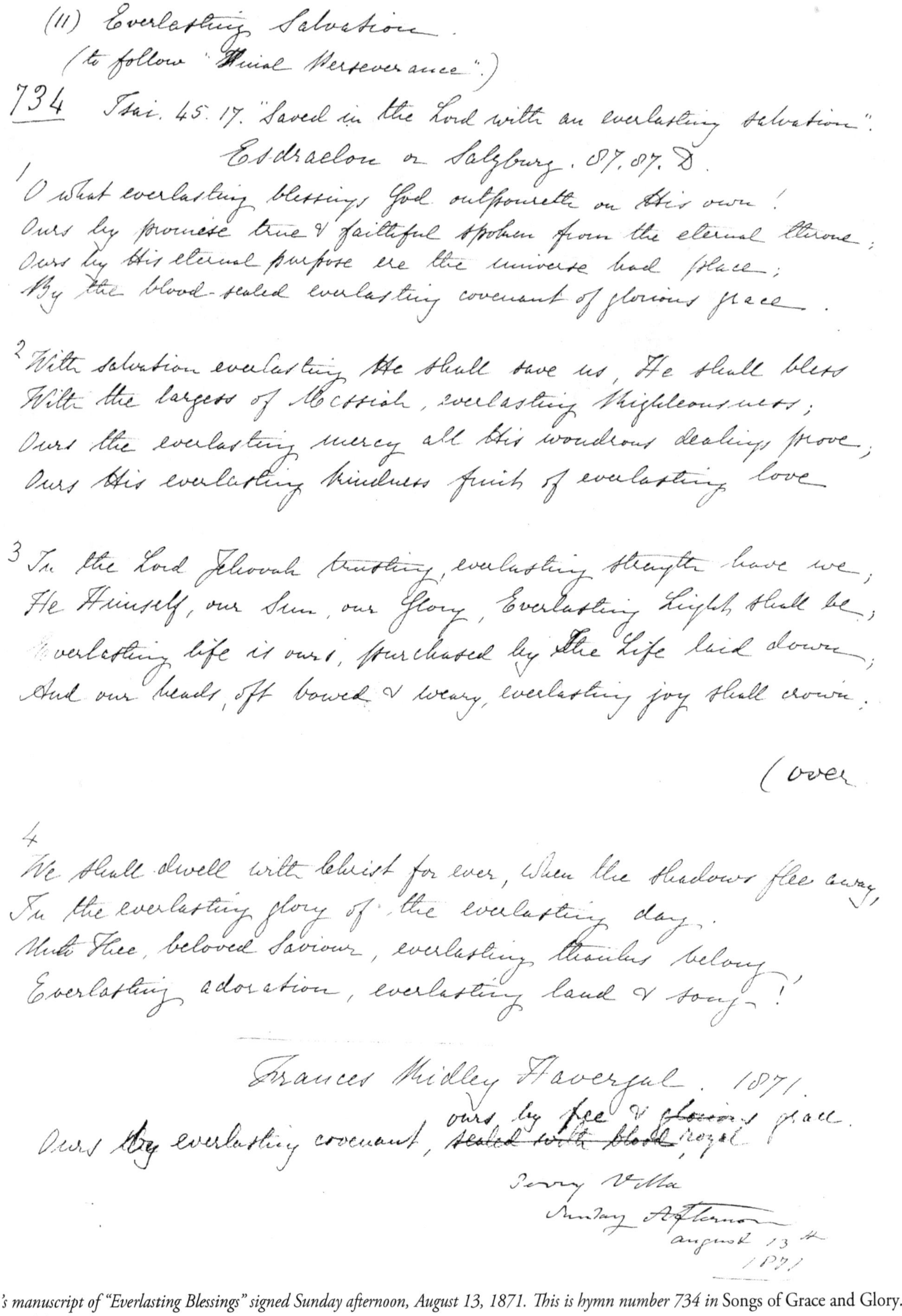

(11) Everlasting Salvation.
(to follow "Final Perseverance".)

734 Isai. 45. 17. "Saved in the Lord with an everlasting salvation".
Esdraelon or Salzburg. 87. 87. D.

1 O what everlasting blessings God outpoureth on His own!
Ours by promise true & faithful spoken from the eternal throne;
Ours by His eternal purpose ere the universe had place;
By the blood-sealed everlasting covenant of glorious grace.

2 With salvation everlasting He shall save us, He shall bless
With the largess of Messiah, everlasting Righteousness;
Ours the everlasting mercy all His wondrous dealings prove;
Ours His everlasting kindness fruit of everlasting love

3 In the Lord Jehovah ~~trusting~~, everlasting strength have we;
He Himself, our Sun, our Glory, Everlasting Light, shall be;
Everlasting life is ours, purchased by The Life laid down;
And our heads, oft bowed & weary, everlasting joy shall crown;

(over

4 We shall dwell with Christ for ever, When the shadows flee away,
In the everlasting glory of the everlasting day.
Unto Thee, beloved Saviour, everlasting thanks belong
Everlasting adoration, everlasting laud & song!

Frances Ridley Havergal. 1871.

Ours ~~by~~ everlasting covenant, ~~sealed with blood~~ ours by free & ~~glorious~~ royal grace.

Perry Villa
Sunday Afternoon
August 13th
1871

F.R.H.'s manuscript of "Everlasting Blessings" signed Sunday afternoon, August 13, 1871. This is hymn number 734 in Songs of Grace and Glory. See page 341 of this book.

Only for Jesus.

Only for Jesus! Lord, keep it for ever
Sealed on the heart & engraved on the life!
Pulse of all gladness & nerve of endeavour,
Secret of rest, & the strength of our strife.

July 1876

F.R.H. wrote this fair copy autograph of her single-verse hymn on page 140 of her Manuscript Book № VIII. *See the printed card on page lxxi.*

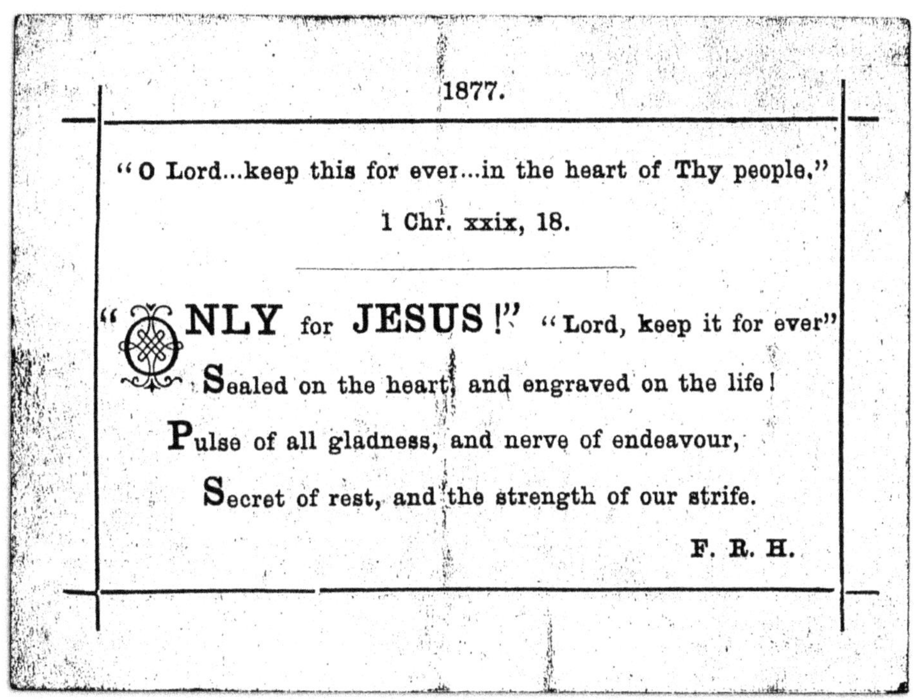

1877.

"O Lord...keep this for ever...in the heart of Thy people."
1 Chr. xxix, 18.

"ONLY for JESUS!" "Lord, keep it for ever"
Sealed on the heart, and engraved on the life!
Pulse of all gladness, and nerve of endeavour,
Secret of rest, and the strength of our strife.

F. R. H.

This was a printed card of Frances' single-verse hymn "Only for Jesus!" Such cards were and are still easy and inexpensive to print and give to many.

This is a manuscript in F.R.H.'s handwriting of the words for hymn number 734 in *Songs of Grace and Glory*. Note that at the bottom she wrote a second draft of the third line of the first stanza. See page 839 of Volume V of the Havergal edition for the finalized, published page with this hymn in S.G.G. Apparently she later changed her mind on the scores, placing her own score "Linus" for this hymn in S.G.G. Very few of her manuscript scores of music have been found (see the list of manuscript scores on page xxvii), but this is a glimpse of her work. Remember that this was the 1870's, when there were no computers, when she would have written by hand every note of every measure of every score for 1,100 hymns. Beyond the labor—with great skill—in preparing all of the music scores and texts for 1,100 hymns, Frances also wrote a number of the hymns newly, specifically for this book, and also composed a number of hymn scores for S.G.G. These words were written by her on August 12, 1871. This is only a glimpse of F.R.H.'s (and also similarly Charles Busbridge Snepp's) long, costly, diligent labor of love to complete *Songs of Grace and Glory*, the most comprehensive hymnbook in the Church of England until that time, and still a true gold-mine for us today.

CONTENTS

Songs of Grace and Glory (the definitive "New and Enlarged Musical Edition" published by James Nisbet & Co. in 1880)

ILLUSTRATIONS

Take my life, & let it be
Consecrated, Lord, to Thee.

Frances Ridley Havergal

This first couplet of the Consecration Hymn and the signature are F.R.H.'s handwriting, placed on the front cover of her sister Maria's biography Memorials of Frances Ridley Havergal *(London: James Nisbet & Co., 1880, found on pages 1–120 of Volume IV of the Havergal edition). See an early manuscript of this hymn on page xliv of Volume V of the Havergal edition.*

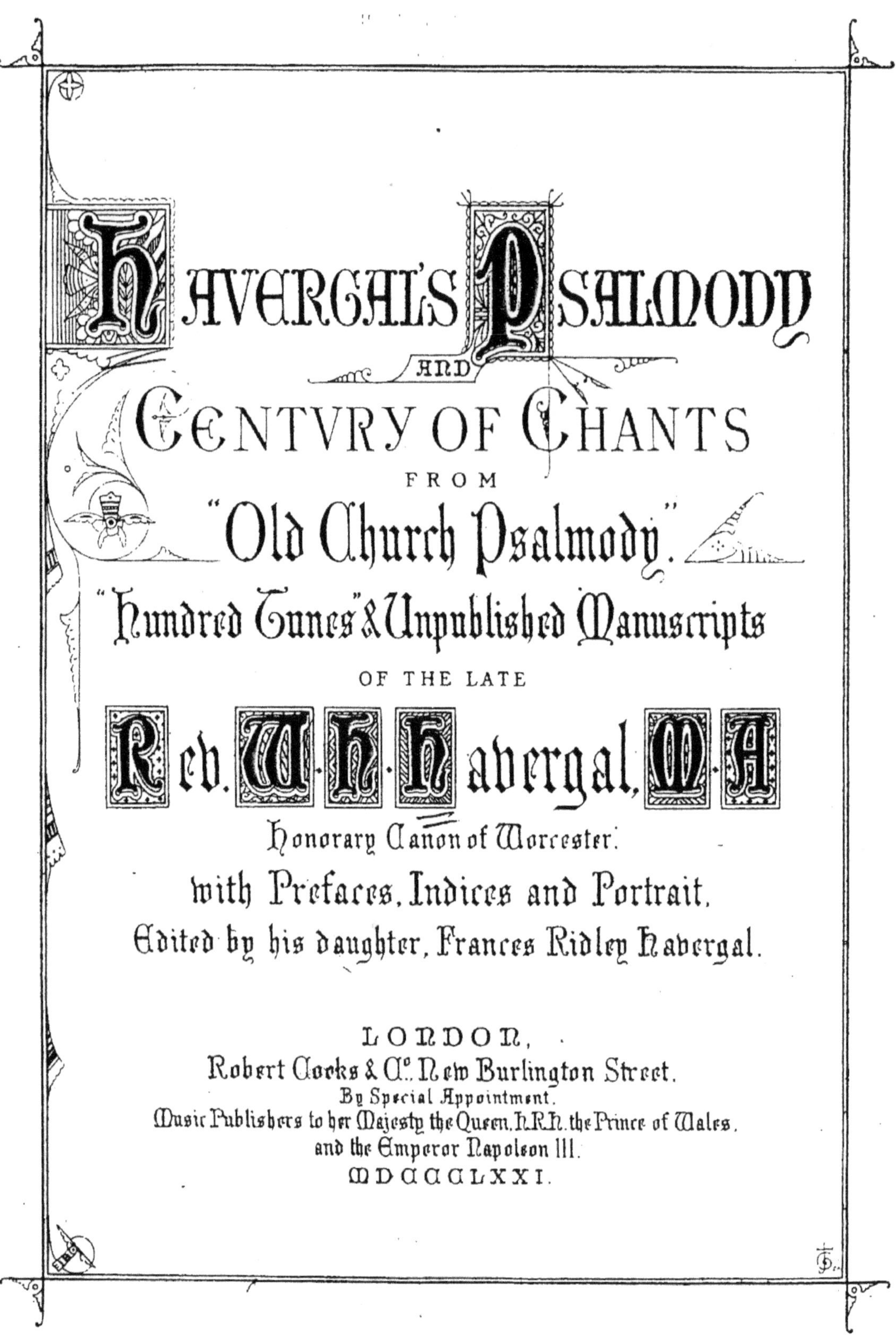

Havergal's Psalmody

and

Century of Chants

from

"Old Church Psalmody."

"Hundred Tunes" & Unpublished Manuscripts

of the late

Rev. W. H. Havergal, M. A.

Honorary Canon of Worcester.

with Prefaces, Indices and Portrait.

Edited by his daughter, Frances Ridley Havergal.

London,

Robert Cocks & Co. New Burlington Street.

By Special Appointment.

Music Publishers to her Majesty the Queen, H.R.H. the Prince of Wales,

and the Emperor Napoleon III.

MDCCCLXXI.

Havergal's Psalmody and Century of Chants *was the foundation for the music scores of the goldmine hymnbook* Songs of Grace and Glory (a very valuable hymnbook though very obscure now, the texts edited by Charles Busbridge Snepp, the music edited by Frances Ridley Havergal). *William Henry Havergal was the foremost church musician and composer of sacred music in England in his generation. Called to be a pastor, he declined a career in music and used music as a benefit to his church ministry, and for rest and pleasure. He would rather write a sermon than compose a score, though few had his ability and love to write and perform music at that level. He was a true scholar both in the Bible, theology, and music, and his ministry to others was a true example of Matthew 22:37–40. When his physical health removed him from pastoral work, he concentrated more on composition of music. See Volume V of the Havergal edition,* Songs of Truth and Love: Music by Frances Ridley Havergal and William Henry Havergal, *which has all of* Havergal's Psalmody and Century of Chants *and also all of* Songs of Grace and Glory.

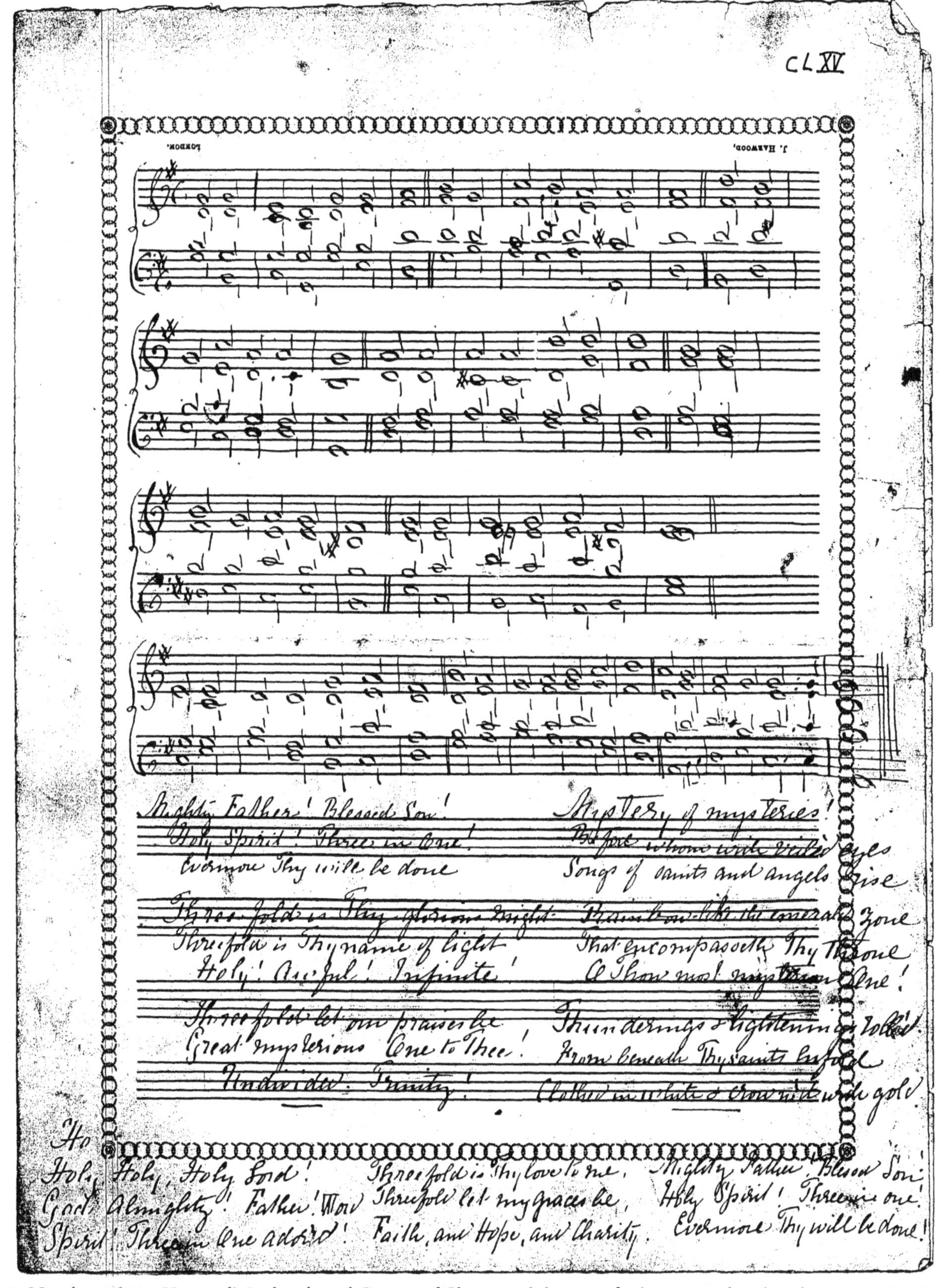

This is Number 163 in *Havergal's Psalmody and Century of Chants*, and the score for hymn number 4 in the companion *Songs of Grace and Glory*. This manuscript was the last music score composed by William Henry Havergal, composed on his last conscious day, Saturday, April 16, 1870. The text by Dr. John S. B. Monsell is symbolic of the Trinity, having three lines in each verse, three verses in each section, and three sections for one hymn. This score was posthumously named "Havergal," and his daughter Frances Ridley Havergal wrote, "The tune with its serene melody and rich harmony is itself an epitome of his musical work" (*Specimen Glasses for the King's Minstrels* by Frances Ridley Havergal, London: Home Words Publishing Office, 1881), original book pages 109–110, page 765 of Volume II of the Havergal edition. See page 60 of this book.

The Consecration Hymn "Take my life"

F.R.H. wrote this hymn on February 4, 1874. She wrote a fair copy autograph of this on pages 14–15 of her Manuscript Book N° VIII, and facsimile copies of these two manuscript pages are found on page xliv after these comments. At the top of her fair copy autograph she wrote, "Yea, let him take all!" (a quotation of part of II Samuel 19:30). Her fair copy autograph in 1874 differs in details from her finalized poem which she published in *Loyal Responses* in 1878, and the words on page 1179 of this volume (and on page 351 of Volume II of the Havergal edition, the original *Loyal Responses* with words only—full of music but without written notes) are definitive. In her handwritten "Index" near the end of this Manuscript Book N° VIII, she listed this with the name "Consecration Hymn,"

Consecration Hymn. 14.

and this name has been used for this hymn since then. Though published previously in leaflets or periodicals, she published this as the First Day of *Loyal Responses* in 1878, and between the title "Consecration Hymn" and the first verse, she gave this quotation from the Anglican *Book of Common Prayer*: "Here we offer and present unto Thee, O Lord, ourselves, our souls and bodies, to be a reasonable, holy, and lively sacrifice unto Thee."

Frances clearly wanted the Consecration Hymn to be sung to her father's hymn score "Patmos," and she wrote this statement in a letter to Charles Henry Purday on December 30, 1878: "I *particularly wish* that hymn ["Take my life"] kept to my dear father's sweet little tune, 'Patmos,' which suits it perfectly." [1]

She wrote this in a letter to a friend:

> Perhaps you will be interested to know the origin of the Consecration hymn, "Take my life." I went for a little visit of five days. There were ten persons in the house, some unconverted and long prayed for, some converted but not rejoicing Christians. He gave me the prayer, "Lord, give me *all* in this house!" And He just *did!* Before I left the house every one had got a blessing. The last night of my visit I was too happy to sleep, and passed most of the night in praise and renewal of my own consecration, and these little couplets formed themselves and chimed in my heart one after another, till they finished with, "*Ever*, ONLY, ALL for Thee!" [2]

In her sister Maria's biography of her, after that quotation, Maria soon quoted Frances from another place:

> Let us sing words which we feel and love, sacrificing everything to clearness of enunciation,[3] and looking up to meet His smile all the while we are singing; our songs will reach more hearts than those of finer voices and more brilliant execution, unaccompanied by His power. A sacred song thus sung often gives a higher tone to the

[1] *Letters by the Late Frances Ridley Havergal* edited by her sister Maria Vernon Graham Havergal (London: James Nisbet & Co., 1885), original book page 311, page 234 of Volume IV of the Havergal edition.

[2] *Memorials of Frances Ridley Havergal* by Maria V. G. Havergal (London: James Nisbet & Co., 1880), original book pages 132–133, page 37 of Volume IV of this edition. Miss Janet Grierson wrote that this was a visit to Areley House (near Stourport, a small city on the River Severn in Worcestershire), the home of Joseph Rogers and his family, relatives of Frances' sister's husband, Henry Crane (on page 1247 of Volume IV, in Chapter 12 of Miss Grierson's book *Singing for Jesus*, published for the first time in Volume IV of this edition). Chapter 12 of *Singing for Jesus* by Miss Grierson has valuable details on this hymn. See also page 1200 of Volume IV of this edition.

[3] This is very important. The true priority should be clarity of communication, that the hearers be able to understand the words and the truth of the words. Both speaking and singing should be to serve, help, benefit others, to show them truth, never to seek to impress anyone with our ability nor to want the praise of men: to help hearers to see Christ, His truth, His glory, never to parade nor magnify ourselves; to point hearers to Him, never to ourselves. Both in speaking and in singing, for individuals and for choirs, there should never be any false "art" that renders unclear the words. The clear communication of truth to needing ones is so great, and will be the priority of true love. I Corinthians 14:19 The New Testament was not written in the Classical Greek of scholars, which many might not be able to follow or understand fully, but in the Koine Greek of the common people, language that dishwashers, laborers, anyone, could understand. The truth of Christ, and the great need of sinners (also the need of believers to understand truth communicated), is so extremely important, and true love will seek to make that truth clear to see, understand and follow. See also F.R.H.'s letter to James Parlane, so valuable, on pages 108–109 of Volume V of the Havergal edition. This is true love as the two commandments say (Matthew 22:37–40), which only the Lord Jesus Christ alone can do in a person. D.C.

evening, and affords, both to singer and listeners, some opportunity of speaking a word for Jesus.

. . . . I was at a large regular London party lately, and I was so happy. He seemed to give me "the secret of His presence," and of course I sang "for Jesus," and did not I have dead silence? Afterwards I had two really important conversations with strangers; one seemed extremely surprised at finding himself *quite easily* drifted from the badinage with which he started into a right-down personal talk about *his* personal danger and *his* only hope for safety; he took it very well, and thanked me. Perhaps that seed may bear fruit. Somehow it is wonderful how the Master manages for me in such cases. I don't think any one can say I force the subject; it just all develops one thing out of another, quite naturally, till very soon they find themselves face to face with eternal things, and the Lord Jesus can be freely "lifted up" before them. I could not *contrive* a conversation thus.[4]

On December 2, 1873, Frances read a pamphlet by Dr. John Tinson Wrenford entitled "All for Jesus," and this pamphlet and a letter by Wrenford to her, in which he wrote about I John 1:7, very profoundly moved and benefitted her. Again, Maria in her *Memorials* quoted Frances:

Yes, it was on Advent Sunday, December 2nd, 1873, I first saw it as a flash of electric light, and what you *see* you can never *unsee*. There must be full surrender before there can be full blessedness. God admits you by the one into the other. He Himself showed me all this most clearly. You know how singularly I have been withheld from attending all conventions and conferences; man's teaching has, consequently, had but little to do with it. First, I was shown that "the blood of Jesus Christ His Son cleanseth us from all sin," and then it was made plain to me that He who had thus cleansed me had power to keep me clean; so I just utterly yielded myself to Him, and utterly trusted Him to keep me.[5]

Wrenford's pamphlet and his letter to her were a source or origin of the Consecration Hymn. Clear in her mind was that full surrender and consecration to Christ meant His keeping of what is committed to Him, and our trusting Him to keep us. On the fifth anniversary of that date, December 2, 1878, she wrote this to Wrenford:

I had a great time early this morning, renewing the never regretted consecration. I seemed led to run over the "Take my life," and could bless Him verse by verse for having led me on to much more definite consecration than even when I wrote it, voice, gold, intellect, etc.[6]

Maria wrote this account:

My dear sister Frances went to Swansea on Thursday, 17th. I sent our good maid M. Farrington with her, as she did not wish me to go; she says that on the way Miss Frances talked so humbly, and that she "felt as if she had no right to go teaching others—such a sinner as I am; but then Mary, I am just trusting for every word." The room was quite full. Mrs. Morgan, not knowing F.'s subject, had chosen a hymn that did not suit it, and my sister always thought it important that hymns should be suitably chosen. As her subject for the evening was from Hosea 3, "I also for thee," (see *Starlight Through the Shadows*), F. said she wished to sing "Precious Saviour, may I live, only for Thee." Mrs. Morgan said they did not know her tune to it ("Onesimus," *S.G.G.* 257 [hymn 257 in *Songs of Grace and Glory*].) F.: "No fear! Do let me just sing one verse alone, and I know they will join." Going to the piano and turning her face to them, she sang with her own bright ringing cheeriness one verse, and then all joined most heartily with her. Mary told me of my sister's soft pleading voice—that her words were intensely tender and entreating. At the close of the meeting, my sister gave to each one a card with her Consecration hymn, "Take my life and let it be Consecrated, Lord, to Thee," specially prepared and printed for this evening (Messrs. Parlane, Paisley, still supply them). Her own name was omitted, and a blank space left for signature. As she gave the cards, she

[4] *Memorials*, original book pages 133–134, pages 37–38 of Volume IV.

[5] *Memorials*, original book pages 126–127, page 36 of Volume IV. Though not fully quoted here, all the details on page 36 of Volume IV are truly valuable. The Scripture that Frances quoted is I John 1:7.

[6] *Memorials*, original book page 269, page 71 of Volume IV.

> asked them to make that hymn a test before God, and if they could really do so, to sign it on their knees at home. Then the hymn was sung to our dear father's tune "Patmos" (No. 145, *S.G.G.*).
>
> It seems to have been a great night of decision to many present. The next morning, before ever her breakfast was finished, one and another came for conversation with my dear sister—a French governess was specially impressed. My sister returned very much exhausted—meetings seemed to take away her little physical strength, and yet she always cheerfully took up any work for her King.[7]

Her last completed book,[8] *Kept for the Master's Use*, was based on the Consecration Hymn, an enlargement and rich presentation of the truths in those twelve couplets.

Another title that has been used for this hymn is "All for Jesus," a title not given by Frances, though she would have surely agreed with the title. Is *all* given, committed, entrusted, to Him? and is all the work His doing, His keeping, His using, none of our own doing but His doing alone? John 15:5, Philippians 4:13, Romans 7:18, I Corinthians 15:10, II Timothy 1:12

This is the finalized text that F.R.H. published as the First Day of *Loyal Responses* in 1878:

Consecration Hymn.

"Here we offer and present unto Thee, O Lord, ourselves, our souls
and bodies,to be a reasonable, holy, and lively sacrifice unto Thee."

Take my life, and let it be
Consecrated, Lord, to Thee.

Take my moments and my days;
Let them flow in ceaseless praise.

Take my hands, and let them move
At the impulse of Thy love.

Take my feet, and let them be
Swift and "beautiful" for Thee.

Take my voice, and let me sing
Always, only, for my King.

Take my lips, and let them be
Filled with messages from Thee.

Take my silver and my gold;
Not a mite would I withhold.

Take my intellect, and use
Every power as Thou shalt choose.

Take my will, and make it Thine;
It shall be no longer mine.

Take my heart, it *is* Thine own;
It shall be Thy royal throne.

Take my love; my Lord, I pour
At Thy feet its treasure-store.

Take myself, and I will be
Ever, *only*, ALL for Thee.

Frances Ridley Havergal

[7] *Letters by the Late Frances Ridley Havergal*, original book pages 326–327, page 238 of Volume IV. This was a "Memorandum" by Maria in *Letters by the Late Frances Ridley Havergal*. (This was April 17, 1879, 47 days before Frances died.)

[8] *Kept for the Master's Use* by F.R.H. (London: James Nisbet & Co., 1879), on pages 417–500 of Volume II of this edition. In the "Prefatory Note" to this book, Maria wrote that Frances "finished revising the proofs of this book shortly before her death on Whit Tuesday, June 3, 1879."

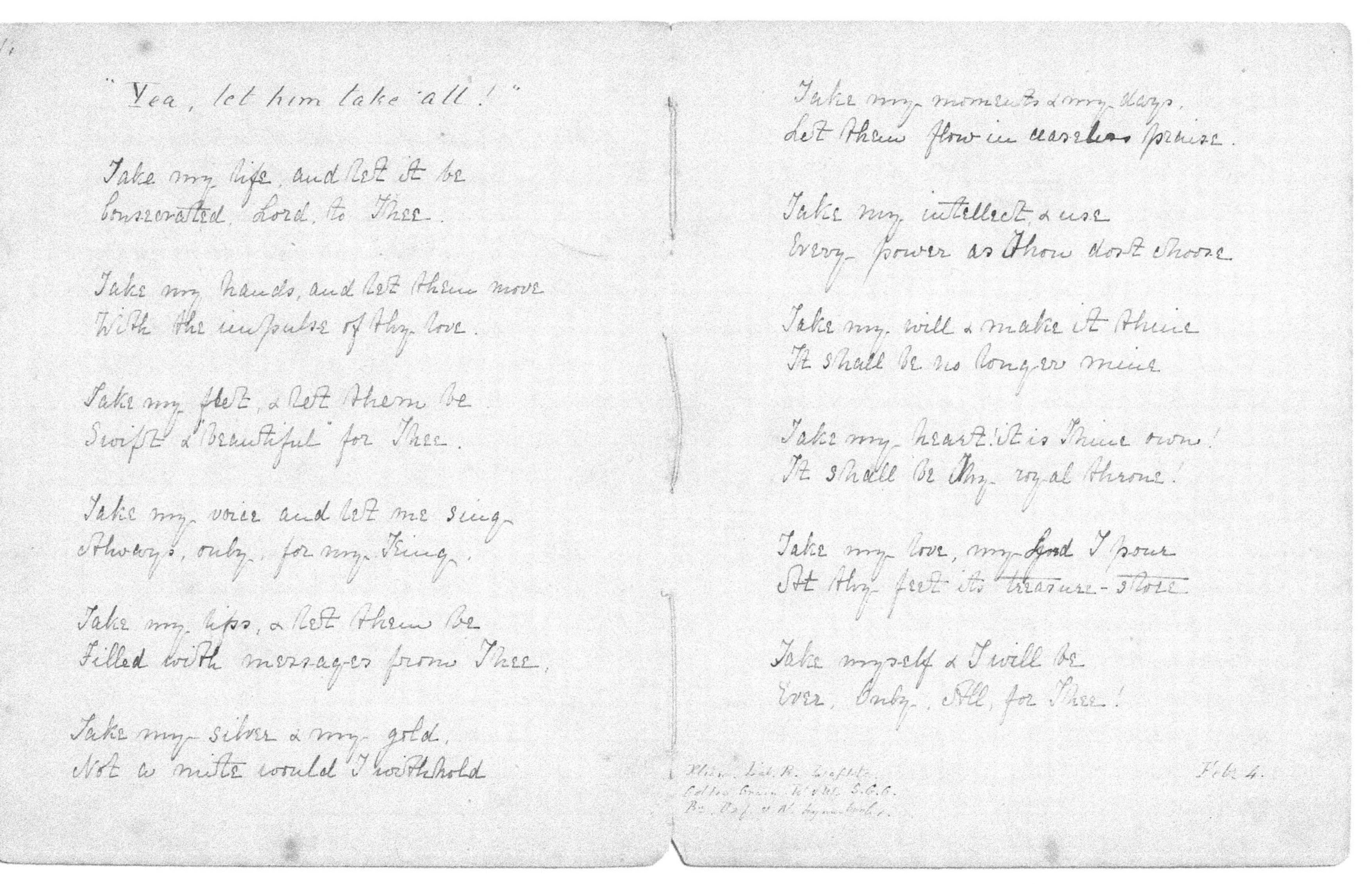

"Yea, let him take all!"

Take my life, and let it be
Consecrated, Lord, to Thee.

Take my hands, and let them move
With the impulse of Thy love.

Take my feet, & let them be
Swift & "beautiful" for Thee.

Take my voice and let me sing
Always, only, for my King.

Take my lips, & let them be
Filled with messages from Thee.

Take my silver & my gold,
Not a mite would I withhold

Take my moments & my days,
Let them flow in ceaseless praise.

Take my intellect, & use
Every power as Thou dost choose.

Take my will & make it Thine
It shall be no longer mine.

Take my heart. It is Thine own!
It shall be Thy royal throne!

Take my love, my God I pour
At Thy feet its treasure-store.

Take myself & I will be
Ever, Only, All, for Thee!

Feb. 4.

This is F.R.H.'s fair copy autograph of the Consecration Hymn in her Manuscript Book Nº VIII. Note that there are small differences in this manuscript and the finalized text published by F.R.H. The title was named "Consecration Hymn." The seventh couplet (beginning "Take my moments") was moved to be the second couplet, and in line 2 of the eighth couplet, "dost" was changed to "shalt." These changes were made by Frances herself, before she published this as the First Day in Loyal Responses.

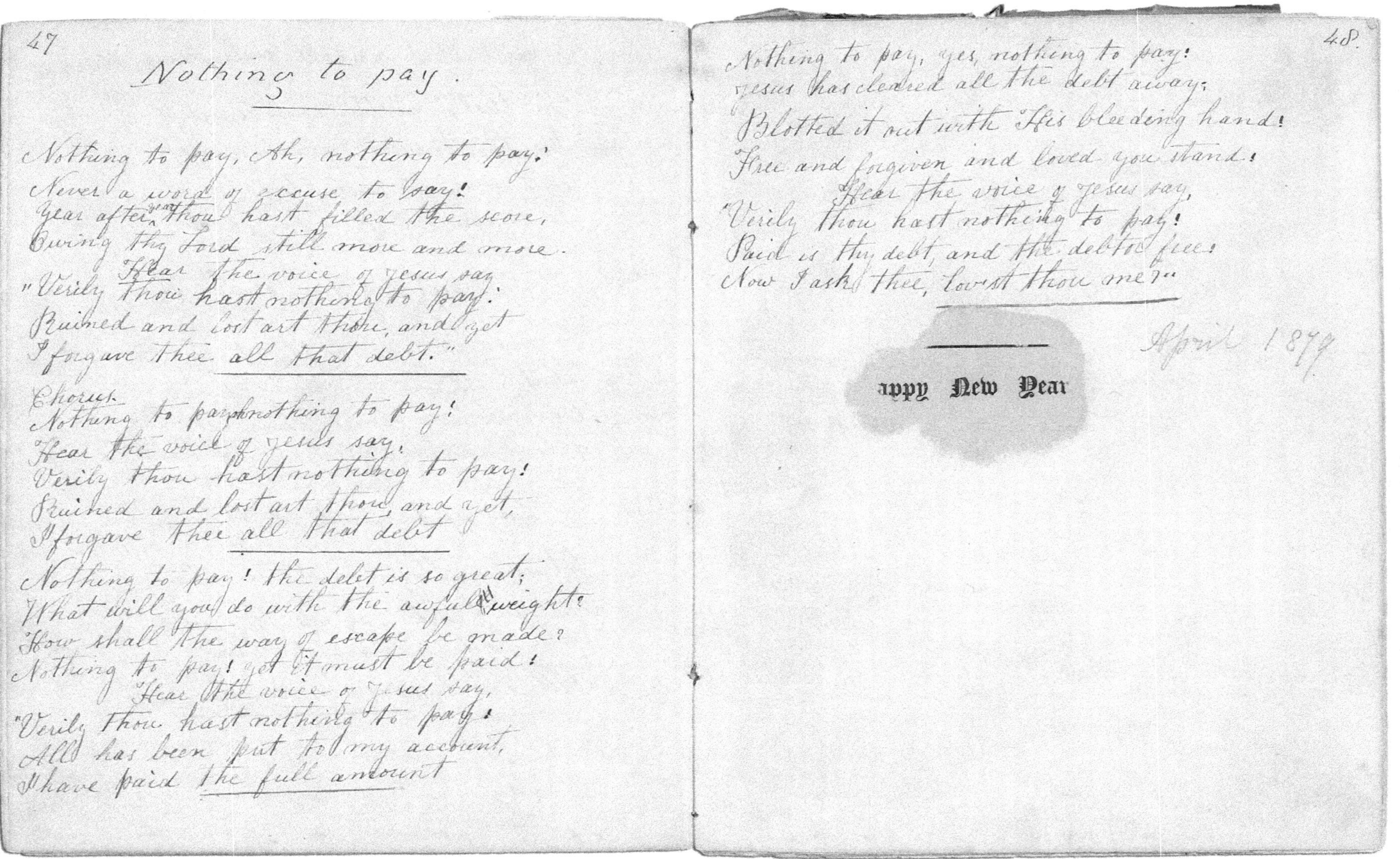

47

Nothing to pay.

Nothing to pay, Ah, nothing to pay;
Never a word of excuse to say!
Year after year thou hast filled the score,
Owing thy Lord still more and more.
Hear the voice of Jesus say,
"Verily thou hast nothing to pay:
Ruined and lost art thou, and yet
I forgave thee all that debt."

Chorus.
Nothing to pay, nothing to pay!
Hear the voice of Jesus say,
Verily thou hast nothing to pay!
Ruined and lost art thou, and yet,
I forgave thee all that debt

Nothing to pay! the debt is so great;
What will you do with the awful weight?
How shall the way of escape be made?
Nothing to pay! yet it must be paid!
Hear the voice of Jesus say,
"Verily thou hast nothing to pay!
All has been put to my account,
I have paid the full amount

48.

Nothing to pay, yes, nothing to pay!
Jesus has cleared all the debt away;
Blotted it out with His bleeding hand!
Free and forgiven and loved you stand!
Hear the voice of Jesus say,
"Verily thou hast nothing to pay!
Paid is thy debt, and the debtor free!
Now I ask thee, lovest thou me?"

April 1879

appy New Year

This is F.R.H.'s manuscript of "Nothing to Pay," apparently one of her last four completed poems (there were only three after this one, in her last Manuscript Book № IX), dated April before she died June 3, 1879. She set this to music, and the score is found on pages 1232–1233 of Volume V of the Havergal edition.

SONGS OF GRACE AND GLORY.

OPINIONS EXPRESSED.

"The external appearance is beautiful, and I can see at a glance that very great care has been bestowed upon the compilation."—THE RIGHT REV. THE LORD BISHOP OF LICHFIELD.

"A very comprehensive and valuable book, and the beauty of its outward form and type leave nothing to be desired."—THE RIGHT REV. THE LORD BISHOP OF WORCESTER.

"In your precious book I find an endless fund of Divine instruction. It is the best 'Preacher's Assistant' I ever met with, next to the Word itself."—JOHN T. MANLEY, Vicar of Tunbridge.

"The *more* I peruse it, the *more* I like it."—MARCUS RAINSFORD, Belgrave Chapel, Eaton Square.

"'SONGS OF GRACE AND GLORY.'—Just the book I wanted—TRUE POETRY, DEEP SPIRITUALITY, GREAT TASTE, and GREAT VARIETY."—H. O. STERLAND, Vicar of St. Edmund's, Gateshead.

"I have carefully read 'Songs of Grace and Glory,' and have no hesitation in saying that the volume is, in my opinion, one of the most admirable and comprehensive collections of Hymns I have ever seen. The labour in research and arrangement undergone by the Editor must have been very great indeed. I shall rejoice to hear of its wide circulation. It is a marvel of cheapness."—R. W. FORREST, Vicar of St. Jude's, South Kensington.

"I like your Collection of Hymns very much."—Rev. J. C. RYLE.

"The selection of *old* Hymns is admirable, and the *new* ones, with which you have enriched your pages, deserve the gratitude of the Church of Christ. Those by Frances Ridley Havergal are particularly pleasing. Their perusal has proved a source of great comfort and instruction to us."—JOHN STEVENSON, D.D. (Author of "The Lord our Shepherd," &c.).

"My brother clergymen are greatly taken with it. It is, without exception, the best ever published. I look at it and at those indices with astonishment. We have been perfectly revelling in the book."—D. A. DOUDNEY, D.D., Incumbent of St. Luke's, Bedminster.

"At Walton, I found the change to your full and faithful Hymn-book most acceptable."—Canon JOHN BABINGTON, Rector of Walton-le-Wolds.

"The demand for 'Songs of Grace and Glory' (just adopted in the writer's church), is so *unprecedented*. They win golden opinions on every side."—C. T. ROLFE, Rector of Shadoxhurst, Kent.

Second Edition, Small Crown 8vo, 3s. 6d., Cloth.

BRUEY, A LITTLE WORKER FOR CHRIST.

BY FRANCES RIDLEY HAVERGAL.

"'Bruey, A Little Worker for Christ' (Nisbet & Co.), is from the well-known pen of the Authoress of 'The Ministry of Song,' &c., Miss Havergal. It draws to the life the experiences of a little girl who, having first given her heart to Christ, devotes herself to doing good to others. Her first effort was in the Sunday-school, but from this she was led on to work for relatives and friends, and among them a cousin Percy, in whom boy nature and habits are vividly depicted. But it is not for individuals alone that Bruey laboured; she is also shown in the light of a missionary collector for Ireland; and, incidentally, a good deal of information about the cause of Irish Evangelization is brought in. The incidents of her collectorship illustrate the difficulties and encouragements of those who engage in that arduous but blessed work. We much rejoice that Miss Havergal has given such a direction to her new and admirable tale."—*Record*, Dec. 6.

Third Edition, now Ready, Small Crown 8vo, 3s. 6d. cloth.

THE MINISTRY OF SONG.

BY FRANCES RIDLEY HAVERGAL.

"A true poet, very rich in thought, and very musical in expression. Her book is vigorous as well as varied in imagery and pictorial power; . . . the tone always elevated and devout." —*Literary Times.*

"Poetical imagination, high intellectual attainment, intense earnestness of heart and purpose, and a remarkable power of melodious expression, present a rare combination. . . . Every poem is a gem; and every gem gathers lustre from its close proximity to the Pearl of Great Price. Her gems of song have become heart treasures."—*Our Own Fireside.*

"Rich in thought, sweet in experience, and most scriptural in doctrine."—*Gospel Magazine.*

"These sacred poems possess the rare and invaluable combinations of religion, genius, and art. They are no mere rhymes, but the masterly renderings of a poet, a seer, a deep thinker."—*Morning Journal.*

LONDON: JAMES NISBET & CO., 21, BERNERS STREET, W.

These are published reviews that were found in a periodical.

29.

TRUST. 223

FIDES. [H. P. 343.]

569 Ps. lv. 23. *"I will trust in Thee."*
Tune FIDES. 65, 65. D. Or HERMAS.

1 JESUS, I will trust Thee, trust Thee with my soul;
Guilty, lost, and helpless, Thou canst make me whole.
There is none in heaven or on earth like Thee:
Thou hast died for sinners—therefore, Lord, for me.

2 Jesus, I may trust Thee, name of matchless worth
Spoken by the angel at Thy wondrous birth;
Written, and for ever, on Thy cross of shame,
Sinners read and worship, trusting in that name.

3 Jesus, I must trust Thee, pondering Thy ways,
Full of love and mercy all Thine earthly days:
Sinners gathered round Thee, lepers sought Thy face—
None too vile or loathsome for a Saviour's grace.

4 Jesus, I can trust Thee, trust Thy written word,
Though Thy voice of pity I have never heard.
When Thy Spirit teacheth, to my taste how sweet—
Only may I hearken, sitting at Thy feet.

5 Jesus, I do trust Thee, trust without a doubt:
"Whosoever cometh, Thou wilt not cast out,"
Faithful is Thy promise, precious is Thy blood—
These my soul's salvation, Thou my Saviour God!

Mary Jane Walker, 1864.

HERMAS.* [H. P. 105.]

See Hymns 1076—1078.

* To this tune its composer, FRANCES RIDLEY HAVERGAL, sang the first verse of this hymn ten minutes only before her death, Tuesday morning, June 3, 1879.

This is a copy of the top two-thirds of page 223 in *Songs of Grace and Glory* (the "New and Enlarged Musical Edition," London: James Nisbet & Co., 1880), the most comprehensive hymnbook till that time in the Church of England, edited by Rev. Charles Busbridge Snepp (texts) and Frances Ridley Havergal (music). Read the asterisked note by Rev. Snepp in this edition after her death: " * To this tune [Hermas] its composer, Frances Ridley Havergal, sang the first verse of this hymn ten minutes only before her death, Thursday morning, June 3, 1879." See also page 779 of Volume V of the Havergal edition.

An undated photograph of William Henry Havergal, with his inscription, and a color portrait of him painted by Solomon Cole in 1845.

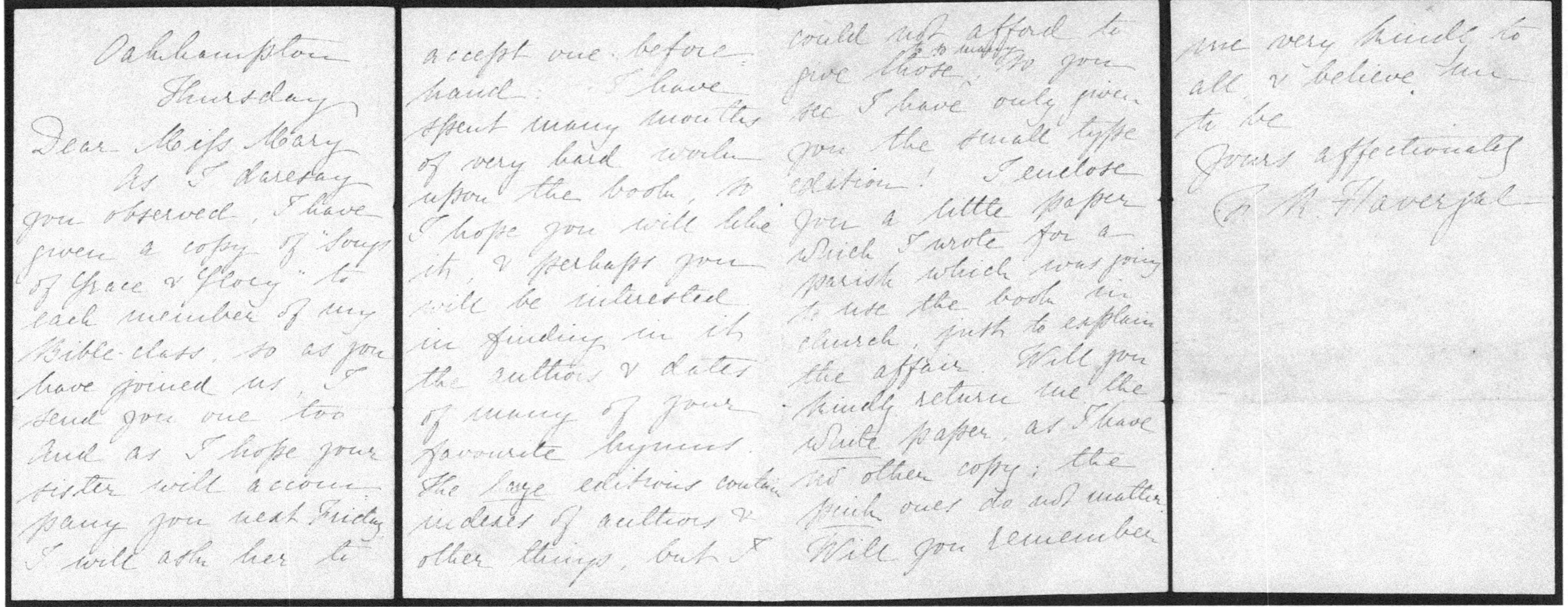

Oakhampton
Thursday

Dear Miss Mary

As I daresay you observed, I have given a copy of "Songs of Grace & Glory" to each member of my Bible class, so as you have joined us, I send you one too. And as I hope your sister will accompany you next Friday, I will ask her to accept one beforehand. I have spent many months of very hard work upon the book, so I hope you will like it, & perhaps you will be interested in finding in it the authors & dates of many of your favorite hymns. The large editions contain indexes of authors & other things, but I could not afford to give those to so many, so you see I have only given you the small type edition! I enclose you a little paper which I wrote for a parish which was going to use the book in church, just to explain the affair. Will you kindly return me the white paper, as I have no other copy; the pink ones do not matter. Will you remember me very kindly to all, & believe me to be

Yours affectionately F. R. Havergal

[Note: The "little paper" which F.R.H. enclosed with this letter is likely the article "A Coming 'Parish Event' " published in the *Home Words Perry Barr Magazine* (on pages 973–976 of Volume II of the Havergal edition).]

This is the original autograph letter that F.R.H. wrote to Rev. Charles Busbridge Snepp the day after her father, William Henry Havergal, died. W.H.H. composed his last score for Rev. Snepp's projected hymnbook Songs of Grace and Glory *on Saturday, April 16, became unconscious the next day (Easter Sunday), and died on Tuesday, April 19, 1870. W.H.H. had been helping Snepp with* Songs of Grace and Glory, *and after his death Frances became the music editor of that so truly valuable hymnbook.*

Dear M[r] Snepp Pyrmont Villa Leamington April 20

My beloved father entered into God's rest at noon yesterday. Early on Easter Sunday morning he was seized with apoplexy & consciousness never returned, so he went home without <u>any</u> suffering, only ceased breathing & was with Jesus.

I write to ask you if you would give me what would now be a very precious treasure – his <u>last</u> tune. He wrote it before breakfast on Saturday, & gave it to me, as he <u>always</u> did all his music, to look over in case of slips of the pen, & I gave it him back with one trifling suggestion as to inner parts. It was the last too that he played to me. Will you give it me? I shall be so grateful for it. <u>Of course</u> you will keep a <u>copy</u>, but it is our dear lst writing that I <u>so</u> long to have that I cannot help asking you for it.

He seemed peculiarly bright & happy all Saturday. God has mingled every possible mercy with this deep sorrow, & it is not the least to be permitted so to <u>see</u> it.

No one but Mamma & I could imagine what the sunset light of this winter has been – his <u>perfect</u> patience & sweetness – he did indeed glorify the Master whom he loved & followed.

Pardon my request. I know you will.

Yours very truly Frances R. Havergal

Poor Hatherly [?] will regret having grieved him. I believe he really loved him, but sadly forgot himself of late.

Songs of Grace and Glory, such a gold-mine, a large treasure chest full of gems, is so valuable and also so extremely obscure today. Few people early in the 21st century even know of or have ever heard of this hymnbook, and very few if any today realize the enormous, costly effort and time that Charles Busbridge Snepp and Frances Ridley Havergal gave to this collection of hymns. Here was true diligence, and much thought, labor, sacrifice in time and effort. In the research on the Havergal edition, no original manuscripts of Rev. Snepp were found, but we can know that he spent countless hours and much thought and effort in the preparation and finalization of S.G.G. Very few of F.R.H.'s manuscript scores of music have been found, but we have important glimpses of their work. Remember that this was the 1870's, when there were no computers, when she would have written by hand every note of every measure of every score for 1,100 hymns. Beyond the labor—with great skill—in preparing all of the music scores and texts for 1,100 hymns, Frances also wrote a number of the hymns newly, specifically for this book, and also composed a number of hymn scores for S.G.G. We have comparatively little from the original papers in their collaboration, but we do have glimpses of F.R.H.'s (and also similarly Charles Busbridge Snepp's) long, costly, diligent work, a true labor of love to complete *Songs of Grace and Glory*, the most comprehensive hymnbook in the Church of England until that time, and still a true gold-mine for us today.

This next quotation from *Memorials of Frances Ridley Havergal* has been given as the quotation number 6 in the set of "Thirty-four Excerpts from Various Books, Quotations by or about Frances Ridley Havergal on Music" (page lii of Volume V of the Havergal edition), but this is included also here before S.G.G.

> It was soon after her father's death that my sister undertook the preparation for the press of "Havergal's Psalmody," which afterwards was largely used in connection with the Rev. C. B. Snepp's Hymnal, "Songs of Grace and Glory," of which full details will be found in the Appendix. The preparation for the work of harmonizing she alludes to in a letter to her friend Mary C. in 1866.
>
>> How I should like to teach you harmony! I do believe I could make it lucid; you can't think what exquisite symmetry there is in chords and intervals, so that I always feel, as well as believe, that man by no means invented harmony, but only found out God's beautiful arrangements in it. As for my own compositions, I am (at some cost of resolution) abstaining entirely. Hiller, of Cologne, recommended me an excellent book, which I got, and determined to write no more till I had gone through it; this I am steadily doing, and enjoy writing the exercises. I suppose, after Hiller's professional opinion, it would be affectation to say I had no talent, and I certainly do feel I have at least a sort of inherited instinct for seeing into harmonies. The way I studied harmony was rather unique; some years ago (at home) I kept a treatise on harmony in my bedroom, read as much as I could conveniently grasp the last thing, and then worked out the exercises in my head before going to sleep. This I did for several weeks, and suppose I must have taken it in very comfortably under this system, inasmuch as I had some work to persuade Hiller that I had gone through no "academical course!"

Frances writes (1870) of difficulties in the work:

> I was so struck this morning with "Thou art the Helper of the fatherless,"—the very first time one of those special orphan promises has come home to me. I had been puzzling over a tune which papa would have decided about in a minute, and missed him so much, when suddenly this verse flashed upon me brightly. I think that even in music the Lord is my helper now; much more in other things.
>
> When composing some tunes at this time, I selected six about which I felt doubtful, and sent them to Sir Frederic Ouseley, asking him to say if they were all right. This he most kindly did; to my great delight he endorsed them every one, and praised them too.

Very prayerfully did she write several hymns for "Songs of Grace and Glory"; and, when she heard from time to time of their being blessed, she wrote in answer to a friend's communication:

> It does seem wonderful that God should so use and bless my hymns; and yet it really does seem as if the seal of His own blessing were set upon them, for so many testimonies have reached me. Writing is *praying* with me, for I never seem to write even a verse by myself, and feel like a little child writing; you know a child would look up at every sentence and say "And what shall I say next?" That is just what I do; I ask that at every line He would give me, not merely thoughts and power, but also every *word*, even the very *rhymes*. Very often I have a most distinct and happy consciousness of direct answers. As you use "Havergal's Psalmody" I thought you might be interested to know a little more about my dear father, so will you accept a "Memorial" of him.
>
> *Literal* "singing for Jesus" is to me, somehow, the most personal and direct commission I hold from my beloved Master; and my opportunities for it are often most curious, and have been greatly blessed; every line in my little poem "Singing for Jesus" is from personal experience. . . .
>
> I was so overwhelmed on Sunday at hearing three of my hymns touchingly sung at Perry Church. I never before realized the high privilege of writing for "the great congregation"; especially 633, "I gave My life for thee" to papa's

tune "Baca"; the others were 120 and 921 in "S.G.G."

(To Margaret W ——.)

. . . Last night they sang "To Him who for our sins was slain," to my little tune "Tryphosa"; it went so deliciously, and choir and congregation really rang out the Alleluias so brightly that it suddenly came over me, as it never did before, what a privilege it is even to have contributed a bit of music for His direct praise. It was a sort of *hush* of praise, all alone with Jesus, for His great goodness. I had no idea "Tryphosa" was such a pretty tune before! . . . [1]

[1] *Memorials of Frances Ridley Havergal* by Maria V. G. Havergal (London: James Nisbet & Co., 1880), pages 103–106. See pages 30–31 of Volume IV of the Havergal edition.

This is a note by F.R.H. to Charles Busbridge Snepp, and also copies of two other closing signatures by her at the ends of other letters. They worked together when she visited Perry Barr (his home and church), and when they were not working together in Perry Barr, there likely was very extensive correspondence between them on numerous details in the work on *Songs of Grace and Glory.*

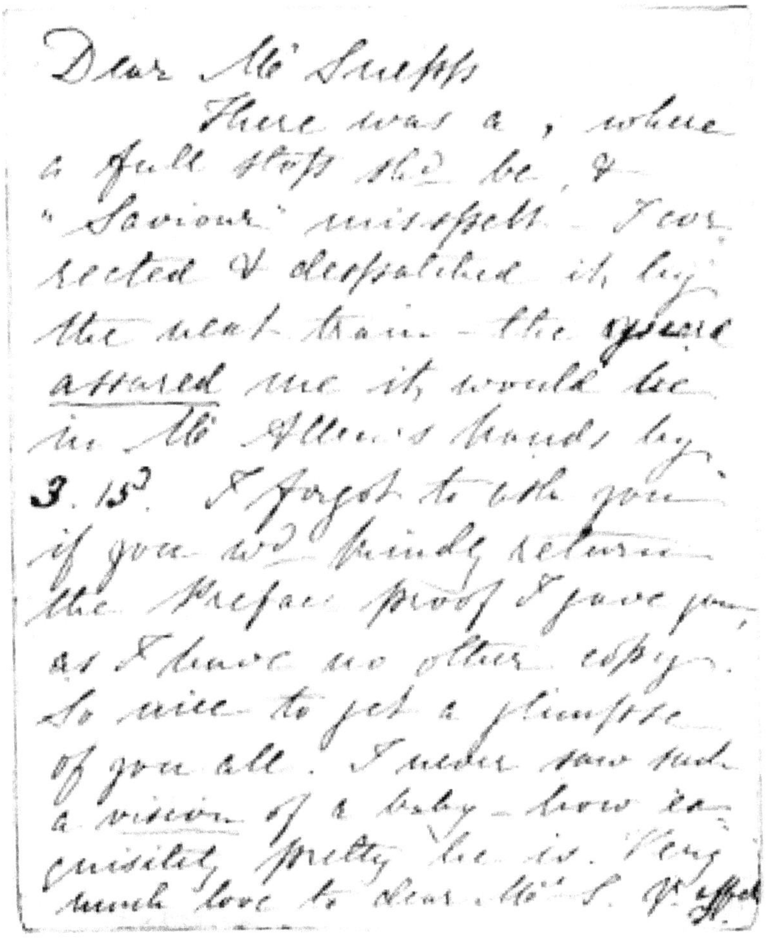

Dear Mr Snepp
There was a , where
a full stop ["full stop" means
period] sh^{d} [should] be, &
"Saviour" misspelt. I cor
rected & despatched it, by
the next train – the guard
assured me it would be
in M. [Mr.] Allen's hands by
3.15. I forgot to ask you
if you w^{d} [would] kindly return
the Preface proof I gave you,
as I have no other copy.
So nice to get a glimpse
of you all. I never saw such
a vision of a baby – how ex
quisitely pretty he is. Very
much love to dear Mrs S. Y^{r} affect F.
[Yours affectionately F.]

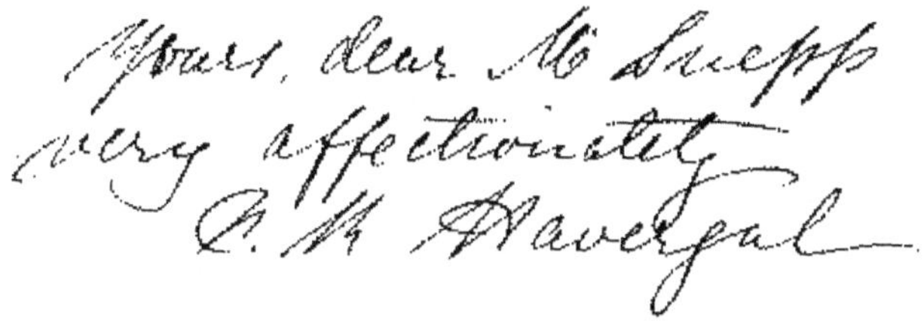

Yours, dear Mr Snepp
very affectionately
F. R. Havergal

Yr affect sister
F.

"I HAVE LOVED THEE WITH AN EVERLASTING LOVE."
"HE HATH SAID, I WILL NEVER LEAVE THEE NOR FORSAKE THEE."

Yours faithfully C. B. Snepp

To the Rev. C. B. Snepp.

I have no hymn, my brother,
Upon your desk to lay,
No song of holy gladness
To bring to you to-day.

To "Songs of Grace and Glory"
No verses sweet and new!
I write not for ten thousand,
I only write for you.

For oh, my heart is singing
A song of quiet praise
To Him who has preserved you,
Upholding all your ways.

To Him who knows our sorrows,
Who knew the orphan's heart,
And sent a friend to cheer it,
And act a brother's part.

So I come before my Father,
My hands in faith uplift,
To fill your cup with gladness
And every perfect gift.

And may His loving-kindness
Crown all with grace for grace
Till in the coming glory
You stand before His face!

And see with light from heaven
Clear-shining on thy ways,
Each pilgrimage petition
Transmuted into praise.

Frances Ridley Havergal,
September, 1871

THE LATE REV. C. B. SNEPP, LL.M.

Saturday Night.

To the same.

Lord, refresh Thy weary servant,
Send him sweet and quiet rest;
Thou hast made him oft a blessing,
Let him now be doubly blest.

Let him feel Thy holy presence
Richly dwelling in his soul,
Every care and every burden
Bid him on Jehovah roll.

Lord, as he for Thee hath spoken,
Now to him, oh do Thou speak!
With Thy still small voice of comfort
Crown the mercies of the week.

May He wake with strength renewed,
Yet again to work for Thee;
Full of Sabbath joy and blessing
Let his spirit always be!

F.R.H. April, 1873

Charles Busbridge Snepp (1823 or 1824–1880). He was 56 when he died June 23, 1880, one year and 20 days after F.R.H. died, and approximately six months after the final, definitive edition of *Songs of Grace and Glory* was published by Nisbet. This portrait was published in an 1880 memorial article by Charles Bullock, "The late Rev. C. B. Snepp, LL.M.: A Record of Life's Closing Hours," published in Bullock's periodical *Home Words for Heart and Hearth.* Below the portrait was written "Drawn by T. C. Scott, from a Photograph by Hennah & Kent, Brighton." and "Engraved by R. & E. Taylor." The oval portrait with the signature was found in *Scriptural Remembrances of a Faithful Pastor: Reverend Charles B. Snepp LL.M.* (London: James Nisbet & Co., 1880).

IN MEMORIAM. F. R. HAVERGAL.

Perry Barr, Near Birmingham.

Dear Mr. Harper,

I know I must not refuse your request to give some short account of our late devoted and beloved Friend, Frances Ridley Havergal—but where to begin and where to end, is no easy matter, for one who has known so much of her private life, and been permitted to labour with her, and trace its hidden workings for the last eight eventful years.

Such years of rapid progress, in knowledge and in grace—in extensive usefulness—in entire consecration—in holy—happy—honoured and successful service for her Saviour and her King!

During a ministerial experience of thirty years—I have never seen such wondrous growth of faith, love, and zeal—still less such marvellous talents consecrated entirely to the Master's service—and laid so humbly at His feet!

When first she came, in June, 1870, to reside with us, at Perry Villa, and to render her much valued help, in the joint editing of *Songs of Grace and Glory*, she did not fully see the Doctrines of "Sovereign Grace"—and "Electing Love." We had several conversations together—but for some time she appeared unable to grasp them—until, one day, a very simple argument drawn from Holy Scripture, was presented with great force and clearness to her mind—and she could no longer withstand it. The passage was from Revelation v. 9. "Thou hast redeemed us to God, out of every kindred, and tongue, and people." This expression "out of" greatly impressed her mind—and looking into her Greek Testament (in which she often delighted) she found the Greek preposition "" [small epsilon with ` over the epsilon and then small kappa] most fully and unmistakably confirmed the doctrine of election—that it was some "out of" every kindred, tongue, and people, who were redeemed to God, by Christ's blood. Hence she became fully convinced of the revealed Truth of God, concerning a personal and special redemption.

From that time she never faltered, and while delighting to proclaim a full and free salvation in Christ Jesus, to every coming, penitent sinner—she also knew that text "no man can come to me except the Father draw him." John vi. 44. And that "All the Father giveth Me shall come to Me," v. 37. And "This is the Father's will that of all which He hath given Me I should lose nothing," v. 39.

About this time she wrote Hymn 398, in *Songs of Grace and Glory*—

"O thou chosen church of Jesus,
Glorious, blessèd, and secure."

Thus recording, most unmistakably, her own belief and confidence in the Doctrine of Election. And indeed, only a short time before her death one of her letters to me fully confirmed this.

Some time ago—when we were searching for a Hymn on the "Everlasting Covenant of Grace," I found several, but none of them came up exactly to the measure and standard I required, whereupon she not only composed one upon the "Covenant of Grace," but brought to bear in that Hymn all the varied, beautiful, and practical lessons to be drawn from it, by every child of God. It is numbered 83 in the New Edition of *Songs of Grace and Glory*, and begins—

"Jehovah's covenant shall endure,
All ordered, everlasting, sure!"

A remarkable little circumstance occurring a little before this will shew her entire dependence on the Lord, and her confidence in prayer. Proofs of *Songs of Grace and Glory* had reached us, up to Hymn 415. My next Hymn was to be on "justification," I was not quite satisfied with the Hymn which was to follow—it was not sufficiently clear and good to illustrate this great truth, I had searched diligently everywhere for a first-class Hymn on this special subject, and was fearing we had to put up with one not quite equal to our wishes. It occurred to me to ask F.R.H. to write one, she replied she could not unless God gave it to her, but added, "If you will pray for me, I will go upstairs to write one." We agreed to do so, and in a very short time she appeared again, in my room, with the Hymn written. It is now numbered 416, and begins in a spirited strain

"Israel of God, awaken!
Church of Christ , arise and shine!"

It is a Hymn most accurately setting forth the glorious doctrine of "Justification by Faith," which as Luther well calls it, is the test of a "Standing or Falling Church ." The first verse contains a burst of praise, the second verse beautifully brings out the plan, the third verse, the blissful results.

Upon another occasion, nearly nine years ago, I have her three short, sweet texts of Holy Scripture, upon the blessed Privileges of Believers. Ephesians i. 6, "Accepted in the Beloved." Colossians i. 28, "Perfect in Christ Jesus." Colossians ii. 10, "Complete in Him." These texts were returned to me, shortly, with that exquisite little Hymn,

"Accepted, perfect, and complete,
For God's inheritance made meet,
How true, how glorious, and how sweet!"

It will be found in No. 725, *Songs of Grace and Glory.*

The beautiful Hymn 432, written a century ago, had been almost lost, save a favourite copy, much prized by "Kent," who had used it so often, and so long, and thumbed it so thoroughly, that the paper was quite worn out in one part, and very difficult to replace with the exact words of the original, whereupon our beloved Friend, catching the very spirit and meaning of the author Andrew Kessell, immediately rectified it, and assigning it to her father's beautiful harmonization of the tune "Exeter," has now made it most complete, and worthy of that glorious subject it represents, "The Church of Christ partaking of His Eternal Glory." It commences—

"Oh! for a burst of praise to God!
Who bought His Church with His own blood,
And will His dear bought right maintain;
Soon shall His voice dispel our gloom,
The marriage of the Lamb is come,
To crown His bride, with Him to reign,
Alleluia."

Further—the results of the Saviour's glorious work for His Church and People are most beautifully represented in her Hymns 431 and 1025. The first of these, illustrating John vi. 37 to 39. John x. 14–16, 27–29. Also John xvii. 2–24, and Hebrews ii. 12, 18. While Hymn 1025, with its magnificent tune (also composed by F.R.H.) represents the final glorious reward awaiting the saints of God, and is beautifully described as "Grace consummated in Glory." The blissful grandeur of which, we doubt not, she is now herself enjoying.

Many other beautiful illustrations might be added, but time fails me, I am compelled to close, and praying for the Divine Blessing upon these words, I remain yours faithfully in Christ Jesus,

Charles B. Snepp,
Vicar of Perry Barr.[1]

[Note: See also Rev. Snepp's letter to F.R.H.'s sister Maria, the 13th quotation in the set of 34 Quotations by or about F.R.H. on Music, on page xxxvi near the front of Volume V of the Havergal edition. This is a valuable letter he wrote after Frances' death, giving important details on her work with him on *Songs of Grace and Glory*.]

[1] "In Memoriam Frances Ridley Havergal" by Charles Busbridge Snepp, in *Wayside Words* A Monthly Magazine edited by Rev. Frederick Harper, M.A., a bound volume for the year 1879 (London: E. Marlborough & Co., 1879), pages 110–113.

Prefaces to *Songs of Grace and Glory* by Charles Busbridge Snepp and Frances Ridley Havergal

Extremely few people today realize the remarkably fine gifts Frances Ridley Havergal had in music. As a performer and as a composer she had a rare level of gifts, and she had rare diligence with her gifts. Her father, Rev. William Henry Havergal, was the foremost church musician and composer of sacred music in England in his generation, and he was a leading advocate for reform in the practice and taste of church music. Rev. Charles Busbridge Snepp, an Anglican pastor, was a hymnologist with a very important collection of hymnbooks, a deep interest in hymns, and a desire to bring out a new, comprehensive hymnal. Snepp had written to William Henry about this project, and on the morning of W.H.H.'s last conscious day, he composed a score for a hymn in Snepp's new project, *Songs of Grace and Glory*. The next day, April 17, 1870, Easter, he was seized with apoplexy and never regained consciousness, dying on April 19. Rev. Snepp after that wrote to his daughter, F.R.H., and later they concluded that she would edit the music for the new hymnal.

Though extremely obscure today, *Songs of Grace and Glory* is a true treasure of worship in song, a gold mine strongly worthy to be republished today, studied by church musicians, and used in worship in our day. Snepp was the architect and leader of the work and the editor of the texts, and F.R.H. prepared and edited all the music. She also wrote words and music to several hymns for this hymnal. This is an enormous and enormously impressive body of work. Frances directly prepared for press the scores of 1,100 hymns, and after she thought that her work was completed on this, she learned that the papers and plates for the Appendix at the printer had been lost in a devastating fire, so that she would need to do all the work on the Appendix again. (See the first part of Chapter 11 of *Memorials of Frances Ridley Havergal*, pages 51–52 of Volume IV of the Havergal edition.) In the British Library, a copy of *Songs of Grace and Glory* is dated 1883 with "Three Hundred and Thirteenth Thousand" on the title page.

The work began with *Havergal's Psalmody and Century of Chants*, a republication of two of William Henry's earlier volumes of hymn scores composed by him, *Old Church Psalmody* (1847) and *A Hundred Psalm and Hymn Tunes* (1859), with other previously unpublished materials by W.H.H. and also a few scores composed by Frances, all edited by F.R.H. and published by Robert Cocks & Co., London, 1871. Cocks published a second and a third edition (the third edition in 1872). James Nisbet & Co. published the fourth edition in 1877, and this is the definitive edition. *Havergal's Psalmody and Century of Chants* was a "Companion Volume to Songs of Grace and Glory." The music in *H.P.C.C.* was the music for the hymns in *Songs of Grace and Glory*. *Songs of Grace and Glory* was published in a number of editions. The first publication, by William Hunt & Co., London, 1872, had 1,025 hymns, and was brought out in eight different formats (varying sizes, leather or cloth covers, 6 indices or 3 indices, with varying prices for each format). Near the back of the hymnal was "Index V. Tunes with Appropriate Hymns." This first publication of *Songs of Grace and Glory* had only the words, without the music, and with this index an organist or pianist could find and play the score for each hymn in *Songs of Grace and Glory* from the "Accompanying Volume" *Havergal's Psalmody and Century of Chants*. Later James Nisbet & Co. published *S.G.G.*, and in 1876 Nisbet published the "Musical Edition" of *Songs of Grace and Glory*. In 1880 Nisbet published a "New and Enlarged Musical Edition" of the hymnbook, a final re-evaluation and preparation of this by F.R.H. Rev. Snepp wrote in his Preface to this 1880 edition: "The musical Editor, the late beloved Frances Ridley Havergal, after composing several New and Beautiful Tunes, and carefully re-arranging the whole, has been called to join the heavenly choir above. Not, however, until she had first bequeathed to the Church of Christ these results of her matured judgment." F.R.H.'s work on *Songs of Grace and Glory* is very valuable, and her collaboration and friendship with Rev. Snepp were very important in her life. Snepp was both her senior colleague and also her dear friend and brother, and they valuably benefitted and enriched each other, both in the work on the hymnbook and in other ways. Both *Havergal's Psalmody and Century of Chants* (the definitive 1877 Fourth Edition by Nisbet) and *Songs of Grace and Glory* (the "New and Enlarged Musical Edition" of 1880 by Nisbet) are to be, if the Lord will, published in facsimile in *Songs of Truth and Love: Music by Frances Ridley Havergal and William Henry Havergal*, Volume V of the Havergal edition. (Volume V also contains other very important music composed by F.R.H.) The Prefaces given next are important to include in this Volume IV of the Havergal edition. First is Rev. Snepp's Preface to the original 1872 Hunt edition of *S.G.G.* Next is his Preface to the Nisbet 1880 "New and Enlarged Musical Edition" of the hymnbook, signed by Snepp December, 1879. Frances died on June 3, 1879, not living longer to write a new Preface to the "New and Enlarged Musical Edition." Thus her 1875 "Original Preface to the Musical Edition" was published in 1880, and that is given next. Her 1871 "Supplementary Remarks" to her new edition of *Havergal's Psalmody and Century of Chants* conclude this section of Volume IV of the Havergal edition. The definitive edition of *Songs of Grace and Glory* was published approximately six months after F.R.H. died (June 3, 1879) and six months before Rev. Snepp died (June 23, 1880). David Chalkley, October 20, 2004

This is Charles Busbridge Snepp's 1871 Preface to the first edition of *Songs of Grace and Glory* (without music). The music for the hymns was provided in the "Companion Volume," *Havergal's Psalmody and Century of Chants.* The Musical Edition of *Songs of Grace and Glory* was published in 1876, the words and music for each hymn together on the same page in the same book.

PREFACE

THIS Hymnal is designed for Private, Family, and Public Worship.

It is sent forth with the prayerful hope that it may please the Great Head of the Church to make use of it—for the spread of His glorious Gospel—the edification of His Church—and the praise of His great and holy Name.

The origin and history of this volume is simply this: The Editor having been interested in the collection of hymns for nearly thirty years (without the least idea of publication), and having been so often refreshed by them, was at length induced to listen to the solicitations of friends, who urged upon him the responsibility of possessing such hymnal treasures, and the duty of making them known to the Church of Christ.

Having no inclination for the extra labour, anxiety, and expense connected with such a work, he at first declined, and it was not until the subject had been repeatedly brought before him, that he consented to discard all personal feeling in the matter, and to undertake the responsibilities connected with it, in the hope of contributing his little quota to the enrichment of the Church of Christ, and, thereby, to the glory of God.

Sir Roundell Palmer's admirable *Book of Praise* was made a first resort, as replete with valuable suggestions. His new arrangement of hymns, and his interesting addition of authors' names and dates, convinced the Editor of the great desirability of adopting some such plan.

He has, however, ventured to construct an entirely new, and in some respects a fuller, arrangement of subjects, endeavouring to represent every doctrine of Holy Scripture, not only those more generally treated of, but the deeper mysteries of the everlasting Covenant of Grace, and the glorious Second Advent of the Messiah.

For this purpose many scarce and valuable works have been examined, some of which—known only to collectors—may be picked up once in a life-time, or borrowed now and then. On the other hand, among authors of the present day, the most recent and beautiful hymns have been carefully sought and added to this collection, while many, by a highly gifted author, have been expressly written for this volume, on subjects of the deepest interest, and on the most precious truths of our holy Faith.

The Holy Scriptures greatly encourage the use of hymns, both by precept and example—both in private and public—both with and without instrumental music.

Singing "praise to God" is the most exalted as well as delightful employment. It approaches nearest to the ceaseless worship of Heaven, where the ten thousand times ten thousand "join in the everlasting song," adoring the Lamb!

God is indeed the author of all the tuneful powers of man. He has designed them for His own glory: "Whoso offereth praise glorifieth Me."

The example of Christ Himself in singing a hymn after the solemnities of the Last Supper may well quicken us to this privilege.

St. Paul connects it with the gift of the Holy Ghost, and exhorts us to be "filled with the Spirit, speaking to yourselves in psalms, and hymns, and spiritual songs, singing and making melody in your hearts to the Lord."

The early Christian Church caught the sacred fire, and their pure and fervent faith shone brightly in the flame of holy song. The very heathen testified of this, and Pliny informs us how, in the days of persecution, the early Christians met together, before the break of day, to sing hymns of praise to Christ as God.

The Rev. J. C. Ryle well says, "A thankful, hymn-singing spirit has always marked the days of a church's prosperity." And surely the growing interest and love for hymns, at the present day, is one of its most cheering and hopeful features.

Only let us be careful to have *Scriptural* hymns—such as clearly teach Divine truth—yea, ALL the truth of Holy Scripture—the complete cycle of Divine revelation—the "*whole* counsel of God;" remembering that *every* truth revealed in Scripture is "given for our learning, and is profitable," whether in prose or verse. Let us, therefore, "TEACH and admonish one another in psalms and hymns and spiritual songs."

The Editor has long felt a growing conviction that a Hymn Book should be a faithful counterpart of God's.

It has, therefore, been the anxious study of the Compiler to represent and teach, in their several parts and places, and in consecutive order, not only the great outlines of Scripture doctrine, but also the more minute detail of each and every branch of Divine truth—from "the Everlasting Covenant"—with all its rich provisions of grace—in a past eternity—to the consummation thereof by the ingathering of the Church of the Redeemed, and their fullness of bliss in an eternity to come. Word, and, in order to be COMPLETE, should carefully and minutely introduce every doctrine of Scripture.

All these momentous truths—one after another—are faithfully represented. And it is hoped that by this epitome of Scripture truth—by this analysis of God's Holy Word—the minds of His people may be instructed, and the glory of His grace proclaimed.

There are three or four ways in which *Songs of Grace and Glory* may help us, and prove a channel of blessing.

First—READING them daily; and perhaps the best method is to go right through the book. Thus, every doctrine and precept of Scripture is brought prominently before the mind—the many hymns under each theme confirming our faith, and enlarging our views.

Secondly—SINGING them daily, at Family Prayer, will afford much pleasure and profit. Many more would thus easily learn to sing, and to cultivate their voices in this, the noblest way in which the human voice (which is our "glory") can possibly be employed. Where they cannot be sung, let them be READ.

Thirdly—Sunday evening enjoyment. In a country parish, where there is no evening service, how delightful to see a Christian household gathered together to spend half an hour, or more, in the holy and happy employment of sacred song, singing hymns suitable to the day or season, and then allowing, as time permits, each one in turn, to hear their own favourite hymn, previously selected. Children, Visitors, and Servants are thus induced to look all through their Hymn Book with great delight and profit, fixing their choice week by week, anticipating the pleasure of their family gathering, and their own sweet Sabbath song!

It would be well if every family would attempt some such plan. Many would be thus gradually learning to take their part in the sacred psalmody of the House of God. The blessing would be manifold and great.

The *Companion Volume* to *Songs of Grace and Glory* will be found to supply tunes for every hymn, easy to learn and remember, and elevating to the musical taste.

Fourthly—The Ministry of Song. The District Visitor, or Christian friend, may minister great comfort and refreshment in singing (or reading) a sweet and holy hymn by the cottage bed-side of the sick, whether of the aged or the young.

This has been beautifully illustrated in *The Ministry of Song*, page 2:

Sing to the little children,
  And they will listen well;
Sing grand and holy music,
  For they can feel its spell.

Sing at the cottage bedside,—
  They have no music there,
And the voice of praise is silent
  After the voice of prayer.

Sing of the gentle Saviour
  In the simplest hymns you know,
And the pain-dimmed eye will brighten
  As the soothing verses flow.

Better than loudest plaudits
  The murmured thanks of such,
For the King will stoop to crown them
  With His gracious "Inasmuch."

When you long to bear the Message
  Home to some troubled breast,
Then sing with loving fervour,
  "Come unto Him, and rest."

Sing on in grateful gladness,
  Rejoice in this good thing
Which the Lord thy God hath given thee,
  The happy power to sing.

F. R. HAVERGAL.

These lines may well stir up the loving district visitor to realize a privilege too seldom thought of, the Ministry of Song.

The practice of LEARNING hymns is far more important than is generally supposed. It has many advantages: it readily strengthens the memory—it instructs and enriches the mind—it raises the affections heavenward—and, in proportion as it is cultivated, it makes us independent of book, light, or eyesight, whether for personal comfort and solace in hours of sorrow and sickness, or for ministration to others, by the choice and holy words we have thus made our own.

Let every Christian seek some attainment in this. And let parents and teachers encourage the practice of learning hymns, next to that of learning God's Holy Word. SONGS OF GRACE AND GLORY are arranged in three parts:

Part I. *The Holy and Ever-blessed "Trinity in Unity."*
Part II. *The Book of God, and the Church of God.*
Part III. *Man, and all prepared for man.*

Every hymn is arranged under its own leading subject, and all the hymns on that subject are brought together, so as to be seen and selected at a glance.

This is carefully summed up and illustrated by Index I.

Index II is a special arrangement of hymns for each service of the Sundays, and Holy Days, in the Ecclesiastical year.

It has been sometimes urged that hymns in which strong expressions of faith and love occur, are not suitable for singing in a mixed congregation. To this it may be replied first, that this Hymnal is expressly designed to afford help for private devotion as well as public worship, and secondly, that there are as strong expressions used in the Psalms of David, every Sunday, in public, by general consent of the Church. To this we take no exception.

So, also, the personal pronoun, in the singular number, is constantly used in the Psalms, whereby we feel fully justified in using it in our public hymns. Moreover, these high expressions of faith and love are often found extremely valuable in assisting the mind to realize a happier state, and stimulating to its attainment.

As regards the LENGTH of some of these hymns, I cannot do better than quote the words of Bishop Wordsworth, in his admirable Preface to his valued hymnal, *The Holy Year.* Bishop Wordsworth thus writes:

IF some of the hymns in the present volume be thought too long for use in public worship, the author would venture to put in a plea for the emancipation of hymnology from its present straitened limits of four or five verses. Comparatively little spiritual good can be effected by such a slender pittance as that. The office of public worship is not only to promote God's glory by prayer and praise, but also to act thereby upon the mind, heart, and life of the worshipper.

To give greater freedom, expansion, and elasticity to hymnology, would be a happy return to primitive usage; and it would minister fresh life to Christian faith and Christian practice.

A hymn which carries the reader on with a flow of thought, and by a suggestion of holy recollection of the past, and of holy aspirations for the future, nourishes the soul with solid and substantial food, is likely to be the *more* edifying.

The Editor acknowledges, with grateful appreciation, the kindness and courtesy of so many authors, including the highest dignitaries of our Church, whose labours have enriched this volume, and who have most generously given permission to reprint. Their names are placed at the foot of every hymn, thereby not only acknowledging the source, but also affording additional interest and pleasure to the reader. In doing this, he is only following the example of our beloved Church, which has directed her officiating ministers to announce the author or source of each chapter, Epistle, or Gospel, read before their congregations.

Sincere thanks are also rendered to those publishers and owners of copyright who have granted permission to use certain hymns.[1]

Also to Mr. D. Sedgwick, of Sun Street, London, warmest thanks are due, for the great assistance rendered in restoring hymns to their originals, and the discovery of so many authors' names and dates, together with much other valuable information. His hymnological library, the great storehouse from which hymn collectors draw material and information, is perhaps the most complete in the world; while his accurate reprints of our older hymn writers are invaluable.

Permission to reprint has been always carefully sought; but should any name, through inadvertency, or inability to discover the address, have been overlooked, the Editor trusts this apology will be accepted, and leave generously conceded.

Havergal's Psalmody, with its 253 beautiful and varied tunes for all metres, has been prepared as *Companion Volume* to *Songs of Grace and Glory*, by the highly gifted daughter of the late Canon Havergal. This eminent composer, and greatest authority on Ecclesiastical Music, was invited to fill the Professorial Chair of Music at Oxford, but that high honour was declined, in order to devote himself more fully to the duties of an Ambassador of Christ. It was only when laid by through illness from direct ministerial work that he allowed himself the enjoyment of musical research and composition, restoring to the Church the treasures of her best age of Psalmody, clothing them in harmonies at once solid and rich, and representing, in his own new tunes, the sobriety and grandeur of the old school, combined with the fervour and sweetness which characterized his own inspiration.

To the Editor of the Hymnal it is a deeply interesting fact that the last tune of this now sainted composer was written early in the morning of his last conscious day on

[1] Acknowledgment has been requested of the source of the following—Hymns by Bishop C. Wordsworth, from his *Holy Year.* Hymn 258, by permission of Rev. R. Brown-Borthwick, from his *Supplementary Hymn and Tune Book.* Hymns 765 and 920, from *Thoughtful Hours*, by H.L.L. Also Messrs. Rivington have granted the free use of hymns by Bishop Mant; and permission has been purchased from Messrs. Longman for translations by Miss C. Winkworth.

earth, expressly for *Songs of Grace and Glory.* It was before eight o'clock in the morning of April 16, 1870—the day before Easter—that the tune was written, in praise of the Holy Trinity, for hymn No. 4, and is rightly named "*Havergal,*" replete with rich and sweetly solemn strains, appropriate to such a momentous season, and truly characteristic of its author.

The Editor of *Havergal's Psalmody* has not only prepared it as the *Companion Volume* to *Songs of Grace and Glory,* but also composed many new tunes, of the same high character as those of her revered and beloved father, to meet the requirements of special metres.

By the same hand many very choice and beautiful hymns have enriched this Hymnal, setting forth, in accordance with Holy Scripture, the higher mysteries of our faith, and the deep experiences of the believer's heart. Much valuable assistance in the general supervision of the work, and carrying it through the press, has also been kindly rendered, greatly lessening the labours and anxieties connected with it; and to Frances Ridley Havergal, the Church of Christ, as well as the Editor of this volume, are greatly indebted.

No labour or expense has been spared to render *Songs of Grace and Glory* useful and comprehensive, both as a work of reference, instruction, and refreshment for individuals and families, and as a practical and complete supply of the requirements for public worship.

The discovery of authors' names and dates to more than 1,000 hymns; the careful comparison with the originals; and the restoration (as far as practical) to those originals; the selection of suitable texts of Holy Scripture for each hymn; the appropriation of suitable tunes; the arrangement of 1,025 hymns under classified subjects; the drawing up of six carefully prepared indices; and the large correspondence involved throughout the whole; all these several items have fully occupied all the spare time at command of the Editor for the last four years, and drawn largely upon health and strength.

On the other hand, the kind and hearty interest expressed with respect to the work has greatly encouraged and stimulated it.

The Editor desires gratefully and affectionately to record a loving and liberal testimonial from a warm-hearted Congregation. This most generous gift from his parishioners and friends was thoughtfully presented in the form of a noble contribution to the furtherance of the object so dear to their pastor's heart, viz., his offering to the Church of Christ these *Songs of Grace and Glory*—these hymnal treasures from many centuries of prayer and praise. By this pleasing mark of oneness of heart and purpose, the Parishioners of Perry Barr will be ever associated with their Pastor in these interesting researches and labours of love.

May it be found at the great day that we have not laboured in vain, nor spent our strength for nought.

"Faithful is He that calleth you, who also will do it."

And to "the God of all Grace"—who has graciously permitted His servant to commence, carry on, and complete this Work and Labour of Love—to the Triune God—the Covenant-keeping—the Faithful God—be all Praise and Glory. Amen.

Charles B. Snepp.

Perry Barr,
November, 1871.

That was Rev. Snepp's Preface to the 1871 First Edition of S.G.G. Next is his Preface to the finalized, definitive edition of *Songs of Grace and Glory* published in 1880.

PREFACE

TO THE NEW AND ENLARGED MUSICAL EDITION OF

"Songs of Grace and Glory."

THE Editors have been occupied a considerable time in preparing this NEW and ENLARGED Musical Edition. And now it is humbly dedicated to the Triune Jehovah, in the prayerful hope that it may be still further used for making known His revealed TRUTH through the refreshing and impressive melodies of holy Song and Tune. No pains or costs have been spared to make it as perfect and complete as our finite powers permit.

The musical Editor, the late beloved FRANCES RIDLEY HAVERGAL, after composing several New and Beautiful Tunes, and carefully re-arranging the whole, has been called to join the heavenly choir above. Not, however, until she had first bequeathed to the Church of Christ these results of her matured judgment.

Several of her New and Beautiful compositions (which are here published for the first time) bear full and ample testimony to high culture and refinement.

The exquisite tune she named "LINUS," composed only a few months before her death, and written both in the minor and major, affords full illustration of this. Nor can we forget to mention the soothing comfort and happiness imparted on her dying couch as she gave utterance to the deep and holy feelings of her soul in singing "Jesus, I will trust Thee," to her own beautiful tune "HERMAS," which has ever been so deservedly popular. The hymn will be found numbered 569 in this and every edition.

Her honoured Father, the late Canon Havergal, led the way in the reform of Church music; and she has well sustained and carried on the great work of raising the musical standard, and introducing a higher tone of grand and holy music for the more reverential worship of the great and holy God. It is no question of mere favourite views, but the laying down of certain great principles for Church music, and protesting against all *secular* strains, whether operatic, light, or tripping. Frances Ridley Havergal warmly advocated the "*higher class*" of sacred music, and only with a protest admitted a few deviations in deference to the wishes of others.

Many will be surprised at the large number of well known and favourite Tunes to be found here. But the truth concerning these ought to be declared. There is scarcely a True Book of any note in the land, but is indebted to, and has made use of Canon Havergal's Tunes and Harmonizations and those of his daughter. I need only mention the well known tune "EVAN," the popularity of which, in England, Scotland, America, and the Colonies, is quite unprecedented; (it was written by Canon Havergal about the year 1867, see note in "Havergal's Psalmody," page 19 in Preface;) while such tunes as Havilah, Hobah, Zaanaim, Shen, and Chesalon, etc., etc., are still more valuable. Among the most beautiful tunes of his daughter must be reckoned Euodias, Hermas, Persis, Tryphosa, St. Paul, and Linus, etc., together with a number of exquisite Hymn Chants.

The present New Edition has involved a large outlay, both of time and thought, which have been humbly offered to the Lord, in the prayerful hope of edifying and refreshing His Church, and thereby promoting His praise and glory.

Meanwhile the Hymns themselves have received a wide circulation, both at home and abroad, both for private devotion as well as family and public worship.

Testimonies, from Churches and Missionaries, have poured in from all parts, speaking of the spiritual help and blessing received through former editions. Letters from India, Australia, and America tell of the great refreshment received. New Zealand, Cape Town, and the Holy Land could also speak of the same.

It is hoped this New Edition may prove still more useful, and the long continued and prayerful efforts be crowned with enlarged blessing.

This work probably forms the largest collection of Hymns and Tunes in the Church of England in one volume. And these Hymns afford the richest variety, adapted to the varying wants and experiences of the Christian life, comprising every doctrine of Holy Scripture and every truth taught by our beloved and scriptural Church. The price also, being so moderate, places it within the reach of all.

Several fine Tunes have been added to this work; many of them written on purpose, others contributed through the kindness of friends.

From the experience of some years, since first bringing out this work, we have been able to make important and useful changes in the selection of Tunes for some of our Hymns. Experience alone can adequately supply such information. And when it is remembered tunes had to be selected and arranged for ELEVEN HUNDRED hymns (!) the task will appear no light and easy matter. GREAT PAINS were bestowed by that eminent servant of God, Frances Ridley Havergal; and she has left a MEMORIAL in THIS as well as in her OTHER works, of that highly gifted mind and refinement of taste with which she was so richly endowed. We had together planned the whole work, and bestowed much time upon the selection of so many tunes of varied metres and characteristics. A few only were left for after determination.

And now what remained to be done after her lamented departure has been both skillfully and kindly carried out by my friend, Septimus Ernest Luke Lillingston, Esq., whose musical genius fully qualified him to watch over and execute the remainder of the work. In corroboration of this our readers are referred to that sublime hymn of Toplady, No. 439, which having seven verses of different lengths, and different metres, had hitherto defied all efforts to compose any grand and suitable tune. This great difficulty is however now fully overcome by Mr. Lillingston, as will be seen in the touching and beautiful Hymn Chant named "Celestial," composed by him and so exquisitely adapted to the words.

Our eleven hundred Hymns are arranged under their appropriate subjects with a Tune printed to each. References to alternative Tunes are also given where desirable.

The FIRST Index (which is, perhaps, the most interesting of all) shows the ARRANGEMENT of Hymns under their own proper subject; and the subjects are taken in consecutive order according to their relative importance, the whole forming a perfect synopsis of the revealed Truths of Holy Scripture.

A carefully revised Index, No. II., shows WHAT HYMNS are more especially suitable for EACH SUNDAY and HOLY DAY throughout the Christian year.

An Index of AUTHORS, No. III., with their respective Hymns, is also given, showing where to find all the Hymns of the various Authors.

In like manner an Index of TUNES, No. IV., alphabetically arranged, shows all the hymns that may be sung to each Tune, and the numerals show where to find them.

ANOTHER Index of TUNES, No. V., arranged according to metre, points out at a glance all the L. M. and C. M. and S. M. and peculiar metres in succession, and their respective Hymns.

Lastly, at end of book, the Sixth Index gives the First Lines of all the Hymns, and where they are to be found.

The eleven tunes given to the Doxologies, being some of most general use and greatest merit, and being placed together, may often be found acceptable for reference, besides their use with the Doxologies.

The Editor cannot but record the kind and gracious Providence of God in raising up one after another to assist him in carrying out this great work. It was thrust upon him many years ago by friends who knew the Hymnal Treasures he possessed, many of them very scarce and valuable. After much reluctance he consented to undertake it; and, amidst great difficulties and numerous pressing engagements, is constrained to bear this testimony, "The Lord hath helped me." Verily the work has grown and reached such dimensions as he never contemplated. Various Editions and Forms, represented by the letters A, B, C, up to S, T, U, have been published; and more than three hundred thousand copies printed.

In many respects it differs from the ordinary Church Hymn Book, since it is prepared for Private and Family Devotion, as well as for Public Worship, thereby presenting the advantage of ONE HYMN BOOK for all purposes both in private and public. The preparation of this work has been particularly helpful, not only through the beautiful hymns themselves, but also in the careful selection and arrangement of them under the many precious doctrines and truths of Holy Scripture.

May the Lord Jehovah vouchsafe to those who shall make use of this volume as rich or still richer and more abundant blessing.

And to the Triune and Covenant God, FATHER, SON, and HOLY GHOST, be devoutly and gratefully ascribed all Honour and Glory and Praise, now, and throughout the countless ages of eternity.

CHARLES B. SNEPP.

Perry Barr,

That was Rev. Snepp's Preface to the definitive edition of *Songs of Grace and Glory* published in 1880. Next is F.R.H.'s Preface to the Musical Edition of S.G.G. first published in 1876.

ORIGINAL PREFACE TO THE MUSICAL EDITION

OF

"Songs of Grace and Glory."

(BY FRANCES RIDLEY HAVERGAL.)

MANY will be surprised at the large number of well-known and favourite tunes in "Havergals' Psalmody." The fact is that "Havergal's Old Church Psalmody" has been the fountain from which editors of subsequent collections have drawn, either at first or second hand, and the original guide to many valuable tune sources, both English and foreign. It was the Columbus of tune-books; the pioneer, not to a New, but to an Old World of musical treasure. *Now*, the route is open and easy.

The retiring and unselfish spirit of its editor, as well as his devotion to yet higher work, prevented that assertion of its true position before the multitude which has always been accorded to it by the highest musical authorities.

The selections from "Havergal's Psalmody" will be found, as experience has proved them to be, easily learnt, greatly liked, and practically adapted for congregational singing. Of one of these, Dr. Lowell Mason, the great American promoter of choral singing, wrote as follows:

> I have lately introduced into my choir, and sung with admirable effect, your tune "Eden." The effect of it was truly magnificent. My choir consists of about sixty singers; the different parts are well sustained, and about equally balanced. I have never heard anything come nearer to my *beau ideal* of Church Music than did the singing of this tune, on a fine Sabbath morning, in a church filled with people. It made a deep impression; and the next day one and another was asking, 'What tune did you sing yesterday morning?' 'Where did you get that tune?' etc. The performance of 'Eden' makes one feel as did Jacob at Luz, and involuntarily exclaim, 'This is none other but the house of God, and this is the gate of heaven.' Wonderful would be the effect of Psalmody were all the people to unite in such lofty and majestic strains."—April 30, 1847.

In order to meet the increasing proportion of "peculiar measures," a number of tunes have been adapted from the Rev. W. H. Havergal's own melodies (chiefly from unpublished MSS.), while, for extra measures which could not be thus supplied, tunes have been added by other hands [F. R. H. and others].

The *name* of each tune at once supplies information as to its origin. Old English, Scotch, or German tunes bear respectively English, Scotch, or German names; those by the Rev. W. H. Havergal are named, with a few exceptions, from the natural geography of the Bible; the tunes added by F. R. H. [Frances Ridley Havergal] are named from "the friends of St. Paul."

"Havergal's Psalmody," a memorial to one whose works do follow him, was originally given to the church by his devoted widow, and "dedicated to his beloved, honoured, and cherished memory." The Large Type or Organ editions of "Havergal's Psalmody" contain Kyries, Glorias, and other additions not included in the present hymnal edition; while editions A and B contain Prefaces and Historical Notes, which are quoted as "a treasury of information and an armoury of defence of the principles of Church Music." A and D include "A Century of Chants." [1]

As the tunes have not been affixed to the hymns without much thought and prayer, and very careful consideration as to which tune will best develop the spirit of each hymn, and emphasize its most important points, it is strongly advised that, generally speaking, the tunes indicated should be adhered to.

On the other hand, as the great aim of making our singing congregational is not attained if too many new tunes are attempted at once, it is well to introduce them *gradually*, repeating each newly learnt tune at short intervals, until quite familiar. It is advisable to begin with a few tunes in such metres as occur abundantly.

The following selection of peculiar metres may be found useful at first, as giving a wide range of hymns. Hermas, for 6 5, 6 5. D.; Zoan I., for spirited and joyous hymns in 7 6, 7 6. D.; and Mahanaim (or Goldbach), for

[1]All of which can be obtained from Nisbet and Co., 21, Berners Street, London.

quieter hymns in the same metre; Lubeck and Patmos, respectively, for the two classes of hymns in 7 7, 7 7; Nassau and Sihor, for 7 7, 7 7, 7 7; Culbach and Frankfort (or Godesberg), for 8 7, 8 7; Zaanaim and Idumea, for 8 7, 8 7, 4 7 (or 8 7, 8 7, 8 7); Magdalene College and Kedron, for 8 8 6. D.; and Paran, for 11 11, 11 11.

1875. FRANCES RIDLEY HAVERGAL.

That was F.R.H.'s Preface to the Musical Edition of S.G.G. first published in 1876. Next is her "Supplementary Remarks" published near the front of *Havergal's Psalmody and Century of Chants* in 1871.

Supplementary Remarks.

1871.

MANY will be surprised at the large number of well-known and favourite tunes in *Havergal's Psalmody.* The fact is, that *Havergal's Old Church Psalmody* has been the fountain from which editors of subsequent collections have drawn—either at first or second hand—and the original guide to many valuable tune-sources, both English and foreign. It was the Columbus of tune-books; the pioneer, not to a New, but to an Old World of musical treasure. *Now*, the route is open and easy.

The retiring and unselfish spirit of its editor, as well as his devotion to yet higher work, prevented that assertion of its true position before the multitude, which has always been accorded to it by the highest musical authorities. "Little more than a sovereign was expended in advertising it;" and only once did he pen a remark upon any unfair treatment of his work. "To the multitudinous applications for permission to reprint tunes from the *Old Church Psalmody* no refusal was ever given, nor was any remuneration named. But the permission, when granted, has not always been duly acknowledged. Some tunes have been properly acknowledged; but others, taken *wholly* or chiefly from the same source, have been printed as though they belonged to the editor of the collection in which they appear. These oversights, which ought not to be made, have too frequently occurred." Also,—"It was due to *Old Church Psalmody* that they who were allowed to borrow its tunes, should likewise have adopted its names."

The selections from "*A Hundred Psalm and Hymn Tunes, by the Rev. W. H. Havergal,*" will be found, as experience has proved them to be, easily learnt, greatly liked, and practically adapted for congregational singing. Of one of these, Dr. Lowell Mason, the great American promoter of choral singing, wrote as follows:—

> I have lately introduced into my choir, and sung with admirable effect, your tune, "ST. NICHOLAS" [now called "EDEN," No. 38 in this volume]. The effect of it was truly magnificent. My choir consists of about sixty singers; the different parts are well sustained, and about equally balanced. I have never heard anything come nearer to my *beau ideal* of Church Music than did the singing of this tune, on a fine Sabbath morning, in a church filled with people. It made a deep impression; and the next day, one and another was asking, "What tune did you sing yesterday morning?" "Where did you get that tune?" etc. The performance of "St. Nicholas" [Eden] makes one feel as did Jacob at Luz, and involuntarily exclaim, "This is none other but the house of God, and this is the gate of heaven." Wonderful would be the effect of the Psalmody were all the people to unite in such lofty and majestic strains.—April 30, 1847.

In order to meet the increasing proportion of "peculiar measures," a number of tunes have been adapted from the Rev. W. H. Havergal's own melodies, (chiefly from unpublished MSS.), while, for extra measures which could not be thus supplied, a few tunes have been added by another hand. The present volume, therefore, contains tunes for all measures in the best modern hymnals. It is, however, specially adapted to the new hymnal, *Songs of Grace and Glory*, with its 1,000 carefully selected hymns, edited by the Rev. C. B. Snepp, to whom the editor of *Havergal's*

Psalmody is greatly indebted for much kind counsel in the work.

Any clergyman or organist will be willingly supplied with a Tuneal Key for whatever hymnal he may wish to use in connection with *Havergal's Psalmody.*

The arrangement of the tunes is strictly metrical. After the regular L.M.'s, C.M.'s, and S.M.'s, the P.M.'s follow *in order of length of measure,* beginning with 5555, and ending with 12 10.[1] When several tunes belong to one measure, they are carefully arranged *in order of character*, beginning with the jubilant, and shading gradually to the plaintive, so that if an alternative tune for any hymn be desired, it will never be far to seek.

[1] (N.B.—15 15, 15 15, will be found under 87, 87 D.)

The nomenclature of *Havergal's Psalmody* is systematic. The *name* of each tune at once supplies information as to its origin. Old English, Scotch or German tunes, bear respectively English, Scotch or German names; those by the Rev. W. H. Havergal are named (with a few exceptions), from the natural geography of the Bible; the added tunes are named from "the friends of St. Paul." No departure from these rules has been made without some necessitating reason.

Amens have been appended for optional use, wherever such a close is not unsuitable to the "suitable words."

May this memorial, to one "whose works do follow" him, be to the glory of his God, who has now "made him most blessed for ever."

F. R. Havergal.

II Chron. 32. 8.
Upon Thy word I rest,
So strong, so sure;
So full of comfort blest,
So sweet, so pure.
The word that changeth not, that faileth never!
My King! I rest upon Thy word for ever.

This is F.R.H.'s fair copy autograph of a verse on II Chronicles 32:8, on page 165 of her Manuscript Book № VIII. This was one of a set of "Verses on Texts" written in 1877. "With him is an arm of flesh; but with us is the Lord our God to help us, and to fight our battles. And the people rested themselves upon the words of Hezekiah king of Judah." II Chronicles 32:8

In this available space, this very late poem by F.R.H. is given, written in April, 1879, before she died June 3, likely one of her last four or five completed poems. Facsimile copies of her rough draft and fair copy autograph of this are given on pages XXVI-XXVII of Volume I of the Havergal edition. The fair copy autograph of a single verse by F.R.H. on II Chronicles 32:8 was written in 1877, the first four lines being the first four lines of the second verse of this very late poem. This was clearly meant to be set to music and sung.

The Scripture cannot be broken.

John 10:35

Upon the Word I rest,
Each pilgrim day;
This golden staff is best
For all the way.
What Jesus Christ hath spoken,
Can*not* be broken!

Upon the Word I rest,
So strong, so sure,
So full of comfort blest,
So sweet, so pure!
The charter of salvation,
Faith's broad foundation.

Upon the Word I stand!
That cannot die!
Christ seals it in my hand.
He cannot lie!
The word that faileth never!
Abiding ever!

Chorus. The Master hath said it! Rejoicing in this,
We ask not for sign or for token;
His word is enough for our confident bliss,—
"The Scripture *cannot* be broken!"

Frances Ridley Havergal

The following article by F.R.H. (found among Havergal manuscripts and papers, date not known, almost surely 1872) was published in the *Perry Barr Magazine*, the parish magazine of St. John's Church in Perry Barr (near Birmingham, now part of Birmingham), where Rev. Charles Busbridge Snepp was the vicar (pastor). In various articles in this periodical, F.R.H. was anonymously named "Our Own Correspondent." She describes the hymnbook *Songs of Grace and Glory* edited by Rev. Snepp and F.R.H. Rev. Snepp was the architect and leader of the work. Frances was very modestly silent about her part in the volume. She was the editor of all the music for the hymnbook, preparing, checking, finalizing every measure of music, an enormous and enormously impressive body of work. She also composed a number of scores and wrote the words of 55 of the hymns for *Songs of Grace and Glory*, and collaborated with Rev. Snepp extensively, invaluably. This was a long, costly, true labor of love by both of them. This hymnbook was first published in 1872 with the words only, and the hymnbook had a "Companion volume," *Havergal's Psalmody and Century of Chants*. This "Companion volume" was published in 1871, edited by F.R.H., and most of the music in it had been composed by her father, Rev. William Henry Havergal, with a few scores composed and added by F.R.H. H.P.C.C. contained the music for all the hymns in *Songs of Grace and Glory*, and with each text of words in S.G.G. was written the number of the score of music for that hymn in the Companion Volume H.P.C.C. In 1876 the "Musical Edition" was published, with both the words and music together in *Songs of Grace and Glory*. This very valuable, richly beneficial hymnal became very obscure, though a copy dated 1883 says "Three Hundred and Thirteenth Thousand" (now in the British Library, London). Though a number of the articles written by her were unsigned, anonymous, here her name Frances Ridley Havergal is printed at the end of this article. Like most of the articles published in periodicals and found among Havergal manuscripts and papers, the date is not known.

PARISH EVENTS.

FROM "OUR OWN CORRESPONDENT."

(*Extract from "Home Words " Perry Barr Magazine.*)

A COMING "PARISH EVENT."

A long anticipated "*Parish Event*" will, it is hoped, take place before the next Magazine reaches all its readers, viz., the introduction of the new hymnal, "*Songs of Grace and Glory*," into the churches and homes of Perry Barr. People ask what it will be like, and how it will differ from other hymn books; so a few words of explanation of the nature and results of their Pastor's long and laborious work for the Church of God in general, and for his parish in particular, may not be out of place.

"Songs of Grace and Glory" contains more than a thousand hymns. Some of them have been treasures of the Church for centuries, others are quite new. All our old favourites will be found in it, as well as many which are even more beautiful and admirable.

The hymns are arranged according to a very perfect and comprehensive scheme of subjects, embracing every Scripture doctrine, every season of our Church's year, every phase of Christian experience, and every duty, sorrow, or joy of our homes. It is not too much to say that there cannot be a throb or a thrill in any heart among us which will not find a true and touching echo in some strain of "*Songs of Grace and Glory.*"

But we must *sing* them! And so, to save all trouble of wondering—"What tune can we have?"—the name of a suitable tune is printed at the top of every hymn. In many cases two tunes are given; so that, if we do not know the first, we have the chance of finding that the second is more familiar. These tunes will all be found in the "*Companion Volume*," advertised at the end of this Magazine.

Who wrote all these hymns?—It is interesting to know; for often the very name of the writer makes us love a hymn the more. We shall know all about it now, for at the foot of each hymn stands not only the name of the author, but the date. So, when a hymn is given out, and we see "Eighth Century," it will surely add to our interest to know that it was sung "to the praise and glory of God" by voices which went up to sing the "New Song" eleven hundred years ago. But it has been no easy thing to find out all these names and dates; and many an hour of patient search or repeated correspondence has been devoted to this by him who has spared no toil to make his work in all respects complete, and worthy of its great object, its dedication to the Triune Jehovah.

Beautiful hymns have often been altered and re-altered till the saintly or sainted writers would hardly know them again; and we feel that, if possible, we should like to have them as they were really written at first. This, again, has cost more labour than any one who had had no share in it would imagine. Mr. Snepp has discovered and restored the original reading of numbers of mutilated hymns. Sometimes, however, our old writers used expressions which are now considered ungrammatical or otherwise faulty; sometimes a line, which might be made to sound all right in reading, was found to be very imperfect for singing, owing to inattention to the correct placing of accented syllables; and sometimes an alteration was such an obvious improvement that, having been adopted by general consent, it would be a pity to return to the original; in these cases alterations have been either made or retained, and this is indicated by (a) placed after the writers' names. Wherever correction has appeared absolutely necessary, the greatest care has been taken to adhere as nearly as possible to the originals

Our beautiful hymns should lead us to love and value all the more the music of God's own Word. So, over every hymn we shall find a text, the key note of the "song" which follows. Often we find that what an earthly writer has taken many lines to express, the One Inspirer has already summed up in a few words; and while the hymn explains the text, the text sums and seals the truth and beauty of the hymn.

Perhaps we think it will take a long time to learn to find our way about such a large collection,—we fancy we shall not be able to find what we want, even if we are sure it is there. This is met by a set of such full and carefully planned indices as no other hymnal can show; so that if we wish to lay our finger upon any particular hymn, text, tune, author and date, subject, or Sunday service, we shall be able to do so in a minute. Special attention, however, should be given to Index No. 1., as, if we study that, the whole scheme of the book will be within our grasp at once.

The outside of "*Songs of Grace and Glory*" will need no introduction, as it is quite attractive enough to stand on its own merits at first sight. There will be seven editions, marked A, B, C, D, E, F, and G, so we shall have plenty of choice. "G" will be wonderfully cheap, as Mr. Snepp will supply it at one shilling, by a sacrifice upon it. That is, we shall get hymns at the rate of very little more than 1*d.* per 100, with strong and handsome binding into the bargain. "A" is a special and very beautiful edition on large paper, intended as a drawing room table or gift book. It is well that this will be in plenty of time for Christmas presents; for what could be a better gift than "*Songs of Grace and Glory*" at that holy and happy season? Far better than useless ornaments, or books which rather hinder than help the "onward and upward" progress. "B", "C", and "D" are in large and clear type, "D" in plain binding, "C" cloth gilt, and "B" very handsome leather gilt; "E" and "F" are smaller, but also very clear type.

Those who have already seen the work, now so nearly completed, cannot but feel that Mr. Snepp is giving, not to his people only, but to his Church and country, a treasure which will outlive the present generation of its singers and readers. The outlay, not merely of money (which is very great), but of far more precious time and health, is not grudged but laid at his Master's feet, in the earnest hope and belief that He will not only accept it, but by the power of His blessing make His servant's work a wide and mighty means of cheering and quickening His people, of spreading the truths of His gospel, and of setting forth His praise from generation to generation.

Frances Ridley Havergal.

[Note: After the facsimile copy of *Songs of Grace and Glory*, the hymn scores within S.G.G. that were composed by F.R.H. are given together as a set, gathered together in one place and copied in facsimile from S.G.G., on pages 1001–1024 of Volume V of the Havergal edition.]

SONGS OF GRACE AND GLORY.

HYMNAL TREASURES OF THE CHURCH OF CHRIST FROM THE SIXTH TO THE NINETEENTH CENTURY.

FULL EDITIONS. Ex. fcap. 8vo.
Containing 1025 *Hymns.*

		s.	d.
A.	Extra size, superior binding, gilt edges. Pulpit, Library, or Gift Edition, crimson, ...	10	0
	Large Type, Seven Indices, and Full Preface.		
AA.	Leather, gilt lettered, crimson or dark purple, ...	6	6
B.	Leather limp, gilt lettered, do.	5	0
C.	Cloth boards, do. dark or bright blue, ...	4	0
CC.	Do. thin, do. Two Indices, no Preface, . . .	3	6
D.	Cloth limp, plain, dark blue, do. . . .	3	0
	Small Type (Nonpareil), Three Indices, Short Preface.		
DD.	Leather, bevelled edges, gilt lettered, crimson, ...	3	0
E.	Leather limp, gilt lettered, ...	2	6
F.	Cloth boards, do. dark blue, ...	1	6
G.	Cloth limp, plain, ...	1	0
	Bourgeois (Medium Type), with Appendix, 1094 *Hymns.*		
T.	Leather limp, gilt lettered, ...	5	0
U.	Cloth boards, do.	4	0
V.	Cloth limp, plain, ...	3	0

PUBLIC WORSHIP EDITIONS.
Containing 520 *Hymns selected from the Full Edition.*
Large Type. Ex. fcap. 8*vo.*

H.	Leather, gilt lettered, crimson or dark purple, ...	3	6
I.	Leather limp, do. do.	3	0
J.	Cloth boards, do. dark, medium, or bright blue, ...	2	6
K.	Cloth limp, plain, do. . . .	2	0
	Medium Type. Super royal 32*mo.*		
L.	Leather, gilt lettered, crimson or dark purple, ...	2	6
M.	Leather limp, do. do.	2	3
N.	Cloth boards, do. dark, medium, or bright blue, ...	1	6
O.	Cloth, ...	1	0
P.	Stiff paper covers, ...	0	9

MUSICAL EDITION. Tunes and Words together, 3s. 6d. in cloth.

SONGS OF GRACE AND GLORY FOR MISSION SERVICES, Etc. Sup. royal 32mo. *Containing* 135 *Hymns selected from the Full Edition.* Price 2d. Cloth, 4d. Gilt, 6d.

CHILDREN'S SONGS OF GRACE AND GLORY. 16mo, square. *Containing* 110 *Hymns selected from the Full Edition.* Price 1½d. Cloth, 4d. Gilt, 6d.

N.B.—*A valuable Appendix of* 69 *Hymns, suited to the special requirements of the present day, may be had bound up with any of the above for* 6*d. extra, except* P, *with which it will be* 3*d. extra, and* F, G, N, *and* O, *with which it will be* 4*d. extra.*

The New and Enlarged Musical Edition of

SONGS OF GRACE AND GLORY

Comprises all the Tunes in Havergal's Psalmody.

4to. Price 6s.

Companion Volume to 'Songs of Grace and Glory.'

HAVERGAL'S PSALMODY AND CENTURY OF CHANTS.

Without Chants. E. 3s.

A SELECTION OF 100 TUNES FROM THE ABOVE, suited to Mission Services and 'Children's Songs of Grace and Glory.' Price 4d. Cloth limp, 6d.

LONDON: JAMES NISBET & CO., 21 BERNERS STREET.

This advertisement page on Songs of Grace and Glory *and* Havergal's Psalmody and Century of Chants *was found at the back of a copy of* Letters by the Late Frances Ridley Havergal, *a copy published by the American publisher Anson D. F. Randolph & Co.*

SONGS OF GRACE AND GLORY:

HYMNAL TREASURES OF THE CHURCH OF CHRIST FROM THE SIXTH TO THE NINETEENTH CENTURY.

	Large Type.	s.	d.		Small Type.	s.	d.
A	Extra size, gilt edges, gift edition	10	0	DD	Leather gilt, bevelled edges	3	0
AA	Leather gilt	6	6	E	Leather limp	2	6
B	Leather limp	5	0	F	Cloth boards, gilt	1	6
C	Cloth boards, gilt	4	0	G	Cloth limp, plain	1	0
D	Cloth limp, plain	3	6				

Music for the Hymns.

COMPANION VOLUME TO "SONGS OF GRACE AND GLORY."

		s.	d.
A	Havergal's Psalmody and Chants, *strong* and handsome binding, prefaces and portraits	6	6
D	Do. do. plain limp cloth, no prefaces, *3s. 6d.* Paper Covers	2	6
	Do. without Chants, B, *5s.*; E, *3s.*; paper covers	2	3

Songs of Grace and Glory. For Private, Family, and Public Worship. Being Hymnal Treasures of the Church of Christ from the Fourth to the Nineteenth Century.

Large type, . 10s., 6s. 6d., 5s., 4s., 3s. 6d., 3s.
Small type, . 3s., 2s. 6d., 1s. 6d., 1s.

Edited by CHARLES B. SNEPP, LL.M., Vicar of Perry Barr.

'SONGS OF GRACE AND GLORY,' to which Havergal's Psalmody forms 'Companion Volume,' contains 1025 Hymns, embracing every Scripture Doctrine, every Church Festival or special occasion, and every phase of Christian life and experience. Suitable tunes, with metres, authors, dates, and texts, are affixed to each hymn; a table of Hymns for Sundays and Holy Days, and seven Indices, facilitate use and reference. *It claims to be the most comprehensive and complete Hymnal in the Church of England.*

ABRIDGED EDITIONS.

PUBLIC WORSHIP EDITION. Containing 520 Hymns. Large and medium type. Price from 9d. to 3s. 6d.

SONGS OF GRACE AND GLORY FOR MISSION SERVICES, Etc. Containing 135 Hymns. Price 2d.; cloth, 4d.; gilt, 6d.

THE CHILDREN'S SONGS OF GRACE AND GLORY. Containing 110 Hymns. Price 1½d.; cloth, 4d.; gilt, 6d.

THE HALFPENNY EDITION. 29 Hymns. Price 3s. 6d. per 100; 30s. per 1000.

For convenience of reference and simultaneous use of all or any of these books, the number to each Hymn remains the same in all the Editions.

London: JAMES NISBET & CO., 21 Berners Street.

These are two more advertisements of S.G.G. The top one was found at the bottom of a page in the Perry Barr Magazine, *a parish magazine for St. John's Church, Perry Barr, near Birmingham, England. The lower one was found in an advertisement page at the end of a copy of F.R.H.'s* The Four Happy Days, *published by Nisbet and dated 1874 on the title page.*

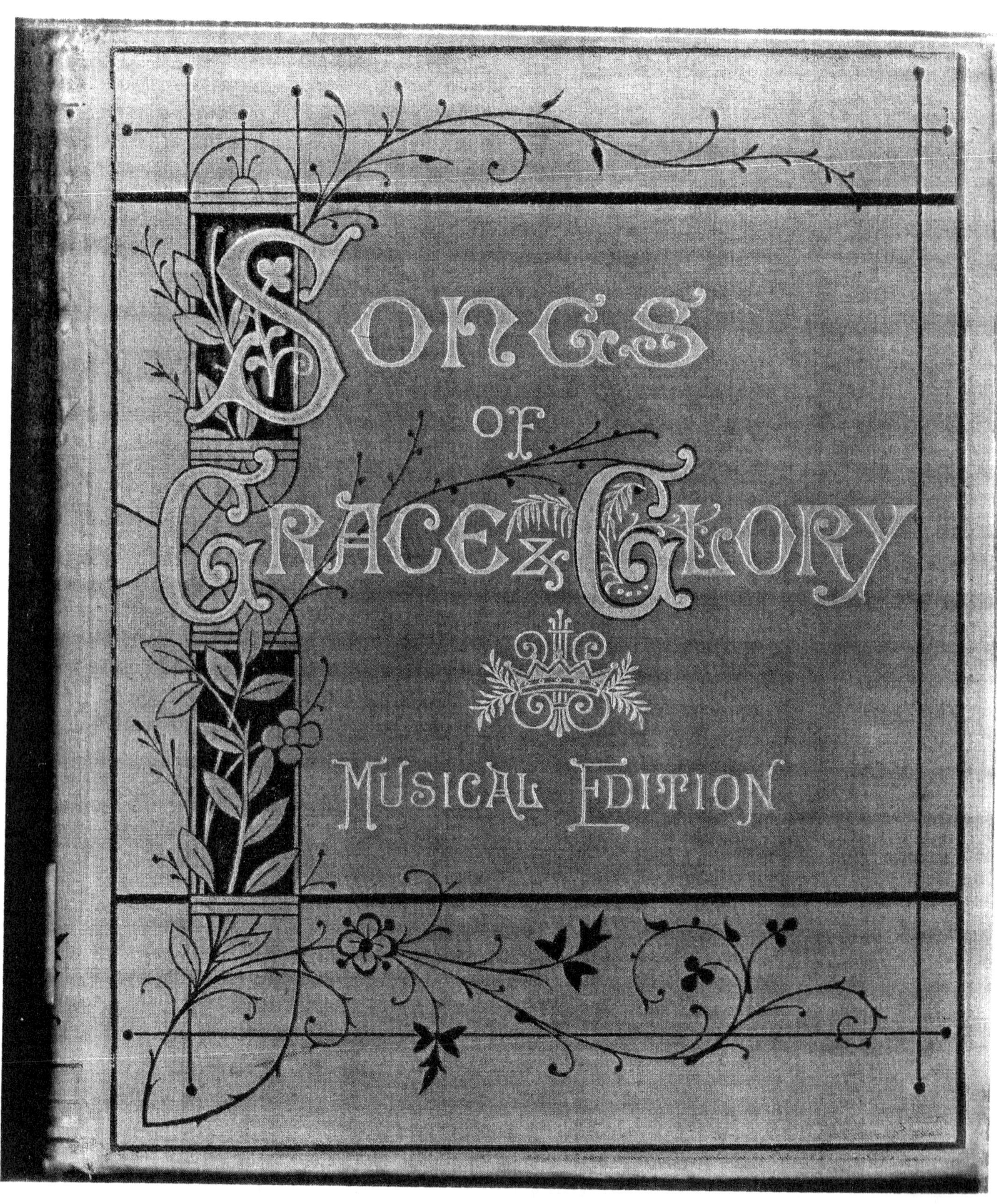
SONGS
OF
GRACE & GLORY
MUSICAL EDITION

SONGS
OF
GRACE AND GLORY.

NEW AND ENLARGED

MUSICAL EDITION.

Hymnal and Musical Treasures of the Church of Christ

FROM MANY CENTURIES.

EDITED BY THE LATE

FRANCES RIDLEY HAVERGAL,

AND

CHARLES B. SNEPP, LL.M.,

Vicar of Perry Barr.

FULL EDITION OF 1100 HYMNS WITH TUNES.

LONDON: JAMES NISBET AND CO., 21, BERNERS STREET.

MDCCCLXXX.

This final, definitive edition (with only a few, possibly 8 or 10, scores not finished by Frances and done by another) was published around six months after she died (June 3, 1879), and around six months before Charles Busbridge Snepp died (June 23, 1880).

Butler & Tanner,
The Selwood Printing Works,
Frome, and London.

[The facing inscription page of *Songs of Grace and Glory* was the desire of all of Snepp's and F.R.H.'s life and works, to glorify God and to help, enrich, bless others, of which "Covenant Blessings" is an example. This is hymn number 83 on page 590 of Volume V of the Havergal edition.

Covenant Blessings

"He hath made with me an everlasting covenant, ordered in all things, and sure." — II Samuel 23 : 5

Jehovah's Covenant shall endure,
All ordered, everlasting, sure!
O child of God, rejoice to trace
Thy portion in its glorious grace.

'T is thine, for Christ is given to be
The Covenant of God to thee:
In Him, God's golden scroll of light,
The darkest truths are clear and bright.

O sorrowing sinner, well He knew,
Ere time began, what He would do!
then rest thy hope within the veil;
His covenant mercies shall not fail.

O doubting one, the Eternal Three
Are pledged in faithfulness for thee;
Claim every promise, sweet and sure,
By covenant oath of God secure.

O waiting one, each moment's fall
Is marked by love that planned them all;
Thy times, all ordered by His hand,
In God's eternal covenant stand.

O feeble one, look up and see
Strong consolation sworn for thee;
Jehovah's glorious arm is shown,
His covenant strength is all thine own.

O mourning one, each stroke of love
A covenant blessing yet shall prove;
His covenant love shall be thy stay;
His covenant grace be as thy day.

O Love that chose, O Love that died,
O Love that sealed and sanctified!
All glory, glory, glory be,
O covenant Triune God, to Thee!

Frances Ridley Havergal, 1871]

To the Glory of God,

THE FATHER—THE SON—AND THE HOLY GHOST,

ONE,

TRIUNE, AND EVER BLESSED JEHOVAH,

AS

REVEALED IN HOLY SCRIPTURE,

IN ALL DIVINE PERFECTIONS,

AND IN COVENANT RELATIONSHIP WITH HIS PEOPLE,

THE "GOD OF ALL GRACE,"

THESE SONGS OF "GRACE AND GLORY"

ARE HUMBLY AND PRAYERFULLY

INSCRIBED.

CONTENTS.

* These Seven Tunes are added in this edition, so that in *one volume* ALL THE TUNES required for every Hymn in every edition of "Songs of Grace and Glory" may here be found complete.

PREFACE

TO THE NEW AND ENLARGED MUSICAL EDITION OF

"Songs of Grace and Glory."

THE Editors have been occupied a considerable time in preparing this NEW and ENLARGED Musical Edition. And now it is humbly dedicated to the Triune Jehovah, in the prayerful hope that it may be still further used for making known His revealed TRUTH through the refreshing and impressive melodies of holy Song and Tune. No pains or costs have been spared to make it as perfect and complete as our finite powers permit.

The musical Editor, the late beloved FRANCES RIDLEY HAVERGAL, after composing several New and Beautiful Tunes, and carefully re-arranging the whole, has been called to join the heavenly choir above. Not, however, until she had first bequeathed to the Church of Christ these results of her matured judgment.

Several of her New and Beautiful compositions (which are here published for the first time) bear full and ample testimony to high culture and refinement.

The exquisite tune she named "LINUS," composed only a few months before her death, and written both in the minor and major, affords full illustration of this. Nor can we forget to mention the soothing comfort and happiness imparted on her dying couch as she gave utterance to the deep and holy feelings of her soul in singing "Jesus, I will trust Thee," to her own beautiful tune "HERMAS," which has ever been so deservedly popular. The hymn will be found numbered 569 in this and every edition.

Her honoured Father, the late Canon Havergal, led the way in the reform of Church music; and she has well sustained and carried on the great work of raising the musical standard, and introducing a higher tone of grand and holy music for the more reverential worship of the great and holy God. It is no question of mere favourite views, but the laying down of certain great principles for Church music, and protesting against all *secular* strains, whether operatic, light, or tripping. Frances Ridley Havergal warmly advocated the "*higher class*" of sacred music, and only with a protest admitted a few deviations in deference to the wishes of others.

Many will be surprised at the large number of well known and favourite Tunes to be found here. But the truth concerning these ought to be declared. There is scarcely a Tune Book of any note in the land, but is indebted to, and has made use of Canon Havergal's Tunes and Harmonizations and those of his daughter. I need only mention the well known tune "EVAN," the popularity of which, in England, Scotland, America, and the Colonies, is quite unprecedented; (it was written by Canon Havergal about the year 1867, see note in "Havergal's Psalmody," page 19 in Preface;) while such tunes as Havilah, Hobah, Zaanaim, Shen, and Chesalon, etc., etc., are still more valuable. Among the most beautiful tunes of his daughter must be reckoned Euodias, Hermas, Persis, Tryphosa, St. Paul, and Linus, etc., together with a number of exquisite Hymn Chants.

The present New Edition has involved a large outlay, both of time and thought, which have been humbly offered to the Lord, in the prayerful hope of edifying and refreshing His Church, and thereby promoting His praise and glory.

Meanwhile the Hymns themselves have received a wide circulation, both at home and abroad, both for private devotion as well as family and public worship.

Testimonies, from Churches and Missionaries, have poured in from all parts, speaking of the spiritual help and blessing received through former editions. Letters from India, Australia, and America tell of the great refreshment received. New Zealand, Cape Town, and the Holy Land could also speak of the same.

It is hoped this New Edition may prove still more useful, and the long continued and prayerful efforts be crowned with enlarged blessing.

This work probably forms the largest collection of Hymns and Tunes in the Church of England in one volume. And these Hymns afford the richest variety, adapted to the varying wants and experiences of the Christian life, comprising every doctrine of Holy Scripture and every truth taught by our beloved and scriptural Church. The price also, being so moderate, places it within the reach of all.

Several fine Tunes have been added to this work; many of them written on purpose, others contributed through the kindness of friends.

From the experience of some years, since first bringing out this work, we have been able to make important and useful changes in the selection of Tunes for some of our Hymns. Experience alone can adequately supply such information. And when it is remembered tunes had to be selected and arranged for ELEVEN HUNDRED hymns (!) the task will appear no light and easy matter. GREAT PAINS were bestowed by that eminent servant of God, Frances Ridley Havergal; and she has left a MEMORIAL in THIS as well as in her OTHER works, of that highly gifted mind and refinement of taste with which she was so richly endowed. We had together planned the whole work, and bestowed much time upon the selection of so many tunes of varied metres and characteristics. A few only were left for after determination.

And now what remained to be done after her lamented departure has been both skilfully and kindly carried out by my friend, Septimus Ernest Luke Lillingston, Esq., whose musical genius fully qualified him to watch over and execute the remainder of the work. In corroboration of this our readers are referred to that sublime hymn of Toplady, No. 439, which having seven verses of different lengths, and different metres, had hitherto defied all efforts to compose any grand and suitable tune. This great difficulty is however now fully overcome by Mr. Lillingston, as will be seen in the touching and beautiful Hymn Chant named "Celestial," composed by him and so exquisitely adapted to the words.

Our eleven hundred Hymns are arranged under their appropriate subjects with a Tune printed to each. References to alternative Tunes are also given where desirable.

The First Index (which is, perhaps, the most interesting of all) shows the ARRANGEMENT of Hymns under their own proper subject; and the subjects are taken in consecutive order according to their relative importance, the whole forming a perfect synopsis of the revealed Truths of Holy Scripture.

A carefully revised Index, No. II., shows WHAT HYMNS are more especially suitable for EACH SUNDAY and HOLY DAY throughout the Christian year.

An Index of AUTHORS, No. III., with their respective Hymns, is also given, showing where to find all the Hymns of the various Authors.

In like manner an Index of TUNES, No. IV., alphabetically arranged, shows all the hymns that may be sung to each Tune, and the numerals show where to find them.

ANOTHER Index of TUNES, No. V., arranged according to metre, points out at a glance all the L. M. and C. M. and S. M. and peculiar metres in succession, and their respective Hymns.

Lastly, at end of book, the Sixth Index gives the First Lines of all the Hymns, and where they are to be found.

The eleven tunes given to the Doxologies, being some of most general use and greatest merit, and being placed together, may often be found acceptable for reference, besides their use with the Doxologies.

The Editor cannot but record the kind and gracious Providence of God in raising up one after another to assist him in carrying out this great work. It was thrust upon him many years ago by friends who knew the Hymnal Treasures he possessed, many of them very scarce and valuable. After much reluctance he consented to undertake it; and, amidst great difficulties and numerous pressing engagements, is constrained to bear this testimony, "The Lord hath helped me." Verily the work has grown and reached such dimensions as he never contemplated. Various Editions and Forms, represented by the letters A, B, C, up to S, T, U, have been published; and more than three hundred thousand copies printed.

In many respects it differs from the ordinary Church Hymn Book, since it is prepared for Private and Family Devotion, as well as for Public Worship, thereby presenting the advantage of ONE HYMN BOOK for all purposes both in private and public. The preparation of this work has been particularly helpful, not only through the beautiful hymns themselves, but also in the careful selection and arrangement of them under the many precious doctrines and truths of Holy Scripture.

May the Lord Jehovah vouchsafe to those who shall make use of this volume as rich or still richer and more abundant blessing.

And to the Triune and Covenant God, FATHER, SON, AND HOLY GHOST, be devoutly and gratefully ascribed all Honour and Glory and Praise, now, and throughout the countless ages of eternity.

PERRY BARR, *December*, 1879. CHARLES B. SNEPP.

ORIGINAL PREFACE TO THE MUSICAL EDITION

OF

"Songs of Grace and Glory."

(BY FRANCES RIDLEY HAVERGAL.)

MANY will be surprised at the large number of well-known and favourite tunes in "Havergal's Psalmody." The fact is that "Havergal's Old Church Psalmody" has been the fountain from which editors of subsequent collections have drawn, either at first or second hand, and the original guide to many valuable tune sources, both English and foreign. It was the Columbus of tune-books; the pioneer, not to a New, but to an Old World of musical treasure. *Now*, the route is open and easy.

The retiring and unselfish spirit of its editor, as well as his devotion to yet higher work, prevented that assertion of its true position before the multitude which has always been accorded to it by the highest musical authorities.

The selections from "Havergal's Psalmody" will be found, as experience has proved them to be, easily learnt, greatly liked, and practically adapted for congregational singing. Of one of these, Dr. Lowell Mason, the great American promoter of choral singing, wrote as follows :—"I have lately introduced into my choir, and sung with admirable effect, your tune 'Eden.' The effect of it was truly magnificent. My choir consists of about sixty singers; the different parts are well sustained, and about equally balanced. I have never heard anything come nearer to my *beau ideal* of Church Music than did the singing of this tune, on a fine Sabbath morning, in a church filled with people. It made a deep impression; and the next day one and another was asking, 'What tune did you sing yesterday morning?' 'Where did you get that tune?' etc. The performance of 'Eden' makes one feel as did Jacob at Luz, and involuntarily exclaim, 'This is none other but the house of God, and this is the gate of heaven.' Wonderful would be the effect of Psalmody were all the people to unite in such lofty and majestic strains."—April 30, 1847.

In order to meet the increasing proportion of "peculiar measures," a number of tunes have been adapted from the Rev. W. H. Havergal's own melodies (chiefly from unpublished MSS.), while, for extra measures which could not be thus supplied, tunes have been added by other hands [F. R. H. and others].

The *name* of each tune at once supplies information as to its origin. Old English, Scotch, or German tunes bear respectively English, Scotch, or German names; those by the Rev. W. H. Havergal are named, with a few exceptions, from the natural geography of the Bible; the tunes added by F. R. H. [Frances Ridley Havergal] are named from "the friends of St. Paul."

"Havergal's Psalmody," a memorial to one whose works do follow him, was originally given to the church by his devoted widow, and "dedicated to his beloved, honoured, and cherished memory." The Large Type or Organ editions of "Havergal's Psalmody" contain Kyries, Glorias, and other additions not included in the present hymnal edition; while editions A and B contain Prefaces and Historical Notes, which are quoted as "a treasury of information and an armoury of defence of the principles of Church Music." A and D include "A Century of Chants." *

As the tunes have not been affixed to the hymns without much thought and prayer, and very careful consideration as to which tune will best develop the spirit of each hymn, and emphasize its most important points, it is strongly advised that, generally speaking, the tunes indicated should be adhered to.

On the other hand, as the great aim of making our singing congregational is not attained if too many new tunes are attempted at once, it is well to introduce them *gradually*, repeating each newly learnt tune at short intervals, until quite familiar. It is advisable to begin with a few tunes in such metres as occur abundantly.

The following selection of peculiar metres may be found useful at first, as giving a wide range of hymns. Hermas, for 6 5, 6 5. D.; Zoan I., for spirited and joyous hymns in 7 6, 7 6. D.; and Mahanaim (or Goldbach), for quieter hymns in the same metre; Lubeck and Patmos, respectively, for the two classes of hymns in 7 7, 7 7; Nassau and Sihor, for 7 7, 7 7, 7 7; Culbach and Frankfort (or Godesberg), for 8 7, 8 7; Zaanaim and Idumea, for 8 7, 8 7, 4 7 (or 8 7, 8 7, 8 7); Magdalene College and Kedron, for 8 8 6. D.; and Paran, for 11 11, 11 11.

1875. FRANCES RIDLEY HAVERGAL.

* All of which can be obtained from Nisbet & Co., 21, Berners Street, London.

ABRIDGEMENT OF ORIGINAL PREFACE
TO
"Songs of Grace and Glory."

A BRIEF statement of a few facts connected with this Hymnal may be desirable.

It is designed for Private, Family, and Public Worship. It was undertaken by request, and is the result of thirty years' collection.

The discovery of authors and dates to more than one thousand hymns; the careful comparison with the originals, and the restoration (as far as practicable) to those originals; the selection of suitable texts of Holy Scripture for each hymn; the appropriation of suitable tunes; the arrangement of 1,025 hymns under classified subjects and Scripture truths; the drawing up of many carefully prepared indices; and the large correspondence involved throughout the whole;—all these several items have fully occupied the spare time at command of the Editor for several years.

The great object of this Hymnal is to spread the glorious gospel of the grace of God, by representing, in sacred verse, all the doctrines of Holy Scripture, including the deeper mysteries of the everlasting Covenant, and the glorious Second Advent of the Messiah. By thus aiding the memory, it may become, through God's blessing, a channel of holy influences on the heart and life.

The Editor acknowledges, with grateful appreciation, the kindness and courtesy of so many authors, including the highest dignitaries of our Church, whose labours have enriched this volume, and who have most generously given permission to reprint.

No labour or expense has been spared to render this Hymnal useful and comprehensive, both as a work of reference, instruction, and refreshment for individuals and families, and as a practical and complete supply of all the requirements for Divine worship.

Every doctrine of Holy Scripture, all the seasons of our ecclesiastical year, and all the hopes and conflicts of the individual believer, have been carefully represented.

May it be found at the Great Day that we have not laboured in vain, nor spent our strength for nought; and to the "God of all Grace," our Triune Covenant and Faithful God, shall be all the "Glory."

PERRY BARR, *November*, 1871.

CHARLES B. SNEPP.

INDEX I.

ARRANGEMENT OF HYMNS.

A FREQUENT REFERENCE TO THIS WILL GREATLY FACILITATE THE SELECTION OF HYMNS FOR ANY SUBJECT OR SERMON.

PART I.

THE HOLY AND EVER-BLESSED "TRINITY IN UNITY."

Theme I. Worship presented to the Triune Jehovah.

(1) Adoration, Hymns 1 to 18.
(2) Invocation, 19—31.
(3) Dedication, 32—40, 1063—1075.

Theme II. The Attributes and Perfections of the Triune Jehovah.

(1) The Being of God, 41.
(2) Infinity, 42. (3) Spirituality, 43.
(4) Eternity, 44, 45. (5) Unity, 46.
(6) Sovereignty, 47. (7) First Cause and Final End, 48.
(8) Dominion, 49. (9) Glory, 50. (10) Wisdom, 51.
(11) Omnipotence, 52. (12) Omniscience, 53.
(13) Goodness, 54. (14) Holiness, 55.
(15) Faithfulness, 56. (16) Omnipresence, 57.
(17) The Pardoning God, 58. (18) Mercy, 59.
(19) Majesty, 60. (20) Kindness, 61.
(21) Love, 62. (22) Unchangeable, 63.
(23) The Names of Jehovah, 64.

Theme III. The Acts of the Triune Jehovah.

(1) The Everlasting Covenant of Grace, 65—85.
(2) Creation, 86—96.
(3) Providence, 97—112.

Theme IV. The Divine Persons of the Triune Jehovah.

I. JEHOVAH—THE FATHER.

(1) His own Essential Blessedness, 113—115.
(2) His Eternal Love to His Eternal Son, 116.
(3) His Choice and Gift of a Church to His Son, 117—119.
(4) His Promise of the Holy Ghost, 120.
(5) The Love of the Father, 121—127.

PART II.

THE BOOK OF GOD, AND THE CHURCH OF GOD.

PART III.

MAN—AND THINGS PROVIDED FOR MAN.

Theme I. Man.

Theme II. The Gospel Proclaimed.

FULL AND FREE SALVATION BY JESUS CHRIST.

Theme III. The Gospel Welcomed and Embraced.

THE LIFE AND HISTORY OF A TRUE BELIEVER.

(9) Desires after Holiness, 530—533, 1043, 1045, 1047, 1066.
(10) Growth in Grace, 534—536.
(11) Prayer, 537—548, 1071.
(12) Watchfulness, 549—551, 1074.
(13) Fasting, 552.
(14) Self-Discipline, 553—556.
(15) Resignation, 557—563.
(16) Patience, 564—566. (17) Trust, 567—570.
(18) Hope, 571—573, 1056.
(19) Full Assurance, 574, 575, 1058.
(20) Support and Comfort, 576—586.
(21) Humility, 587, 588. (22) Love, 589—596.
(23) Almsgiving, 597, 598.
(24) Praise, 599—632.
(25) Zeal, 633—641. (26) Courage, 642—646, 1062.
(27) Peace and Joy, 647—667, 1036.

II. PRIVILEGES ENJOYED.

(1) Union with Christ, 668—674.
(2) Adoption, 675—679. (3) Pardon, 680—684.
(4) Justification, 685, 686. (5) Sanctification, 687.
(6) Fellowship with the Father and with His Son, 688—710.
(7) Direction and Guidance, 711—714.
(8) Everlasting Love, 715—722.
(9) Security in Christ, 723—728, 1070.
(10) Final Perseverance, 729—733, 1080—1083.
(11) Everlasting Salvation, 734, 1043.

III. TALENTS IMPROVED.

(1) Time, 735. (2) Tongue, 736, 737.
(3) Influence, 738. (4) Wealth, 739, 740.

IV DUTIES FULFILLED.

(1) Social and Relative, 741, 742.
(2) Christian Fellowship, 743.
(3) Mutual Forbearance, 744, 745.
(4) Saints and Martyrs—their Holy Example, 746—752.
(5) Angels—Ministering Spirits, 753—755.

Theme IV. Ambassadors for Christ.

(1) Consecration and Ordination, 756, 757.
(2) Ministers of Christ and Stewards of the Mysteries of God, 758—764.
(3) Fellow Helpers, 765—768.
(4) Sunday School Teachers, 769—771.
(5) District Visitors, 772, 773.

Theme V. The Two Sacraments.

(1) Baptism, 774—778.
(2) The Lord's Supper, 779—791, 1086—1089.

Theme VI. The Lord's Day.

(1) Opening of the Lord's Day, 792—798.
(2) Opening of Public Worship, 799—808.
(3) Before the Sermon, 809—814.

(4) Close of Public Worship, 815—818.
(5) Close of the Lord's Day, 819—822.
(6) Deprived of Public Worship, 823, 824.
(7) Restored to Public Worship, 825.

THEME VII. Special Services.

(1) Foundation or Consecration of a Church, 826, 827, 1044.
(2) Choir Meetings, 828.
(3) Prayer Meetings, 829—836.
(4) Times of Refreshing, 837—841.
(5) Mothers' Meetings, 842, 843.

THEME VIII. National Occasions.

(1) National Hymns, 844—849.
(2) Harvest, 850—856.
(3) War and Peace, 857—859.
(4) National Fast and Humiliation, 860—862.
(5) National Thanksgiving and Rejoicing, 863.
(6) Prayer for those at Sea, 864.

THEME IX. Missions.

I. AT HOME.

(1) Schools, 865, 866.
(2) Mission Services, 867—869.
(3) Hospital Sunday, 870, 1035.

II. ABROAD.

(1) Jews, 871—874. (2) Gentiles, 875—884.

THEME X. Times and Seasons.

I. SEASONS OF THE DAY.

(1) Morning, 885—888. Saturday Morning, 889.
(2) Evening, 890—903. Saturday Evening, 904, 905.
(3) Midnight, 906—908.

II. THE YEAR.

(1) Opening of the Year, 909—913, 1076—1079.
(2) Close of the Year, 914—917.
(3) Year of Jubilee, 918, 919.

III. SEASONS OF LIFE.

(1) Birthdays, 920—922, 1076—1079.
(2) Childhood and Youth, 923—948.
(3) Confirmation, 949—957.
(4) Marriage, 958—960.
(5) Thanksgiving after Childbirth, 961.
(6) Sickness, 962—968.
(7) More Fruit, 969, 970.
(8) Old Age, 971, 972.
(9) Death, 973—978.
(10) Burial, 979—983.

IV. THE LIFE TO COME.

(1) The First Resurrection—of the Saints, 984—987.
(2) The General Resurrection, 988—991.

(3) The Great Day of Judgment, 992—999.
(4) The State of the Lost, 1000.
(5) The New Jerusalem, 1001, 1002.
(6) The New Heavens and Earth, 1003.
(7) Heaven, 1004—1018.

THEME XI. Eternity.

(1) The Mediatorial Kingdom delivered up to the Father, 1019.
(2) The Solemnities of Eternity, 1020, 1021.
(3) The Praises of Eternity, 1022—1024.
(4) Grace consummated in Glory, 1025, 1093, 1094.

GOD ALL IN ALL.

THEME XII. Doxologies. *(These are in this edition transferred to the close of all the hymns.)*

APPENDIX.

Part I. GOSPEL ECHOES. Hymns 1026 to 1042.
,, II. FAITH HYMNS. Hymns 1043 to 1062.
,, III. CONSECRATION HYMNS. Hymns 1063 to 1075.

Birthdays, New Years, and Anniversaries	Hymns	1076 to 1079
"Preserved in Christ"	,,	1080 to 1083
To Refresh the Missioner	,,	1084
Sickness, or Hospital Sundays	,,	1085
The Lord's Supper	,,	1086 to 1089
The Second Advent	,,	1090, 1091
Farewell	,,	1092
Glory: Present	,,	1093
Glory: Future	,,	1094

To this edition are added Seven Hymns from "Songs of Grace and Glory for the Young," in order that TUNES *may be here provided for all.*

No. 54	in "Songs of	Grace and	Glory for	the Young."	Subject:	"Our Saviour's Care."
,, 55	,,	,,	,,	,,	,,	"The Little Ones."
,, 87	,,	,,	,,	,,	,,	"Work for Jesus."
,, 97	,,	,,	,,	,,	,,	"Sing of Jesus."
,, 116	,,	,,	,,	,,	,,	"The Sabbath."
,, 131	,,	,,	,,	,,	,,	"Talents."
,, 133	,,	,,	,,	,,	,,	"Perseverance."

DOXOLOGIES.

INDEX II.

HYMNS ARRANGED FOR THE SUNDAYS AND HOLY DAYS OF THE CHRISTIAN YEAR.

	MORNING.				AFTERNOON.		EVENING.			
Sundays of Advent:—										
First	294	1090	*Pt.* ii.	299	297	301	300	298	336	1091
Second	397	396	301	293	305	388	384	310	382	395
Third	992	993	757	760	187	758	991	758	429	431
Fourth	204	135	*Pt.* ii.	1088	150	313	533	320	948	1044
Christmas Day, Dec. 25	199	202	195	*Pt.* ii.	200	201	197	204	205	203
December 26	149	752	747							
December 27	4	592	747							
December 28	438	751	747							
Sunday after Christmas	164	191	608	1076	203	916	198	917	573	914
The Circumcision of Christ, New Year's Day, Jan. 1	1078	212	164	162						
First Sunday in the Year	911	921	1067	913	910	912	1077	1078	932	1080
The Epiphany, Jan. 6	207	210	211	206			167	209	887	*Pt.* ii.
Sundays after Epiphany:—										
First	207	210	211	208	319	878	206	165	877	919
Second	883	900	163	621	875	881	120	661	660	901
Third	329	221	1043	415	403	*Pt.* ii.	323	222	613	612
Fourth	578	579	142	713	151	379	529	581	708	576
Fifth	420	730	664	665	144	728	629	116	419	423
Sixth	676	677	*Pt.* ii.	675	801	143	687	425	682	681
Septuagesima	50	89	1003	91	87	95	342	90	341	330
Sexagesima	133	569	811	813	469	454	517	722	702	721
Quinquagesima	605	589	595	594	591	592	496	572	596	589
Ash Wednesday	499	501	500	862						
Sundays in Lent:—										
First	499	477	503	*Pt.* ii.	479	468	470	501	500	462
Second	488	703	704	705	182	183	537	539	732	711
Third	549	550	633	535	575	577	465	466	715	1065
Fourth	451	486	677	*Pt.* ii.	548	490	475	476	14	471
Fifth	242	239	275	241	521	532	350	70	*Pt.* ii.	*Pt.* ii.
Sunday before Easter	225	226	228	283	216	229	129	240	599	227
Monday in Passion Week	221	241	607							
Tuesday " "	220	633	235							
Wednesday " "	806	166	229							
Thursday " "	230	*Pt.* ii.	*Pt.* iii.							
Good Friday	233	239	236	235	166	784	240	234	241	242

HYMNS ARRANGED FOR THE SUNDAYS.

	MORNING.				AFTERNOON.		EVENING.			
Easter Even	244	245	246	717						
Easter Day	248	258	254	257	148	255	249	253	250	256
Easter Monday	256	251	254							
Easter Tuesday	261	253	250							
Sundays after Easter:—										
First	254	261	259	258	806	311	251	271	*Pt.* ii.	260
Second	214	600	934	177	153	462	730	179	618	607
Third	291	366	506	*Pt.* ii.	405	404	407	410	957	*Pt.* ii.
Fourth	349	42	44	367	954	80	1007	33	38	700
Fifth	528	32	398	734	278	733	800	286	717	902
Ascension Day	264	*Pt.* ii.	266		284	289	265	270	268	
Sunday after Ascension Day	265	264	*Pt.* ii.	282	267	274	321	275	288	*Pt.* ii.
Whitsunday	361	*Pt.* ii.	368	350	355	369	343	346	378	*Pt.* ii.
Monday in Whitsun Week	373	371	372							
Tuesday in Whitsun Week	354	362	370							
Trinity Sunday	1	3	4	11	21	7	2	*Pt.* ii.	12	900
After Trinity:—										
First	24	14	23	17	149	15	30	29	16	22
Second	28	522	193	467	25	26	611	642	1086	*Pt.* ii.
Third	653	754	755	8	524	34	562	753	444	558
Fourth	1009	536	302	340	559	1006	1010	953	1011	1008
Fifth	803	633	1072	36	322	327	638	640	639	326
Sixth	984	1025	1012	1024	433	435	1001	*Pt.* ii.	*Pt.* iii.	*Pt.* iv.
Seventh	473	489	428	426	827	667	191	810	734	407
Eighth	65	120	101	432	112	98	828	47	103	606
Ninth	623	184	194	939	570	441	601	707	698	891
Tenth	797	363	483	494	587	610	488	569	485	493
Eleventh	77	835	413	617	668	670	429	573	572	956
Twelfth	804	695	696	671	718	723	20	*Pt.* ii.	29	725
Thirteenth	799	646	986	987	113	109	181	568	425	27
Fourteenth	795	*Pt.* ii.	614	1002	637	974	831	106	66	832
Fifteenth	108	105	721	423	636	624	603	608	839	817
Sixteenth	137	716	324	*Pt.* ii.	971	130	665	653	666	821
Seventeenth	792	78	448	442	918	472	846	969	*Pt.* ii.	463
Eighteenth	726	549	706	421	176	729	656	838	732	953
Nineteenth	370	692	*Pt.* ii.	682	354	145	372	400	398	956
Twentieth	627	424	428	628	840	841	824	654	650	1005
Twenty-First	626	644	645	635	655	658	966	968	990	819
Twenty-Second	647	725	431	446	331	314	438	434	974	991
Twenty-Third	691	1013	*Pt.* ii.	1015	337	839	1020	1041	*Pt.* ii.	1021
Twenty-Fourth *	1023	704	1049	*Pt.* ii.	62	63	430	1025	121	1019
Sunday next before Advent	417	173	416	685	317	316	949	735	304	1003

* If *more* Sundays before Advent, see Hymns for Fifth and Sixth Sundays after Epiphany.

Note.—The Proper Lessons, Collect, Epistle, or Gospel, will be found to have suggested the key-note for each day, thus preserving the unity of the service, whenever hymns specially appropriate to the sermon have not been selected.

	MORNING.		
St. Andrew's Day, November 30	949	489	747
St. Thomas, December 21	524	251	747
Conversion of St. Paul, January 25	554	765	747
Presentation of Christ in the Temple, February 2	216	687	32
St. Matthias' Day, February 24	757	758	747
The Annunciation, March 25	137	162	164
St. Mark's Day, April 25	670	744	747
St. Philip and St. James, May 1	187	637	747
St. Barnabas the Apostle, June 11	366	533	747
St. John Baptist, June 24	499	149	747
St. Peter's Day, June 29	399	398	747
St. James the Apostle, July 25	506	*Pt.* ii.	747
St. Bartholomew, August 24	396	712	747
St. Matthew, September 21	949	739	747
St. Michael and All Angels, September 29	753	754	755
St. Luke the Evangelist, October 18	170	696	747
St. Simon and St. Jude, October 28	810	1044	747
All Saints' Day, November 1	748	438	749

A SECOND LIST OF SUGGESTED HYMNS,

WITH THEIR APPROPRIATE TUNES, WHEN VARIATIONS ARE DESIRED.

Hymn.	*Tune.*	*Hymn.*	*Tune.*	*Hymn.*	*Tune.*	*Hymn.*	*Tune.*	*Hymn.*	*Tune.*
39	Gilboa.	387	Succoth.	526	Nassau.	683	Jordan.	1018	Sheba.
49	Lubeck.	399	Mahanaim.	531	Gershom.	701	Goldbach, Pt.I.	1022	St. Dunstan.
59	Paran.	401	Bevan.	534	Old Ten. Com.	710	Beulah.	1045	Hobah.
67	St. Michael.	436	Jordan.	540	Thyatira.	742	Merom.	1048	Urbane.
68	Eden.	439	Celestial.	543	Evan I.	772	Boston.	1055	Evan I.
69	Moriah.	453	Altorf.	545	Sardis.	798	Melcombe.	1056	"Better farther on."
72	French.	456	St. George.	546	Gethsemane.	808	Narenza.	1057	Urbane.
73	Hanover.	458	Faith.	556	Harts.	820	St. Gregory.	1059	"The Great Physician."
74	Kedron.	459	Church Triumphant.	564	St.Chrysostom.	822	Thyatira.	1060	Everton.
76	Franconia.	461	Gloucester.	565	Expectation.	834	Melcombe.	1061	"More to follow."
81	Crescens.	479	Vienna.	567	St. Ethelburga.	868	Evan II.	1070	"Safe in the arms."
84	MagdaleneColl.	481	Purday.	582	Smyrna.	897	Laodicea.	1071	"Sweet hour of prayer."
100	Vienna.	504	Beulah.	586	Godesberg.	905	Kedron.	1092	Dismissal.
127	Moriah.	508	Honidon.	632	Goshen.	925	Patmos.	1093	Zoan I.
134	Moscow.	511	Armageddon.	649	Eirene.	929	St. Theodulph.		
281	Stuttgard.	513	St.Chrysostom.	663	Boston.	938	Sternberg.		
338	Mizpeh.	516	Gethsemane.	669	Besor.	941	Munich.		
375	St. Asaph.	518	Sardis.	674	Frankfort.	967	Sternberg.		
376	Old Ten Com.	523	Crasselius.	679	Godesberg.	970	Linus.		
385	Maon.			680	Gilboa.	1017	Aristarchus.		

For MISSION SERVICES see many in the above List. Also 1026 to 1094.

For CHILDREN'S SERVICES see Hymns 923 to 957. Also "Songs of Grace and Glory for the Young," containing 178 Hymns.

INDEX III.

INDEX OF AUTHORS AND THEIR HYMNS.

INDEX OF AUTHORS AND THEIR HYMNS. xxi

INDEX OF AUTHORS AND THEIR HYMNS.

HYMNS TRANSLATED, AND NAMES OF TRANSLATORS.

INDEX IV.

TUNES, ALPHABETICALLY ARRANGED.

*(Where a * is affixed, the tune has been altered more or less, to meet the peculiar structure of the hymn.)*

Tune.	Metre.	Composer, or Source.	Hymns.
Abilene	77, 77	Rev. W. H. Havergal	853.
All Saints	87, 87, 77	German	288, 313, 339, 881.
Alpha	L. M. D.	C. H. Purday	119.
Altorf, *or* Luther's Hymn	87, 87, 887; or 88, 888	Old Church Psalmody	*453, 988, 1021.
Amana	S. M.	Rev. W. H. Havergal	139.
Amplias	64, 66	Frances Ridley Havergal	898.
Angels' Song	88, 88, 88	Old Church Psalmody	759.
Apphia	98, 98	Frances Ridley Havergal	87 in "S. G. G. for the Young."
Aquila	9998, 8888	Frances Ridley Havergal	642, *1094.
Archippus	C. M.	Frances Ridley Havergal	324, 413.
Aristarchus	8888	Frances Ridley Havergal	724, 906, 1017.
Armageddon	S. M.	Rev. W. H. Havergal	372, 511, 802, 1012.
Arnon	66, 84	Rev. W. H. Havergal (Adapted F. R. H.)	166.
Arran	C. M.	Rev. W. H. Havergal	631, 940.
Augsburg	87, 87. D.	Old Church Psalmody	232.
Aven	S. M.	Rev. W. H. Havergal	242, 260, 435, 627, 665, 799, 952.
Baca	66, 66, 66	Rev. W. H. Havergal (Adapted F. R. H.)	633.
Baden I., *or* Nuremberg	87, 87, 44, 87	Old Church Psalmody	557.
Baden II., *or* Nuremberg	88, 88, 47.	Old Church Psalmody	599.
Bashan	66, 66	Rev. W. H. Havergal	108, 386, 691, 787.
Bedford	C. M.	Old Church Psalmody	75, 112, 576, 584, 776, 950.
Besor	C. M.	Rev. W. H. Havergal	137, 300, 559, 560, 571, 590, 669, 761.
Bethabara	888, 6	Rev. W. H. Havergal	110.
Bethany	86, 84	Rev. W. H. Havergal	367.
Bethaven	C. M. D.	Rev. W. H. Havergal	903, 920.
Bether	C. M.	Rev. W. H. Havergal	464.
Beulah	64, 64, 6664	Rev. W. H. Havergal	504, 710, 1027.
Bevan	66, 66, 88.	Sir John Goss	401, 918.
Bohemia	65, 65. D.	German	964.
Boston	76, 76. D.	Dr. Lowell Mason	663, *772, 937.
Bremen	87, 87	Old Church Psalmody	861.
Bridehead	886	Rev. A. H. D. Troyte	316, 492, 591.
"Bright Jewels"	11 11, 11 11	William F. Sherwin	97 in "S. G. G. for the Young."
Caithness	C. M.	Old Church Psalmody	218, 219, 220.
Calvary	10 lines 7s; or 7777. D.	Rev. W. H. Havergal (Adapted F. R. H.)	231.
Canterbury	87, 87	Rev. C. J. Latrobe	863.
Carmel	C. M.	Rev. W. H. Havergal	53, 214, 215, 243, 245, 500, 527, 528, 530, 548, 979.
Carpus	888, 4	Frances Ridley Havergal	572.
Cassel	87, 87, 77	Old Church Psalmody	303, 693, 694, 745.

TUNES, ALPHABETICALLY ARRANGED.

Tune.	Metre.	Composer, or Source.	Hymns.
Celestial	Hymn Chant	S. E. L. Lillingston	439.
Chaldea	888	Rev. W. H. Havergal (Adapted F. R. H.)	251, 261.
Chesalon	C. M.	Rev. W. H. Havergal	65, 129, 204, 337, 382, 419, 426, 427, 601, 603, 667, 985.
Christmas Carols	... ...	Rev. W. H. Havergal	923, 943, 944, 945.
Church Triumphant	L. M.	Rev. J. W. Elliott	152, 402, 437, 459, 1023.
Civitas Regis Magni	87, 87, 87.	Dr. Gauntlett	295, 336, 405, 671, 996.
Claudia	65, 65	Frances Ridley Havergal	547.
"Coming to the Cross"	77, 77. D.	W. G. Fischer	1047.
Conway	10 10, 10 10	Old Church Psalmody	345.
Corfe Mullen	87, 87, 47.	Rev. J. R. Matthews	314, 321, 612.
Corpus Christi	98, 98	Rev. — Paget	789.
Crasselius, *or* Winchester New	L. M.	Old Church Psalmody	13, 25, 82, 86, 148, 194, 225, 271, 272, 332, 412, 523, 615, 748, 844, 875, 1007.
Crescens	11 8, 11 8	Frances Ridley Havergal	79, 81.
Crete	L. M.	Rev. W. H. Havergal	756.
Crüger	76, 76. D.	German	116, 330.
Culbach	87, 87	Old Church Psalmody	1, 63, 351, 422, 433, 613, 739, 1040.
Cyprus	L. M.	Rev. W. H. Havergal	43, 138, 154, 457, 699, 743, 973, 1088.
Cyrene	S. M.	Rev. W. H. Havergal	676, 782.
Dalmatia	L. M.	Rev. W. H. Havergal	370, 1085.
Damaris	66, 66	Frances Ridley Havergal	396.
Darwell	66, 66, 88.	Rev. J. Darwell	188, 224, 257, 611, 827.
Deptford	10 10, 10 10	Orlando Gibbons	196, 446.
Dies Iræ	888	Frances Ridley Havergal	994.
Dimon	C. M.	Rev. W. H. Havergal (Composed in a Dream)	190, 360, 714.
Dismissal	87, 87, 87.	W. L. Viner	470, 817, 818, 895, 1092.
Dix	77, 77, 77.	German	206, 207, 836.
Dortmund	L. M.	Old Church Psalmody	756.
Dundee, *or* Windsor	C. M.	Old Church Psalmody	451, 862.
Durham	77, 77	Old Litany	664, 819.
Eastham	76, 86. D.	Rev. Sir F. Ouseley	986.
Eaton	88, 88, 88.	S. Wyvill	181, 343, 538, 690, 718, 720, 775, 864.
Ebronah	10 10, 10 10	Rev. W. H. Havergal	697.
Eden	C. M.	Rev. W. H. Havergal	68, 97, 99, 126, 266, 331, 441, 487, 794, 926.
Edgbaston	65, 65. D.	Rev. J. R. Matthews	163.
"Ein feste Burg"	87, 87, 6666, 7	Martin Luther	623.
Eirene	11 10, 11 10; or 11 10, 11 10, 10 10	Frances Ridley Havergal	29, 292, 648, 649, 708, 971, 1084.
Elah	C. M.	Rev. W. H. Havergal	172.
Epaphroditus	13 11, 13 12	Frances Ridley Havergal	982.
Epenetus	13 6, 13 13, 13 15	Frances Ridley Havergal	165.
Ephesus	Hymn Chant	Rev. W. H. Havergal	738, 766.
Ephron	C. M.	Rev. W. H. Havergal	297, 298.
Esdraelon	87, 87. D.	Rev. W. H. Havergal (Arranged F. R. H.)	130, 146, 282, 349, 395, 608.
Eunice	10 10, 10 10.	Frances Ridley Havergal	54 in "S. G. G. for the Young."
Euodias	84, 84, 8884	Frances Ridley Havergal	101, 428.
Euphrates	L. M.	Rev. W. H. Havergal	158, 159, 226, 333.
Evan I.	C. M.	Rev. W. H. Havergal	169, 185, 187, 541, 543, 568, 647, 658, 672, 707, 737, 791, 924, 1055.
Evan II.	C. M. D.	Rev. W. H. Havergal	488, 868.
Everton	87, 87. D.	Sir Henry Smart	7, *348, 636, 1060.
Exeter	888. D.	Old Church Psalmody	432.
Expectation	S. M. D.	C. H. Purday	565.

Tune.	Metre.	Composer, or Source.	Hymns.
FAITH	118, 118	C. H. Purday	458.
FARRANT	C. M.	Old Church Psalmody	448, 499, 515, 517, 588.
FIDES	65, 65. D.	... ...	569, 947, 969.
FILITZ	777, 5	German	132.
FORTUNATUS	88, 88, 68, 88, 68	Frances Ridley Havergal	116 in "S. G. G. for the Young."
FRANCONIA	S. M.	Old Church Psalmody	76, 497, 539, 562, 643, 751, 764, 912, 1076.
FRANKFORT	87, 87	Old Church Psalmody	62, 150, 369, 646, 674, 709, 785, 1032.
FRENCH, *or* DUNDEE	C. M.	Old Church Psalmody	72, 160, 161, 171, 241, 505, 507, 688, 780, 1074.
FREYLINGHAUSEN	87, 87. D.	German	16, 328, 361, 403.
FUGAL	S. M.	Rev. H. E. Havergal	760, 763.
GAIUS	11 10, 11 10	Frances Ridley Havergal	614.
GALILEE	L. M.	Rev. W. H. Havergal	57.
GENNESARET	L. M.	Rev. W. H. Havergal	51, 736.
GERSHOM	88, 118	Rev. J. Knowles	531.
GETHSEMANE	L. M.	Rev. W. H. Havergal	37, 170, 212, 475, 476, 502, 514, 516, 546.
GIBBONS	77, 77	Old Church Psalmody	96, 290, 310, 587, 656.
GILBOA	L. M.	Rev. W. H. Havergal	28, 39, 143, 144, 305, 340, 341, 509, 680, 757, 879, 951.
GLOUCESTER	C. M.	Old Church Psalmody	15, 307, 461 with chorus.
GODESBERG	87, 87	Old Church Psalmody	586, 662, 679, 790, 813, 816, 831, 902, 949, 1051.
GOLDBACH	76, 76; or 76, 76. D.	Old Church Psalmody	193, 366, 704, 747, 795, 930, 972, 974, 1049, 1065.
GOLDBACH, Part I. only.	76, 76	Old Church Psalmody	701, 719, 723, 781, 933, 963, 1001 (Part I.), 1078.
GÖLDEL	L. M.	Old Church Psalmody	277.
GOLDSTERN	76, 76. D.	German	111, 317.
GOSHEN	76, 76	Rev. W. H. Havergal	524, 632, 854, 1015, 1081.
GOTHA	87, 87	H.R.H. the late Prince Consort	285, 315, 784.
GOZAN	77, 87	Rev. W. H. Havergal (Adapted F. R. H.)	11, 12, 157.
GROSVENOR	65, 65. D.	Dr. C. Steggall	955.
HALLE	88, 88, 88	German	377.
HAMBURG	87, 87. D.	Old Church Psalmody	236.
HANOVER, *or* CROFT'S 104th	10 10, 11 11	Old Church Psalmody	73, 510, 583.
HARTS	77, 77	Benjamin Milgrove	88, 388, 556, 566.
HAVERGAL	777, 777, 777	Rev. W. H. Havergal	4.
HAVERGAL, Part I. only.	777	Rev. W. H. Havergal	352, 786.
HAVILAH	87, 87, 87	Rev. W. H. Havergal	38, 85, 210, 211, 301, 302, 400, 407, 414, 447, 809, 810, 837, 984.
HEATHLANDS	77, 77, 77	Sir Henry Smart	609.
HEBRON	L. M.	Rev. W. H. Havergal	34, 71, 178, 383.
HERMAS	65, 65. D.	Frances Ridley Havergal	258, 265, 569, 851, 911, 932, 956.
HERMON	L. M.	Rev. W. H. Havergal	216, 227, 234, 235, 445, 542, 544, 585, 746, 858, 874.
HESHBON, *or* PARRACOMBE	77, 77. D.	Rev. W. H. Havergal	440.
HOBAH	11 11, 11 11	Rev. W. H. Havergal	*653, 846, *1045, 1058, 1067, 1077.
"HOLD THE FORT"	85, 85. D.	P. P. Bliss	1062.
HOLY VOICES	87, 87. D.	James E. Langran	284.
HONIDON	77, 77. D.	Rev. J. R. Matthews	508, 702.
HURSLEY	L. M.	German	83.
"I HAVE ENTERED THE VALLEY"	118, 118	W. G. Fischer	1064.
IDUMEA	87, 87, 87	Rev. W. H. Havergal (Adapted F. R. H.)	177, 203, 293, 322, 468, 469, 650, 654, 884, 1033, 1037.

TUNES, ALPHABETICALLY ARRANGED.

Tune.	Metre.	Composer, or Source.	Hymns.
IONA	C. M.	Rev. W. H. Havergal	56, 323, 489, 637, 797, 848.
"IT IS BETTER FARTHER ON"	97, 87, 87, 87	... ...	1056.
"JESUS OF NAZARETH"	88, 88, 89.	T. E. Perkins	1039.
JEZREEL	888, 4	Rev. W. H. Havergal	102, 962 (Part I.).
JORDAN	886. D.	Rev. W. H. Havergal	128, 147, 408, 418, 436, 683, 811.
JULIUS	447, 887	Frances Ridley Havergal	89.
JUNIA	56, 56	Frances Ridley Havergal	131 in "S. G. G. for the Young."
KADESH	7777. D.; or 10 lines 7s	Rev. W. H. Havergal	92, 824, 850, 946, 1003.
KEDAR	C. M.	Rev. W. H. Havergal	40, 155, 156, 859, 873.
KEDRON	886. D.	Rev. W. H. Havergal	36, 74, 121, 183, 374, 485, 715, 758, 905, 922, 959, *1083.
KENT	C. M.	Old Church Psalmody	80, 247, 404, 651, 652, 961, 977, 1006.
"KNOCKING"	77, 87, 87.	G. F. Root	1053.
KÖCKER	76, 76	German	55 in "S. G. G. for the Young."
LAODICEA	Hymn Chant	Frances Ridley Havergal	141, 365, 563, 659, 692, 894, 897.
LEBANON	86, 86, 88	Rev. W. H. Havergal	442, 833.
LEIPSIC	L. M.	Old Church Psalmody	41, 117, 118, 554, 555.
LILLINGSTON	11 11 11, 5.	S. E. L. Lillingston	847.
LINUS	87, 87. D.; or 1515, 1515	Frances Ridley Havergal	415, 416, 438, 506, 520, 533, 639, 734, 753, 968 (major and minor), 970, 1043, *1087.
LOIS	83, 83, 888, 33	Frances Ridley Havergal	493.
LONDON NEW, *or* NEWTON	C. M.	Old Church Psalmody	283, 495, 634, 670, 800.
LUBECK	77, 77	Old Church Psalmody	49, 60, 200, 213, 249, 311, 610, 629, 887, 1016.
LUCIUS	86, 889	Frances Ridley Havergal	1041.
LUSATIA	87, 87, 447	Old Church Psalmody	27.
LUXEMBURG	77, 77	Old Church Psalmody	965.
MAGDALENE COLLEGE	886. D.	Old Church Psalmody	84, 113, 133, 136, 201, 259, 289, 535, 604.
MAGDEBURG	87, 87, 87	German	135, 304, 327, 463, 711, 1014, 1086.
MAHANAIM	76, 76. D.	Rev. W. H. Havergal	5, 95, 253, 274, 399, 490, 682, 703, 957, 1001 (Part III.), *1013, 1046.
MAMRE	88, 88, 88; or 98, 98, 88	Rev. W. H. Havergal	31, 104, 494, *960, 987.
MANNHEIM	87, 87, 87	German	237, 981.
MAON	88, 88, 88	Rev. W. H. Havergal	58, 273, 280, 291, 385, 394, 684, 729.
MASSAH	S. M. D.	Rev. W. H. Havergal	270.
MEDIA	87, 87, 87	Rev. W. H. Havergal	805.
MELCOMBE	L. M.	Old Church Psalmody	221, 240, 373, 443, 685, 686, 769, 770, 773, 779, 783, 796, 798, 801, 832, 834, 841, 885, 954, 1073.
MEROM	887, 887	Rev. W. H. Havergal (Adapted F. R. H.)	252, 742.
MIDIAN	86, 86, 4	Rev. W. H. Havergal (Adapted F. R. H.)	478.
MILES LANE	C. M.	W. Shrubsole	324.
MINDEN	76, 76, 77	Old Church Psalmody	142.
MIZPEH	6666, 88	Rev. W. H. Havergal	338, 727.
MORAVIA	S. M.	Old Church Psalmody	312, 344, 550.
"MORE TO FOLLOW"	76, 76. D.	P. P. Bliss	1061.
MORIAH	6666, 88	Rev. W. H. Havergal	69, 127, 209, 287.
MOSCOW	664, 6664	Old Church Psalmody	30, 134, 192, 430, 852, 877, 990.
MUNICH	76, 76. D.	German	8, 712, 806, *941.
NARENZA	S. M.	Old Church Psalmody	294, 522, 638, 808, 840.

Tune.	Metre.	Composer, or Source.	Hymns.
NASSAU	77, 77, 77 . .	Old Church Psalmody .	2, 32, 195, 410, 420, *526.
NATIONAL ANTHEM .	664, 6664 . .	Dr. John Bull . .	845.
NAYLAND, *or* ST. STEPHEN	C. M. . . .	Rev. W. Jones . .	140, 145, 379, 460, 596, 598, 814.
NIMRIM	64, 64, 664 . .	Rev. W. H. Havergal .	706.
NOTTINGHAM, *or* ST. MAGNUS	C. M. . . .	Old Church Psalmody .	107, 434, 620, 730, 849.
"NUN DANKET ALLE GOTT"	67, 67, 6666 . .	Johann Crüger . .	606.
"OH THAT WILL BE JOYFUL"	776, 67 . . .	... ...	928.
OLD 25TH . . .	S. M. D. . . .	Old Church Psalmody .	306.
OLD 81ST . . .	C. M. D. . . .	Old Church Psalmody .	483, 752.
OLD 100TH . . .	L. M. . . .	Old Church Psalmody .	18, 45, 61, 91, 93, 114, 131, 602, 624, 625, 826.
OLD 124TH . . .	10 10 10, 10 10 . .	Old Church Psalmody .	914.
OLD NUNC DIMITTIS .	C. M. D. . . .	Old Church Psalmody .	561.
OLD TEN COMMANDMENTS	L. M. . . .	Old Church Psalmody .	9, 10, 46, 48, 376, 380, 532, 534, 580.
OLDENBURG . . .	77, 77 . . .	Old Church Psalmody .	356.
OLYMPAS . . .	76, 76, 7776 . .	Frances Ridley Havergal	635.
"ONE MORE DAY'S WORK"	76, 556, 46 . .	R. Lowry . . .	1069.
ONESIMUS . . .	74, 74. D. . .	Frances Ridley Havergal	695.
ORIEL	87, 87, 87 . .	German. . . .	342, 605, 871.
PARAN	10 10, 11 11; or 11 11, 11 11	Rev. W. H. Havergal .	50, 59, 173, 299, 411, 423, 581, 698, 992, 993, *1050, 1066.
PATMOS	77, 77 . . .	Rev. W. H. Havergal .	22, 151, 179, 278, 355, 384, 491, 592, 618, 640, 717, 815, 835, 842, 843, 910, *925, 935, 936, 953, 1047, 1052, 1072.
PATROBAS . . .	77, 77. . . .	Frances Ridley Havergal	1026.
PEDAL TUNE . . .	88, 88, 88 . .	Rev. H. E. Havergal .	616, 1044.
PENIEL	L. M. . . .	Rev. W. H. Havergal .	700, 901.
PEOR	11 11, 10 10; or 11 11, 11 11	Rev. W. H. Havergal .	308, 318, *976.
PERGAMOS . . .	Hymn Chant . .	Frances Ridley Havergal	70, 90, 597.
PERSIS	87, 87, 3 . . .	Frances Ridley Havergal	120, 689, 721, 839, 1036.
PHARPAR . . .	77, 77, 77 . .	Rev. W. H. Havergal .	268.
PHEBE	77, 66 . . .	Frances Ridley Havergal	1068.
PHILADELPHIA . .	Hymn Chant . .	Frances Ridley Havergal	33, 246, 477, 716, 735, 765, 1079.
PHILEMON . . .	888, 7 . . .	Frances Ridley Havergal	197, *892, *893, *907, 1005.
PISGAH	77, 77 . . .	Rev. W. H. Havergal .	184, 199, 248, 267, 326, 626, 1019.
PLEYEL	77, 77 . . .	German. . . .	916.
PRAGUE	85, 85; or 85, 83 .	Old Church Psalmody .	595.
PSALM 148TH, O. V. .	6666, 4444 . .	Old Church Psalmody .	804.
PURDAY	87, 87, 77 . .	C. H. Purday . .	*481, 519, 771, 865.
PYRMONT . . .	10 10, 10 10 . .	German. . . .	696.
RABENLEI . . .	65, 65 . . .	German. . . .	934.
RATISBON . . .	77, 77, 77 . .	Old Church Psalmody .	19, 363, 381, 675.
REDHEAD . . .	77, 77, 77 . .	R. Redhead . . .	244.
REGENT SQUARE . .	87, 87, 87 . .	Sir Henry Smart . .	256, 948.
REPHAIM . . .	77, 77 . . .	Rev. W. H. Havergal .	255, 269.
RIPON	10 10, 11 11 . .	Old Church Psalmody .	628.
"SAFE IN THE ARMS" .	76, 76. D. . .	W. H. Doane . .	1070.
SALISBURY . . .	C. M. . . .	Old Church Psalmody .	222, 223, 391, 392, 393, 421, 425, 486, 754.
SALMON	78, 78 . . .	Rev. W. H. Havergal . (Adapted F. R. H.)	250.
SALZBURG . . .	87, 87. D. . .	Old Church Psalmody .	17, 20, 21, 866, 867, 921, 1029.

xxviii *TUNES, ALPHABETICALLY ARRANGED.*

Tune.	Metre.	Composer, or Source.	Hymns.
Samaria	77, 77. D.	Rev. W. H. Havergal (Adapted F. R. H.)	750.
Samos	777, 3	Rev. W. H. Havergal (Adapted F. R. H.)	549.
Sardis	Hymn Chant	Frances Ridley Havergal	35, 64, 175, 378, 518, 545, 552, 558, *579, 641, 705, 749.
Saxony	L. M.	Old Church Psalmody	296, 452, 762, 978, 997, 1020.
Seir	77, 77. D.	Rev. W. H. Havergal	6, *357, 812, 975.
Sharon	87, 87	Dr. Boyce	882.
Sheba	6666. D.	Rev. W. H. Havergal (Adapted F. R. H.)	1018.
Shen	87, 87. D.	Rev. W. H. Havergal (Adapted F. R. H.)	47, 254, 264, 398, 406.
Shenir I.	777, 5	Rev. W. H. Havergal (Adapted F. R. H.)	589, 900.
Shenir II.	77, 77	Rev. W. H. Havergal	350, 353, 593, 722, 777, 829, 830, 896, 917.
Sihor	77, 77, 77	Rev. W. H. Havergal (Adapted F. R. H.)	229, 230, 462, 474, 570, 768, 788, 856, 904, 991, 1028.
Siloam	77, 77	Rev. W. H. Havergal	482, 484, 998.
Silvanus	86, 86, 86.	Frances Ridley Havergal	567.
Sirion	87, 87.	Rev. W. H. Havergal	182.
Sitnah	87, 87	Rev. W. H. Havergal	205.
Smyrna	Hymn Chant	Rev. W. H. Havergal	263, 465, 553, 578, 582, 889, 1082.
Sorek	87, 87	Rev. W. H. Havergal	98, 167, 308.
Sosthenes	10 11, 11 11, 12 11	Frances Ridley Havergal	424, 498, 621.
Southgate	84, 84, 8884	Rev. F. Southgate	890.
St. Alphege	76, 76	Dr. Gauntlett. From Church Hymn and Tune Book	454, 958, 1001 (Part II.).
St. Ann	C. M.	Old Church Psalmody	94, 389, 390, 594, 741, 807.
St. Asaph	87, 87. D.	W. S. Bambridge	375, 660.
St. Barnabas	65, 65. D.	Frances Ridley Havergal	964, 980.
St. Barnabas II.	86, 86, 88	Rev. H. E. Havergal	740.
St. Botolph	Hymn Chant	S. E. L. Lillingston	1022.
St. Bride	S. M.	Old Church Psalmody	501, 503, 512, 983, 999, 1000.
St. Chrysostom	C. M.	Rev. W. H. Havergal	329, 513, 529, 564, 661, 687, 728, 774, 1002, 1034, 1054.
St. David	C. M.	Old Church Psalmody	109.
St. Dunstan	10 10, 7	S. E. L. Lillingston	1022.
St. Ethelburga	Hymn Chant	S. E. L. Lillingston	567.
St. Flavian	C. M.	Ravenscroft	228.
St. George (Gauntlett).	S. M.	Dr. Gauntlett. From Church Hymn and Tune Book.	106, 456.
St. Gregory	L. M.	German.	186, 820, 821, 888, 909.
St. Hilda	77, 77. D.	Rev. J. R. Matthews	577.
St. James	C. M.	Old Church Psalmody	417.
St. John's	66, 66, 88	Rev. W. H. Havergal	115, 275, 276, 645, 1030.
St. Mary, *or* Hackney	C. M.	Old Church Psalmody	238, 449, 450, 455, 551, 860.
St. Michael	S. M.	Old Church Psalmody	67, 180, 872.
St. Peter	C. M.	A. R. Reinagle	103, 162.
St. Paul	87, 887, 7777	Frances Ridley Havergal	44, 600, 1025, 1090.
St. Silas	5555, 6565	Frances Ridley Havergal	*536, 644.
St. Theodulph	76, 76. D.	German.	929.
St. Werbergh	87, 87, 87	German.	233, 480, 733.
Stephanas	83, 83, 888, 33	Frances Ridley Havergal	239.
Sternberg	11 10, 11 10	Old Church Psalmody	42, 208, 666, 731, 938, 939, 967, 1091.
Stobel	664, 6664	Old Church Psalmody	496, 880.
Stuttgard	87, 87	Old Church Psalmody	281, 681, 803, 838, 927, 1035.
Succoth	87, 87, 77.	Rev. W. H. Havergal (Adapted F. R. H.)	23, 153, 387, 444, 870, 1010.

Tune.	Metre.	Composer, or Source.	Hymns.
SWABIA	S. M.	Old Church Psalmody	24, 26, 77, 78, 354, 358, 359, 409, 431, 575, 767, 793, 869, 1008, 1009, 1089.
"SWEET HOUR OF PRAYER"	L. M.	B. Bradbury	1071.
TALLIS'S CANON	L. M.	Old Church Psalmody	886, 899.
TALLIS, *or* TALLIS'S ORDINAL	C. M.	Old Church Psalmody	52, 54, 55, 346, 347, 362, 364, 371, 744, 778.
TEKOA	87, 87, 87; or 87, 87, 447	Rev. W. H. Havergal	857, 989.
TERTIUS	11 11, 11 11 5	Frances Ridley Havergal	525.
"THE GREAT PHYSICIAN"	87, 87, 7776	Rev. J. H. Stockton	1059.
THYATIRA	Hymn Chant	Frances Ridley Havergal	466, 540, 573, 657, 673, 822, 823, 908, 962 (Part II.), 1063.
"'TIS A LESSON YOU SHOULD HEED"	75, 7775	S. E. L. Lillingston	133 in "S. G. G. for the Young."
TRISAGION	11 12, 12 10	Rev. W. H. Havergal	3.
TROPHIMUS	669	Frances Ridley Havergal	726.
TROYTE	Hymn Chant	Rev. A. H. D. Troyte	262, 279, 891.
TRYPHENA	888	Frances Ridley Havergal	725.
TRYPHOSA	886	Frances Ridley Havergal	286, 368.
URBANE	85, 83	Frances Ridley Havergal	966, 1057.
URBANE, Part II.	85, 83. D.	Frances Ridley Havergal	1048.
VENITE ADOREMUS	12 10, 11 10	Rev. W. H. Havergal	202, 473.
VIENNA	77, 77	Old Church Psalmody	100, 105, 168, 217, 479, 521, 537, 668, 915.
WALDECK	L. M.	Old Church Psalmody	87, 124, 125, 619.
WINCHESTER	C. M.	Old Church Psalmody	123, 467, 574, 655, 678, 1004, 1031.
WINTON	C. M.	Rev. H. E. Havergal	174, 319.
WORCESTER	Hymn Chant	Rev. W. H. Havergal	66.
"YET THERE IS ROOM!"	10 10, 10 10	Ira D. Sankey	1042.
YORK	C. M.	Old Church Psalmody	122, 334, 630, 825.
ZAANAIM	87, 87, 87, or 447	Rev. W. H. Havergal	14, 164, 176, 320, 471, 472, 607, 677, 713, 878, 919, 1024, 1075, 1080.
ZARED I.	85, 85, 7775	Rev. W. H. Havergal	198.
ZARED II.	85, 85, 843	Rev. W. H. Havergal	828.
ZION	88, 88, 88	Rev. W. H. Havergal	429, 617, 792.
ZOAN I.	76, 76. D.	Rev. W. H. Havergal	149, 189, 191, 732, 855, 876, 883, 913, 942, 1001 (Part IV.), 1011, 1038, *1093.
ZOAN II.	77, 87. D.	Rev. W. H. Havergal (Adapted F. R. H.)	325, 335, 397, *931.
ZOHELETH	87, 87, 887	Rev. W. H. Havergal	622, 995.
ZOPHIM	55, 77, 776	Rev. W. H. Havergal	755.

INDEX V.

TUNES ARRANGED ACCORDING TO METRE.

*(Where a * is affixed, the tune has been altered more or less, to meet the peculiar structure of the hymn.)*

LONG METRE.

Double Long Metre.

COMMON METRE.

Double Common Metre.

SHORT METRE.

Double Short Metre.

TUNES ARRANGED ACCORDING TO METRE.

Metres—	Tunes—	Hymns—
76, 76, 77	MINDEN	142.
76, 76. D.	BOSTON	663, *772, 937.
	CRÜGER	116, 330.
	GOLDBACH	193, 366, 704, 747, 795, 930, 972, 974, 1049, 1065.
	GOLDSTERN	111, 317.
	MAHANAIM	5, 95, 253, 274, 399, 490, 682, 703, 957, 1001 (Part III.),* 1013, 1046.
	"MORE TO FOLLOW"	1061.
	MUNICH	8, 712, 806, *941.
	"SAFE IN THE ARMS"	1070.
	ST. THEODULPH	929.
	ZOAN I.	149, 189, 191, 732, 855, 876, 883, 913, 942, 1001 (Part IV.), 1011, 1038, *1093.
76, 76, 7776	OLYMPAS	635.
76, 86. D.	EASTHAM	986.
77, 66	PHEBE	1068.
777	HAVERGAL, Part I. only	352, 786.
777, 3	SAMOS	549.
777, 5	FILITZ	132.
	SHENIR I.	589, 900.
77, 77	ABILENE	853.
	DURHAM	664, 819.
	GIBBONS	96, 290, 310, 587, 656.
	HARTS	88, 388, 556, 566.
	LUBECK	49, 60, 200, 213, 249, 311, 610, 629, 887, 1016.
	LUXEMBURG	965.
	OLDENBURG	356.
	PATMOS	22, 151, 179, 278, 355, 384, 491, 592, 618, 640, 717, 815, 835, 842, 843, 910, *925, 935, 936, 953, 1047, 1052, 1072.
	PATROBAS	1026.
	PISGAH	184, 199, 248, 267, 326, 626, 1019.
	PLEYEL	916.
	REPHAIM	255, 269.
	SHENIR II.	350, 353, 593, 722, 777, 829, 830, 896, 917.
	SILOAM	482, 484, 998.
	VIENNA	100, 105, 168, 217, 479, 521, 537, 668, 915.
77, 77, 77.	DIX	206, 207, 836.
	HEATHLANDS	609.
	NASSAU	2, 32, 195, 410, 420, *526.
	PHARPAR	268.
	RATISBON	19, 363, 381, 675.
	REDHEAD	244.
	SIHOR	229, 230, 462, 474, 570, 768, 788, 856, 904, 991, 1028.
77, 77. D.	"COMING TO THE CROSS"	1047.
	HESHBON, *or* PARRACOMBE	440.
	HONIDON	508, 702.
or 10 lines 7s	KADESH	92, 824, 850, 946, 1003.
	SAMARIA	750.
	SEIR	6, *357, 812, 975.
	ST. HILDA	577.
777, 777, 777	HAVERGAL	4.
10 lines 7s; or 77 77. D.	CALVARY	231.
77, 87.	GOZAN	11, 12, 157.
77, 87, 87	"KNOCKING"	1053.
77, 87. D.	ZOAN II.	325, 335, 397, *931.
776, 67	"OH THAT WILL BE JOYFUL"	928.
78, 78.	SALMON	250.
83, 83, 888, 33.	LOIS	493.
	STEPHANAS	239.
84, 84, 8884	EUODIAS	101, 428.
	SOUTHGATE	890.

TUNES ARRANGED ACCORDING TO METRE.

Metres—	*Tunes*—	*Hymns*—
886 D.	JORDAN	128, 147, 408, 418, 436, 683, 811.
	KEDRON	36, 74, 121, 183, 374, 485, 715, 758, 905, 922, 959, *1083.
	MAGDALENE COLLEGE	84, 113, 133, 136, 201, 259, 289, 535, 604.
887, 887	MEROM	252, 742.
888 (Iambic)	CHALDEA	251, 261.
	TRYPHENA	725.
888 (Trochaic)	DIES IRÆ	994.
888, 4.	CARPUS	572.
	JEZREEL	102, 962 (Part I.).
888, 6.	BETHABARA	110.
888, 7	PHILEMON	197, *892, *893, *907, 1005.
8888	ARISTARCHUS	724, 906, 1017.
88, 88, 47	BADEN II., *or* NUREMBERG	599.
88, 88, 68, 88, 68	FORTUNATUS	116 in "S. G. G. for the Young."
88, 88, 88	ANGELS' SONG	759.
	EATON	181, 343, 538, 690, 718, 720, 775, 864.
	HALLE	377.
or 98, 98, 88	MAMRE	31, 104, 494, *960, 987.
	MAON	58, 273, 280, 291, 385, 394, 684, 729.
	PEDAL TUNE	616, 1044.
	ZION	429, 617, 792.
888. D.	EXETER	432.
88, 88, 89	"JESUS OF NAZARETH"	1039.
88, 118	GERSHOM	531.
97, 87, 87, 87	"IT IS BETTER FARTHER ON"	1056.
98, 98	APPHIA	87 in "S. G. G. for the Young."
	CORPUS CHRISTI	789.
9998, 8888	AQUILA	642, *1094.
10 10, 7	ST. DUNSTAN	1022.
10 10, 10 10	CONWAY	345.
	DEPTFORD	196, 446.
	EBRONAH	697.
	EUNICE	54 in "S. G. G. for the Young."
	PYRMONT	696.
	"YET THERE IS ROOM!"	1042.
10 10 10, 10 10	OLD 124TH	914.
10 10, 11 11	HANOVER, *or* CROFT'S 104th	73, 510, 583.
or 11 11, 11 11	PARAN	50, 59, 173, 299, 411, 423, 581, 698, 992, 993, *1050, 1066.
	RIPON	628.
10 11, 11 11, 12 11	SOSTHENES	424, 498, 621.
11 8, 11 8	CRESCENS	79, 81.
	"I HAVE ENTERED THE VALLEY"	1064.
11 10, 11 10	GAIUS	614.
	STERNBERG	42, 208, 666, 731, 938, 939, 967, 1091.
or 11 10, 11 10, 10 10	EIRENE	29, 292, 648, 649, 708, 971, 1084.
11 11 11, 5	LILLINGSTON	847.
11 11, 10 10; or 11 11, 11 11	PEOR	308, 318, *976.
11 11, 11 11	"BRIGHT JEWELS"	97 in "S. G. G. for the Young."
	HOBAH	*653, 846, *1045, 1058, 1067, 1077.
11 11, 11 11, 5	TERTIUS	525.
11 12, 12 10	TRISAGION	3.
12 9, 11 9	FAITH	458.
12 10, 11 10	VENITE ADOREMUS	202, 473.
13 6, 13 6, 13 13, 13 15	EPENETUS	165.
13 11, 13 12	EPAPHRODITUS	982.

HYMN CHANTS.

	Tunes—	*Hymns—*
For L. M., C. M., or S. M.	Ephesus	738, 766.
	Smyrna	263, 465, 553, 578, 582, 889, 1082.
	Worcester	66.
For other Measures of four lines	Pergamos	70, 90, 597.
	Thyatira	466, 540, 573, 657, 673, 822, 823, 908, 962 (Part II.), 1063.
	Troyte	262, 279, 891.
	Sardis	35, 64, 175, 378, 518, 545, 552, 558, *579, 641, 705, 749.
For other Measures of five lines	Philadelphia	33, 246, 477, 716, 735, 765, 1079.
For other Measures of six lines	Laodicea	141, 365, 563, 659, 692, 894, 897.

For Hymn 439	Celestial.
„ 567	St. Ethelburga
„ 1022	St. Botolph.

Christmas Carols . . . 923, 943, 944, 945.

EXPLANATIONS.

Numerals in Brackets indicate the subdivisions of each subject.
Numerals, thus [H. P. 191], on the right hand of the Tunes, indicate the number of the Tune in the Companion Volume, "HAVERGAL'S PSALMODY."
Small numerals over first line of Hymn indicate the METRE.
(*a.*) signifies some *necessary* alteration, either by Usage, Euphony, or Grammar.
(*tr.*) signifies Translator.

SYNOPSIS OF MEASURES.

L.M. Long Measure	8 8 8 8.
L.M. D. Long Measure doubled . . .	8 8 8 8 : 8 8 8 8.
C.M. Common Measure	8 6 8 6.
C.M. D. Common Measure doubled . .	8 6 8 6 : 8 6 8 6.
S.M. Short Measure	6 6 8 6.
S.M. D. Short Measure doubled. . .	6 6 8 6 : 6 6 8 6.
Old 25th Psalm. S.M. D.	6 6 8 6 : 6 6 8 6.
Old 81st Psalm. C.M. D.	8 6 8 6 : 8 6 8 6.
Old 100th Psalm. L.M.	8 8 8 8.
Old 124th Psalm	10 10 10, 10 10.

P.M. Peculiar Measure, varying metres, from 5 5 to 15 15, etc., etc.

Part I.—The Holy and Ever-blessed Trinity in Unity.

Theme I.—Worship.

CULBACH. [H. P. 181.]

(1) ADORATION.

1 Isa. vi. 1. *"I saw , the Lord sitting upon a throne."* Tune Culbach. 87, 87.

1 BRIGHT the vision that delighted
Once the sight of Judah's seer;
Sweet the countless tongues united
To entrance the prophet's ear.

2 Round the Lord in glory seated,
Cherubim and seraphim
Filled His temple, and repeated
Each to each the' alternate hymn:

3 "Lord, Thy glory fills the heaven,
Earth is with its fulness stored;
Unto Thee be glory given,
Holy, Holy, Holy Lord!"

4 Heaven is still with glory ringing,
Earth takes up the angels' cry,
"Holy, Holy, Holy,"—singing,
"Lord of hosts, the Lord most high!"

5 With His seraph train before Him,
With His Holy Church below,
Thus conspire we to adore Him,
Bid we thus our anthem flow.

6 Thus, Thy glorious name confessing,
We adopt Thy angels' cry,
"Holy, Holy, Holy,"—blessing
Thee, "the Lord of hosts most high!"

Bishop Mant, 1837.

NASSAU. [H. P. 155.]

2 Tune Nassau. 77, 77, 77.
Isa. vi. 3. *"Holy, Holy, Holy."*

1 HOLY, Holy, Holy Lord,
God of hosts, Eternal King,
By the heavens and earth adored;
Angels and archangels sing,
Chanting everlastingly
To the Blessèd Trinity.

2 Since by Thee were all things made,
And in Thee do all things live,
Be to Thee all honour paid,
Praise to Thee let all things give,
Singing everlastingly
To the Blessèd Trinity.

3 Thousands, tens of thousands, stand,
Spirits blest, before Thy throne,
Speeding thence at Thy command;
And, when Thy behests are done,
Singing everlastingly
To the Blessèd Trinity.

4 Cherubim and seraphim
Veil their faces with their wings;
Eyes of angels are too dim
To behold the King of kings,
While they sing eternally
To the Blessèd Trinity.

Part II.

5 Thee, apostles, prophets, Thee,
Thee, the noble martyr band
Praise with solemn jubilee;
Thee, the church in every land,
Singing everlastingly
To the Blessèd Trinity.

6 In Thy name baptized are we,
With Thy blessing are dismissed;
And Thrice-holy chant to Thee
In the holy eucharist;
Life is one Doxology
To the Blessèd Trinity.

7 To the Father, and the Son,
Who for us did deign to die,
And to God the Holy One,
Who the church doth sanctify;
Sing we with glad jubilee,
Hallelujah! Lord, to Thee.

8 Hallelujah! Lord, to Thee—
Father, Son, and Holy Ghost,
Godhead One, and Persons Three,
Join us with the heavenly host,
Singing everlastingly
To the Blessèd Trinity.

Bishop Christopher Wordsworth, 1862.

TRISAGION. [H. P. 249.]

3 Rev. iv. 8. "*They rest not . . . saying, Holy, Holy, Holy.*" Tune TRISAGION. 11 12, 12 10.

1 HOLY, Holy, Holy, Lord God Almighty!
Early in the morning our song shall rise to Thee;
Holy, Holy, Holy! merciful and mighty!
God in Three Persons, Blessèd Trinity!

2 Holy, Holy, Holy! all the saints adore Thee,
Casting down their golden crowns around the glassy sea,
Cherubim and seraphim falling down before Thee,
Which wert and art, and evermore shalt be.

3 Holy, Holy, Holy! though the darkness hide Thee,
Though the eye of sinful man Thy glory may not see,
Only Thou art holy, there is none beside Thee,
Perfect in power, in love, and purity.

4 Holy, Holy, Holy, Lord God Almighty!
All Thy works shall praise Thy name, in earth, and sky, and sea;
Holy, Holy, Holy! Merciful and Mighty!
God in Three Persons, Blessèd Trinity!

Bishop Heber, 1827.

HAVERGAL. [H. P. 163.]

4 Col. ii. 2. "*The mystery of God, and of the Father, and of Christ.*" Tune HAVERGAL. 777.

1 MIGHTY Father! Blessèd Son!
Holy Spirit! Three in One!
Evermore Thy will be done!

2 Threefold is Thy glorious might,
Threefold is Thy name of light,
Holy! Awful! Infinite!

3 Threefold let our praises be,
Great mysterious One, to Thee!
Undivided Trinity!

4 Mystery of mysteries!
Before whom with veilèd eyes
Songs of saints and angels rise.

5 Rainbow-like the emerald zone
That encompasseth Thy throne,
O Thou most mysterious One!

6 Thunderings and lightnings, rolled
From beneath, Thy saints enfold,
Clothed in white, and crowned with gold.

7 Holy, Holy, Holy Lord!
God Almighty! Father! Word!
Spirit! Three in One adored!

8 Threefold is Thy love to me,
Threefold let my graces be,
Faith, and Hope, and Charity.

9 Mighty Father! Blessèd Son!
Holy Spirit! Three in One!
Evermore Thy will be done.

J. S. B. Monsell, LL.D., 1863.

Note the Symbolic Form—Three lines harmonizing in each verse;—three verses in each division;—three divisions making one hymn.

ADORATION OF THE HOLY TRINITY. 3

MAHANAIM. [H. P. 129.]

5 Tune Mahanaim. 76, 76. D.
Eph. iv. 5. "*One Lord, one faith.*"

1 O HOLY! Holy Father,
O Christ ascended high,
O pure celestial Spirit,
Eternal Trinity!
We, with Thy countless seraphs,
We, with Thy saints in light,
Bow down in adoration,
And praise Thee day and night.

2 One life pervades Thy ransomed
Within the golden gate,
And those who still are pilgrims,
And for their glory wait.
The shouts of triumph yonder,
The plaintive songs of earth,
Flow from the Spirit's presence;
Both own a heavenly birth.

3 O wondrous, living union!
The saints are one with Thee,
Thou Fountain of their being,
Mysterious Trinity!
No power on earth,—or Satan,
Can separate Christ's sheep,
For which He gave the ransom,
And which He 's pledged to keep!

4 Then teach us, Lord, to worship
With loving hearts to-day;
And whilst we sing Thy praises,
And learn in faith to pray,
Help us to feel our union
With *all* who know Thy name,
And glory in Jehovah,
Unchangeably the same!

William Pennefather, 1871.

SEIR (Mount). [H. P. 161.]

6 Ps. lxv. 1. "*Praise waiteth for Thee, O God.*"
Tune Seir. 77, 77. D.

1 HOLY, Holy, Holy Lord!
Self-existent Deity!
By the hosts of heaven adored,
Teach us how to worship Thee.
Only uncreated Mind,
Wonders in Thy nature meet,
Perfect unity combined
With society complete.

2 All perfection dwells in Thee,
Now to us obscurely known;
Three in One, and One in Three,
Great Jehovah, God alone.
Be our all, O Lord Divine!
Father, Saviour, vital Breath!
Body, spirit, soul, be Thine,
Now, and at, and after death.

3 Glorious Thou in holiness,
When Thou didst Thy right maintain;
Truth and grace at once express
When Thine only Son was slain.
Here was deepest wisdom seen;
Here the richest stores of grace;
Mildest love, and vengeance keen;
Oh how bright their mingled rays!

4 Fearful Thou in praises, too,
Loving Saviour, slaughtered Lamb!
We with joy and reverence view
All Thy glory, all Thy shame.
Be Thy death the death of sin;
Be Thy life the sinner's plea;
Save me, teach me, rule within—
Prophet, Priest, and King to me!

5 Wonder-working Spirit! Thine
Is the mighty grace we sing;
Set on us Thy seal Divine,
Safely to Thy kingdom bring:
Mortify each sinful deed,
Daily strengthen every grace;
Lead us, urge us on with speed,
And let GLORY crown the race!

John Ryland, D.D., 1796.

EVERTON. [H. P. 308.]

7 Eph. ii. 18. *"We . . . have access."* Tune EVERTON. 87, 87. D. Or SALZBURG.

1 GRACIOUS God of our salvation,
Thee, in Christ, we would adore;
Standing in the high relation
Of Thy sons for evermore:
We, by sin, were separated
From our Father's face awhile;
But we now are new-created,
By His sweet, returning smile.

2 Now the Spirit keeps us moving
To our Father's holy throne;
Through the Saviour sweetly proving
How for sin He did atone!
Now, instead of threatening thunder,
And of life an endless loss,
We enjoy the peaceful wonder
Of our dear Redeemer's cross.

3 To the Father, by the Spirit,
Now a sweet access we find,
Through the Saviour's matchless merit,
He is most divinely kind:
Now in praises to the Saviour
Let our sacred song ascend;
And, the best of all behaviour,
Honour our Almighty Friend.

4 Now to Him who has redeemed us
With His precious sacrifice,
And the Holy Ghost who seals us,
For the Father in the skies,
Let us join in endless praises,
To the' eternal THREE in ONE,
For the grace and blood that raises
Us to God, through Christ His Son.

Thomas Row, 1817.

MUNICH. [H. P. 279.]

3 Rom. xiii. 11. *"Now is our salvation nearer than when we believed."* Tune MUNICH. 76, 76. D. Or MAHANAIM.

1 YON shining shore *is* nearer!
The saints in robes of light,
With harps and golden vials,
Are almost within sight!
Hark! at the mighty anthem,
That rolls across the sea,
"We give Thee praise and glory,
Eternal Trinity!"

2 "A little while" they've left us,
To tread the desert sand;
But Jesus is beside us,
We march at His command;
And soon our dusty raiment
We'll lay, for aye, aside,
And, with our Saviour's likeness,
We shall be glorified!

3 Amidst our tears and conflicts,
We almost can discern
The radiant Throne before us,—
"The lamps" that ever burn,—
The Father's dazzling glory,—
The Lamb whose blood was shed,—
The living, kingly Jesus,
Who once for us was dead!

4 We come to-day to worship,
We bring our gifts to Thee,
Our hearts, our gold, our praises,
Thou blessèd Trinity!
Alas! too long, our idols
Have hid Thee from our sight;
Help us to cast them from us,
And henceforth "walk in light!"

William Pennefather, 1871.

OLD "TEN COMMANDMENTS' TUNE." [H. P. 15.]

9 Tune OLD TEN COMMANDMENTS. L.M. Or GÖLDEL.
1 John v. 7. *"There are Three that bear record."*

1 ALL hail, Adorèd Trinity!
All hail, Eternal Unity!
O God the Father, God the Son,
And God the Spirit, ever One.

2 Behold, to Thee, this festal day
We meekly pour our thankful lay;
Oh let our work accepted be,
That sweetest work of praising Thee.

3 Three Persons praise we evermore,
One only God our hearts adore;
In Thy sure mercy, ever kind,
Oh may we our protection find.

4 O Trinity! O Unity!
Be present as we worship Thee;
With songs that angels sing to Thee,
Unite our hymns of jubilee.

J. D. Chambers (tr.), 1857.

10 Tune OLD TEN COMMANDMENTS. L. M.
2 Cor. xiii. 14. *"Grace . . . Love . . . Communion."*

1 O TRIUNE GOD! O King of Kings!
All-glorious ONE, mysterious THREE!
Archangels bow with veiling wings,
Adoring where they cannot see.

2 Yet we the Trinity can praise
In Unity, through Christ our King;
Our grateful hearts and voices raise
In faith and love, while thus we sing:—

3 Glory to God the Father be,
Because He sent His Son to die;
Glory to God the Son, that He
Did with such willingness comply;

4 Glory to God the Holy Ghost,
Who to our hearts this love reveals:
Thus God, Triune, to sinners lost,
Salvation sends, procures, and seals.

Joseph Hart, 1759.—*ver.* 1, *F. R. H.*

GOZAN (River of). [H. P. 165.]

11 Tune GOZAN. 77, 87. Or ZOAN II.
Rev. i. 5. *"Unto Him that loved us."*

1 ETERNAL Hallelujahs
Be to the Father given,
Who loved His own—ere time began,
And marked them out for heaven.

2 Anthems of equal glory
Ascribe we to the SAVIOUR;
Who lived and died—that we, His Bride,
Might live with Him for ever.

3 Hail! co-eternal SPIRIT,
Thy church's new Creator!
The saints He seals—their fear dispels,
And sanctifies their nature.

4 We laud the glorious TRIAD,
The mystic One in essence;
Till called to join—the hosts that shine
In His immediate Presence.

5 Faithful is He that promised,
And stands engaged to save us;
The Triune Lord—has passed His word
That He will never leave us.

6 A kingdom He assigned us,
Before the world's foundation:
Thou God of grace—be Thine the praise,
And ours the consolation!

Augustus M. Toplady, 1774.

12 Tune GOZAN. 77, 87. D.
Eph. i. 4. *"He hath chosen us in Him."*

1 THOU God of grace, our Father,
We now rejoice before Thee,
Thy children we—and loved by Thee;
'Tis meet we should adore Thee!
As Thine Thou didst foreknow us,
For such was Thine election,
And Thou hast shown—to us Thine own—
Thy fulness of affection.

2 In Jesus Thou didst choose us
Before the world's foundation,
Ere Adam's fall—involved us all
In guilt and condemnation.
Thy purpose and election,
In spite of all our failing,
Have firmly stood—and by the blood
Of Christ are made availing.

3 The grace of this salvation
The Holy Ghost hath taught us;
By Him we're healed—for He revealed
How Jesu's blood hath bought us.
Soon all the church in glory,
In its predestined station,
Shall bless Thy name—with Christ the Lamb,
Thou God of all salvation!

S. P. Tregelles, LL.D., 1837.

CRASSELIUS; *or*, WINCHESTER NEW. [H. P. 3.]

13

Ps. cl. 2. *"His excellent greatness."* Tune CRASSELIUS. L. M.

1 PARENT of all, whose love displayed
Still rules the world Thy bounty made,
Fain would we raise the hymn to Thee,
In Substance One, in Person Three.

2 Fain would we chant to Thee the song,
Which through the ages all along
Is chanted by Thy heavenly train,
And earth resounds to heaven again.

3 Taught by Thy word, this festal day,
Our homage of true faith we pay;
Oh, in that faith preserve us still,
And shield us evermore from ill:

4 That still our lips Thy praise may show,
And with Thy Holy Church below,
Above with Thy angelic host,
Sing Father, Son, and Holy Ghost.

Bishop Mant (tr.), 1837.

ZAANAIM (Plain of). [H. P. 191.]

14

Eph. i. 3. *"All spiritual blessings . . . in Christ."* Tune ZAANAIM. 87, 87, 47.

1 O MY Lord, how great the wonders
Thy rich grace has wrought for me!
On Thy love my spirit ponders,
Praising, magnifying Thee;
Hallelujah!
To the great ETERNAL THREE!

2 I was once far off—a stranger—
Guilty, helpless, deaf, and blind;
Jesus rescued me from danger,
And renewed my heart and mind:
Precious Saviour!
How compassionate and kind!

3 Quickened by His Holy Spirit,
Covered with His righteousness,
He has said I shall inherit
Everlasting life and bliss:
Blessèd Jesus!
How my soul exults in this!

4 He has all my sins forgiven,
Paid my debt and set me free,
Vanquished hell, and opened heaven,
And prepared a place for me:
My Redeemer
Loved me from eternity.

5 Yea, He says He'll never leave me,
But, when all His will is done,
To His kingdom He'll receive me,
As the partner of His throne;
Then I'll praise Him,
While eternity rolls on!

Joseph Irons, 1825.

ADORATION OF THE HOLY TRINITY.

GLOUCESTER. [H. P. 40.]

15 2 Cor. i. 3. "*Blessed be God.*" Tune GLOUCESTER. C. M.

1 THOU dear and great mysterious THREE,
For ever be adored,
For all the endless grace we see
In our Redeemer stored.

2 The Father's ancient grace we sing,
That chose us in our Head;
Ordaining Christ, our God and King,
To suffer in our stead.

3 The sacred Son, in equal strains,
With reverence we address,
For all His grace, and dying pains,
And splendid righteousness.

4 With tuneful tongue the Holy Ghost
For His great work we praise,
Whose power inspires the blood-bought host,
Their grateful voice to raise.

5 Thus, the eternal Three in One
We join to praise, for grace
And endless glory through the Son,
As shining from His face.

Thomas Row, 1817.

FREYLINGHAUSEN. [H. P. 306.]

16 2 Cor. iv. 6. "*The glory of God in the face of Jesus Christ.*" Tune FREYLINGHAUSEN. 87, 87. D. Or SHEN.

1 GOD in Three appears all glorious,
In the everlasting One;
Shines the fulness of the Godhead,
In the person of the Son;
Reigns in Thee the great Jehovah,
Reigns in all-victorious grace,
Shows His all-transporting beauties,
Through the bleeding Prince of Peace.

2 Sing we all the Lord of Glory,
Sing the mercy pure and free,
Mercy flowing from the fountain
Of the everlasting Three;
Equal all, and all united,
In the One eternal God,
Shining all with equal splendour,
Through the rich atoning blood.

3 May we all, with admiration,
Roll the cheering truth along,
Three in One be all the chorus,
Three in One be all the song.
Come, Thou Triune God and Saviour,
Now descend in purest love,
Sing we then with holy ardour,
Sing our way to realms above.

Richard Burnham, 1796.

SALZBURG. [H. P. 203.]

17 1 John iii. 1. *"Behold what manner of love!"*

Tune SALZBURG. 87, 87. D.

1 SEE, oh see! what love the Father
Hath bestowed upon our race,
How He bends, with sweet compassion,
Over us His beaming face!
See how He His best and dearest
For the very worst hath given,
His own Son for us poor sinners;
See, oh see! the love of Heaven!

2 See, oh see! what love the Saviour
Also hath on us bestowed,
How He bled for us and suffered,
How He bare the heavy load!
On the cross, and in the garden,
Oh! how sore was His distress!
Is not this a love that passeth
Aught that tongue can e'er express?

3 See, oh see! what love is shown us
Also by the Holy Ghost!
How He strives with us poor sinners,
Even when we sin the most!
Teaching, comforting, correcting,
Where He sees it needful is!
Oh, what heart would not be thankful
For a three-fold love like this?

C. J. P. Spitta, 1833; *R. Massie (tr.)*, 1860.

THE OLD 100th TUNE. [H. P. 1.]

18 2 Cor. ix. 14. *"The exceeding grace of God."*

Tune OLD HUNDREDTH. L. M.

1 HOW can a mortal tongue express,
Almighty Lord, Thine endless praise;
Or, how can we Thy throne address,
And be accepted in our lays?

2 Through Jesus, our Redeemer, we
Our cheerful, humble praises bring,
For all the endless grace we see
In Him, our Saviour and our King.

3 For grace that saves our souls from hell,
Accept, dear Lord, our grateful song;
And let us join, Thy grace to tell,
Until we reach the heavenly throng.

4 For grace that ends in glory bright,
We bless Thee, Triune God of love,
For now, by faith, we see the light
Of that celestial world above.

5 For grace, that formed the wondrous plan
Of our deliverance from the dead,
And chose us in the Glory-Man,
We give Thee praise through Him who bled.

6 For grace, with endless glory joined,
We bless the Father and the Son;
And praise the Spirit, who we find
Reveals our glorious Three in One.

Thomas Row, 1817.

RATISBON. [H. P. 157.]

(2) INVOCATION.

19 Tune RATISBON. 77, 77, 77.
Mark xiv. 36. "*He said*, ABBA, FATHER."

1 "ABBA!" gentle Jesus prayed,
Kneeling in the garden shade;
"Father!" Christ the' anointed King
Cried out in His suffering;
"Abba, Father!" sighed the Son,
"Not My will, but Thine be done."

2 "Jesus!" Jewish voices cry,
"Save from sin and misery!"
"Christ!" by Gentile hearts adored,
"Save us, our anointed Lord!"
"Abba, Father!" it is done,
All in Jesus Christ are one.

3 "Abba!" to Thy bosom take
Sin-cleansed souls, for "Jesu's" sake;
"Father!" in our utmost need
We the "Christ" within us plead;
"Abba, Father!" day by day
We through "Jesus Christ" do pray.

4 "Jesus"—for the Jewish tribes,
On the top-stone Love inscribes,
"Christ"—for all the Gentile race,
Graving on its other face:
"Jesus Christ!"—the Corner-stone!
Making all the building one!

J. S. B. Monsell, LL.D., 1866.

20 Tune SALZBURG. 87, 87. D.
(*Repeat last half for Chorus.*)
Rom. viii. 15. "*We cry, Abba, Father.*"

1 ABBA, Father! Lord, we call Thee,
Hallowed name! from day to day;
'Tis Thy children's right to know Thee,
None but children Abba say.
This high privilege we inherit,
First Thy gift, and then Christ's blood;
God the Spirit, to our spirit,
Witnesseth we are sons of God.
Chorus.—Abba, Father! still we call Thee,
Abba sounds through all our host;
All in heaven and earth adore Thee,
FATHER, SON, and HOLY GHOST.

2 Abba's love first gave us being,
When, in Christ, in that vast plan,
Abba chose the church in Jesus,
Long before the world began!
Oh! what love the Father bore us!
Oh! how precious in His sight!
When He gave His church to Jesus;
Jesus! His whole soul's delight!
Chorus.—Abba, Father! etc.

PART II.]

3 Though our nature's fall in Adam
Seemed to shut us out from God,
Thus it was His counsel brought us
Nearer still through Jesu's blood:
By the plan Himself had formèd,
Ere like sheep we went astray;
They, said God, shall call Me Father,
Nor from Me shall turn away.
Chorus.—Abba, Father! etc.

4 And the richest stores of pardon
God sets forth in Christ His Son;
With the Spirit's grace to guide us,
Safe to bring His children home.
Abba, Father! makes all certain,
Both by word, by oath, and blood;
Abba saith, "They are My people,"
And they say, "The Lord's my God."
Chorus.—Abba, Father! etc.

5 Hence through all our changing seasons,
Trouble, sorrow, sickness, woe;
Nothing changeth God's affection,
Abba's love will bring us through.
Soon shall all Thy blood-bought children
Round Thy throne their anthems raise;
And in songs of rich salvation
Shout to Abba endless praise!
Chorus.—Abba, Father! etc.

Robert Hawker, D.D., 1827.

21 Tune SALZBURG. 87, 87. D.
Gal. iv. 6. "*Because ye are sons.*"

1 ABBA, Father! we approach Thee
In our Saviour's precious name;
We, Thy children, here assembling,
Now Thy promised blessings claim:
From our sins His blood has washed us,
'Tis through Him our souls draw nigh;
And Thy Spirit too hath taught us,
Abba, Father! thus to cry.

2 Once as prodigals we wandered,
In our folly far from Thee;
But Thy grace, o'er sin abounding,
Rescued us from misery.
Clothed in garments of salvation,
At Thy table in our place,
We rejoice, and Thou rejoicest
In the riches of Thy grace.

3 Abba, Father! all adore Thee,
All rejoice in heaven above:
While in us they learn the wonders
Of Thy wisdom, grace, and love.
Soon before Thy throne assembled,
All Thy children shall proclaim
Glory, everlasting glory,
Be to God and to the Lamb!

James George Deck, 1838.

PATMOS. [H. P. 147.]

22 Isa. liv. 13. *"All thy children shall be taught of the Lord."* Tune PATMOS. 77, 77. Or GIBBONS.

1 HOLY Father! let Thy love
 Rest upon us from above;
All Thy children deign to own,
Teach them to approach Thy throne.

2 Precious Saviour! Zion's King,
Of Thy glorious work we sing;
Reign amidst Thy chosen race,
Spread the triumphs of Thy grace.

3 Kind Preceptor! we expect
Promised grace for God's elect;
Make the Saviour's fulness known;
Sanctify and teach Thine own.

4 Triune God! Thy covenant love
Faithful to the end shall prove;
All things rest on Thy decree,
Glory to the' Eternal Three!

Joseph Irons, 1825.

SUCCOTH (Valley of). [H. P. 189.]

Hal - le - lu - jah, Hal - le - lu - jah.
Hal - - - le - lu - jah.

23 John xvii. 23. *"Thou hast loved them, as Thou hast loved Me."* Tune SUCCOTH. 87, 87, 77.

1 HOLY Father! we address Thee—
 Loved in Thy belovèd Son;
Holy Son of God, we bless Thee,
 Boundless grace hath made us one;
Holy Spirit, aid our songs,
This glad work to Thee belongs.

2 Wondrous was Thy love, O Father!
 Wondrous Thine, O Son of God!
Vast the love that bruised and wounded,
 Vast the love that bore the rod;
Holy Spirit, still reveal
How those stripes alone can heal.

3 Gracious Father! Thy good pleasure
 Is to love us as Thy Son,
Meting out the self-same measure,
 Since Thou seest us as one.
Blessèd Jesus! loved are we,
As the Father loveth Thee.

4 Hallelujah! we are hasting
 To our Father's house above;
By the way our souls are tasting
 Rich and everlasting love;
In Jehovah is our boast,
Father, Son, and Holy Ghost!

Mary Bowly, 1847.

SWABIA. [H. P. 82.]

24 Ps. xxxiv. 3. *"O magnify the Lord with me."* Tune Swabia. S. M.

1 WE sing the Father's love—
We trust the Saviour's grace—
The Holy Spirit's power we prove,
Amidst the chosen race.

2 We give the Father praise—
We glorify the Son—
We bless the Spirit for His grace,
Which makes salvation known.

3 'Twas God the Father chose
Our souls in God the Son;
And God the Holy Ghost bestows
All blessings from the throne.

4 A Triune God we own,
In daily songs of praise;
In Persons Three, in Essence One
The God of sovereign grace!

Joseph Irons, 1825.

CRASSELIUS; *or*, **WINCHESTER NEW.** [H. P. 3.]

25 Tune Crasselius. L. M.
Ps. cv. 3. *"Glory ye in His holy name."*

1 FATHER! we glory in Thy choice—
Saviour! we in Thy work rejoice—
O Holy Ghost! Thy power we sing;
Thou, Triune God, art Zion's King.

2 Father! 'tis in Thy love we rest—
Saviour! in Thee our souls are blest—
O Holy Ghost! Thy power we own,
Which made Jehovah's glory known.

3 The Father, Son, and Holy Ghost,
Adored by all the heavenly host,
Is Zion's Triune God and King!
Let all the church His glory sing!

Joseph Irons, 1825.

26 Tune Swabia. S. M.
2 Cor. iii. 18. *"The glory of the Lord."*

1 FATHER! in whom we live,
In whom we are and move,
The glory, praise, and power receive,
Of Thy creating love.

2 Let all the angel throng
Give thanks to God on high;
While earth repeats the joyful song,
And echoes through the sky.

3 Incarnate Deity!
Let all the ransomed race
Render in thanks their lives to Thee
For Thy redeeming grace.

4 The grace to sinners showed,
Ye heavenly choirs, proclaim;
And cry "Salvation to our God!
Salvation to the Lamb!"

5 Spirit of Holiness!
Let all Thy saints adore
Thy sacred energy, and bless
Thy heart-renewing power.

6 Not angel tongues can tell
Thy love's ecstatic height,
The glorious joy unspeakable,
The beatific sight!

7 Eternal Triune Lord!
Let all the hosts above,
Let all the sons of men, record
And dwell upon Thy love.

8 When heaven and earth are fled
Before Thy glorious face,
Sing all the saints Thy love hath made
Thine everlasting praise!

Charles Wesley, 1747.

LUSATIA. [H. P. 199.]

27 Ps. lxxiii. 24. "Thou shalt guide me with Thy counsel." Tune LUSATIA. 87, 87, 87.

1 LEAD us, heavenly Father, lead us
O'er the world's tempestuous sea;
Guide us, guard us, keep us, feed us,
For we have no help but Thee:
Yet possessing—every blessing,
If our God our Father be.

2 Saviour, breathe forgiveness o'er us;
All our weakness Thou dost know;
Thou didst tread this earth before us,
Thou didst feel its keenest woe:
Lone and dreary—faint and weary,
Through the desert Thou didst go.

3 Spirit of our God, descending,
Fill our hearts with heavenly joy;
Love, with every passion blending,
Pleasure that can never cloy:
Thus provided—pardoned, guided,
Nothing can our peace destroy!

James Edmeston, 1820.

GILBOA (Mount). [H. P. 11.]

28 1 John v. 7. "The Father, the Word, and the Holy Ghost." Tune GILBOA. L. M. Or BAVARIA.

1 FATHER of heaven! whose love profound
A ransom for our souls hath found,
Before Thy throne we sinners bend;
To us Thy pardoning love extend.

2 Almighty Son! Incarnate Word!
Our Prophet, Priest, Redeemer, Lord,
Before Thy throne we sinners bend;
To us Thy saving grace extend.

3 Eternal Spirit! by whose breath
The soul is raised from sin and death,
Before Thy throne we sinners bend;
To us Thy quickening power extend.

4 Jehovah! Father, Spirit, Son!
Mysterious Godhead! Three in One!
Before Thy throne we sinners bend;
Grace, pardon, life to us extend!

J. Cooper, 1812.

EIRENE. [H. P. 246.]

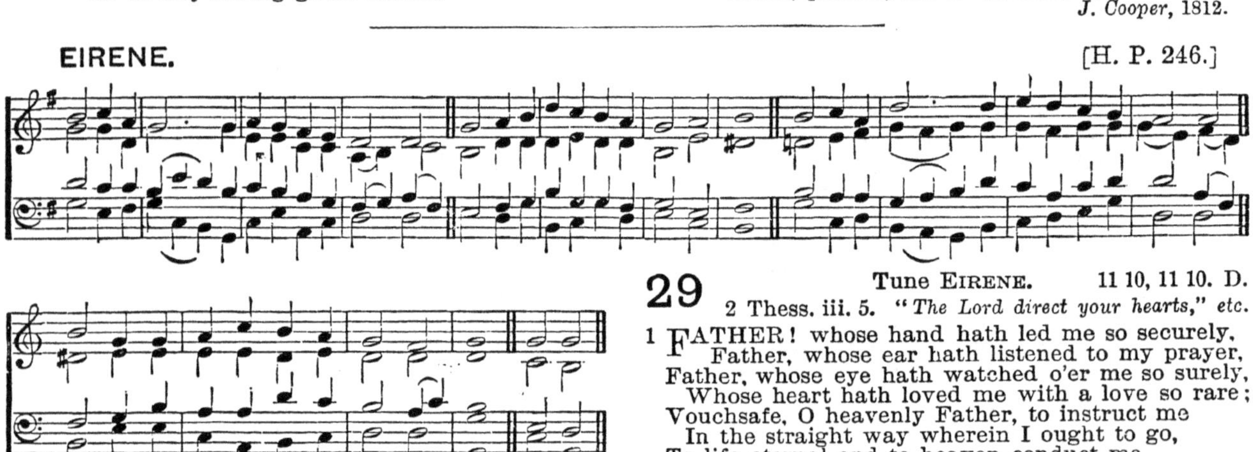

29 Tune EIRENE. 11 10, 11 10. D.
2 Thess. iii. 5. "The Lord direct your hearts," etc.

1 FATHER! whose hand hath led me so securely,
Father, whose ear hath listened to my prayer,
Father, whose eye hath watched o'er me so surely,
Whose heart hath loved me with a love so rare;
Vouchsafe, O heavenly Father, to instruct me
In the straight way wherein I ought to go,
To life eternal and to heaven conduct me,
Through health and sickness, and through weal and woe.

2 O my Redeemer! who hast my redemption
Purchased, and paid for, by Thy precious blood;
Thereby procuring an entire exemption
From the dread wrath and punishment of God:
Thou who hast saved my soul from condemnation,
Redeem it also from the power of sin,
Be Thou the Captain still of my salvation,
Through whom alone I can the victory win.

3 O Holy Ghost! who from the Father flowest—
And from the Son, oh teach me how to pray!
Thou, who the love and peace of God bestowest,
With faith and hope inspire and cheer my way;
Direct, control, and sanctify each motion
Within my soul, and make it thus to be
Prayerful, and still, and full of deep devotion,
A holy temple, worthy, Lord, of Thee!

C. J. P. Spitta, 1833; *R. Massie* (*tr.*), 1860.

30 Tune Moscow. 664, 6664.

Ps. xlv. 1. "*My heart is inditing a good matter.*"

1 COME, Thou almighty King!
Help us Thy name to sing,
Help us to praise!
Father, all-glorious,
O'er all victorious!
Come, and reign over us,
Ancient of days!

2 Come, Thou incarnate Word!
Gird on Thy mighty sword,
Our prayer attend!
Come and Thy people bless,
And give Thy word success;
Spirit of holiness,
On us descend!

3 Come, Holy Comforter!
Thy sacred witness bear,
In this glad hour:
Thou who almighty art,
Now rule in every heart,
And ne'er from us depart,
Spirit of power!

4 To the great One in Three
Eternal praises be
Hence evermore!
His sovereign majesty
May we in glory see,
And to eternity
Love and adore!

C. Wesley's Leaflets, 1757.

31 Ps. xvi. 2. "*Thou art my Lord.*" Tune Mamre. 88, 88, 88.

1 LORD God of gods, before whose throne
Stand storms and fire, oh what shall we
Return to Heaven that is our own,
When all the world belongs to Thee!
We have no offering to impart,
But praises and a wounded heart.

2 O Thou that sitt'st in heaven, and seest
My deeds without, my thoughts within,
Be Thou my Prince, be Thou my Priest,
Command my soul and cure my sin;
How bitter my afflictions be,
I care not, so I rise to Thee.

3 Fountain of light and living breath,
Whose mercies never fail nor fade,
Fill me with life that hath no death,
Fill me with light that hath no shade;
Appoint the remnant of my days
To see Thy power and sing Thy praise.

4 What I possess or what I crave,
Brings no content, great God, to me,
If what I would, or what I have
Be not possessed and blessed in Thee;
What I enjoy, oh make it mine,
In making me, that have it, Thine.

John Quarles (*restored*), 1654.

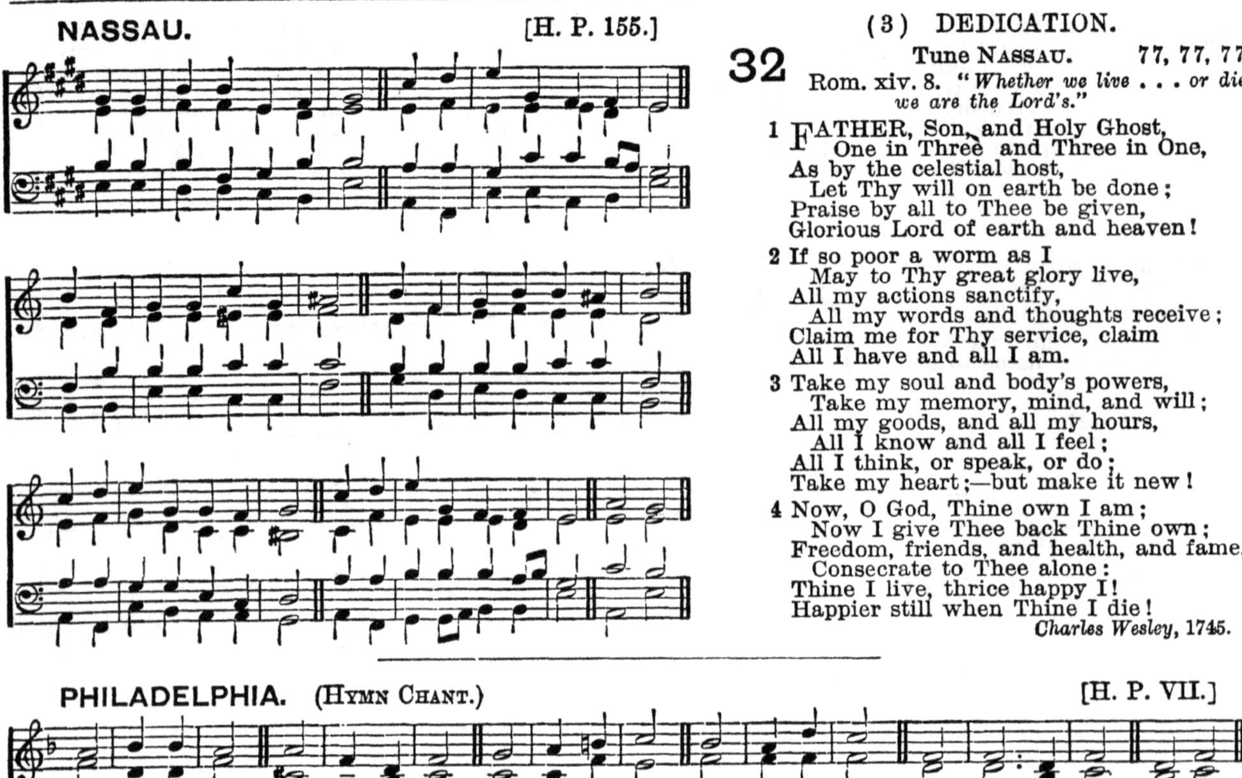

(3) DEDICATION.

32 Tune NASSAU. 77, 77, 77.

Rom. xiv. 8. *"Whether we live . . . or die, we are the Lord's."*

1 FATHER, Son, and Holy Ghost,
One in Three and Three in One,
As by the celestial host,
Let Thy will on earth be done;
Praise by all to Thee be given,
Glorious Lord of earth and heaven!

2 If so poor a worm as I
May to Thy great glory live,
All my actions sanctify,
All my words and thoughts receive;
Claim me for Thy service, claim
All I have and all I am.

3 Take my soul and body's powers,
Take my memory, mind, and will;
All my goods, and all my hours,
All I know and all I feel;
All I think, or speak, or do;
Take my heart;—but make it new!

4 Now, O God, Thine own I am;
Now I give Thee back Thine own;
Freedom, friends, and health, and fame,
Consecrate to Thee alone:
Thine I live, thrice happy I!
Happier still when Thine I die!

Charles Wesley, 1745.

33 Ps. cxvi. 16. *"O Lord, truly I am Thy servant."* Tune, Hymn Chant PHILADELPHIA. 88, 886.

1 O LORD, Thy heavenly grace impart,
And fix my frail, inconstant heart;
Henceforth my chief desire shall be
To dedicate myself to Thee;
To Thee, my God, to Thee!

2 Whate'er pursuits my time employ,
One thought shall fill my heart with joy;
That silent, secret thought shall be,
That all my hopes are fixed on Thee;
On Thee, my God, on Thee!

3 Thy glorious eye pervadeth space;
Thou'rt present, Lord, in every place;
And wheresoe'er my lot may be,
Still shall my spirit cleave to Thee;
To Thee, my God, to Thee!

4 Renouncing every worldly thing,
Safe 'neath the covert of Thy wing,
My sweetest thought henceforth shall be,
That all I want I find in Thee;
In Thee, my God, in Thee!

J. F. Oberlin, 1820; *Caroline Wilson* (*tr.*), 1829.

34 Ps. cxix. 94. *"I am Thine, save me!"* Tune HEBRON. L. M. Or GILBOA.

1 O GOD, Thy mercy, vast and free,
Has turned my happy soul to Thee:
Still round me let that mercy shine,
And save me, Lord, for I am Thine!

2 Thy truth display; Thy power reveal;
Oh let me now Thy presence feel:
Give me the joys of love Divine;
Oh save me, Lord, for I am Thine.

3 From self, from Satan, and from sin,
From foes without, and fears within,
Though they against me all combine,
Oh save me, Lord, for I am Thine!

4 And when in glory I appear,
And sing with the redeemèd there,
Then shall this work of joy be mine,
To praise that love which made me Thine!

Samuel Medley, 1800. (*a.*)

SARDIS. (Hymn Chant.) [H. P. VI.]

35 Heb. xiii. 5. *"He hath said, I will never leave thee."* Tune, Hymn Chant Sardis.

1 BY Thee, Jesu, will I stay,
Evermore Thy servant stand;
From Thee, my feet shall never stray,
But I will go where points Thy hand.

2 Thou! life of all the life that's mine,
My soul's core-sap and vital power,
As to its branch from out the vine
Flows sap of life from hour to hour.

3 Stay near me through this heat and glow;
Stay near, too, when my day sinks down,
And long the evening shadows grow,
And the dark night comes stealing on.

4 Lay in blessing, then, Thy hand
On my weary, weakly head;
Saying, "Rest, child! to the land
Thy faith hath sought thou shalt be led."

5 Stay near me; in Thine arms enfold,
When most the chill of death I dread;
Chill, like the sharp and bitter cold,
Ere dawns in heaven the morning red.

6 When darkness shall mine eyes o'ertake,
Light Thou my spirit through the gloom,
That unto me the morn may break
As breaks to him the exile's home.

C. J. P. Spitta; John B. Walter (tr.), 1868.

KEDRON (Brook). [H. P. 213.]

36 Acts ix. 6. *"Lord, what wilt Thou have me to do?"* Tune Kedron. 886, 886.

1 LORD, Thou hast won, at length I yield;
My heart, by mighty grace compelled,
Surrenders all to Thee;
Against Thy terrors long I strove;
But who can stand against Thy love?
Love conquers even me!

2 If Thou hadst bid Thy thunders roll,
And lightnings flash, to blast my soul,
I still had stubborn been:
But mercy has my heart subdued;
A bleeding Saviour I have viewed,
And now I hate my sin.

3 Now, Lord, I would be Thine alone;
Come, take possession of Thine own,
For Thou hast set me free;
Released from Satan's hard command,
See all my powers waiting stand
To be employed by Thee.

4 My will conformed to Thine would move;
On Thee, my hope, desire, and love,
In fixed attention join;
My hands, my eyes, my ears, my tongue,
Have Satan's servants been too long,
But now they shall be Thine!

John Newton, 1779.

GETHSEMANE. [H. P. 28.]

37 Luke x. 42. *"Mary hath chosen that good part."* Tune GETHSEMANE. L. M.

1 BESET with snares on every hand,
In life's uncertain path I stand:
Saviour Divine, infuse Thy light,
To guide my doubtful footsteps right.

2 Engage this roving, treacherous heart
To fix on Mary's better part,
To scorn the trifles of a day
For joys that none can take away.

3 Then let the wildest storms arise;
Let tempests mingle earth and skies:
No fatal shipwreck shall I fear,
But all my treasures with me bear.

4 If Thou, my Jesus, still be nigh,
Cheerful I live, and joyful die;
Secure, when mortal comforts flee,
To find ten thousand worlds in Thee!

Philip Doddridge, D.D., 1755.

HAVILAH. [H. P. 192.]

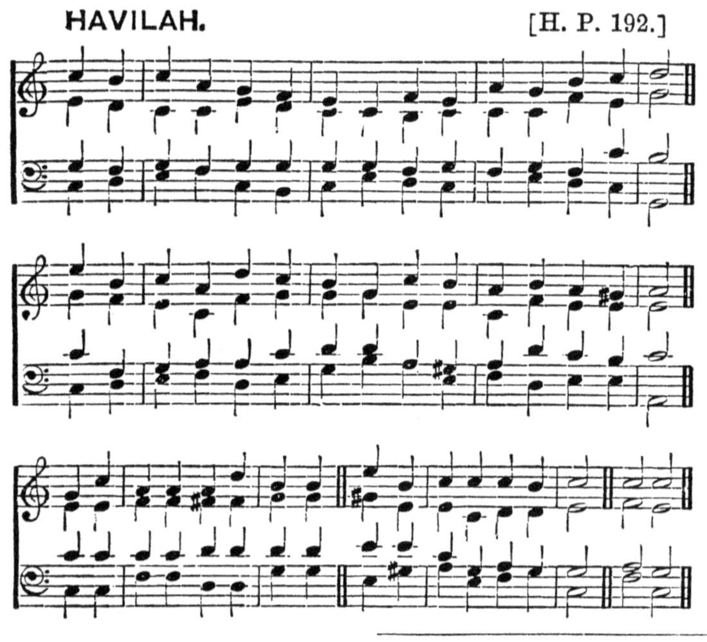

38 Tune HAVILAH. 87, 87, 47.
Ps. cviii. 1. *"My heart is fixed; I will sing."*

1 GRACIOUS Lord, my heart is fixèd,
Sing I will, and sing of Thee,
Since the cup that justice mixèd
Thou didst drink, and drink for me:
Great Deliverer!
Thou hast set the prisoner free.

2 Many were the chains that bound me,
But the Lord has loosed them all;
Arms of mercy now surround me,
Favours these, nor few nor small:
Saviour, keep me!
Keep Thy servant lest he fall.

3 Fair the scene that lies before me,
Life eternal Jesus gives;
While He waves His banner o'er me,
Peace and joy my soul receives:
Sure His promise!
I shall live because He lives.

4 When the world would bid me leave Thee,
Telling me of shame and loss,
Saviour, guard me lest I grieve Thee,
Lest I cease to love Thy cross:
This is treasure!
All the rest I count but dross!

Thomas Kelly, 1809.

GILBOA (Mount). [H. P. 11.]

39 Acts viii. 39. *"He went on his way rejoicing."* Tune GILBOA. L. M. Or BAVARIA.

1 O HAPPY day! when first we felt
Our souls with deep contrition melt,
And saw our sins, of crimson guilt,
All cleansed by blood on Calvary spilt.

2 O happy day! when first Thy love
Began our grateful hearts to move;
And gazing on Thy wondrous cross,
We saw all else as worthless dross.

3 O happy day! when we no more
Shall grieve Thee whom our souls adore;
When sorrows, conflicts, fears, shall cease,
And all our trials end in peace.

4 O happy day! when we shall see
And fix our longing eyes on Thee—
On Thee, our Light, our Life, our Love,
Our all below, our heaven above.

5 O happy day of cloudless light,
Eternal day without a night!
Lord, when shall we its dawning see,
And spend it all in praising Thee?

6 Come, Saviour, come, oh quickly come!
Take us, Thy waiting people, home:
We long to stand around Thy throne,
And know Thee as ourselves are known.

James George Deck, 1837.

KEDAR. [H. P. 42.]

40 Ps. cxix. 57. "*Thou art my portion, O Lord.*" Tune KEDAR. C. M.

1 FROM pole to pole let others roam,
And search in vain for bliss;
My soul is satisfied at home,
The Lord my portion is.

2 Jesus—who on His glorious throne
Rules heaven, and earth, and sea—
Is pleased to claim me for His own,
And gives Himself to me.

3 His person fixes all my love,
His blood removes my fear;
And while He pleads for me above,
His arm preserves me here.

4 His word of promise is my food,
His Spirit is my guide;
Thus daily is my strength renewed,
And all my wants supplied.

5 For Him I count as gain each loss,
Disgrace for Him, renown;
Well may I glory in His cross,
While He prepares my crown!

John Newton, 1779.

See Hymns 949—957, 1063—1075.

THEME II.—The Attributes of the Ever-Blessed Trinity.

LEIPSIC. [H. P. 19.]

THE BEING OF GOD.

41 Ps. xiv. 1. "*The fool hath said in his heart, There is no God.*" Tune LEIPSIC. L. M.

1 "THERE is a God"—all nature cries,
All knowledge proves "there is a God":
"There is no God," the fool replies,
Whose heart is duller than the clod.

2 The grateful clod, refreshed with rains,
Pours flowers along its Maker's path;
But the fool's heart a fool's remains,
Untouched by love—unmoved by wrath.

3 And yet the wretch himself deceives;
While fiends believe, and trembling fly,
He trembles though he disbelieves;
And conscience gives his life the lie.

4 Can guilt, can madness further go?
Yes, his—who God in works denies;
Whose creed saith "Yes," whose life says "No":
Am I more holy, just, and wise?

5 My soul, sink down in shame and grief;
So fair without, so foul within;
Thy faith is specious unbelief,
Thy righteousness self-righteous sin.

6 O God! Thou art, Thou surely art,
And those who truly seek Thee find;
Put Thou Thy laws into my heart,
In mercy write them on my mind.

7 Light in Thy light I long to see,
Thy glory in Thy goodness trace:
Ah! then reveal Thy Son in me;
Through faith may I be saved by grace!

James Montgomery, 1853.

STERNBERG. [H. P. 245.]

42 THE INFINITY OF GOD.

Tune STERNBERG. 11 10, 11 10.

Ps. cxxxix. 6. "*Too wonderful for me.*"

1 HOLY and Infinite! Viewless, Eternal!
Veiled in the glory that none can sustain,
None comprehendeth Thy being supernal,
Nor can the heaven of heavens contain.

2 Holy and Infinite! limitless, boundless,
All Thy perfections, and powers, and praise!
Ocean of mystery! awful and soundless
All Thine unsearchable judgments and ways!

3 King of Eternity! what revelation
Could the created and finite sustain,
But for Thy marvellous manifestation,
Godhead incarnate in weakness and pain!

4 Therefore archangels and angels adore Thee,
Cherubim wonder, and seraphs admire;
Therefore we praise Thee, rejoicing before Thee,
Joining in rapture the heavenly choir.

5 Glorious in holiness, fearful in praises,
Who shall not fear Thee, and who shall not laud?
Anthems of glory Thy universe raises,
Holy and Infinite! Father and God!

Frances Ridley Havergal, 1872.

CYPRUS. [H. P. 26.]

43 THE SPIRITUALITY OF GOD.

John iv. 24. "*God is a Spirit.*" Tune CYPRUS. L. M.

1 WHAT know we, Holy God, of Thee,
Thy being and Thine essence pure?
Too bright the very mystery
For mortal vision to endure.

2 We only know Thy word sublime,
Thou art a Spirit! Perfect! One!
Unlimited by space or time,
Unknown but through the' eternal Son.

3 By change untouched, by thought untraced,
And by created eye unseen,
In *Thy great present* is embraced
All that shall be, all that hath been.

4 O Father of our spirits, now
We seek Thee in our Saviour's face;
In truth and spirit we would bow,
And worship where we cannot trace.

Frances Ridley Havergal, 1872.

44 THE ETERNITY OF GOD.

Tune ST. PAUL. 87, 887, 77, 77.

1 Tim. i. 17. "*The King, eternal, immortal, invisible.*"

1 KING, Eternal and Immortal!
We, the children of an hour,
Bend in lowly adoration,
Rise in raptured admiration,
At the whisper of Thy power.
Myriad ages in Thy sight
Are but as the fleeting day;
Like a vision of the night,
Worlds may rise and pass away.

2 All Thy glories are eternal,
None shall ever pass away;
Truth and mercy all-victorious,
Righteousness and love all-glorious,
Shine with everlasting ray:

ST. PAUL. [H. P. 253.]

All-resplendent, ere the light
Bade primeval darkness flee:
All-transcendent, through the flight
Of eternities to be.

3 Thou art God from everlasting,
And to everlasting art!
Ere the dawn of shadowy ages,
Dimly guesssed by angel sages,
Ere the beat of seraph-heart;
Thou, Jehovah, art the same,
And Thy years shall have no end;
Changeless nature, changeless name,
Ever Father, God, and Friend.

Frances Ridley Havergal, 1872.

THE OLD 100th TUNE. [H. P. 1.]

45 Ps. xc. 2. "*From everlasting to everlasting Thou art God.*" Tune Old Hundredth. L. M.

1 LORD! Thou hast been Thy children's God,
All-powerful, wise, and good, and just,
In every age their safe abode,
Their hope, their refuge, and their trust.

2 Before Thy word gave nature birth,
Or spread the starry heavens abroad,
Or formed the varied face of earth,
From everlasting Thou art God.

Anne Steele, 1760.

OLD "TEN COMMANDMENTS' TUNE." [H. P. 15.]

THE UNITY OF GOD.

46 Deut. vi. 4. "*The Lord our God is one Lord.*" Tune Old Ten Commandments. L. M.

1 ETERNAL God! Almighty Cause
Of earth, and seas, and worlds unknown;
All things are subject to Thy laws,
All things depend on Thee alone.

2 Thy glorious Being singly stands,
Of all within itself possest,
Controlled by none in Thy commands,
And in Thyself completely blest.

3 To Thee alone ourselves we owe;
Let heaven and earth due homage pay;
All other gods we disavow,
Deny their claims, renounce their sway.

4 Lord! spread Thy name through heathen lands;
Their idol deities dethrone;
Reduce the world to Thy commands;
And reign, as Thou art, God alone!

Simon Browne, 1720. (*a.*)

SHEN (The Rock). [H. P. 201.]

THE SOVEREIGNTY OF GOD.

47 Ps. xlvi. 10. "*Be still, and know that I am God.*" Tune SHEN. 15 15, 15 15.

1 GOD Almighty! King of nations! earth Thy footstool, heaven Thy throne!
Thine the greatness, power, and glory, Thine the kingdom, Lord, alone!
Life and death are in Thy keeping, and Thy will ordaineth all:
From the armies of Thy heavens to an unseen insect's fall.

2 Reigning, guiding, all-commanding, ruling myriad worlds of light;
Now exalting, now abasing, none can stay Thy hand of might!
Working all things by Thy power, by the counsel of Thy will,
Thou art God! enough to know it, and to hear Thy word: "Be still!"

3 In Thy sovereignty rejoicing, we Thy children bow and praise,
For we know that kind and loving, just and true, are all Thy ways:
While Thy heart of sovereign mercy, and Thine arm of sovereign might,
For our great and strong salvation in Thy sovereign grace unite.

Frances Ridley Havergal, 1872.

OLD "TEN COMMANDMENTS' TUNE." [H. P. 15.]

GREAT FIRST CAUSE AND FINAL END.

48 Rom. xi. 36. "*Of Him, and through Him, and to Him, are all things.*" Tune OLD TEN COMMANDMENTS. L. M.

1 CAUSE of all causes, and the Source
Whence universal being sprang;
Thou wast ere time began its course,
Or morning stars Thy praises sang.

2 Existing through all ages, Thou
The deeds of every age canst tell;
All things above—all things below,
And in the dreadful gloom of hell.

3 Through the vast regions of the air,
The trackless wilderness of space,
The worlds and systems wandering there
Thine everlasting arms embrace.

4 Thou First, Thou Last, Thou Cause, and End
Of all that is, or e'er shall be;
To Thee, their Source, all beings tend,
All things that are exist for Thee!

Thomas Raffles, D.D., 1812.

THE DOMINION OF GOD.

49 Dan. iv. 35. "*He doeth according to His will.*" Tune LUBECK. 7 7, 7 7. Or SEIR.

1 GLORIOUS, high, and lofty One!
Self-existent, matchless God!
Stands immovable Thy throne,
Empires totter at Thy nod. Hallelujah.

2 Ranks of angels waiting stand
To obey Thy sovereign will;
Listening to Thy dread command,
Winged Thy counsels to fulfil. Hallelujah.

3 Saints before Thee sweetly sing,
And Thy grand perfections praise;
Heaven's eternal arches ring
With Thy glorious acts of grace. Hallelujah.

4 Moving in unbounded space,
Worlds of light beneath Thee shine;
Round the earth perform their race,
And o'er nations stretch their line. Hallelujah.

5 Countless oceans float in air,
Guided by Thy skilful hand;
By Thy order lightnings glare,
Thunders roar at Thy command. Hallelujah.

6 Mighty winds, the gentle breeze,
Summer's drought, the vernal shower,
Limpid streams, and raging seas,
All proclaim Thy sovereign power. Hallelujah.

PART II.

7 At Thy pleasure nations rise,
Kings their pompous power display;
And before Thy flaming eyes
Kings and nations melt away. Hallelujah.

8 Thou array'st the broad campaign,
All in bloody horrors, Lord!
Troops contend, are wounded, slain
At Thy all-commanding word. Hallelujah.

9 Haughty lords and humble swains
From Thy will derive their birth;
Thy eternal power maintains
All the varied tribes on earth. Hallelujah.

10 Fish that shoot along the flood,
Strong and savage beasts that prowl
Round the lonely, trackless wood,
All are under Thy control. Hallelujah.

11 All the feathered tribes that sing,
As they hop from spray to spray,
Or ascend on active wing,
Thy amazing skill display. Hallelujah.

LUBECK. [H. P. 139.]

Hal - le - lu - jah, Hal - le - lu - jah!

12 Works of wonder Thou hast wrought,
Wondrous counsels to fulfil;
Every creature, action, thought,
Is subservient to Thy will! Hallelujah.

Job Hupton, 1806.

PARAN (Wilderness of). [H. P. 241.]

THE GLORY OF GOD.

50 Ps. cxlv. 10. "*All Thy works shall praise Thee, O Lord.*" Tune PARAN. 10 10, 11 11.

1 O WORSHIP the King, All glorious above!
O gratefully sing His power and His love!
Our Shield and Defender—The Ancient of Days,
Pavilioned in splendour, And girded with praise.

2 O tell of His might, O sing of His grace,
Whose robe is the light, Whose canopy space;
His chariots of wrath Deep thunder-clouds form,
And dark is His path On the wings of the storm.

3 This earth, with its store Of wonders untold,
Almighty! Thy power Hath founded of old;
Hath stablished it fast By a changeless decree,
And round it hath cast, Like a mantle the sea.

4 Thy bountiful care, What tongue can recite?
It breathes in the air, It shines in the light;
It streams from the hills, It descends to the plain,
And sweetly distils In the dew and the rain.

5 Frail children of dust, And feeble as frail,
In Thee do we trust, Nor find Thee to fail;
Thy mercies how tender, How firm to the end,
Our Maker, Defender, Redeemer, and Friend!

6 O measureless Might! Ineffable Love!
While angels delight To hymn Thee above,
The humbler creation, Though feeble their lays,
With true adoration Shall lisp to Thy praise!

Sir Robert Grant, 1839.

GENNESARET. [H. P. 17.]

THE WISDOM OF GOD.

51 Job xxxvi. 5. "*Behold, God is mighty . . . in wisdom.*" Tune GENNESARET. L. M. Or CYPRUS

1 WAIT, O my soul, thy Maker's will;
Tumultuous passions, all be still;
Nor let a murmuring thought arise!
His ways are just, His counsels wise.

2 He in the thickest darkness dwells,
Performs His work, the cause conceals;
But though His methods are unknown,
Judgment and truth support His throne.

3 In heaven, and earth, and air, and seas,
He executes His firm decrees;
And by His saints it stands confessed
That what He does is ever best.

4 Wait then, my soul, submissive wait,
Prostrate before His awful seat;
And, 'midst the terrors of His rod,
Trust in a wise and gracious God!

Benjamin Beddome, 1818.

TALLIS'S ORDINAL. [H. P. 44.]

THE OMNIPOTENCE OF GOD.

52 Ps. cvii. 29. "*He maketh the storm a calm.*" Tune TALLIS. C. M. Or EPHRON.

1 THE Lord our God is full of might,
The winds obey His will;
He speaks, and in his heavenly height
The rolling sun stands still.

2 Arise, ye waves, and o'er the land
With threatening aspect roar,
The Lord uplifts His awful hand,
And chains you to the shore.

3 Howl, winds of night, your force combine!
Without His high behest,
Ye shall not, in the mountain pine,
Disturb the sparrow's nest.

4 His voice sublime is heard afar,
In distant peals it dies;
He yokes the whirlwind to His car,
And sweeps the howling skies.

5 Ye nations, bend, in reverence bend;
Ye monarchs, wait His nod,
And bid the choral song ascend
To celebrate our God!

Henry Kirke White, 1806.

CARMEL (Mount). [H. P. 69.]

THE OMNISCIENCE OF GOD.

53 Jer. xvii. 10. "*I the Lord search the heart.*" Tune CARMEL. C. M.

1 GOD knows our secret thoughts and words,
And all our actions too;
Nor can a cloud conceal them from
His penetrating view.

2 A boundless and mysterious deep
His own perfections are;
And yet He knows the wondrous depth
That dwells profoundly there.

3 He knows the heavenly world on high,
And every angel there;
Nor can a seraph be without
His knowledge and His care.

4 The earth, and hell, with all their train,
Are open to His sight;
And all the dark designs of both
He'll shortly bring to light.

5 In knowledge unconfined He fixed
His grand designs of grace;
With all the plans of providence
To save the chosen race.

6 In all His holy, wondrous plan,
No error can arise;
Ten thousand things unknown to us
Are plain before His eyes!

Thomas Row, 1817.

THE GOODNESS OF GOD.

54 Tune Tallis. C. M.

Ps. xxxi. 19. "*O how great is Thy goodness!*"

1 THE goodness of our glorious God
Is wonderfully bright;
His goodness will we sound abroad,
At morning, noon, and night.

2 Good is the Lord to all mankind,
Relieving their complaints;
But the best things He has designed
For His believing saints.

3 Eternal good He'll freely pour
On Israel's chosen race,
And all His goodness they adore,
And triumph in His grace.

4 O Lord, Thy goodness now display,
Through the Redeemer's blood;
Constraining all Thy saints to say,
That "God is truly good!"

5 And may Thy goodness, dearest Lord,
Lead us to mourn for sin;
Keep us obedient to Thy word,
And give the heaven within.

6 And when we soar above the skies,
Beyond the glooms of night,
Thy goodness will we ever praise,
Through all the realms of light!

Richard Burnham, 1794.

See Hymn 87.

THE HOLINESS OF GOD.

55 Tune Tallis. C. M.

Exod. xv. 11. "*Glorious in holiness.*"

1 HOLY and reverend is the name
Of our eternal King!
"Thrice holy Lord," the angels cry,
"Thrice holy," let us sing.

2 The deepest reverence of the mind,
Pay, O my soul! to God;
Lift, with thy hands, a holy heart
To His sublime abode.

3 With sacred awe pronounce His name,
Whom words nor thoughts can reach,
A contrite heart shall please Him more
Than noblest forms of speech.

4 Thou holy God, preserve my soul
From all pollution free;
The pure in heart are Thy delight,
And they Thy face shall see!

John Needham, 1768.

IONA. [H. P. 37.]

THE FAITHFULNESS OF GOD.

56 Ps. lxxxix. 1. "*I will make known Thy faithfulness.*" Tune Iona. C. M. Or Gloucester.

1 BEGIN, my tongue, some heavenly theme,
And speak some boundless thing;
The mighty works, or mightier name,
Of our eternal King.

2 Tell of His wondrous faithfulness,
And sound His power abroad;
Sing the sweet promise of His grace,
And our performing God.

3 Engraved as in eternal brass
The mighty promise shines;
Nor can the powers of darkness rase
Those everlasting lines.

4 His every word of grace is strong
As that which built the skies;
The voice that rolls the stars along
Speaks all the promises.

5 Oh! might I hear Thy heavenly tongue
But whisper "Thou art Mine!"
Those gentle words should raise my song
To notes almost Divine.

6 How would my leaping heart rejoice,
And think my heaven secure!
I trust the all-creating Voice,
And faith desires no more!

Isaac Watts, D.D., 1709.

GALILEE. [H. P. 25.]

THE OMNIPRESENCE OF GOD.

57 Ps. cxxxix. 7. "*Whither shall I flee from Thy presence?*" Tune GALILEE. L. M. Or DALMATIA.

1 FATHER and Friend! Thy light, Thy love
Beaming through all Thy works we see;
Thy glory gilds the heavens above,
And all the earth is full of Thee.

2 Thy voice we hear—Thy presence feel,
Whilst Thou, too pure for mortal sight,
Involved in clouds—invisible,
Reignest the Lord of life and light.

3 We know not in what hallowed part
Of the wide heavens Thy throne may be,
But this we know, that where Thou art,
Strength, wisdom, goodness, dwell with Thee.

4 And through the various maze of time,
And through infinity of space,
We follow Thy career sublime,
And all Thy wondrous footsteps trace.

5 Thy children shall not faint or fear,
Sustained by this delightful thought,
Since Thou their God art everywhere,
They cannot be where Thou art not!

Sir John Bowring, LL.D., 1824.

MAON (Wilderness of). [H. P. 229.]

THE PARDONING GOD.

58 Neh. ix. 17. "*A God ready to pardon.*" Tune MAON. 88, 88, 88.

1 GREAT God of wonders! all Thy ways
Are matchless, Godlike, and Divine;
But the fair glories of Thy grace
More Godlike and unrivalled shine:
Who is a pardoning God like Thee?
Or who has grace so rich and free?

2 Crimes of such horror to forgive,
Such guilty, daring worms to spare;
This is Thy grand prerogative,
And none shall in the honour share:
Who is a pardoning God like Thee?
Or who has grace so rich and free?

3 In wonder lost, with trembling joy
We take the pardon of our God;
Pardon for crimes of deepest dye;
A pardon bought with Jesus' blood:
Who is a pardoning God like Thee?
Or who has grace so rich and free?

4 Oh! may this strange, this matchless grace,
This Godlike miracle of love,
Fill the wide earth with grateful praise,
And all the' angelic choirs above:
Who is a pardoning God like Thee?
Or who has grace so rich and free?

President Samuel Davies, 1769.

See Hymns 680—684.

PARAN (Wilderness of). [H. P. 241.]

THE MERCY OF GOD.

59 Ps. lxxxix. 1. "*I will sing of the mercies of the Lord for ever.*" Tune PARAN. 11 11, 11 11.

1 THY mercy, my God, is the theme of my song,
The joy of my heart and the boast of my tongue;
Thy free grace alone, from the first to the last,
Hath won my affections, and bound my soul fast.

2 Without Thy sweet mercy, I could not live here,
Sin soon would reduce me to utter despair,
But through Thy free goodness my spirits revive,
And He that first made me still keeps me alive.

3 Thy mercy is more than a match for my heart,
Which wonders to feel its own hardness depart;
Dissolved by Thy goodness, I fall to the ground,
And weep to the praise of the mercy I've found.

4 Thy mercy is endless, most tender and free;
No sinner need doubt, since 'tis given to me:
No merit will buy it, nor sin stop its course;
Good works are the fruits of its freeness and force.

5 Thy mercy in Jesus exempts me from hell;
Its glories I'll sing, and its wonders I'll tell;
'Twas Jesus, my Friend, when He hung on the tree,
That opened the channel of mercy for me.

6 Great Father of mercies! Thy goodness I own,
And the covenant love of Thy crucified Son;
All praise to the Spirit, whose whisper Divine
Seals mercy, and pardon, and righteousness mine!

John Stocker, 1776. (*a.*)

LUBECK. [H. P. 139.]

Hal - le - lu - jah, Hal - le - lu - jah!

THE MAJESTY OF GOD.

60 Tune LUBECK. 77, 77.

Ps. xciii. 1. "*He is clothed with majesty.*"

1 GLORY to the' eternal King,
Clad in majesty supreme!
Let all heaven His praises sing,
Let all worlds His power proclaim.
Hallelujah.

2 Through eternity He reigns
In unbounded realms of light:
He the universe sustains
As an atom in His sight.
Hallelujah.

3 Suns on suns, through boundless space,
With their systems move or stand;
Or, to occupy their place,
New orbs rise at His command.
Hallelujah.

4 Kingdoms flourish, empires fall,
Nations live, and nations die,
All forms nothing, nothing all—
At the movement of His eye.
Hallelujah.

5 Oh let my transported soul
Ever on His glories gaze!
Ever yield to His control,
Ever sound His lofty praise!
Hallelujah.

Benjamin Francis, 1787.

THE OLD 100th TUNE. [H. P. 1.]

THE KINDNESS OF GOD.

61 Ps. lii. 1. *"The goodness of God endureth continually."* Tune OLD HUNDREDTH. L. M.

1 GIVE thanks to God, He reigns above;
  Kind are His thoughts, His name is love;
His mercy ages past have known,
And ages long to come shall own.

2 Let the redeemèd of the Lord
The wonders of His grace record;
How great His works; how kind His ways!
Let every tongue pronounce His praise!

Isaac Watts, D.D., 1719.

FRANKFORT. [H. P. 183.]

LOVE AND WISDOM.

62 1 John iv. 8. *"God is love."* Tune FRANKFORT. 87, 87.

1 GOD is love, His mercy brightens
  All the path in which we rove;
Bliss He wakes, and woe He lightens;
  God is wisdom, God is love.

2 Chance and change are busy ever,
  Man decays, and ages move;
But His mercy waneth never;
  God is wisdom, God is love.

3 E'en the hour that darkest seemeth
  Will His changeless goodness prove;
From the mist His brightness streameth,
  God is wisdom, God is love.

4 He with earthly cares entwineth
  Hope and comfort from above;
Everywhere His glory shineth;
  God is wisdom, God is love!

Sir John Bowring, LL.D., 1825.

See Hymns 121—127, 189—194.

CULBACH. [H. P. 181.]

THE UNCHANGEABLE GOD.

63 Jer. xxxi. 3. *"I have loved thee with an everlasting love."* Tune CULBACH. 87, 87.

1 GREAT Jehovah's love endureth,
  Then away with all complaints!
His unchanging love secureth
  Crowns of glory for the saints.

2 May we all be ever learning
  How it shines in Christ the Lamb,
Never knows a shade of turning,
  But in Him abides the same.

3 This great truth yields heavenly pleasure
  To the feeble and the faint,
Ever proves a solid treasure
  To the weak and weary saint.

4 What a spring of consolation
  Is the Lord's abounding grace;
And what blissful contemplation
  This affords the chosen race.

5 Father! help us now to ponder
  On Thy never-ceasing love;
Fill us with transporting wonder
  While its boundless joys we prove!

Richard Burnham, 1794.

SARDIS. (Hymn Chant.) [H. P. VI.]

THE NAMES OF JEHOVAH.

64

Exod. vi. 3. "*My name Jehovah.*" Tune, Hymn Chant Sardis. 10 10, 10 10.

1 "JEHOVAH ELOHIM!" Creator Great,
Who art with glorious attributes arrayed;
To Thee by heaven and earth and all therein,
Be everlasting praise and worship paid!
Gen. ii. 4.

2 "JEHOVAH JIREH!" who our ruin saw,
And as a ransom did Thyself provide;
As guilty sinners we would fly to Thee,
And in Thy bosom from Thine anger hide.
Gen. xxii. 14.

3 "JEHOVAH ROPHI!"—sick, diseased with sin,
We come to Thee who canst our sickness heal;
Oh touch and cleanse each plague-spot of our souls,
And grant us life and strength within to feel.
Exod. xv. 26.

4 "JEHOVAH NISSI!"—in the midst of foes,
The glorious banner of Thy love unfurled
Waves o'er our heads,—yea, Thou our Banner art,
By faith in whom we overcome the world.
Exod. xvii. 15.

5 "JEHOVAH SHALOM!"—Thou who art "our Peace,"
Oh whisper calm to every troubled heart:
Say to the raging waters, "Peace, be still!"
And make each unbelieving fear depart.
Jud. vi. 24.

6 "JEHOVAH TZIDKENU!"—we love that name,
Which bids us know, while pardoning, Thou art just,
"The Lord our Righteousness" shall be our song,
"The Lord our Righteousness" our only trust.
Jer. xxiii. 6.

7 "JEHOVAH SHAMMAH!" soon, oh! soon descend,
And make this earth again Thy blest abode,
Bid sin and sorrow cease, and come and reign,
Our ever-gracious, ever-present God!
Ezek. xlviii. 35.

Christina Forsyth, 1858.

Theme III.—The Acts of the Triune Jehovah.

CHESALON (Mount). [H. P. 35.]

(1) THE EVERLASTING COVENANT OF GRACE.

65

Rom. xi. 36. "*Of Him, and through Him, and to Him, are all things.*" Tune Chesalon. C. M.

1 ARISE, my soul, in songs to own
Thy faithful covenant God;
Of Him, through Him, to Him alone
Salvation now record.

2 Of God the Father's sovereign choice,
Of God the Saviour's grace,
Of God the Spirit's quickening voice,
Live all the chosen race.

3 Through God the Father's faithfulness,
Through God the Spirit's might,
Through God the Saviour's righteousness,
We gain the realms of light.

4 To God the Father praise belongs,
To God the Son we sing,
To God the Holy Ghost the throng
Of saints shall glory bring!

Joseph Irons, 1825.

WORCESTER. (Hymn Chant.) *Recte et Retro.* [H. P. No. I.]

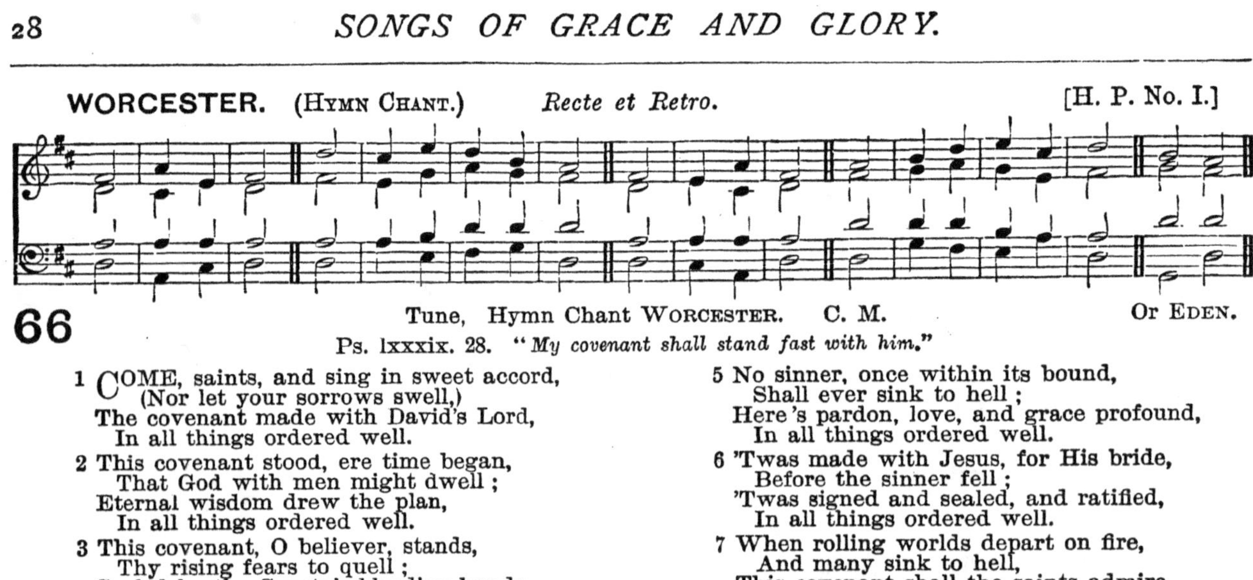

66

Tune, Hymn Chant Worcester. C. M. Or Eden.

Ps. lxxxix. 28. "*My covenant shall stand fast with him.*"

1 COME, saints, and sing in sweet accord,
(Nor let your sorrows swell,)
The covenant made with David's Lord,
In all things ordered well.

2 This covenant stood, ere time began,
That God with men might dwell;
Eternal wisdom drew the plan,
In all things ordered well.

3 This covenant, O believer, stands,
Thy rising fears to quell;
Sealed by thy Surety's bleeding hands,
In all things ordered well.

4 Ere Adam stretched his hand to take
That fruit by which he fell,
This covenant stood, for Jesu's sake,
In all things ordered well.

5 No sinner, once within its bound,
Shall ever sink to hell;
Here's pardon, love, and grace profound,
In all things ordered well.

6 'Twas made with Jesus, for His bride,
Before the sinner fell;
'Twas signed and sealed, and ratified,
In all things ordered well.

7 When rolling worlds depart on fire,
And many sink to hell,
This covenant shall the saints admire,
In all things ordered well.

8 In glory, soon, with Christ their King,
His saints shall surely dwell;
And this blest covenant ever sing,
In all things ordered well!

John Kent, 1803.

ST. MICHAEL. [H. P. 85.]

67

2 Tim. i. 9. "*Grace given us in Christ Jesus before the world began.*" Tune St. Michael. S. M.

1 THE covenant of free grace,
As made with Christ our Head,
Is stored with precious promises,
By which our souls are fed.

2 The solemn oath of God
Confirms each promise true,
And Jesus, with His precious blood,
Has sealed the covenant too.

3 Hence all our comforts flow,
And balm for every fear;
Oh may we by experience know,
How choice, how rich they are!

Gospel Magazine, 1778.

EDEN. [H. P. 38.]

68

Rom. xi. 36. "*Of Him, and through Him, and to Him, are all things.*" Tune Eden. C. M. Or Nottingham.

1 OF Israel's covenant God I boast,
As part of Israel's stock;
The Father, Son, and Holy Ghost,
Are my eternal rock.

2 Of Him beloved before the fall,
Through Him salvation came;
To Him I owe my life—my all;
All glory to His name!

3 Of Him I gain a right to heaven,
Through Him I'm justified,
To Him my helpless soul is given,
And with Him glorified.

4 Of Him I love to speak and sing,
Through Him I've joy and peace,
To Him my guilt and shame I bring,
And triumph in His grace.

5 Of Him I daily grace receive,
Through Him my joys abound,
To Him I bow, in Him believe,
With Him I shall be crowned.

6 My Father's everlasting love,
My Saviour's precious name,
My Teacher's unction from above,
Let all the church proclaim!

Joseph Irons, 1825.

MORIAH (Mount). [H. P. 119.]

69

Tune MORIAH. 6666, 88.

Ps. lxxxix. 3. "*I have made a covenant with My chosen.*"

1 WITH David's Lord and ours,
A covenant once was made,
Whose bonds are firm and sure,
Whose glories ne'er shall fade;
Signed by the sacred Three in One,
Jehovah—Father, Spirit, Son.

2 Firm as the lasting hills,
This covenant shall endure,
Whose potent *shalls* and *wills*
Make every blessing sure:
When ruin shakes all nature's frame,
Its every word shall stand the same.

3 Here, when thy feet shall fall,
Believer, thou shalt see
Grace to restore thy soul,
And pardon, full and free;
Thee with delight shall God behold,
A sheep restored to Zion's fold.

4 And when through Jordan's flood
Thy God shall bid thee go,
His arm shall thee defend,
And vanquish every foe;
And in this covenant thou shalt view
Sufficient strength to bear thee through.

John Kent, 1803.

PERGAMOS. (HYMN CHANT.) [H. P. No. IV.]

70

Ps. lxxxix. 1. "*I will sing of the mercies of the Lord for ever.*" Hymn Chant PERGAMOS. 66, 84. D. Or ARNON.

1 THE God of Abraham praise,
Who reigns enthroned above,
Ancient of everlasting days,
And God of love!
Jehovah, great I AM!
By earth and heaven confessed;
I bow and bless the sacred Name,
For ever blest!

2 The God of Abraham praise,
At whose supreme command
From earth I rise and seek the joys
At His right hand:
I all on earth forsake,
Its wisdom, fame, and power;
And Him my only portion make,
My shield and tower.

3 The God of Abraham praise,
Whose all-sufficient grace
Shall guide me all my happy days
In all His ways:
He calls a worm His friend,
He calls Himself my God!
And He shall save me to the end,
Through Jesu's blood.

4 He by Himself hath sworn,
I on His oath depend:
I shall, on eagles' wings upborne,
To heaven ascend:
I shall behold His face,
I shall His power adore,
And sing the wonders of His grace
For evermore!

PART II.

5 Though nature's strength decay,
And earth and hell withstand,
To Canaan's bounds I urge my way
At His command:
The watery deep I pass
With Jesus in my view,
And through the howling wilderness
My way pursue.

6 The goodly land I see,
With peace and plenty blest;
A land of sacred liberty,
And endless rest:
There milk and honey flow;
And oil and wine abound:
And trees of life for ever grow,
With mercy crowned.

7 There dwells the Lord our King,
The Lord our Righteousness!
Triumphant o'er the world and sin,
The Prince of Peace!
On Zion's sacred height
His kingdom still maintains:
And glorious with His saints in light
For ever reigns!

8 He keeps His own secure,
He guards them by His side,
Arrays in garments white and pure
His spotless bride;
With streams of sacred bliss,
With groves of living joys,
With all the fruits of paradise,
He still supplies.

PART III.

9 Before the Great Three-One
They all exulting stand,
And tell the wonders He hath done
Through all their land:
The listening spheres attend,
And swell the growing fame;
And sing, in songs which never end,
The wondrous Name.

10 The God who reigns on high
The great archangels sing:
And "Holy, holy, holy," cry,
"Almighty King!
Who was and is the same,
And evermore shall be;
Jehovah, Father, great I AM,
We worship Thee."

11 Before the Saviour's face
The ransomed nations bow,
O'erwhelmed at His almighty grace,
For ever new:
He shows His prints of love;
They kindle to a flame,
And sound, through all the world above,
The slaughtered Lamb.

12 The whole triumphant host
Give thanks to God on high,
"Hail Father, Son, and Holy Ghost!"
They ever cry:
Hail, Abraham's God, and mine!
(I join the heavenly lays;)
All might and majesty are Thine,
And endless praise!

Thomas Olivers, 1772.

HEBRON. [H. P. 12.]

71 Rom. iv. 16. "*The promise . . . sure to all the seed.*" Tune HEBRON. L. M.

1 GRACE is Jehovah's sovereign will,
In an eternal covenant sure:
Which for His seed He will fulfil
Longer than sun and moon endure.

2 Grace is a firm but friendly hand,
Put forth by God to save His own;
And by that grace, through faith, we stand
Adoring at our Father's throne.

3 Lord, help us on Thy grace to stand,
And every trial firm endure;
Preservèd by Thy sovereign hand,
And by Thine oath and covenant sure.

4 Thy willingness to save Thy seed,
Is as they stand in Christ their Head:
No act Thy grace can supersede,
For Thine must live, though they were dead.

5 Thanks, everlasting thanks be given
To God, to Christ, for matchless grace;
And to that Dove, who seals for heaven
All who shall sing Jehovah's praise.

John Stevens, 1808.

FRENCH; *or*, DUNDEE. [H. P. 65.]

72 Rom. iii. 24. "*Justified freely by His grace.*"

Tune FRENCH. C. M.

1 LOVE was the great self-moving cause,
From whence salvation came;
Free grace, the channel where it flows,
Eternally the same.

2 Free grace, thy peerless glories beamed
Before the Day Star rose!
Angels elect, and men redeemed,
Thy fame can ne'er disclose.

3 Free grace the Christian's charter is,
The royal grant of Heaven;
In this he finds his righteousness,
And sees his sins forgiven.

4 Free grace hath heights and depths unknown,
Beyond what seraphs know;
'Tis high as heaven's eternal throne,
And deep as hell below.

5 Free grace can cleanse the foulest stains,
That red like crimson prove;
It flowed from our Redeemer's veins,
In drops of endless love.

6 Free grace they sing before the throne,
Without one jarring sound;
The Lamb's redeeming blood, they own,
Their mighty ransom found.

7 Free grace, we'll count thy wonders o'er,
And lift thy glories high;
We hope, at last, on Jordan's shore,
In thine embrace to die!

John Kent, 1803. (*a.*)

HANOVER; *or*, MODERN 104TH. [H. P. 239.]

73 Tune HANOVER. 10 10, 11 11.

Zeph. iii. 17. "*He will rest in His love.*"

1 SALVATION by grace, how charming the song!
With seraphim join, the theme to prolong;
'Twas planned by Jehovah in council above,
Who to everlasting shall rest in His love.

2 This covenant of grace all blessings secures;
Believer, rejoice, for all things are yours:
And God from His purpose shall never remove,
But love thee, and bless thee, and rest in His love.

3 But when, like a sheep that strays from the fold,
To Jesus thy Lord thy love shall grow cold,
Think not He'll reject thee, but rather reprove,
Yet though He correct thee, He'll rest in His love!

John Kent, 1803.

KEDRON (Brook). [H. P. 213.]

74 Rom. viii. 30. *"Whom He did predestinate, . . . them He also glorified."* Tune KEDRON. 886. D.

1 BRIGHT from the mysteries of God,
With beams of mercy all abroad
Shines His electing love;
Sweet to the chosen of the Lord,
To those whom His eternal word
Appoints to bliss above.

2 In chains of sin before enthralled,
The chosen by free grace are called,
And from their sin they cease;
And, justified by faith, they find
The only comfort of the mind,
The Spirit's holy peace.

3 When Death, that mighty king of fear,
Proclaims their time is finished here,
(To them a glorious hour!)
With joy the summons they embrace,
To meet Emmanuel face to face,
Partakers of His power.

4 Triumphantly they take their flight
To realms of everlasting light,
Washed in a Saviour's blood:
A Saviour, whom they'll ever praise,
When shouting in seraphic lays
Salvation to our God!

Philip Gell's Collection, 1826.

BEDFORD. [H. P. 66.]

75 Isa. lvi. 4. *"Take hold of My covenant."* Tune BEDFORD. C. M.

1 'TIS mine, the covenant of His grace,
And every promise mine;
All sprung from everlasting love,
And sealed by blood Divine.

2 On my unworthy favoured head
Its blessings all unite;
Blessings more numerous than the stars,
More lasting and more bright.

3 That covenant the last accent claims
Of this poor faltering tongue,
And that shall the first notes employ
Of my celestial song!

Philip Doddridge, D.D., 1755.

FRANCONIA. [H. P. 87.]

76

Eph. i. 4. *"He hath chosen us in Christ."* Tune FRANCONIA. S. M.

1 "YOU have not chosen Me,"
The Lord our Saviour said:
But He hath chosen us, we see,
And raised us from the dead.

2 We must not once suppose
That we the difference make
Between ourselves, and such as those
Who do not grace partake.

3 God's sovereign choice alone
Has set His saints apart;
And we by faith rejoice to own
It wrought our change of heart.

4 Has not the Lord of all
A most undoubted right
To choose whom He will love, and call
To live with Him in light?

5 Can mortals e'er arraign
The Ruler of the skies?
Or have a reason to complain
He is not just and wise?

6 We know that Thou art just;
We know that Thou art wise;
And so we humbly wait and trust
Till clearer light arise

7 O Lord! we would adore
The grace that made us Thine;
And praise Thy name, as sinners poor,
For favour so Divine!

Thomas Row, 1817. (*a.*)

SWABIA. [H. P. 82.]

77

Tune SWABIA. S. M.

Eph. ii. 8. *"By grace are ye saved."*

1 GRACE! 'tis a charming sound!
Harmonious to the ear:
Heaven with the echo shall resound,
And all the earth shall hear.

2 Grace first contrived a way
To save rebellious man,
And all the steps that grace display,
Which drew the wondrous plan!

3 Grace first inscribed my name
In God's eternal book:
'Twas grace that gave me to the Lamb,
Who all my sorrows took.

4 Grace taught my soul to pray,
And pardoning love to know;
'Twas grace that kept me to this day,
And will not let me go.

5 Grace all the work shall crown,
Through everlasting days:
It lays in heaven the topmost stone,
And well deserves the praise!

P. Doddridge, D.D., 1755; *A. M. Toplady*, 1776.

78

Tune SWABIA. S. M.

1 Cor. xv. 10. *"By the grace of God I am what I am."*

1 FREE grace! melodious sound!
How it delights my ear:
It cheers my soul, revives my hope,
And drowns my every fear!

2 Through grace I conquer hell,
And break infernal chains!
Through grace my soul aspires to heaven,
Where the Redeemer reigns.

3 Grace the good work begins,
And grace completes the same;
Grace shall constrain my soul to raise
Hosannas to the Lamb.

4 From His abounding grace
I daily draw supplies;
Grace is the never-ceasing spring
Of all my sacred joys.

5 And when we meet our Lord
In yon celestial throng,
Grace shall inspire our souls to sing,
And grace be all our song!

Richard Burnham, 1794. (*a.*)

79 Tune Crescens. 118, 118.

Eph. i. 3. "*Blessed be the God and Father of our Lord Jesus Christ.*"

CRESCENS. [H. P. 244.]

1 IN songs of sublime adoration and praise,
Ye pilgrims to Zion above,
Break forth, and extol the great Ancient of Days,
His rich and distinguishing love.

2 His love, from eternity fixed upon you,
Broke forth and discovered its flame,
When each with the cords of His kindness He drew,
And brought you to love His great name.

3 Oh, had He not pitied the state you were in,
Your bosoms His love had ne'er felt;
You all would have lived, would have died too, in sin,
And sunk with the load of your guilt.

4 What was there in you that could merit esteem,
Or give the Creator delight?
"'Twas even so, Father," Thy love did redeem,
"Because it seemed good in Thy sight."

5 'Twas all of Thy grace we were brought to obey,
While others were suffered to go;
The road which, by nature, we chose as our way,
Leads only to regions of woe.

6 Then give Him the glory all due to His name,
To Him all the glory belongs;
Be yours the high joy still to sound forth His fame,
And crown Him with jubilant songs!

George Keith, 1787. (*a.*)

KENT. [H. P. 63.]

80 Ps. lxxxix. 34. "*My covenant will I not break.*" Tune Kent. C. M. Or Kedar.

1 MY God! the covenant of Thy love
Abides for ever sure;
And in its matchless grace I feel
My happiness secure.

2 What though my house be not with Thee
As nature could desire!
To nobler joys than nature gives
Thy servants all aspire.

3 Since Thou, the everlasting God,
My Father art become,
Jesus my Guardian and my Friend,
And heaven my final home;

4 I welcome all Thy sovereign will,
For all that will is love;
And, when I know not what Thou dost,
I wait the light above.

5 Thy covenant in the darkest gloom
Shall heavenly rays impart,
Which, when my eyelids close in death,
Shall warm my chilling heart!

Philip Doddridge, D.D., 1755.

---

81 Rom. xi. 7. "*The election hath obtained it.*" Tune Crescens. 118, 118.

1 ETERNAL election preserves me secure,
I live by that sovereign decree;
Redeemed by my Saviour, and called by His power,
I worship the covenant Three!

2 'Tis grace unexpected my spirit now sings,
Emerging from regions of night;
My heart, put in tune by celestial things,
Gives praise for the dawning of light.

3 From chambers of death and defilement I rise,
My robes of pollution lay by;
New clothed by my Saviour, approved in His eyes,
I sing of His friendship with joy.

4 I did not suppose it, but now I believe,
He died as a Surety for me;
Through His crucifixion, by faith I receive
Salvation completed and free.

5 When Adam our father revolted and fell,
Mankind became guilty and dead;
Free grace still prevented from falling to hell
The members who stood in their Head.

6 Their union, eternal, could not be destroyed,
Though ruin came in by offence;
For love everlasting sent Jesus, who died,
And bore their iniquity hence!

John Stevens, 1808.

CRASSELIUS; *or*, WINCHESTER NEW. [H. P. 3.]

82 Rom. viii. 29. *"He also did predestinate."* Tune CRASSELIUS. L. M. Or TALLIS'S CANON.

1 I SING the gracious fixed decree,
Passed by the great Eternal Three,
In council held in heaven above:
The Lord's predestinating love.

2 All that concerns the chosen race,
In nature, providence, and grace,
Where they shall dwell, and when remove,
Fixed by predestinating love.

3 Their calling, growth, and robes they wear,
Their conflicts, trials, daily care,
Are, for them, well arranged above,
By God's predestinating love.

4 In this let Zion's sons rejoice,
Their God will not revoke His choice;
Nor sin, nor death, nor hell, can move
His firm predestinating love.

5 This is our bulwark of defence,
Nor foes, nor friends, shall drive us hence:
In life, and death, and realms above,
We 'll sing predestinating love!

Joseph Irons, 1825.

HURSLEY. [H. P. 260.]

83 2 Sam. xxiii. 5. *"He hath made with me an everlasting covenant, ordered in all things, and sure."* Tune HURSLEY. L. M. Or GILBOA.

1 JEHOVAH'S covenant shall endure,
All ordered, everlasting, sure!
O child of God, rejoice to trace
Thy portion in its glorious grace.

2 'Tis thine, for Christ is given to be
The covenant of God to thee;
In Him, God's golden scroll of light,
The darkest truths are clear and bright.

3 O sorrowing sinner, well He knew,
Ere time began, what He would do!
Then rest thy hope within the veil;
His covenant mercies shall not fail.

4 O doubting one, the' eternal Three
Are pledged in faithfulness for thee;
Claim every promise, sweet and sure,
By covenant oath of God secure.

5 O waiting one, each moment's fall
Is marked by Love that planned them all;
Thy times, all ordered by His hand,
In God's eternal covenant stand.

6 O feeble one, look up and see
Strong consolation sworn for thee;
Jehovah's glorious arm is shown,
His covenant strength is all thine own.

7 O mourning one, each stroke of love
A covenant blessing yet shall prove;
His covenant love shall be thy stay;
His covenant grace be as thy day.

8 O Love that chose, O Love that died,
O Love that sealed and sanctified,
All glory, glory, glory be,
O covenant, Triune God, to Thee!

Frances Ridley Havergal, 1872.

---

84 Zech. iv. 7. *"Shoutings, crying, Grace, grace unto it."* Tune MAGDALENE COLLEGE. 886. D.

1 HARK! how the blood-bought host above
Conspire to praise redeeming love
In sweet harmonious strains;
And while they strike their golden lyres,
This glorious theme each bosom fires,
That grace triumphant reigns.

2 Join thou, my soul, for thou canst tell
How grace Divine broke up thy cell,
And loosed thy native chains;
And still, from that auspicious day,
How oft art thou constrained to say,
That grace triumphant reigns.

3 When David fell, in days of old,
This brought the wanderer to the fold,
A prisoner in his chains;
Now free from sin, a virgin soul,
To sing, while endless ages roll,
That grace triumphant reigns.

4 Grace, till the tribes redeemed by blood
Are brought to know themselves and God,
Her empire shall maintain;
To call, when He appoints the day,
And from the mighty takes the prey,
Shall grace triumphant reign.

5 When called to meet the King of Dread,
Should love compose my dying bed,
And grace my soul sustain;
Then, ere I quit this mortal clay,
I'll raise my fainting voice, and say,
Let grace triumphant reign!

John Kent, 1803.

85 Tune Havilah. 87, 87, 47.

Rom. viii. 29. *"He also did predestinate."*

1 ARE the saints predestinated
By the purposes of grace?
They can never be frustrated,
God will have His chosen race;
In His kingdom,
All His saints shall see His face.

2 Are the saints predestinated
To a kingdom and a crown?
Then they shall be new-created,
God will send His Spirit down
To transform them
To the image of His Son.

3 Are the saints predestinated
To their mansions built above?
This rich blessing emanated
From Jehovah's sovereign love;
His affection
Never, never shall remove.

4 Yes, we are predestinated!
'Tis asserted by the King;
With this precious truth elated,
We will of His mercy sing;
Home to glory
Jesus will His subjects bring!

Joseph Irons, 1825.

(2) CREATION.

86 Ps. xix. 1. *"The heavens declare the glory of God."* Tune Crasselius. L. M. D.

1 THE spacious firmament on high,
With all the blue ethereal sky,
And spangled heavens, a shining frame,
Their great Original proclaim.
The' unwearied sun, from day to day,
Does his Creator's power display,
And publishes to every land
The work of an Almighty hand.

2 Soon as the evening shades prevail,
The moon takes up the wondrous tale,
And nightly to the listening earth
Repeats the story of her birth;
Whilst all the stars that round her burn,
And all the planets in their turn,
Confirm the tidings, as they roll,
And spread the truth from pole to pole.

3 What, though in solemn silence all
Move round the dark terrestrial ball;
What, though no real voice or sound
Amidst their radiant orbs be found?
In reason's ear they all rejoice,
And utter forth a glorious voice,
For ever singing, as they shine,
"The hand that made us is Divine!"

Joseph Addison, 1712.

WALDECK. [H. P. 4.]

87 Ps. cxix. 68. "*Thou art good.*" Tune WALDECK. L. M.

1 YES, God is good; in earth and sky,
From ocean-depths and spreading wood,
Ten thousand voices seem to cry,
"God made us all, and God is good."

2 The sun that keeps his trackless way,
And downward pours his golden flood,
Night's sparkling hosts, all seem to say,
In accents clear, that God is good.

3 The merry birds prolong the strain,
Their song with every spring renewed;
And balmy air, and falling rain,
Each softly whisper, "God is good."

4 I hear it in the rushing breeze;
The hills that have for ages stood,
The echoing sky and roaring seas,
All swell the chorus, "God is good."

5 Yes, God is good, all nature says,
By God's own hand with speech endued;
And man, in louder notes of praise,
Should sing for joy that God is good.

6 For all Thy gifts we bless Thee, Lord;
But chiefly for our heavenly food,
Thy pardoning grace, Thy quickening word;
These prompt our song, that "God is good!"

John Hampden Gurney, 1838.

HARTS. [H. P. 284.]

88 Ps. cxlv. 10. "*All Thy works shall praise Thee.*" Tune HARTS. 77, 77. Or REPHAIM.

1 HARK! my soul, how everything
Strives to serve our bounteous King,
Each a double tribute pays,
Sings its part, and then obeys.

2 Nature's chief and sweetest quire
Him with cheerful notes admire;
Chanting every day their lauds,
While the grove their song applauds.

3 Though their voices lower be,
Streams have too their melody;
Night and day they warbling run,
Never pause, but still sing on.

4 All the flowers that gild the spring
Hither their still music bring;
If Heaven bless them, thankful they
Smell more sweet, and look more gay.

5 Wake, for shame, my sluggish heart,
Wake, and gladly sing thy part;
Learn of birds, and springs, and flowers,
How to use thy nobler powers.

6 Live for ever, glorious Lord!
Live, by all Thy works adored!
One in Three, and Three in One,
Thrice we bow to Thee alone!

John Austin, 1668.

JULIUS. [H. P. 266.]

rall.

89 Tune JULIUS. 87, 887.

Ps. cxlviii. 13. "*Let them praise the name of the Lord.*"

1 ANGELS holy,
High and lowly,
Sing the praises of the Lord!
Earth and sky, all living nature,
Man, the stamp of thy Creator,
Praise ye, praise ye, God the Lord!

2 Sun and moon bright,
Night and noonlight,
Starry temples azure-floored;
Cloud and rain, and wild winds' madness,
Sons of God that shout for gladness,
Praise ye, praise ye, God the Lord!

3 Ocean hoary,
Tell His glory,
Cliffs, where tumbling seas have roared!
Pulse of waters, blithely beating,
Wave advancing, wave retreating,
Praise ye, praise ye, God the Lord!

4 Rock and high land,
Wood and island,
Crag, where eagle's pride hath soared;
Mighty mountains, purple-breasted,
Peaks cloud-cleaving, snowy-crested,
Praise ye, praise ye, God the Lord!

5 Rolling river,
Praise Him ever,
From the mountain's deep vein poured;
Silver fountain, clearly gushing,
Troubled torrent, madly rushing,
Praise ye, praise ye, God the Lord!

6 Praise Him ever,
Bounteous Giver;
Praise Him, Father, Friend, and Lord!
Each glad soul, its free course winging,
Each glad voice, its free song singing,
Praise the great and mighty Lord!

John Stuart Blackie, 1857.

PERGAMOS. (Hymn Chant.) [H. P. No. IV.]

90

Ps. cxlviii. 1. "*Praise ye the Lord.*"

Tune, Hymn Chant Pergamos.

1 THE strain upraise of jóy and praise, Allelúia!
To the glory of their King shall the ransomed
péople sing, Alleluia!

2 And the choirs that dwell on high shall re-echo
thróugh the sky, Alleluia!
They through the fields of Paradise who roam, the
blessed ones, repeat through thát bright home,
Alleluia!

3 The planets glittering on their héavenly way,
The shining constellations, jóin and say,
Alleluia! Alleluia!

4 Ye clouds that onward sweep, ye winds on pinions
light,
Ye thunders, echoing loud and deep, ye lightnings
wíldly bright,
In sweet consént unite Your Alleluia!

5 Ye floods and ocean billows, ye storms and winter
snow,
Ye days of cloudless beauty, hoar frost and súmmer
glow;
Ye groves that wave in spring, and glorious fórest,
sing Alleluia!

6 First let the birds, with painted plumage gay, exalt
their great Creator's práise, and say, Alleluia!
Then let the beasts of earth, with varying strain,
join in creation's hymn, and crý again,
Alleluia!

7 Here let the mountains thunder fórth sonorous,
Alleluia!
There let the valleys sing in géntler chorus,
Alleluia!

8 Thou jubilant abyss of ócean, cry Alleluia!
Ye tracts of earth and continénts, reply Alleluia!

9 To God, who all creátion made,
The frequent hymn be dúly paid;
Alleluia! Alleluia!

10 This is the strain, the eternal strain, the Lord
Almíghty loves; Alleluia!
This is the song, the heavenly song, that Christ
Himsélf approves; Alleluia!

11 Wherefore we sing, both heart and vóice awaking,
Alleluia!
And children's voices echo, ánswer making,
Alleluia!

12 Now from all men bé outpoured
Alleluia tó the Lord;
With Alleluia évermore
The Son and Spirit wé adore.

13 Praise be done to the Thrée in One;
Alleluia! Alleluia! Alleluia!

Godeschalcus, circa 940; *John Mason Neale, D.D. (tr.)*, 1851.

Note.—Printed thus to facilitate chanting.

THE OLD 100th TUNE. [H. P. 1.]

91

Ps. c. 3. "*It is He that hath made us.*"

Tune Old Hundredth. L. M.

1 BEFORE Jehovah's awful throne,
Ye nations bow with sacred joy;
Know that the Lord is God alone,
He can create, and He destroy.

2 His sovereign power, without our aid,
Made us of clay, and formed us men;
And when like wandering sheep we strayed,
He brought us to His fold again.

3 We'll crowd Thy gates with thankful songs,
High as the heavens our voices raise;
And earth, with her ten thousand tongues,
Shall fill Thy courts with sounding praise.

4 Wide as the world is Thy command,
Vast as eternity Thy love;
Firm as a rock Thy truth must stand,
When rolling years shall cease to move!

Isaac Watts, D.D., 1719 (*a. by John Wesley*).

KADESH. [H. P. 159.]

92 Ps. xcvi. 1. "*O sing unto the Lord a new song.*" Tune KADESH. 77, 77, 77, 77, 77.

1 COME, oh come! in pious lays
Sound we God Almighty's praise;
Hither bring, in one consent,
Heart, and voice, and instrument:
Music add of every kind;
Sound the trump, the cornet wind,
Strike the viol, touch the lute,
Let not tongue nor string be mute;
Nor a creature dumb be found
That hath either voice or sound.

2 Let those things which do not live
In still music praises give;
Lowly pipe, ye worms that creep
On the earth or in the deep:
Loud aloft your voices strain,
Beasts and monsters of the main;
Birds, your warbling treble sing;
Clouds, your peals of thunder ring;
Sun and moon, exalted higher,
And bright stars, augment the choir.

3 Come, ye sons of human race,
In this chorus take your place,
And amid the mortal throng
Be you masters of the song:
Angels and supernal powers,
Be the noblest tenor yours:
Let, in praise of God, the sound
Run a never-ending round,
That our song of praise may be
Everlasting, as is He.

4 From earth's vast and hollow womb
Music's deepest bass may come;
Seas and floods, from shore to shore,
Shall their counter-tenors roar:
To this concert, when we sing,
Whistling winds, your descants bring;
That our song may over-climb
All the bounds of place and time,
And ascend, from sphere to sphere,
To the great Almighty's ear.

5 So from heaven on earth He shall
Let His gracious blessings fall;
And this huge wide orb we see
Shall one choir, one temple be;
Where in such a praiseful tone
We will sing what He hath done,
That the cursèd fiends below
Shall thereat impatient grow:
Then, oh come, in pious lays
Sound we God Almighty's praise!

George Wither, 1641.

THE OLD 100th TUNE. [H. P. 1.]

93 Gen. i. 1. "*In the beginning God created the heaven and the earth.*" Tune OLD HUNDREDTH. L. M.

1 IN the beginning, God said "Be!"
And all things were—heaven, earth, and sea:
God, in the end, once more will say,
"Perish!" and all shall pass away.

2 But Thou, O Lord! for ever art:
The orb of Thine eternity
Is one great whole, without a part;
Past, present, future, meet in Thee.

3 Convinced of sin, my soul would bend
Before Thee in the lowest dust;
Yet to Thy throne by prayer ascend,
With trembling awe and childlike trust.

4 Oh look in loving-kindness down
On a frail worm with Thee at strife;
Eternal death were in Thy frown,
Thy smile will be eternal life!

James Montgomery, 1853.

ST. ANN. [H. P. 52.]

94 Ps. civ. 24. *"In wisdom hast Thou made them all."* Tune St. Ann. C. M.

1 I SING the' almighty power of God,
That made the mountains rise,
That spread the flowing seas abroad,
And built the lofty skies.

2 I sing the wisdom that ordained
The sun to rule the day:
The moon shines full at His command,
And all the stars obey.

3 I sing the goodness of the Lord,
That filled the earth with food;
He formed the creatures with His word,
And then pronounced them good.

4 Lord, how Thy wonders are displayed
Where'er I turn mine eye;
If I survey the ground I tread,
Or gaze upon the sky!

5 There's not a plant or flower below,
But makes Thy glories known;
And clouds arise, and tempests blow,
By order from Thy throne.

6 Creatures, as numerous as they be,
Are subject to Thy care;
There's not a place where we can flee
But God is present there.

7 In heaven He shines with beams of love,
With wrath in hell beneath;
'Tis on His earth I stand or move,
And 'tis His air I breathe.

8 His hand is my perpetual guard;
He keeps me with His eye;
Why should I then forget the Lord,
Who is for ever nigh?

Isaac Watts, D.D., 1715.

MAHANAIM. [H. P. 129.]

95 Gen. i. 10. *"God saw that it was good."* Tune Mahanaim. 76, 76. D. Or Crüger.

1 'TWAS God that made the ocean,
And laid its sandy bed;
He gave the stars their motion,
And built the mountain's head:
He made the rolling thunder,
The lightning's forkèd flame;
His works are full of wonder,
All-glorious is His name.

2 And must it not surprise us
That One, so high and great,
Should see, and not despise us
Poor sinners, at His feet?
Yet day by day He gives us
Our raiment and our food;
In sickness He relieves us,
And is in all things good.

3 But things that are far greater
His mighty hand hath done;
And sent us blessings sweeter,
Through Christ His only Son;
Who, when He saw us dying
In sin and sorrow's night,
On wings of mercy flying,
Came down with life and light.

4 He gives His word to teach us
Our danger and our wants;
And kindly doth beseech us
To take the life He grants.
His Holy Spirit frees us
From Satan's deadly power;
Leads us by faith to Jesus,
And makes His glory ours!

Church Sunday School Hymn Book, 1868.

GIBBONS. [H. P. 148.]

96 Gen. i. 31. "*Behold, it was very good.*" Tune GIBBONS. 77, 77.

1 PRAISE the High, the Holy One!
God o'er all, the First, the Last:
For He spake, and it was done;
He commanded, it stood fast.

2 At His word, from darkness light,
Harmony from discord broke;
Weakness started into might,
Beauty out of dust awoke:

3 Fire and water, air and earth,
Heard His voice and hushed their strife;
Death itself, by wondrous birth,
Grew the parent of all life.

4 Plant, and flower, and herb, and tree,
Sprang spontaneous from the sod;
Sun and moon, and land and sea,
Day and night, beheld their God.

5 Fishes, fowls upon the wing,
Beasts, and all that creep or fly,
Every breathing, moving thing,
Peopled forest, flood, and sky.

6 But while all was fair and good,
All accordant to His will,
None their Maker understood,
Mind and thought were wanting still.

7 God, His glory to display,
With His image crowned the whole,
Breathed His Spirit into clay,
And made man a living soul.

8 Hallelujah! praise the One
God o'er all, the First, the Last:
For He spake, and it was done;
He commanded, it stood fast!

James Montgomery, 1851.

See Hymns 50, 116, 341—343, 604, 622, 1003.

EDEN. [H. P. 38.]

(3) PROVIDENCE.

97 Ps. iv. 8. "*Thou, Lord, only makest me dwell in safety.*" Tune EDEN. C. M. Or YORK.

1 LORD! in the day Thou art about
The paths wherein I tread;
And in the night, when I lie down,
Thou art about my bed.

2 While others in God's prisons lie,
Bound with affliction's chain,
I walk at large, secure and free
From sickness and from pain.

3 'Tis Thou dost crown my hopes and plans
With good success each day:
This crown, together with myself,
At Thy blest feet I lay.

4 Oh let my house a temple be,
That I and mine may sing
Hosanna to Thy majesty,
And praise our heavenly King!

John Mason, 1683; *John Hampden Gurney*, 1851.

SOREK (Valley of). [H. P. 184.]

98 Ps. cxix. 65. "*Thou hast dealt well with Thy servant.*" Tune SOREK. 87, 87.

1 OH how kindly hast Thou led me,
Heavenly Father, day by day!
Found my dwelling, clothed, and fed me,
Furnished friends to cheer my way!

2 Didst Thou bless me, didst Thou chasten,
With Thy smile, or with Thy rod,
'Twas that still my step might hasten
Homeward, heavenward, to my God!

3 Oh how slowly have I often
Followed where Thy hand would draw!
How Thy kindness failed to soften!
How Thy chastening failed to awe!

4 Make me for Thy rest more ready,
As Thy path is longer trod;
Keep me in Thy friendship steady,
Till Thou call me home, my God!

Thomas Grinfield, 1836.

99 Ps. xxxiv. 1. *"I will bless the Lord at all times."* Tune EDEN. C. M. Or WINCHESTER.

1 O LORD! I would delight in Thee,
And on Thy care depend;
To Thee in every trouble flee,
My best—my only Friend!

2 When all created streams are dried,
Thy fulness is the same;
May I with this be satisfied,
And glory in Thy name!

3 Why should the soul a drop bemoan,
Who has a fountain near;
A fountain which will ever run
With water sweet and clear?

4 No good in creatures can be found,
But may be found in Thee;
I must have all things, and abound,
While God is God to me.

5 Oh that I had a stronger faith,
To look within the veil;
To credit what my Saviour saith,
Whose word can never fail!

6 He that has made my heaven secure,
Will here all good provide;
While Christ is rich, can I be poor?
What can I want beside?

7 O Lord! I cast my care on Thee,
I triumph and adore:
Henceforth my great concern shall be
To love and please Thee more!

John Ryland, D.D., 1777.

VIENNA. [H. P. 149.]

100 Ps. xxxi. 15. *"My times are in Thy hand."* Tune VIENNA. 77, 77.

1 SOVEREIGN Ruler of the skies,
Ever gracious, ever wise!
All my times are in Thy hand,
All events at Thy command.

2 His decree who formed the earth,
Fixed my first and second birth;
Parents, native place, and time,
All appointed were by Him.

3 He that formed me in the womb,
He shall guide me to the tomb;
All my times shall ever be
Ordered by His wise decree.

4 Times of sickness, times of health;
Times of penury and wealth;
Times of trial and of grief;
Times of triumph and relief.

5 Times the tempter's power to prove;
Times to taste a Saviour's love;
All must come, and last, and end,
As shall please my heavenly Friend.

6 Plagues and deaths around me fly;
Till He bids, I cannot die;
Not a single shaft can hit,
Till the God of love thinks fit.

7 O Thou Gracious, Wise, and Just,
In Thy hands my life I trust!
Have I somewhat dearer still?
I resign it to Thy will.

8 May I always own Thy hand—
Still to the surrender stand;
Know that Thou art God alone;
I and mine are all Thine own.

9 Thee at all times will I bless;
Having Thee I all possess:
How can I bereavèd be,
Since I cannot part with Thee!

John Ryland, D.D., 1777.

EUODIAS. [H. P. 255.]

101 2 Kings iv. 26. *"It is well."* Tune EUODIAS. 84, 84, 8884.

1 THROUGH the love of God our Saviour,
All will be well;
Free and changeless is His favour,
All, all is well!
Precious is the blood that healed us;
Perfect is the grace that sealed us;
Strong the hand stretched out to shield us;
All must be well!

2 Though we pass through tribulation,
All will be well;
Ours is such a full salvation,
All, all is well!
Happy, still in God confiding;
Fruitful, if in Christ abiding;
Holy, through the Spirit's guiding:
All must be well!

3 We expect a bright to-morrow,
All will be well;
Faith can sing through days of sorrow,
All, all is well!
On our Father's love relying,
Jesus every need supplying,
Both in living and in dying,
All must be well!

Mary Bowly, 1847.

JEZREEL (Valley of). [H. P. 220.]

102 John xiii. 7. *"What I do thou knowest not now."* Tune JEZREEL. 88, 84. Or Hymn Chant SARDIS.

1 WE cannot always trace the way,
Where Thou, our gracious Lord, dost move;
But we can always surely say
That Thou art Love.

2 When fear its gloomy cloud will fling
O'er earth, our souls to heaven above
As to their sanctuary spring;
For Thou art Love.

3 When mystery shrouds our darkened path,
We'll check our dread, our doubts reprove;
In this our soul sweet comfort hath,
That Thou art Love.

4 Yes, Thou art Love—a truth like this
Can every gloomy thought remove,
And turn all tears or woes to bliss;
Our God is Love!

Sir John Bowring, LL.D., 1824.

ST. PETER. [H. P. 263.]

103 Ps. lxxvii. 19. *"Thy footsteps are not known."* Tune ST. PETER. C. M. Or LONDON NEW.

1 GOD moves in a mysterious way,
His wonders to perform;
He plants His footsteps in the sea,
And rides upon the storm.

2 Deep in unfathomable mines
Of never-failing skill,
He treasures up His bright designs,
And works His sovereign will.

3 Ye fearful saints, fresh courage take:
The clouds ye so much dread
Are big with mercy, and shall break
In blessings on your head.

4 Judge not the Lord by feeble sense,
But trust Him for His grace;
Behind a frowning providence
He hides a smiling face.

5 His purposes will ripen fast,
Unfolding every hour;
The bud may have a bitter taste,
But sweet will be the flower.

6 Blind unbelief is sure to err,
And scan His work in vain:
God is His own interpreter,
And He will make it plain!

William Cowper, 1774.

104 Tune MAMRE. 88, 88, 88. Or MAON.
Deut. viii. 2. *"Thou shalt remember all the way."*

1 THUS far on life's perplexing path,
Thus far Thou, Lord, our steps hast led;
Snatched from the world's pursuing wrath,
Unharmed, though floods hung o'er our head;
Like ransomed Israel on the shore,
Here then we pause, look back, adore.

2 Strangers and pilgrims here below,
Like all our fathers in their day,
We to the land of promise go,
Lord, by Thine own appointed way:
Still guide, illumine, cheer our flight,
In cloud by day, in fire by night.

MAMRE (Plain of). [H. P. 226.]

3 When we have numbered all our years,
  And stand at length on Jordan's brink,
Though the flesh fail with mortal fears,
  Oh let not then the spirit sink;
But, strong in faith, and hope, and love,
Plunge through the stream to rise above!

James Montgomery, 1825.

VIENNA. [H. P. 149.]

105 John vi. 31. *"He gave them bread from heaven."* Tune VIENNA. 77, 77.

1 DAY by day the manna fell;
  Oh! to learn this lesson well:
Still by constant mercy fed,
Give me, Lord, my daily bread.

2 Day by day, the promise reads:
Daily strength for daily needs;
Cast foreboding fears away;
Take the manna of to-day.

3 Lord, my times are in Thy hand;
All my sanguine hopes have planned
To Thy wisdom I resign,
And would make Thy purpose mine.

4 Thou my daily task shalt give:
Day by day to Thee I live;
So shall added years fulfil,
Not my own—my Father's will.

5 Fond ambition, whisper not;
Happy is my humble lot;
Anxious, busy cares, away!
I'm provided for to-day.

6 Oh! to live exempt from care
By the energy of prayer;
Strong in faith, with mind subdued,
Yet elate with gratitude!

Josiah Conder, 1836.

ST. GEORGE. [H. P. 265.]

106 Isa. iii. 10. *"Say ye to the righteous, It shall be well."* Tune ST. GEORGE. S. M. Or CYRENE.

1 WHAT cheering words are these!
  Their sweetness who can tell?
In time and to eternal days,
  'Tis with the righteous well.

2 Well, when they see His face,
  Or sink amidst the flood;
Well, in affliction's thorny maze,
  Or on the mount with God.

3 'Tis well when joys arise,
  'Tis well when sorrows flow,
'Tis well when darkness veils the skies,
  And strong temptations blow.

4 'Tis well when at His throne
  They wrestle, weep, and pray,
'Tis well when at His feet they groan,
  Yet pray their wants away.

5 'Tis well when they can sing
  As sinners bought with blood,
And when they touch the mournful string,
  And mourn an absent God.

6 'Tis well when on the mount
  They feast on dying love,
And 'tis as well, in God's account,
  When they the furnace prove!

John Kent, 1803.

NOTTINGHAM; *or*, ST. MAGNUS. [H. P. 39.]

107 Ps. ciii. 1. *"Bless the Lord, O my soul."*

Tune Nottingham. C. M.

1 WHEN all Thy mercies, O my God,
My rising soul surveys,
Transported with the view, I'm lost
In wonder, love, and praise!

2 Oh how shall words, with equal warmth,
The gratitude declare
That glows within my ravished heart!
But Thou canst read it there.

3 To all my weak complaints and cries
Thy mercy lent an ear,
Ere yet my feeble thoughts had learnt
To form themselves in prayer.

4 When in the slippery paths of youth
With heedless steps I ran,
Thine arm unseen conveyed me safe,
And led me up to man.

5 Through hidden dangers, toils, and deaths
It gently cleared my way;
And through the pleasing snares of vice,
More to be feared than they.

6 When worn with sickness, oft hast Thou
With health renewed my face;
And when in sin and sorrow sunk,
Revived my soul with grace.

7 Through every period of my life
Thy goodness I'll pursue;
And after death, in distant worlds,
The glorious theme renew.

8 When nature fails, and day and night
Divide Thy works no more,
My ever grateful heart, O Lord!
Thy mercy shall adore.

9 Through all eternity to Thee
A joyful song I'll raise;
But oh! eternity's too short
To utter all Thy praise!

Joseph Addison, 1712.

BASHAN (Hill of). [H. P. 112.]

108 Ps. cvii. 7. *"He led them forth by the right way."* Tune Bashan. 66, 66.

1 THY way, not mine, O Lord,
However dark it be!
Lead me by Thine own hand,
Choose out the path for me.

2 Smooth let it be or rough,
It will be still the best;
Winding or straight, it leads
Right onward to Thy rest.

3 I dare not choose my lot;
I would not, if I might:
Choose Thou for me, my God,
So shall I walk aright.

4 The kingdom that I seek
Is Thine; so let the way
That leads to it be Thine;
Else I must surely stray.

5 Take Thou my cup, and it
With joy or sorrow fill,
As best to Thee may seem;
Choose Thou my good and ill;

6 Choose Thou for me my friends,
My sickness or my health;
Choose Thou my cares for me,
My poverty or wealth.

7 Not mine—not mine the choice,
In things or great or small;
Be Thou my Guide, my Strength,
My Wisdom, and my All!

Horatius Bonar, D.D., 1856.

ST. DAVID. [H. P. 60.]

109 1 Sam. iii. 18. *"It is the Lord."* Tune St. David. C. M.

1 IT is the Lord—enthroned in light—
Whose claims are all Divine;
Who hath an undisputed right
To govern me and mine.

2 It is the Lord. Should I distrust
Or contradict His will,
Who cannot do but what is just,
And must be righteous still?

3 It is the Lord—who gives me all—
My health my friends, my ease;
And of His bounties may recall
Whatever part He please.

4 It is the Lord—who can sustain
Beneath the heaviest load:
From Him assistance I obtain,
To tread the thorny road.

5 It is the Lord—whose matchless skill
Can from afflictions raise
Blessings, eternity to fill
With ever-growing praise.

6 It is the Lord—my covenant God,
Thrice blessèd be His name,
Whose gracious promise, sealed with blood,
Must ever be the same.

Thomas Greene, 1780.

BETHABARA. [H. P. 222.]

110

John xv. 4. "*Abide in Me, and I in you.*" Tune BETHABARA. 8 8 8, 6.

1 O HOLY Saviour, Friend unseen,
Since on Thine arm Thou bidd'st us lean,
Help us, throughout life's changing scene,
By faith to cling to Thee.

2 Blest with this fellowship Divine,
Take what Thou wilt, we'll not repine;
E'en as the branches to the vine,
Our souls will cling to Thee.

3 Without a murmur we dismiss
Our former dreams of earthly bliss;
Our joy, our consolation this,
Each hour to cling to Thee.

4 Though faith and hope may oft be tried,
We ask not, need not, aught beside:
So safe, so calm, so satisfied,
The souls that cling to Thee!

5 They fear not Satan nor the grave,
They know Thee near and strong to save,
Nor dread to cross e'en Jordan's wave,
Because they cling to Thee.

6 Blest be our lot, whate'er befall!
What can disturb, or who appal,
While as our Strength, our Rock, our All,
Saviour, we cling to Thee?

Charlotte Elliott, 1834.

GOLDSTERN. [H. P. 280.]

111

Ps. xlii. 5. "*Why art thou cast down?*" Tune GOLDSTERN. 7 6, 7 6. D. Or MUNICH.

1 WHY restless, why so weary,
My soul, why so cast down?
Is all around thee dreary?
And hath the cross no crown?
Where is the God that found thee,
Who once could make thee glad
His arms are still around thee;
Then wherefore art thou sad?

2 Oh, trust the Lord, who bought thee!
Oh, trust the sinner's Friend!
The wondrous love that sought thee
Will keep thee to the end;
'Twill give a glorious morrow
To this thy night of pain,
And make thy dews of sorrow
Like sunshine after rain.

John S. B. Monsell, LL.D., 1837.

BEDFORD. [H. P. 66.]

112 Ps. xxxiv. 1. *"I will bless the Lord at all times."* Tune BEDFORD. C. M.

1 THROUGH all the changing scenes of life,
In trouble and in joy,
The praises of my God shall still
My heart and tongue employ.

2 Of His deliverance I will boast,
Till all who are distrest
From my example comfort take,
And charm their griefs to rest.

3 The hosts of God encamp around
The dwellings of the just;
Protection He affords to all
Who make His name their trust.

4 Oh make but trial of His love!
Experience will decide
How blest are they, and only they,
Who in His truth confide.

5 Fear Him, ye saints! and you will then
Have nothing else to fear;
Make you His service your delight—
Your wants shall be His care.

6 While hungry lions lack their prey,
The Lord will food provide
For such as put their trust in Him,
And see their needs supplied!

Tate and Brady, 1696.

See Hymns 562, 583, 606, 663.

THEME IV.—The Divine Persons of the Ever-Blessed Trinity.

JEHOVAH—THE FATHER.

MAGDALENE COLLEGE. [H. P. 210.]

(1) HIS OWN ESSENTIAL BLESSEDNESS.

113 Exod. iii. 14. *"I am that I am."* Tune MAGDALENE COLLEGE. 8 8 6. D.

1 ASPIRE, my soul, to yonder throne,
Where sits the Infinite Unknown,
The self-existent One;
Whose being no beginning knows,
The brightness of whose glory flows
Through His belovèd Son.

2 'Tis His to fill immensity;
No object can escape His eye,
Nor thought His mind elude;
All things were by His wisdom planned
All are supported by His hand;
And all at once are viewed.

3 Justice and mercy, truth and love,
Shine from His glorious throne above,
As Israel's covenant Lord;
In Persons three—in Essence one—
He is the sovereign Lord alone,
And be His name adored.

4 With Him is no futurity;
He stands enwrapt in purity;
Unchangeably the same:
God over all, for ever blessed,
The Fount of joy, the Fount of rest;
And holy is His name!

Joseph Irons, 1825. (*a.*)

114 Ps. xciii. 1. *"The Lord reigneth."* Tune OLD HUNDREDTH. L. M. Or WALDECK.

1 JEHOVAH reigns! His throne is high;
His robes are light and majesty;
His glory shines with beams so bright,
No mortal can sustain the sight.

2 His terrors keep the world in awe;
His justice guards His holy law;
His love reveals a smiling face;
His truth and promise seal the grace.

THE OLD 100th TUNE. [H. P. 1.]

3 Through all His works His wisdom shines,
And baffles Satan's deep designs;
His power is sovereign to fulfil
The noblest counsels of His will.

4 And will this glorious Lord descend
To be my Father and my Friend?
Then let my song with angels' join;
Heaven is secure, if God be mine!

Isaac Watts, D.D., 1709.

---

115 1 Tim. vi. 16. "*Dwelling in the light which no man can approach unto.*"

Tune St. John. 6666, 88.
Or Gopsal; or Moriah.

ST. JOHN. [H. P. 272.]

1 O GLORIOUS God and King,
O gracious Father, hear
The praise our hearts would bring
To Thee, who, ever near,
Yet in eternity dost dwell,
Immortal and invisible.

2 Around Thee all is light,
And rest of perfect love,
And glory full and bright,
All human thought above;
Thyself the Fountain infinite
Of all ineffable delight.

3 O depth of holy bliss,
Essential and Divine,
What thought can measure this—
Thy joy, *Thy* glory,—Thine!
Yet such our treasure evermore—
Thy fulness is Thy children's store.

4 O Father, Thy great grace
We magnify and praise;
Called to that blessèd place,
With Thee through endless days
Thy joy to share, Thy joy to be,
Thy glory all unveiled to see!

Frances Ridley Havergal, 1872.

See Hymn 46.

---

(2) HIS ETERNAL LOVE TO HIS BELOVED SON.

116 Tune Crüger. 76, 76. D.
Or Mahanaim.

Prov. viii. 30. "*I was daily His delight.*"

CRÜGER. [H. P. 276.]

1 "ERE God had built the mountains,
Or raised the fruitful hills;
Before He filled the fountains,
That feed the running rills;
In Me, from everlasting,
The wonderful I AM
Found pleasures never wasting,
And Wisdom is My name.

2 "When, like a tent to dwell in,
He spread the skies abroad,
And swathed about the swelling
Of ocean's mighty flood,
He wrought by weight and measure;
And I was with Him then:
Myself the Father's pleasure,
And Mine the sons of men."

3 Thus Wisdom's words discover
Thy glory and Thy grace,
Thou everlasting Lover
Of our unworthy race!
Thy gracious eye surveyed us
Ere stars were seen above:
In wisdom Thou hast made us,
And died for us in love.

4 And couldst Thou be delighted
With creatures such as we,
Who, when we saw Thee, slighted,
And nailed Thee to a tree?
Unfathomable wonder,
And mystery Divine!
The voice that speaks in thunder,
Says, "Sinner, I am thine!"

William Cowper, 1779.

(3) THE CHOICE AND GIFT OF THE CHURCH, BY THE FATHER, TO HIS SON.

117 Jer. xxxi. 3. "*Yea, I have loved thee.*"
Tune Leipsic. L. M.

1 'TWAS with an everlasting love
That God His own elect embraced,
Before He made the worlds above,
Or earth on her huge columns placed.

2 Long ere the sun's refulgent ray
Primeval shades of darkness drove,
They on His sacred bosom lay,
Loved with an everlasting love.

3 Then, in the glass of His decrees,
Christ and His bride appeared as one:
Her sin, by imputation, His,
Whilst she in spotless splendour shone.

4 O love, how high thy glories swell,
How great, immutable, and free!
Ten thousand sins, as black as hell,
Are swallowed up, O love, in thee!

5 Believer, here thy comfort stands,
From first to last salvation's free;
And everlasting love demands
An everlasting song from thee!

John Kent, 1803.

118 Eph. i. 4. "*Chosen in Him before the foundation of the world.*"
Tune Leipsic. L. M.

1 WHO can the distant period trace,
When God, to glorify His grace,
And magnify His love to man,
Drew forth redemption's wondrous plan?

2 God's own Elect, was Christ proclaimed,
Then all His mystic members named,
One glorious Head, one body there,
Who should at last one glory share.

3 In God's decree her form He viewed,
All beauteous in His eyes she stood,
Presented through the' eternal name,
Betrothed in love, and free from blame.

4 Not as she stood, in Adam's fall,
When guilt and ruin covered all,
But as she'll stand another day,
Fair as the sun's meridian ray.

5 O glorious grace! mysterious plan,
Too great for angels' mind to scan;
Our thoughts are lost, our numbers fail;
All hail, redeeming love! all hail!

John Kent, 1823.

119 1 Pet. i. 2. "*Elect according to the foreknowledge of God.*" Tune Alpha. L. M. D.

1 BEFORE the' Almighty Power began
To form the wondrous frame of man;
Before He hung the lights on high,
And made them sparkle o'er the sky;
Before He gave the mountains birth,
Or shaped the yet unfounded earth,
God all His ransomed people knew,
And in His love He chose them too.

2 Chose them in Christ, that they should prove
The trophies of His dying love;
Chose them through faith, that precious grace
Which bears the fruits of righteousness;
Chose them that they on earth should shine
The image of His face Divine;
Chose them, like jewels, from the world,
When it should be to ruin hurled.

3 But, oh, no tongue can ever tell
The grace that is unsearchable!
Angels that fell were passèd by
When Christ for mortals came to die.
The poor shall wear the' immortal crown
That decks few brows of high renown;
And vilest sinners be forgiven,
To raise the loudest songs in heaven!

Ingram Cobbin, 1828.

See Hymns 398—492.

PERSIS. [H. P. 187.]

(4) THE PROMISE BY THE FATHER, OF THE HOLY GHOST, THROUGH THE SON.

120 Ps. lxxxvii. 7. *"All my springs are in Thee."* Tune PERSIS. 8 7, 8 7.

1 HEAR the Father's ancient promise!
Listen, thirsty, weary one!
"I will pour My Holy Spirit
On Thy chosen seed, O Son."
Promise to the Lord's Anointed,
Gift of God to Him for thee!
Now, by covenant appointed,
All thy springs in Him shall be.

2 Springs of life in desert places
Shall thy God unseal for thee;
Quickening and reviving graces,
Dew-like, healing, sweet and free.
Springs of sweet refreshment flowing,
When thy work is hard or long,
Courage, hope, and power bestowing,
Lightening labour with a song.

3 Springs of peace, when conflict heightens,
Thine uplifted eye shall see;
Peace that strengthens, calms, and brightens,
Peace, itself a victory.
Springs of comfort, strangely springing
Through the bitter wells of woe;
Founts of hidden gladness, bringing
Joy that earth can ne'er bestow.

4 Thine, O Christian, is this treasure,
To thy risen Head assured!
Thine in full and gracious measure,
Thine by covenant secured!
Now arise! His word possessing,
Claim the promise of the Lord;
Plead through Christ for showers of blessing,
Till the Spirit be outpoured!

Frances Ridley Havergal, 1870.

(5) GOD IS LOVE.

121 Rom. v. 8. *"God commendeth His love toward us."*
Tune KEDRON. 886. D.

KEDRON (Brook). [H. P. 213.]

1 SUPREMELY sweet is sovereign love,
That brought the Saviour from above,
To agonize and die;
Its aim in Jesus was to bless
His children with His righteousness;
'Tis finished, hear Him cry!

2 The love of God is firm and sure,
In Christ it made us so secure,
That hell may rage in vain;
Love keeps us ever one with Him,
And brought Him fully to redeem,
That we might rise and reign.

3 Jehovah's love shall brightly shine
Upon us, richly to refine,
Through Jesu's bleeding cross;
In Christ we ever must remain,
And here possess eternal gain,
By His amazing loss.

4 This love shall make us ever blest,
And guide us to the realms of rest,
Where Jesus reigns on high;
In this great love we place our trust,
And in its praises sing we must
At last above the sky!

Thomas Row, 1817.

YORK. [H. P. 45.]

122 Eph. i. 3. *"Blessed with all spiritual blessings . . in Christ."* Tune YORK. C. M.

1 SING to the Lord, whose matchless love
A sure foundation lays,
To take a people to Himself,
And form them for His praise.

2 In grateful strains His counsel sing,
For thus His counsel runs;
To choose, adopt, redeem, and bring
To glory all His sons.

3 Let sweet adoption lead the song,
Election swell the strain,
While promises the theme prolong,
And joys celestial reign.

4 'Tis yours who know His mighty love,
To sing on themes like these;
When He the heartfelt joy imparts,
No other subjects please.

5 His ways how wonderful to trace,
By which His love is shown
To sinners, saved by richest grace,
Who worship at His throne!

William Wales Horne, 1823.

E

WINCHESTER. [H. P. 46.]

123 Hos. xiv. 4. "*I will love them freely.*" Tune WINCHESTER. C. M. Or NOTTINGHAM.

1 WHAT boundless and unchanging love
God has bestowed on saints;
'Tis this shall tune their harps above,
And banish their complaints.

2 Love placed their souls in Jesu's hand,
Who rescued them from hell:
By His unchanging love they stand,
And with Him hope to dwell.

3 'Twas love that brought them to His feet,
And melted every heart:
His love shall make their bliss complete,
And ne'er from them depart.

4 The drawings of His love shall bring
Their souls up to His throne:
Of His eternal love to sing,
With rapture here unknown!

Joseph Irons, 1819.

WALDECK. [H. P. 4.]

124 1 John iii. 1. "*Behold what manner of love.*" Tune WALDECK. L. M. Or OLD TEN COMMANDMENTS.

1 JEHOVAH'S love first chose His saints;
Love listens now to their complaints;
Love paid their debt incurred by sin;
Love breaks their hearts, and enters in.

2 Thus Father, Son, and Holy Dove,
The Three in One, a God of Love,
Engaged in covenant for our sake:
This threefold cord can never break.

3 'Tis held in God our Saviour's hand;
Suspended by His own command,
It reaches to the gates of hell,
And rescues souls, with Him to dwell.

4 Nor sin nor Satan can devour
The soul that feels its vital power;
It will not, cannot, lose its hold.
Eternal joys it will unfold!

Joseph Irons, 1819.

125 John xvii. 23. "*Thou hast loved them as Thou hast loved Me.*" Tune WALDECK. L. M.

1 WHO can e'er fathom God's rich love?
Not all the heavenly hosts above;
The brightest angel ne'er can trace
The end of great Jehovah's grace.

2 None can e'er know its vast extent,—
No, not the most exalted saint;
Its length, its breadth, its depth, its height,
Is far beyond a creature's sight.

3 How rich, how free, is love Divine!
Oh, how resplendent doth it shine!
Its bursting glory charms the saints,
And banishes their sad complaints.

4 The highest pleasures we can prove
Flow from this great and glorious love;
Oh, 'tis a most delightful thing,
Infinite love to chant and sing.

5 Dear Lord! descend from Thy bright throne,
And now to us Thy love make known;
To every soul Thyself proclaim,
And let us feel the heavenly flame.

6 God of all grace, to Thee we pray;
More of Thy love, and more, display;
And when we join the heavenly throng,
Infinite love shall be our song!

Richard Burnham, 1803.

EDEN. [H. P. 38.]

126 Rom. v. 5. "*The love of God.*" Tune EDEN. C. M.

1 HOW truly glorious is the love
Of all the glorious Three,—
Eternal, boundless, sovereign, pure,
Unchangeable, and free!

2 The Father's love sent Jesus down
From His own bright abode;
The Saviour, in His wondrous love,
His life for ours bestowed.

3 Drawn by the Spirit's love, we rise,
And breathe for things above,
More swift than eagles' rapid flight,
To see eternal love.

4 We pray, repent, believe, obey,
And joy with those above;
Admire, adore, and shout, and sing
Of everlasting love.

5 Soon may we soar to worlds of light—
On hills of glory shine;
And sing of pure eternal love,
In raptures all Divine!

Richard Burnham, 1803. (*a.*)—*ver.* 2, *F. R. H.*

MORIAH (Mount). [H. P. 119.]

See Hymns 17, 62, 63, 102, 715–722.

127

1 John iv. 16. "*God is love.*"
Tune MORIAH. 6666, 88.
Or BEVAN.

1 LOVE will I ever sing—
Sing of its ancient date;
Love is the flowing spring
Of blessings truly great:
Love is the pure immortal food;
Love is the height and depth of God.

2 Love is my comely dress,
My glory and my crown,
My life, my joy, my peace,
My heaven, and my throne:
Love is the pure immortal food;
Love is the height and depth of God.

3 Lord, may I soon be caught
Up to the realms above,
And there be better taught
The glories of Thy love,
And feast on this immortal food,
And triumph in the love of God!

Richard Burnham, 1796.

JEHOVAH—THE SON.

JORDAN. [H. P. 211.]

(1) HIS DEITY.

128

John i. 1. "*In the beginning was the Word.*" Tune JORDAN. 886. D.

1 HAIL, Thou eternal Logos, hail!
Before whose glory angels veil
Their rapture-beaming eyes:
Our grateful spirits hold Thee dear;
To Thee we breathe the ardent prayer,
And hallelujahs rise.

2 Yes: while incessant shouts of praise
Break from angelic ranks, and raise
The concert of the blessed;
While all that tread the starry road
Announce the dear Redeemer God,
Be it on earth confessed.

3 Being of beings! Lord of all!
While yonder lucid orbs that roll
Declare the great I AM,
We recollect the holy word,
Where all the names and works of God
Are given to the Lamb.

4 Thy works, Thy wondrous works, display
The attributes of Deity,
And spell the sacred name:
Jehovah! Jesus! reigning Cause!
Yes, at Thy mighty fiat rose
This universal frame.

5 Redeeming Lord, to Thee we bow:
Bless Thy rejoicing people now
With wisdom from above;
Come, with Thy vesture dipped in blood;
Appear a very present God,—
A God of perfect love!

Admiral Richard Kempenfelt, 1777.

CHESALON (Mount). [H. P. 35.]

129

Matt. xxi. 9. "*Hosanna in the highest.*" Tune CHESALON. C. M.

1 HOSANNA! raise the pealing hymn
To David's Son and Lord;
With cherubim and seraphim
Exalt the' Incarnate Word.

2 Hosanna! Lord, our feeble tongue
No lofty strains can raise:
But Thou wilt not despise the young,
Who meekly chant Thy praise.

3 Hosanna! Sovereign, Prophet, Priest;
How vast Thy gifts, how free!
Thy blood, our life; Thy word, our feast;
Thy name, our only plea.

4 Hosanna! Master, lo we bring
Our offerings to Thy throne;
Nor gold, nor myrrh, nor mortal thing,
But hearts to be Thine own.

5 Hosanna! once Thy gracious ear
Approved a lisping throng:
Be gracious still, and deign to hear
Our poor but grateful song.

6 O Saviour, if, redeemed by Thee,
Thy temple we behold,
Hosannas through eternity
We'll sing to harps of gold!

William Henry Havergal, 1833.

ESDRAELON. [H. P. 202.]

130

Matt. iii. 17. "*This is My beloved Son.*" Tune ESDRAELON. 87, 87. D.

1 LAMB of God! our souls adore Thee
While upon Thy face we gaze;
There the Father's love and glory
Shine in all their brightest rays.
Thine almighty power and wisdom
All creation's works proclaim:
Heaven and earth alike confess Thee,
As the ever-great "I AM."

2 Lamb of God! Thy Father's bosom
Ever was Thy dwelling-place;
His delight, in Him rejoicing,
One with Him in power and grace.
Oh, what wondrous love and mercy!
Thou didst lay Thy glory by,
And for us didst come from heaven
As the Lamb of God to die.

3 Lamb of God! when we behold Thee
Lowly in the manger laid;
Wandering as a homeless stranger,
In the world Thy hands had made;
When we see Thee in the garden
In Thine agony of blood—
At Thy grace we are confounded,
Holy, spotless Lamb of God!

4 When we see Thee as a victim,
Bound to the accursèd tree,
For our guilt and folly stricken,
All our judgment borne by Thee,
Lord, we own, with hearts adoring,
Thou hast loved us unto blood;
Glory, glory everlasting,
Be to Thee, Thou Lamb of God!

James George Deck, 1838.

131

Col. i. 16. "*By Him were all things created that are in heaven, and that are in earth.*" Tune OLD HUNDREDTH. L. M.

1 WHAT is that grand, that awful name,
Whose blazing glories round us shine?
Who can His mighty works rehearse,
Who spake and built the universe?

2 Not Gabriel's tongue His fame can tell,
His ways are quite unsearchable!
Such are the beauties of His face,
None can His full perfection trace.

3 His presence fills both space and time;
His knowledge reaches every clime;
His wisdom guards and guides the whole,
From nature's centre to the pole.

THE OLD 100th TUNE. [H. P. 1.]

4 Know you, ye saints, this wondrous name,
Whose glories heaven and earth proclaim?
Who? what is He? Oh, strange to tell,
'Tis our beloved Immanuel!

5 This Great First, Last, Beginning, End,
No stretch of thought can comprehend;
In wonder lost, will we adore
That name which angels can't explore!

Augustus M. Toplady, 1776.

132 Isa. lxiii. 1. "*Mighty to save.*"
Tune Filitz. 777, 5. Or Shenir I.

FILITZ. [H. P. 283.]

1 LORD of mercy and of might,
Maker, Teacher, Infinite,
Of mankind the life and light,
Jesus, hear and save.

2 Who, when sin's tremendous doom
Gave creation to the tomb,
Didst not scorn the Virgin's womb,
Jesus, hear and save.

3 Mighty Monarch, Saviour mild,
Humbled to a mortal child,
Captive, beaten, bound, reviled,
Jesus, hear and save.

4 Throned above celestial things,
Borne aloft on angels' wings,
Lord of lords, and King of kings,
Jesus, hear and save.

5 Who shall yet return from high,
Robed in might and majesty,
Hear us, help us when we cry;
Jesus, hear and save.

Bishop Heber, 1811.

MAGDALENE COLLEGE. [H. P. 210.]

133 Ps. cxlv. 10. "*Thy saints shall bless Thee.*" Tune Magdalene College. 886. D.

1 DRAW near, ye saints, with sweetest praise,
Melodious notes, and rapturous lays;
In adoration join:
Before His throne, beneath His feet,
In whom salvation's wonders meet,
And blessings all combine!

2 To Christ our light, our life, and praise,
Eternal strength and righteousness,
Adoring homage pay:
He calls for loudest praise from us,
Who died and saved us from the curse,
And bore our sins away!

3 Lo! God with us, what glories shine!
Here all the attributes Divine
Refulgently unite;
The glories of His truth and grace,
His justice and His holiness,
Angelic praise excite!

4 Since they in ecstasies above
Adore the grace, the wondrous love,
Of our Incarnate God;
What ardent praises shall we bring,
Who louder far than angels sing,
For we are bought with blood!

William Wales Horne, 1823.

134

Rev. v. 12. "*Worthy is the Lamb.*"

Tune Moscow. 664, 6664.

1 GLORY to God on high!
Let earth and skies reply,
Praise ye His name!
His love and grace adore,
Who all our sorrows bore;
Sing aloud evermore,
Worthy the Lamb!

2 Jesus, our Lord and God,
Bore sin's tremendous load,
Praise ye His name.
Tell what His arm hath done,
What spoils from death He won;
Sing His great name alone;
Worthy the Lamb!

While they around the throne
Cheerfully join in one,
Praising His name:
Ye, who have felt His blood,
Sealing your peace with God,
Sound His dear fame abroad;
Worthy the Lamb!

4 Join all ye ransomed race,
Our holy Lord to bless,
Praise ye His name:
In Him we will rejoice,
And make a joyful noise,
Shouting with heart and voice,
Worthy the Lamb!

5 What though we change our place,
Yet we shall never cease
Praising His name:
To Him our songs we bring,
Hail Him our gracious King,
And without ceasing sing,
Worthy the Lamb!

6 Then let the host above,
In realms of endless love,
Praise His dear name:
To Him ascribèd be
Honour and majesty,
Through all eternity;
Worthy the Lamb!

James Allen, 1761. (*a.*)

135

Luke ii. 14. "*Glory to God in the highest.*"

Tune MAGDEBURG. Or ZAANAIM.

1 MIGHTY God! while angels bless Thee,
May an infant lisp Thy name!
Lord of men, as well as angels,
Thou art every creature's theme:
Hallelujah, Hallelujah. Hallelujah, Amen.

2 Lord of every land and nation,
Ancient of eternal days!
Sounded through the wide creation
Be Thy just and lawful praise;
Hallelujah, Hallelujah. Hallelujah, Amen.

3 For the grandeur of Thy nature,
Grand beyond a seraph's thought:
For created works of power,
Works with skill and kindness wrought:
Hallelujah, Hallelujah. Hallelujah, Amen.

4 For Thy providence, that governs
Through Thine empire's wide domain;
Wings an angel, guides a sparrow;
Blessèd be Thy gentle reign:
Hallelujah, Hallelujah. Hallelujah, Amen.

5 But Thy rich, Thy free redemption,
Dark through brightness all along!
Thought is poor, and poor expression:
Who dare sing that awful song?
Hallelujah, Hallelujah. Hallelujah, Amen.

PART II.

6 Brightness of the Father's glory,
Shall Thy praise unuttered lie?
Fly, my tongue, such guilty silence!
Sing the Lord who came to die:
Hallelujah, Hallelujah. Hallelujah, Amen.

7 Did archangels sing Thy coming?
Did the shepherds learn their lays?
Shame would cover me ungrateful,
Should my tongue refuse to praise:
Hallelujah, Hallelujah. Hallelujah, Amen.

8 From the highest throne in glory,
To the cross of deepest woe;
All to ransom guilty captives:
Flow, my praise, for ever flow:
Hallelujah, Hallelujah. Hallelujah, Amen.

9 Go, return, immortal Saviour;
Leave Thy footstool, take Thy throne;
Thence return, and reign for ever,
Be the kingdom all Thy own:
Hallelujah, Hallelujah. Hallelujah, Amen.

Robert Robinson, 1774.

MAGDALENE COLLEGE. [H. P. 210.]

136 Ps. lxxii. 19. "*Blessed be His glorious name for ever.*" Tune MAGDALENE COLLEGE. 886. D.

1 LONG as I live I'll sing the Lamb,
The God, the Man, the Great I AM·
His wondrous person view!
As God He loves—as Man He dies,
As God and Man all grace supplies,
And gives all glory too.

2 He is my Glory, He my Head,
The First-begotten from the dead,
All glory now He wears;
He, who was first of human kind,
Retains me ever in His mind,
Witness the name He bears.

3 His cries and tears are now all o'er,
Once dead, He lives, and bleeds no more;
My soul hath seen Him rise
In faith's bright vision to His rest;
Conqueror of sin, He now is raised
Again above the skies.

4 One work remains for Christ to do,
To bring His chosen people through
The terrors of the grave:
Then He'll appear both God and Man,
The Head and End of wisdom's plan,
And mighty, too, to save.

5 And when this last great work is done,
And all His saints are upwards gone
To their eternal home;
The reigning Lamb will feast their eyes.
With love's triumphant victories:
Amen! Lord Jesus, come!

John Stevens, 1808.

See Hymns 195, 199, 200, 202, 493.

(2) THE NAMES AND TITLES OF CHRIST.

ALPHABETICALLY ARRANGED.

BESOR (Brook). [H. P. 51.]

137 Phil. ii. 9. "*A name which is above every name.*" Tune BESOR. C.M. Or EVAN.

1 THERE is a Name I love to hear;
I love to sing its worth;
It sounds like music in mine ear,
The sweetest name on earth.

2 It tells me of a Saviour's love,
Who died to set me free:
It tells me of His precious blood,
The sinner's perfect plea.

3 It tells me of a Father's smile
Beaming upon His child:
It cheers me through this little while,
Through desert, waste, and wild.

4 Jesus, the name I love so well,
The name I love to hear:
No saint on earth its worth can tell,
No heart conceive how dear.

5 This name shall shed its fragrance still,
Along this thorny road,
Shall sweetly smooth the rugged hill,
That leads me up to God.

6 And there with all the blood-bought throng,
From sin and sorrow free,
I'll sing the new eternal song
Of Jesus' love to me!

Frederick Whitfield, 1857.

CYPRUS. [H. P. 26.]

ADVOCATE.

138 1 John ii. 1. "*We have an Advocate.*" Tune Cyprus. L. M.

1 LOOK up, my soul, with cheerful eye,
See where the great Redeemer stands;
The glorious Advocate on high,
With precious incense in His hands.

2 He sweetens every humble groan,
He recommends each broken prayer;
Recline thy hope on Him alone,
Whose power and love forbid despair.

3 Teach my weak heart, O gracious Lord,
With stronger faith to call Thee mine;
Bid me pronounce the blissful word,
My Father, God, with joy Divine!

Anne Steele, 1760.

AMANA (Mount). [H. P. 84.]

ADVOCATE.

139 Heb. ix. 24. "*Now to appear in the presence of God for us.*" Tune Amana. S. M.

1 AWAKE, my warmest powers,
To sing the Saviour's love;
Since He appears upon the throne,
Our Advocate above.

2 His all-obedient life
Fulfilled the Father's laws;
This is the ground on which He lives
To plead His people's cause.

3 Their names upon His breast
Before the throne He bears;
And our unworthy nature now
This glorious Person wears.

4 His all-atoning death,
And sacrifice Divine,
Prevails to send salvation down
To such a soul as mine.

5 To all that venture near,
In His eternal name,
His power to save, and sanctify,
Shall ever prove the same.

6 With such a glorious plea,
He never prayed in vain;
The Father hears, and Christ receives
The purchase of His pain.

Thomas Row, 1822.

NAYLAND; *or*, ST. STEPHEN. [H. P. 47.]

ADVOCATE.

140 John xvii. 9. "*I pray for them.*" Tune Nayland. C. M.

1 AWAKE! sweet gratitude, and sing
The' ascended Saviour's love;
Sing how He lives to carry on
His people's cause above.

2 With cries and tears He offered up
His humble suit below;
But with authority He asks,
Enthroned in glory now.

3 For all that come to God by Him,
Salvation He demands;
Points to their names upon His breast,
And spreads His wounded hands.

4 His sweet atoning sacrifice
Gives sanction to His claim:
"Father, I will that all My saints
Be with Me where I am:

5 "By their salvation, recompense
The sorrows I endured;
Just to the merits of Thy Son,
And faithful to Thy word."

6 Eternal life, at His request,
To every saint is given:
Safety below, and, after death,
The plenitude of heaven.

Augustus M. Toplady, 1771.

See Hymns 275—281.

LAODICEA. (Hymn Chant.) [H. P. No. VIII.]

ALL IN ALL.

141 Col. ii. 9. "*In Him dwelleth all the fulness.*"

Tune, Hymn Chant Laodicea. 66, 86, 88.

1 I NEED no other plea
  With which to' approach my God,
Than His own mercy, boundless, free,
  Through Christ on man bestowed,
A Father's love, a Father's care
Receives and answers every prayer.

2 I need no other priest
  Than One High Priest above;
His intercession ne'er has ceased
  Since first I knew His love:
Through that my faith shall never fail,
E'en when I pass through death's dark vale.

3 I need no human ear
  In which to pour my prayer;
My great High Priest is ever near,
  On Him I cast my care:
To Him, Him only, I confess,
Who can alone absolve and bless.

4 I need no works by me
  Wrought with laborious care,
To form a meritorious plea
  The bliss of heaven to share:
Christ's finished work, through boundless grace,
Has there secured my dwelling-place!

Part II.

5 I need no prayers to saints,
  Beads, relics, martyrs' shrines;
Hardships 'neath which the spirit faints,
  Yet still, sore burdened, pines:
Christ's service yields my soul delight,
Easy His yoke, His burden light.

6 I need no other book
  To guide my steps to heaven,
Than that on which I daily look,
  By God's own Spirit given;
For this, when He illumes our eyes,
Unto salvation makes us wise.

7 I need no holy oil
  To' anoint my lips in death;
No priestly power my guilt to' assoil,
  And ease my parting breath;
Long since, those words bade fear to cease,
"Thy faith hath saved thee; go in peace."

8 I need no priestly mass,
  No purgatorial fires,
My soul to' anneal, my guilt to' efface,
  When this brief life expires.
Christ died my endless life to win,
His blood has cleansed me from all sin.

9 I need no other dress,
  I urge no other claim,
Than His imputed righteousness;
  In Him complete I am.
Heaven's portals at that word fly wide,
No passport do I need beside!

Charlotte Elliott, 1863.

ALL IN ALL.

142 Col. iii. 11. "*Christ is all, and in all.*"

Tune Minden. 76, 76, 77.

MINDEN. [H. P. 126.]

1 JESUS, Sun and Shield art Thou,
  Sun and Shield for ever!
Never canst Thou cease to shine,
  Cease to guard us never.
Cheer our steps as on we go,
Come between us and the foe.

2 Jesus, Bread and Wine art Thou,
  Wine and Bread for ever!
Never canst Thou cease to feed
  Or refresh us, never.
Feed we still on bread Divine,
Drink we still this heavenly wine.

3 Jesus, Love and Life art Thou,
  Life and Love for ever!
Ne'er to quicken shalt Thou cease,
  Or to love us never.
All of life and love we need
Is in Thee, in Thee indeed.

4 Jesus, Peace and Joy art Thou,
  Joy and Peace for ever!
Joy that fades not, changes not,
  Peace that leaves us never.
Joy and peace we have in Thee,
Now and through eternity.

5 Jesus, Song and Strength art Thou,
  Strength and Song for ever!
Strength that never can decay,
  Song that ceaseth never.
Still to us this strength and song
Through eternal days prolong!

Horatius Bonar, D.D., 1861.

GILBOA (Mount). [H. P. 11.]

ALL IN ALL.

143 Rev. xix. 12. *"On His head were many crowns."* Tune GILBOA. L. M. Or DALMATIA.

1 SAVIOUR, I read with grateful joys
The names Thy holy word employs
To charm my heart and calm my fears,
To show Thy lovely characters.

2 Water of life; of life the Tree;
The Bread of life art Thou to me!
The Light of life, the Living Way,
The Sun of everlasting day!

3 The Rock of strength, the Corner stone,
The Branch of God, Plant of renown,
The Morning Star, the precious Pearl,
The "Chiefest," and "the All in All!"

4 Prophet, and Priest, and Prince, and King,
And First, and Last, Thy praise we sing:
Through life we'll bless Thee, and, again,
Ceaseless, in heaven! Amen, Amen!

Benjamin Samuel Hollis, 1849.

ALL IN ALL.

144 Col. ii. 10. *"Ye are complete in Him."* Tune GILBOA. L. M.

1 IN Christ, I've all my soul's desire;
His Spirit does my heart inspire
With boundless wishes large and high,
And Christ will all my wants supply.

2 Christ is my Hope, my Strength, and Guide;
For me He bled, and groaned, and died:
He is my Sun, to give me light;
He is my soul's supreme delight.

3 Christ is the source of all my bliss,
My Wisdom and my Righteousness;
My Saviour, Brother, and my Friend,
On Him alone I now depend.

4 Christ is my King, to rule and bless,
And all my troubles to redress;
He's my salvation and my all,
Whate'er on earth shall me befal.

5 Christ is my strength and portion too;
My soul in Him can all things do;
Through Him I triumph o'er the grave,
And Satan, death, and hell outbrave!

W. G., 1790; *and John Dobell,* 1866.

NAYLAND; *or,* ST. STEPHEN. [H. P. 47.]

ALL IN ALL.

145 Tune NAYLAND. C. M.
Ps. lxxiii. 25. *"There is none upon earth that I desire beside Thee."*

1 COMPARED with Christ, in all beside
No comeliness I see;
The one thing needful, dearest Lord,
Is to be one with Thee.

2 The sweetness of Thy dying love
Into my soul convey;
Thyself bestow; for Thee alone,
My All in All, I pray.

3 Less than Thyself will not suffice
My comfort to restore;
More than Thyself I cannot crave,
Nor canst Thou give me more.

4 Loved of my God, for Him again
With love intense I burn;
Chosen of Thee, ere time began,
I choose Thee in return.

5 Whate'er consists not with Thy will,
Oh teach me to resign;
I'm rich to all the' intents of bliss,
Since Thou, O God, art mine!

Augustus M. Toplady, 1772.

See Hymn 489.

ALPHA AND OMEGA.

146 Rev. i. 11. *"I am Alpha and Omega."* Tune ESDRAELON. 87, 87. D.

1 JESUS is our God and Saviour,
Guide, and Counsellor, and Friend,
Bearing all our misbehaviour,
Kind and loving to the end.
Trust Him; He will not deceive us,
Though we hardly of Him deem:
He will never, never leave us,
Nor will let us quite leave Him.

2 View Him in the doleful garden;
View Him on the bloody tree,
Dearly purchasing a pardon
For His people, full and free.
View Him now in heaven sitting,
Interceding for us there;
Not a moment intermitting
His compassion and His care.

3 Nothing but Thy blood, O Jesus,
Can relieve us from our smart;
Nothing else from guilt release us;
Nothing else can melt the heart.
Law and terrors do but harden,
All the while they work alone;
But a sense of blood-bought pardon
Soon dissolves a heart of stone.

PART II.

4 Jesus, all our consolations
Flow from Thee, the sovereign good;
Love, and faith, and hope, and patience,
All are purchased by Thy blood.
From Thy fulness we receive them;
We have nothing of our own:
Freely Thou delight'st to give them
To the needy, who have none!

5 Teach us, by Thy patient Spirit,
How to mourn, and not despair;
Let us, leaning on Thy merit,
Wrestle hard with God in prayer.
Whatsoe'er afflictions seize us,
They shall profit, if not please;
But defend, defend us, Jesus,
From security and ease.

6 Softly to Thy garden lead us,
To behold Thy bloody sweat;
Though Thou from the curse hast freed us,
Let us not the cost forget.
Be Thy groans and cries rehearsèd
By the Spirit in our ears,
Till we, viewing Him we've piercèd,
Melt in sympathetic tears!

Joseph Hart, 1759.

See Hymn 236.

AMEN.

147 Rev. iii. 14. "*The Amen.*" Tune JORDAN. 886. D.

1 WE bless Thee, O Thou great Amen!
Jehovah's pledge to sinful men,
Confirming all His word;
No promises are doubtful then,
For all are yea and all amen,
In Jesus Christ our Lord.

Chorus.—Secured in this, the church on high,
And all below, unceasing cry
Amen! Amen! Amen!
To Thee, O Lord, all praise is given,—
The loud response of earth and heaven:
All hail, Thou great Amen.

2 Sweet ordinance of God to bless,
By Him, the Lord our Righteousness,—
By Him, I say again:
This mighty Word makes all things sure,
Through life, in death, and evermore,
In Him, the great Amen. *Chorus.*

3 O faithful Witness of our God,
Who came by water and by blood,
Proving the Holy One;
Thy record must for ever stand,
Of life eternal from God's hand,
And all in Thee, His Son. *Chorus.*

PART II.

4 Sweetly Thy Verilys we hear,
For God's Amen dispels all fear,
Thy faithfulness it proves;
And while such grace from God is shown,
To God's Amen we add our own,
Our So-be-it God loves. *Chorus.*

5 Ye saints of God, in age or youth,
Who swear by Him, the God of truth,
By Him, I say again;
Make Him whom God hath made to you,
Your Alpha and Omega too,
God's Christ is your Amen. *Chorus.*

6 Nor less above, ye heavenly host,
To Father, Son, and Holy Ghost,
Give praise, through Him with men;
For of Him, through Him, by Him, sure
The church shall glory evermore
In Him, the great Amen. *Chorus.*

Robert Hawker, D.D., 1831.

CRASSELIUS; *or*, WINCHESTER NEW. [H. P. 3.]

BREAKER.

148 Mic. ii. 13. "*The Breaker is come up before them.*"

Tune CRASSELIUS. L. M. Or OLD HUNDREDTH.

1 SING the dear Saviour's glorious fame,
Who bears the Breaker's wondrous name;
Sweet name, and it becomes Him well,
Who breaks down sin, guilt, death, and hell.

2 A mighty Breaker surely He,
Who broke my chains, and set me free;
A gracious Breaker to my soul;
He breaks, and oh! He makes me whole.

3 He breaks through every gloomy cloud,
Which can my soul with darkness shroud;
He breaks the bars of every snare,
Which hellish foes for me prepare.

4 He breaks the gates of hardened brass,
To bring His faithful word to pass;
And though with ponderous iron barred,
The Breaker's love they can't retard.

5 Great Breaker, oh! Thy love impart,
Daily, to break my stony heart;
Oh, break it, Lord, and enter in,
And break, oh break, the power of sin!

Samuel Medley, 1789.

ZOAN I. (Field of). [H. P. 127.]

CAPTAIN OF SALVATION.

149 Heb. ii. 10. "*The Captain of their salvation.*"

Tune ZOAN I. 76, 76. D.

1 STAND up! stand up for Jesus!
Ye soldiers of the cross;
Lift high His royal banner,
It must not suffer loss;
From victory unto victory
His army shall be led,
Till every foe is vanquished,
And Christ is Lord indeed.

2 Stand up! stand up for Jesus!
The trumpet call obey;
Forth to the mighty conflict
In this His glorious day;
Ye that are men, now serve Him,
Against unnumbered foes;
Let courage rise with danger,
And strength to strength oppose.

3 Stand up! stand up for Jesus!
Stand in His strength alone;
The arm of flesh will fail you—
Ye dare not trust your own:
Put on the gospel armour,
And, watching unto prayer,
Where duty calls, or danger,
Be never wanting there.

4 Stand up! stand up for Jesus!
The strife will not be long;
This day the noise of battle,
The next the victor's song:
To him that overcometh
A crown of life shall be,
He with the King of glory
Shall reign eternally.

See Hymn 432.

George Duffield, 1858.

CONSOLATION.

150 Luke ii. 25. "*The consolation of Israel.*"

Tune FRANKFORT. 87, 87.

1 COME, Thou long-expected Jesus,
Born to set Thy people free;
From our fears and sins release us,
Let us find our rest in Thee:

2 Israel's strength and consolation,
Hope of all the saints Thou art;
Dear desire of every nation,
Joy of every longing heart.

FRANKFORT. [H. P. 183.]

3 Born Thy people to deliver;
Born a child, and yet a King:
Born to reign in us for ever,
Now Thy gracious kingdom bring:

4 By Thine own eternal Spirit,
Rule in all our hearts alone:
By Thine all-sufficient merit,
Raise us to Thy glorious throne!

Charles Wesley, 1744.

PATMOS. [H. P. 147.]

EMMANUEL.

151

Matt. i. 23. "*Emmanuel . . . God with us.*" Tune PATMOS. 77, 77.

1 SWEETER sounds than music knows
Charm me in Emmanuel's name:
All her hopes my spirit owes
To His birth, and cross, and shame.

2 When He came, the angels sung
"Glory be to God on high!"
Lord, unloose my stammering tongue;
Who should louder sing than I?

3 Did the Lord a man become
That He might the law fulfil,
Bleed and suffer in my room,
And canst thou, my tongue, be still?

4 No: I must my praises bring,
Though they worthless are and weak;
For should I refuse to sing,
Sure the very stones would speak.

5 O my Saviour, Shield, and Sun,
Shepherd, Brother, Husband, Friend—
Every precious name in One!
I will love Thee without end!

John Newton, 1779.

CHURCH TRIUMPHANT. [H. P. 258.]

FORERUNNER.

152

Heb. vi. 20. "*The Forerunner is for us entered.*" Tune CHURCH TRIUMPHANT. L.M. Or CRASSELIUS.

1 FAR, far beyond these lower skies,
Up to the glories all His own;
Where we, by faith, lift up our eyes,
There Jesus, our Forerunner, 's gone.

2 High on His throne of heavenly light,
Eternal glory He sustains;
While saints and angels bless the sight:
There Jesus, our Forerunner, reigns.

3 He lives salvation to impart
From sin and Satan's cursèd wiles;
With love eternal in His heart:
There Jesus, our Forerunner, smiles.

4 Before His heavenly Father's face,
For every saint He intercedes;
And with infallible success,
There Jesus, our Forerunner, pleads.

5 But, oh, 'tis this completes the whole,
And all its bliss and glory proves,
That while eternal ages roll,
There Jesus, our Forerunner, loves!

Samuel Medley, 1789.

SUCCOTH (Valley of). [H. P. 189.]

Hal - le - lu - jah, Hal - le - lu - jah.
Hal - - - le - lu - jah.

FRIEND.

153 Prov. xviii. 24. *"There is a friend that sticketh closer than a brother."* Tune SUCCOTH. 87, 87, 77.

1 ONE there is above all others,
Well deserves the name of Friend;
His is love beyond a brother's,
Costly, free, and knows no end:
They who once His kindness prove
Find it everlasting love.

2 Which of all our friends, to save us,
Could or would have shed his blood?
But our Jesus died to have us
Reconciled in Him to God:
This was boundless love indeed!
Jesus is a friend in need.

3 When He lived on earth abasèd,
Friend of sinners was His name;
Now above all glories raisèd,
He rejoices in the same;
Still He calls them brethren, friends,
And to all their wants attends.

4 Oh, for grace our hearts to soften!
Teach us, Lord, at length to love:
We, alas! forget too often
What a Friend we have above:
But when home our souls are brought,
We shall love Thee as we ought.

John Newton, 1779.

CYPRUS. [H. P. 26.]

FRIEND.

154 Matt. xi. 19. *"A friend of . . sinners."* Tune CYPRUS. L. M.

1 POOR, weak, and worthless, though I am,
I have a rich almighty Friend;
Jesus, the Saviour, is His name:
He freely loves, and without end.

2 He ransomed me from hell with blood,
And by His power my foes controlled:
He found me wandering far from God,
And brought me to His chosen fold.

3 He cheers my heart, my wants supplies,
And says that I shall shortly be
Enthroned with Him above the skies;
Oh, what a Friend is Christ to me!

4 But ah! my inmost spirit mourns;
And well my eyes with tears may swim,
To think of my perverse returns;
I've been a faithless friend to Him.

5 Sure, were not I most vile and base,
I could not thus my Friend requite:
And were not He the God of grace,
He'd frown and spurn me from His sight!

John Newton, 1779.

KEDAR. [H. P. 42.]

FRIEND.

155

Cant. v. 16. "*This is my friend.*" Tune KEDAR. C. M. Or NOTTINGHAM.

1 A FRIEND there is—your voices join,
Ye saints, to praise His name!
Whose truth and kindness are Divine,
Whose love—a constant flame.

2 When most we need His helping hand,
This Friend is always near;
With heaven and earth at His command,
He waits to answer prayer.

3 His love no end or measure knows,
No change can turn its course;
Immutably the same it flows
From one eternal source.

4 When frowns appear to veil His face,
And clouds surround His throne,
He hides the purpose of His grace,
To make it better known.

5 And, if our dearest comforts fall
Before His sovereign will,
He never takes away our all,
Himself He gives us still!

6 Our sorrows in the scale He weighs,
And measures out our pains;
The wildest storm His word obeys,
His word its rage restrains!

Joseph Swain, 1792.

See Hymn 941.

HEAD.

156

Eph. iv. 15. "*The Head, even Christ.*" Tune KEDAR. C. M.

1 JESUS, I sing Thy matchless grace,
That calls a worm Thine own;
Gives me among Thy saints a place
To make Thy glories known.

2 Allied to Thee, our vital Head,
We act, and grow, and thrive:
From Thee divided, each is dead
When most he seems alive.

3 Thy saints on earth, and those above,
Here join in sweet accord:
One body all in mutual love,
And Thou our common Lord.

4 Oh! may my faith each hour derive
Thy Spirit with delight;
While death and hell in vain shall strive
This bond to disunite.

5 Thou the whole body wilt present
Before Thy Father's face;
Nor shall a wrinkle or a spot
Its beauteous form disgrace!

Philip Doddridge, D.D., 1755.

GOZAN (River of). [H. P. 165.]

HEAD OF THE CHURCH.

157

Eph. i. 22. "*Head over all things to the Church.*" Tune GOZAN. 77, 87. D. Or ZOAN II.

1 HEAD of the church triumphant,
We joyfully adore Thee;
Till Thou appear, Thy members here
Shall sing like those in glory:
We lift our hearts and voices,
With blest anticipation,
And cry aloud, And give to God
The praise of our salvation.

2 While in affliction's furnace,
And passing through the fire,
Thy love we praise, In grateful lays,
Which ever brings us nigher;
We clap our hands, exulting
In Thine almighty favour;
The love Divine That made us Thine
Shall keep us Thine for ever.

3 Thou dost conduct Thy people
Through torrents of temptation;
Nor will we fear, While Thou art near,
The fire of tribulation:
The world, with sin and Satan,
In vain our march opposes,
By Thee we shall Break through them all,
And sing the song of Moses.

4 By faith we see the glory
To which Thou shalt restore us,
The world despise, For that high prize
Which Thou hast set before us.
And, if Thou count us worthy,
We each, with dying Stephen,
Shall see Thee stand At God's right hand,
To call us up to heaven!

Charles Wesley, 1745.

See Hymns 444, 744.

EUPHRATES. [H. P. 2.]

HIDING-PLACE.

158 Isa. xxxii. 2. "*An Hiding-place.*" Tune EUPHRATES. L. M.

1 AWAKE, sweet harp of Judah, wake!
Retune thy strings for Jesu's sake;
We sing the Saviour of our race,
The Lamb, our shield, and Hiding-place.

2 When God's right arm is bared for war,
And thunders clothe His cloudy car,
Where—where—oh! where shall man retire,
To' escape the horror of His ire?

3 'Tis He—the Lamb—to Him we fly,
While the dread tempest passes by:
God sees His Well-belovèd's face,
And spares us in our Hiding-place.

4 While yet we sojourn here below,
Pollutions still our hearts o'erflow:
Fallen, abject, mean—a sentenced race,
We deeply need a Hiding-place.

5 Yet courage! days and years will glide,
And we shall lay these clods aside;
Shall be baptized in Jordan's flood,
And washed in Jesu's cleansing blood.

6 Then pure, immortal, sinless, freed,
We through the Lamb shall be decreed;
Shall meet the Father face to face,
And need no more a Hiding-place.

Henry Kirke White, 1806.

HIDING-PLACE.

159 Ps. xxxii. 7. "*Thou art my Hiding-place.*" Tune EUPHRATES. L. M. Or GILBOA.

1 HAIL! sovereign love, that first began
The scheme to rescue fallen man!
Hail! matchless, free, eternal grace,
That gave my soul a Hiding-place.

2 Against the God that rules the sky,
I fought with hand uplifted high,
Despised the method of His grace,
Secure without a Hiding-place.

3 Enwrapt in thick Egyptian night,
And loving darkness more than light,
I madly ran my sinful race,
Too proud to seek a Hiding-place.

4 But lo! a gracious voice I heard,
And mercy's heavenly form appeared;
She led me on with smiling face,
To Jesus as my Hiding-place.

5 On Him the tenfold vengeance fell,
That must have sunk a world to hell;
He bore it for His chosen race,
And thus became their Hiding-place.

6 A few more rolling suns at most
Will land me safe on Canaan's coast;
There I shall see Him face to face,
Jesus, my glorious Hiding-place.

Jehoiada Brewer, 1776.

FRENCH; *or* DUNDEE. [H. P. 65.]

HIGH PRIEST.

160 Heb. vi. 20. "*An High Priest for ever.*" Tune FRENCH. C. M. Or LONDON NEW.

1 NOW let our cheerful eyes survey
Our great High Priest above,
And celebrate His constant care,
And sympathetic love.

2 Though raised to a superior throne,
Where angels bow around,
And high o'er all the shining train,
With matchless honours crowned;

3 The names of all His saints He bears
Deep graven on His heart;
Nor shall the meanest Christian say,
That he hath lost his part.

4 So, gracious Saviour! on my breast
May Thy dear name be worn,
A sacred ornament and guard,
To endless ages borne!

Philip Doddridge, D.D., 1755.

JESUS.

161 Phil. ii. 10. *"At the name of Jesus every knee should bow."* Tune FRENCH. C. M. Or BETHER.

1 JESUS, in Thy transporting name,
What blissful glories rise!
Jesus! the angels' sweetest theme,
The wonder of the skies!

2 Didst Thou forsake Thy radiant crown,
And boundless realms of day,
Aside Thy robes of glory thrown,
To dwell with feeble clay?

3 Victorious love! can language tell
The wonders of Thy power,
Which conquered all the force of hell
In that tremendous hour?

4 Is there a heart that will not bend
To Thy Divine control?
Descend, O sovereign love, descend,
And melt that stubborn soul!

Anne Steele, 1760.

ST. PETER. [H. P. 263.]

JESUS.

162 Cant. i. 3. *"Thy Name is as ointment poured forth."* Tune ST. PETER. C. M. Or FRENCH.

1 HOW sweet the name of Jesus sounds,
In a believer's ear!
It soothes his sorrows, heals his wounds,
And drives away his fear.

2 It makes the wounded spirit whole,
And calms the troubled breast;
'Tis manna to the hungry soul,
And to the weary, rest.

3 Dear Name! the rock on which I build,
My shield and hiding-place;
My never-failing treasury, filled
With boundless stores of grace.

4 By Thee my prayers acceptance gain,
Although with sin defiled;
Satan accuses me in vain,
And I am owned a child.

5 Jesus, my Shepherd, Husband, Friend,
My Prophet, Priest, and King;
My Lord, my Life, my Way, my End,
Accept the praise I bring.

6 Weak is the effort of my heart,
And cold my warmest thought;
But when I see Thee as Thou art,
I'll praise Thee as I ought.

7 Till then I would Thy love proclaim
With every fleeting breath;
And may the music of Thy name
Refresh my soul in death!

John Newton, 1779.

JESUS.

163 Ps. xxxvi. 9. *"With Thee is the fountain of life."*

Tune EDGBASTON. 65, 65. D.
Or HERMAS.

EDGBASTON. [H. P. 270.]

1 ERE each morning breaketh,
I would see Thy face,
Jesus! Precious Saviour!
Jesus! King of Grace!
For my thirsty spirit
Longs to drink again
Of the living river
Flowing through this plain.

2 Hark! how sweet its music,
As it dashes by,
Clear and fresh as ever,
In its melody.
From the crystal city,
From the throne on high,
It has leaped to succour
Sinners lest they die!

3 Flowing where the desert
Looks most parched and bare,
There its shining wavelets
Sparkle everywhere!
We, with dying thousands,
Would again partake
Of this crystal river,
It our thirst can slake!

4 It the drooping pastures
Can refresh and bless,
And with fragrant blossoms
Clothe the wilderness!
Oh! Thou living Spirit,
Give us of Thy dew;
Then our souls, like gardens,
Will yield fruit anew!

William Pennefather, 1871.

ZAANAIM (Plain of). [H. P. 191.]

JESUS.

164 Phil. ii. 9. *"A Name which is above every name."*
Tune Zaanaim. 87, 87, 87. Or Teman.

1 TO the Name of our salvation
Laud and honour let us pay;
Which for many a generation
Hid in God's foreknowledge lay,
But with holy exultation
We may sing aloud to-day.

2 Jesus is the Name we treasure;
Name beyond what words can tell;
Name of gladness, Name of pleasure,
Ear and heart delighting well;
Name of sweetness passing measure,
Saving us from sin and hell.

3 'Tis the Name for adoration,
Name for songs of victory,
Name for holy meditation
In this vale of misery,
Name for joyful veneration
By the citizens on high.

4 'Tis the Name that whoso preacheth
Speaks like music to the ear;
Who in prayer this Name beseecheth
Sweetest comfort findeth near;
Who its perfect wisdom reacheth
Heavenly joy possesseth here.

5 Therefore we, in love adoring,
This most blessèd Name revere;
Holy Jesus, Thee imploring
So to write it in us here
That hereafter, heavenward soaring,
We may sing with angels there!

John M. Neale, D.D., 1851. (a.)

EPENETUS. [H. P. 254.]

Tell it out a-mong the hea-then that the Lord is King! Tell it out! Tell it out! Tell it out! . . . Tell it out a-mong the na-tions, bid them
Tell it out! Tell it out! that the Lord is King! Tell it out! . . . . Tell it out! Tell it out! Tell it out! bid them
shout and sing! Tell it out! Tell it out! Tell it out!
Fine. Tell it out with a-do-ra-tion that He shall in-crease;
Tell it out! . . . . that He shall in-crease;
Tell it out with a-do-ra-tion that He shall in-crease; That the migh-ty King of Glo-ry is the
shout and sing! Tell it out! Tell . . . it out! Tell it out! . . . . that He shall in-crease;
D.S.
King of Peace; Tell it out with ju-bi-la-tion though the waves may roar, That He sit-teth on the wa-ter-floods, our King for e-ver-more. Tell it

KING.

165 Ps. xcvi. 10. (P.B.V.) *"Tell it out among the heathen that the Lord is King."*

Tune Epenetus. 13 6, 13 6, 13 13, 13 15.

[1 TELL it out among the heathen that the Lord is King!
Tell it out! Tell it out!
Tell it out among the nations, bid them shout and sing!
Tell it out! Tell it out!]
Tell it out with adoration that He shall increase;
That the mighty King of Glory is the King of Peace;
Tell it out with jubilation, though the waves may roar,
That He sitteth on the water-floods, our King for evermore!
[Tell it out among the heathen that the Lord is King, etc.]

2 Tell it out among the heathen that the Saviour reigns!
Tell it out! Tell it out!
Tell it out among the nations, bid them burst their chains!
Tell it out! Tell it out!
Tell it out among the weeping ones that Jesus lives;
Tell it out among the weary ones what rest He gives:
Tell it out among the sinners that He came to save;
Tell it out among the dying that He triumphed o'er the grave.
[Tell it out among the heathen that the Lord is King, etc.]

3 Tell it out among the heathen Jesus reigns above!
Tell it out! Tell it out!
Tell it out among the nations that His reign is love!
Tell it out! Tell it out!
Tell it out among the highways and the lanes at home;
Tell it out across the mountains and the ocean foam!
Like the sound of many waters let our glad shout be,
Till it echo and re-echo from the islands of the sea!
[Tell it out among the heathen that the Lord is King, etc.]

Frances Ridley Havergal, 1872.

LAMB OF GOD.

166 Tune Arnon. 66, 84.
John i. 29. *"Behold the Lamb of God."*

1 BEHOLD the Lamb of God!
Behold, believe, and live:
Behold His all-atoning blood,
And life receive.

2 Look from thyself to Him,
Behold Him on the tree:
What though the eye of faith be dim,
He looks on thee.

3 That meek, that languid eye,
Turns from Himself away;
Invites the trembling sinner nigh,
And bids him stay.

4 Stay with Him near the tree,
Stay with Him near the tomb;
Stay till the risen Lord you see,
Stay, till He come!

Charles Sabine, 1857.

See Hymn 130.

ARNON (The River). [H. P. 118.]

SOREK (Valley of). [H. P. 184.]

LIGHT.

167 John viii. 12. *"I am the Light of the world."*

Tune Sorek. 87, 87.

1 LIGHT of those, whose dreary dwelling
Borders on the shades of death,
Come, and, by Thyself revealing,
Dissipate the clouds beneath:

2 The new heaven and earth's Creator,
In our deepest darkness rise,
Scattering all the night of nature,
Pouring day upon our eyes.

3 Still we wait for Thine appearing;
Life and joy Thy beams impart,
Chasing all our fears, and cheering
Every poor, benighted heart.

4 Come, and manifest the favour
God hath for our ransomed race;
Come, Thou dear exalted Saviour,
Come, apply Thy saving grace.

5 Save us in Thy great compassion,
O Thou mild pacific Prince:
Give the knowledge of salvation,
Give the pardon and the peace.

6 By Thine all-sufficient merit
Every burdened soul release!
By the teachings of Thy Spirit
Guide us into perfect peace!

Charles Wesley, 1744. (*a.*)

See Hymns 206—211.

VIENNA. [H. P. 149.]

MELCHIZEDEK.

168 Heb. vii. 2. "*King of Salem, which is, King of Peace.*" Tune VIENNA. 77, 77.

1 KING of Salem, bless my soul!
Make a wounded sinner whole;
King of righteousness and peace,
Let not Thy sweet visits cease!

2 Come, refresh this soul of mine
With Thy sacred bread and wine!
All Thy love to me unfold,
Half of which cannot be told.

3 Hail! Melchizedek, Divine;
Great High Priest, Thou shalt be mine;
All my powers before Thee fall;
Take not tithe, but take them all!

John Wingrove, 1785.

EVAN I. [H. P. 54.]

MELCHIZEDEK.

169 Heb. vii. 17. "*A Priest for ever.*" Tune EVAN I. C. M. Or EDEN.

1 THOU dear Redeemer, dying Lamb,
We love to hear of Thee;
No music like Thy hallowed name,
Nor half so sweet can be.

2 Oh! may we ever hear Thy voice
In mercy to us speak;
And in our Priest we will rejoice,
Thou great Melchizedek.

3 Our Jesus shall be still our theme,
While in this world we stay:
We 'll sing our Jesu's lovely name,
When all things else decay.

4 When we appear in yonder cloud,
With all His favoured throng,
Then will we sing more sweet, more loud,
And Christ shall be our song!

John Cennick, 1745. (*a.*)

GETHSEMANE. [H. P. 28.]

PHYSICIAN.

170 Jer. xvii. 14. "*Heal me, O Lord.*" Tune GETHSEMANE. L. M.

1 DEEP are the wounds which sin hath made:
Where shall the sinner find a cure?
In vain, alas! is nature's aid,
The work exceeds all nature's power.

2 Sin, like a raging fever, reigns
With fatal strength in every part;
The dire contagion fills the veins,
And spreads its poison to the heart.

3 And can no sovereign balm be found,
And is no kind physician nigh,
To ease the pain, and heal the wound,
Ere life and hope for ever fly?

4 There is a great Physician near;
Look up, O fainting soul, and live:
See in His heavenly smiles appear
Such ease as nature cannot give.

See Hymn 454.

5 See, in the Saviour's dying blood,
Life, health, and bliss abundant flow;
'Tis only this dear sacred flood
Can ease thy pain and heal thy woe.

6 Sin throws in vain its pointed dart,
For here a sovereign cure is found;
A cordial for the fainting heart,
A balm for every painful wound!

Anne Steele, 1760.

FRENCH; *or*, DUNDEE. [H. P. 65.]

PRIEST.

171 Zech. vi. 13. "*A Priest upon His throne.*" Tune French. C. M.

1 JESUS, in Thee our eyes behold
A thousand glories more
Than the rich gems and polished gold
The sons of Aaron wore.

2 The first their own burnt-offerings brought,
To purge themselves from sin;
Thy life was pure, without a spot,
And all Thy nature clean.

3 Fresh blood as constant as the day
Was on their altar spilt;
But Thy one offering takes away
For ever all our guilt.

4 Their priesthood ran through several hands,
For mortal was their race;
Thy never-changing office stands
Eternal as Thy days.

5 Once in the circuit of a year,
With blood, but not his own,
Aaron within the veil appears,
Before the golden throne.

6 But Christ by His own powerful blood
Ascends above the skies,
And in the presence of our God
Shows His own sacrifice.

7 Jesus, the King of Glory, reigns
On Zion's heavenly hill;
Looks like a lamb that has been slain,
And wears His priesthood still.

8 He ever lives to intercede
Before His Father's face:
Give Him, my soul, thy cause to plead,
Nor doubt the Father's grace!

Isaac Watts, D.D., 1709.

ELAH (Valley of). [H. P. 34.]

And crown Him, crown Him, crown Him Prince of Peace.

PRINCE OF PEACE.

172 Isa. ix. 6. "*The Prince of Peace.*"
Tune Elah. C. M.

1 LET saints on earth their anthems raise,
Who taste the Saviour's grace:
With those above proclaim His praise,
And crown Him Prince of Peace!

2 Praise Him who laid His glory by
For man's apostate race;
Praise Him who stooped to bleed and die,
And crown Him Prince of Peace!

3 We soon shall reach the heavenly shore,
To view His glorious face,
His name for ever to adore,
And crown Him Prince of Peace!

Jonathan Evans, 1784.

PARAN (Wilderness of). [H. P. 241.]

THE LORD OUR RIGHTEOUSNESS.

173 Jer. xxiii. 6. "*The Lord our Righteousness.*"

Tune Paran. 11 11, 11 11.

1 I ONCE was a stranger to grace and to God,
I knew not my danger, and felt not my load;
Though friends spoke in rapture of Christ on the tree,
Jehovah Tsidkenu was nothing to me.

2 I oft read with pleasure, to soothe or engage,
Isaiah's wild measure and John's simple page;
But e'en when they pictured the blood-sprinkled tree,
Jehovah Tsidkenu seemed nothing to me.

3 Like tears from the daughter of Zion that roll,
I wept when the waters went over His soul;
Yet thought not that my sins had nailed to the tree
Jehovah Tsidkenu—'twas nothing to me.

4 When free grace awoke me, by light from on high,
Then legal fears shook me, I trembled to die;
No refuge, no safety in self could I see—
Jehovah Tsidkenu my Saviour must be.

5 My terrors all vanished before the sweet name;
My guilty fears banished, with boldness I came
To drink at the fountain, life-giving and free—
Jehovah Tsidkenu is all things to me.

6 Jehovah Tsidkenu! my treasure and boast,
Jehovah Tsidkenu! I ne'er can be lost;
In Thee I shall conquer, by flood and by field,
My cable, my anchor, my breastplate and shield!

7 E'en treading the valley, the shadow of death,
This watchword shall rally my faltering breath;
For while from life's fever my God sets me free,
Jehovah Tsidkenu my death-song shall be.

Robert Murray M'Cheyne, 1834.

See Hymns 416, 685.

SAVIOUR.

174 Titus iii. 4. "*The kindness and love of God our Saviour.*"

Tune Winton. C. M.

WINTON. [H. P. 262.]

1 THE Saviour! Oh what endless charms
Dwell in the blissful sound!
Its influence every fear disarms,
And spreads sweet comfort round.

2 Here pardon, life, and joys Divine
In rich effusion flow,
For guilty rebels lost in sin,
And doomed to endless woe.

3 The' Almighty Framer of the skies
Stooped to our mean abode;
While angels viewed with wondering eyes,
And hailed the' incarnate God.

4 Oh! the rich depths of love Divine!
Of grace a boundless store!
Permit me, Lord, to call Thee mine!
I cannot wish for more.

5 On Thee alone my hope relies,
Beneath Thy cross I fall,
My Lord, my life, my sacrifice,
My Saviour, and my all!

Anne Steele, 1760.

SARDIS. (Hymn Chant.) [H. P. VI.]

SAVIOUR.

175 Luke i. 47. "*My spirit hath rejoiced in God my Saviour.*"

Tune, Hymn Chant Sardis. 8 8 8, 3.

1 IN form I long had bowed the knee,
But nought attractive then could see
To win my wayward heart to Thee,
My Saviour!

2 Yet oft I trembled when I thought
How I had sold myself for nought,
But still against Thy love I fought,
My Saviour!

3 When self-accused I trembling stood,
I promised fair, as any could,
But never counted on Thy blood,
My Saviour!

4 Too soon the promise vain I proved
That sinners make while sin is loved,
But still to Thee this heart ne'er moved,
My Saviour!

5 To pleasure prone, I thought it hard
From pleasure's path to be debarred,
Nor pleasure sought from Thy regard,
My Saviour!

6 At length, despairing to be free,
A willing slave I meant to be;
'Twas then Thou didst appear for me,
My Saviour!

7 Thou, whom I had so long withstood,
Thou didst redeem my soul with blood,
And Thou hast brought me to my God,
My Saviour!

8 Through storms and waves of conflict past,
Thy potent arm has held me fast,
And Thou wilt save me to the last,
My Saviour!

9 And when I reach the happy shore
I hope to rest, but not before,
And never to offend Thee more,
My Saviour!

Thomas Kelly, 1804.

ZAANAIM (Plain of). [H. P. 191.]

SAVIOUR.

176 2 Tim. i. 9. "*Who hath saved us, and called us.*" Tune Zaanaim. 87, 87, 47.

1 JESUS is our great salvation,
Worthy of our best esteem!
He has saved His favoured nation:
Join to sing aloud to Him!
He has called us,
Christ alone can us redeem.

2 When, involved in sin and ruin,
And no helper there was found,
Jesus our distress was viewing;
Grace did more than sin abound:
He has called us,
With salvation in the sound.

3 Save us from a mere profession!
Save us from hypocrisy;
Give us, Lord, the sweet possession
Of Thy righteousness and Thee:
Best of favours!
None compared with this can be.

4 Free election, known by calling,
Is a privilege Divine:
Saints are kept from final falling;
All the glory, Lord, be Thine;
All the glory,
All the glory, Lord, is Thine!

See Hymn 191.

John Adams, 1776.

SHEPHERD.

177 John x. 27, 28. *"My sheep . . . shall never perish."*

Tune Idumea. 8 7, 8 7, 4 7.

1 SHEPHERD of the chosen number,
They are safe whom Thou dost keep;
Other shepherds faint and slumber,
And forget to watch the sheep;
Watchful Shepherd!
Thou dost wake while others sleep.

2 When the lion came, depending
On his strength to seize his prey,
Thou wert there, Thy sheep defending,
Thou didst then Thy power display;
Mighty Shepherd!
Thou didst turn the foe away.

3 When the Shepherd's life was needful
To redeem the sheep from death,
Of their safety ever heedful,
Thou for them didst yield Thy breath;
Faithful Shepherd!
Love like Thine no other hath.

Thomas Kelly, 1809.

IDUMEA. [H. P. 193.]

HEBRON. [H. P. 12.]

SHEPHERD.

178 Ezek. xxxiv. 23. *"I will set up one Shepherd over them."* Tune Hebron. L. M.

1 JESUS, the Shepherd of the sheep,
Thy little flock in safety keep;
The flock for which Thou camest from heaven,
The flock for which Thy life was given.

2 O guard Thy sheep from beasts of prey,
And guide them that they never stray:
Cherish the young, sustain the old,
Let none be feeble in Thy fold.

3 Secure them from the scorching beam,
And lead them to the living stream;
In verdant pastures let them lie,
And watch them with a Shepherd's eye.

4 O may Thy sheep discern Thy voice,
And in its sacred sound rejoice:
From strangers may they ever flee,
And know no other guide but Thee.

5 Lord, bring Thy sheep that wander yet,
And let the number be complete;
Then let Thy flock from earth remove,
And occupy the fold above!

Thomas Kelly, 1804.

PATMOS. [H. P. 147.]

SHEPHERD.

179 John x. 11. *"I am the good Shepherd."* Tune Patmos. 7 7, 7 7. Or Chios.

1 LOVING Shepherd of Thy sheep,
Keep me, Lord, in safety keep;
Nothing can Thy power withstand,
None can pluck me from Thy hand.

2 Loving Shepherd! Thou didst give
Thine own life that I might live;
May I love Thee day by day,
Gladly Thy sweet will obey!

3 Loving Shepherd! ever near,
Teach me still Thy voice to hear;
Suffer not my step to stray
From the strait and narrow way.

4 Where Thou leadest me I go,
Walking in Thy steps below:
Then before Thy Father's throne,
Jesu! claim me for Thine own!

Jane E. Leeson, 1842.

ST. MICHAEL. [H. P. 85.]

180 SHEPHERD.

John x. 14. "*I know My sheep.*" Tune ST. MICHAEL. S. M.

1 MY soul, with joy attend,
While Jesus silence breaks;
No angel's harp such music yields,
As what my Shepherd speaks.

2 "I know My sheep," He cries,
"My soul approves them well;
Vain is the treacherous world's disguise,
And vain the rage of hell.

3 "I freely feed them now
With tokens of My love;
But richer pastures I prepare,
And sweeter streams above.

4 "Unnumbered years of bliss
I to My sheep will give;
And, while My throne unshaken stands,
Shall all My chosen live.

5 "This tried Almighty hand
Is raised for their defence;
Where is the power shall reach them there?
Or what shall force them thence?"

6 Enough, my gracious Lord,
Let faith triumphant cry;
My heart can on this promise live,
Can on this promise die!

Philip Doddridge, D.D., 1755.

EATON. [H. P. 313.]

181 SHEPHERD.

Ps. xxiii. 1. "*The Lord is my Shepherd*" Tune EATON. 88, 88, 88. Or MAON.

1 THE Lord my pasture shall prepare,
And feed me with a Shepherd's care;
His presence shall my wants supply,
And guard me with a watchful eye:
My noonday walks He will attend,
And all my midnight hours defend.

2 When in the sultry glebe I faint,
Or on the thirsty mountains pant,
To fertile vales and dewy meads
My weary, wandering steps He leads,
Where peaceful rivers, soft and slow,
Amid the verdant landscape flow.

3 Though in a bare and rugged way
Through devious lonely wilds I stray,
Thy presence shall my pains beguile;
The barren wilderness shall smile,
With sudden green and herbage crowned;
And streams shall murmur all around.

4 Though in the paths of death I tread,
With gloomy horrors overspread,
My steadfast heart shall fear no ill,
For Thou, O Lord, art with me still:
Thy friendly hand shall give me aid,
And guide me through the dreadful shade!

Joseph Addison, 1712.

See Hymns 511, 934.

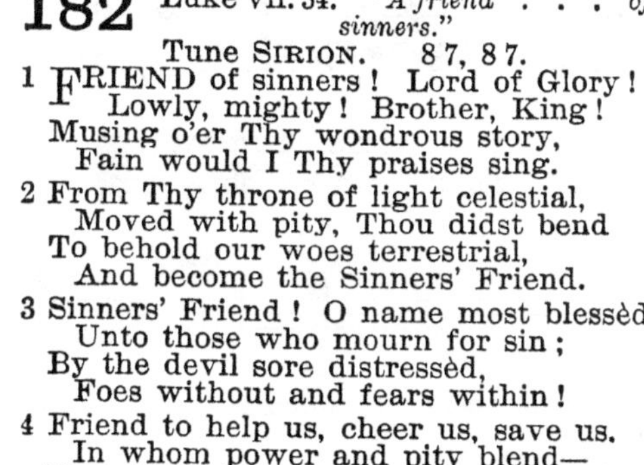

182 SINNERS' FRIEND.

Luke vii. 34. "*A friend . . . of sinners.*"

Tune SIRION. 87, 87.

1 FRIEND of sinners! Lord of Glory!
Lowly, mighty! Brother, King!
Musing o'er Thy wondrous story,
Fain would I Thy praises sing.

2 From Thy throne of light celestial,
Moved with pity, Thou didst bend
To behold our woes terrestrial,
And become the Sinners' Friend.

3 Sinners' Friend! O name most blessèd
Unto those who mourn for sin;
By the devil sore distressèd,
Foes without and fears within!

4 Friend to help us, cheer us, save us,
In whom power and pity blend—
Praise we must, the grace which gave us
Jesus Christ, the Sinners' Friend!

Newman Hall, 1858.

SIRION (Mount). [H. P. 180.]

Hal - le - lu - jah, Hal - le - lu - jah.

KEDRON (Brook). [H. P. 213.]

SUBSTITUTE.

183 2 Cor. v. 21. "*He hath made Him to be sin for us, who knew no sin.*" Tune KEDRON. 886. D. Or BRIDEHEAD.

1 FROM whence this fear and unbelief?
Hath not the Father put to grief
His spotless Son for me?
And will the righteous Judge of men
Condemn me for that debt of sin,
Which, Lord, was charged on Thee?

2 Complete atonement Thou hast made,
And to the utmost farthing paid
Whate'er Thy people owed:
Nor can His wrath on me take place,
If sheltered in Thy righteousness,
And sprinkled with Thy blood.

3 If my discharge Thou hast procured,
And freely in my room endured
The whole of wrath Divine:
Payment God cannot twice demand,
First at my bleeding Surety's hand,
And then again at mine.

4 Turn then, my soul, unto thy rest;
The merits of thy great High Priest
Have bought thy liberty:
Trust in His efficacious blood,
Nor fear thy banishment from God,
Since Jesus died for thee!

Augustus M. Toplady, 1775.

SURETY.

184 Heb. vii. 22. "*Jesus . . . made a Surety.*"
Tune PISGAH. 77, 77. Or LUBECK.

PISGAH (Mount). [H. P. 137.]

Hal - le - lu - jah, Hal - le - lu - jah!

1 CHRIST exalted is our song,
Hymned by all the blood-bought throng;
To His throne our shouts shall rise,
God with us by sacred ties.

2 Shout, believer, to thy God,
He hath once the winepress trod;
Peace procured by blood Divine,
Cancelled all thy sins, and mine.

3 Here thy bleeding wounds are healed,
Sin condemned, and pardon sealed;
Grace her empire still maintains;
Christ without a rival reigns.

4 Through corruption, felt within,
Darkness, deadness, guilt, and sin,
Still to Jesus turn thine eyes,
Israel's Hope and Sacrifice.

5 In thy Surety thou art free,
His dear hands were pierced for thee;
With His spotless vesture on,
Holy as the Holy One.

6 Oh! the heights, the depths of grace,
Shining with meridian blaze;
Here the sacred records show
Sinners black, but comely too.

7 Saints dejected, cease to mourn;
Faith shall soon to vision turn;
Ye the kingdom shall obtain,
And with Christ exalted reign!

John Kent, 1803.

EVAN I. [H. P. 54.]

TRUE VINE.

185

John xv. 1. "*I am the true Vine.*" Tune EVAN I. C. M.

1 JESUS, immutably the same,
Thou true and living Vine,
Around Thy all-supporting stem
My feeble arms I twine.

2 Quickened by Thee, and kept alive,
I flourish and bear fruit;
My life I from Thy sap derive,
My vigour from Thy root.

3 I can do nothing without Thee;
My strength is wholly Thine:
Withered and barren should I be,
If severed from the Vine.

4 Upon my leaf when parched with heat
Refreshing dew shall drop;
The plant which Thy right hand hath set
Shall ne'er be rooted up.

5 Each moment watered by Thy care,
And fenced with power Divine,
Fruit to eternal life shall bear
The feeblest branch of Thine!

Augustus M. Toplady, 1771.

ST. GREGORY. [H. P. 259.]

THE WAY.

186

John xiv. 6. "*I am the Way.*" Tune ST. GREGORY. L. M.

1 JESUS, my all, to heaven is gone,
He whom I fix my hopes upon;
His track I see, and I'll pursue
The narrow way, till Him I view.

2 The way that holy prophets went,
The road that leads from banishment,
The King's highway of holiness,
I'll go, for all His paths are peace.

3 No stranger may proceed therein,
No lover of the world and sin;
Wayfaring men, to Canaan bound,
Shall only in the way be found.

4 This is the way I long have sought,
And mourned because I found it not;
My grief and burden long have been,
Because I could not cease from sin.

5 The more I strove against its power,
I sinned and stumbled but the more;
Till late I heard my Saviour say,
"Come hither, soul! I am the Way!"

6 Lo! glad I come: and Thou, blest Lamb
Shalt take me to Thee, as I am.
Nothing but sin have I to give;
Nothing but love shall I receive.

7 Now will I tell to sinners round
What a dear Saviour I have found;
I'll point to Thy redeeming blood,
And say, "Behold the Way to God!'

John Cennick, 1743. (*a.*)

THE WAY.

187

John xiv. 6. "*I am the Way.*" Tune EVAN I. C. M.

1 THOU art the Way: to Thee alone
From sin and death we flee,
And he who would the Father seek,
Must seek Him, Lord, by Thee.

2 Thou art the Truth: Thy word alone
Sound wisdom can impart;
Thou only canst inform the mind,
And purify the heart.

3 Thou art the Life: the rending tomb
Proclaims Thy conquering arm;
And those who put their trust in Thee
Nor death nor hell shall harm.

4 Thou art the Way, the Truth, the Life;
Grant us that Way to know,
That Truth to keep, that Life to win,
Whose joys eternal flow!

Bishop George W. Doane, 1856.

ABOVE EVERY NAME.

188 Phil. ii. 9. "*A Name which is above every name.*"

Tune DARWELL. 6 6 6 6, 8 8.

1 JOIN all the glorious names
Of wisdom, love, and power,
That mortals ever knew,
That angels ever bore;
All are too mean to speak His worth,
Too mean to set my Saviour forth.

2 But oh what gentle terms,
What condescending ways,
Doth our Redeemer use
To teach His heavenly grace!
Mine eyes with joy and wonder see
What forms of love He bears for me.

3 Arrayed in mortal flesh
The Covenant-Angel stands,
And holds the promises
And pardons in His hands:
Commissioned from His Father's throne
To make His grace to mortals known.

4 Great Prophet of my God!
My tongue would bless Thy name:
By Thee the joyful news
Of our salvation came;
The joyful news of sins forgiven,
Of hell subdued, and peace with heaven.

PART II.

5 Be Thou my Counsellor,
My Pattern, and my Guide,
And through this desert land
Still keep me near Thy side:
Oh let my feet ne'er run astray,
Nor rove, nor seek the crooked way.

6 I love my Shepherd's voice:
His watchful eye shall keep
My wandering soul among
The thousands of His sheep:
He feeds His flock, He calls their names,
His bosom bears the tender lambs.

7 To this dear Surety's hand
Will I commit my cause;
He answers and fulfils
His Father's broken laws;
Behold my soul at freedom set!
My Surety paid the dreadful debt.

8 Jesus, my great High Priest,
Offered His blood and died;
My guilty conscience seeks
No sacrifice beside;
His powerful blood did once atone,
And now it pleads before the throne.

PART III.

9 My Advocate appears
For my defence on high,
The Father bows His ear,
And lays His thunder by;
Not all that hell or sin can say,
Shall turn His heart, His love away.

10 My dear Almighty Lord,
My Conqueror and my King,
Thy sceptre, and Thy sword,
Thy reigning grace I sing;
Thine is the power; behold I sit
In willing bonds before Thy feet.

11 Now let my soul arise,
And tread the tempter down:
My Captain leads me forth
To conquest and a crown;
A feeble saint shall win the day,
Though death and hell obstruct the way.

12 Should all the hosts of death,
And powers of hell unknown,
Put their most dreadful forms
Of rage and mischief on;
I shall be safe, for Christ displays
Superior power, and guardian grace.

Isaac Watts, D.D., 1709.

---

(3) THE DIVINE LOVE OF CHRIST.

189 Titus iii. 4. "*The kindness and love of God our Saviour.*" Tune ZOAN I. 7 6, 7 6. D.

1 LOVE caused Thine incarnation,
Love brought Thee from on high;
Thy thirst for our salvation—
This made Thee come to die;
Oh! love beyond all measure!
Wherewith Thou didst embrace
The victims of the pressure
Of sin and its disgrace.

2 Not sinful man's endeavour,
Nor any mortal's care,
Could draw that sovereign favour
To sinners in despair;
Uncalled, Thou camest with gladness
Us from the fall to raise,
And change our grief and sadness
To songs of joy and praise!

Paul Gerhardt, 1653; *J. C. Jacobi* (*tr.*), 1722.

DIMON (Waters of). [H. P. 64.]

190 Eph. v. 2. "*Christ also hath loved us.*"

Tune DIMON. C. M. Or ST. ANN.

1 O BLESSED Saviour! is Thy love
So great, so full, so free?
Fain would we give our hearts, our minds,
Our lives, our all, to Thee.

2 We love Thee for the glorious work
That in Thyself we see,
We love Thee for the shameful cross
Endured so patiently.

3 No man of greater love can boast
Than for his friend to die;
Thou for Thine enemies wast slain—
What love with Thine can vie?

4 Thou in the very form of God,
With heavenly glory crowned,
Thou didst partake of human flesh,
Beset with sorrows round.

5 Thou wouldst like sinful man be made
In everything but sin,
That we as like Thee might become
As we unlike have been;—

6 Like Thee in faith, in meekness, love,
In every heavenly grace,
From glory unto glory changed,
Till we behold Thy face!

Joseph Stennett, 1697.

ZOAN I. (Field of). [H. P. 127.]

191 1 Pet. i. 8. "*Whom having not seen, ye love.*"

Tune ZOAN I. 7 6, 7 6. D.

1 O SAVIOUR, precious Saviour,
Whom yet unseen we love,
O Name of might and favour,
All other names above:
We worship Thee, we bless Thee,
To Thee alone we sing;
We praise Thee, and confess Thee
Our holy Lord and King!

2 O Bringer of salvation,
Who wondrously hast wrought,
Thyself the revelation
Of love beyond our thought:
We worship Thee, we bless Thee,
To Thee alone we sing;
We praise Thee, and confess Thee
Our gracious Lord and King!

3 In Thee all fulness dwelleth,
All grace and power Divine;
The glory that excelleth,
O Son of God, is Thine:
We worship Thee, we bless Thee,
To Thee alone we sing;
We praise Thee, and confess Thee
Our glorious Lord and King!

4 O grant the consummation
Of this our song above,
In endless adoration
And everlasting love:
Then shall we praise and bless Thee,
Where perfect praises ring,
And evermore confess Thee
Our Saviour and our King!

Frances Ridley Havergal, 1870.

192 Ps. ciii. 20. "*Bless the Lord, ye His angels that excel in strength.*"

MOSCOW. [H. P. 107.]

Tune Moscow. 6 6 4, 6 6 6 4.

1 PRAISE God, ye seraphs bright,
Praise Him, ye sons of light,
Jesus adore!
What earthly choirs can swell,
What mortal tongue can tell,
Thy love, Immanuel,
God evermore?

2 Yet must *we* lisp Thy praise,
Though but in human lays,
Jesus Most High!
Didst Thou not leave Thy throne,
And to this world come down,
To bear our curse alone,—
To bleed and die!

3 Come, saints, in God rejoice,
Lift up a mighty voice,
Sing to the Lamb!
For us His blood was shed,—
For us He left the dead,
His foes discomfited!
Praise the I AM!

4 Now at the Father's hand,—
While countless angels stand
Waiting His word,
Christ sits in majesty!
In Him humanity
Is one with Deity,—
Praise ye the Lord!

5 Soon shall we see His face,
Wearing no mournful trace,—
Oh, what a sight!
Soon shall we hear Him say,
"Come, waiting child, away,
Lo! *now* has dawned the day
That knows *not* night!"

William Pennefather, 1871.

GOLDBACH. [H. P. 130.]

193 Matt. xi. 28. "*Come unto Me.*"

Tune Goldbach. 7 6, 7 6. D.

1 "COME unto Me, ye weary,
And I will give you rest."
O blessèd voice of Jesus,
Which comes to hearts oppressed!
It tells of benediction,
Of pardon, grace, and peace;
Of joy that hath no ending,
Of love which cannot cease.

2 "Come unto Me, dear children,
And I will give you light."
O loving voice of Jesus,
Which comes to cheer the night!
Our hearts were filled with sadness,
And we had lost our way;
But morning brings us gladness,
And songs the break of day.

3 "Come unto Me, ye fainting,
And I will give you life."
O peaceful voice of Jesus,
Which comes to end our strife!
The foe is stern and eager,
The fight is fierce and long;
But Thou hast made us mighty,
And stronger than the strong.

4 "And whosoever cometh,
I will not cast him out."
O patient voice of Jesus,
Which drives away our doubt;
Which calls us, very sinners,
Unworthy though we be
Of love so free and boundless,
To come, dear Lord, to Thee.

William Chatterton Dix, 1867.

194 Isa. lxiii. 7. "*The lovingkindnesses of the Lord.*"

Tune Crasselius. L. M.

1 AWAKE, my soul, in joyful lays,
And sing thy great Redeemer's praise;
He justly claims a song from me—
His loving-kindness, oh! how free!

2 He saw me ruined in the fall,
Yet loved me notwithstanding all;
He saved me from my lost estate—
His loving-kindness, oh! how great!

CRASSELIUS; *or*, WINCHESTER NEW. [H. P. 3.]

3 Though numerous hosts of mighty foes,
Though earth and hell, my way oppose,
He safely leads my soul along—
His loving-kindness, oh! how strong!

4 When trouble, like a gloomy cloud,
Has gathered thick and thundered loud,
He near my soul has always stood—
His loving-kindness, oh! how good!

5 I often feel my sinful heart
Prone from my Jesus to depart;
But though I have Him oft forgot,
His loving-kindness changes not!

6 Soon shall I pass the gloomy vale,
Soon all my mortal powers must fail;
Oh! may my last expiring breath
His loving-kindness sing in death!

7 Then let me mount and soar away
To the bright world of endless day;
And sing with rapture and surprise
His loving-kindness in the skies!

Samuel Medley, 1785.

See Hymns 215, 715—722, 930, 935.

(4) THE INCARNATION.

195 Luke ii. 10. "*Good tidings of great joy.*"
Tune NASSAU. 7 7, 7 7, 7 7.

NASSAU. [H. P. 155.]

1 SING, oh sing, this blessèd morn,
Unto us a Child is born,
Unto us a Son is given,
God Himself comes down from heaven;
Sing, oh sing, this blessèd morn,
Jesus Christ to-day is born.

2 Jesus Christ, the King of kings,
Maker of all worldly things,
Now descends from heaven to earth,
To restore us by His birth;
Sing, oh sing, etc.

3 God of God, and Light of light,
Comes with mercies infinite;
Joining, in a wondrous plan,
Heaven to earth, and God to man;
Sing, oh sing, etc.

4 God with us, Emmanuel,
Deigns for ever now to dwell;
He on Adam's fallen race
Sheds the fulness of His grace;
Sing, oh sing, etc.

5 Truth and mercy show their face,
And with loving kiss embrace;
Righteousness looks down from heaven,
God is pleased, and man forgiven;
Sing, oh sing, etc.

PART II.

6 God comes down that man may rise,
Lifted far above the skies;
He is Son of Man, that we
Sons of God in Him may be;
Sing, oh sing, etc.

7 Human flesh is now become
Christ's abode, the Godhead's home;
Royal palace, sacred shrine
For the Majesty Divine;
Sing, oh sing, etc.

8 Now we rise, from prison free;
On we march to victory,
Joyful banners are unfurled;
'Tis the birthday of the world;
Sing, oh sing, etc.

9 Now behold the rising Sun
Hath His glorious race begun;
Now the Bridegroom from above
Weds the Bride, with heavenly love;
Sing, oh sing, etc.

10 Oh renew us, Lord, we pray,
With Thy Spirit day by day;
That we ever one may be
With the Father, and with Thee;
Sing, oh sing, etc.

11 Sing, oh sing, this blessèd morn,
Jesus Christ to-day is born;
Glory to the Father give,
Praise the Son in whom we live;
Glory to the Spirit be,
Godhead One, and Persons Three. Amen.

Bishop Christopher Wordsworth, 1862.

196 Luke ii. 10. *"I bring you good tidings."*

Tune Deptford. 10 10, 10 10, 10 10.

1 CHRISTIANS, awake, salute the happy morn
Whereon the Saviour of mankind was born;
Rise to adore the mystery of love,
Which hosts of angels chanted from above;
With them the joyful tidings were begun,
Of God Incarnate, and the Virgin's Son.

2 Oh! may we keep and ponder in our mind
God's wondrous love in saving lost mankind;
Trace we the Babe, who hath retrieved our loss,
From the poor manger to the bitter cross!
Tread in His steps, assisted by His grace,
Till man's first heavenly state again take place.

DEPTFORD. [H. P. 315.]

3 Then may we hope, the' angelic hosts among,
To join, redeemed, a glad, triumphant throng;
He that was born upon this joyful day
Around us all His glory shall display;
Saved by His love incessant we shall sing
Eternal praise to heaven's Almighty King!

John Byrom, 1761.

PHILEMON. [H. P. 223.]

197 Luke ii. 11. *"A Saviour, which is Christ the Lord."* Tune Philemon. 8 8 8, 7.

1 BRING to Christ your best oblation,
Grateful hearts and adoration,
Join in songs of gratulation,
Christian people, on this day.

2 Sin and hell may look astounded,
Death and devil be confounded;
We, in whom grace hath abounded,
Cast all griefs and fears away.

3 See the precious Gift God giveth!
His own Son, who ever liveth:
He who in His name believeth
Shall be savèd through His grace.

4 Oh how great was His compassion,
Thus to come in human fashion,
And to visit with salvation
Our poor sin-polluted race!

5 Jacob's Star, desired for ages,
Guides from far the Eastern sages;
The old dragon fumes and rages,
When he sees the woman's Seed.

6 Long we sat in bitter anguish,
In a dungeon left to languish;
Jesus comes our foe to vanquish,
Bursts our bonds, and we are freed!

7 Blessèd hour! when full confession
First we made of our transgression,
And obtained a free remission,
Jesus, through Thy precious blood!

8 Smile upon us, heavenly Stranger,
Cradled in a lowly manger,
Bring us from this world of danger,
To Thyself, our Lord and God!

Paul Gerhardt, 1659; *R. Massie (tr.)*, 1864.

198 Luke ii. 14. *"On earth peace."*

Tune Zared I. 8 5, 8 5, 7 7 7, 5.

1 JESUS, from the skies descending,
Lies a babe on earth!
Seraphs, o'er the manger bending,
Hail the wondrous birth!
Lo! the watchful shepherds hear
Sounds of joy with holy fear;
Haste to gaze; then, far and near,
Spread the tidings forth.

2 'Tis to open sweet communion
'Twixt the earth and skies;
'Tis to bind all hearts in union,
God an infant lies!
Gaze upon that placid brow,
And while ye admiring bow,
Holy love to cherish, vow,
Till all discord dies.

ZARED I. [H. P. 172.]

3 Oh, let every heart adore Him!
Peace and love o'erflow!
Anger, hatred, sink before Him,
To your depths below!
Be no sound beneath the sky;
Be no glance from mortal eye;
Be no thought, no feeling, nigh,
Brethren should not know!

Thomas Davis, 1846.

199

Luke ii. 14. *"Glory to God."*
Tune Pisgah. 77, 77.

1 Hark, the herald angels sing,
Glory to the new-born King,
"Peace on earth, and mercy mild;
God and sinners reconciled."

2 Joyful, all ye nations, rise,
Join the triumph of the skies;
Hail the heaven-born Prince of Peace!
Hail the Sun of Righteousness!

3 Veiled in flesh the Godhead see;
Hail the' Incarnate Deity;
Pleased as man with men to' appear,
Jesus our Immanuel here.

4 Mild He lays His glory by;
Born that men no more might die;
Born to raise the sons of earth;
Born to give them second birth.

5 Come, Desire of Nations, come!
Fix in us Thy humble home;
Rise, the woman's promised Seed,
Bruise in us the serpent's head.

6 Glory to the new-born King!
Let us all the anthem sing,
"Peace on earth, and mercy mild;
God and sinners reconciled!"

Charles Wesley, 1739.

PISGAH (Mount). [H. P. 137.]

Hal - le - lu - jah, Hal - le - lu - jah!

LUBECK. [H. P. 139.]

Hal - le - lu - jah, Hal - le - lu - jah!

200

Isa. ix. 6. *"Unto us a Child is born."*
Tune Lubeck. 77, 77.

1 Bright and joyful is the morn,
For to us a Child is born:
From the highest realms of heaven
Unto us a Son is given.

2 On His shoulder He shall bear
Power and majesty, and wear,
On His vesture and His thigh,
Names most awful, names most high.

3 Wonderful in counsel He,
The Incarnate Deity:
Sire of ages ne'er to cease,
King of kings, and Prince of Peace.

4 Come and worship at His feet,
Yield to Christ the homage meet,
From His manger to His throne,
Homage due to God alone!

James Montgomery, 1819.

MAGDALENE COLLEGE. [H. P. 210.]

201 Luke ii. 14. "*Glory to God in the highest.*" Tune MAGDALENE COLLEGE. 8 8 6. D. Or KEDRON.

1 HOW sweet the notes of yonder choir,
While Gabriel's words their hearts inspire,
The subject so Divine:
To Zion's daughters now declare,
For you is born the promised Heir
Of David's royal line.

2 'Tis not the noise of war we hear,
Nor garments rolled in blood we fear,
On this auspicious morn;
Judgment and mercy both conspire
With love to set our souls on fire:
"To us a Child is born."

3 In David's city long foretold,
The Son of David now behold,
Desire of nations He;
The Mighty God, the Prince of Peace,
Whose government shall never cease,
In Bethlehem's Babe we see.

4 'Tis "God with us, Emmanuel,"
With new-strung harps the tidings swell;
He'll bring His banished home.
The once loved nation's sceptre broke,
Fulfilled the words the prophet spoke,
The gathering Shiloh's come!

5 As Jacob's Star behold Him shine,
As Israel's Sceptre all Divine;
"His own received Him not;"
Yet in His temple shall He stand,
A priest with incense in His hand,
To plead for those He bought.

6 Then catch the notes of yonder choir,
While listening seraphim admire;
Let love our hearts inflame;
And since "to us a Child is born,"
We'll sing on this auspicious morn,
That Jesus is His name!

John Kent, 1841.

VENITE ADOREMUS. [H. P. 250.]

202 Luke ii. 15. "*Let us now go even unto Bethlehem.*" Tune VENITE ADOREMUS. 12 10, 11 10.

1 O COME, all ye faithful, joyfully triumphant;
To Bethlehem haste ye with glad accord;
Lo! in a manger lies the King of angels;
O come, let us adore Him, CHRIST THE LORD.

2 Though true God of true God, Light of Light eternal,
The womb of a Virgin He hath not abhorred:
Son of the Father, not made but begotten;
O come, let us adore Him, CHRIST THE LORD.

3 Raise, raise, choirs of angels! songs of loudest triumph,
Through heaven's wide courts be your praises poured;
Now to our God be glory in the highest;
O come, let us adore Him, CHRIST THE LORD.

4 Amen! Lord, we bless Thee, born for our salvation;
O Jesu! for ever be Thy name adored;
Word of the Father, late in flesh appearing;
O come, let us adore Him, CHRIST THE LORD!

Adeste Fideles, 15th Century; W. Mercer. (r.)

---

203 Luke ii. 13. "*A multitude of the heavenly host.*"

Tune IDUMEA. 8 7, 8 7, 4 7.

1 ANGELS, from the realms of glory,
Wing your flight o'er all the earth,
Ye who sang creation's story,
Now proclaim Messiah's birth;
Come and worship,
Worship Christ, the new-born King.

2 Saints, before the altar bending,
Waiting long with hope and fear,
Suddenly the Lord descending
In His temple shall appear;
Come and worship,
Worship Christ, the new-born King.

3 Sinners, wrung with true repentance,
Doomed for guilt to endless pains,
Justice now repeals the sentence,
Mercy calls you—break your chains;
Come and worship,
Worship Christ, the new-born King.

James Montgomery, 1819.

CHESALON (Mount). [H. P. 35.]

204 Luke i. 72. "*To perform the mercy promised.*"

Tune CHESALON. C. M.

1 HARK, the glad sound, the Saviour comes,
The Saviour promised long!
Let every heart prepare a throne,
And every voice a song.

2 On Him the Spirit, largely poured,
Exerts its sacred fire;
Wisdom and might, and zeal and love,
His holy breast inspire.

3 He comes, the prisoners to release,
In Satan's bondage held;
The gates of brass before Him burst,
The iron fetters yield.

4 He comes, from thickest films of vice
To clear the mental ray;
And on the eyeballs of the blind
To pour celestial day.

5 He comes, the broken heart to bind,
The bleeding soul to cure;
And with the treasures of His grace
To' enrich the humble poor.

6 Our glad hosannas, Prince of Peace!
Thy welcome shall proclaim;
And heaven's eternal arches ring
With Thy belovèd name!

Philip Doddridge, D.D., 1755.

SITNAH (Well of). [H. P. 179.]

Hal - le - lu - jah, Hal - le - lu - jah!

See Hymns 132, 135, 943—948.

205 Luke ii. 9-11. *"The glory of the Lord."*
Tune SITNAH. 87, 87. Or SIRION.

1 HARK! what mean those holy voices,
Sweetly sounding in the skies!
Lo! the' angelic host rejoices:
Loudest Hallelujahs rise.
Hallelujah!

2 Listen to the wondrous story
Which they chant in hymns of joy;
"Glory in the highest, glory;
Glory be to God most high.
Hallelujah!

3 "Peace on earth, good will from heaven,
Reaching far as man is found;
Souls redeemed and sins forgiven,
Loud our golden harps shall sound.
Hallelujah!

4 "Christ is born: the great Anointed!
Heaven and earth His glory sing!
O receive whom God appointed
For your Prophet, Priest, and King.
Hallelujah!

5 "Hasten, mortals, to adore Him,
Learn His name and taste His joy,
Till in heaven ye sing before Him,
Glory be to God most high!"
Hallelujah!

6 Let us learn the wondrous story
Of our great Redeemer's birth,
Spread the brightness of His glory,
Till it cover all the earth.
Hallelujah!

John Cawood, 1816.

DIX. [H. P. 287.]

(5) THE EPIPHANY.

206 Luke i. 78. *"The Day-spring from on high."*
Tune DIX. 77, 77, 77. Or SIHOR.

1 CHRIST, whose glory fills the skies,
Christ, the true, the only Light,
Sun of Righteousness, arise,
Triumph o'er the shades of night;
Day-spring from on high, be near;
Day-star, in my heart appear!

2 Dark and cheerless is the morn,
Unaccompanied by Thee;
Joyless is the day's return,
Till Thy mercy's beams I see;
Till they inward light impart,
Glad my eyes and warm my heart.

3 Visit then this soul of mine,
Pierce the gloom of sin and grief,
Fill me, Radiancy Divine;
Scatter all my unbelief;
More and more Thyself display,
Shining to the perfect day!

Charles Wesley, 1740.

207 Matt. ii. 2. *"We have seen His Star."*
Tune DIX. 77, 77, 77.

1 AS with gladness men of old
Did the guiding star behold;
As with joy they hailed its light,
Leading onward, beaming bright:
So, most gracious Lord, may we
Evermore be led to Thee.

2 As with joyful steps they sped
To that lowly manger-bed,
There to bend the knee before
Him whom heaven and earth adore:
So may we with willing feet
Ever seek the mercy-seat.

3 As they offered gifts most rare
At that manger rude and bare:
So may we with holy joy,
Pure and free from sin's alloy,
All our costliest treasures bring,
Christ, to Thee, our heavenly King.

4 Holy Jesus, every day
Keep us in the narrow way;
And, when earthly things are past,
Bring our ransomed souls at last
Where they need no star to guide,
Where no clouds Thy glory hide.

5 In the heavenly country bright
Need they no created light:
Thou its light, its joy, its crown,
Thou its sun which goes not down:
There for ever may we sing
Hallelujahs to our King!

William Chatterton Dix, 1861.

208

Rev. xxii. 16. "*I am the bright and morning Star.*"

Tune STERNBERG. 11 10, 11 10.

1 BRIGHTEST and best of the sons of the morning!
Dawn on our darkness and lend us thine aid!
Star of the East, the horizon adorning,
Guide where our infant Redeemer is laid!

2 Cold on His cradle the dewdrops are shining,
Low lies His bed with the beasts of the stall;
Angels adore Him, in slumber reclining,
Maker, and Monarch, and Saviour of all!

3 Say, shall we yield Him, in costly devotion,
Odours of Edom and offerings Divine?
Gems of the mountain and pearls of the ocean,
Myrrh from the forest or gold from the mine?

4 Vainly we offer each ample oblation,
Vainly with gifts would His favour secure;
Richer by far is the heart's adoration,
Dearer to God are the prayers of the poor!

5 Brightest and best of the sons of the morning!
Dawn on our darkness and lend us thine aid!
Star of the East, the horizon adorning,
Guide where our infant Redeemer is laid!

Bishop Heber, 1811.

209

Luke ii. 32. "*A Light to lighten the Gentiles.*"

Tune MORIAH. 6 6 6 6, 4 4 4 4.

1 IN doubt and dread dismay,
'Midst superstition's gloom,
The heathen grope their way,
And joyless reach the tomb:
No holy light, No balmy ray
Of gospel day Has blessed their sight.

2 Then, Star of life, arise!
And on Thy healing wing,
With blood of sacrifice,
Thy great salvation bring:
Let heathen lands Thy brightness see;
O set them free From cruel bands.

3 With searching beams explore
The dark strongholds of sin;
And on the prisoners pour
Transforming light within:
Bright Morning Star! Unveil Thy face,
And shed Thy grace In realms afar.

4 O Jesus, Light of Life!
Arouse the world from sleep;
Send love in place of strife,
And joy to those who weep:
Great King of kings! Thy Spirit give;
Let Gentiles live Beneath Thy wings!

William Henry Havergal, 1837.

210 2 Pet. i. 19. "*Until the day dawn, and the Day Star arise.*" Tune HAVILAH. 87, 87, 47. Or ZAANAIM.

1 WIDELY, 'midst the slumbering nations,
Darkness holds his despot sway;
Cruel in his habitations,
Ruthless o'er his prostrate prey.
Star of Bethlehem!
Rise and beam in conquering day!

2 Light of Life, our sole Defender,
Rise, with healing on Thy wing;
Rise, in all Thy soothing splendour;
Rise, and earth with joy shall sing!
Israel's Glory!
Gentiles call Thee "Lord and King."

3 Christians, haste! the morn is breaking;
Darkness wheels his downward flight;
But, your polished armour taking,
Stand! nor quit the waning fight.
Great Redeemer!
Guard us with Thy shield of light.

4 Onward, Christians, onward pressing,
Triumph in the Crucified!
Endless honour, rest, and blessing,
Wait you at His radiant side.
Cease not, cease not,
Till you see Him glorified!

William Henry Havergal, 1828.

HAVILAH. [H. P. 192.]

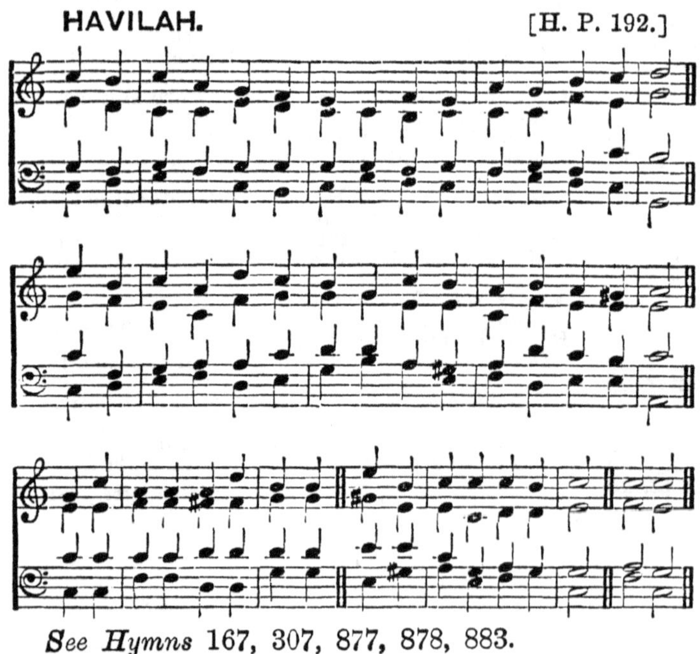

See Hymns 167, 307, 877, 878, 883.

211 Mal. iv. 2. "*The Sun of Righteousness.*" Tune HAVILAH. 87, 87, 87.

1 BRIGHTER than meridian splendour,
Beams Messiah's spotless fame;
Him we hail our firm Defender,
Him let every tongue proclaim.
He is precious,
He is gracious,
He for ever is the same.

2 Lord of glory! Source of favour!
Bid Thy heralds take their stand;
Let Thy name's reviving savour
Wake each dark and drowsy land.
Saviour, hear us;
Speak and cheer us,
When we lift the suppliant hand.

3 Thou art all! and all adore Thee,
Where they hymn one ceaseless song;
Soon shall earth, subdued before Thee,
Peal Thy name her tribes among.
Sons of glory,
Chant the story,
And your deep Amen prolong!

William Henry Havergal, 1830.

GETHSEMANE. [H. P. 28.]

(6) THE CIRCUMCISION OF CHRIST.

212 Luke ii. 21. "*When eight days were accomplished.*" Tune GETHSEMANE. L. M.

1 O BLESSED day, when first was poured
The blood of our redeeming Lord!
O blessèd day, when first began
His sufferings borne for sinful man!

2 Scarce entered on this life of woe,
His infant blood begins to flow;
A foretaste of His death He feels,
An earnest of His love reveals.

3 The law's great Maker for our aid
Obedient to the law is made;
Henceforth a holier law prevails,
The law of love, which never fails.

4 Lord, circumcise our hearts, we pray,
And take what is not Thine away;
Write Thine own name within our hearts,
Thy law upon our inmost parts!

Besnault, 1726; *John Chandler* (*tr.*), 1837.

213 Matt. i. 21. *"Thou shalt call His name Jesus, for He shall save His people from their sins."*

Tune Lubeck. 77, 77.

1 CONQUERING kings their titles take
From the foes they captive make;
Jesus, by a nobler deed,
From the thousands He hath freed.

2 Jesu's only name is given
Unto mortals under heaven,
Which can make the dead arise,
And exalt them to the skies.

3 Joyfully for Jesu's name
Bear the cross, endure the shame:
Joyfully for Him to die
Is not death, but victory.

4 Jesu, who dost condescend
To be called the sinner's Friend,
Hear us as to Thee we pray,
Glorying in Thy name to-day.

5 Glory to the Father be,
Glory, Holy Son, to Thee,
Glory to the Holy Ghost,
From the saints and angel-host!

John Chandler (tr.), 1837. (a.)

LUBECK. [H. P. 139.]

Hal - le - lu - jah, Hal - le - lu - jah!

CARMEL (Mount). [H. P. 69.]

(7) CHRIST OUR EXAMPLE.

214 Heb. xii. 2. *"Looking unto Jesus."*

Tune Carmel. C. M.

1 LORD, as to Thy dear cross we flee,
And plead to be forgiven,
So let Thy life our pattern be,
And form our souls for heaven.

2 Help us, through good report and ill,
Our daily cross to bear;
Like Thee, to do our Father's will,
Our brethren's griefs to share.

3 Let grace our selfishness expel,
Our earthliness refine;
And kindness in our bosoms dwell,
As free and true as Thine.

4 If joy shall at Thy bidding fly,
And grief's dark day come on,
We, in our turn, would meekly cry,
"Father, Thy will be done."

5 Kept peaceful in the midst of strife,
Forgiving and forgiven,
Oh! may we lead the pilgrim's life,
And follow Thee to heaven!

John Hampden Gurney, 1838.

215 Heb. xii. 3. *"Consider Him."*

Tune Carmel. C. M. D. Or Old Nunc Dimittis.

1 HE came, whose embassy was peace,
He left His throne above,
To prove if enmity would cease
Beneath the power of love.
He came, whose errand was to give;
His hand was opened wide,
Yea, at our need, that we might live,
He gave Himself—and died.

2 What had the world for Him? 'twas meet
To answer love with love,
With signs of thankful joy to greet
The Stranger from above.
For Him! with all its proud array,
Of kingdom, palace, tower?
He was a wanderer each day,
A mourner every hour.

3 For Him! with all its glory spread
Before its Maker's sight;
He had not where to lay His head—
That wearied head, by night.
For Him! His days were almost past,
His sorrows well-nigh o'er?
But lo, the world will give at last,
From its abundant store!

4 The shameful cross, the piercing thorn,
The vinegar and gall!
The world gives these with cruel scorn,
And He endures them all.
O world! that cross doth still proclaim,
On earth—in heaven above,
The story of thy guilt and shame,
The wonders of His love!

Mary Jane Walker, 1855.

HERMON. [H. P. 27.]

216 John xiii. 15. *"I have given you an example."* Tune HERMON. L. M. Or CYPRUS.

1 MY dear Redeemer and my Lord,
 I read my duty in Thy word;
But in Thy life the law appears
Drawn out in living characters.

2 Such was Thy truth, and such Thy zeal,
Such deference to Thy Father's will,
Such love, and meekness so Divine,
I would transcribe and make them mine.

3 Cold mountains and the midnight air
Witnessed the fervour of Thy prayer;
The desert Thy temptation knew,
Thy conflict and Thy victory too.

4 Be Thou my pattern; make me bear
More of Thy gracious image here;
Then God the Judge shall own my name
Amongst the followers of the Lamb!

Isaac Watts, D.D., 1709.

VIENNA. [H. P. 149.]

217 Matt. ix. 9. *"Follow Me."* Tune VIENNA. 77, 77.

1 FATHER of eternal grace,
 May we all resemble Thee:
Meekly beaming in our face,
 May the world Thine image see.

2 Happy only in Thy love,
 Poor, unfriended, or unknown;
Fix our thoughts on things above,
 Stay our hearts on Thee alone.

3 Humble, holy, all resigned
 To Thy will—Thy will be done!
Give us, Lord, the perfect mind
 Of Thy well-belovèd Son.

4 Counting gain and glory loss,
 May we tread the path He trod;
Bear with Him on earth our cross,
 Rise with Him to Thee, our God!

James Montgomery, 1819.

See Hymns 555, 933.

CAITHNESS. [H. P. 56.]

(8) THE COMPASSION AND SYMPATHY OF CHRIST.

218 Titus iii. 4. *"The kindness and love of God our Saviour."* Tune CAITHNESS. C. M.

1 PLUNGED in a gulf of dark despair
 We wretched sinners lay,
Without one cheerful beam of hope,
 Or spark of glimmering day.

2 With pitying eyes, the Prince of Grace
 Beheld our helpless grief;
He saw, and—O amazing love!
 He came to our relief.

3 Down from the shining seats above
 With joyful haste He fled,
Entered the grave in mortal flesh,
 And dwelt among the dead.

4 He spoiled the powers of darkness thus,
 And brake our iron chains;
Jesus hath freed our captive souls
 From everlasting pains.

5 Oh! for this love let rocks and hills
 Their lasting silence break,
And all harmonious human tongues
 The Saviour's praises speak.

6 Angels, assist our mighty joys,
 Strike all your harps of gold;
But when you raise your highest notes,
 His love can ne'er be told!

Isaac Watts, D.D., 1709.

219 Matt. viii. 17. "*Himself took our infirmities.*" Tune CAITHNESS. C. M.

1 HOW condescending, and how kind,
Was God's eternal Son!
Our misery reached His heavenly mind,
And pity brought Him down.

2 When justice, by our sins provoked,
Drew forth its dreadful sword,
He gave His soul up to the stroke
Without a murmuring word.

3 He sank beneath our heavy woes,
To raise us to His throne;
There's ne'er a gift His hand bestows,
But cost His heart a groan.

4 This was compassion like a God,
That when the Saviour knew
The price of pardon was His blood,
His pity ne'er withdrew.

5 Now though He reigns exalted high,
His love is still as great;
Well He remembers Calvary,
Nor lets His saints forget.

6 Here let our hearts begin to melt,
While we His death record,
And, with our joy for pardoned guilt,
Mourn that we pierced the Lord!

Isaac Watts, D.D., 1709.

220 Isa. liii. 4. "*He hath borne our griefs.*" Tune CAITHNESS. C. M. Or CARMEL.

1 A PILGRIM through this lonely world,
The blessèd Saviour passed;
A mourner all His life was He,
A dying Lamb at last.

2 That tender heart that felt for us,
For us its life-blood gave;
It found on earth no resting-place,
Save only in the grave.

3 Such was our Lord. And shall we fear
The cross with all its scorn?
Or love a faithless, evil world,
That wreathed His brow with thorn?

4 No! facing all its frowns or smiles,
Like Him, obedient still,
We homeward press, through storm or calm,
To yon celestial hill.

5 In tents we dwell amid the waste,
Nor turn aside to roam
In folly's paths, nor seek our rest
Where Jesus had no home.

6 Dead to the world, with Him who died
To win our hearts, our love,
We, risen with our risen Head,
In spirit dwell above.

7 By faith His boundless glory there
Our wondering eyes behold,
Those glories which eternal years
Shall never all unfold!

Sir Edward Denny, 1837.

MELCOMBE. [H. P. 24.]

221 Heb. iv. 15. "*Touched with the feeling of our infirmities.*" Tune MELCOMBE. L. M. Or GETHSEMANE.

1 WHERE high the heavenly temple stands,
The house of God not made with hands,
A great High Priest our nature wears;
The Guardian of mankind appears.

2 He who, for men, their Surety stood,
And poured on earth His precious blood,
Pursues in heaven His mighty plan;
The Saviour and the Friend of man.

3 Though now ascended up on high,
He bends on earth a Brother's eye;
Partaker of the human name,
He knows the frailty of our frame.

4 Our Fellow-sufferer yet retains
A fellow-feeling of our pains;
And still remembers, in the skies,
His tears, His agonies, and cries.

5 In every pang that rends the heart
The Man of Sorrows hath a part;
He sympathises with our grief,
And to the sufferer sends relief.

6 With boldness, therefore, at the throne,
Let us make all our sorrows known,
And ask the aid of heavenly power
To keep us in the evil hour.

Michael Bruce, 1770. (a.)

SALISBURY. [H. P. 62.]

222 Heb. iv. 16. *"Grace to help in time of need."* Tune SALISBURY. C. M.

1 WITH joy we meditate the grace
  Of our High Priest above;
His heart is filled with tenderness,
  His very name is love.

2 Touched with a sympathy within,
  He knows our feeble frame;
He knows what sore temptations mean,
  For He has felt the same.

3 But spotless, innocent, and pure,
  Our great Redeemer stood;
While Satan's fiery darts He bore,
  And did resist to blood.

4 He, in the days of feeble flesh,
  Poured out His cries and tears,
And though exalted, feels afresh
  What every member bears.

5 He'll never quench the smoking flax,
  But raise it to a flame;
The bruisèd reed He never breaks,
  Nor scorns the meanest name.

6 Then boldly let our faith address
  His mercy and His power;
We shall obtain delivering grace
  In each distressing hour!

Isaac Watts, D.D., 1709.

See *Hymn* 280.

(9) JESUS SEEN OF ANGELS.

223 1 Tim. iii. 16. *"Seen of angels."* Tune SALISBURY. C. M.

1 BEYOND the glittering starry skies,
  Far as the' eternal hills,
There, in the boundless worlds of light,
  Our dear Redeemer dwells.

2 Immortal angels, bright and fair,
  In countless armies shine!
At His right hand, with golden harps,
  They offer songs Divine.

3 In all His toils and dangerous paths
  They did His steps attend,
Oft paused, and wondered how at last
  This scene of love would end.

4 And when the powers of hell combined
  To fill His cup of woe,
Their pitying eyes beheld His tears
  In bloody anguish flow.

5 As on the' accursèd tree He hung,
  And darkness veiled the sky,
They saw, aghast, that awful sight,—
  The Lord of glory die!

6 Anon He bursts the gates of death,
  Subdues the tyrant's power;
They saw the' illustrious Conqueror rise,
  And hailed the blessèd hour.

7 They brought His chariot from above,
  To bear Him to His throne;
Waved their triumphant wings, and cried,
  "The glorious work is done."

8 My soul the joyful triumph feels,
  And thinks the moments long
Ere she her Saviour's glory sees,
  And joins the rapturous song!

James Fanch, 1776; *Daniel Turner*, 1791. (*a.*)

224 Ps. xci. 11. *"He shall give His angels charge over thee."*
Tune DARWELL. 6666, 4444.

DARWELL. [H. P. 274.]

1 YE bright, immortal throng
  Of angels round the throne,
Join with our feeble song
  To make the Saviour known:
On earth ye knew His wondrous grace;
His beauteous face In heaven ye view.

2 Ye saw the heaven-born Child
  In human flesh arrayed,
Benevolent and mild,
  While in the manger laid:
And praise to God, And peace on earth,
For such a birth, Proclaimed aloud.

3 Ye, in the wilderness,
  Beheld the tempter spoiled,
Well known in every dress,
  In every combat foiled:
And joyed to crown The Victor's head,
When Satan fled Before His frown.

4 Around the bloody tree
  Ye pressed with strong desire,
That wondrous sight to see,
  The Lord of life expire:
And, could your eyes Have known a tear,
Had dropped it there In sad surprise.

5 Around His sacred tomb
A willing watch ye kept;
Till the blest moment came
To waken Him that slept:
Then rolled the stone, And all adored
Your rising Lord, With joy unknown.

6 When all arrayed in light
The shining Conqueror rode,
Ye hailed His rapturous flight
Up to the throne of God;
And waved around Your golden wings,
And struck your strings Of sweetest sound.

7 The warbling notes pursue,
And louder anthems raise;
While mortals sing with you
Their own Redeemer's praise:
And thou, my heart, With equal flame,
And joy the same, Perform thy part!

Philip Doddridge, D.D., 1755.

See Hymns 753—755.

CRASSELIUS; *or*, WINCHESTER NEW. [H. P. 3.]

(10) THE SUFFERINGS AND SIN-ATONING DEATH OF CHRIST.

Passion Week.

225

Zech. ix. 9. "*Behold, thy King cometh.*"

Tune CRASSELIUS. L. M.

1 RIDE on! ride on in majesty!
Hark! all the tribes Hosanna cry!
O Saviour meek, pursue Thy road,
With palms and scattered garments strowed.

2 Ride on! ride on in majesty!
In lowly pomp ride on to die!
O Christ! Thy triumphs now begin
O'er captive death and conquered sin!

3 Ride on! ride on in majesty!
The wingèd squadrons of the sky
Look down with sad and wondering eyes
To see the' approaching Sacrifice!

4 Ride on! ride on in majesty!
Thy last and fiercest strife is nigh;
The Father, on His sapphire throne,
Expects His own anointed Son!

5 Ride on! ride on in majesty!
In lowly pomp ride on to die!
Bow Thy meek head to mortal pain!
Then take, O God, Thy power, and reign!

Dean Henry Hart Milman, D.D., 1827.

226

Matt. xxi. 15. "*Children . . . saying, Hosanna to the Son of David.*"

Tune EUPHRATES. L. M.

1 WHAT are those soul-reviving strains,
Which echo thus from Salem's plains?
What anthems loud, and louder still,
So sweetly sound from Zion's hill?
Hosanna, Hosanna, Amen!

2 Lo! 'tis an infant chorus sings
Hosanna to the King of kings:
The Saviour comes! and babes proclaim
Salvation sent in Jesu's name.
Hosanna, Hosanna, Amen!

3 Nor these alone their voice shall raise,
For we will join this song of praise;
Still Israel's children forward press
To hail the Lord their Righteousness.
Hosanna, Hosanna, Amen!

4 Messiah's name shall joy impart
Alike to Jew and Gentile heart:
He bled for us—He bled for you,
And we will sing Hosanna too.
Hosanna, Hosanna, Amen!

EUPHRATES. [H. P. 2.]

Hosanna! Hosanna! Hosanna! A-men, A-men.

5 Proclaim Hosannas loud and clear;
See David's Son and Lord appear!
All praise on earth to Him be given,
And glory shout through highest heaven!
Hosanna, Hosanna, Amen.

James Montgomery, 1820.

HERMON. [H. P. 27.]

227 John xii. 3. "*Mary . . . anointed the feet of Jesus.*" Tune HERMON. L. M.

1 ONCE did the ointment's rich perfume
Anoint the blessèd Saviour's feet:
Lord, let our trembling hearts presume
To bring a sacrifice as sweet.

2 We would with humble joy adore,
And prostrate at Thy footstool bend;
Nor costly ointments need we pour
In honour to the Sinners' Friend.

3 He asks the offering of the heart;
He deigns to' accept the contrite tear;
Oh! may we bear a humble part,
And bring our best affections here!

4 How blest was Martha's dear abode,
With Jesus for her constant Guest;
We, too, may entertain our God,
And banquet at His gospel-feast.

5 Like Lazarus, at the table meet,
Where faith presents her dying Lord;
Like Mary, sit at Jesu's feet,
To learn instruction from His word.

6 Blessèd Redeemer! Glorious King!
Nourish our souls with grace Divine!
Receive the sacrifice we bring,
And make our hearts supremely Thine!

Professor Scholefield's "Passion Week," 1836.

ST. FLAVIAN. [H. P. 264.]

228 Luke ix. 51. "*He stedfastly set His face to go to Jerusalem.*" Tune ST. FLAVIAN. C. M. D.
OR OLD NUNC DIMITTIS.

1 SEE what unbounded zeal and love
Inflamed the Saviour's breast,
When stedfast towards Jerusalem
His urgent way He pressed.
Good will to man and zeal for God
His every thought engross:
He longs to be baptized with blood,
He thirsts to reach the cross.

2 With all His sufferings full in view,
And woes to us unknown,
Forth to the work His spirit flew,
'Twas love that urged Him on:
By His obedience unto death
See paradise restored,
And fallen man brought face to face
With his forgiving Lord.

3 Prepare us, Lord, to view Thy cross,
Who all our griefs hast borne;
To look on Thee, whom we have pierced,
To look on Thee, and mourn:
While thus we mourn, may we rejoice;
And as Thy cross we see,
May each exclaim, in faith and hope,
"The Saviour died for me!"

William Cowper, 1779; *and Thomas Cotterill,* 1819.

Gethsemane.

229 Phil. iii. 10. "*The fellowship of His sufferings.*" Tune SIHOR. 77, 77, 77. OR RATISBON.

1 GO to dark Gethsemane,
Ye that feel the tempter's power;
Your Redeemer's conflict see;
Watch with Him one bitter hour;
Turn not from His griefs away;
Learn of Jesus Christ to pray.

2 Follow to the judgment-hall,
View the Lord of life arraigned;
Oh, the wormwood and the gall!
Oh, the pangs His soul sustained!
Shun not suffering, shame, or loss;
Learn of Him to bear the cross.

3 Calvary's mournful mountain climb;
There, adoring at His feet,
Mark that miracle of time,
God's own sacrifice complete.
"It is finished!" hear Him cry;
Learn of Jesus Christ to die.

4 Early hasten to the tomb,
Where they laid His breathless clay;
All is solitude and gloom:
Who hath taken Him away?
Christ is risen! He meets our eyes;
Saviour, teach us so to rise!

James Montgomery, 1825.

230

John xviii. 2. "*Jesus ofttimes resorted thither.*"

Tune SIHOR. 77, 77, 77.

1 JESUS, while He dwelt below,
As Divine historians say,
To a place would often go;
Near to Kedron's brook it lay:
In this place He loved to be,
And 'twas named Gethsemane.

2 'Twas a garden, as we read,
At the foot of Olivet;
Low, and proper to be made
The Redeemer's lone retreat;
When from noise He would be free,
Then He sought Gethsemane.

3 Thither, by their Master brought,
His disciples likewise came;
There the heavenly truths He taught
Often set their hearts on flame;
Therefore they, as well as He,
Visited Gethsemane.

4 Here they oft conversing sat,
Or might join with Christ in prayer:
Oh what blest devotion that,
When the Lord Himself is there!
All things to them seemed to' agree
To endear Gethsemane.

5 Here no strangers durst intrude;
But the Prince of Peace could sit,
Cheered with sacred solitude,
Wrapped in contemplation sweet;
Yet how little could they see
Why He chose Gethsemane!

PART II.

6 Full of love to man's lost race,
On His conflict much He thought;
This He knew the destined place,
And He loved the sacred spot;
Therefore 'twas He liked to be
Often in Gethsemane.

7 They, His followers, with the rest,
Had incurred the wrath Divine;
And their Lord, with pity pressed,
Longed to bear their load—and mine;
Love to them, and love to me,
Made Him love Gethsemane.

8 Many woes had He endured,
Many sore temptations met,
Patient, and to pains inured:
But the sorest trial yet
Was to be sustained in thee,
Gloomy, sad Gethsemane!

9 Came at length the dreadful night,
Vengeance with its iron rod
Stood, and with collected might
Bruised the harmless Lamb of God!
See, my soul, thy Saviour see,
Groaning in Gethsemane!

10 View Him in that olive-press,
Pouring forth His sacred blood!
View thy Maker's deep distress!
Hear the sighs and groans of God!
Then reflect what sin must be,
Gazing on Gethsemane!

SIHOR (River). [H. P. 158.]

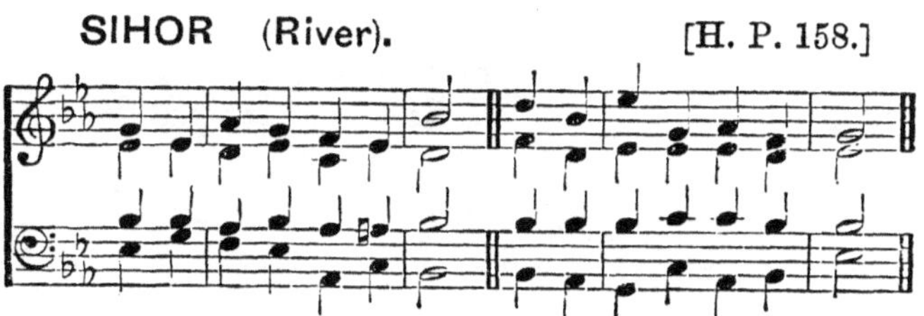

11 Oh what wonders love has done!
But how little understood!
God well knows, and God alone,
What produced that sweat of blood!
Who can thy deep wonders see?
Wonderful Gethsemane!

PART III.

12 There my God bore all my guilt:
This through grace can be believed;
But the horrors which He felt
Are too vast to be conceived;
None can penetrate through thee,
Doleful, dark Gethsemane!

13 Gloomy garden, on thy beds,
Washed by Kedron's waters foul,
Grow most rank and bitter weeds:
Think on these, my sinful soul!
Wouldst thou sin's dominion flee?
Call to mind Gethsemane!

14 Eden, from each flowery bed,
Did for man short sweetness breathe;
Soon, by Satan's counsel led,
Man wrought sin, and sin wrought death:
But of life the healing tree
Grows in rich Gethsemane.

15 Sins against a holy God;
Sins against His righteous laws;
Sins against His love, His blood;
Sins against His name and cause:
Sins immense as is the sea—
Hide me, O Gethsemane!

16 Saviour, all the stone remove
From my flinty frozen heart;
Thaw it with the beams of love,
Pierce it with the blood-dipped dart,
Wound the heart that wounded Thee;
Melt it in Gethsemane!

Joseph Hart, 1759.

CALVARY. [H. P. 164.]

231 Matt. xxvii. 54. "*Truly this was the Son of God.*" Tune CALVARY. 77, 77, 77, 77, 77.

1 BOUND upon the' accursèd tree,
Faint and bleeding, who is He?
By the eyes so pale and dim,
Streaming blood and writhing limb,
By the flesh with scourges torn,
By the crown of twisted thorn,
By the side so deeply pierced,
By the baffled burning thirst,
By the drooping death-dewed brow,
Son of Man! 'tis Thou, 'tis Thou!

2 Bound upon the' accursèd tree,
Dread and awful, who is He?
By the sun at noonday pale,
Shivering rocks and rending veil,
Earth that trembles at His doom,
By the saints who burst their tomb,
By Eden, promised ere He died
To the felon at His side,
Lord! our suppliant knees we bow,
Son of God! 'tis Thou, 'tis Thou!

PART II.

3 Bound upon the' accursèd tree,
Sad and dying, who is He?
By the last and bitter cry,
The ghost given up in agony;
By the lifeless body laid
In the chamber of the dead;
By the mourners come to weep
Where the bones of Jesus sleep;
Crucified! we know Thee now;
Son of Man! 'tis Thou, 'tis Thou!

4 Bound upon the' accursèd tree,
Dread and awful, who is He?
By the prayer for them that slew,
"Lord! they know not what they do!"
By the spoiled and empty grave,
By the souls He died to save,
By the conquest He hath won,
By the saints before His throne,
By the rainbow round His brow,
Son of God! 'tis Thou, 'tis Thou!

Dean Milman, D.D., 1827.

AUGSBURG. [H. P. 206.]

232 Isa. liii. 4. "*Stricken, smitten of God, and afflicted.*" Tune AUGSBURG. 87, 87. D.

1 "STRICKEN, smitten, and afflicted,"
See Him dying on the tree!
'Tis the Christ by man rejected!
Yes, my soul, 'tis He! 'tis He!
'Tis the long-expected Prophet,
David's Son, yet David's Lord:
Proofs I see sufficient of it:
'Tis a true and faithful word.

2 Tell me, ye who hear Him groaning,
Was there ever grief like His?
Friends through fear His cause disowning,
Foes insulting His distress.
Many hands were raised to wound Him,
None would interpose to save;
But the awful stroke that found Him
Was the stroke that justice gave.

3 Ye who think of sin but lightly,
Nor suppose the evil great,
Here may view its nature rightly,
Here its guilt may estimate.
Mark the Sacrifice appointed!
See who bears the awful load!
'Tis the Word, the Lord's Anointed,
Son of Man, and Son of God.

4 Here we have a firm foundation;
Here 's the refuge of the lost:
Christ 's the rock of our salvation;
His the name of which we boast.
Lamb of God for sinners wounded!
Sacrifice to cancel guilt!
None shall ever be confounded,
Who on Him their hopes have built!

Thomas Kelly, 1804.

233 John xix. 30. "*It is finished.*"
Tune St. Werbergh. 8 7, 8 7, 4 7.

1 HARK! the voice of love and mercy
Sounds aloud from Calvary!
See! it rends the rocks asunder,
Shakes the earth and veils the sky!
"It is finished!"
Hear the dying Saviour cry!

2 "It is finished!" Oh what pleasure
Do these precious words afford!
Heavenly blessings, without measure,
Flow to us from Christ the Lord:
"It is finished!"
Saints, the dying words record.

3 Finished! all the types and shadows
Of the ceremonial law!
Finished! all that God had promised;
Death and hell no more shall awe:
"It is finished!"
Saints, from hence your comfort draw.

4 Tune your harps anew, ye seraphs,
Join to sing the pleasing theme;
All on earth, and all in heaven,
Join to praise Emmanuel's name!
Hallelujah!
Glory to the bleeding Lamb!

Jonathan Evans, 1784.

ST. WERBERGH. [H. P. 304.]

HERMON. [H. P. 27.]

234 1 Cor. xv. 3. "*Christ died for our sins.*"
Tune Hermon. L. M. Or Gennesaret.

1 HE dies! the Friend of sinners dies;
Lo! Salem's daughters weep around:
A solemn darkness veils the skies,
A sudden trembling shakes the ground.

2 Come, saints, and trace in sad review
His grief who groaned beneath your load:
He gave His precious life for you,
The ransom of your soul, to God.

3 But, lo! the Lord forsakes the tomb;
In vain His foes forbid His rise;
Angelic legions guard Him home,
And shout Him welcome to the skies.

4 Cease, cease your tears, ye saints, and tell
How high your great Deliverer reigns;
Sing how He spoiled the hosts of hell,
And led His captive, Death, in chains.

5 Say, "Live for ever, wondrous King,
Born to redeem, and strong to save";
Then ask of Death, "Oh, where 's thy sting,
And where thy victory, boasting Grave?"

Ver. 1, *John Wesley; Isaac Watts, D.D.*, 1706.

235 Gal. vi. 14. "*Glory . . . in the cross of our Lord Jesus Christ.*"
Tune Hermon. L. M. Or Gethsemane.

1 WHEN I survey the wondrous cross
On which the Prince of Glory died,
My richest gain I count but loss,
And pour contempt on all my pride.

2 Forbid it, Lord, that I should boast,
Save in the death of Christ, my God;
All the vain things that charm me most,
I sacrifice them to His blood.

3 See from His head, His hands, His feet,
Sorrow and love flow mingled down!
Did e'er such love and sorrow meet,
Or thorns compose so rich a crown?

4 Were the whole realm of nature mine,
That were a present far too small;
Love so amazing, so Divine,
Demands my soul, my life, my all!

Isaac Watts, D.D., 1709.

HAMBURG. [H. P. 205.]

236 Heb. iv. 14. *"We have a great High Priest."* Tune HAMBURG. 87, 87. D.

1 GREAT High Priest, we view Thee stooping,
With our names upon Thy breast,
In the garden, groaning, drooping,
To the ground with horrors pressed.
Weeping angels stood confounded
To behold their Maker thus;
And can we remain unwounded,
When we know 'twas all for us?

2 On the cross Thy body broken
Cancels every penal tie;
Tempted souls, produce this token,
All demands to satisfy.
All is finished; do not doubt it;
But believe your dying Lord;
Never reason more about it;
Only take Him at His word.

3 Lord! we fain would trust Thee solely;
'Twas for us Thy blood was spilt,
Bruisèd Bridegroom, take us wholly;
Take and make us what Thou wilt.
Thou hast borne the bitter sentence
Passed on man's devoted race;
True belief and true repentance
Are Thy gifts, Thou God of Grace!

Joseph Hart, 1759.

MANNHEIM. [H. P. 303.]

237 Isa. xlv. 22. *"Look unto Me, and be ye saved."* Tune MANNHEIM. 87, 87. D. Or HAMBURG.

1 SEE the blessèd Saviour dying
On the cross for ruined man;
There the willing spotless Victim,
Working out redemption's plan;
Listen to His loving accents,
"Father, oh forgive!" He cries:
Hark, again He speaks, "'Tis finished!"
Ere He bows His head and dies.

2 With this cruel death before Him,
Every insult, pang, foreseen,
Nought could move Him from His purpose,
No dismay could intervene;
Yea, and through the contradiction
Nothing could His calmness move;
Oh! the wondrous depths eternal
Of His own almighty love.

3 Love which made Him, "Prince of Glory,"
Come to die, the "Sinner's Friend,"
Love beyond the reach of mortals'
Deepest thoughts to comprehend.
Sinner, make this love thy portion,
Slight not love so vast and free;
Still unblest, if unforgiven,
Come, the Saviour calleth thee!

Albert Midlane, 1865.

238 John xix. 16. *"They took Jesus, and led Him away."* Tune ST. MARY. C. M.

1 FROM Salem's gate advancing slow,
A stricken One behold!
What means this majesty of woe,
Mysterious, manifold?

2 Despised, rejected, wounded now,
Bowed 'neath a cross of shame,
With visage marred, with bleeding brow,
Know ye the Sufferer's name?

3 O Man of Sorrows!—Is this He
Who human form should wear,
And with transgressors numbered be,
Our mighty sins to bear?

ST. MARY'S; *or,* **HACKNEY.** [H. P. 73.]

4 Yes, now I know 'tis He! 'tis He!
Christ Jesus, God's dear Son;
Wrapt in mortality to die
For crimes that I have done.

5 O Son of God, who unto death
Hast loved, so lovèd me,
Henceforth be all my life and breath
Devoted unto Thee.

William Batty, 1757.—*ver.* 2, 3, 5, *F. R. H.*

239

1 Thess. iv. 14. *"We believe that Jesus died."*
Tune Stephanas. 8 3, 8 3, 8 8 8, 3 3.

STEPHANAS. [H. P. 168.]

1 THERE is a word I fain would speak;
Jesus died.
O eyes that weep, and hearts that break:
Jesus died.
No music from the quivering string
Could such sweet sounds of rapture bring,
Oh! may I always love to sing,
Jesus died, Jesus died.

2 Though Satan seeks my soul to have:
Jesus died.
Yes, Jesus died my soul to save,
Jesus died.
The holy Lord, the bleeding Lamb,
The Crucified, the Great I Am:
There's life in every lovely name.
Jesus died, Jesus died.

3 And now I need not fear to pray:
Jesus died.
He washes all my sins away:
Jesus died.
He washes all my sins away,
He is the Life, the Truth, the Way;
And now to all men I can say,
Jesus died, Jesus died.

4 'Twill soothe my heart with death in view—
Jesus died.
And bear me that cold river through:
Jesus died.
That word will heaven's bright gate unclose,
Release me from my mortal woes,
And bear me where Thy glory glows:
Jesus died, Jesus died.

Paxton Hood, 1862.

MELCOMBE. [H. P. 24.]

240

Rom. vi. 8. *"If we be dead with Christ, we believe that we shall also live with Him."* Tune Melcombe. L. M.

1 WE sing the praise of Him who died,
Of Him who died upon the cross;
The sinner's hope let men deride,
For this we count the world but loss.

2 Inscribed upon the cross we see,
In shining letters, "God is love."
He bears our sins upon the tree,
He brings us mercy from above.

3 The cross! it takes our guilt away,
It holds the fainting spirit up;
It cheers with hope the gloomy day,
And sweetens every bitter cup.

4 It makes the coward spirit brave,
And nerves the feeble arm for fight:
It takes the terror from the grave,
And gilds the bed of death with light.

5 The balm of life, the cure of woe,
The measure and the pledge of love;
The sinner's refuge here below,
The angel's theme in heaven above.

Thomas Kelly, 1815.

H

FRENCH; *or*, DUNDEE. [H. P. 65.]

241 Zech. xiii. 1. "*A Fountain opened for sin.*" Tune FRENCH. C. M. Or LONDON NEW.

1 THERE is a fountain filled with blood
Drawn from Emmanuel's veins;
And sinners plunged beneath that flood
Lose all their guilty stains.

2 The dying thief rejoiced to see
That fountain in his day;
And there have I, though vile as he,
Washed all my sins away!

3 Dear dying Lamb, Thy precious blood
Shall never lose its power
Till all the ransomed church of God
Be saved to sin no more.

4 E'er since, by faith, I saw the stream
Thy flowing wounds supply,
Redeeming love has been my theme,
And shall be till I die.

5 Then in a nobler, sweeter song,
I'll sing Thy power to save,
When this poor lisping, stammering tongue
Lies silent in the grave!

6 Lord, I believe Thou hast prepared,
Unworthy though I be,
For me a blood-bought free reward,
A golden harp for me.

7 'Tis strung and tuned for endless years,
And formed by power Divine,
To sound in God the Father's ears
No other name but Thine!

William Cowper, 1772.

AVEN (Plain of). [H. P. 79.]

242 1 John i. 7. "*The blood of Jesus Christ His Son cleanseth us from all sin.*" Tune AVEN. S. M.

1 NOT all the blood of beasts,
On Jewish altars slain,
Could give the guilty conscience peace,
Or wash away the stain.

2 But Christ, the heavenly Lamb,
Takes all our sins away;
A Sacrifice of nobler name,
And richer blood than they.

3 My faith would lay her hand
On that dear head of Thine,
While like a penitent I stand,
And there confess my sin.

4 My soul looks back to see
The burdens Thou didst bear
When hanging on the cursèd tree,
And hopes her guilt was there.

5 Believing, we rejoice
To see the curse remove;
We bless the Lamb with cheerful voice,
And sing His bleeding love!

Isaac Watts, D.D., 1709.

CARMEL (Mount). [H. P. 69.]

243 Heb. ix. 22. "*Without shedding of blood is no remission.*" Tune CARMEL. C. M.

1 ALAS! and did my Saviour bleed,
And did my Sovereign die?
Would He devote that sacred head
For such a worm as I?

2 Was it for crimes that I had done
He groaned upon the tree?
Amazing pity! grace unknown!
And love beyond degree!

3 Well might the sun in darkness hide,
And shut his glories in,
When God, the mighty Maker, died
For man the creature's sin.

4 Thus might I hide my blushing face,
While His dear cross appears,
Dissolve my heart in thankfulness,
And melt my eyes to tears.

5 But drops of grief can ne'er repay
The debt of love I owe;
Here, Lord, I give myself away;
'Tis all that I can do!

Isaac Watts, D.D., 1709.

See Hymn 965.

(11) THE BURIAL OF CHRIST.

Easter Eve.

244 John xix. 42. "*There laid they Jesus.*"
Tune REDHEAD. 77, 77, 77.

REDHEAD. [H. P. 288.]

1 RESTING from His work to-day,
In the tomb the Saviour lay;
Still He slept, from head to feet
Shrouded in the winding sheet,
Lying in the rock alone,
Hidden by the sealèd stone.

2 Late at even there was seen,
Watching long, the Magdalene;
Early, ere the break of day,
Sorrowful, she took her way
To the holy garden glade,
Where her buried Lord was laid.

3 So with Thee, till life shall end,
I would solemn vigil spend;
Let me hew Thee, Lord, a shrine
In this rocky heart of mine,
Where, in pure embalmèd cell,
None but Thou may ever dwell.

4 Myrrh and spices will I bring,
True affection's offering:
Close the door from sight and sound
Of the busy world around;
And in patient watch remain
Till my Lord appear again!

Thomas Whytehead, 1812.

---

245 Matt. xxviii. 6. "*Come, see the place where the Lord lay.*" Tune CARMEL. C. M. Or FARRANT.

1 COME, see the place where Jesus lies:
The last sad rite is done;
With aching hearts, and weeping eyes,
The faithful few are gone.

2 They washed with tears each bloody trace
On those dear limbs that lay;
Then spread the napkin o'er His face,
And turned and went away.

3 By the sealed stone, with grounded spears,
The guards their vigil keep:
They wist not other eyes than theirs
Watch o'er the Saviour's sleep.

4 All heaven above, all hell beneath—
Bright hope, and blank dismay—
Look on, to see if grisly death
Can hold his mighty prey.

5 Now, grisly death, thy powers combine!
Now gird thee to the strife!
Yet needs there stronger arm than thine
To keep the Lord of life.

6 'Tis done! O death, thy Victor-guest
Hath smoothed thy visage grim!
O grave! thou place of blessèd rest
To all who sleep in Him!

Thomas Edwards Hankinson, **1843.**

PHILADELPHIA. (HYMN CHANT.) [H. P. VII.]

246 1 Cor. xv. 4. "*He was buried.*" Tune, Hymn Chant PHILADELPHIA. 447, 76.

1 SO rest—my Rest!
Thou ever blest!
Thy grave with sinners making:
By Thy precious death, from sin
My dead soul awaking!

2 Here hast Thou lain,
After much pain,
Life of my life reposing!
Round Thee now a rock-hewn grave,
Rock of Ages, closing.

3 Breath of all breath!
I know from death
Thou wilt my soul awaken!
Wherefore should I dread the grave,
Or my faith be shaken?

4 To me the tomb
Is but a room,
Where I lie down in Jesus!
Who by death hath conquered death,
Safely there receives us!

5 The body dies,
(Nought else) and lies
In dust, until victorious
From the grave, it shall arise,
Beautiful and glorious!

6 Meantime I will,
My Jesus, still
Deep in my bosom lay Thee,
Musing on Thy death; in death
Be with me, I pray Thee.

S. Frank, 1710; *Richard Massie (tr.),* 1856.

KENT. [H. P. 63.]

247 Matt. xiii. 35. *"I will open My mouth in parables."* Tune KENT. C. M.

1 UPON the sixth day of the week
The first man had his birth,
In God's own image bright and pure
Created from the earth.

2 Upon the sixth day of the week
The Second Adam died,
And by the Second Adam's death
Man was revivified.

3 Upon the seventh day of the week
God from His works did rest,
And on that holy Sabbath day
The works of God were blessed.

4 Upon the seventh day of the week
Christ in the grave did rest.
The grave is now a holy place;
A sabbath for the blest.

5 By tasting the forbidden tree
Man fell in Paradise;
Upon the tree Christ tasted death,
And by His death we rise.

6 Christ in a garden buried lay,
Which spring flowers did adorn;
And there our Resurrection bloomed
On the bright Easter morn.

7 The grave itself a garden is,
Where loveliest flowers abound:
For Christ our amaranthine Life
Sprang from the holy ground.

8 He by the Spirit once was born
Pure from the Virgin's womb,
And by the Spirit once again
Born from the virgin tomb.

9 Oh give us grace to die to sin,
That we, O Lord, may have
A holy, happy rest with Thee,
A sabbath, in the grave.

10 Oh may we buried be with Thee,
And with Thee, Lord, arise
To an eternal Easter-day
Of glory in the skies!

Bishop Christopher Wordsworth, 1862.

(12) THE RESURRECTION OF CHRIST.

Easter.

248 Luke xxiv. 34. *"The Lord is risen indeed."*
Tune PISGAH. 7 7, 7 7. Or LUBECK.

1 JESUS Christ is risen to-day—
Our triumphant holy day;
Who did once upon the cross
Suffer to redeem our loss. Hallelujah!

2 Hymns of praise then let us sing
Unto Christ our heavenly King;
Who endured the cross and grave,
Sinners to redeem and save. Hallelujah!

3 But the pains which He endured,
Our salvation have procured:
Now above the sky He's king,
Where the angels ever sing. Hallelujah!

4 Sing we to our God above
Praise eternal as His love;
Praise Him, all ye heavenly host,
Father, Son, and Holy Ghost. Hallelujah!

From Latin Hymn of 15th Century.

PISGAH (Mount). [H. P. 137.]

Hal - le - lu - jah, Hal - le - lu - jah!

LUBECK. [H. P. 139.]

249 Mark xvi. 6. *"He is risen."*
Tune LUBECK. 7 7, 7 7. Or ABILENE.

1 "CHRIST, the Lord, is risen to-day,"
Sons of men and angels say:
Raise your songs and triumphs high;
Sing, ye heavens! thou earth, reply. Hallelujah!

2 Love's redeeming work is done,
Fought the fight, the battle won;
Lo! our sun's eclipse is o'er;
Lo! he sets in blood no more. Hallelujah!

3 Vain the stone, the watch, the seal;
Christ hath burst the gates of hell;
Death in vain forbids His rise;
Christ hath opened Paradise, Hallelujah!

4 Lives again our glorious King!
Where, O Death! is now thy sting?
Once He died, our souls to save;
Where thy victory, O Grave? Hallelujah!

5 Soar we now where Christ hath led,
Following our exalted Head;
Made like Him, like Him we rise;
Ours the cross, the grave, the skies. Hallelujah!

6 Hail the Lord of earth and heaven!
Praise to Thee from both be given;
Thee we greet triumphant now,
Hail, the Resurrection, Thou!
Hallelujah! Amen.

Charles Wesley, 1739.

Hal - le - lu - jah, Hal - le - lu - jah!

SALMON (Hill of). [H. P. 167.]

250

Rev. i. 18. *"I am He that liveth."*
Tune SALMON. 7 8, 7 8.

1 JESUS lives! no longer now
Can thy terrors, Death, appal us;
Jesus lives! by this we know
Thou, O Grave, canst not enthral us.
Alleluia!

2 Jesus lives! henceforth is death
But the gate of life immortal;
This shall calm our trembling breath,
When we pass its gloomy portal.
Alleluia!

3 Jesus lives! for us He died:
Then alone to Jesus living,
Pure in heart may we abide,
Glory to our Saviour giving. Alleluia!

4 Jesus lives! our hearts know well
Nought from us His love can sever;
Life, nor death, nor powers of hell
Tear us from His keeping ever. Alleluia!

5 Jesus lives! to Him the throne
Over all the world is given:
May we go where He is gone,
Rest and reign with Him in heaven. Alleluia!

6 Praise the Father; praise the Son,
Who to us new life hath given;
Praise the Spirit, Three in One,
All in earth and all in heaven. Alleluia!

C. F. Gellert, 1757; *F. E. Cox* (*tr.*), 1841.

251

Ps. cxviii. 24. *"This is the day which the Lord hath made, we will rejoice and be glad in it."*
Tune CHALDEA. 8 8 8.

1 O SONS and daughters, let us sing!
The King of Heaven, the glorious King,
O'er death to-day rose triumphing. Alleluia!

2 On Sunday morn, at break of day,
The faithful women went their way
To seek the tomb where Jesus lay. Alleluia!

3 An angel clad in white they see,
Who sat and spake unto the three,
"Your Lord doth go to Galilee." Alleluia!

4 That night the' apostles met in fear;
Amidst them came the Lord most dear,
And said, "My peace be on all here." Alleluia!

5 When Didymus the tidings heard,
He doubted if it were the Lord,
Until He came and spake the word: Alleluia!

6 "My piercèd side, O Thomas, see;
My hands, My feet, I show to thee;
Nor faithless, but believing be." Alleluia!

7 No longer Thomas then denied;
He saw the feet, the hands, the side;
"Thou art my Lord and God," he cried. Alleluia!

8 How blest are they who do not see,
And yet whose faith is firm in Thee,
For they shall live eternally. Alleluia!

CHALDEA. [H. P. 216.]

9 On this most holy day of days,
To Thee our heart and voice we raise
In laud, and jubilee, and praise. Alleluia!

10 Glory to Father, and to Son
Who has for us the victory won,
And Holy Ghost; blest Three in One. Alleluia!

Twelfth Century; tr. John Mason Neale, D.D., 1861.

252 Luke xxiv. 27. "*He expounded in all the Scriptures the things concerning Himself.*"

Tune MEROM. 887. D.

1 IN Thy glorious Resurrection,
Lord, we see a world's erection,
Man in Thee is glorified.
Bliss, for which the patriarchs panted,
Joys, by holy psalmists chanted,
Now in Thee are verified!

2 Oracles of former ages,
Veiled in dim prophetic pages,
Now lie open to the sight;
Now the types, which glimmered darkling
In the twilight gloom, are sparkling
In the blaze of noonday light.

3 Isaac from the wood is risen;
Joseph issues from the prison;
See the Paschal Lamb which saves;
Israel through the sea is landed,
Pharaoh and his hosts are stranded,
And o'erwhelmèd in the waves.

4 See the cloudy pillar leading,
Rock refreshing, manna feeding;
Joshua fights and Moses prays;
See the lifted wave-sheaf, cheering
Pledge of harvest-fruits appearing,
Joyful dawn of happy days.

PART II.

5 Samson see at night uptearing
Gaza's brazen gates, and bearing
To the top of Hebron's hill;
Jonah comes from stormy surges,
From his three-days' grave emerges,
Bids beware of coming ill.

6 So Thy Resurrection's glory
Sheds a light on ancient story;
And it casts a forward ray,
Beacon light of solemn warning,
To the dawn of that great Morning
Ushering in the Judgment day.

7 Ever since Thy death and rising
Thou the nations art baptizing
In Thy death's similitude;
Dead to sin, and ever dying,
And our members mortifying,
May we walk with life renewed!

8 Forth from Thy first Easter going,
Sundays are for ever flowing
Onward to a boundless sea;
Lord, may they for Thee prepare us,
On a holy river bear us
To a calm eternity!

Bishop Christopher Wordsworth, 1862.

253 John xi. 25. "*I am the Resurrection, and the Life.*"

Tune MAHANAIM. 76, 76. D.

1 ALL hail, Thou Resurrection!
All hail, Thou Life and Light!
All hail, Thou Self Perfection,
Sole Source of grace and might!
Thy church, O Christ, now greets Thee,
Uprising from the grave
And every eye that meets Thee
Beholds Thee strong to save.

2 All hail, belovèd Jesus!
For Thou, indeed, art He
Whose death from sin now frees us,
Whose life brings liberty.
Hence, let our faith embrace Thee
With warmest hand and eye,
And then delight to trace Thee
Ascending up on high.

3 O Saviour, come in glory
To raise Thy holy dead,
And end redemption's story,
With crowns upon Thy head.
Then robed in white before Thee,
Without one stain or tear,
Shall all Thy saints adore Thee,
Midst wonder, love, and fear.

William Henry Havergal, 1867.

SHEN (The Rock). [H. P. 201.]

254

1 Pet. i. 3. "*A lively hope by the Resurrection.*" Tune SHEN. 15 15, 15 15.

1 HALLELUJAH! Hallelujah! Hearts to heaven and voices raise!
Sing to God a hymn of gladness, sing to God a hymn of praise!
He who on the cross a Victim for the world's salvation bled,
Jesus Christ, the King of Glory, now is risen from the dead.

2 Now the iron bars are broken, Christ from death to life is born,
Glorious life, and life immortal, on this holy Easter morn:
Christ has triumphed, and we conquer by His mighty enterprise,
We with Him to life eternal by His resurrection rise.

3 Christ is risen, Christ the first-fruits of the holy harvest-field,
Which will all its full abundance at His second coming yield;
Then the golden ears of harvest will their heads before Him wave,
Ripened by His glorious sunshine, from the furrows of the grave.

4 Christ is risen; we are risen! Shed upon us heavenly grace,
Rain and dew and gleams of glory from the brightness of Thy face,
That we, Lord, with hearts in heaven, here on earth may fruitful be,
And by angel-hands be gathered, and be ever safe with Thee.

5 Hallelujah! Hallelujah! Glory be to God on high;
Hallelujah to the Saviour, who has gained the victory;
Hallelujah to the Spirit, Fount of Love and Sanctity;
Hallelujah! Hallelujah! to the Triune Majesty!

Bishop Christopher Wordsworth, 1862.

255

Acts xvii. 3. "*Christ must needs have . . risen again.*"

Tune REPHAIM. 77, 77. Or LUBECK.

1 CHRIST the Lord is risen again,
Christ hath broken every chain;
Hark, angelic voices cry,
Singing evermore on high— Hallelujah!

2 He who gave for us His life,
Who for us endured the strife,
Is our Paschal Lamb to-day;
We too sing for joy and say Hallelujah!

3 He who bore all pain and loss,
Comfortless upon the cross,
Lives in glory now on high,
Pleads for us and hears our cry. Hallelujah!

4 He who slumbered in the grave
Is exalted now to save;
Now through Christendom it rings
That the Lamb is King of kings. Hallelujah!

5 Now He bids us tell abroad
How the lost may be restored,
How the penitent forgiven,
How we too may enter heaven. Hallelujah!

6 Thou our Paschal Lamb indeed;
Christ, Thy ransomed people feed;
Take our sins and guilt away,
Let us sing by night and day, Hallelujah!

Michael Weiss, 1531; *C. Winkworth (tr.),* 1858.

REPHAIM (Valley of). [H. P. 141.]

Hal - le - lu - jah, Hal - le - lu - jah!

256 Mark xvi. 6. *"Behold the place where they laid Him."*

Tune Regent Square. 87, 87, 47.

1 COME, ye saints, look here and wonder,
See the place where Jesus lay;
He has burst His bands asunder;
He has borne our sins away;
Joyful tidings!
Yes, the Lord is risen to-day.

2 Jesus triumphs! sing ye praises:
By His death He overcame:
Thus the Lord His glory raises;
Thus He fills His foes with shame:
Sing ye praises!
Praises to the Victor's name.

3 Jesus triumphs! countless legions
Come from heaven to meet their King:
Soon in yonder blessèd regions
They shall join His praise to sing.
Songs eternal
Shall through heaven's high arches ring.

Thomas Kelly, 1809.

---

257 Eph. iv. 8. *"He led captivity captive."*

Tune Darwell. 6666, 88.

1 THE happy morn is come;
Triumphant o'er the grave,
The Saviour leaves the tomb,
Omnipotent to save:
Captivity is captive led;
For Jesus liveth, that was dead.

2 Who now accuseth them,
For whom their Ransom died?
Who now shall those condemn
Whom God hath justified?
Captivity is captive led;
For Jesus liveth, that was dead.

3 Christ hath the ransom paid;
The glorious work is done;
On Him our help is laid,
By Him our victory won:
Captivity is captive led;
For Jesus liveth, that was dead!

Thomas Haweis, LL.D., 1792.

---

258 Matt. xxviii. 8. *"They departed from the sepulchre with great joy."* Tune Hermas. 65, 65. D.

1 "WELCOME, happy morning!" Age to age shall say;
Hell to-day is vanquished, heaven is won to-day!
Lo! the Dead is living, God for evermore!
Him their true Creator all His works adore!
"Welcome, happy morning!" Age to age shall say;
Hell to-day is vanquished, heaven is won to-day!

2 Earth with joy confesses, clothing her for spring,
All good gifts returned with her returning King;
Bloom in every meadow, leaves on every bough,
Speak His sorrow ended, hail His triumph now.
Welcome, happy morning! etc.

3 Months in due succession, days of lengthening light,
Hours and passing moments praise Thee in their flight;
Brightness of the morning, sky, and fields, and sea,
Vanquisher of darkness, bring their praise to Thee!
Welcome, happy morning! etc.

4 Maker and Redeemer, Life and Health of all,
Thou, from heaven beholding human nature's fall,
Of the Father's Godhead true and only Son,
Manhood to deliver, manhood didst put on.
Welcome, happy morning! etc.

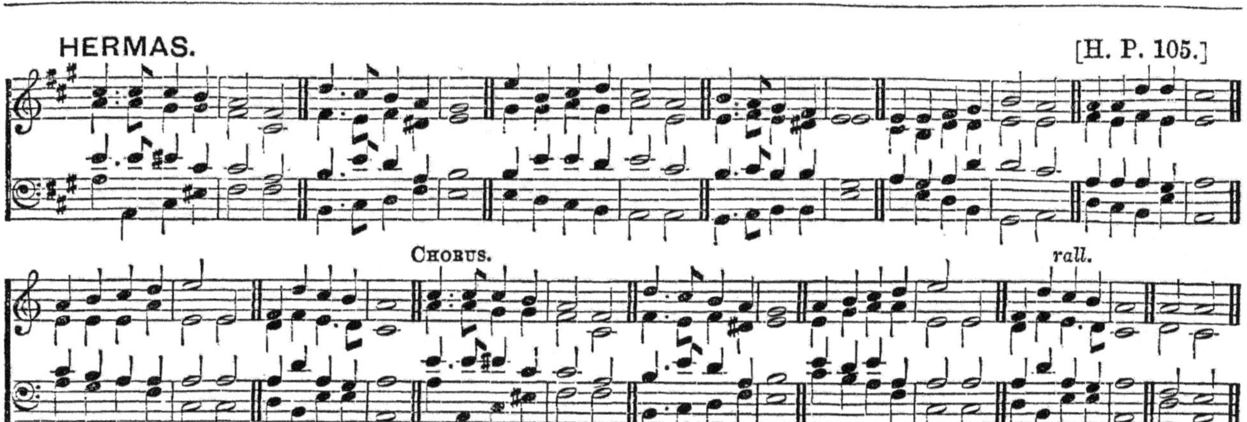

5 Thou, of life the Author, death didst undergo,
Tread the path of darkness, saving strength to show;
Come then, True and Faithful, now fulfil Thy word;
'Tis Thine own third morning; rise, my buried Lord!
Welcome, happy morning! etc.

6 Loose the hearts long prisoned, bound with Satan's chain;
All that now is fallen raise to life again;
Show Thy face in brightness, bid the nations see;
Bring again our daylight: day returns with Thee.
Welcome, happy morning! etc.

Venantius Fortunatus, Sixth Century; John Ellerton (tr.), 1869.

259

John xx. 20. "*Then were the disciples glad.*"

Tune Magdalene College. 886. D.

1 COME, see the place where Jesus lay,
And hear angelic watchers say,
"He lives who once was slain;
Why seek the living 'midst the dead?
Remember how the Saviour said
That He would rise again."

2 O joyful sound! O glorious hour!
When Jesus, by almighty power,
Revived and left the grave.
In all His works behold Him great!
Before, almighty to create!
Almighty now to save!

3 "The First Begotten from the dead,"
Behold Him risen, His people's Head!
To make their life secure.
They too, like Him, shall yield their breath,
Like Him, shall burst the bands of death:
Their resurrection sure.

4 Why should His people now be sad?
None have such reason to be glad,
As reconciled to God.
Jesus, the mighty Saviour, lives;
To them eternal life He gives,
The purchase of His blood.

5 Why should His people fear the grave?
Since Jesus will their spirits save,
And raise their bodies too.
What though this earthly house shall fail?
Almighty power will yet prevail,
And build it up anew.

6 Ye ransomed, let your praise resound,
And in your Master's work abound,
Steadfast, immovable:
Be sure your labour 's not in vain;
Your bodies shall be raised again,
No more corruptible!

Thomas Kelly, 1809. (*a.*)

AVEN (Plain of). [H. P. 79.]

260 Luke xxiv. 34. "*The Lord is risen indeed.*" Tune AVEN. S. M.

1 "THE Lord is risen indeed!"
And are the tidings true?
Yes, they beheld the Saviour bleed,
And saw Him living too.

2 "The Lord is risen indeed,"
Then Justice asks no more;
Mercy and Truth are now agreed,
Who stood opposed before.

3 "The Lord is risen indeed,"
Then is His work performed,
The captive Surety now is freed,
And death, our foe, disarmed.

4 "The Lord is risen indeed,"
Then hell has lost his prey;
With Him is risen the ransomed seed,
To reign in endless day.

5 "The Lord is risen indeed,"
He lives to die no more;
He lives, the sinner's cause to plead,
Whose curse and shame He bore.

6 "The Lord is risen indeed,"
This yields my soul a plea;
He bore the punishment decreed,
And satisfied for me.

7 "The Lord is risen indeed";
Attending angels, hear,
Up to the courts of heaven with speed
The joyful tidings bear.

8 Then take your golden lyres,
And strike each cheerful chord;
Join, all the bright celestial choirs,
To sing our risen Lord!

Thomas Kelly, 1804.

---

261 Ps. lvii. 8. "*Awake up, my glory.*" Tune CHALDEA. 888.

1 THE strife is o'er, the battle done,
The triumph of the Lord is won,
Oh! let the song of praise be sung— Alleluia!

2 The powers of death have done their worst,
And Jesus hath His foes dispersed;
Let shouts of praise and joy outburst— Alleluia!

3 On that third morn He rose again,
In glorious majesty to reign;
Oh! let us swell the joyful strain— Alleluia!

4 He closed the yawning gates of hell,
The bars from heaven's high portals fell;
Let songs of joy His triumphs tell— Alleluia!

5 Lord, by the stripes which wounded Thee,
From death's dread sting Thy servants free,
That we may live and sing to Thee, Alleluia!

Twelfth Century; tr. Francis Pott, 1860.

CHALDEA. [H. P. 216.]

Sunday before Ascension Day.

HYMN CHANT (Troyte's). [H. P. 311.]

262 John xiv. 18. "*I will not leave you comfortless.*" Tune TROYTE'S HYMN CHANT. 888, 4.

1 THOU bidd'st us "visit in distress
The widow and the fatherless";
And wilt Thou leave us comfortless?
Wilt Thou depart?

2 Wilt Thou, O Lord, Thy church forsake?
Must she a widow's garment take?
Wilt Thou Thy children orphans make?
O grief of heart!

3 No: Christ will visit in distress
The widow and the fatherless;
Seeming to leave you comfortless,
He loves you most.

4 For He departs, that He may send
Another Comforter and Friend,
To tarry with you till the end:
The Holy Ghost.

5 At Thy first birth, Thou, Lord, didst wait,
And forty days from it didst date,
And then Thy Zion's temple gate
Did welcome Thee.

6 Old age with joy saw Thee appear,
And widowhood found comfort there;
Perhaps the doves, then offered, were
A prophecy.

7 And now the fortieth from Thy birth,
To endless life, from womb of earth,
Will be a day of joy and mirth
In realms above.

8 For though Thy earthly course will end,
To Zion's gates Thou wilt ascend,
To be our great High Priest, and send
The Heavenly Dove.

9 Why then this sorrow and dismay?
'Tis good that He should go away;
He goes, that He for you may pray,
And never cease;

10 He goes as man, that you may see
By faith His present Deity;
That here the Comforter may be,
And give you peace!

Bishop Christopher Wordsworth, 1862.

Rogation Days, being the Monday, Tuesday, and Wednesday before Ascension Day.

SMYRNA. (Hymn Chant.) *Double Counterpoint.* [H. P. No. III.]

263 1 Tim. ii. 1, 2. *"I exhort . . that supplications, prayers, intercessions, and giving of thanks, be made for all men."*

Tune, Hymn Chant Smyrna. S. M. Or Armageddon.

1 FATHER, we humbly pray
To Thee in whom we live;
Our countless sins, for Jesu's sake,
Forgive, O Lord, forgive!

2 We have unthankful been
For all Thy tender care;
Thy indignation we deserve;
But spare, O Father, spare!

3 The creatures of Thy hand
Made for Thy glory are;
But we Thy creatures have abused:
Spare us, O Father, spare!

4 From plague and pestilence,
From famine, fire, and sword,
From storm and flood, from dearth and drought,
Deliver us, O Lord!

5 From hard and stubborn hearts,
That scorn Thy holy Word,
From discord, strife, and heresy,
Deliver us, O Lord!

6 With genial rains and dews
Enrich the circling year,
With golden sunshine and fresh breeze;
Hear us, O Father, hear!

7 Sheepfolds and garners fill,
The homestead and the stall;
Orchards and gardens crown with fruits,
Maker and Lord of all!

Part II.

8 Love in our households breathe;
Hearts ready to obey
As in Thy sight, and as to Thee,
Give us, O Lord, we pray.

9 Bless, Lord, our gracious Queen,
With Thy best bounties bless;
Grant her a long and glorious reign
In peace and quietness.

10 Bless, Lord, Thy holy Church,
With heavenly graces bless,
That it may flourish and abound
In love and godliness.

11 Bishops and Clergy bless;
Holy, and grave, and wise,
Faithful and zealous, may they be
In all their ministries.

12 Our ancient minsters bless,
Where deep-toned organs peal;
And village churches among trees,
Where humble peasants kneel.

13 Our schools of learning bless,
Our Colleges and Halls;
May piety and wisdom dwell
Alway within their walls!

14 Counsel in Senates give,
Justice and Law maintain;
And make contentment in all hearts
And loyalty to reign.

Part III.

15 Our Fleets and Armies bless
With courage from on high;
And in all just and righteous wars
Give them the victory.

16 The Widow desolate,
The Children fatherless,
All who in grief and sorrow are,
O comfort, Lord, and bless.

17 The erring and in sin,
All, Lord, who from Thee stray,
Bring them, O bring them back again,
To Thy most holy way.

18 All who to heathen climes
Go forth and preach Thy Word,
And bear glad tidings of good things,
Speed them, and help them, Lord!

19 May all who sit in gloom
Thy glorious light behold;
One faith, one Father, and one Lord,
One Shepherd and one fold!

20 So may we all with Christ
To highest heaven ascend,
And Hallelujahs sing to Thee
Through ages without end!

Bishop Christopher Wordsworth, 1862.

SHEN (The Rock). [H. P. 201.]

(13) THE ASCENSION OF CHRIST.

264 Ps. xxiv. 7. "*The King of Glory shall come in.*"
Tune SHEN. 15 15, 15 15.

1 SEE the Conqueror mounts in triumph, see the King in royal state,
Riding on the clouds His chariot, to His heavenly palace gate;
Hark, the quires of angel voices joyful Hallelujahs [sing,
And the portals high are lifted, to receive their heavenly King.

2 Who is this that comes in glory, with the trump of jubilee?
Lord of battles, God of armies, He has gained the [victory;
He who on the cross did suffer, He who from the grave arose,
He has vanquished sin and Satan, He by death has spoiled His foes.

3 While He raised His hands in blessing, He was parted from His friends;
While their eager eyes behold Him, He upon the clouds ascends;
He who walked with God, and pleased Him, preaching truth and doom to come,
He, our Enoch, is translated to His everlasting home.

4 Now our heavenly Aaron enters, with His blood, within the veil;
Joshua now is come to Canaan, and the kings before Him quail;
Now He plants the tribes of Israel in their promised resting place; [grace.
Now our great Elijah offers double portion of His

5 Thou hast raised our human nature in the clouds to God's right hand,
There we sit in heavenly places, there with Thee in glory stand;
Jesus reigns, adored by angels; man with God is on the throne;
Mighty Lord, in Thine Ascension we by faith behold our own!

PART II.

6 Holy Ghost, Illuminator, shed Thy beams upon our eyes;
Help us to look up with Stephen, and to see beyond the skies,
Where the Son of man in glory standing is at God's right hand,
Beckoning on His martyr army, succouring His faithful band.

7 See Him, who is gone before us, heavenly mansions to prepare,
See Him, who is ever pleading for us, with prevailing prayer;
See Him, who with sound of trumpet and with His angelic train,
Summoning the world to judgment, on the clouds will come again!

8 Lift us up from earth to heaven, give us wings of faith and love,
Gales of holy aspirations wafting us to realms above;
That with hearts and minds uplifted, we with Christ our Lord may dwell,
Where He sits enthroned in glory, in His heavenly citadel.

9 So at last, when He appeareth, we from out our graves may spring,
With our youth renewed like eagles, flocking round our heavenly King,
Caught up on the clouds of heaven, and may meet Him in the air,
Rise to realms where He is reigning, and may reign for ever there.

10 Glory be to God the Father, glory be to God the Son,
Dying, risen, ascending for us, who the heavenly realm has won; [Three,
Glory to the Holy Spirit; to one God in Persons
Glory both in earth and heaven, glory, endless glory be.

Bishop Christopher Wordsworth, 1862.

265 Eph. iv. 8. "*He ascended up on high.*" Tune HERMAS. 6 5, 6 5. D.

1 GOLDEN harps are sounding,
Angel voices ring,
Pearly gates are opened,—
Opened for the King;
Christ, the King of Glory,
Jesus, King of Love,
Is gone up in triumph
To His throne above.

2 He who came to save us,
He who bled and died,
Now is crowned with glory
At His Father's side.
Never more to suffer,
Never more to die:
Jesus, King of Glory,
Is gone up on high.

3 Praying for His children,
In that blessèd place,
Calling them to glory,
Sending them His grace:
His bright home preparing,
Faithful ones, for you;
Jesus ever liveth,
Ever loveth too.

Chorus.—All His work is ended, Joyfully we sing,
Jesus hath ascended! Glory to our King!

Frances Ridley Havergal, 1871.

266 Ps. xxiv. 8. "*Who is this King of Glory?*" Tune Eden. C. M.

1 LIFT up your heads, eternal
Unfold, to entertain [gates;
The King of glory—see, He comes,
With His celestial train!
Who is the King of glory? Who?
The Lord for strength renowned:
In battle mighty; o'er His foes
Eternal Victor crowned!

2 Lift up your heads, ye heavenly
In state to entertain [gates,
The King of glory—lo! He comes,
With all His ransomed train!
Who is the King of glory? Who?
The Lord of hosts renowned;
Triumphant over sin and death,
Eternal Victor crowned!

Tate and Brady, 1696.

267 Luke xxiv. 51. "*While He blessed them, He was parted from them, and carried up into heaven.*"

Tune Pisgah. 7 7, 7 7. Or Lubeck.

1 HAIL the day that sees Him rise,
Parted from our wishful eyes!
Christ, awhile to mortals given,
Re-ascends His native heaven:

2 There the glorious triumph waits;
Lift your heads, eternal gates!
Wide unfold the radiant scene,
Take the King of glory in.

3 See, the heaven its Lord receives!
Yet He loves the earth He leaves;
Though returning to His throne,
Still He calls mankind His own.

4 See, He lifts His hands above!
See, He shows the prints of love!
Hark, His gracious lips bestow
Blessings on His church below!

5 Still for us He intercedes;
Still His death prevailing pleads;
Near Himself prepares our place,
Harbinger of human race.

6 What, though parted from our sight,
Far beyond yon azure height!
Grant our hearts may thither rise,
Following Thee beyond the skies.

7 Ever upward let us move,
On the wings of faith and love;
Looking when our Lord shall come,
Longing for our heavenly home.

8 There we shall with Thee remain,
Partners of Thine endless reign;
There Thy face unclouded see,
Find our heaven of heavens in Thee!

Charles Wesley, 1739. (*a.*)

268 Heb. ii. 9. *"Crowned with glory and honour."*
Tune PHARPAR. 77, 77, 77. Or NASSAU.

1 GLORY, glory to our King!
Crowns unfading wreathe His head.
Jesus is the name we sing;
Jesus risen from the dead;
Jesus, Conqueror o'er the grave;
Jesus, mighty now to save.

2 Jesus is gone up on high;
Angels come to meet their King;
Shouts triumphant rend the sky,
While the Victor's praise they sing:
"Open now, ye heavenly gates!
'Tis the King of glory waits."

3 Now behold Him high enthroned!
Glory beaming from His face;
By adoring angels owned,
God of holiness and grace:
Oh for hearts and tongues to sing,
"Glory, glory to our King."

4 Jesus, on Thy people shine!
Warm our hearts and tune our tongues!
That with angels we may join,
Share their bliss and swell their songs.
Glory, honour, praise, and power,
Lord, be Thine for evermore!

Thomas Kelly, 1804.

PHARPAR (River). [H. P. 156.]

REPHAIM (Valley of). [H. P. 141.]

Hal - le - lu - jah, Hal - le - lu - jah!

269 Eph. iv. 8. *"He led captivity captive, and gave gifts unto men."*
Tune REPHAIM. 77, 77.

1 SING, O heavens! O earth, rejoice!
Angel harp and human voice,
Round Him, as He rises, raise
Your ascending Saviour's praise.
Hallelujah!

2 Bruisèd is the serpent's head,
Hell is vanquished, death is dead;
And to Christ, gone up on high,
Captive is captivity.
Hallelujah!

3 All His work and warfare done,
He into His heaven is gone,
And beside His Father's throne
Now is pleading for His own:
Hallelujah!

4 Asking gifts for sinful men,
That He may come down again,
And, the fallen to restore,
In them dwell for evermore.
Hallelujah!

5 Sing, O heavens! O earth, rejoice!
Angel harp and human voice,
Round Him, in His glory, raise
Your ascended Saviour's praise.
Hallelujah!

John S. B. Monsell, LL.D., 1863.

270 Ps. lxviii. 18. *"Thou hast ascended on high."*
Tune MASSAH. S. M. D.

1 THOU art gone up on high,
To mansions in the skies;
And round Thy throne unceasingly
The songs of praise arise.
But we are lingering here
With sin and care oppressed;
Lord, send Thy promised Comforter,
And lead us to Thy rest.

MASSAH (The Rock). [H. P. 96.]

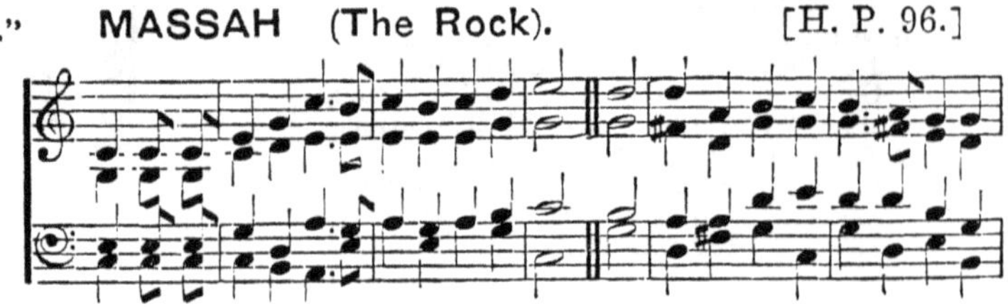

2 Thou art gone up on high;
  But Thou didst first come down,
Through earth's most bitter agony
  To pass unto Thy crown;
And girt with griefs and fears
  Our onward course must be;
But only let that path of tears
  Lead us at last to Thee!

3 Thou art gone up on high;
  But Thou shalt come again,
With all the bright ones of the sky
  Attendant in Thy train.
Oh, by Thy saving power
  So make us live and die,
That we may stand, in that dread hour,
  At Thy right hand on high!

Emma Toke, 1851.

CRASSELIUS; *or*, WINCHESTER NEW. [H. P. 3.]

271

Job xix. 25. *"I know that my Redeemer liveth."* Tune CRASSELIUS. L. M. Or WALDECK. Or HEBRON.

1 I KNOW that my Redeemer lives!
  What comfort this sweet sentence gives!
He lives! He lives! who once was dead;
He lives, my ever-living Head!

2 He lives—triumphant from the grave,
He lives—eternally to save,
He lives—all glorious in the sky,
He lives—exalted there on high.

3 He lives—to bless me with His love,
He lives—to plead for me above,
He lives—my hungry soul to feed,
He lives—to help in time of need.

4 He lives—to grant me rich supply,
He lives—to guide me with His eye,
He lives—to comfort me, when faint,
He lives—to hear my soul's complaint.

5 He lives—to crush the power of hell,
He lives—that He may in me dwell,
He lives—to heal, and make me whole,
He lives—to guard my feeble soul.

PART II.

6 He lives—to silence all my fears,
He lives—to stay and wipe my tears,
He lives—to soothe my troubled heart,
He lives—all blessings to impart.

7 He lives—my kind, my faithful Friend,
He lives—and loves me to the end,
He lives—and while He lives, I 'll sing,
He lives—my Prophet, Priest, and King.

8 He lives—and grants me daily breath,
He lives—and I shall conquer death,
He lives—my mansion to prepare,
He lives—to bring me safely there.

9 He lives—all glory to His name!
He lives—my Jesus, still the same!
Oh! the sweet joy this sentence gives,
"I know that my Redeemer lives!"

Samuel Medley, 1800.

272

Rom. viii. 33. *"Who shall lay anything to the charge of God's elect?"* Tune CRASSELIUS. L. M. Or HEBRON. Or OLD HUNDREDTH.

1 WHO shall the Lord's elect condemn?
  'Tis God that justifies their souls;
And mercy, like a mighty stream,
  O'er all their sins divinely rolls.

2 Who shall adjudge the saints to hell?
  'Tis Christ that suffered in their stead;
And the salvation to fulfil,
  Behold Him rising from the dead!

3 He lives! He lives! and sits above,
  For ever interceding there;
Who shall divide us from His love?
  Or what shall tempt us to despair?

4 Shall persecution, or distress?
  Famine, or sword, or nakedness?
He, that hath loved us, bears us through,
  And makes us more than conquerors too.

5 Not all that men on earth can do,
  Nor powers on high, nor powers below,
Shall cause His mercy to remove,
  Or wean our hearts from Christ, our love!

Isaac Watts, D.D., 1709.

MAON (Wilderness of). [H. P. 229.]

273 John xiv. 2. *"I go to prepare a place for you."* Tune MAON. 8 8, 8 8, 8 8.

1 AND art Thou, gracious Master, gone,
A mansion to prepare for me?
Shall I behold Thee on Thy throne,
And there for ever sit with Thee?
Then let the world approve or blame,
I'll triumph in Thy glorious name.

2 Should I, to gain the world's applause,
Or to escape its angry frown,
Refuse to countenance Thy cause,
And make Thy people's lot my own,
What shame would fill me in that day
When Thou Thy glory wilt display!

3 And what is man, or what his smile?
The terror of his anger what?
Like grass he flourishes awhile,
But soon his place shall know him not.
Through fear of such a one shall I
The Lord of heaven and earth deny?

4 No; let the world cast out my name,
And vile account me if it will,
If to confess my Lord be shame,
Oh, then would I be viler still!
For Thee, my God, I all resign,
Content that I can call Thee mine.

5 What transport then will fill my heart,
When Thou my worthless name wilt own,
When I shall see Thee as Thou art,
And know as I myself am known;
When I, from sin and sorrow free,
Shall have eternal rest with Thee!

Thomas Kelly, 1840.

MAHANAIM. [H. P. 129.]

274 Rev. i. 5, 6. *"Unto Him that loved us . . be glory and dominion for ever."* Tune MAHANAIM. 7 6, 7 6. D.

1 O LORD, who now art seated
Above the heavens on high
(The gracious work completed
For which Thou cam'st to die),
To Thee our hearts are lifted,
While pilgrims wandering here,
For Thou art truly gifted
Our every grief to share.

2 We know that Thou hast bought us,
And washed us in Thy blood;
We know Thy grace has brought us
As "kings and priests to God":
We know that soon the morning,
Long looked for, hasteth near,
When we, at Thy returning,
In glory shall appear.

3 O Lord, Thy love's unbounded!
So full, so sweet, so free!
Our thoughts are all confounded
Whene'er we think of Thee.
For us Thou cam'st from heaven,
For us to bleed and die,
That, purchased and forgiven,
We might ascend on high.

4 Oh, let this love constrain us
To give our hearts to Thee;
Let nothing henceforth pain us,
But that which paineth Thee.
Our joy, our one endeavour,
Through suffering, conflict, shame—
To serve Thee, gracious Saviour,
And magnify Thy name.

James George Deck, 1837.

(14) THE INTERCESSION OF CHRIST.

ST. JOHN. [H. P. 272.]

275 Heb. iv. 14. "*A great High Priest that is passed into the heavens, Jesus the Son of God.*"

Tune St. John. 6666, 88. Or Mizpeh.

1 THE' atoning work is done;
The Victim's blood is shed;
And Jesus now is gone,
His people's cause to plead:
He stands in heaven, their great High Priest,
And bears their names upon His breast.

2 He sprinkles with His blood
The mercy-seat above;
For justice had withstood
The purposes of love;
But justice now objects no more,
And mercy yields her boundless store.

3 No temple made with hands
His place of service is;
In heaven itself He stands,—
A heavenly Priesthood His!
In Him the shadows of the law
Are all fulfilled, and now withdraw.

4 And though awhile He be
Hid from the eyes of men,—
His people look to see
Their great High Priest again:
In brightest glory He will come,
And take His waiting people home!

Thomas Kelly, 1806.

276 1 John ii. 1. "*We have an Advocate.*" Tune St. John. 6666, 88. Or Moriah.

1 ARISE, my soul, arise;
Shake off thy guilty fears:
The bleeding Sacrifice
In my behalf appears.
Before the throne my Surety stands:
My name is written on His hands.

2 He ever lives above,
For me to intercede;
His dear redeeming love,
His precious blood, to plead:
That blood hath saved a guilty race,
And sprinkles now the throne of grace.

3 The Father hears Him pray,—
His dear Anointed One:
He cannot turn away
The presence of His Son:
His Spirit answers to the blood,
And tells me I am born of God.

4 My God is reconciled;
His pardoning voice I hear:
He owns me for His child;
I can no longer fear:
With confidence I now draw nigh,
And Father, Abba Father, cry.

Charles Wesley, 1742.

GÖLDEL. [H. P. 7.]

277 Heb. ix. 24. "*In the presence of God for us.*" Tune Göldel. L. M.

1 HE lives, the great Redeemer lives!
What joy the blest assurance gives!
And now before His Father, God,
Pleads the full merit of His blood.

2 Repeated crimes awake our fears,
And justice armed with frowns appears;
But in the Saviour's beaming face
Sweet mercy smiles, and all is peace.

3 In every dark distressful hour,
When sin and Satan join their power,
Let this dear hope repel the dart,—
That Jesus bears us on His heart.

4 Great Advocate, Almighty Friend,
On Thee alone our hopes depend;
Our cause can never, never fail,
For Jesus pleads, and must prevail!

Anne Steele, 1760.

PATMOS. [H. P. 147.]

278 Rom. viii. 34. "*Christ . . . also maketh intercession for us.*"

Tune Patmos. 77, 77.

1 PRAYING soul, dismiss thy fear:
Joy and peace will soon appear:
To the throne of grace draw nigh;
Jesus intercedes on high.

2 Come before thy Father's throne,
Make thy wants and sorrows known;
Never, never doubt His love;
Jesus intercedes above.

3 Let the world and Satan frown;
This should never cast thee down:
All is working for thy good;
Jesus intercedes with blood.

4 Do corruptions rise and rage?
Learn from God's inspirèd page,
Reigning grace shall sin subdue;
Jesus intercedes for you.

5 He has made thy cause His own;
He is Priest upon His throne;
Thou shalt gain eternal bliss;
Jesus intercedes for this.

Joseph Irons, 1825.

HYMN CHANT (Troyte's). [H. P. 311.]

279

John xvii. 9. "*I pray for them.*" Tune TROYTE'S HYMN CHANT. 888, 6.

1 O THOU, the contrite sinner's Friend,
Who, loving, lov'st him to the end,
On this alone my hopes depend,—
That Thou wilt plead for me!

2 When, weary in the Christian race,
Far off appears my resting place,
And fainting I mistrust Thy grace,
Then, Saviour, plead for me!

3 When I have erred and gone astray,
Afar from Thine and wisdom's way,
And see no glimmering guiding ray,
Still, Saviour plead for me!

4 When Satan, by my sins made bold,
Strives from Thy cross to loose my hold,
Then with Thy pitying arms enfold,
And plead, oh plead for me!

5 And when my dying hour draws near,
Darkened with anguish, guilt, and fear,
Then to my fainting sight appear,
Pleading in heaven for me!

6 When the full light of heavenly day
Reveals my sins in dread array,
Say Thou hast washed them all away;
Oh say Thou plead'st for me!

Charlotte Elliott, 1845.

MAON (Wilderness of). [H. P. 229.]

280

John xiv. 1. "*Let not your heart be troubled.*" Tune MAON. 88, 88, 88.

1 WHEN gathering clouds around I view,
And days are dark, and friends are few,
On Him I lean, who not in vain
Experienced every human pain;
He sees my wants, allays my fears,
And counts and treasures up my tears.

2 If aught should tempt my soul to stray
From heavenly wisdom's narrow way;
To fly the good I would pursue,
Or do the sin I would not do:
Still He, who felt temptation's power,
Shall guard me in that dangerous hour.

3 If vexing thoughts within me rise,
And, sore dismayed, my spirit dies,
Still He, who once vouchsafed to bear
The sickening anguish of despair,
Shall sweetly soothe, shall gently dry,
The throbbing heart, the streaming eye.

4 When sorrowing o'er some stone I bend,
Which covers all that was a friend,
And from his hand, his voice, his smile,
Divides me for a little while,
Thou, Saviour, mark'st the tears I shed,
For Thou didst weep o'er Lazarus dead.

5 And, oh, when I have safely passed
Through every conflict—but the last,
Still, Lord, unchanging, watch beside
My dying bed—for Thou hast died;
Then point to realms of cloudless day,
And wipe the latest tear away!

Sir Robert Grant, 1806.

281

Heb. vii. 25. "*He ever liveth to make intercession.*" Tune STUTTGARD. 87, 87.

1 NOW I know the great Redeemer,
Know He lives, and spreads His fame;
Lives—and all the heavens adore Him;
Lives—and earth resounds His name.

2 Yes, I know Messiah liveth,—
Lives, and prays, and pleads for me;
Lives, and loves, and smiles, and blesses;
Lives—and sets my spirit free.

3 My Redeemer lives within me,
Lives—and heavenly life conveys;
Lives—and glory now surrounds me;
Lives—and I His name shall praise.

4 Pardon, peace, and full salvation
From my living Saviour flow;
Light, and life, and consolation,
All the good I e'er can know.

STUTTGARD. [H. P. 182.]

5 Ah, how kind is my Redeemer;
He's my ever-living Friend;
He will never, never leave me;
But will love me to the end.

6 Soon shall I behold my Saviour;
He who lives and reigns above,
Lives—and I shall live for ever,
Live and sing redeeming love!

See Hymns 138—140.

Richard Burnham, 1794.

ESDRAELON. [H. P. 202.]

(15) THE MEDIATORIAL GLORY OF CHRIST.

282 1 Pet. iii. 22. *"Angels, and authorities, and powers, being made subject unto Him."* Tune ESDRAELON. 87, 87. D.

1 LAMB of God! Thou now art seated
High upon Thy Father's throne;
All Thy gracious work completed,
All Thy mighty victory won:
Every knee in heaven is bending
To the Lamb for sinners slain;
Every voice and harp is swelling,
"Worthy is the Lamb to reign."

2 Lord, in all Thy power and glory,
Still Thy thoughts and eyes are here!
Watching o'er Thy ransomed people,
To Thy gracious heart so dear:
Thou for us art interceding;
Everlasting is Thy love!
And a blessed rest preparing
In our Father's house above.

3 Lamb of God! Thou soon in glory
Wilt to this sad earth return;
All Thy foes shall quake before Thee,
All that now despise Thee, mourn:
Then Thy saints shall rise to meet Thee,—
With Thee in Thy kingdom reign;
Thine the praise, and Thine the glory,
Lamb of God for sinners slain!

James George Deck, 1838.

LONDON NEW; *or*, NEWTON. [H. P. 55.]

283 Heb. ii. 9. *"Crowned with glory and honour."* Tune LONDON NEW. C. M. Or NOTTINGHAM.

1 THE Head that once was crowned with thorns
Is crowned with glory now;
A royal diadem adorns
The mighty Victor's brow.

2 The highest place that heaven affords
Is His, is His by right,
"The King of kings and Lord of lords,"
And heaven's eternal light.

3 The joy of all who dwell above,
The joy of all below
To whom He manifests His love,
And grants His name to know.

4 To them, the cross with all its shame,
With all its grace, is given;
Their name an everlasting name,
Their joy the joy of heaven.

5 They suffer with their Lord below,
They reign with Him above;
Their profit and their joy to know
The mystery of His love.

6 The cross He bore is life and health,
Though shame and death to Him;
His people's hope, His people's wealth,
Their everlasting theme!

Thomas Kelly, 1820.

HOLY VOICES. [H. P. 309.]

284 Col. ii. 10. "*The Head of all Principality and power.*" Tune HOLY VOICES. 8 7, 8 7. Or SALZBURG.

1 HAIL! Thou once despisèd Jesus!
Hail! Thou Galilean King!
Thou didst suffer to release us,
Thou didst free salvation bring:
Hail! Thou agonising Saviour,
Bearer of our sin and shame!
By Thy merits we find favour,
Life is given through Thy name.

2 Paschal Lamb, by God appointed,
All our sins on Thee were laid,
By almighty love anointed,
Thou hast full atonement made.
All Thy people are forgiven,
Through the virtue of Thy blood;
Opened is the gate of heaven;
Peace is made 'tween man and God.

3 Jesus, hail! enthroned in glory,
There for ever to abide!
All the heavenly hosts adore Thee,
Seated at Thy Father's side.
There, for sinners Thou art pleading,
There, Thou dost our place prepare;
Ever for us interceding,
Till in glory we appear.

4 Worship, honour, power, and blessing,
Thou art worthy to receive!
Loudest praises, without ceasing,
Meet it is for us to give.
Help, ye bright angelic spirits!
Bring your sweetest, noblest lays;
Help to sing our Saviour's merits;
Help to chant Emmanuel's praise!

John Bakewell, 1757; Augustus M. Toplady, 1776.

GOTHA. [H. P. 296.]

285 Rev. xix. 1. "*I heard a great voice of much people in heaven.*" Tune GOTHA. 8 7, 8 7.

1 HARK! the notes of angels singing—
Glory, glory to the Lamb!
All in heaven their tribute bringing,
Raising high the Saviour's name.

2 Ye for whom His life is given,
Sacred themes to you belong,
Come, assist the choir of heaven,
Join the everlasting song.

3 Saints and angels, thus united,
Songs imperfect still must raise;
Though despised on earth and slighted,
Jesus is above all praise.

4 See, the' angelic hosts have crowned Him,
Jesus fills the throne on high:
Countless myriads, hovering round Him,
With His praises rend the sky.

5 Filled with holy emulation,
Let us vie with those above;
Sweet the theme—a free salvation!
Fruit of everlasting love.

6 Endless life in Him possessing,
Let us praise His glorious name,
Glory, honour, power, and blessing,
Be for ever to the Lamb!

Thomas Kelly, 1806.

TRYPHOSA. [H. P. 209.]

286 Rev. v. 9. *"Thou hast redeemed us to God by Thy blood."* Tune TRYPHOSA. 8 8 6.

1 TO Him who for our sins was slain,
To Him, for all His dying pain,
Sing we Alleluia!

2 To Him, the Lamb, our Sacrifice,
Who gave His life our ransom-price,
Sing we Alleluia!

3 To Him who died, that we might die
To sin, and live with Him on high,
Sing we Alleluia!

4 To Him who rose, that we might rise,
And reign with Him beyond the skies,
Sing we Alleluia!

5 To Him who now for us doth plead,
And helpeth us in all our need,
Sing we Alleluia!

6 To Him who doth prepare on high
Our home in immortality,
Sing we Alleluia!

7 To Him be glory evermore!
Ye heavenly hosts, your Lord adore!
Sing we Alleluia!

8 To Father, Son, and Holy Ghost,
One God most great, our joy and boast,
Sing we Alleluia! Amen.

Arthur T. Russell, 1851.

---

287 Rev. xix. 1. *"Salvation, and glory, and honour, and power, unto the Lord our God."*

Tune MORIAH. 6 6 6 6. 8 8.

MORIAH (Mount). [H. P. 119.]

1 REJOICE, the Lord is King!
Your God and King adore!
Mortals, give thanks and sing,
And triumph evermore.
Lift up your heart, lift up your voice,
Rejoice, again I say, rejoice.

2 Jesus, the Saviour, reigns
The God of truth and love;
When He had purged our stains
He took His seat above.
Lift up your heart, lift up your voice,
Rejoice, again I say, rejoice.

3 His kingdom cannot fail,
He rules o'er earth and heaven;
The keys of death and hell
Are unto Jesus given.
Lift up your heart, lift up your voice,
Rejoice, again I say, rejoice.

4 He sits at God's right hand,
Till all His foes submit,
And bow to His command,
And fall beneath His feet.
Lift up your heart, lift up your voice,
Rejoice, again I say, rejoice.

5 He all His foes shall quell,
Shall all our sins destroy,
And every bosom swell
With pure seraphic joy.
Lift up your heart, lift up your voice,
Rejoice, again I say, rejoice.

6 Rejoice, in glorious hope,
Jesus our Lord shall come,
And take His brethren up
To their eternal home:
We soon shall hear the' archangel's voice:
How then shall all His saints rejoice!

Charles Wesley, 1745.

288 Rev. xiv. 2. "*I heard the voice of harpers harping with their harps.*"

Tune ALL SAINTS. 8 7, 8 7, 7 7.

1 HARK! ten thousand harps and voices
Sound the note of praise above!
Jesus reigns, and heaven rejoices:
Jesus reigns, the God of love:
Lo! He sits on yonder throne;
Jesus rules the world alone.

2 Well may angels bright and glorious
Sing the praises of the Lamb;
While on earth, He prayed victorious;
Now, He bears a matchless name:
Well may angels sing of Him,
Heaven supplies no richer theme.

3 Come, ye saints, unite your praises
With the angels round His throne;
Soon we hope our Lord will raise us
To the place where He is gone.
Meet it is that we should sing
Glory, glory to our King.

4 Sing how Jesus came from heaven,
How He bore the cross below;
How all power to Him is given;
How He reigns in glory now:
'Tis a great and endless theme:
Oh 'tis sweet to sing of Him!

PART II.

5 Jesus, hail, whose glory brightens
All above, and gives it worth.
Lord of life, Thy smile enlightens,
Cheers, and charms Thy saints on earth
When we think of love like Thine,
Lord, we own it love Divine!

6 King of glory, live for ever,
Thine an everlasting crown:
Nothing from Thy love shall sever
Those whom Thou hast made Thine own!
Happy objects of Thy grace,
Destined to behold Thy face.

7 Saviour, hasten Thine appearing!
Bring, oh bring the glorious day,
When, the awful summons hearing,
Heaven and earth shall pass away:
Then, with golden harps, we'll sing—
Glory, glory to our King!

Thomas Kelly, 1806.

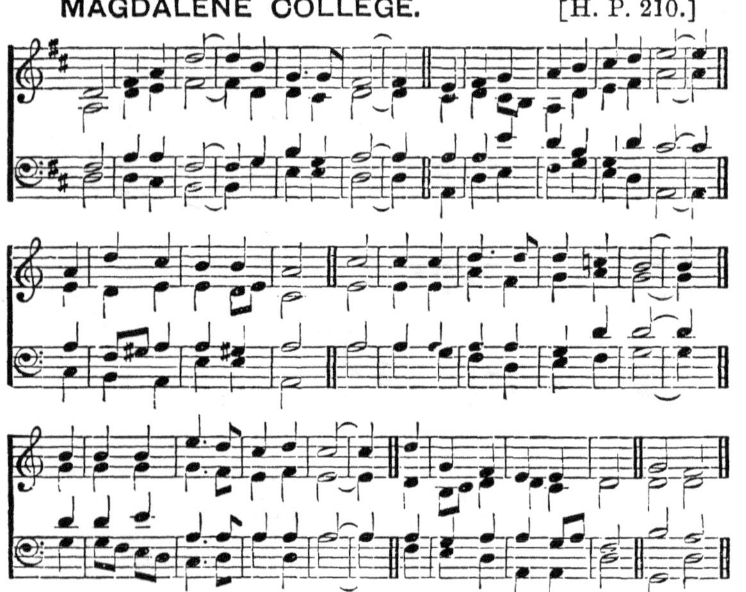

289 Rev. v. 12. "*Worthy is the Lamb.*"
Tune MAGDALENE COLLEGE. 8 8 6. D.
Or KEDRON.

1 O BLESSED Jesus! Lamb of God!
Who hast redeemed us with Thy blood
From sin, and death, and shame—
With joy and praise, Thy people see
The crown of glory won by Thee,
And worthy Thee proclaim.

2 Exalted by the Father's love,
All thrones, and powers, and names above—
On earth below or heaven;
Wisdom and riches, power Divine,
Blessing and honour, Lord, are Thine—
All things to Thee are given.

3 Head of the church! Thou sittest there,
Thy bride shall all Thy glory share—
Thy fulness, Lord, is ours:
Our life Thou art—Thy grace sustains,
Thy strength in us the victory gains,
O'er sin and Satan's powers.

4 Soon shall the day of glory come,
Thy bride shall reach the Father's home,
And all Thy beauty see;
And oh! what joy to see Thee shine,
To hear Thee own us, Lord, as Thine,
And ever dwell with Thee!

James George Deck, 1846.

290 Zech. vi. 13. "*A Priest upon His throne.*" Tune GIBBONS. 7 7, 7 7.

1 BRETHREN, let us join to bless
Christ the Lord, our Righteousness!
Let our praise to Him be given,
High at God's right hand in heaven.

2 Son of God! to Thee we bow:
Thou art Lord, and only Thou!
Thou the woman's promised Seed,
Glory of Thy church, and Head.

3 Thee the angels ceaseless sing;
Thee we praise, our Priest and King;
Worthy is Thy name of praise,
Full of glory, full of grace.

4 We, Thy favoured flock, adore
Thee, the Lord, for evermore;
Ever with us show Thy love,
Till we join with those above!

John Cennick, 1742.

GIBBONS. [H. P. 148.]

(16) THE SECOND ADVENT OF CHRIST.

291 John xvi. 16. *"A little while, and ye shall see Me."*

Tune Maon. 88, 88, 88.

1 "A LITTLE while," our Lord shall come,
And we shall wander here no more;
He 'll take us to our Father's home,
Where He for us hath gone before—
To dwell with Him, to see His face,
And sing the glories of His grace.

2 "A little while"—He 'll come again!
Let us the precious hours redeem;
Our only grief to give Him pain,
Our joy to serve and follow Him.
Watchful and ready may we be,
As those who long their Lord to see.

3 "A little while"—'twill soon be past:
Why should we shun the shame and cross?
Oh! let us in His footsteps haste,
And count for Him all else but loss!
Oh, how will recompense His smile,
The sufferings of this "little while"!

4 "A little while"—come, Saviour, come!
For Thee Thy bride has tarried long;
Take Thy poor wearied pilgrims home,
To sing the new eternal song;
To see Thy glory, and to be
In everything conformed to Thee!

James George Deck, 1838.

MAON (Wilderness of). [H. P. 229.]

EIRENE. [H. P. 246.]

292 John xvi. 18. *"What is this that He saith, A little while?"*

Tune Eirene. 11 10, 11 10.

1 OH! for the peace which floweth as a river,
Making life's desert places bloom and smile!
Oh! for the faith to grasp heaven's bright "for ever,"
Amid the shadows of earth's "little while"!

2 "A little while" for patient vigil-keeping,
To face the stern, to wrestle with the strong;
"A little while," to sow the seed with weeping,
Then bind the sheaves, and sing the harvest song.

3 "A little while," to wear the weeds of sadness,
To pace with weary step through miry ways;
Then to pour forth the fragrant oil of gladness,
And clasp the girdle round the robe of praise.

4 "A little while," 'mid shadow and illusion,
To strive, by faith, love's mysteries to spell;
Then read each dark enigma's bright solution,
Then hail sight's verdict, "He doeth all things well!"

5 "A little while," the earthen pitcher taking
To wayside brooks, from far-off fountains fed;
Then the cool lip its thirst for ever slaking
Beside the fulness of the Fountain-head.

6 "A little while," to keep the oil from failing;
"A little while," faith's flickering lamp to trim;
And then, the Bridegroom's coming footsteps hailing,
To haste to meet Him with the bridal hymn.

7 And He who is Himself the Gift and Giver—
The future glory and the present smile,
With the bright promise of the glad "for ever,"
Will light the shadows of the "little while."

Jane Crewdson, 1863.

IDUMEA. [H. P. 193.]

NARENZA. [H. P. 80.]

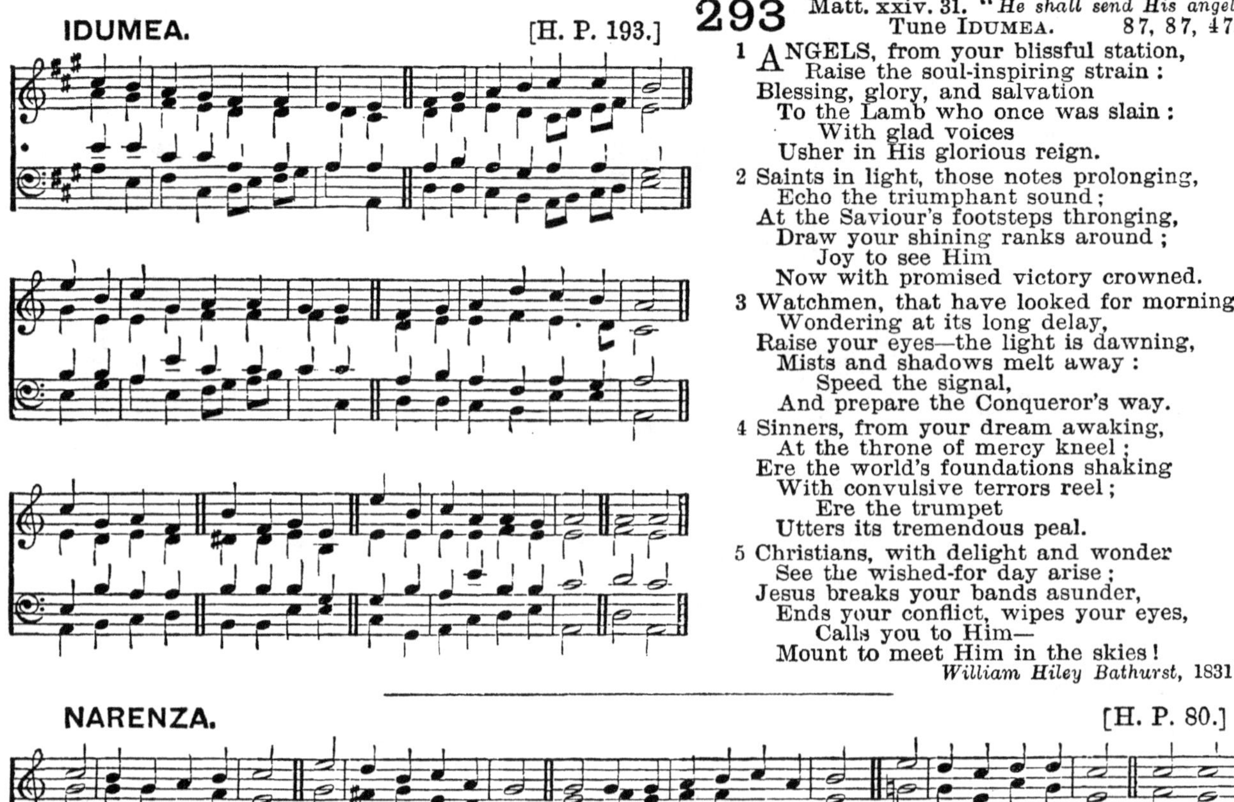

293 Matt. xxiv. 31. "*He shall send His angels.*"
Tune Idumea. 87, 87, 47.

1 Angels, from your blissful station,
Raise the soul-inspiring strain:
Blessing, glory, and salvation
To the Lamb who once was slain:
With glad voices
Usher in His glorious reign.

2 Saints in light, those notes prolonging,
Echo the triumphant sound;
At the Saviour's footsteps thronging,
Draw your shining ranks around;
Joy to see Him
Now with promised victory crowned.

3 Watchmen, that have looked for morning,
Wondering at its long delay,
Raise your eyes—the light is dawning,
Mists and shadows melt away:
Speed the signal,
And prepare the Conqueror's way.

4 Sinners, from your dream awaking,
At the throne of mercy kneel;
Ere the world's foundations shaking
With convulsive terrors reel;
Ere the trumpet
Utters its tremendous peal.

5 Christians, with delight and wonder
See the wished-for day arise;
Jesus breaks your bands asunder,
Ends your conflict, wipes your eyes,
Calls you to Him—
Mount to meet Him in the skies!

William Hiley Bathurst, 1831.

294 Rev. xxii. 20. "*Come, Lord Jesus.*" Tune Narenza. S. M.

1 Come, Lord, and tarry not,
Bring the long looked-for day;
Oh! why these years of waiting here,
These ages of delay?

2 Come, for Thy saints still wait;
Daily ascends their sigh;
The Spirit and the bride say, Come;
Dost Thou not hear the cry?

3 Come, for creation groans,
Impatient of Thy stay;
Worn out with these long years of ill,
These ages of delay.

4 Come, for the corn is ripe;
Put in Thy sickle now;
Reap the great harvest of the earth:
Sower and Reaper Thou!

5 Come in Thy glorious might,
Come with the iron rod,
Disperse Thy foes before Thy face,
Most mighty Son of God.

6 Come, and make all things new;
Build up this ruined earth;
Restore our faded paradise,
Creation's second birth.

7 Come, and begin Thy reign
Of everlasting peace;
Come, take the kingdom to Thyself,
Great King of Righteousness!

Horatius Bonar, D.D., 1857.

295 Phil. iv. 5. "*The Lord is at hand!*"
Tune Civitas Regis. 87, 87, 47.

1 Christ is coming! let creation
Bid her groans and travail cease;
Let the glorious proclamation
Hope restore, and faith increase—
Maranatha! * [* *i.e.* "Our Lord cometh."]
Come, Thou blessèd Prince of Peace!

2 Earth can now but tell the story
Of Thy bitter cross and pain,
She shall yet behold Thy glory,
When Thou comest back to reign.
Maranatha!
Let each heart repeat the strain!

CIVITAS REGIS MAGNI. [H. P. 301.]

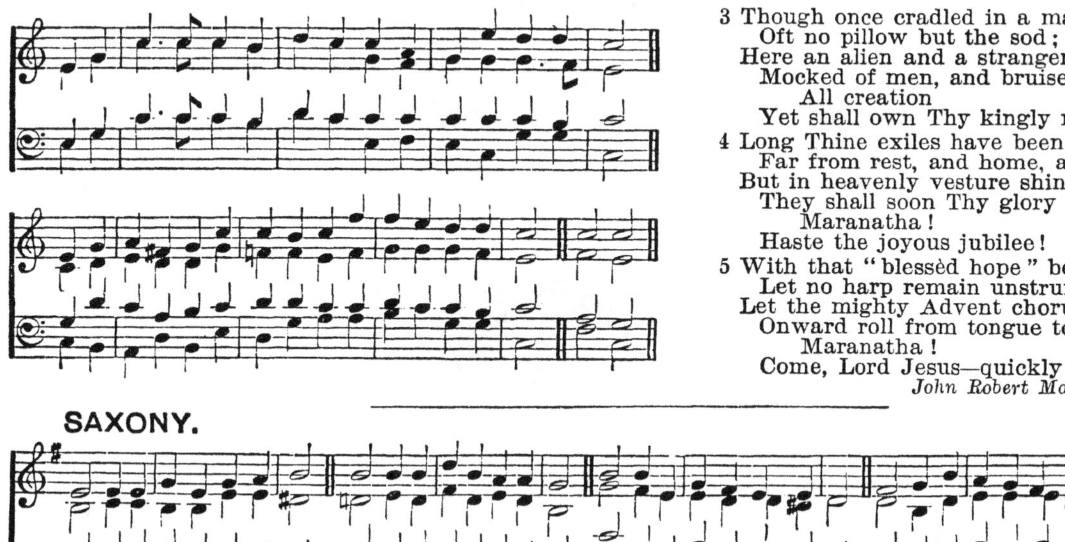

3 Though once cradled in a manger,
Oft no pillow but the sod;
Here an alien and a stranger,
Mocked of men, and bruised of God—
All creation
Yet shall own Thy kingly rod.

4 Long Thine exiles have been pining,
Far from rest, and home, and Thee;
But in heavenly vesture shining,
They shall soon Thy glory see—
Maranatha!
Haste the joyous jubilee!

5 With that "blessèd hope" before us,
Let no harp remain unstrung,
Let the mighty Advent chorus
Onward roll from tongue to tongue—
Maranatha!
Come, Lord Jesus—quickly come!

John Robert Macduff, D.D., 1853.

SAXONY. [H. P. 32.]

296 Zech. xiv. 5. *"The Lord my God shall come."* Tune Saxony. L. M.

1 THE Lord will come! the earth shall quake;
The mountains from their centre shake;
And, withering from the vault of night,
The stars withdraw their feeble light.

2 The Lord will come! but not the same
As once in lowly form He came—
A silent Lamb to slaughter led,
The bruised, the suffering, and the dead.

3 The Lord will come! a dreadful form,
With wreath of flame and robe of storm,
On cherub wings and wings of wind,
Anointed Judge of all mankind.

4 Can this be He, once wont to stray,
A pilgrim on the world's highway,
By power oppressed, and mocked by pride,
The Nazarene—the Crucified?

5 Go, tyrants! to the rocks complain!
Go, seek the mountain's cleft in vain!
But faith, victorious o'er the tomb,
Shall sing for joy—the Lord is come!

Bishop Heber, 1811.

EPHRON. [H. P. 57.]

297 Cant. v. 2. *"I sleep, but my heart waketh."*
Tune Ephron. C. M. Or London New.

1 CHILDREN of light, awake! awake!
Ye slumbering virgins, rise!
Go, meet the royal Bridegroom now,
And show that ye are wise.

2 Like foolish virgins, ye have failed
Your holy watch to keep;
And lo, He comes, and almost finds
Your languid souls asleep!

3 Through love, the Man of Sorrows oft
Hath watched and wept for you;
Then gave away His life, to prove
That all that love was true.

4 Then wake, for lo, the midnight cry
Of warning in the air
Bids all His church, to greet Him now,
Their dying lamps prepare!

Sir Edward Denny, 1838.

298 Cant. ii. 13. *"Arise, My love, My fair one, and come away."*
Tune Ephron. C. M. Or Besor.

1 BRIDE of the Lamb, rejoice! rejoice!
Thy midnight watch is past,
True to His promise, lo, 'tis He!
The Saviour comes at last.

2 His heart, amid the blest repose
And glories of the throne,
With love's unwearied care, hath made
Thy sorrows all its own.

3 Through days and nights of suffering, taught
For human woe to feel,
He only, with unerring skill,
Thy wounded heart could heal.

4 And now, at length, behold He comes
To claim thee from above,
In answer to the ceaseless call
And deep desire of love.

5 Go then, thou loved and blessèd one,
Thou drooping mourner, rise!
Go—for He calls thee now to share
His dwelling in the skies.

6 For thee, His royal bride—for thee,
His brightest glories shine:
And, happier still, His changeless heart,
With all its love, is thine!

Sir Edward Denny, 1848.

PARAN (Wilderness of). [H. P. 241.]

299 Rev. xxii. 20. "*Surely I come quickly.*" Tune PARAN. 12 11, 12 11.

1 LORD Jesus, come quickly, Thy bride is preparing
In garments of glory before Thee to stand;
Her dimmed eyes are straining to catch Thine appearing,
Her heart bursts in rapture—"My Lord is at [hand."

2 Why linger His steps, like the morning's dawn blushing?
To heaven like the sunlight, to earth like the [dew;
Poor perishing sinners, His garment-hem touching,
Stay the Lord on His path to the house of the Jew.

3 Yet hasten, we pray Thee, Thy kingdom of glory;
Prepare Thine elect one, Thy blood-purchased bride;
Her bliss waits completion, rejoicing before Thee,
Till robed, crowned, and jewelled, she sits by Thy side.

4 Before Thy bright footsteps the clouds part asunder;
Thy foes, from the heavens, in terror depart;
While worlds stand astonished, and angels shall wonder
At all Thou hast wrought for the bride of Thine [heart.

5 Then come, Lord, come quickly, the groans of creation
Respond to the tears which Thy people have shed
O'er the hope, long deferred, of their blest consummation
Of glory and bliss with their covenant Head.

6 Then take, Lord, Thy kingdom, and come in Thy glory;
Make the scene of Thy sorrows the place of Thy [throne;
Complete all the blessing which ages in story
Have told of the triumphs so justly Thine own!

J. Groom, Leaflet, 1847.

BESOR (Brook). [H. P. 51.]

300 Cant. ii. 14. "*Sweet is Thy voice.*" Tune BESOR. C. M.

1 BRIDE of the Lamb! awake, awake!
Why sleep for sorrow now?
The hope of glory, Christ is thine,
A child of glory thou!

2 Thy spirit through the lonely night,
From earthly joy apart,
Hath sighed for One that's far away,
The Bridegroom of thy heart.

3 But see, the night is waning fast,
The breaking morn is near;
And Jesus comes with voice of love,
Thy drooping heart to cheer.

4 He comes! for oh, His yearning heart
No more can bear delay,
To scenes of full unmingled joy
To call His bride away.

5 This earth, the scene of all His woe,
A homeless wild to thee,
Full soon upon His heavenly throne
Its rightful King shall see.

6 Thou too shalt reign; He will not wear
His crown of joy alone;
And earth His royal bride shall see
Beside Him on the throne.

7 Then weep no more; 'tis all thine own,
His crown, His joy Divine;
And, sweeter far than all beside,
He, He Himself is thine!

Sir Edward Denny, 1837.

301 Rev. i. 7. "*Behold, He cometh with clouds.*" Tune HAVILAH. 87, 87, 47. Or ST. WERBERGH.

1 LO! He comes with clouds descending,
Once for favoured sinners slain;
Thousand, thousand saints attending,
Swell the triumph of His train;
Hallelujah!
God appears on earth to reign.

2 Every eye shall now behold Him,
Robed in dreadful majesty;
Those who set at nought and sold Him,
Pierced, and nailed Him to the tree,
Deeply wailing,
Shall the true Messiah see.

3 Every island, sea, and mountain,
Heaven and earth, shall flee away;
All who hate Him, must, confounded,
Hear the trump proclaim the day:
Come to judgment!
Come to judgment, come away!

4 Now redemption, long expected,
See in solemn pomp appear!
All His saints, by men rejected,
Now shall meet Him in the air:
Hallelujah!
See the day of God appear.

5 Yea, Amen, let all adore Thee,
High on Thine eternal throne!
Saviour, take the power and glory,
Claim the kingdom for Thine own:
Oh come quickly!
Hallelujah! come, Lord, come!

John Cennick, 1752; *C. Wesley*, 1758; *Martin Madan*, 1760.

HAVILAH. [H. P. 192.]

302

Rev. xxii. 20. "*Even so, come, Lord Jesus.*"
Tune HAVILAH. 87, 87, 47.

1 SAVIOUR, hasten Thine appearing,
Take Thy waiting people home;
This sweet hope, our spirits cheering
While we in the desert roam,
Makes Thy people
Strangers here till Thou dost come.

2 Lord, how long shall Thy creation
Groan and travail sore in pain;
Waiting for its sure salvation,
When Thou shalt in glory reign;
And, like Eden,
This sad earth shall bloom again?

3 Gather, Lord, Thy chosen nation,
Israel's long afflicted race;
Let them find Thy free salvation,
Own and trust Thy wondrous grace;
And, adoring,
Look on Thy once marrèd face.

4 Reign, oh reign, Almighty Saviour!
Heaven and earth in one unite;
Make it known, that in Thy favour
There alone is life and light;
When we see Thee,
We shall have unmixed delights!

James George Deck, 1846.

CASSEL. [H. P. 190.]

303

Matt. xxiv. 42. "*Watch, therefore; for ye know not what hour your Lord doth come.*"
Tune CASSEL. 87, 87, 77.

1 NOTHING know we of the season
When the world shall pass away;
But we know the saints have reason
To expect a glorious day,
When the Saviour will return,
And His people cease to mourn.

2 While a careless world is sleeping,
Then it is the day will come;
Mirth will then be turned to weeping,
Sinners then must meet their doom;
But the people of the Lord
Shall obtain their bright reward.

3 Oh what sacred joys await them!
They shall see the Saviour then;
Those who now oppose and hate them
Never can oppose again;
Brethren, let us think of this:
All is ours, if we are His.

4 Waiting for the Lord's returning,
Be it ours His word to keep;
Let our lamps be always burning;
Let us watch while others sleep;
We're no longer of the night;
We are children of the light.

5 Being of the favoured number
Whom the Saviour calls His own,
'Tis not meet that we should slumber,
Nothing should be left undone:
This should be His people's aim,
Still to glorify His name!

Thomas Kelly, 1809.

MAGDEBURG. [H. P. 300.]

304 Cant. viii. 14. *"Make haste, my Beloved."* Tune MAGDEBURG. 8 7, 8 7, 4 7. Or IDUMEA.

1 FLY, ye seasons, fly still faster;
Let the glorious day come on,
When we shall behold our Master
Seated on His heavenly throne;
Then the Saviour
Shall descend to claim His own.

2 What is earth with all its treasures
To the joy the gospel brings?
Well may we resign its pleasures,
Jesus gives us better things;
All His people
Draw from heaven's eternal springs.

3 But if here we taste of pleasure,
What will heaven itself afford?
There our joy will know no measure;
There we shall behold our Lord;
There His people
Shall obtain their bright reward.

4 Fly, ye seasons, fly still faster;
Swiftly bring the glorious day;
Jesus, come, our Lord and Master!
Come from heaven without delay;
Take Thy people,
Take, oh take us hence away!

Thomas Kelly, 1809.

GILBOA (Mount). [H. P. 11.]

305 Cant. ii. 17. *"Until the day break."*
Tune GILBOA. L. M.

1 'TIS night—but oh, the joyful morn
Will soon our waiting spirits cheer:
Yon gleams of coming glory warn
Thy saints, O Lord, that Thou art near.

2 Lord of our hearts, beloved of Thee,
Weary of earth, we sigh to rest,
Supremely happy, safe and free,
For ever on Thy tender breast.

3 To see Thee, love Thee, feel Thee near,
Nor dread, as now, Thy transient stay;
To dwell beyond the reach of fear
Lest joy should wane or pass away.

4 Children of hope, belovèd Lord!
In Thee we live, we glory now;
Our joy, our rest, our great reward,
Our diadem of beauty, Thou!

5 And when exalted, Lord, with Thee,
Thy royal throne at length we share,
To everlasting Thou shalt be
Our diadem, our glory there!

Sir Edward Denny, 1838.

306 Rev. vi. 10. *"How long, O Lord?"*
Tune OLD 25TH. S. M. D.

1 THE church has waited long
Her absent Lord to see;
And still in loneliness she waits,
A friendless stranger she.
Age after age has gone,
Sun after sun has set,
And still, in weeds of widowhood,
She weeps, a mourner yet.
Come then, Lord Jesus, come!

2 Saint after saint on earth
Has lived, and loved, and died;
And as they left us one by one,
We laid them side by side.
We laid them down to sleep,
But not in hope forlorn—
We laid them but to ripen there
Till the last glorious morn.
Come then, Lord Jesus, come!

OLD 25th. [H. P. 97.]

3 The serpent's brood increase,
The powers of hell grow bold,
The conflict thickens, faith is low,
And love is waxing cold.
How long, O Lord our God,
Holy, and true, and good,
Wilt Thou not judge Thy suffering church,
Her sighs, and tears, and blood!
Come then, Lord Jesus, come!

4 We long to hear Thy voice,
To see Thee face to face,
To share Thy crown and glory then,
As now we share Thy grace.
Should not the loving bride
The absent Bridegroom mourn?
Should she not wear the weeds of grief
Until her Lord return?
Come then, Lord Jesus, come!

5 The whole creation groans,
And waits to hear that voice
That shall restore her comeliness,
And make her wastes rejoice.
Come, Lord, and wipe away
The curse, the sin, the stain,
And make this blighted world of ours
Thine own fair world again.
Come then, Lord Jesus, come!

Horatius Bonar, D.D., 1845.

GLOUCESTER. [H. P. 40.]

307

2 Pet. i. 19. "*Until the day dawn, and the Day Star arise.*" Tune GLOUCESTER. C. M.

1 THE gloomy night will soon be past,
The morning will appear;
The rays of blessèd light at last
Each waiting eye will cheer.

2 Thou bright and Morning Star, Thy light
Will to our joy be seen;
Thou, Lord, wilt meet our longing sight
Without a cloud between.

3 Ah, yes! Lord Jesus, Thou, whose heart
Still for Thy saints doth care;
We shall behold Thee as Thou art,
Thy perfect likeness bear.

4 Thy love sustains us on our way,
While pilgrims here below;
Thou dost, O Saviour, day by day,
The suited grace bestow.

5 But oh! the more we learn of Thee,
And Thy rich mercy prove,
The more we long Thy face to see,
And fully know Thy love.

6 Then shine, Thou bright and Morning Star,
Dispel the dreary gloom;
Oh! take from sin and grief afar,
Thy blood-bought people home!

Samuel Prideaux Tregelles, LL.D., 1855.

308

Rom. xiii. 12. "*The night is far spent.*"
Tune PEOR. 10 11, 11 11. Or PARAN.

1 THE night is far spent, the day is at hand;
Already the dawn may be seen in the sky;
Rejoice then, ye saints, 'tis your Lord's own command;
Rejoice, for the coming of Jesus draws nigh.

2 How bright will it be, when Jesus appears!
How welcome to those who have shared in His cross!
A crown incorruptible then will be theirs,
A rich compensation for suffering and loss.

3 Affliction is light compared to the day
Of glory that then will from heaven be revealed!
The Saviour is coming, His people may say,
The Lord whom we look for, our Sun and our Shield.

4 Oh pardon us, Lord, that love to Thy name
Is faint, with so much our affections to move!
Our deadness shall fill us with grief and with shame,
So much to be loved and so little to love!

5 Oh kindle within us a holy desire,
Like that which was found in Thy people of old!
Who felt all Thy love, and whose hearts were on fire,
While waiting in patience Thy face to behold!

Thomas Kelly, 1836. (*a.*)

PEOR (Mount). [H. P. 242.]

SOREK (Valley of). [H. P. 184.]

309 Heb. x. 25. *"Ye see the day approaching."* Tune SOREK. 8 7, 8 7. Or FRANKFORT.

1 LORD, we see the day approaching,
When Thou wilt again appear;
Sinners, still Thy garments touching,
Stay Thee in Thy coming here.

2 Hid in heaven is all our treasure,
Patience now becomes Thy saints;
Lord, we wait Thy gracious pleasure,
Faith should silence all complaints.

3 Through the wilderness we wander,
Troubled oft, but not distressed;
Seek we glory?—it is yonder,
Suffering pledges future rest.

4 Coming judgments round us darken,
Human hearts may fail or fear;
But to Thee alone we hearken,
"Your redemption draweth near."

5 Make each waiting child obedient,
Stay our anxious hearts on this:
If Thy going were "expedient,"
Surely Thy return is bliss.

6 Our own Lord is coming hither,
Light in darkness, joy in grief;
Hope deferred would quickly wither
Hearts that had not this relief.

7 All we need is deep affection,
Singleness of eye and heart,
Strength to own Thee in rejection;
Grace sufficient, Lord, impart!

Mary Bowly, 1847.

GIBBONS. [H. P. 148.]

310 Isa. xxi. 11. *"Watchman, what of the night?"* Tune GIBBONS. 7 7, 7 7. Or VIENNA.

1 WATCHMAN! tell us of the night,
What its signs of promise are.
Traveller! o'er yon mountain's height
See that glory-beaming star.

2 Watchman! does its beauteous ray
Aught of hope or joy foretell?
Traveller! yes; it brings the day,
Promised day of Israel.

3 Watchman! tell us of the night;
Higher yet that star ascends.
Traveller! blessedness and light,
Peace and truth, its course portends.

4 Watchman! will its beams alone
Gild the spot that gave them birth?
Traveller! ages are its own;
See! it bursts o'er all the earth.

5 Watchman! tell us of the night,
For the morning seems to dawn.
Traveller! darkness takes its flight;
Doubt and terror are withdrawn.

6 Watchman! let thy wanderings cease;
Hie thee to thy quiet home.
Traveller! lo, the Prince of Peace,
Lo, the Son of God, is come!

Sir John Bowring, LL.D., 1825.

LUBECK. [H. P. 139.]

311 Rev. vii. 12. *"Blessing, and glory, . . and honour, and power, be unto our God for ever."* Tune LUBECK. 7 7, 7 7.

1 SEE the ransomed millions stand,
Palms of conquest in their hand;
This before the throne their strain,
"Hell is vanquished, death is slain;

2 Blessing, honour, glory, might,
Are the Conqueror's native right;
Thrones and powers before Him fall;
Lamb of God, and Lord of all."

3 Hasten, Lord, the promised hour!
Come in glory and in power!
Still Thy foes are unsubdued:
Nature sighs to be renewed.

4 Time has nearly reached its sum;
All things, with Thy bride, say "Come";
Jesus, whom all worlds adore,
Come, and reign for evermore.

Josiah Conder, 1836.

MORAVIA. [H. P. 83.]

312 Isa. xxi. 12. "*If ye will inquire, inquire ye.*"

Tune Moravia. S. M.

1 ENQUIRE, my soul, enquire!
 What doth the watchman say?
Is the one Object of desire
 Already on His way?

2 What doth the watchman say,
 Whose cry the slumberer wakes?
"The night hath nearly passed away;
 And lo! the morning breaks.

3 "The night is coming, too!
 A night of speechless woe;
But there shall be no night to you—
 To you who Jesus know.

4 "Come, whosoever will,
 Ere God's right hand He leaves:
He waits till He His bosom fill
 With all His precious sheaves!

5 "God speaks, shall I be dumb?
 Watch that your lamps may burn;
Come, all ye weary wanderers, come!
 Return to God! return!"

6 Take up the watchman's word:
 Repeat the midnight cry:
"Prepare to meet the coming Lord;
 The time is drawing nigh."

7 The hours with eager flight
 Pass on till He appear,
That moment of unknown delight
 Will soon, will soon be here.

Mary Bowly, 1847.

---

313 1 Thess. iv. 16. "*The Lord Himself shall descend.*"

Tune All Saints. 87, 87, 77. Or Succoth.

1 WELCOME sight! the Lord descending!
 Jesus in the clouds appears;
Lo! the Saviour comes, intending
 Now to dry His people's tears.
Lo! the Saviour comes to reign:
Welcome to His waiting train.

2 Long they mourned their absent Master;
 Long they felt like men forlorn;
Bid the seasons fly still faster,
 While they sighed for His return:
Lo! the period comes at last;
All their sorrows now are past.

3 Now from home no longer banished,
 They are going to their rest;
Though the heavens and earth have vanished,
 With their Lord they shall be blest:
Blest with Him His saints shall be;
Blest throughout eternity!

4 Happy people! grace unbounded,
 Grace alone, exalts you thus:
Be ashamed, and be confounded;
 Sing for ever—"Not to us,
Not to us be glory given—
Glory to the God of heaven!"

Thomas Kelly, 1809.

ALL SAINTS. [H. P. 298.]

314 Rev. xix. 6. "*I heard as it were the voice of a great multitude.*"

Tune CORFE MULLEN. 87, 87, 47.
Or ZAANAIM.

1 LO! He cometh! countless trumpets
Blow to raise the sleeping dead!
'Mid ten thousand saints and angels,
See the great exalted Head!
Hallelujah!
Welcome, welcome, Son of God!

2 Full of joyful expectation,
Saints behold their Lord appear;
Truth and justice go before Him;
Now the joyful sentence hear!
Hallelujah!
Welcome sounds throughout the air!

3 Come, ye blessèd of My Father,
Enter into life and joy!
Banish all your fears and sorrows,
Endless praise be your employ!
Hallelujah!
Welcome, welcome to the skies.

4 Now at once they rise to glory,
Jesus brings them to the King;
There, with all the hosts of heaven,
They eternal anthems sing:
Hallelujah!
Boundless glory to the Lamb!

John Cennick, 1752. (*a.*)

315 Rev. v. 11-13. "*Worthy is the Lamb.*" Tune GOTHA. 87, 87. Or CULBACH.

1 HARK! ten thousand voices crying,
"Lamb of God!" with one accord;
Thousand, thousand saints replying,
Wake at once the echoing chord.

2 "Praise the Lamb," the chorus waking,
All in heaven together throng,
Loud and far, each tongue partaking,
Rolls around the endless song.

3 Grateful incense this, ascending
Ever to the Father's throne;
Every knee to Jesus bending,
All the mind in heaven is one:

4 All the Father's counsels claiming
Equal honour to the Son;
All the Son's effulgence, beaming,
Makes the Father's glory known.

5 By the Spirit all pervading,
Hosts unnumbered round the Lamb,
Crowned with light and joy unfading,
Hail Him as the great "I AM."

6 Joyful now the whole creation
Rests in undisturbed repose,
Blest in Jesu's full salvation,
Sorrow now, nor thraldom knows.

John Nelson Darby, 1837.

316 Mal. iii. 2. "*Who may abide the day of His coming?*" Tune BRIDEHEAD. 886. D.

1 WHEN Thou, my righteous Judge, shalt come
To fetch Thy ransomed people home,
Shall I among them stand?
Shall such a worthless worm as I,
Who sometimes am afraid to die,
Be found at Thy right hand?

2 I love to meet among them now,
Before Thy gracious feet to bow,
Though vilest of them all:
But can I bear the piercing thought,
What if my name should be left out,
When Thou for them shalt call?

3 Prevent it, Saviour, by Thy grace;
Be Thou, O Lord, my hiding-place,
In this the' accepted day.
Thy pardoning voice, oh let me hear,
To still my unbelieving fear;
Nor let me fall, I pray.

4 Let me among Thy saints be found,
Whene'er the' archangel's trump shall sound,
And see Thy smiling face:
Then with what rapture shall I sing,
While heaven's resounding mansions ring
With shouts of sovereign grace!

Selina Countess of Huntingdon's Collection, 1774; *C. Wesley*. (*a.*)

GOLDSTERN. [H. P. 280.]

317 Zech. i. 12. "*O Lord of Hosts, how long?*"

Tune GOLDSTERN. 7 6, 7 6. D. Or GOLDBACH.

1 HOW long, O Lord our Saviour,
Wilt Thou remain away?
Our hearts are growing weary
At Thy so long delay;
Oh! when shall come the moment,
When, brighter far than morn,
The sunshine of Thy glory
Shall on Thy people dawn?

2 How long, O gracious Master,
Wilt Thou Thy household leave?
So long hast Thou now tarried,
Few Thy return believe:
Immersed in sloth and folly,
Thy servants, Lord, we see;
And few of us stand ready
With joy to welcome Thee.

3 How long, O heavenly Bridegroom,
How long wilt Thou delay?
And yet how few are grieving,
That Thou dost absent stay!
Thy very Bride her portion
And calling hath forgot,
And seeks for ease and glory,
Where Thou, her Lord, art not.

4 Oh! wake Thy slumbering virgins;
Send forth the solemn cry,
Let all Thy saints repeat it—
"The Bridegroom draweth nigh!"
May all our lamps be burning,
Our loins well girded be,
Each longing heart preparing
With joy Thy face to see!

James George Deck, 1837.

PEOR (Mount). [H. P. 242.]

318 Joel ii. 1. "*The day of the Lord cometh.*"

Tune PEOR. 11 11, 11 11, 11 11.

1 TIME'S sun is fast setting, its twilight is nigh,
Its evening is falling in cloud o'er the sky,
Its shadows are stretching in ominous gloom;
Its midnight approaches, the midnight of doom.
Then haste, sinner, haste, there is mercy for thee,
And wrath is preparing—flee, lingerer, flee!

2 Rides forth the fierce tempest on the' wing of the cloud;
The moan of the night-blast is fitful and loud;
The mountains are heaving, the forests are bowed,
The ocean is surging, earth gathers its shroud.
Then haste, sinner, haste, etc.

3 The vision is nearing—the Judge and the throne!—
The voice of the angel proclaims, "It is done."
On the whirl of the tempest its Ruler shall come,
And the blaze of His glory flash out from its gloom.
Then haste, sinner, haste, etc.

4 With clouds He is coming! His people shall sing,
With gladness they hail Him Redeemer and King,
The iron rod wielding—the rod of His ire,
He cometh to kindle earth's last fatal fire!
Then haste, sinner, haste, etc.

Horatius Bonar, D.D., 1844.

K

319 Rev. ii. 28. *"I will give him the Morning Star."*

Tune WINTON. C. M. Or NOTTINGHAM.

WINTON. [H. P. 262.]

1 LIGHT of the lonely pilgrim's heart,
 Star of the coming day!
Arise, and, with Thy morning beams,
 Chase all our griefs away.

2 Come, blessèd Lord! bid every shore
 And answering island sing
The praises of Thy royal name,
 And own Thee as their King.

3 Bid the whole earth, responsive now
 To the bright world above,
Break forth in rapturous strains of joy,
 In memory of Thy love.

4 Lord, Lord, Thy fair creation groans,
 The air, the earth, the sea,
In unison with all our hearts,
 And calls aloud for Thee.

5 Come then, with all Thy quickening power,
 With one awakening smile,
And bid the serpent's trail no more
 Thy beauteous realms defile.

6 Thine was the cross, with all its fruits
 Of grace and peace Divine:
Be Thine the crown of glory now,
 The palm of victory Thine!

Sir Edward Denny, 1848.

[H. P. 191.]

320 Mal. iii. 1. *"The Lord, whom ye seek, shall suddenly come to His temple."* Tune ZAANAIM. 87, 87, 47.

1 SAVIOUR, come, Thy friends are waiting,
 Waiting for the final day;
Thence their promised glory dating,
 Come, and bear Thy saints away.
 Come, Lord Jesus,
 Thus Thy waiting people pray.

2 Base the wish, and vain the' endeavour,
 While on earth to find our rest;
Till we see Thy face, we never
 Shall or can be fully blest;
 In Thy presence
 Nothing shall our peace molest.

3 Lord, we wait for Thine appearing;
 "Tarry not," Thy people say;
Bright the prospect is, and cheering,
 Of beholding Thee that day;
 When our sorrow
 Shall for ever pass away.

4 Till it comes, oh keep us steady;
 Keep us walking in Thy ways;
At Thy call may we be ready,
 And our heads with triumph raise;
 Then with angels
 Sing Thine everlasting praise!

See Hymns 210, 211, 1090, 1091.

Thomas Kelly, 1820.

---

(17) THE CORONATION OF CHRIST—KING OF KINGS.

321 Rev. xix. 16. *"King of kings, and Lord of lords."* Tune CORFE MULLEN. 87, 87, 47. Or ZAANAIM.

1 LOOK, ye saints, the sight is glorious,
 See the "Man of Sorrows" now;
From the fight returned victorious,
 Every knee to Him shall bow:
 Crown Him, crown Him;
 Crowns become the Victor's brow.

2 Crown the Saviour, angels, crown Him:
 Rich the trophies Jesus brings:
In the seat of power enthrone Him,
 While the vault of heaven rings:
 Crown Him, crown Him;
 Crown the Saviour "King of kings."

CORFE MULLEN. [H. P. 297.]

3 Sinners in derision crowned Him,
Mocking thus the Saviour's claim;
Saints and angels crowd around Him,
Own His title, praise His name:
Crown Him, crown Him;
Spread abroad the Victor's fame.

4 Hark! those bursts of acclamation!
Hark! those loud triumphant chords!
Jesus takes the highest station:
Oh what joy the sight affords!
Crown Him, crown Him;
"King of kings, and Lord of lords!"

Thomas Kelly, 1806.

322 Rev. xix. 12. *"On His head were many crowns."*

Tune Idumea. 87, 87, 47. Or Zaanaim.

1 BRIGHT with all His crowns of glory,
See the royal Victor's brow;
Once for sinners marred and gory,
See the Lamb exalted now;
While before Him
All His ransomed brethren bow.

2 Blessèd morning! long expected,
Lo, they fill the peopled air,
Mourners once, by man rejected,
They, with Him exalted, there
Sing His praises,
And His throne of glory share.

3 Judah! Lo, thy royal Lion
Reigns on earth, a conquering King:
Come, ye ransomed tribes, to Zion,
Love's abundant offering bring;
There behold Him,
And His ceaseless praises sing.

4 King of kings! let earth adore Him,
High on His exalted throne;
Fall, ye nations, fall before Him,
And His righteous sceptre own:
All the glory
Be to Him, and Him alone.

Sir Edward Denny, 1837.

IDUMEA. [H. P. 193.]

IONA. [H. P. 37.]

323 Isa. xxiv. 23. *"The Lord of Hosts shall reign in Mount Zion."* Tune Iona. C. M.

1 ISLES of the deep, rejoice! rejoice!
Ye ransomed nations, sing
The praises of your Lord and God,
The triumphs of your King.

2 He comes—and at His mighty word
The clouds are fleeting fast;
And o'er the land of promise, see,
The glory breaks at last.

3 There He, upon His ancient throne,
His power and grace displays;
While Salem, with its echoing hills,
Sends forth the voice of praise.

4 Streams of Divine, unfailing joy,
Whose sweetness none can know
But the redeemed, the blood-bought soul,
Through all creation flow.

5 Oh! let His praises fill the earth,
While all the blest above,
In strains of loftier triumph still,
Speak only of His love.

6 Sing, ye redeemed; before the throne,
Ye white-robed myriads, fall;
Sing—for the Lord of glory reigns,
The Christ—the Heir of all.

Sir Edward Denny, 1848.

ARCHIPPUS. [H. P. 34A.]

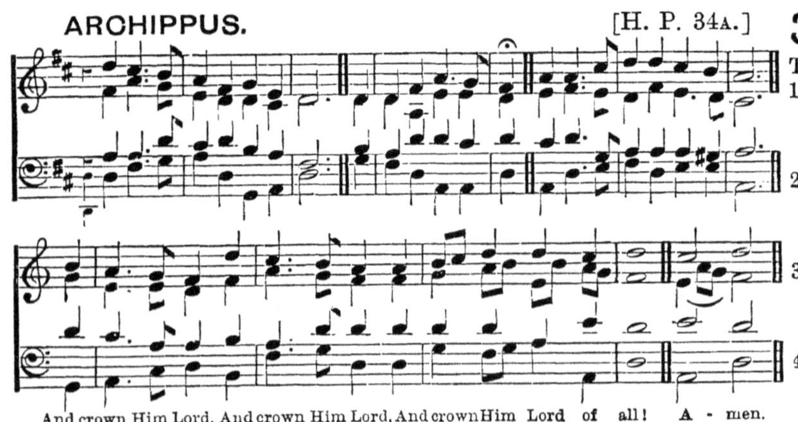
And crown Him Lord, And crown Him Lord, And crown Him Lord of all! A - men.

324 Rev. xix. 16. "*King of kings, and Lord of lords.*"

Tune ARCHIPPUS. C.M. Or MILES' LANE.

1 ALL hail the power of Jesu's name!
  Let angels prostrate fall:
Bring forth the royal diadem,
  To crown Him Lord of all.

2 Let high-born seraphs tune the lyre,
  And as they tune it, fall
Before His face, who tunes their choir,
  And crown Him Lord of all.

3 Crown Him, ye morning stars of light,
  Who fixed this floating ball;
Now hail the Strength of Israel's might,
  And crown Him Lord of all.

4 Crown Him, ye martyrs of your God,
  Who from His altar call;
Extol the stem of Jesse's rod,
  And crown Him Lord of all.

PART II.

5 Ye seed of Israel's chosen race,
  Ye ransomed of the fall,
Hail Him who saves you by His grace,
  And crown Him Lord of all.

6 Hail Him, ye heirs of David's line,
  Whom David Lord did call;
The God Incarnate—Man Divine;
  And crown Him Lord of all.

7 Sinners! whose love can ne'er forget
  The wormwood and the gall,
Go—spread your trophies at His feet,
  And crown Him Lord of all.

8 Let every tribe, and every tongue,
  That bound creation's ball,
Now shout in universal song
  The crownèd Lord of all.

9 Oh that, with yonder sacred throng,
  We at His feet may fall;
There join the everlasting song,
  And crown Him Lord of all!

Edward Perronet, 1780; *ver.* 2, *Anon.*; *ver.* 9, *Dr. Rippon.*

MILES' LANE. [H. P. 261.]

ZOAN II. (Field of.) [H. P. 166.]

325 Zech. xiv. 4. "*His feet shall stand upon the Mount of Olives.*" Tune ZOAN II. 77, 87. D.

1 LO! 'tis the heavenly army,
  The Lord of hosts attending;
'Tis He—the Lamb, The great I AM,
  With all His saints descending.
To you, ye kings and nations,
  Ye foes of Christ, assembling,
The hosts of light, Prepared for fight,
  Come with the cup of trembling.

2 Joy to His ancient people!
  Your bonds He comes to sever;
And now 'tis done! The Lord hath won,
  And ye are free for ever.
Joy to the ransomed nations!
  The foe, the ravening lion,
Is bound in chains While Jesus reigns
  King of the earth, in Zion.

3 Joy to the church triumphant,
The Saviour's throne surrounding;
They see His face, Adore His grace
O'er all their sin abounding:
Crowned with the mighty Victor,
His royal glory sharing;
Each fills a throne, His name alone
To heaven and earth declaring.

4 Praise to the Lamb for ever!
Bruised for our sin, and gory,
Behold His brow, Encircled now
With all His crowns of glory—
Beneath His love reposing,
The whole redeemed creation
Is now at rest, For ever blest,
And sings His great salvation.

Sir Edward Denny, 1838.

326

Tune PISGAH. 77, 77.

Rev. xiv. 14. "*On His head a golden crown.*"

PISGAH (Mount). [H. P. 137.]

Hal - le - lu - jah, Hal - le - lu - jah!

1 CROWNS of glory ever bright
Rest upon the Victor's head:
Crowns of glory are His right,
His, "who liveth and was dead."

2 Jesus fought and won the day;
Such a day was never fought;
Well His people now may say,
See what God, our God, has wrought!

3 He subdued the powers of hell;
In the fight He stood alone;
All His foes before Him fell,
By His single arm o'erthrown.

4 They have fallen to rise no more:
Final is the foes' defeat:
Jesus triumphed by His power,
And His triumph is complete.

5 His the fight, the arduous toil;
His the honours of the day;
His the glory and the spoil;
Jesus bears them all away!

6 Now proclaim His deeds afar;
Fill the world with His renown:
His alone the Victor's car;
His the everlasting crown.

Thomas Kelly, 1806.

MAGDEBURG. [H. P. 300.]

327

Ps. xlv. 3. "*Gird Thy sword upon Thy thigh, O most Mighty, with Thy glory and Thy majesty.*"

Tune MAGDEBURG. 87, 87, 47. Or HAVILAH.

1 LET us sing the King Messiah,
King of righteousness and peace!
Hail Him, all His happy subjects,
Never let His praises cease;
Ever hail Him,
Never let His praises cease.

2 How transcendent are Thy glories!
Fairer than the sons of men!
While Thy blessèd mediation
Brings us back to God again:
Blest Redeemer,
How we triumph in Thy reign!

3 Gird Thy sword on, mighty Hero!
Make Thy word of truth Thy car:
Prosper in Thy course majestic;
All success attend Thy war!
Gracious Victor,
Let mankind before Thee bow!

4 Majesty, combined with meekness,
Righteousness and peace unite,
To ensure Thy blessèd conquests:
On, great Prince, assert Thy right!
Ride triumphant,
All around the conquered globe!

5 Blest are all that touch Thy sceptre,
Blest are all that own Thy reign;
Freed from sin, that worst of tyrants,
Rescued from its galling chain.
Saints and angels,
All who know Thee, bless Thy reign.

John Ryland, D.D., 1790.

FREYLINGHAUSEN. [H. P. 306.]

(18) THE MILLENNIAL REIGN OF CHRIST.

328 Zech. xiv. 9. *"The Lord shall be King over all the earth."* Tune FREYLINGHAUSEN. 87, 87. D. Or SHEN.

1 ZION'S King shall reign victorious,
All the earth shall own His sway,
He will make His kingdom glorious,
He will reign through endless day:
What though none on earth assist Him?
God requires no help from man;
What though all the world resist Him?
God will realize His plan.

2 Nations now from God estrangèd
Then shall see a glorious light,
Night to day shall then be changèd,
Heaven shall triumph in the sight:
See the ancient idols falling!
Worshipped once, but now abhorred;
Men on Zion's King are calling,
Zion's King, by all adored.

3 Then shall Israel, long dispersèd,
Mourning seek the Lord their God,
Look on Him whom once they piercèd,
Own and kiss the chastening rod:
Then all Israel shall be savèd,
War and tumult then shall cease,
While the greater Son of David
Rules a conquered world in peace.

4 Mighty King, Thine arm revealing,
Now Thy glorious cause maintain,
Bring the nations help and healing,
Make them subject to Thy reign:
Angels, in their lofty station,
Praise Thy name, Thou Only Wise;
Oh, let earth, with emulation,
Join the triumph of the skies.

Thomas Kelly, 1806.

329 Isa. lx. 18. *"Thou shalt call thy walls Salvation, and thy gates Praise."*
Tune ST. CHRYSOSTOM. C. M.

1 WAKE, harp of Zion, wake again,
Upon thine ancient hill,
On Jordan's long deserted plain,
By Kedron's lowly rill.

2 The hymn shall yet in Zion swell,
That sounds Messiah's praise,
And Thy loved name, Emmanuel,
As once in ancient days.

3 For Israel yet shall own her King,
For her salvation waits,
And hill and dale shall sweetly sing,
With praise in all her gates.

4 Oh hasten, Lord, these promised days,
When Israel shall rejoice;
And Jew and Gentile join in praise,
With one united voice!

James Edmeston, 1846.

ST. CHRYSOSTOM. [H. P. 53.]

330 Ps. lxxii. 17. *"All nations shall call Him blessed."* Tune CRÜGER. 76, 76. D. Or ZOAN I.

1 HAIL to the Lord's Anointed;
Great David's greater Son;
Hail in the time appointed,
His reign on earth begun!
He comes to break oppression,
To set the captive free;
To take away transgression,
And rule in equity.

2 He shall come down like showers
Upon the fruitful earth;
And love, joy, hope, like flowers,
Spring in His path to birth:
Before Him on the mountains,
Shall Peace, the herald, go;
And righteousness, in fountains,
From hill to valley flow.

3 Arabia's desert-ranger
To Him shall bow the knee,
The Ethiopian stranger
His glory come to see;
With offerings of devotion
Ships from the Isles shall meet,
To pour the wealth of ocean
In tribute at His feet.

CRÜGER. [H. P. 276.]

4 Kings shall fall down before
  Him,
 And gold and incense bring,
All nations shall adore Him,
 His praise all people sing:
For He shall have dominion
 O'er river, sea, and shore,
Far as the eagle's pinion
 Or dove's light wing can soar.

5 For Him shall prayer unceas-
  ing,
 And daily vows, ascend;
His kingdom still increasing,
 A kingdom without end:
The mountain dew shall nourish
 A seed in weakness sown,
Whose fruit shall spread and
  flourish,
 And shake like Lebanon.

6 O'er every foe victorious,
 He on His throne shall rest;
From age to age more glorious,
 All-blessing and all-blest.
The tide of time shall never
 His covenant remove;
His name shall stand for ever,
 That name to us is—Love!

James Montgomery, 1822.

EDEN. [H. P. 38.]

331

Rev. xi. 15. *"He shall reign for ever and ever."*

Tune EDEN. C. M.

1 FOR ever and for ever, Lord,
 Thy kingdom shall endure;
Thy holy, lofty, sovereign word
 Its glory doth secure.

2 Bring on, bring on the promised day,
 Oh speed its eagle wing;
When earth, like heaven, shall Thee obey,
 And all the nations sing!

3 Grant us in firmest faith to stand,
 Full certain of the end;
And with Thy valiant little band
 Thine ancient truth defend.

4 O Jesu, be Thy cross our all,
 Thy crown our highest meed;
Nor saint nor angel will we call
 To help in time of need.

5 Thy Spirit give, and we will then
 Return Thee fervent praise;
And when Thou shalt come back again,
 A nobler song we'll raise!

William Henry Havergal, 1866.

CRASSELIUS; *or,* WINCHESTER NEW. [H. P. 3.]

332

Ps. lxxii. 19. *"Let the whole earth be filled with His glory; Amen, and Amen."* Tune CRASSELIUS. L. M. Or OLD HUNDREDTH.

1 JESUS shall reign where'er the sun
 Doth his successive journeys run;
His kingdom stretch from shore to shore,
Till moons shall wax and wane no more.

2 To Him shall endless prayer be made,
And praises throng to crown His head;
His name like sweet perfume shall rise
With every morning sacrifice.

3 People and realms of every tongue
Dwell on His love with sweetest song;
And infant voices shall proclaim
Their early blessings on His name.

4 Blessings abound where'er He reigns,
The prisoner leaps to lose his chains,
The weary find eternal rest,
And all the sons of want are blessed.

5 Where He displays His healing power,
Death and the curse are known no more;
In Him the tribes of Adam boast
More blessings than their father lost.

6 Let every creature rise and bring
Peculiar honours to our King;
Angels descend with songs again,
And earth repeat the loud Amen!

Isaac Watts, D.D., 1719.

EUPHRATES. [H. P. 2.]

Hosanna! Hosanna! Hosanna! A-men, A-men.

333 Rev. xi. 15. *"The kingdoms of this world are become the kingdoms of our Lord."*

Tune EUPHRATES. L. M.

1 SOON may the last glad song arise,
Through all the millions of the skies—
That song of triumph, which records
That all the earth is now the Lord's!

2 Let thrones, and powers, and kingdoms be
Obedient, mighty God, to Thee!
And over land, and stream, and main,
Wave Thou the sceptre of Thy reign!

3 Oh that that anthem soon might swell,
And host to host the triumph tell—
That not one rebel heart remains,
But over all the Saviour reigns!

Josiah Pratt's Psalms and Hymns, 1829.

YORK. [H. P. 45.]

334 Isa. ii. 2. *"The mountain of the Lord's house shall be established."* Tune YORK. C. M.

1 BEHOLD! the mountain of the Lord
In latter days shall rise
On mountain tops, above the hills,
And draw the wondering eyes.

2 To this the joyful nations round,
All tribes and tongues, shall flow;
"Up to the hill of God," they 'll say,
"And to His house we 'll go."

3 The beam that shines from Zion's hill
Shall lighten every land;
The King who reigns in Salem's towers
Shall all the world command.

4 Among the nations He shall judge;
His judgments truth shall guide;
His sceptre shall protect the just,
And quell the sinner's pride.

5 No strife shall rage, nor hostile feuds
Disturb those peaceful years;
To ploughshares men shall beat their swords,
To pruning-hooks their spears.

6 No longer hosts, encountering hosts,
Shall crowds of slain deplore;
They hang the trumpet in the hall,
And study war no more.

7 Come then! O come from every land,
To worship at His shrine,
And, walking in the light of God,
With holy beauties shine!

Scripture Songs, 1751, altered by Michael Bruce, 1768.

ZOAN II. (Field of.) [H. P. 166.]

335 Rev. xx. 4. *"They lived and reigned with Christ a thousand years."* Tune ZOAN II. 77, 87. D.

1 BREAK forth, O earth, in praises!
Dwell on His wondrous story;
The Saviour's name And love proclaim—
The King who reigns in glory.
See on the throne beside Him,
O'er all her foes victorious,
His royal Bride For whom He died,
Like Him for ever glorious.

2 Ye of the seed of Jacob!
Behold the royal Lion
Of Judah's line, In glory shine,
And fill His throne in Zion.
Blest with Messiah's favour,
A ransomed holy nation,
Your offerings bring To Christ your King,
The God of your salvation.

3 Come, O ye kings! ye nations,
With songs of gladness hail Him,
Ye Gentiles all, Before Him fall,
The royal Priest in Salem.
O'er hell and death triumphant,
Your conquering Lord hath risen,
His praises sound, Whose power hath bound
Your ruthless foe in prison.

4 Hail to the King of glory:
Head of the new creation—
Thy ways of grace We love to trace,
And praise Thy great salvation.
Thy heart was pressed with sorrow,
The bonds of death to sever,
To make us free, That we might be
Thy crown of joy for ever.

Sir Edward Denny, 1838.

336 Rev. xxii. 20. "*Even so, come, Lord Jesus.*"
Tune Civitas Regis. 8 7, 8 7, 4 7. Or Idumea.

CIVITAS REGIS MAGNI. [H. P. 301.]

1 "COME, Lord Jesus! O come quickly!"
Oft has prayed the mourning Bride:
"Lo!" He answers, "I come quickly!"
Who His coming may abide?
All who loved Him,
All who longed to see His day!

2 "Come," He saith, "ye heirs of glory;
Come, ye purchase of My blood;
Claim the kingdom now before you;
Rise, and fill the mount of God,
Fixed for ever
Where the Lamb on Zion stands."

3 See! ten thousand burning seraphs
From their thrones as lightnings fly;
"Take," they cry, "your seats above us,
Nearest Him who rules the sky!"
Patient sufferers,
How rewarded are ye now!

4 In full triumph see them marching
Through the gates of massy light,
While the city walls are sparkling
With meridian glory bright!
O how lovely
Are the dwellings of the Lamb!

5 Hosts angelic all adore Him,
Circling round His orient seat;
Elders cast their crowns before Him,
Fall and worship at His feet;
O how holy
And how reverend is Thy name!

6 Hail, Thou Alpha and Omega!
First and Last of all alone!
He that is, and was, and shall be,
And beside whom there is none!
Take the glory,
Great Eternal Three in One.

Thomas Olivers, 1757.

CHESALON (Mount). [H. P. 35.]

337 Luke i. 32. "*The Lord God shall give unto Him the throne of His Father David.*" Tune Chesalon. C. M. Or Eden.

1 'TIS He—the mighty Saviour comes,
The victory now is won,
And lo, the throne of David waits
For David's royal Son.

2 Thou blessèd Heir of all the earth!
Ascend Thine ancient throne,
And bid the willing nations now
Thy peaceful sceptre own.

3 Shine forth in all Thy glory, Lord,
That man at length may see
That joy, so long estranged from earth,
Can only spring from Thee.

4 O happy day! 'tis come at last,
The reign of death is o'er;
And sin that marred our sweetest joys
Shall grieve our hearts no more.

5 Washed in Thy blood, the tribes of earth,
With all the blest above,
Shall dwell in peace, united now,
One family of love.

6 Fruit of Thy toil, Thou bleeding Lamb!
These joys we owe to Thee,
Then take the glory, Lord!—'tis Thine!
And shall for ever be!

Sir Edward Denny, 1838.

338 Isa. xxxv. 1. *"The desert shall rejoice, and blossom as the rose."*

Tune MIZPEH. 6666, 88.

MIZPEH (Valley of). [H. P. 120.]

1 JOY to the ransomed earth!
  Messiah fills the throne;
His all-excelling worth,
  Ye joyful nations, own.
Ye sons of men, break forth and sing
The praises of your God and King!

2 Behold! the desert smiles
  To hear His welcome voice,
And all the listening isles
  Beneath His love rejoice.
Ye dwellers in the islands, sing
The glories of your heavenly King!

3 To gain a royal crown
  Of glory for His Bride,
The foe He trampled down,
  And conquered when He died.
O earth, rejoice! break forth and sing
The conquests of your dying King!

4 Rejoice beneath the eye
  Of Jesus and His Bride,
His Queen, enthroned on high,
  In glory at His side!
Blest in His love, ye nations, sing
Hosanna to your glorious King!

Sir Edward Denny, 1838.

ALL SAINTS. [H. P. 298.]

339 Isa. lxiii. 1. *"Who is this that cometh from Edom?"*

Tune ALL SAINTS. 87, 87, 77.

1 "WHO is this that comes from Edom?"
  All His raiment stained with blood,
To the slave proclaiming freedom,
  Bringing and bestowing good;
Glorious in the garb He wears,
Glorious in the spoils He bears.

2 'Tis the Saviour, now victorious,
  Travelling onward in His might
'Tis the Saviour, O how glorious
  To His people is the sight!
Jesus now is strong to save,
Mighty to redeem the slave.

3 Why that blood His raiment staining?
  'Tis the blood of many slain;
Of His foes there 's none remaining,
  None the contest to maintain;
Fallen they are, no more to rise,
All their glory prostrate lies.

4 This the Saviour has effected,
  By His mighty arm alone;
See the throne for Him erected,
  'Tis an everlasting throne;
'Tis the great reward He gains,
Glorious fruit of all His pains.

5 Mighty Victor, reign for ever,
  Wear the crown so dearly won;
Never shall Thy people, never
  Cease to sing what Thou hast done:
Thou hast fought Thy people's foes;
Thou wilt heal Thy people's woes!

Thomas Kelly, 1806.

GILBOA (Mount). [H. P. 11.]

340 Isa. ix. 6. *"His name shall be called the Prince of Peace."* Tune GILBOA. L. M.

1 PEACE to the world! the Lord is come;
  Its days of conflict now are o'er;
The Prince of Peace ascends the throne,
  And war has ceased from shore to shore!

2 Joy to the earth! Messiah reigns!
  Earth's diadems are on His brow;
Its rebel kingdoms are become
  His everlasting kingdom now.

3 Rest to the nations, blessèd rest!
The storm is hushed above, below:
Joy to creation; welcome sound!
After six thousand years of woe.

4 The earth again is Paradise,
The desert blossoms as the rose,
Far happier place than Eden this,
Far brighter, sweeter days than those!

5 Oh! long expected, absent long,
Star of creation's troubled gloom!
Let heaven and earth break forth in song,
Messiah, Saviour, art Thou come?

6 For Thou hast bought us with Thy blood,
And Thou wast slain to set us free;
Thou mad'st us kings and priests to God,
And we shall reign on earth with Thee!

Horatius Bonar, D.D., 1844.

See Hymns 621, 918, 919.

341 Acts iii. 19. "*Times of refreshing . . from the Lord.*"
Tune Gilboa. L.M. Or Crasselius.

1 O WHAT a bright and blessèd world
This groaning earth of ours will be,
When, from its throne the tempter hurled,
Shall leave it all, O Lord, to Thee!

2 But brighter far, that world above,
Where we, as we are known, shall know;
And, in the sweet embrace of love,
Reign o'er this ransomed earth below.

3 O blessèd Lord! with weeping eyes
That blissful hour we wait to see;
While every worm or leaf that dies
Tells of the curse, and calls for Thee.

4 Come, Saviour, then, o'er all below
Shine brightly from Thy throne above;
Bid heaven and earth Thy glory know,
And all creation feel Thy love.

Sir Edward Denny, 1838.

JEHOVAH—THE HOLY GHOST.

ORIEL. [H. P. 302.]

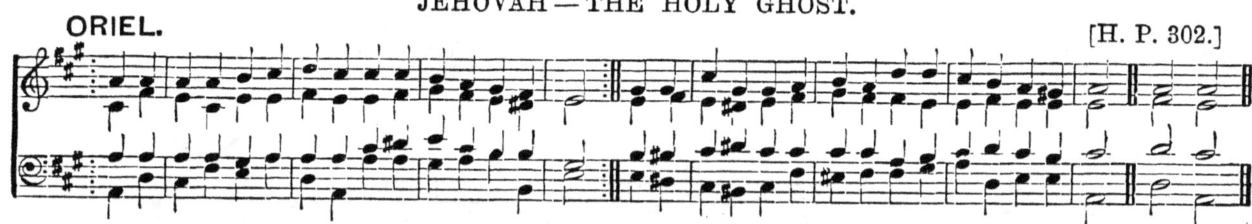

(1) HIS DEITY SEEN IN CREATION.

342 Job xxxiii. 4. "*The Spirit of God hath made me.*" Tune Oriel. 87, 87, 47.

1 ERE the world, with light invested,
Rose from its primeval sleep,
Gloom and desolation rested
On the surface of the deep:
Earth and ocean
Formed one rude and shapeless heap.

2 There the Holy Spirit moving,
Wide His fostering pinions spread;
Till, beneath His power improving,
Nature seemed no longer dead;
Light and beauty
Rose to crown her radiant head.

3 Blessèd Spirit, we implore Thee,
Yet once more Thy succour lend;
Scatter the thick clouds before Thee,
Which through all the earth extend;
On all nations
Bid the light of life descend.

4 See what sin, and what delusion,
In this wretched world are found:
Stay the torrent of confusion,
Ere it spreads destruction round:
Where sin triumphed,
Now let grace and truth abound.

William Hiley Bathurst, 1831.

343 Gen. i. 2. "*The Spirit of God moved upon the face of the waters.*"
Tune Eaton. 88, 88, 88. Or Angels' Song.

1 CREATOR Spirit, by whose aid
The world's foundations first were laid,
Come visit every humble mind,
Come pour Thy joy on all mankind:
From sin and sorrow set us free,
And make us temples meet for Thee.

2 O Source of uncreated light!
The Father's promised Paraclete!
Thrice holy Fount, thrice holy Fire,
Our hearts with heavenly love inspire:
Come, and Thy sacred unction bring,
To sanctify us while we sing.

3 Plenteous of grace descend from high,
Rich in Thy sevenfold energy;
Make us eternal truths receive,
And practise all that we believe:
Give us Thyself, that we may see
The Father and the Son by Thee.

4 Immortal honours, endless fame,
Attend the' Almighty Father's name:
The Saviour Son be glorified,
Who for lost man's redemption died:
And equal adoration be,
Eternal Paraclete, to Thee.

Latin Hymn, about Seventh Century;
(tr.) John Dryden, 1693.

EATON. [H. P. 313.]

MORAVIA. [H. P. 83.]

(2) DISTINCT PERSONALITY.

344 Heb. x. 15. "*The Holy Ghost also is a witness.*" Tune MORAVIA. S. M.

1 TO God the Holy Ghost,
The Lord of truth and grace,
The church on earth, the heavenly host,
Ascribe eternal praise.

2 He Wills, and Speaks, and Acts,
For God and sinful men:
And writes, within us, gospel facts,
With an immortal pen.

3 The things of God most deep,
He Searches and Reveals:
And when, by Him, for sin we weep,
Our souls, through faith, He Heals.

4 To Him are all things Known,
And here His Godhead shines,
He brings the truth from Jesu's throne
In bright celestial lines.

5 His glories let us tell,
His Name be all-adored,
As God distinct, yet one as well,
Within the Triune Lord.

Thomas Row, 1817. (*a.*)

CONWAY. [H. P. 234.]

(3) PROCEEDING FROM THE FATHER AND THE SON.

345 John xv. 26. "*The Comforter, . . . whom I will send unto you from the Father.*"
Tune CONWAY. 10 10, 10 10. Or DEPTFORD.

1 HAIL, Holy Spirit, bright immortal Dove!
Great Spring of light, of purity and love;
Proceeding from the Father and the Son,
Distinct from Both, and yet with Both but One.

2 O Lord, from Thee one kind and quickening ray
Will pierce the gloom and re-enkindle day;
Will warm the frozen heart with love Divine,
And with its Maker's image make it shine.

3 O shed Thine influence, and Thy power exert;
Clear my dark mind, and thaw my icy heart;
Pour on my drowsy soul celestial day,
And heavenly life to all its powers convey.

Simon Browne, 1720.

TALLIS'S ORDINAL. [H. P. 44.]

(4) NAMES AND TITLES EXPRESSING HIS WORK.

DIVINE.

346 Titus iii. 5. "*The renewing of the Holy Ghost.*"
Tune TALLIS. C. M.

1 SPIRIT Divine! attend our prayers,
And make this house Thy home;
Descend with all Thy gracious powers,
O come, Great Spirit, come!

2 Come as the light—to us reveal
Our emptiness and woe;
And lead us in those paths of life
Where all the righteous go.

3 Come as the fire—and purge our hearts,
Like sacrificial flame;
Let our whole soul an offering be
To our Redeemer's name.

4 Come as the dew—and sweetly bless
  This consecrated hour;
May barrenness rejoice to own
  Thy fertilising power.

5 Come as the dove—and spread Thy wings,
  The wings of peaceful love;
And let Thy church on earth become
  Blest as the church above.

6 Come as the wind—with rushing sound
  And Pentecostal grace;
That all of woman born may see
  The glory of Thy face.

7 Spirit Divine! attend our prayers,
  Make this lost world Thy home;
Descend with all Thy gracious powers;
  O come, Great Spirit, come!

Andrew Reed, D.D., 1842.

ETERNAL.

347 Heb. ix. 14. "*Christ . . . through the Eternal Spirit offered Himself.*" Tune TALLIS. C.M. Or GLOUCESTER.

1 ETERNAL Spirit, by whose power
  Are burst the bands of death,
On our cold hearts Thy blessings shower,
  And stir them with Thy breath.

2 'Tis Thine to point the heavenly way,
  Each rising fear control,
And with a warm enlivening ray
  To melt the icy soul.

3 'Tis Thine to cheer us when distressed,
  To raise us when we fall,
To calm the doubting troubled breast,
  And aid when sinners call.

4 'Tis Thine to bring God's sacred word,
  And write it on our heart;
There its reviving truths record,
  And there its peace impart.

5 Almighty Spirit, visit thus
  Our hearts, and guide our ways;
Pour down Thy quickening grace on us,
  And tune our lips to praise.

William Hiley Bathurst, 1831.

EVERTON. [H. P. 308.]

HOLY GHOST

348 John xiv. 16. "*He shall give you another Comforter.*" Tune EVERTON. 87, 87, 77, 88.

1 HOLY GHOST, dispel our sadness,
  Pierce the clouds of sinful night:
Come, Thou Source of sweetest gladness,
  Breathe Thy life, and spread Thy light!
  Loving Spirit, God of Peace,
  Great Distributer of grace,
Rest upon this congregation!
Hear, O hear, our supplication!

2 From that height which knows no measure,
  As a gracious shower descend;
Bringing down the richest treasure
  Man can wish, and God can send:
  O Thou Glory, shining down
  From the Father and the Son,
Grant us Thy illumination!
Rest upon this congregation.

PART II.

3 Come, Thou best of all donations
  God can give, or we implore;
Having Thy sweet consolations,
  We need wish for nothing more.
  Come, with unction and with power;
  On our souls Thy graces shower;
Author of the new creation,
Make our hearts Thy habitation.

4 Known to Thee are all recesses
  Of the earth and spreading skies;
Every sand the shore possesses,
  Thy omniscient mind descries:
  Holy Fountain, wash us clean,
  Both from error and from sin;
Make us fly what Thou refusest,
And delight in what Thou choosest.

5 Manifest Thy love for ever;
  Fence us in on every side;
In distress be Thou our Helper,
  Guard and teach, support and guide:
  Let Thy kind, effectual grace
  Turn our feet from evil ways:
Show Thyself our New Creator,
And conform us to Thy nature!

Paul Gerhardt, 1653; *Augustus M. Toplady*, 1776.

ESDRAELON. [H. P. 202.]

INSPIRER.

349 Acts ii. 4. "*They were all filled with the Holy Ghost.*"
Tune ESDRAELON. 87, 87. D.

1 HOLY GHOST, inspire our praises!
Shed abroad the Saviour's love.
While we sing the name of Jesus
Deign on every heart to move;
Source of sweetest consolation,
Breathe Thy peace on all below;
Bless, O bless this congregation!
Bid our hearts with love o'erflow.

2 Come with heavenly inspiration,
Jesus in our souls reveal!
Manifest His great salvation,
As Thine own our spirits seal!
Light Divine, on darkness shining,
Deign the light of truth to give;
Every grace and joy combining,
May we to Thy glory live!

3 Hail! ye spirits bright and glorious,
High exalted round the throne!
Now with you we join in chorus,
And your Lord we call our own.
God to us His Son hath given:
Saints, your noblest anthems raise!
All in earth and all in heaven,
Sing the great Jehovah's praise!

Basil Woodd, 1800.

SHENIR II. (Mount.) [H. P. 151.]

ILLUMINATOR.

350 1 Cor. xii. 7. "*The manifestation of the Spirit.*" Tune SHENIR II. 77, 77. Or VIENNA.

1 HOLY GHOST, with light Divine,
Shine upon this heart of mine;
Chase the shades of night away,
Turn the darkness into day.

2 Holy Ghost, with power Divine,
Cleanse this guilty heart of mine;
Long has sin without control
Held dominion o'er my soul.

3 Holy Ghost, with joy Divine,
Cheer this saddened heart of mine;
Bid my many woes depart,
Heal my wounded, bleeding heart.

4 Holy Spirit, all Divine,
Dwell within this heart of mine;
Cast down every idol throne;
Reign supreme, and reign alone!

Andrew Reed, D.D., 1817.

CULBACH. [H. P. 181.]

REVEALER.

351 Matt. iii. 11. "*He shall baptize you with the Holy Ghost, and with fire.*" Tune CULBACH. 87, 87.

1 HOLY GHOST, whose fire celestial
Light and life Divine imparts,
Come, and dwell in breasts terrestrial;
Heaven reveal in all our hearts.

2 Come and pour, in blest effusion,
Heavenly unction from above;
Scattering wide, in rich diffusion,
Comfort, life, and fire of love.

3 Keep Thy church in holy union;
Foes remove, give peace at home:
Source of peace and sweet communion,
Where Thou art no ill can come.

4 Teach us humbly to adore Thee,
While on earth we pass our days;
Thence transport our souls to glory,
Lost in wonder, love, and praise!

Thomas Cotterill, 1815.

HAVERGAL. [H. P. 163.]

COMFORTER.

352 John xiv. 26. "*The Comforter, which is the Holy Ghost.*" Tune HAVERGAL. 777.

1 HOLY GHOST! my Comforter!
Now from highest heaven appear,
Shed Thy gracious radiance here.

2 Thou the heart's most precious Guest,
Thou of comforters the best,
Give to us, Thy people, rest.

3 Cleanse, through Christ, from sinful stain;
O'er the parchèd heart, oh! rain,
And the wounded heal from pain.

4 Bend the stubborn will to Thine,
Melt the cold with fire Divine,
Erring hearts aright incline!

5 Grant us, Lord, who cry to Thee,
Steadfast in the faith to be,
Give Thy gifts of charity.

6 May we live in holiness,
And in death find happiness,
And abide with Thee in bliss!

17th Century, (tr.) Catherine Winkworth, 1855.

SANCTIFIER.

353 2 Thess. ii. 13. "*Sanctification of the Spirit.*" Tune SHENIR II. 77, 77. Or LUXEMBURG.

1 HOLY SPIRIT, from on high,
Bend on us a pitying eye;
Animate the drooping heart,
Bid the power of sin depart.

2 Light up every dark recess
Of our heart's ungodliness;
Show us every devious way,
Where our steps have gone astray:

3 Teach us with repentant grief
Humbly to implore relief;
Then the Saviour's blood reveal,
All our deep disease to heal.

4 May we daily grow in grace,
And pursue the heavenly race,
Trained in wisdom, led by love,
Till we reach our rest above!

William Hiley Bathurst, 1831.

SWABIA. [H. P. 82.

SPIRIT OF POWER.

354 2 Tim. i. 7. "*The spirit . . of power.*" Tune SWABIA. S. M.

1 O HOLY SPIRIT, come,
And Jesu's love declare:
Oh tell us of our heavenly home,
And guide us safely there.

2 Our unbelief remove
By Thine almighty breath;
Oh work the wondrous work of love,
The mighty work of faith.

3 Come with resistless power,
Come with almighty grace,
Come with the long expected shower,
And fall upon this place!

Oswald Allen, 1862.

PATMOS. [H. P. 147.]

SPIRIT OF GRACE.

355 Zech. xii. 10. "*I will pour . . . the spirit of grace.*" Tune PATMOS. 77, 77. Or VIENNA.

1 GRACIOUS Spirit, power Divine!
Let Thy light around us shine:
All our guilty fears remove;
Fill us with Thy peace and love.

2 Pardon to the contrite give;
Bid the wounded sinner live;
Lead us to the Lamb of God,
Cleanse us with His precious blood.

3 Earnest Thou of heavenly rest,
Soothe and heal the troubled breast;
Life and joy and peace impart,
Sanctifying every heart.

4 Guardian Spirit, lest we stray,
Keep us in our heavenly way;
Bring us to Thy courts above,
Realms of light, and bliss and love.

John Stocker, 1777; *Thomas Cotterill,* 1820.

OLDENBURG. [H. P. 146.]

HOLY SPIRIT.

356 1 John ii. 27. *"The anointing which ye have received."* Tune OLDENBURG. 77, 77. Or PATMOS.

1 HOLY SPIRIT, in my breast
Grant that lively faith may rest,
And subdue each rebel thought
To believe what Thou hast taught!

2 When around my sinking soul
Gathering waves of sorrow roll,
Spirit blest, the tempest still,
And with hope my bosom fill!

3 Holy Spirit, from my mind
Thought, and wish, and will unkind,
Deed and word unkind, remove,
And my bosom fill with love!

4 Faith, and hope, and charity,
Comforter, descend from Thee;
Thou the' anointing Spirit art,
These Thy gifts to us impart;

5 Till our faith be lost in sight,
Hope be swallowed in delight,
Love return to dwell with Thee,
In the threefold Deity!

Bishop Mant, 1837.

SEIR - (Mount). [H. P. 161.]

SPIRIT OF GLORY.

357 1 Pet. iv. 14. *"The Spirit of glory and of God resteth upon you."* Tune SEIR (adapted). 7777, 5777.

1 HOLY SPIRIT, gently come,
Raise us from our fallen state,
Fix Thy everlasting home
In the hearts Thou didst create.
Gift of God most High,
Visit every troubled breast!
Life and light and love supply;
Give our spirits perfect rest!

2 Heavenly unction from above,
Comforter of weary saints,
Fountain, Life, and Fire of Love,
Hear, and answer our complaints!
Thee, we humbly pray,
Spirit of the Living God,
Now Thy sevenfold grace display,
Shed our Saviour's love abroad!

3 Now Thy quickening influence bring,
On our spirits sweetly move;
Open every mouth to sing
Jesu's everlasting love!
Lighten every heart;
Drive our enemies away;
Joy and peace to us impart;
Lead us in the heavenly way!

4 Take the things of Christ, and show
What our Lord for us hath done;
May we God the Father know
Only in and through the Son:
Nothing will we fear,
Though to wilds and deserts driven,
While we feel Thy presence near,
Witnessing our sins forgiven.

5 Glory be to God alone,
God, whose hand created all!
Glory be to God the Son,
Who redeemed us from our fall!
To the Holy Ghost
Equal praise and glory be,
When the course of time is lost,
Lost in wide eternity!

William Hammond, 1745.

SWABIA. [H. P. 82.]

THE SPIRIT COMPARED TO THE WIND.

358 Cant. iv. 16. "*Awake, O north wind; and come, thou south.*" Tune SWABIA. S. M.

1 AWAKE, O heavenly Wind,
Thou Spirit most Divine,
Come blow upon Thy garden here,
And make its graces shine.

2 Let every fruitful plant
And fragrant spice be seen,
To make the garden of our God
Most pleasant and serene.

3 Come, sweet celestial Dove,
In Thy reviving gales,
And tune our souls to sing the Lamb,
Whose kindness never fails.

4 Let His sweet name perfume
The garden of Thy care;
And fill our songs and every breath
With Thy delightful air!

Thomas Row, 1817.

359 Acts ii. 4. "*They were all filled with the Holy Ghost.*" Tune SWABIA. S. M.

1 LORD God, the Holy Ghost,
In this accepted hour,
As on the day of Pentecost,
Descend in all Thy power.

2 We meet with one accord,
In our appointed place,
And wait the promise of our Lord,
The Spirit of all grace.

3 Like mighty, rushing wind
Upon the waves beneath,
Move with one impulse every mind,
One soul, one feeling breathe.

4 The young, the old, inspire
With wisdom from above;
And give us hearts and tongues of fire,
To pray and praise and love.

5 Spirit of light, explore,
And chase our gloom away,
With lustre shining more and more
Unto the perfect day.

6 Spirit of truth, be Thou,
In life and death, our Guide;
O Spirit of adoption, now
May we be sanctified.

James Montgomery, 1825.

DIMON (Waters of). [H. P. 64.]

DOVE.

360 Eph. i. 13. "*Ye were sealed with that Holy Spirit.*" Tune DIMON. C. M. Or FARRANT.

1 WHY should the children of a King
Go mourning all their days?
Great Comforter, descend and bring
Some tokens of Thy grace.

2 Dost Thou not dwell in all the saints,
And seal the heirs of heaven?
When wilt Thou banish my complaints,
And show my sins forgiven?

3 Assure my conscience of her part
In the Redeemer's blood,
And bear Thy witness with my heart
That I am born of God.

4 Thou art the earnest of His love,
The pledge of joys to come,
And Thy soft wings, celestial Dove,
Will safe convey me home!

Isaac Watts, D.D., 1709.

FREYLINGHAUSEN. [H. P. 306.]

(5) THE DAY OF PENTECOST.

361 Eph. iv. 8. "*When He ascended up on high, He led captivity captive, and gave gifts unto men.*"

Tune FREYLINGHAUSEN. 87, 87. D. Or SALZBURG.

1 WHEN the Lord of Hosts ascended
To His heavenly citadel,
Soon the Holy Ghost descended,
Sent by Him, with men to dwell;
Sign of Christ's Inauguration
In the kingdom of His power,
Largess of His Coronation,
Royal bounty, promised dower.

2 When the faithful were assembled
On the day of Pentecost,
Rushed the wind, the place it trembled,
Came from heaven the Holy Ghost;
Golden shower of consecration,
Tongues of fire were on them shed;
And that holy dedication
Made an altar of each head.

3 Now the festive Pentecostal
Harvest-home of souls they keep;
With his sickle each apostle
Whitening fields goes forth to reap;
God with holy flame from heaven
Writes on hearts the law of love;
Jubilee of sins forgiven
Sounds its trumpet from above.

4 Holy Ghost, Divine Creator,
Who didst on the waters move;
Holy Ghost, Regenerator,
Author of all life and love;
Holy Ghost, Illuminator,
Who didst then with fire baptize;
Holy Ghost, great Renovator,
Come, the world evangelize.

PART II.

5 Not in fire from heaven descending,
Not in earthquake, nor in shower,
Not in wind the mountains rending,
Now, O Lord, we seek Thy power;
But in holy aspirations
Do we seek and find Thee, Lord,
And in quiet meditations
On Thy everlasting word.

6 Guide of erring, go before us;
Breeze in heat, refresh our soul;
Shed Thy genial lustre o'er us;
Balm of sickness, make us whole;
In the hour of trouble hear us;
After labour give repose;
In the days of sickness, cheer us;
Guard in danger from our foes.

7 Strengthen, warm, and purify us;
From the bands of sin release;
Comfort, counsel, sanctify us;
Give us love and joy and peace;
Patience, faith, and resignation
Breathe upon us with Thy breath;
Give us heavenly consolation
In the solemn hour of death.

8 So when earth with fruit aboundeth,
And shall angel reapers see,
And the great archangel soundeth
God's eternal jubilee,
We may join their gratulation,
And to Father and to Son,
And to Spirit, adoration
Ever give, blest Three in One!

Bishop Christopher Wordsworth, 1862.

TALLIS'S ORDINAL. [H. P. 44.]

362 1 Cor. xii. 11. "*The selfsame Spirit, dividing to every man severally as He will.*" Tune TALLIS. C. M.

1 NOT bound by chains, nor pent in cells,
Of person or of place,
But, like the air, untrammelled blow
The breezes of Thy grace.

2 The Spirit is not tied to means,
But sovereign is and free;
But when Thou hast prescribed the means,
Tied to those means are we.

3 We love the means, for they are Thine,
Which heavenly life impart;
They channels are, through which it flows;
But Thou the Fountain art.

4 The vessel of our thirsting hearts
To Thee in them we bring;
O grant us, Lord, in heaven to drink
Of Thine eternal spring!

Bishop Christopher Wordsworth, 1862.

363 Zech. x. 1. "*Ask ye of the Lord rain.*"
Tune Ratisbon. 77, 77, 77.

1 QUICKEN, Lord, Thy church and me;
Send the promised Spirit down;
Holy One, Eternal Three,
All Thy former mercies crown:
Father, Son, and Holy Ghost,
Send another Pentecost!

2 Let the living fire descend,
Cloven tongues on every head,
Tongues which all may comprehend—
Speak Thy life into the dead!
Suddenly the power of grace
Send from heaven, and fill this place.

3 Send the rushing mighty wind,
Give the utterance Divine;
Let us know the Spirit's mind;
Let us speak in words of Thine:
Send a pure baptismal shower—
Tongues of fire, and words of power!

4 As of old, so be it now,
Now the glorious scene repeat;
See Thy humbled people bow,
Waiting lowly at Thy feet,
Crying all with one accord,
Send the promised Spirit, Lord!

5 First on the believing few,
Then in widening power unfurled,
Gathering, as the deluge grew,
Pour Thy Spirit on the world;
Bright in panoply Divine
Bid Thy church arise and shine!

RATISBON. [H. P. 157.]

6 Jesus! glorious Victor, come,
Thou whose right it is to reign;
Call Thine ancient people home,
Paradise restore again:
Father, Son, and Holy Ghost,
Send another Pentecost! *Benjamin Gough*, 1864.

364 Zeph. iii. 9. "*Then will I turn to the people a pure language.*" Tune Tallis. C. M.

1 ONCE all the nations were as one,
For all did speak one speech;
But pride said, "Let us build a tower,
Whose top to heaven may reach."

2 Another tower and city now
Is builded, Lord, by Thee;
Thy Zion, not built up by pride,
But by humility.

3 One Lord, one faith, one baptism
The holy city knows;
And thence one gospel in the streams
Of every language flows.

4 Give us Thy Holy Spirit, Lord;
No pride nor strife be ours;
Not Babel-builders may we be,
But strengthen Zion's towers.

5 Soon may we in Thy Zion dwell,
Jerusalem above;
Where but one language will be heard,
And that one language—Love.

6 With joyful song and jubilee
This holy time we greet;
And praise the Father, and the Son,
And heavenly Paraclete!
Bishop Christopher Wordsworth, 1862.

LAODICEA. (Hymn Chant.) [H. P. No. VIII.]

(6) HIS WORK OF GRACE UPON THE SOUL.

365 John xiv. 17. "*He dwelleth with you, and shall be in you.*"
Hymn Chant VIII., Laodicea. 88, 88, 66.

1 O HOLY Comforter, I hear
Thy blessèd Name with throbbing heart,
Pressed oft with sorrow, sin, and fear,
And pierced with many a venomed dart:
Come, Messenger Divine,
Come, cheer this heart of mine.

2 O Holy Comforter, I know
Thou art not to dull sense revealed;
Thou com'st unseen as the sweet flow
Of the soft wind that woos the field:
Breathe, Messenger Divine,
Breathe on this soul of mine.

3 O Holy Comforter, Thy light
Is light eternal and serene;
Shine Thou, and on my ravished sight
Visions shall break of things unseen:
Come, Messenger Divine,
Make these bright glimpses mine.

4 O Holy Comforter, Thy grace
Is life, and help, and hope, and power:
By this I can each cross embrace,
Can triumph in the darkest hour:
Come, Messenger Divine,
Thy strength of grace be mine.

5 O Holy Comforter, Thy peace,
The peace of God, impart and keep
Unruffled till life's tumults cease,
And all its angry tempests sleep:
Come, Messenger Divine,
Thy perfect peace be mine.
Ray Palmer, D.D., 1865.

GOLDBACH. [H. P. 130.]

366 John xvi. 7. *"If I go not away, the Comforter will not come."* Tune GOLDBACH. 76, 76. D.

1 DRAW, Holy Spirit, nearer,
And in our hearts abide;
O make our judgment clearer,
Our minds inform and guide.
O come, Thou great Renewer,
Touch heart and lip with fire,
Make every bosom truer,
Our aims and objects higher.

2 O come, Thou true Consoler,
Thou fire, that warms the cold,
The haughty breast's controller,
O come and make us bold:
On all sides danger threatens;
Lord, to our succour come,
And arm us with the weapons
Of early Christendom.

3 Hard unbelief and folly
The truth of God deny:
O arm us, Lord most holy,
With weapons from on high;
With faith that never falters,
Unmoved by fear or praise,
With love that never alters,
And hope in darkest days.

4 We need a free confession
In this our lukewarm age,
A frank and full profession,
In spite of scorn and rage;
To friend alike and foeman,
On this or heathen ground,
To every man and woman,
The gospel trump to sound.

5 Give power to those who witness
And preach Thy holy word,
That all may taste its sweetness,
And rally round their Lord.
Be this our preparation,
A heart and tongue of fire!
That this our proclamation
May speed as we desire!

C. J. P. Spitta, 1833; *Richard Massie (tr.)*, 1860.

BETHANY. [H. P. 174.]

367 John xiv. 16. *"I will pray the Father, and He shall give you another Comforter."* Tune BETHANY. 86, 84.

1 OUR blest Redeemer, ere He breathed
His tender, last farewell,
A Guide, a Comforter, bequeathed,
With us to dwell.

2 He comes, the mystic heavenly Dove,
With sheltering wings outspread,
The holy balm of peace and love
On earth to shed.

3 He comes, sweet influence to impart,
A gracious, willing Guest,
Where He can find one humble heart
Wherein to rest.

4 And His that gentle voice we hear,
Soft as the breath of even,
That checks each fault, that calms each fear,
And speaks of heaven.

5 And every virtue we possess,
And every victory won,
And every thought of holiness,
Are His, alone!

6 Spirit of purity and grace,
Our weakness, pitying, see:
Oh make our hearts Thy dwelling-place,
And meet for Thee!

Harriet Auber, 1829.

TRYPHOSA. [H. P. 209.]

(7) FAITHFUL TO HIS COVENANT.

368

Heb. x. 15, 23. "*The Holy Ghost. . . He is faithful that promised.*" Tune TRYPHOSA. 8 8 6.

1 TO Thee, O Comforter Divine,
For all Thy grace and power benign,
Sing we Alleluia!

2 To Thee, whose faithful love had place
In God's great Covenant of Grace,
Sing we Alleluia!

3 To Thee, whose faithful voice doth win
The wandering from the ways of sin,
Sing we Alleluia!

4 To Thee, whose faithful power doth heal,
Enlighten, sanctify, and seal,
Sing we Alleluia!

5 To Thee, whose faithful truth is shown
By every promise made our own,
Sing we Alleluia!

6 To thee, our Teacher and our Friend,
Our faithful Leader to the end,
Sing we Alleluia!

7 To Thee, by Jesus Christ sent down,
Of all His gifts the sum and crown,
Sing we Alleluia!

8 To Thee, who art with God the Son
And God the Father ever One,
Sing we Alleluia!

Frances Ridley Havergal, 1872.

FRANKFORT. [H. P. 183.]

369

John xvi. 14. "*He shall glorify Me.*" Tune FRANKFORT. 8 7, 8 7.

1 NOW, Thou faithful, gentle Spirit,
Make the glorious Saviour known,
In His all-prevailing merit,
From His high and heavenly throne.

2 Holy Spirit, we remember,
Thou art faithful still to guide
To our gracious great Defender,
Where we seek our souls to hide.

3 Thou dost guide us to the fountain
Of the Saviour's precious blood;
Lead us, Lord, to Calvary's mountain,
Where He poured the cleansing flood.

4 Thou dost show the great relation
That our perfect heavenly Head
Manifested in salvation,
When He mingled with the dead!

Thomas Row, 1817.

DALMATIA. [H. P. 20.]

(8) PRAYER FOR THE OUTPOURING OF THE HOLY SPIRIT.

370

Ps. xliii. 3. "*O send out Thy light and Thy truth.*" Tune DALMATIA. L. M. Or MELCOMBE.

1 COME, gracious Spirit, heavenly Dove,
With light and comfort from above:
Be Thou our Guardian, Thou our Guide,
O'er every thought and step preside.

2 The light of truth to us display,
That we may know and choose Thy way;
Plant holy fear in every heart,
That we from God may ne'er depart.

3 Conduct us safe, conduct us far
From every sin and hurtful snare;
Lead us to Christ, the living Way,
Nor let us from His pastures stray.

4 Lead us to holiness, the road
That we must take to dwell with God;
Lead us to God, our final rest,
To be with Him for ever blessed!

Simon Browne, 1720. (a.)

TALLIS'S ORDINAL. [H. P. 44.]

371 Ps. lxxx. 18. *"Quicken us, and we will call upon Thy name."* Tune TALLIS. C. M.

1 COME, Holy Spirit, heavenly Dove,
With all Thy quickening powers
Kindle a flame of sacred love
In these cold hearts of ours.

2 Look how we grovel here below,
Fond of these earthly toys;
Our souls—how heavily they go,
To reach eternal joys!

3 In vain we tune our formal songs,
In vain we strive to rise;
Hosannas languish on our tongues,
And our devotion dies.

4 Dear Lord, and shall we ever be
In this low, lifeless state?
Our love so faint, so cold to Thee,
And Thine to us so great!

5 Come, Holy Spirit, heavenly Dove,
With all Thy quickening powers!
Come, shed abroad a Saviour's love,
And that shall kindle ours!

Isaac Watts, D.D., 1709.

ARMAGEDDON (Valley of) [H. P. 90.]

372 John xiv. 26. *"The Holy Ghost, whom the Father will send in My name."* Tune ARMAGEDDON. S. M.

1 COME, Holy Spirit, come,
Let Thy bright beams arise,
Dispel all sorrow from our minds,
All darkness from our eyes.

2 Cheer our desponding hearts,
Thou heavenly Paraclete;
Give us to lie, with humble hope,
At our Redeemer's feet.

3 Revive our drooping faith,
Our doubts and fears remove,
And kindle in our breasts the flame
Of never-dying love.

4 Convince us of our sin,
Then lead to Jesu's blood,
And to our wondering view reveal
The secret love of God.

5 'Tis Thine to cleanse the heart,
To sanctify the soul;
To pour fresh life in every part,
And new-create the whole.

6 Dwell therefore in our hearts,
Our minds from bondage free;
Then we shall know, and praise, and love
The Father, Son, and Thee!

Joseph Hart, 1759.

MELCOMBE. [H. P. 24.]

373 Rom. viii. 26. *"The Spirit also helpeth our infirmities."* Tune MELCOMBE. L. M.

1 COME, Holy Spirit! calm my mind,
And fit me to approach my God;
Remove each vain, each worldly thought,
And lead me to Thy blest abode.

2 Hast Thou imparted to my soul
A living spark of heavenly fire?
Oh, kindle now the sacred flame;
With fervent love my soul inspire.

3 Impress upon my wandering mind
The love that Christ for sinners bore;
Then mourn the wounds my sins produced,
And my redeeming God adore.

4 A brighter faith and hope impart,
And let me now the Saviour see;
Oh, soothe and cheer my burdened heart,
And bid my spirit rest in Thee!

John Stewart, 1803.

KEDRON (Brook). [H. P. 213.]

374 Ezek. xxxvii. 9. "*Come from the four winds, O Breath, and breathe upon these slain.*" Tune KEDRON. 8 8 6. D.

1 DESCEND from heaven, celestial Dove,
With flames of pure seraphic love
Our ravished breasts inspire.
O Fount of joy, bless'd Paraclete,
Warm our cold hearts with heavenly heat,
And set our souls on fire.

2 Breathe on these bones, so dry and dead;
Thy sweetest, softest influence shed
In all our hearts abroad.
Point out the place where grace abounds:
Direct us to the bleeding wounds
Of our incarnate God.

3 Conduct, bless'd Guide, Thy sinner-train
To Calvary, where the Lamb was slain;
And with us there abide.
Let us our loved Redeemer meet,
Weep o'er His piercèd hands and feet,
And view His wounded side.

4 Thou with the Father and the Son
Art that mysterious Three-in-One,
God bless'd for evermore;
Whom though we cannot comprehend,
Feeling Thou art the sinner's Friend,
We love Thee, and adore!

Joseph Hart, 1759.

ST. ASAPH. [H. P. 307.]

375 2 Cor. i. 22. "*The earnest of the Spirit.*" Tune ST. ASAPH. 8 7, 8 7. D. Or SALZBURG.

1 COME, Thou all-inspiring Spirit,
Into every longing heart!
Bought for us by Jesu's merit,
Now Thy blissful Self impart:
Sign our uncontested pardon;
Wash us in the' atoning blood;
Make our hearts a watered garden;
Fill our thirsting souls with God.

2 If Thou gav'st the' enlarged desire,
Which for Thee we ever feel,
Now our panting souls inspire,
Now our cancelled sin reveal:
Claim us for Thy habitation;
Dwell within our hallowed breast;
Seal us heirs of full salvation,
Fitted for our heavenly rest.

3 Give us quietly to tarry,
Till for all Thy glory meet,
Waiting, like attentive Mary,
Happy at the Saviour's feet;
Keep us from the world unspotted,
From all earthly passions free,
Wholly to Thyself devoted,
Fixed to live and die for Thee.

4 Wrestling on in mighty prayer,
Lord, we will not let Thee go,
Till Thou all Thy mind declare,
All Thy grace on us bestow:
Peace, the seal of sin forgiven,
Joy, and perfect love, impart,
Present, everlasting heaven,
All Thou hast, and all Thou art!

Charles Wesley, 1767. (a.)

376 Eph. iii. 16. *"Strengthened with might by His Spirit."* Tune Old Ten Commandments. L. M. Or Melcombe.

1 Come, gracious Lord, descend and dwell
By faith and love in every breast;
Then shall we know, and taste, and feel
The joys that cannot be expressed.

2 Come fill our hearts with inward strength;
Make our enlargèd souls possess
And learn the height, and breadth, and length
Of Thine unmeasurable grace.

3 Now to the God whose power can do
More than our thoughts or wishes know,
Be everlasting honours done
By all the church, through Christ His Son!

Isaac Watts, D.D., 1709.

377 Exod. xxxiii. 18. *"I beseech Thee, show me Thy glory."*
Tune Halle. 88, 88, 88. Or Maon.

1 Lord, show Thy glory, as of old,
The work of heavenly love display;
And let our longing eyes behold
Another Pentecostal day:
Our fervent wishes deign to crown,
And send Thy quickening Spirit down.

2 Thou seest, Lord, how far we stray,
Oppressed with ills we cannot flee;
How sin hath drawn our hearts away
From peace, from happiness, and Thee;
Thy gracious Spirit, Lord, bestow,
And snatch us from the depth of woe.

3 Encompassed with a host of foes,
Our strength is small, our danger nigh;
Where can we find some brief repose,
Or whither for protection fly?
O Lord, Thy mighty Spirit send,
Our hearts to strengthen and defend.

4 Now let a brighter day begin
Than ever yet was witnessed here;
Bid darkly-gathering clouds of sin
Before Thy presence disappear:
Reign in each heart; in every place
Set up the empire of Thy grace!

William Hiley Bathurst, 1831.

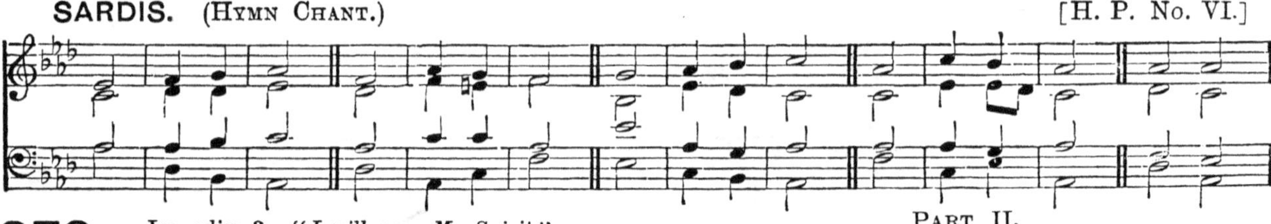

378 Isa. xliv. 3. *"I will pour My Spirit."*
Hymn Chant VI., Sardis. 10 10, 10 10.

1 O Holy Spirit! now descend on me,
As showers of rain upon a thirsty ground;
Cause me to flourish as a spreading tree,
May all Thy precious fruits in me be found.

2 Be Thou my Teacher—to my soul reveal
The length, breadth, depth, and height of Jesus' love,
And on my soul Thy blest instructions seal,
Raising my thoughts and heart to things above.

3 Be Thou my Comforter—when I'm distressed,
Oh gently soothe my sorrows, calm my grief:
Help me to find upon my Saviour's breast,
In every hour of trial, sure relief.

4 Be Thou my Guide into all truth Divine,
Give me increasing knowledge of my God;
Show me the glories that in Jesus shine,
And make my heart the place of His abode!

Part II.

5 Be Thou my Intercessor—teach me how
To pray according to God's holy will;
Cause me with deep and strong desire to glow,
And my whole soul with heavenly longings fill.

6 Be Thou my Earnest of eternal rest,
And witness with me I am God's own child,
With His unchanging love and favour blest,
By Jesu's merits fully reconciled.

7 Be Thou my Sanctifier—dwell within,
And purify and cleanse my every thought,
Subdue the power of each besetting sin,
And be my will to sweet submission brought.

8 Be Thou my Quickener—in me revive
Each drooping grace, so prone to fade and die;
Help me on Jesus day by day to live,
And loosen more and more each earthly tie.

9 Blest Spirit! I would yield myself to Thee,
Do for me more than I can ask or think;
Let me Thy holy habitation be,
And daily deeper from Thy fulness drink!

Christina Forsyth, 1861.

See Hymns 120, 756—759, 809, 811, 875.

PART II.—The Book of God, and the Church of God.

THEME I.—The Holy Scriptures—the Revelation of the Triune Jehovah.

NAYLAND; *or*, ST. STEPHEN. [H. P. 47.]

(1) INSPIRATION.

379 Acts i. 16. *"The Holy Ghost, by the mouth of David, spake."* Tune NAYLAND. C. M. Or EDEN.

1 THE Spirit breathes upon the word,
And brings the truth to sight,
Precepts and promises afford
A sanctifying light.

2 A glory gilds the sacred page,
Majestic, like the sun;
It gives a light to every age—
It gives, but borrows none.

3 The Hand that gave it still supplies
The gracious light and heat;
Its truths upon the nations rise—
They rise, but never set.

4 Let everlasting thanks be Thine,
For such a bright display
As makes a world of darkness shine
With beams of heavenly day.

5 My soul rejoices to pursue
The steps of Him I love,
Till glory breaks upon my view
In brighter worlds above!

William Cowper, 1779.

OLD "TEN COMMANDMENTS' TUNE." [H. P. 15.]

380 2 Tim. iii. 16. *"All Scripture is given by inspiration of God."* Tune OLD TEN COMMANDMENTS. L. M.

1 ETERNAL Spirit! 'twas Thy breath
The oracles of truth inspired,
And kings, and holy seers of old,
With strong prophetic impulse fired.

2 Filled with Thy great almighty power,
Their lips with heavenly science flowed;
Their hands a thousand wonders wrought,
Which bore the signature of God.

3 The powers of earth, and hell, in vain
Against the sacred word combine;
Thy providence through every age
Securely guards the Book Divine.

4 Thee, its great Author, Source of light,
Thee, its Preserver, we adore;
And humbly ask a ray from Thee,
Its hidden wonders to explore!

Elizabeth Scott, 1860.

---

381 2 Pet. i. 21. *"Holy men of God spake as they were moved by the Holy Ghost."*
Tune RATISBON. 77, 77, 77.

1 DOES the Lord of glory speak
To His creatures here below;
And may souls so frail and weak
All His gracious dealings know?
Does the blessèd Bible bring
Tidings from our heavenly King?

2 Oh with what intense desire
Should we search that sacred book!
Here our zeal should never tire;
Here we should delight to look
For the rules by mercy given,
To conduct our souls to heaven.

3 Shall not he that humbly seeks
All the light of truth discern?
Do we not, when Jesus speaks,
Feel our hearts within us burn?
For His soul-reviving voice
Bids the mourner now rejoice.

4 Lord, Thy teaching grace impart,
That we may not read in vain;
Write Thy precepts on our heart,
Make Thy truths and doctrines plain:
Let the message of Thy love
Guide us to Thy rest above!

William Hiley Bathurst, 1831.

RATISBON. [H. P. 157.]

CHESALON (Mount). [H. P. 35.]

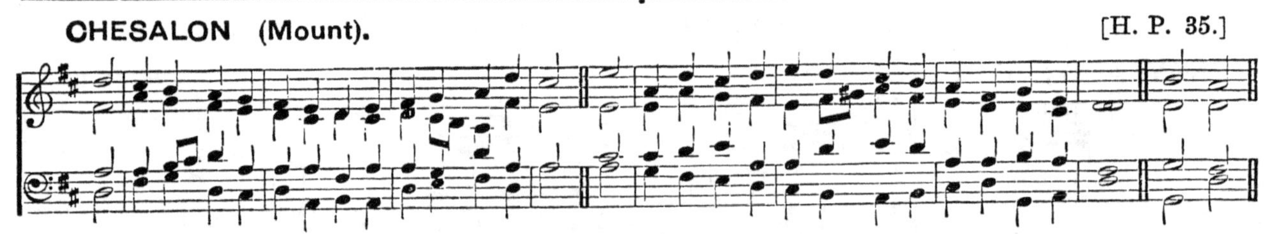

(2) EXCELLENCY.

382

Ps. cxix. 105. *"Thy word is a lamp unto my feet."*

Tune CHESALON. C. M.

1 LAMP of our feet, whereby we trace
Our path when wont to stray;
Stream from the fount of heavenly grace,
Brook by the traveller's way:

2 Bread of our souls, whereon we feed,
True manna from on high;
Our guide and chart, wherein we read
Of realms beyond the sky:

3 Pillar of fire, through watches dark,
And radiant cloud by day;
When waves would whelm our tossing bark,
Our anchor and our stay:

4 Word of the everlasting God,
Will of His glorious Son;
Without thee how could earth be trod,
Or heaven itself be won?

5 Lord, grant us all aright to learn
The wisdom it imparts;
And to its heavenly teaching turn
With simple, childlike hearts!

Bernard Barton, 1836.

HEBRON. [H. P. 12.]

383

Jer. xv. 16. *"Thy word was unto me the joy and rejoicing of mine heart."* Tune HEBRON. L. M. Or WALDECK.

1 I LOVE the sacred book of God,
No other can its place supply;
It points me to the saints' abode,
It gives me wings, and bids me fly.

2 Sweet book! in thee my eyes discern
The image of my absent Lord;
From thine illumined page I learn
The joys His presence will afford.

3 In thee I read my title clear
To mansions never to decay;
My Lord! oh when will He appear,
And bear His prisoner far away!

4 Then shall I need thy light no more,
For nothing shall be then concealed;
When I have reached the heavenly shore,
The Lord Himself will stand revealed.

5 When 'midst the throng celestial placed,
The bright Original I see,
From which thy sacred page was traced,
Sweet book! I've no more need of thee.

6 But while on earth, thou shalt supply
His place, and tell me of His love;
I'll read with faith's discerning eye,
And get a taste of joys above.

7 I know His Spirit breathes in thee,
To animate His people here;
May thy sweet truths prove life to me,
Till in His presence I appear!

Thomas Kelly, 1804.

PATMOS. [H. P. 147.]

384

Deut. vi. 6. *"These words . . . shall be in thine heart."* Tune PATMOS. 77, 77.

1 HOLY Bible, Book Divine,
Precious treasure, thou art mine;
Mine, to tell me whence I came;
Mine, to teach me what I am;

2 Mine, to chide me when I rove;
Mine, to show a Saviour's love;
Mine art thou, to guide my feet;
Mine to judge, condemn, acquit;

3 Mine, to comfort in distress,
If the Holy Spirit bless;
Mine, to show by living faith
Man can triumph over death;

4 Mine, to tell of joys to come,
Light and life beyond the tomb;
Holy Bible, Book Divine,
Precious treasure, thou art mine!

John Burton, 1805.

MAON (Wilderness of). [H. P. 229.]

385

Ps. cxix. 24. "*Thy testimonies also are my delight.*" Tune MAON. 88, 88, 88.

1 WHEN quiet in my house I sit,
Thy book is my companion still;
My joy Thy sayings to repeat,
Talk o'er the records of Thy will,
And search the oracles Divine,
Till every heart-felt word be mine.

2 Oh may the gracious words Divine
Subject of all my converse be:
So will the Lord His follower join,
And walk and talk Himself with me;
So shall my heart His presence prove,
And burn with everlasting love.

3 Oft as I lay me down to rest,
Oh may the reconciling word
Sweetly compose my weary breast!
While, on the bosom of my Lord,
I sink in blissful dreams away,
And visions of eternal day.

4 Rising to sing my Saviour's praise,
Thee may I publish all day long;
And let Thy precious word of grace
Flow from my heart, and fill my tongue;
Fill all my life with purest love,
And join me to the church above!

Charles Wesley, 1762. (*a.*)

BASHAN (Hill of). [H. P. 112.]

386

Matt. iv. 7. "*It is written again.*" Tune BASHAN. 66, 66.

1 FIVE pebbles from the brook
The shepherd David drew;
One of those five he took,
And proud Goliath slew.

2 He went forth all alone,
No armour had he on;
But with a sling and stone
The victory he won.

3 There is a holy stream,
By God's pure wellspring fed;
Bright polished pebbles gleam,
Like jewels, in its bed

4 The Bible is that brook;
The five books of God's law
Jesus, our David, took,
And one from them did draw.

5 With that, and that alone,
He went to meet the foe;
And with that single stone
He laid the tempter low.

6 Sing praises to our Lord,
Glad Hallelujahs sing,
Who conquered by His word;
Our Captain and our King.

7 Lord, arm us with that word,
With faith in Thee our shield;
We need no other sword,
Teach us that sword to wield.

8 Help us like Thee to fight,
Oh give us victory;
So may we put to flight
Our ghostly enemy.

9 To Father and the Son,
And, Holy Ghost, to Thee,
Eternal Three in One,
Eternal glory be!

Bishop Christopher Wordsworth, 1862.

SUCCOTH (Valley of). [H. P. 189.]

Hal - le - lu - jah, Hal - le - lu - jah.
Hal - - - le - lu - jah.

387 Ps. cxix. 103. *"How sweet are Thy words unto my taste."* Tune SUCCOTH. 87, 87, 77.

1 PRECIOUS Bible! what a treasure
  Does the word of God afford!
All I want for life or pleasure,
  Food and medicine, shield and sword:
    Let the world account me poor,
    Having this, I need no more.

2 Food, to which the world's a stranger,
  Here my hungry soul enjoys;
Of excess there is no danger,
  Though it fills it never cloys:
    On a dying Christ I feed,
    He is meat and drink indeed!

3 When my faith is faint and sickly,
  Or when Satan wounds my mind,
Cordials to revive me quickly,
  Healing medicines, here I find:
    To the promises I flee,
    Each affords a remedy.

4 In the hour of dark temptation,
  Satan cannot make me yield;
For the word of consolation
  Is to me a mighty shield;
    While the Scripture-truths are sure,
    From his malice I'm secure.

5 Vain his threats to overcome me,
  When in faith I take the sword;
Then with ease I drive him from me,
  Satan trembles at the word:
    'Tis a sword for conquest made,
    Keen the edge, and strong the blade.

6 Shall I envy then the miser,
  Doating on his golden store?
Sure I am, or should be, wiser—
  I am rich, 'tis he is poor:
    Jesus gives me in His word
    Food and medicine, shield and sword.

John Newton, 1774.

HARTS. [H. P. 284.]

388 John v. 39. *"Search the Scriptures."* Tune HARTS. 77, 77.

1 PRECIOUS Bible, what a store
  For the sons of men to' explore:
Precious Christ, it speaks of Thee;
Give us eyes Thyself to see.

2 Precious Bible, what a friend,
All my footsteps to attend;
All my wants it can supply;
For it brings the Saviour nigh.

3 Precious Bible, what a field!
Precious fruits its furrows yield:
Wide extent, and fertile ground,
Verdant pastures here are found.

4 Precious Bible, what a mine!
Full of promises Divine:
I would all thy wealth explore,
And thy Author, God, adore!

Joseph Irons, 1816.

(3) SUFFICIENCY.

389 Ps. cxix. 54. *"Thy statutes have been my songs."* Tune ST. ANN. C. M.

1 FATHER of mercies, in Thy word
  What endless glory shines!
For ever be Thy name adored
  For these celestial lines.

2 Here may the wretched sons of want
  Exhaustless riches find;
Riches, above what earth can grant,
  And lasting as the mind.

ST. ANN. [H. P. 52.]

3 Here the fair tree of knowledge grows,
And yields a free repast;
Sublimer sweets than nature knows
Invite the longing taste.

4 Here the Redeemer's welcome voice
Spreads heavenly peace around,
And life, and everlasting joys,
Attend the blissful sound.

5 Oh may these heavenly pages be
My ever dear delight;
And still new beauties may I see,
And still increasing light.

6 Divine Instructor, gracious Lord,
Be Thou for ever near:
Teach me to love Thy sacred word,
And view my Saviour there!

Anne Steele, 1760.

390 Ps. cxix. 130. "*The entrance of Thy words giveth light.*" Tune St. Ann. C.M. Or York. Or Bedford.

1 HOW shall the young secure their hearts,
And guard their lives from sin?
Thy word, O Lord, the way imparts
To keep the conscience clean.

2 When once it enters to the mind,
It spreads such light abroad,
The meanest may instruction find,
And raise their thoughts to God.

3 'Tis like the sun, a heavenly light,
That guides us all the day;
And through the dangers of the night,
A lamp to lead our way.

4 Thy word is everlasting truth;
How pure is every page!
Oh may it guard our earliest youth,
And cheer our latest age!

Isaac Watts, D.D., 1719.

SALISBURY. [H. P. 62.]

391 Ps. cxix. 97. "*Oh how love I Thy law!*" Tune Salisbury. C. M.

1 OH! how I love Thy holy law!
'Tis daily my delight;
And thence my meditations draw
Divine advice by night.

2 How doth Thy word my heart engage!
How well employ my tongue!
And in my trying pilgrimage
Yields me a heavenly song.

3 Am I a stranger, or at home,
'Tis my perpetual feast:
Not honey dropping from the comb
So much allures the taste.

4 No treasures so enrich the mind,
Nor shall Thy word be sold
For loads of silver well-refined,
Nor heaps of choicest gold.

5 When nature sinks and spirits droop,
Thy promises of grace
Are pillars to support my hope,
And there I write Thy praise!

Isaac Watts, D.D., 1719.

392 Ps. xviii. 28. "*Thou wilt light my candle.*" Tune Salisbury. C. M.

1 HOW precious is the Book Divine,
By inspiration given!
Bright as a lamp its doctrines shine,
To guide our souls to heaven.

2 It sweetly cheers our drooping hearts,
In this dark vale of tears;
Life, light, and joy its truth imparts,
And quells our rising fears.

3 This lamp, through all the tedious night
Of life, shall guide our way;
Till we behold the clearer light
Of everlasting day.

John Fawcett, 1782.

393 Ps. cxix. 140. "*Thy word is very pure.*" Tune Salisbury. C. M.

1 LORD, I have made Thy word my choice,
My lasting heritage;
There shall my noblest powers rejoice,
My warmest thoughts engage!

2 I'll read the histories of Thy love,
And keep Thy laws in sight,
While through the promises I rove
With ever fresh delight.

3 'Tis a broad land of wealth unknown,
Where springs of life arise,
Seeds of immortal bliss are sown,
And hidden glory lies.

4 The best relief that mourners have,
It makes their sorrows blest;
And bids them look beyond the grave,
To an eternal rest!

Isaac Watts, D.D., 1719.

MAON (Wilderness of). [H. P. 229.]

394 Ps. cxix. 130. *"The entrance of Thy words giveth light."* Tune MAON. 88, 88, 88.

1 UNFOLD, O Lord, to us unfold
The wonders of the sacred page;
The things by prophets sung of old,
And handed down from age to age;
The things that Jesus said and did,
And all that from the world lies hid.

2 The child-like spirit, Lord, impart,
That with implicit faith receives
The living word, and in the heart
Deposits that which it believes;
There, Lord, to work Thy sovereign will,
And all Thy pleasure to fulfil! *Thomas Kelly,* 1806.

ESDRAELON. [H. P. 202.]

395 Ps. cxix. 172. *"My tongue shall speak of Thy word."* Tune ESDRAELON. 87, 87. D.

1 PRECIOUS volume! what thou doest,
Other books attempt in vain;
Plainest, fullest, sweetest, truest,
All our good from thee we gain!
How thy living words refresh us!
Words of truth and grace they are;
Than the finest gold more precious,
Than the honey sweeter far.

2 What lay hid from ancient sages,
What they sought, but failed to find,
This, unfolded in thy pages,
Now appears to all mankind.
Far too high for man to reach it,
'Tis revealed from heaven above;
God Himself alone could teach it:
'Tis the mystery of love.

3 Precious volume! all revealing,
All that we have need to know:
Nothing from our view concealing,
That can profit here below.
Hope we have: this hope is cheering,
That the things we know not now,
In the day of His appearing,
Christ will to His people show! *Thomas Kelly,* 1806.

DAMARIS.

396 Ps. cxix. 89. *"For ever, O Lord, Thy word is settled in heaven."* Tune DAMARIS. 66, 66.

1 LORD, Thy Word abideth,
And our footsteps guideth;
Who its truth believeth
Light and joy receiveth.

2 When our foes are near us,
Then Thy Word doth cheer us,
Word of consolation,
Message of salvation.

3 When the storms are o'er us,
And dark clouds before us,
Then its light directeth,
And our way protecteth.

4 Who can tell the pleasure,
Who recount the treasure,
By Thy Word imparted
To the simple-hearted?

5 Word of mercy, giving
Succour to the living;
Word of life, supplying
Comfort to the dying!

6 Oh, that we discerning
Its most holy learning,
Lord, may love and fear Thee,
Evermore be near Thee!
The Rev. Sir Henry Williams Baker, 1861.

ZOAN II. (Field of.) [H. P. 166.]

397 Ps. cxix. 11. *"Thy word have I hid in mine heart."* Tune ZOAN II. 7 6, 8 6, 8 6, 8 6.

1 WE won't give up the Bible,
God's Holy Book of truth;
The blessèd staff of hoary age,
The guide of early youth;
The lamp that sheds a glorious light
On, else—a dreary road!
The voice that speaks a Saviour's love,
And leads us home to God.

2 We won't give up the Bible;
For it alone can tell
The way to save our ruined souls
From Satan, sin, and hell;
The guilty sinner here may learn—
The Gentile and the Jew—
To wash his robes in Jesu's blood,
From sins of every hue.

3 We won't give up the Bible,
For pleasure or for pain;
We'll buy the truth, and sell it not
For all that we might gain.
Though men should try to take our prize,
By guile and cruel might,
May we maintain the truth in love,
And God defend the right!

4 We won't give up the Bible,
But spread it far and wide,
Until its saving voice be heard
Beyond the rolling tide;
Till all shall know its gracious power,
And, with one voice and heart,
Resolve that from God's holy word
We'll never, never part!

William M. Whittemore, D.D., 1841, and John Gregg Bishop.

See Hymn 712.

THEME II.—The Church of the Triune Jehovah as revealed in Holy Scripture.

ITS THREEFOLD ASPECT—PAST—PRESENT—FUTURE.

I.—FORESEEN BY JEHOVAH FROM ALL ETERNITY.

SHEN (The Rock). *HIS ELECT CHURCH.* [H. P. 201.]

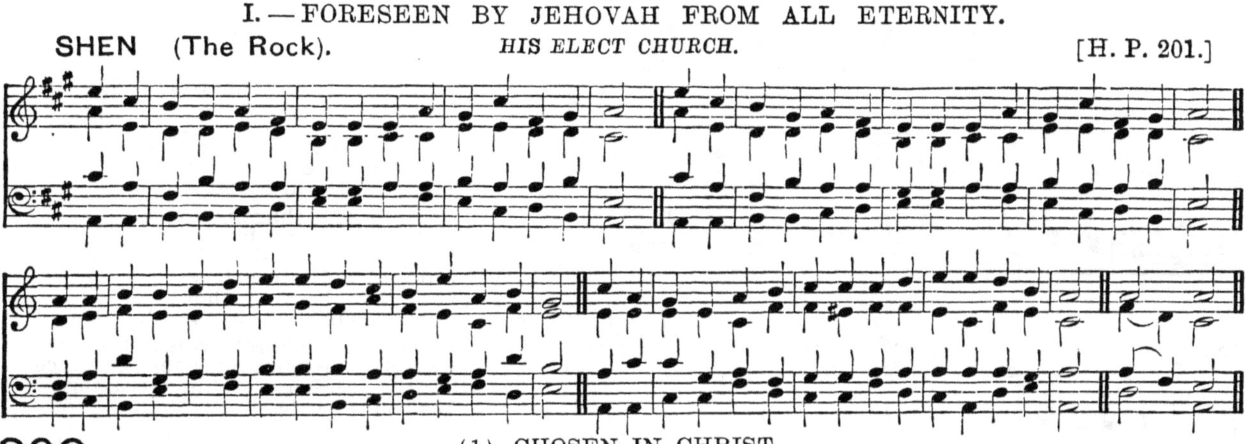

398 (1) CHOSEN IN CHRIST.

Eph. i. 4. *"He hath chosen us in Him before the foundation of the world."* Tune SHEN. 15 15, 15 15.

1 O THOU chosen church of Jesus, glorious, blessèd, and secure,
Founded on the One Foundation, which for ever shall endure;
Not thy holiness or beauty can thy strength and safety be,
But the everlasting love wherewith Jehovah lovèd thee.

2 Chosen—by His own good pleasure, by the counsel of His will,
Mystery of power and wisdom working for His people still:
Chosen—in thy mighty Saviour, ere one ray of quickening light
Beamed upon the chaos waiting for the Word of sovereign might.

3 Chosen—through the Holy Spirit, through the sanctifying grace
Poured upon His precious vessels, meetened for the heavenly place:
Chosen—to show forth His praises, to be holy in His sight:
Chosen—unto grace and glory, chosen unto life and light.

4 Blessèd be the God and Father of our Saviour Jesus Christ,
Who hath blessed us with such blessings all uncounted and unpriced!
Let our high and holy calling, and our strong salvation, be
Theme of never-ending praises, God of sovereign grace, to Thee!

Frances Ridley Havergal, 1871.

MAHANAIM. [H. P. 129.]

399 Eph. v. 25. "*Christ also loved the church, and gave Himself for it.*" Tune MAHANAIM. 76, 76. D.

1 THE Church's one Foundation
Is Jesus Christ her Lord,
She is the new creation
By water and the Word;
From heaven He came, and sought
To be His holy bride, [her
With His own blood He bought her,
And for her life He died.

2 Elect from every nation,
Yet one o'er all the earth,
The charter of salvation,
One Lord, one Faith, one Birth;
One holy Name she blesses,
Partakes one holy food,
And to one hope she presses,
With every grace endued.

3 Though with a scornful wonder,
Men see her sore opprest,
By schisms rent asunder,
By heresies distrest;
Yet saints their watch are keeping,
Their cry goes up, "How long?"
And soon their night of weeping
Shall be the morn of song.

4 'Mid toil and tribulation,
And tumult of her war,
She waits the consummation
Of peace for evermore;
Till with the vision glorious
Her longing eyes are blest,
And the great church, victorious,
Shall be the church at rest.

5 Yet she on earth hath union
With God, the Three in One;
And mystic, sweet communion
With those whose rest is won.
O happy ones and holy!
Lord, give us grace that we
Like them, the meek and lowly,
On high may dwell with Thee.

Samuel John Stone, 1865.

HAVILAH. [H. P. 192.]

400 Isa. liii. 11. "*He shall see of the travail of His soul.*"
Tune HAVILAH. 87, 87, 47.

1 JESUS saw His church, elected,
And betrothed her as His own;
She shall never be rejected,
But be partner of His throne!
How He loved her!
Long ere time or sin were known.

2 Jesus saw His church, when falling
Into ruin and disgrace:
When her state was most appalling,
Stood as Surety in her place;
How He loved her!
Thus to magnify His grace.

3 Jesus saw His church, enslaved,
In her guilt, and far from God;
But, resolved she should be saved,
Interposed His precious blood:
How He loved her!
Thus to suffer for her good.

4 Jesus saw His church, when straying,
Brought her back by sovereign grace;
Now He sees her watching—praying—
Waiting to behold His face:
Still He loves her!
And in heaven prepares her place!

Joseph Irons, 1825.

401 Acts xiii. 48. "*As many as were ordained to eternal life believed.*"
Tune BEVAN. 6666, 88.

1 THE people of the Lord
Were chosen in their Head,
To all eternal good,
Before the worlds were made;
Elect to know the Prince of Peace,
And taste the riches of His grace.

BEVAN. [H. P. 273.]

2 Elect to faith and hope,
To purity and love,
To all the life of God,
To all the things above;
Elect to prove salvation sure,
Elect to reign for evermore.

3 Grace, grace alone appears
In His eternal choice;
It cheers the humble saint,
And makes the soul rejoice:
Its endless glory shines so bright,
It makes obedience all delight.

4 Now, Lord, to us reveal
Thy all-confirming grace;
And may we all pursue
The shining paths of peace;
Press onward to the joys above,
And ever sing electing love!

Richard Burnham, 1796. (*a.*)

CHURCH TRIUMPHANT. [H. P. 258.]

402

2 Tim. i. 9. "*Grace which was given us in Christ Jesus before the world began.*"

Tune CHURCH TRIUMPHANT. L. M.

1 NOW to the power of God supreme
Be everlasting honours given;
He saves from hell (we bless His name),
He calls our wandering feet to heaven.

2 Not for our duties or deserts,
But of His own abounding grace,
He works salvation in our hearts,
And forms a people for His praise.

Isaac Watts, D.D., 1709.

See Hymns 117—119.

FREYLINGHAUSEN. [H. P. 306.]

(2) PRECIOUS.

403

Ps. lxxxvii. 3. "*Glorious things are spoken of thee.*"

Tune FREYLINGHAUSEN. 87, 87. D.

1 GLORIOUS things of thee are spoken,
Zion, city of our God!
He, whose word cannot be broken,
Formed thee for His own abode:
On the Rock of Ages founded,
What can shake thy sure repose?
With salvation's walls surrounded,
Thou mayest smile at all thy foes.

2 See! the stream of living waters,
Springing from eternal love,
Well supply thy sons and daughters,
And all fear of want remove:
Who can faint while such a river
Ever flows their thirst to' assuage?
Grace which, like the Lord, the Giver,
Never fails from age to age.

3 Round each habitation hovering,
See the cloud and fire appear!
For a glory and a covering,
Showing that the Lord is near:
Thus deriving from their banner
Light by night, and shade by day,
Safe they feed upon the manna
Which He gives them when they pray!

PART II.

4 Blest inhabitants of Zion,
Washed in the Redeemer's blood,
Jesus, whom their souls rely on,
Makes them kings and priests to God.
'Tis His love His people raises
Over self to reign as kings;
And as priests, His solemn praises
Each for a thank-offering brings.

5 Saviour, if of Zion's city
I through grace a member am,
Let the world deride or pity,
I will glory in Thy name:
Fading is the worldling's pleasure,
All his boasted pomp and show!
Solid joys and lasting treasure
None but Zion's children know!

John Newton, 1779.

M

KENT. [H. P. 63.]

404 Isa. xliii. 4. "*Since thou wast precious in My sight.*" Tune Kent. C. M.

1 NOW let Jehovah's covenant love
To saints employ my breath;
Its constancy shall always prove
The same, in life and death.

2 Beloved and precious in His sight,
Before all worlds they stood,
Their souls were always His delight,
They cost Him precious blood.

3 Yes, they are precious while they live,
And precious when they die;
So precious, that to them He'll give
Most precious crowns on high.

4 So precious that His grace and power
Conspire to make them blest;
So precious at their dying hour,
He takes them to His breast.

5 So precious that He has engraved
Their names upon His hand;
So precious that they shall be saved,
And in His presence stand.

6 Hear, O my soul, what Jesus saith,
Nor tremble to depart;
For all His saints, in life and death,
Are precious to His heart!

Joseph Irons, 1825.

---

405 Ps. cxxv. 2. "*As the mountains are round about Jerusalem, so the Lord is round about His people.*"

Tune Civitas Regis. 87, 87, 47. Or Havilah.

CIVITAS REGIS MAGNI. [H. P. 301.]

1 ZION stands by hills surrounded:
Zion kept by power Divine:
All her foes shall be confounded,
Though the world in arms combine.
Happy Zion!
What a favoured lot is thine!

2 Every human tie may perish;
Friend to friend unfaithful prove;
Mothers cease their own to cherish;
Heaven and earth at last remove:
But no changes
Can attend Jehovah's love.

3 Zion's Friend in nothing alters,
Though all others may and do:
His is love that never falters,
Always to its object true.
Happy Zion!
Crowned with mercies ever new.

4 If thy God should show displeasure,
'Tis to save and not destroy:
If He punish, 'tis in measure;
'Tis to rid thee of alloy.
Be thou patient;
Soon thy grief shall turn to joy.

5 In the furnace God may prove thee,
Thence to bring thee forth more bright;
But can never cease to love thee:
Thou art precious in His sight:
God is with thee,
God thine everlasting light.

Thomas Kelly, 1806.

---

406 Ps. cxxxii. 13. "*The Lord hath chosen Zion.*" Tune Shen. 87, 87. D.

1 ZION is Jehovah's dwelling;
There "the King of kings" appears:
Hers is glory far excelling
All the worldling sees or hears.
Zion's walls are everlasting,
Formed through endless years to shine;
Strength and beauty, never wasting,
Show their origin Divine.

SHEN (The Rock). [H. P. 201.]

2 Zion claims peculiar honour:
High distinction marks her lot:
Light eternal shines upon her;
Hers a sun that faileth not.
Zion's city hath foundations:
God Himself hath raised her walls;
She survives the wreck of nations;
Zion stands, whatever falls.

3 Happy they who, now discerning
Zion's glory, thither move!
Earth with all its honours spurning,
Zion is the place they love.
There the Lord, His face disclosing,
Fills His people's hearts with joy;
While, from all their toils reposing,
Bliss is theirs without alloy.

4 Brethren, let the prospect cheer us;
Fair the lot that 's cast for us:
When we call, our God will hear us:
Happy who are favoured thus!
Let the timid fear no longer:
What though earth and hell oppose?
He who pleads our cause is stronger,
Stronger far than all our foes!

Thomas Kelly, 1806.

---

407 Jer. xxxi. 3. "*Yea, I have loved thee with an everlasting love.*"

Tune HAVILAH. 87, 87, 47.

HAVILAH. [H. P. 192.]

1 LOVED with love from everlasting,
Lord, Thy church must rest secure;
Bought with blood, by grace now quickened;
Their eternal peace is sure.
Happy people,
Loved, and bought, and called by grace.

2 Yet, amidst a world of follies,
With a nature vile and base,
Oft assailed by fierce temptations,
How we need Thy mighty grace!
Dangers threaten;
Lord, uphold us in Thy fear.

3 Never safe but when protected
By Thy providence and love;
Leave us not, but daily keep us,
Till we see Thy face above.
Keep us, Jesus,
As the apple of Thine eye.

4 Keep us, Lord, from hard presumption,
Keep us, too, from unbelief;
When assailed by dark temptation,
Send us succour and relief.
Keep, O keep us,
Till our pilgrimage is o'er.

5 Keep us that our lives may praise Thee,
May we live to honour Thee;
And, when called to pass the river,
May we then Thy presence see.
Jesus, keep us,
Till in heaven we sing Thy grace!

Septimus Sears, 1865.

JORDAN. [H. P. 211.]

408 Num. xxiii. 20. *"Behold I have received commandment to bless."* Tune JORDAN. 886. D.

1 COME let us stand as Balaam stood,
And mark the people blessed of God
In Israel's tents below;
How goodly is their dwelling-place,
How happy is the favoured race,
Whom He vouchsafes to know.

2 The sons of Israel stand alone;
Jehovah claims them for His own;
His cause and theirs the same:
He saved them from the tyrant's hand,
Allots to them a pleasant land,
And calls them by His name.

3 His arm protects, His presence guides,
His love for all their need provides;
With peace and hope they're blest:
Preserved by their almighty Friend,
Till all their toils and trials end
In everlasting rest! *Edward Osler*, 1836.

SWABIA. [H. P. 82.]

409 Isa. xliii. 1. *"Fear not, for I have redeemed thee."* Tune SWABIA. S. M.

1 ZION, beloved of God,
No more to doubts incline;
Hear the sweet accents of His word:
"Fear not, for thou art Mine."

2 "Ere chaos heard My voice,
Or stars began to shine,
Thou wast the object of My choice,
And ever shalt be Mine.

3 "I bought thee with My blood,
I save thee when foes combine, [stood,
I'll conquer, though thou hast with-
And make thee wholly Mine."

4 And may my soul thus claim
A blessing so Divine?
I will exult in Jesu's name,
And know that He is mine!
Joseph Irons, 1819.

410 Deut. xxxiii. 29. *"Happy art thou, O Israel."* Tune NASSAU. 77, 77, 77.

NASSAU. [H. P. 155.]

1 SONS of Zion, lift your eyes
Upward to your native skies;
Now ascend the azure height,
To your city wrapt in light.
Free of Zion's city, you
Keep your freedom still in view;

2 Tread in faith the streets of gold,
Love's rich fountain now behold,
Pluck the fruit of life's fair tree,
Drink the stream that flows for thee;
Bow before the golden throne,
Christ your rightful monarch own.

3 Tread around salvation's wall,
Tell the towers that cannot fall;
Count ye well her bulwarks strong,
Make her safety now your song.
Though in Meshech's land ye dwell,
There of Zion you may tell.

4 God of might, the power bestow
On Thy feeble sons below;
Now on faith's strong wing to fly,
Upward toward our native sky;
Fetch from glimpses of our home
Strength the wilderness to roam;

5 Grace to prove to all around
Zion's sons we shall be found;
Zion's sons on earth by faith,
Zion's citizens at death;
Zion's songsters in that day
When all tears are wiped away!
Septimus Sears, 1865.

PARAN (Wilderness of). [H. P. 241.]

411 Num. xxiii. 23. "*Surely there is no enchantment against Jacob.*" Tune PARAN. 11 11, 11 11.

1 O PEOPLE, selected by sovereign love,
Through free grace elected to glory above;
What cause for uniting your voices to sing,
What cause for delighting in Jesus your King!

2 What nation so blessèd, so honoured of God?
Your sins all atoned for by Calvary's blood;
Your sorrows removed, and your wants all supplied,
By Him that has loved you and bought you beside.

3 Though foes should assail you on every hand,
Your King will not fail you—beside you He'll stand;
He's near to defend you, and ne'er will depart;
No power shall rend you away from His heart!

Septimus Sears, 1865.

CRASSELIUS; *or*, WINCHESTER NEW. [H. P. 3.]

(3) COMPLETE.

412 John vi. 37. "*All that the Father giveth Me shall come to Me.*" Tune CRASSELIUS. L. M.

1 ALL hail, Thou great Redeemer, hail!
We know Thy promise cannot fail;
Thy ransomed family shall come
To their prepared eternal home.

2 Shall come! this truth demands a song
From all the blest returning throng;
Satan must yield his long-held prey
When Jesus bids them come away.

3 Nor sins, nor doubts, nor foes can keep
The least of Jesu's ransomed sheep;
They shall come to His sacred fold,
Whom He engaged to save of old.

4 His name, His honour, and His blood,
Are pledged to bring them home to God:
And all His church shall come, and prove
Jehovah's free unchanging love!

Joseph Irons, 1825.

413 John xvii. 2. "*That He should give eternal life to as many as Thou hast given Him.*"
Tune ARCHIPPUS. C. M.

1 HARK! how the choir around the [throne
Adore their glorious King!
They drink full draughts of bliss un- [known,
And Hallelujah sing.

2 They range through heaven's unmeasured plain,
And find new cause for praise;
See more of Jesus, and again
Loud Hallelujahs raise.

3 Anon, the pearly gates unfold,
An heir of bliss draws nigh;
Again they strike their harps of gold,
And Hallelujah cry.

4 Another sinner born of God
Makes heaven's vast concave ring;
Again they Jesu's love record,
And Hallelujah sing.

5 At last the ransomed throng complete
Is glorified throughout:
Again they bow at Jesu's feet,
And Hallelujah shout.

ARCHIPPUS. [H. P. 34A.]

And Hal - le - lu - jah, Hal - le - lu - jah, Hal - le - lu - jah sing! A - men.

6 Ere long we hope to join the throng
Who bow before the King;
And in one everlasting song
Our Hallelujah bring.

Joseph Irons, 1825.

414 John vii. 38. "*Rivers of living water.*"
Tune HAVILAH. 87, 87, 47.

1 SEE from Zion's fountain rises
Life's full stream, whose rolling tide
All impediment despises,
Swelling high and spreading wide;
Life abounding—
Life from Jesus crucified.

2 Barren sands, and lofty mountains,
Open channels for its course;
And all other streams and fountains
Dry away before its force:
This is daily
Well supplied from Christ its source.

3 Flow, ye waves, to every nation,
Every tribe, and every tongue,
Till the blessings of salvation
Visit all the ransomed throng,
And the Saviour's
Praises through the earth are sung.

4 Saviour, let Thy gospel river
Spread its blessings all around;
Loudest songs to Thee, the Giver,
Shall throughout Thy church resound,
And for ever
Lord of all Thou shalt be crowned.

Joseph Irons, 1816. (*a.*)

II.—REDEEMED AND GATHERED OUT FROM THE WORLD.

HIS CHURCH MILITANT.

(1) CALLED.

415 Heb. iii. 1. "*Partakers of the heavenly calling.*"
Tune ESDRAELON. 1515, 1515.

1 HOLY brethren, called and chosen by the Sovereign Voice of might,
See your high and holy calling, out of darkness into light!
Called according to His purpose, and the riches of His love,
Won to listen by the leading of the gentle heavenly Dove.

2 Called to suffer with our Master, patiently to run His race;
Called a blessing to inherit, called to holiness and grace;
Called to fellowship with Jesus, by the Ever-faithful One;
Called to His eternal glory, to the kingdom of His Son.

3 Whom He calleth He preserveth, and His glory they shall see;
He is faithful that hath called you; He will do it, fear not ye!
Therefore, holy brethren, onward! make your heavenly calling sure;
For the prize of this high calling, bravely to the end endure.

Frances Ridley Havergal, 1872.

(2) JUSTIFIED.

416 Jer. xxxiii. 16. "*She shall be called, The Lord our Righteousness.*"
Tune ESDRAELON. 1515, 1515.

1 ISRAEL of God, awaken! Church of Christ, arise and shine!
Mourning garb and soilèd raiment henceforth be no longer thine!
For the Lord thy God hath clothed thee with a new and glorious dress,
With the garments of salvation, with the robe of righteousness.

2 By the grace of God the Father, thou art freely justified,
Through the great redemption purchased by the blood of Him who died;
By His life, for thee fulfilling God's command exceeding broad,
By His glorious resurrection, seal and signet of thy God.

3 Therefore justified for ever by the faith which He hath given,
Peace, and joy, and hope abounding, smooth thy trial path to heaven:
Unto Him betrothed for ever, who thy life shall crown and bless,
By His name thou shalt be callèd, Christ, "The Lord our Righteousness!"

Frances Ridley Havergal, 1871.

ST. JAMES. [H. P. 49.]

417

Jer. xxiii. 6. "*This is His name whereby He shall be called,* THE LORD OUR RIGHTEOUSNESS."
Tune ST. JAMES. C. M.

1 SAVIOUR Divine, we know Thy name,
And in that name we trust!
Thou art the Lord our Righteousness
Thou art Thy people's boast!

2 'Tis not by works of righteousness
Which our own hands have done;
But we are saved by sovereign grace
Abounding through His Son.

3 'Tis from the mercy of our God
That all our hopes begin;
'Tis by the water and the blood,
Our souls are washed from sin.

4 'Tis through the purchase of His death
Who hung upon the tree,
The Spirit is sent down to breathe
On such dry bones as we.

5 Raised from the dead, we live anew;
And, justified by grace,
We shall appear in glory too,
And see our Father's face!

See Hymns 685, 686.

Isaac Watts, D.D., 1709; *and Philip Doddridge, D.D.*, 1755.

JORDAN. [H. P. 211.]

418

(3) SEPARATED FROM THE WORLD.

John xv. 19. "*I have chosen you out of the world.*" Tune JORDAN. 886. D.

1 AWAKE! awake! ye saints of God,
Redeemed and cleansed with precious blood,
In Christ pronouncèd just;
Your beauteous garments daily wear,
Let your true dignity appear,
Shake off the earthly dust.

2 Why should this world delight you so?
Why grovel in the dust below?
Your portion is in heaven.
Oh hear your glorious Bridegroom say,
"Rise up, My love, and come away,
Eternal life is given."

3 Beloved of Jesus, heirs of bliss,
Haste through this dreary wilderness,
Regardless of its toys;
A few more steps will bring us through,
Then we shall Jesus's glories view,
In everlasting joys!

See Hymns 504—509.

Joseph Irons, 1825.

CHESALON (Mount). [H. P. 35.]

419

(4) NEVER SEPARATED FROM CHRIST.

Rom. viii. 38, 39. "*Neither death nor life . . . shall be able to separate us.*"
Tune CHESALON. C. M. Or LONDON NEW.

1 BLEST truth! the church and
Christ are one,
In bonds the most secure;
No separation! precious thought,
While endless years endure.

2 No separation, is proclaimed
In God's unerring word:
Christ is not of His bride ashamed,
Then let her own her Lord.

3 No separation! cheers my heart,
And bids my fears subside;
My soul and Jesus cannot part,
For me He lived and died.

4 No separation! precious thought,
Then Christ is with me here,
And home to heaven I must be
brought,
For Jesus Christ is there.

5 No separation! this decree
Of everlasting love
Is fixed by the eternal Three,
And never can remove!

Joseph Irons, 1825.

NASSAU. [H. P. 155.]

420 Rom. viii. 35. "*Who shall separate us from the love of Christ?*"

Tune NASSAU. 77, 77, 77.

1 HALLELUJAH! who shall part
Christ's own church from Christ's own heart?
Sever from the Saviour's side
Souls for whom the Saviour died?
Cast one precious jewel down
From Emmanuel's blood-bought crown?

2 Hallelujah! shall the sword
Part us from our glorious Lord?
Trouble dire or dark disgrace
From His heart our names erase?
Famine, nakedness, or hate,
Us from Jesus separate?

3 Hallelujah! life nor death,
Powers above, nor powers beneath,
Satan's might, nor hell's dark gloom,
Things which are, nor things to come,
Men nor angels, e'er shall part
Christ's own church from Christ's own heart!

William Dickinson, 1846.

SALISBURY. [H. P. 62.]

(5) PRESERVED IN CHRIST.

421 Jude 1. "*Preserved in Jesus Christ.*"

Tune SALISBURY. C. M.

1 HOW safe are all the chosen race,
Preserved in Christ their Head,
Before He calls them by His grace,
And after calling led.

2 Preserved in Christ, and taught to love
His name, His saints, His word:
Preserved to gain a throne above,
And praise and love the Lord.

3 Preserved when earth and hell oppose,
Preserved in life and death,
Preserved when wrath destroys their foes,
And victory crowns their faith.

4 Preserved 'midst Satan's fiery darts,
Through all this wilderness:
Preserved from vile depravèd hearts,
For everlasting bliss.

Joseph Irons, 1825.

CULBACH. [H. P. 181.]

422 Isa. xxvii. 3. "*I will water it every moment: lest any hurt it, I will keep it night and day.*"

Tune CULBACH. 87, 87.

1 LORD, what blessèd consolation
Do Thy promises supply!
In the season of temptation,
Is not Thy assistance nigh?

2 Art Thou not a strong Defender
Of Thy church from all her foes?
Shall the citadel surrender,
Though assailed by rudest blows?

3 No, the Rock on which she's founded
Stands immovably secure:
Though by enemies surrounded,
She shall flourish and endure.

4 Vain are all their boasted numbers,
Marshalled forth in stern array;
For Thine eye, that never slumbers,
Keepeth her by night and day.

5 Lord, our resolution's taken;
We would share the lot of those
Who, though by the world forsaken,
On Thy constant love repose.

6 May Thy Spirit safely guide us
Through the dangers of our road;
And in happier worlds provide us
With a peaceable abode!

William Hiley Bathurst, 1831.

PARAN (Wilderness of). [H. P. 241.]

423

Isa. xli. 10. "*Fear thou not; for I am with thee.*" Tune PARAN. 11 11, 11 11.

1 HOW firm a foundation, ye saints of the Lord,
Is laid for your faith in His excellent word!
What more can He say than to you He hath said,
You—who unto Jesus for refuge have fled?

2 "Fear not, I am with thee, oh, be not dismayed!
For I am thy God, and will still give thee aid;
I'll strengthen thee, help thee, and cause thee to stand,
Upheld by My righteous, omnipotent hand.

3 "When through the deep waters I call thee to go,
The rivers of sorrow shall not overflow:
For I will be with thee, thy troubles to bless,
And calm with My presence thy deepest distress.

4 "And when through the fire thy pathway shall lie,
My grace all-sufficient shall be thy supply;
The flame shall not hurt thee; I only design
Thy dross to consume and thy gold to refine."

5 The soul that on Jesus hath leaned for repose,
He will not, He will not desert to his foes;
That soul, though all hell should endeavour to shake,
Jehovah will never, no, never forsake!

George Keith, 1787. (a.)

SOSTHENES. [H. P. 243.]

424

Exod. xv. 4. "*Pharaoh's chariots and his host hath He cast into the sea.*" Tune SOSTHENES. 10 11, 11 11, 12 11.

1 SOUND the loud timbrel o'er Egypt's dark sea,
Jehovah hath triumphed, His people are free!
Sing, for the pride of the tyrant is broken:
His chariots and horsemen, all splendid and brave,
How vain was their boasting! The Lord hath but spoken,
And chariots and horsemen are sunk in the wave.
Sound, etc.

2 Praise to the Conqueror, praise to the Lord;
His word was our arrow—His breath was our sword:
Who shall return to tell Egypt the story
Of those she sent forth in the hour of her pride?
The Lord hath looked out from His pillar of glory,
And all her brave thousands are dashed in the tide!
Sound, etc.

Thomas Moore, 1816.

See Hymns 728—734.

(6) MADE LIKE CHRIST.

425

Gal. iv. 19. "*Until Christ be formed in you.*" Tune SALISBURY. C. M. Or ST. PETER.

1 O JESUS CHRIST, grow Thou in me,
And all things else recede!
My heart be daily nearer Thee,
From sin be daily freed.

2 Each day let Thy supporting might
My weakness still embrace;
My darkness vanish in Thy light,
Thy life my death efface.

3 In Thy bright beams which on me fall,
Fade every evil thought:
That I am nothing, Thou art all,
I would be daily taught.

4 More of Thy glory let me see,
Thou Holy, Wise, and True!
I would Thy living image be,
In joy and sorrow too.

5 Fill me with gladness from above,
Hold me by strength Divine;
Lord, let the glow of Thy great love
Through my whole being shine.

6 Make this poor self grow less and less,
Be Thou my life and aim;
Oh, make me daily through Thy grace
More meet to bear Thy name!

Johann Caspar Lavater, 1801; *H. B. Smith* (*tr.*), 1869.

See Hymns 190, 214—217.

III.—HEREAFTER TO BE GLORIFIED, AND PRESENTED AS THE BRIDE ADORNED FOR HER KING.

HIS CHURCH TRIUMPHANT.

CHESALON (Mount). [H. P. 35.]

(1) CONTINUING IN HIS PRESENCE.

426 Ps. cxix. 89. "*For ever, O Lord, Thy word is settled in heaven.*" Tune CHESALON. C. M.

1 FOR ever! oh, delightful word!
My God for ever lives:
For ever shall my song record
The blessings which He gives.

2 For ever firm His covenant stands,
For ever sure His oath;
For ever safe in Jesu's hands,
My soul and body both.

3 For ever justified by grace,
For ever loved of God;
For ever blest in Christ's embrace,
For ever with the Lord.

4 For ever singing Jesu's love,
For ever owned as His;
For ever triumphing above,
For ever crowned with bliss!

Joseph Irons, 1825.

427 John xiv. 3. "*That where I am, there ye may be also.*" Tune CHESALON. C. M.

1 IN yonder realms, where Jesus reigns
Upon His Father's throne,
Each ransomed soul a mansion gains,
And claims it as his own.

2 Built on His purposes of love,
Prepared by hands Divine,
Within the Father's house above,
Where endless glories shine.

3 Is there, dear Lord, a place for me,
Prepared and freely given?
Where Jesus is, I long to be,
For there I find my heaven!

Joseph Irons, 1819.

(2) REJOICING IN HIS UNCHANGING LOVE.

428 Rev. v. 9. "*They sung a new song.*"
Tune EUODIAS. 84, 84, 8884.

EUODIAS. [H. P. 255.]

1 'TIS the church triumphant singing,
Worthy the Lamb;
Heaven throughout with praises ringing,
Worthy the Lamb.
Thrones and powers before Him bending,
Odours sweet with voice ascending
Swell the chorus never ending,
Worthy the Lamb.

2 Every kindred, tongue, and nation,
Worthy the Lamb;
Join to sing the great salvation,
Worthy the Lamb.
Loud as mighty thunders roaring
Floods of mighty waters pouring,
Prostrate at His feet adoring:
Worthy the Lamb.

3 Harps and songs for ever sounding,
Worthy the Lamb;
Mighty grace o'er sin abounding,
Worthy the Lamb.
By His blood He dearly bought us;
Wandering from the fold He sought us,
And to glory safely brought us:
Worthy the Lamb!

4 Sing with blest anticipation,
Worthy the Lamb;
Through the vale of tribulation,
Worthy the Lamb.
Sweetest notes, all notes excelling,
On the theme for ever dwelling,
Still untold, though ever telling:
Worthy the Lamb!

John Kent, 1803.

ZION. [H. P. 312.]

429 Rev. xiv. 3. *"They sung as it were a new song before the throne."*

Tune Zion. 88, 88, 88.

1 Hark! how the glorious hosts above,
Around the great Jehovah's throne,
Enjoying His eternal love,
The Author of their glory own;
Without a jarring note they sing,
"Salvation to our God" and King.

2 Brought home by rich and sovereign grace,
From every nation, tribe, and tongue,
They bow before Jehovah's face,
And join the everlasting song;
Without a sorrow, fear, or doubt,
"Salvation to our God" they shout.

3 Arrayed in robes of righteousness,
With glorious crowns, and harps of gold,
Among them Jesus dwells to bless;
His matchless glory they behold;
And as they gaze, repeat their songs,
"Salvation to our God" belongs.

4 Oh, when shall we among them stand,
In Jesu's righteousness complete,
Obtain our place at His right hand,
And cast our crowns before His feet?
We'll join the heavenly chorus then,
"Salvation to our God!" Amen!

Joseph Irons, 1825.

430 Rev. i. 5, 6. *"Unto Him that loved us . . . be glory and dominion for ever and ever."*

Tune Moscow. 664, 6664.

MOSCOW. [H. P. 107.]

1 Behold the saints of God,
Redeemed with precious blood,
Free grace record!
In Jesus crucified,
For evermore confide,
For you He lived and died;
Praise ye the Lord!

2 He loved your souls so well,
He rescued you from hell,
And life restored:
Sing of His sovereign grace,
His blessèd footsteps trace,
Still gazing on His face;
Praise ye the Lord!

3 To Him all glory give,
Upon His fulness live,
And trust His word;
Low at His footstool fall,
Upon Him daily call,
And own Him Lord of all;
Praise ye the Lord!

4 By all the host of heaven,
And sinners here forgiven,
Christ is adored;
To our all-glorious King
We will our tribute bring,
And thus for ever sing
Praise ye the Lord!

Isaac Bridgman, 1830.

(3) PARTAKING OF HIS ETERNAL GLORY.

431 Heb. ii. 13. *"Behold I and the children which God hath given Me."*

Tune Swabia. S. M.

1 Our Saviour and our King,
Enthroned and crowned above,
Shall with exceeding gladness bring
The children of His love.

SWABIA. [H. P. 82.]

2 All that the Father gave
His glory shall behold;
Not one whom Jesus came to save
Is missing from His fold.

3 He shall confess His own
From every clime and coast,
Before His Father's glorious throne,
Before the angel host.

4 "O righteous Father, see,
In spotless robes arrayed,
Thy chosen gifts of love to Me,
Before the worlds were made.

5 "By new creation Thine,
By purpose and by grace,
By right of full redemption Mine,
Faultless before Thy face.

6 "As Thou hast lovèd Me,
So hast Thou lovèd them;
Thy precious jewels they shall be,
My glorious diadem!"

Frances Ridley Havergal, 1871.

EXETER. [H. P. 230.]

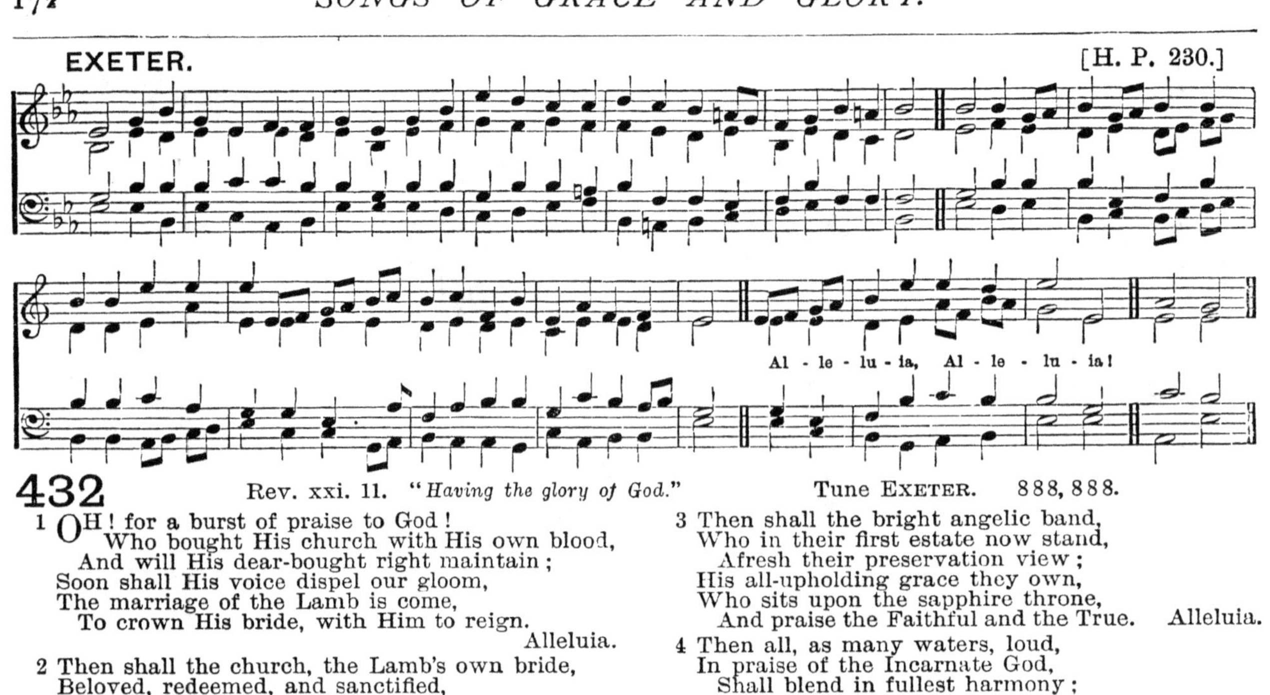

432 Rev. xxi. 11. "*Having the glory of God.*" Tune EXETER. 888, 888.

1 OH! for a burst of praise to God!
Who bought His church with His own blood,
And will His dear-bought right maintain;
Soon shall His voice dispel our gloom,
The marriage of the Lamb is come,
To crown His bride, with Him to reign.
Alleluia.

2 Then shall the church, the Lamb's own bride,
Beloved, redeemed, and sanctified,
All glorious in His glory be;
While He who all her sorrows bore,
Blessing and blessèd evermore,
The travail of His soul shall see. Alleluia.

3 Then shall the bright angelic band,
Who in their first estate now stand,
Afresh their preservation view;
His all-upholding grace they own,
Who sits upon the sapphire throne,
And praise the Faithful and the True. Alleluia.

4 Then all, as many waters, loud,
In praise of the Incarnate God,
Shall blend in fullest harmony;
Redeeming love shall swell the song,
While endless ages roll along
A glorious eternity! Alleluia.

Andrew Kessel, 1787. (*a.* 1871.)

CULBACH. [H. P. 181.]

433 Isa. lx. 19. "*The Lord shall be . . . an everlasting light, and thy God thy glory.*" Tune CULBACH. 87, 87.

1 HEAR what God the Lord hath spoken:
"O My people, faint and few;
Comfortless, afflicted, broken,
Fair abodes I build for you;

2 "Thorns of heartfelt tribulation
Shall no more perplex your ways;
You shall name your walls Salvation,
And your gates shall all be Praise.

3 "Ye no more your suns descending,
Waning moons no more, shall see;
But, your griefs for ever ending,
Find eternal noon in Me.

4 "God shall rise, and, shining o'er you,
Change to day the gloom of night;
He, the Lord, shall be your glory,
God your everlasting light!"

William Cowper, 1779.

NOTTINGHAM; *or*, ST. MAGNUS. [H. P. 39.]

THE CHURCH FURTHER DESCRIBED.—IV. ITS EXTENT.

(1) A LITTLE FLOCK.

434 Luke xii. 32. "*Fear not, little flock; for it is your Father's good pleasure to give you the kingdom.*" Tune NOTTINGHAM. C. M.

1 A LITTLE flock! So calls He thee.
Who bought thee with His blood;
A little flock, disowned of men,
But owned and loved of God.

2 Church of the everlasting God,
The Father's gracious choice,
Amidst the voices of this earth
How feeble is thy voice!

3 A little flock! 'tis well, 'tis well;
Such be her lot and name;
Through ages past it has been so,
And now 'tis still the same.

4 But the chief Shepherd comes at length;
Her feeble days are o'er;
No more a handful on the earth,
A little flock no more;

5 No more a lily among thorns,
Weary, and faint, and few,
But countless as the stars of heaven,
Or as the early dew.

6 Then entering the' eternal halls
In robes of victory,
That mighty multitude shall keep
The joyous jubilee.

7 Unfading palms they bear aloft,
Unfaltering songs they sing,
Unending festival they keep,
In presence of the King!

Horatius Bonar, D.D., 1856.

AVEN (Plain of). [H. P. 79.]

435

Jer. xxiii. 3. "*I will gather the remnant of My flock.*" Tune AVEN. S. M.

1 HARK! 'tis the Shepherd's voice,
Who with His flock appears;
He bids the tender lambs rejoice,
And banish all their fears.

2 "A little flock" below,
You shall to glory rise:
"Fear not," your Father will bestow
A kingdom in the skies.

3 "Fear not, ye little flock,"
Whom Jesus Christ redeems;
'Tis yours to feed beside that Rock,
Which sends forth living streams.

4 "Fear not"; believe His word;
You are to Jesus given;
'Tis "the good pleasure" of the Lord
To bring you safe to heaven!

Joseph Irons, 1819.

JORDAN. [H. P. 211.]

436

Luke xii. 32. "*Fear not, little flock.*" Tune JORDAN. 886. D.

1 FEAR not, O little flock, the foe
Who madly seeks your overthrow,
Nor dread his rage and power:
What though your courage sometimes faints,
His seeming triumph o'er God's saints
Lasts but a little hour.

2 Be of good cheer; your cause belongs
To Him who can avenge your wrongs;
Then leave it to your Lord;
Though hidden yet from all our eyes,
He sees the Gideon who shall rise
To save us and His word.

3 As true as God's own word is true
Nor earth nor hell with all their crew
Against us shall prevail.
A jest and byword are they grown;
God is with us, we are His own,
Our victory cannot fail.

4 Amen, Lord Jesus, grant our prayer:
Great Captain, now Thine arm make bare:
Fight for us once again:
So shall the saints and martyrs raise
A mighty chorus to Thy praise,
World without end. Amen.

Gustavus Adolphus' battle-hymn, by Altenburg, 1631: *Catherine Winkworth (tr.)*, 1855.

CHURCH TRIUMPHANT. [H. P. 258.]

(2) NEVERTHELESS "A COUNTLESS MULTITUDE."

437 Rev. xiv. 1. "*Lo, a Lamb stood on the mount Sion, and with Him an hundred forty and four thousand.*"
Tune CHURCH TRIUMPHANT. L. M. Or CRASSELIUS.

1 I LOOKED, and to my raptured eyes
Saw Zion's holy mount arise;
And on its heavenly summit stood
The Lamb once slain—the Lamb of God.

2 Twelve times twelve thousand saints around
Were with unearthly glories crowned;
Marked on their brows a wondrous name,
That name, the Father of the Lamb.

3 I heard from heaven a mighty voice,
Like waters' rush, or thunders' noise;
And unseen harpers from on high
Harped with their harps loud notes of joy.

4 Before the throne, before the throng
Of ransomed saints, arose their song:
That sweet new song which none might name
But those blest followers of the Lamb.

5 These are the pure, of heavenly birth,
Cleansed from their native stain of earth;
Redeemed to God, of mortal clay,
His consecrated first-fruits they.

6 Freed from the fault and guilt of sin,
No guile is found their hearts within;
Before the' eternal throne approved
Through Him, whom unto death they loved.

7 And now their glorious Lord, where'er
He goes, their footsteps follow near;
Nor ever part they from the side
Of Him, the Lamb, the Crucified!

Professor Scholefield, D.D., 1836.

LINUS. [H. P. 336.]

438 Rev. vii. 9. "*A great multitude, which no man could number.*" Tune LINUS. 15 15, 15 15.
Or HOLY VOICES.

1 HARK! the sound of holy voices, chanting at the crystal sea,
Hallelujah! Hallelujah! Hallelujah! Lord, to Thee.
Multitude, which none can number, like the stars, in glory stands
Clothed in white apparel, holding palms of victory in their hands.

2 Patriarch, and holy prophet, who prepared the way of Christ,
King, apostle, saint, confessor, martyr, and evangelist,
Saintly maiden, godly matron, widows who have watched to prayer,
Joined in holy concert, singing to the Lord of all, are there.

3 They have come from tribulation, and have washed their robes in blood,
Washed them in the blood of Jesus; tried they were, and firm they stood;
Mocked, imprisoned, stoned, tormented, sawn asunder, slain with sword,
They have conquered death and Satan, by the might of Christ the Lord.

4 Marching with Thy cross their banner, they have triumphed following
Thee, the Captain of salvation, Thee their Saviour and their King;
Gladly, Lord, with Thee they suffered; gladly, Lord, with Thee they died;
And by death to life immortal they were born, and glorified.

5 Now they reign in heavenly glory, now they walk in golden light,
Now they drink, as from a river, holy bliss, yea infinite;
Love and peace they taste for ever; and all truth and knowledge see
In the beatific vision of the blessèd Trinity!

6 God of God, the One-begotten, Light of light, Emmanuel,
In whose body joined together all the saints for ever dwell,
Pour upon us of Thy fulness, that we may for evermore
God the Father, God the Son, and God the Holy Ghost adore!

Bishop Christopher Wordsworth, 1862.

439

Rev. v. 11. "*Ten thousand times ten thousand, and thousands of thousands.*"

1 I SAW, and lo! a | countless throng,
The' elect of every | nation, name and tongue,
Assembled round the | everlasting throne;

With robes of white endued, the righteous | ness of God!
And each a palm sustained in | his victorious hand;
When thus the bright me | lodious choir begun:

"Salvation | to Thy name,
Eternal God, and | co-eternal Lamb!
In power, in glory, | and in essence, One!"

2 So sang the saints! The' an | gelic train
Second the anthem | with a loud Amen;
(These in the outer circle stood, the | saints were nearest God;)

And prostrate fall, with glory | overpowered,
And hide their | faces with their wings,
And thus ad | dress the King of kings:

"All hail! by Thy triumphant | church adored!
Blessing and thanks and honour too are Thy supreme, Thy | everlasting due,
Our Triune Sovereign, | our propitious Lord!"

3 While I beheld the' a | mazing sight,
A seraph pointed | to the saints in white,
And told me who they | were, and whence they came:

"These are they whose lot below was persecution, | pain, and woe;
These are the chosen purchased flock, who | ne'er their Lord forsook;
Through His imputed | merit free from blame;

Redeemed from | every sin; [clean,
And, as thou seest, whose | garments were made
Washed in the blood of | yon exalted Lamb.

4 "Saved by His righteous | ness alone,
Spotless they | stand before the throne,
And in the' ethereal | temple chant His praise:

Himself among them deigns to dwell, and face to face His | light reveal:
Hunger and thirst, as heretofore, and pain and | heat, they know no more,
Nor need, as once, the | sun's prolific rays:

Emmanuel here His | people feeds,
To streams of | joy perennial leads, [face."
And wipes, for ever wipes, the | tears from every

CELESTIAL. (Hymn Chant.)

For Verses 1, 2, 3, 4, 6, 7. *Three-line Chant.*

Part II.

5 Happy the souls released from fear,
And safely landed there!
Some of the shining number | once I knew,
And travelled with them here:

Nay some, my elder brethren now,
Set later out for heaven, my | junior saints below:
Long after me, they heard the | call of grace
Which waked them | into righteousness:

How have they got beyond!
Converted last, yet | first with glory crowned!
Little, once, I thought that these would first the | summit gain,
And leave me far behind, slow | journeying through the plain.

For Verse 5. *Four lines.*

6 Loved while on earth! nor less | beloved, though
Think not I | envy you your crown: [gone!
No! If I could, I | would not call you down!

Though slower is my pace, to you I'll | follow on,
Leaning on | Jesus all the way;
Who, now and then, lets fall a ray of | comfort from His throne:

The shinings of His grace soften my passage through the | wilderness;
And vines, nectareous, | spring where briers grew;
The sweet unveilings of His face make me, at times, near | half as blest as you!

Oh! might His beauty feast my | ravished eyes,
His gladdening | presence ever stay,
And cheer me | all my journey through!

But soon the clouds return; my | triumph dies;
Damp vapours | from the valley rise,
And hide the hill of | Zion from my view.

Part III.

7 Spirit of Light! thrice | holy Dove!
Brighten my sense of | interest in that love
Which knew no birth, and | never shall expire!

Electing goodness | firm and free,
My whole sal | vation hangs on thee,
Eldest and fairest daughter | of eternity!

Redemption, grace, and | glory too,
Our bliss a | bove, and hopes below,
From her, their | parent fountain, flow.

Ah! tell me, Lord, that Thou hast | chosen me!
Thou who hast kindled my intense desire, fulfil the wish Thy | influence did inspire,
And let me | my election know!

Then, when Thy summons bids me | come up higher,
Well pleased I | shall from life retire,
And join the burning hosts, be | held at distance now!

A-men.

Augustus M. Toplady, 1759—1774.

Note.—Printed thus to facilitate chanting.

HESHBON; *or*, PARRACOMBE. [H. P. 160.]

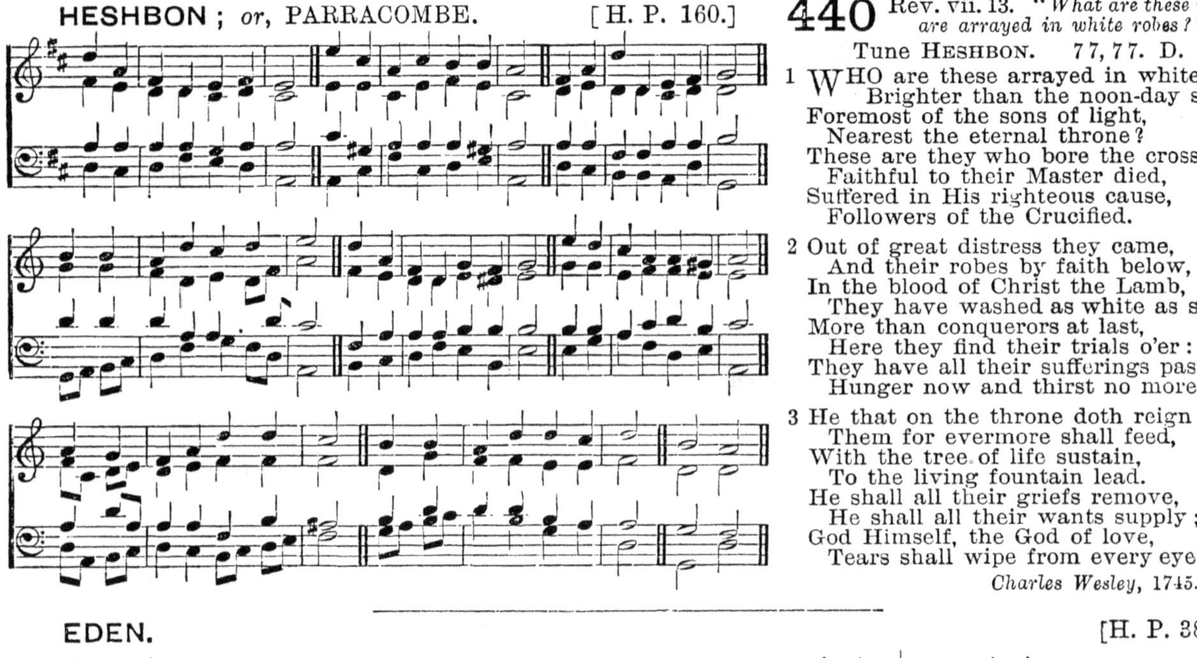

440 Rev. vii. 13. "*What are these which are arrayed in white robes?*"

Tune HESHBON. 77, 77. D.

1 WHO are these arrayed in white,
 Brighter than the noon-day sun,
Foremost of the sons of light,
 Nearest the eternal throne?
These are they who bore the cross,
 Faithful to their Master died,
Suffered in His righteous cause,
 Followers of the Crucified.

2 Out of great distress they came,
 And their robes by faith below,
In the blood of Christ the Lamb,
 They have washed as white as snow.
More than conquerors at last,
 Here they find their trials o'er:
They have all their sufferings passed,
 Hunger now and thirst no more.

3 He that on the throne doth reign
 Them for evermore shall feed,
With the tree of life sustain,
 To the living fountain lead.
He shall all their griefs remove,
 He shall all their wants supply;
God Himself, the God of love,
 Tears shall wipe from every eye!

Charles Wesley, 1745. (*a.*)

EDEN. [H. P. 38.]

441 (3) AMPLITUDE—OUT OF EVERY KINDRED, AND TONGUE, AND PEOPLE, AND NATION.

Rev. vii. 9. "*Of all nations, and kindreds, and people.*" Tune EDEN. C. M.

1 SING we the song of those who stand
 Around the' eternal throne,
Of every kindred, clime, and land,
 A multitude unknown.

2 Life's poor distinctions vanish here;
 To-day the young, the old,
Our Saviour and His flock appear
 One Shepherd and one fold.

3 Toil, trial, suffering, still await
 On earth the pilgrim throng;
Yet learn we, in our low estate,
 The church triumphant's song.

4 "Worthy the Lamb for sinners slain!"
 Cry the redeemed above,
"Blessing and honour to obtain,
 And everlasting love."

5 "Worthy the Lamb!" on earth we sing,
 "Who died our souls to save!
Henceforth, O Death! where is thy sting?
 Thy victory, O Grave?"

6 Then Hallelujah! power and praise
 To God in Christ be given;
May all who now this anthem raise
 Renew this strain in heaven!

James Montgomery, 1819.

442 1 Cor. x. 17. "*We, being many, are one bread.*"

Tune LEBANON. 86, 86, 88.

1 HOW sweet to think that all who love
 The Saviour's precious name,
Who look by faith to Him above,
 And own His gentle claim,
Though severed wide by land or sea,
Are members of one family.

2 Christians who dwell on snow-clad ground,
 Or on the burning strand,
And those whose happy home is found
 In our fair, peaceful land,
Are linked by more than earthly tie,
And form one lovely family.

3 "Our Father," is the hallowed sound
 They breathe from day to day!

LEBANON. [H. P. 177.]

Trained by His love, their steps are found
In the same heavenward way;
Their joys are one, alike their fears,
The same bright hope their exile cheers.

4 Yes, they are one—though some, we know,
Have reached the home of love;
But those who yet remain below
Are one with those above:
In that bright world are mansions fair,
And all will soon be gathered there!

Harriet Whittemore, 1836.

MELCOMBE. [H. P. 21.]

443 Rev. vii. 15. "*Therefore are they before the throne of God.*" Tune MELCOMBE. L. M.

1 LO! round the throne, at God's right hand,
The saints in countless myriads stand,
Of every tongue redeemed to God,
Arrayed in garments washed in blood.

2 Through tribulation great they came;
They bore the cross, despised the shame;
From all their labours now they rest,
In God's eternal glory blest.

3 Hunger and thirst they feel no more;
Nor sin, nor pain, nor death deplore;
The tears are wiped from every eye,
And sorrow yields to endless joy.

4 They see the Saviour face to face,
And sing the triumphs of His grace;
Him day and night they ceaseless praise:
To Him their loud Hosannas raise.

5 Oh may we tread the sacred road
That holy saints and martyrs trod;
Wage to the end the glorious strife,
And win, like them, the crown of life!

Rowland Hill, 1783; *and T. Cotterill*, 1810.

THE CHURCH FURTHER DESCRIBED. — V. ITS NAMES AND TITLES.

(1) THE BODY OF CHRIST.

444 Eph. i. 22, 23. "*Head over all things to the church, which is His body.*"
Tune SUCCOTH. 87, 87, 77. Or CASSEL.

1 JOINED to Christ in mystic union,
We Thy members, Thou our Head,
Sealed by deep and true communion,
Risen with Thee, who once were dead—
Saviour, we would humbly claim
All the power of this Thy name.

2 Instant sympathy to brighten
All their weakness and their woe,
Guiding grace their way to lighten,
Shall Thy loving members know;
All their sorrows Thou dost bear,
All Thy gladness they shall share.

3 Make Thy members every hour
For Thy blessèd service meet;
Earnest tongues, and arms of power,
Skilful hands, and hastening feet,
Ever ready to fulfil
All Thy word, and all Thy will.

4 Everlasting life Thou givest,
Everlasting love to see;
They shall live because Thou livest,
And their life is hid with Thee.
Safe Thy members shall be found,
When their glorious Head is crowned!

See Hymn 156. *Frances Ridley Havergal*, 1871.

SUCCOTH (Valley of). [H. P. 189.]

N

HERMON. [H. P. 27.]

(2) THE BRIDE OF CHRIST—THE LAMB'S WIFE.

445

Hos. ii. 19, 20. "*I will betroth thee unto Me for ever.*" Tune HERMON. L. M.

1 BETROTHED in love, ere time began,
His blood-bought bride with Jesus see;
Made by eternal union One,
Who was, and is, and is to be.

2 Thus He became her covenant Head;
Charged with her sin the Saviour stands,
To do and suffer, in her stead,
All that the righteous law demands.

3 A glorious church, from blemish free,
She shall appear before the throne,
Christ's everlasting joy to be,
His everlasting love her own!

John Kent, 1803—*ver.* 3, *F. R. H.*

See Hymns 289, 298—300, 317, 335, 338.

(3) THE CHURCH OF GOD.

DEPTFORD. [H. P. 315.]

446

Acts xx. 28. "*The church of God.*"
Tune DEPTFORD. 10 10, 10 10.

1 "THE Church of God," amazing, precious thought!
That sinners, vile and outcast, should be brought,
Renewed in heart, and cleansed by Jesu's blood,
To form the body of the "Church of God."

2 The Church is one, it has one glorious Head,
And by one Spirit through this waste is led;
And nourishment from Christ, on high, bestowed,
Together binds in one the "Church of God."

3 United to her risen Head above,
Even now she knows the sweetness of His love;
His power is hers to help her on the road—
Bride of the Lamb—Church of the living God!

4 Soon will He come, and take His Church away—
And oh, sweet thought! fast hastens on the day,
When He will stand with all His saints avowed
Head of the Church—the purchased "Church of God!"

Albert Midlane, 1864.

(4) THE TEMPLE OF THE HOLY GHOST.

HAVILAH. [H. P. 192.]

447

2 Cor. vi. 16. "*Ye are the temple of the living God.*"
Tune HAVILAH. 87, 87, 47.

1 RISING on the one Foundation,
Planned and built by God alone,
See His chosen habitation,
Christ Himself the Corner-stone.
Holy temple!
King Messiah's priestly throne.

2 While in Christ the building groweth,
Fitly framed of polished stones,
All its matchless glory floweth
From the blood which there atones.
In this temple
God Himself our worship owns.

3 Lo! the ark, the priest, the altar,
Incense, bread, and sacred fire,
Sacrifice for each defaulter,
Joyful praise and holy choir;
God's own temple,
Chosen rest, and His desire!

4 Are we living stones, united
To the temple of the Lord?
Then in us He hath delighted,
And His love we shall record.
In His temple
Be His holy name adored!

Joseph Irons, 1825. (*a.* 1871.)

FARRANT. [H. P. 67.]

(5) THE HOUSEHOLD OF FAITH.

448 Eph. iii. 15. "*The whole family in heaven and earth.*" Tune FARRANT. C. M.

1 COME let us join our friends above,
That have obtained the prize,
And on the eagle wings of love,
To joy celestial rise.

2 The saints on earth, and those above,
But one communion make;
Joined to their Lord in bonds of love,
All of His grace partake.

3 One family, we dwell in Him:
One church, above, beneath;
Though now divided by the stream—
The narrow stream, of death.

4 One army of the living God,
To His command we bow;
Part of the host have crossed the flood,
And part are crossing now.

5 Lo! thousands to their endless home
Are swiftly borne away;
And we are to the margin come,
And soon must launch as they.

6 Lord Jesus, be our constant Guide;
Then when the word is given,
Bid death's cold flood its waves divide,
And land us safe in heaven!

Charles Wesley, 1759. (*a.*)—*ver.* 2, *Isaac Watts, D.D.*

See Hymn 1092.

PART III.—Man, and Things Provided for Man.

THEME I.—Man.

ST. MARY'S; *or*, HACKNEY. [H. P. 73.]

(1) FALLEN.

449 Eph. ii. 3. "*By nature the children of wrath.*" Tune ST. MARY. C. M.

1 HOW helpless guilty nature lies,
Unconscious of its load!
The heart unchanged can never rise
To happiness and God.

2 Can aught beneath a power Divine
The stubborn will subdue?
'Tis Thine, Eternal Spirit, Thine,
To form the heart anew.

3 'Tis Thine the passions to recall,
And upwards bid them rise;
And make the scales of error fall
From reason's darkened eyes.

4 To chase the shades of death away,
And bid the sinner live;
A beam of heaven, a vital ray,
'Tis Thine alone to give.

5 Oh change these sinful hearts of ours,
And give them life Divine!
Then shall our passions and our powers,
Almighty Lord, be Thine!

Anne Steele, 1760.

450 Gen. vi. 5. "*Only evil continually.*" Tune ST. MARY. C. M.

1 ALAS! by nature how depraved!
How prone to every ill!
Our lives to Satan how enslaved!
How obstinate our will!

2 And can such sinners be restored,
Such rebels reconciled?
Can grace itself the means afford
To make a foe a child?

3 Yes, grace has found the wondrous means,
Which shall effectual prove,
To cleanse us from our countless sins,
And teach our hearts to love.

4 Jesus for sinners undertakes,
And died that we may live;
His blood a full atonement makes,
And cries aloud, "Forgive!"

John Newton, 1779.

DUNDEE; *or*, WINDSOR. [H. P. 72.]

(2) SINFUL.

451

Isa. liii. 6. "*All we, like sheep, have gone astray.*" Tune DUNDEE. C. M.

1 ALMIGHTY Father, God of grace!
We all, like sheep astray,
In folly from Thy paths have turned,
Each to his sinful way.

2 Sins of omission and of act
Through all our lives abound:
Alas! in thought, in word, in deed,
No health in us is found.

3 Oh spare us, Lord, in mercy spare!
Our contrite souls restore,
Through Him who suffered on the cross,
And man's transgression bore.

4 And grant, O Father, for His sake,
That we through all our days
A just and godly life may lead,
To Thine eternal praise!

T. Cotterill, 1812.

SAXONY. [H. P. 32.]

452

Ps. li. 5. "*I was shapen in iniquity.*" Tune SAXONY. L. M.

1 LORD, I am vile, conceived in sin,
And born unholy and unclean;
Sprung from the man whose guilty fall
Corrupts his race, and taints us all.

2 Soon as we draw our infant breath,
The seeds of sin grow up for death;
Thy law demands a perfect heart;
We are defiled in every part.

3 Great God, create my heart anew,
And form my spirit pure and true;
Oh make me wise betimes to see
My danger and my remedy.

4 Jesus, my Lord, Thy blood alone
Hath power sufficient to atone;
Thy blood can make me white as snow;
No Jewish types could cleanse me so.

5 While guilt disturbs and breaks my peace,
Nor flesh nor soul hath rest or ease;
Lord, let me hear Thy pardoning voice,
And make my broken bones rejoice!

Isaac Watts, D.D., 1719.

453

Heb. xii. 1. "*The sin which doth so easily beset us.*"
Tune ALTORF (repeating last two lines).
87, 887, 88.

ALTORF; *or*, LUTHER'S HYMN [H. P. 208.]

1 THAT cherished sin—'twill cost thee dear;
Each spring of comfort stealing;
Thy God in mercy will not hear,
Nor wilt thou find His presence near,
While there is double dealing.
Reject the thought, that peace within
Can harmonise with Achan's sin.

2 That cherished sin will paralyse
Each effort grace is making;
The sickly plant of fervour dies,
If God withholds His rich supplies,
The wayward child forsaking.
In honesty approach the throne,
Or grapple with thy foes alone.

3 That cherished sin will close the gate
To realms of glory leading,
And leave thee to the hopeless fate
Of those who wake, alas! too late,
And die, on folly feeding.
Oh! pause in time—and count the cost,
Before thy precious soul is lost!

From J. Groom's Leaflets, 1846.

ST. ALPHEGE. [H. P. 275.]

454

Luke xv. 24. "*He was lost, and is found.*"

Tune St. Alphege. 7 6, 7 6. D.

1 HOW lost was our condition,
  Till Jesus made us whole!
There is but one Physician
  Can heal the sin-sick soul.
In sin and death He found us,
  He snatched us from the grave:
To tell to all around us
  His wondrous power to save.

2 The dying, risen Jesus,
  Seen by the eye of faith,
At once from anguish frees us,
  And frees the soul from death.
How gracious this Physician!
  His help He'll freely give;
He makes no hard condition,
  He bids us look and live!

John Newton, 1779.

See Hymn 170.

ST. MARY'S; *or*, HACKNEY. [H. P. 73.]

(3) MORTAL.

455

Amos iv. 12. "*Prepare to meet thy God.*"

Tune St. Mary. C. M.

1 BENEATH our feet, and o'er our head,
  Is equal warning given;
Beneath us lie the countless dead,
  Above us is the heaven!

2 Their names are graven on the stone,
  Their bones are in the clay;
And ere another day is gone,
  Ourselves may be as they.

3 Death rides on every passing breeze,
  He lurks in every flower;
Each season has its own disease,
  Its peril every hour.

4 Turn, mortal, turn! thy danger know:
  Where'er thy foot can tread,
The earth rings hollow from below,
  And warns thee of her dead!

5 Turn, Christian, turn! thy soul apply
  To truths divinely given;
The bones, that underneath thee lie,
  Shall live for hell or heaven.

Bishop Heber, 1827.

ST. GEORGE. [H. P. 265.]

456

Prov. xxvii. 1. "*Boast not thyself of to-morrow.*"

Tune St. George. S. M.

1 TO-MORROW, Lord, is Thine,
  Lodged in Thy sovereign hand;
And if its sun arise and shine,
  It shines by Thy command.

2 The present moment flies,
  And bears our life away;
Oh, make Thy servants truly wise,
  That we may live to-day!

3 Since on this wingèd hour
  Eternity is hung,
Waken by Thine almighty power
  The aged and the young.

4 One thing demands our care;
  Oh, be it still pursued!
Lest, slighted once, the season fair
  Should never be renewed.

5 To Jesus may we fly,
  Swift as the morning light,
Lest life's young golden beams should die
  In sudden, endless night!

Philip Doddridge, D.D., 1755.

CYPRUS. [H. P. 26.]

457 Ps. xxxix. 4. *"Make me to know mine end."* Tune Cyprus. L. M.

1 ALMIGHTY Maker of my frame!
Teach me the measure of my days;
Teach me to know how frail I am,
And spend the remnant to Thy praise.

2 My days are shorter than a span,
A little point my life appears;
How frail at best is dying man!
How vain are all his hopes and fears!

3 Vain his ambition, noise, and show;
Vain are the cares which rack his mind;
He heaps up treasures mixed with woe,
And dies, and leaves them all behind.

4 Oh, be a nobler portion mine!
My God, I bow before Thy throne:
Earth's fleeting treasures I resign,
And fix my hopes on Thee alone!

Anne Steele, 1760.

See Hymns 735, 978.

THEME II.—The Gospel Proclaimed.

FULL AND FREE SALVATION BY JESUS CHRIST.

(1) ITS EXCELLENCE.

FAITH. [H. P. 337.]

458 Isa. xlv. 22. *"Look unto Me, and be ye saved."*
Tune Faith. 12 9, 11 9.

1 THERE is life for a look at the Crucified One;
There is life at this moment for thee;
Then look, sinner—look unto Him, and be saved—
Unto Him who was nailed to the tree.

2 It is not thy tears of repentance, or prayers,
But the blood, that atones for the soul;
On Him then, who shed it, believing at once,
Thy weight of iniquities roll.

3 His anguish of soul on the cross hast thou seen?
His cry of distress hast thou heard?
Then why, if the terrors of wrath He endured,
Should pardon to thee be deferred?

4 We are healed by His stripes; wouldst thou add to the word?
And He is our Righteousness made:
The best robe of heaven He bids thee put on;
Oh, couldst thou be better arrayed?

5 Then doubt not thy welcome, since God has declared
There remaineth no more to be done;
That once in the end of the world He appeared,
And completed the work He begun.

6 But take, with rejoicing, from Jesus at once
The life everlasting He gives;
And know, with assurance, thou never canst die,
Since Jesus, thy Righteousness, lives.

7 There is life for a look at the Crucified One;
There is life at this moment for thee;
Then look, sinner—look unto Him, and be saved,
And know thyself spotless as He!

Amelia Matilda Hull, 1860.

CHURCH TRIUMPHANT. [H. P. 258.]

459 Isa. lxiii. 5. *"Mine own arm brought salvation."* Tune Church Triumphant. L. M. Or Gilboa.

1 SALVATION is of God alone,
The glorious plan is all His own;
In love He formed the great design,
And here His grace and wisdom shine.

2 Salvation is of God alone:
One only Victim could atone
For human guilt; that victim He
Who claims with God equality.

3 Salvation is of God alone;
'Tis He who breaks the heart of stone,
Who makes self-righteousness to cease,
And gives the troubled conscience peace.

4 Salvation is of God alone;
'Tis He who leads His people on;
'Tis He who makes their burdens light,
And shields them in the day of fight.

5 Salvation is of God alone;
This truth let all His people own,
And to His name the praise be given
By saints on earth, and saints in heaven!

Thomas Kelly, 1851.

NAYLAND; *or*, ST. STEPHEN. [H. P. 47.]

Ps. lxxxv. 10. "*Mercy and truth are met together; righteousness and peace have kissed each other.*"

460

Tune NAYLAND. C. M. Or TALLIS.

1 SALVATION! what a glorious plan,
How suited to our need!
The grace, that raises fallen man,
Is wonderful indeed!

2 'Twas wisdom formed the vast design
To ransom us when lost;
And love's unfathomable mine
Provided all the cost.

3 Strict justice, with approving look,
The holy covenant sealed;
And truth, and power, both undertook
The whole should be fulfilled.

4 Truth, wisdom, justice, power, and love,
In all their glory shone,
When Jesus left the courts above,
And died to save His own.

5 Truth, wisdom, justice, power, and love,
Are equally displayed,
Now Jesus reigns enthroned above,
Our Advocate, our Head!

John Newton, 1779.

GLOUCESTER (WITH CHORUS). [H. P. 40.]

461

Heb. ii. 3. "*So great salvation.*"

Tune GLOUCESTER (and Chorus). C. M.

1 SALVATION! O the joyful sound!
'Tis pleasure to our ears!
A sovereign balm for every wound,
A cordial for our fears.
Glory, honour, praise, and power,
Be unto the Lamb for ever!
Jesus Christ is our Redeemer,
Hallelujah! praise the Lord.

2 Salvation! let the echo fly
The spacious earth around;
While all the armies of the sky
Conspire to raise the sound!
Glory, honour, praise, and power, etc.

3 Salvation! O Thou bleeding Lamb,
To Thee the praise belongs;
Salvation shall inspire our hearts,
And dwell upon our tongues!
Glory, honour, praise, and power, etc.

Isaac Watts, D.D., 1709—*chorus and third stanza, Anon.*, 1774.

462 1 Cor. x. 4. "*That Rock was Christ.*"
Tune SIHOR. 77, 77, 77. Or REDHEAD.

SIHOR (River). [H. P. 158.]

1 ROCK of Ages, cleft for me,
Let me hide myself in Thee!
Let the water and the blood,
From Thy riven side which flowed,
Be of sin the double cure,
Cleanse me from its guilt and power.

2 Not the labours of my hands
Can fulfil Thy law's demands:
Could my zeal no respite know,
Could my tears for ever flow,
All for sin could not atone:
Thou must save, and Thou alone!

3 Nothing in my hand I bring;
Simply to Thy cross I cling;
Naked, come to Thee for dress;
Helpless, look to Thee for grace;
Foul, I to the fountain fly:
Wash me, Saviour, or I die!

4 While I draw this fleeting breath—
When mine eyes shall close in death—
When I soar through tracts unknown—
See Thee on Thy judgment throne—
Rock of Ages, cleft for me,
Let me hide myself in Thee!

Augustus M. Toplady, 1776.

See Hymns 174—176, 232—243.

MAGDEBURG. [H. P. 300.]

(2) ITS PROMISES.

463 Ps. cxliv. 15. "*Happy is that people.*" Tune MAGDEBURG. 87, 87, 47. Or HAVILAH.

1 O THE happiness arising
From the life of grace within,
When the soul is realizing
Conquests over hell and sin:
Happy moments!
Heavenly joys on earth begin.

2 On the Saviour's fulness living,
All His saints obtain delight;
With the strength which He is giving,
They can wrestle, they can fight:
Happy moments!
When King Jesus is in sight.

3 Nearer, nearer, to Him clinging,
Let my helpless soul be found;
All my sorrows to Him bringing,
May His grace in me abound;
Happy moments!
With new covenant blessings crowned.

4 All the world has nothing charming;
Foes and sorrows flee away:
Nor is death itself alarming,
Jesus took its sting away:
Happy moments!
Dawning of eternal day!

Joseph Irons, 1819.

BETHER (Mountains of). [H P. 36.]

464 Ps. lxxxix. 15. "*Blessed is the people that know the joyful sound.*" Tune BETHER. C. M.

1 BLEST are the souls that hear and know
The gospel's joyful sound!
Peace shall attend the path they go,
And light their steps surround.

2 Their joy shall bear their spirits up,
Through their Redeemer's name;
His righteousness exalts their hope,
Nor Satan dares condemn.

3 The Lord, our glory and defence,
Strength and salvation gives:
Israel, thy God for ever reigns,
Thy God for ever lives!

Isaac Watts, D.D., 1719.

SMYRNA. (Hymn Chant.) *Double Counterpoint.* [H. P. No. III.]

(3) INVITATIONS.

465

Rev. xxii. 17. "*Whosoever will.*"

Tune, Hymn Chant Smyrna. 888, 6.

1 JUST as thou art, without one trace
Of love, or joy, or inward grace,
Or meetness for the heavenly place,
O guilty sinner, come!

2 Thy sins I bore on Calvary's tree!
The stripes, thy due, were laid on Me,
That peace and pardon might be free:
O wretched sinner, come!

3 Burdened with guilt, wouldst thou be blest?
Trust not the world; it gives no rest:
I bring relief to hearts oppressed:
O weary sinner, come!

4 Come, leave thy burden at the cross;
Count all thy gains but empty dross;
My grace repays all earthly loss:
O needy sinner, come!

5 Come, hither bring thy boding fears,
Thy aching heart, thy bursting tears;
'Tis mercy's voice salutes thine ears,
O trembling sinner, come!

6 "The Spirit and the Bride say, Come;"
Rejoicing saints re-echo, Come;
Who faints, who thirsts, who will, may come;
Thy Saviour bids thee come!

Russell Sturgis Cook, 1850.

THYATIRA. (Hymn Chant.) [H. P. No. V.]

466

Jer. iii. 22. "*Behold, we come unto Thee.*"

Tune, Hymn Chant Thyatira. Or Bethabara.

1 JUST as I am—without one plea,
But that Thy blood was shed for me,
And that Thou bidd'st me come to Thee,
O Lamb of God, I come.

2 Just as I am—and waiting not
To rid my soul of one dark blot,
To Thee, whose blood can cleanse each spot,
O Lamb of God, I come.

3 Just as I am—though tossed about
With many a conflict, many a doubt,
Fightings within, and fears without,
O Lamb of God, I come.

4 Just as I am—poor, wretched, blind,
Sight, riches, healing of the mind,
Yea, all I need, in Thee to find,
O Lamb of God, I come.

5 Just as I am—Thou wilt receive,
Wilt welcome, pardon, cleanse, relieve;
Because Thy promise I believe,
O Lamb of God, I come.

6 Just as I am—(Thy love unknown
Has broken every barrier down)
Now, to be Thine, yea, Thine alone,
O Lamb of God, I come.

7 Just as I am—of that free love
The breadth, length, depth, and height to prove,
Here for a season, then above,
O Lamb of God, I come!

Charlotte Elliott, 1841.

WINCHESTER. [H. P. 46.]

467

Luke xiv. 22. "*Yet there is room.*"

Tune Winchester. C. M. Or Kedar.

1 COME, sinner, to the gospel feast;
Oh! come without delay;
For there is room in Jesu's breast
For all who will obey.

2 There's room in God's eternal love
To save thy precious soul!
Room in the Spirit's grace above
To heal, and make thee whole.

3 There's room within the church redeemed
With blood of Christ Divine.
Room in the white-robed throng convened,
For that dear soul of thine.

4 There's room in heaven among the choir,
And harps and crowns of gold,
And glorious palms of victory there,
And joys that ne'er were told.

5 There's room around thy Father's board
For thee and thousands more:
Oh! come, and welcome, to the Lord:
Yea, come this very hour!

F. D. Huntingdon, 1843.

468 Matt. xi. 29. *"Take My yoke upon you."*
Tune Idumea. 87, 87, 47. Or Media.

1 Come, ye souls by sin afflicted,
Bowed with fruitless sorrow down;
By the broken law convicted,
Through the cross behold the crown.
Look to Jesus—
Mercy flows through Him alone.

2 Take His easy yoke and wear it,
Love will make obedience sweet;
Christ will give you strength to bear it,
While His wisdom guides your feet
Safe to glory,
Where His ransomed captives meet.

3 Blessèd are the eyes that see Him;
Blest the ears that hear His voice:
Blessèd are the souls that trust Him,
And in Him alone rejoice;
His commandments
Then become their happy choice!

Joseph Swain, 1792.

469 John vi. 37. *"Him that cometh to Me, I will in no wise cast out."*
Tune Idumea. 87, 87, 47.

1 Come, and welcome, to the Saviour,
He in mercy bids thee come:
Come, be happy in His favour,
Longer from Him do not roam;
Come, and welcome,
Come to Jesus, sinner, come!

2 Come, and welcome; rise to glory,
Leave this passing world behind:
Christ will spread His banner o'er thee,
Thou in Him a friend shalt find;
Come, and welcome,
To a Saviour good and kind.

3 Come, and welcome: do not linger,
Make thy happy choice to-day;
True, thou art a guilty sinner,
But He'll wash thy sins away:
Come, and welcome,
Time admits of no delay!

Albert Midlane, 1865.

470 Matt. xi. 28. *"Come unto Me, all ye that labour and are heavy laden, and I will give you rest."*
Tune Dismissal. 87, 87, 47. Or Havilah.

1 Come, ye sinners, poor and wretched,
Weak and wounded, sick and sore;
Jesus ready stands to save you,
Full of pity joined with power;
He is able,
He is willing; doubt no more.

2 Come, ye needy, come, and welcome,
God's free bounty glorify;
True belief, and true repentance,
Every grace that brings us nigh,
Without money,
Come to Jesus Christ, and buy.

3 Let not conscience make you linger,
Nor of fitness fondly dream;
All the fitness He requireth,
Is to feel your need of Him:
This He gives you;
'Tis the Spirit's rising beam.

4 Come, ye weary, heavy laden,
Lost and ruined by the fall;
If you tarry till you're better
You will never come at all.
Not the righteous,
Sinners Jesus came to call.

5 Lo! the' incarnate God, ascended,
Pleads the merit of His blood;
Venture on Him, venture wholly,
Let no other trust intrude:
None but Jesus
Can do helpless sinners good.

6 Saints and angels, joined in concert,
Sing the praises of the Lamb;
While the blissful seats of heaven
Sweetly echo with His name,
Hallelujah!
Sinners here may sing the same!

Joseph Hart, 1759.

ZAANAIM (Plain of.) [H. P. 191.]

471

Mark x. 49. "*Rise, He calleth thee.*"
Tune ZAANAIM. 8 7, 8 7, 4 7.

1 HARK! the voice of Jesus calling,
 "Come, thou laden, come to Me:
I have rest and peace to offer;
 Rest, poor labouring one, for thee:
 Take salvation,
 Take it now, and happy be."

2 Yes, though high in heavenly glory,
 Still the Saviour calls to thee;
Faith can hear His gracious accents—
 "Come, thou laden, come to Me;
 Take salvation,
 Take it now, and happy be."

3 Soon that Voice will cease its calling,
 Now it speaks, and speaks to thee
Sinner, heed the gracious message,
 To the blood for refuge flee;
 Take salvation,
 Take it now, and happy be.

4 Life is found alone in Jesus,
 Only there 'tis offered thee—
Offered without price or money,
 'Tis the gift of God sent free;
 Take salvation,
 Take it now, and happy be!

Albert Midlane, 1865.

472

Isa. lv. 1. "*Ho, every one that thirsteth, come ye to the waters.*"
Tune ZAANAIM. 8 7, 8 7, 4 7. Or IDUMEA.

1 HO, ye thirsty! parched and fainting,
 Here are waters, turn and see!
To the thirstiest, poorest, vilest,
 Without money, all is free—
 Thirsty sinner!
 Drink and stay not, 'tis for thee.

2 Ho, ye weary! toiling, burdened,
 With a world of woes oppressed;
Come! it is thy Lord invites thee,
 Lay thy head upon My breast.
 Weary sinner!
 Come to Jesus, come and rest.

3 Ho, ye wounded! bruisèd, broken,
 Come, and health Divine receive;
Look to Him who heals the wounded,
 He alone can healing give.
 Wounded sinner!
 Look to Jesus, look and live!

Horatius Bonar, D.D., 1844.

VENITE ADOREMUS. [H. P. 250.]

473

Matt. xi. 28. "*Come unto Me.*"
Tune VENITE ADOREMUS. 12 10, 11 10.

1 OH come, ye that labour and are heavy laden,
 Come ye to Jesus for rest and peace.
Lo! now He calls, and lovingly invites us.
Oh come and fall before Him, Christ the Lord.

2 Jesus is willing! waiting to be gracious;
And none that come will He cast out.
Dying—He proves His love, all love surpassing.
Oh come and fall before Him, Christ the Lord.

3 Jesus is able! from the grave arising,
Lo! He proclaimeth His power to save.
He that is with us is more than all against us,
Oh come and fall before Him, Christ the Lord.

4 Saviour of sinners, Chosen of the Father,
On Thee alone all our trust we build.
Thou art alone a Saviour all-sufficient,
Our hearts we bow before Thee, Christ the Lord.

5 Blessing and honour, glory and dominion,
Be to the Lamb once for sinners slain.
Oh! may we join the everlasting chorus,
And bow with them before Him, Christ the Lord!

Edward Harland, 1867.

474 John xii. 32. "*If I be lifted up, . . will draw all men unto Me.*"

Tune SIHOR. 77,77,77.

1 FROM the cross uplifted high,
 Where the Saviour deigns to die,
What melodious sounds I hear,
Bursting on my ravished ear!
Love's redeeming work is done;
Come, and welcome, sinner, come.

2 Spread for thee the festal board,
See with richest dainties stored;
To thy Father's bosom pressed,
Yet again a child confessed,
Never from His house to roam,
Come, and welcome, sinner, come.

3 Soon the days of life shall end;
Lo, I come, your Saviour, Friend,
Safe your spirits to convey
To the realms of endless day,
Up to My eternal home.
Come, and welcome, sinner, come.

Thomas Haweis, 1792.

See Hymns 166, 193, 515.

(4) EXPOSTULATIONS.

475 Rev. iii. 20. "*Behold I stand at the door, and knock.*"

Tune GETHSEMANE. L. M.

1 BEHOLD! a Stranger at the door!
 He gently knocks, has knocked before;
Has waited long; is waiting still:
You treat no other friend so ill.

2 But will He prove a friend indeed?
He will: the very Friend you need:
The Man of Nazareth, 'tis He,
With garments dyed at Calvary.

3 O lovely attitude! He stands
With melting heart and bleeding hands;
O matchless kindness! and He shows
This matchless kindness to His foes!

4 Admit Him, ere His anger burn,
His feet depart, and ne'er return.
Admit Him, or the hour's at hand
When at His door denied you'll stand.

5 Yet know (nor of the terms complain)
Where Jesus comes He comes to reign;
To reign, and with no partial sway;
Thoughts must be slain that disobey.

6 Sovereign of souls! Thou Prince of Peace,
Oh, may Thy gentle reign increase:
Throw wide the door, each willing mind,
And be His empire all mankind!

See Hymn 1053. *Joseph Grigg*, 1765.

476 Hos. xiv. 1. "*Return unto the Lord thy God.*"

Tune GETHSEMANE. L. M. Or HERMON.

1 RETURN, O wanderer! return!
 And seek an injured Father's face:
Those warm desires that in thee burn
 Were kindled by reclaiming grace.

2 Return, O wanderer! return!
 And seek a Father's melting heart,
Whose pitying eyes thy grief discern,
 Whose hand can heal thine inward smart.

3 Return, O wanderer! return!
 He heard thy deep repentant sigh;
He saw thy softened spirit mourn,
 When no intruding ear was nigh.

4 Return, O wanderer! return!
 Thy Saviour bids thy spirit live;
Go to His bleeding feet, and learn
 How freely Jesus can forgive.

5 Return, O wanderer! return!
 And wipe away the falling tear;
'Tis God who says, "No longer mourn,"
 'Tis mercy's voice invites thee near.

6 Return, O wanderer! return!
 Regain thy lost, lamented rest;
Jehovah's love for thee doth yearn
 To clasp His children to His breast!

William Bengo Collyer, 1812.

477 Gen. xix. 17. "*Escape for thy life.*"

Tune, Hymn Chant PHILADELPHIA. 88, 88, 4.

1 HASTE, traveller, haste, the night comes on,
 And many a shining hour is gone;
The storm is gathering in the west,
And thou art far from home and rest:
 Haste, traveller, haste!

2 Oh, far from home thy footsteps stray:
Christ is the Life, and Christ the Way,
And Christ the Light—yon setting sun
Sinks ere the morn is scarce begun:
 Haste, traveller, haste!

PHILADELPHIA. (Hymn Chant.) [H. P. VII.]

3 The rising tempest sweeps the sky,
The rain descends, the winds are high;
The waters swell, and death and fear
Beset thy path—no refuge near:
Haste, traveller, haste!

4 Oh yes, a shelter you may gain,
A covert from the wind and rain,
A hiding-place, a rest, a home,
A refuge from the wrath to come:
Haste, traveller, haste!

5 Then linger not in all the plain,
Flee for thy life, the mountain gain;
Look not behind, make no delay,
Oh, speed thee, speed thee on thy way:
Haste, traveller, haste!

6 Poor, lost, benighted soul, art thou
Willing to find salvation now?
There yet is hope—hear mercy's call—
Truth, life, light, way, in Christ is all!
Haste to Him, haste!

William Bengo Collyer, 1829.

MIDIAN. [H. P. 175.]

478

Isa. lv. 7. *"Let him return unto the Lord."*

Tune Midian. 86, 86, 4.

1 RETURN, O wanderer, to thy home,
Thy Father calls for thee!
No longer now an exile roam
In guilt and misery!
Return, return!

2 Return, O wanderer, to thy home,
'Tis Jesus calls for thee:
The Spirit and the bride say, Come:
Oh, now for refuge flee!
Return, return!

3 Return, O wanderer, to thy home,
'Tis madness to delay:
There are no pardons in the tomb,
And brief is mercy's day.
Return, return!

Thomas Hastings, 1834.

VIENNA. [H. P. 149.]

479

2 Cor. vi. 2. *"Behold, now is the accepted time."* Tune Vienna. 77, 77. Or Luxemburg.

1 HASTEN, sinner, to be wise,
Stay not for the morrow's sun;
Longer wisdom you despise,
Harder is she to be won.

2 Hasten, mercy to implore,
Stay not for the morrow's sun,
Lest thy season should be o'er
Ere this evening's stage be run.

3 Hasten, sinner, to return,
Stay not for the morrow's sun,
Lest thy lamp should fail to burn
Ere the work of grace is done.

4 Hasten, sinner, to be blest,
Stay not for the morrow's sun,
Lest perdition thee arrest
Ere the morrow is begun.

5 Lord, do Thou the sinner turn!
Rouse him from his senseless state;
Let him not Thy counsel spurn,
Rue his fatal choice too late!

Thomas Scott, 1773.

480 Jer. xxvii. 13. "*Why will ye die?*"
Tune St. Werbergh. 87, 87, 47.

1 SINNERS, will you scorn the message
Sent in mercy from above?
Every sentence, oh how tender!
Every line is full of love!
Listen to it,
Every line is full of love.

2 Hear the heralds of the gospel
News from Zion's King proclaim,
To each rebel sinner—"Pardon,
Free forgiveness in His name;"
How important!
"Free forgiveness in His name."

3 Tempted souls, they bring you succour;
Fearful hearts, they quell your fears,
And with news of consolation
Chase away the falling tears:
Tender heralds!
Chase away the falling tears.

4 Who hath our report believed?
Who received the joyful word?
Who embraced the news of pardon
Offered to you by the Lord?
Can you slight it,
Spoken to you by the Lord?

5 O ye angels! hovering round us,
Waiting spirits! speed your way;
Hasten to the court of Heaven,
Tidings bear without delay:
"Rebel sinners
Glad the message will obey!"

Jonathan Allen, 1801.

ST. WERBERGH. [H. P. 304.]

PURDAY. [H. P. 338.]

481 Gal. vi. 10. "*As we have therefore oppor tunity.*"
Tune Purday. 87, 87, 77, 77.

1 MARK that long dark line of shadows,
Stretching far into the past:
Every day it seems to lengthen;
Whither does it tend at last?
Each one added to the hosts
From the present moment flies;
These are time's forgotten ghosts—
Fleeted opportunities.

2 Characters of light or darkness
Gabriel's pen from each requires
God records, if man forgets them,
Numbers each as each expires;
And the awful spectres all
At the day of doom will rise,
Witnesses at Heaven's call—
Fleeted opportunities.

3 Buried powers of good unmeasured,
Hardly present did ye seem,
Yet I thought I should have treasured,
When ye vanished like a dream.
Crushing now my sinful soul,
All your weight upon it lies;
Jesu's blood must o'er you roll,
Fleeted opportunities.

4 Oh, my soul! no further lengthen,
Wilfully, this ghostly train;
Rise, and seek for grace to strengthen.
Where 'twas never sought in vain.
Lost, this hour but adds another
To those solemn witnesses:
Every living soul's thy brother—
Mark thine opportunities!

Ellen Ranyard, 1861.

482 Matt. xii. 43. "*Seeking rest, and findeth none.*" Tune Siloam. 77, 77.

1 SINNER, is thy heart at rest?
Is thy bosom void of fear?
Art thou not by guilt oppressed?
Speaks not conscience in thy ear?

2 Can this world afford thee bliss?
Can it chase away thy gloom?
Flattering, false, and vain it is;
Tremble at the worldling's doom!

SILOAM (Pool of). [H. P. 153.]

3 Long the gospel thou hast spurned,
Long delayed to love thy God,
Stifled conscience, nor hast turned,
Still refused the Saviour's blood.

4 Think, O sinner, on thy end;
See the judgment-day appear,
Thither must thy spirit tend,
There thy solemn sentence hear.

5 Wretched, ruined, helpless soul,
To a Saviour's blood apply;
He alone can make thee whole,
Fly to Jesus, sinner, fly!

Jared Bell Waterbury, 1830.

OLD 81st. [H. P. 75.]

483 Matt. xxiii. 37. "*How often would I have gathered thy children together!*"

Tune Old Eighty-first. C. M. D. Or Evan II.

1 JERUSALEM, Jerusalem! enthronèd once on high,
Thou favoured home of God on earth, thou heaven below the sky!
Now brought to bondage with thy sons, a curse and grief to see,
Jerusalem, Jerusalem! our tears shall flow for thee.

2 Oh! hadst thou known thy day of grace, and flocked beneath the wing
Of Him who called thee lovingly, thine own anointed King,
Then had the tribes of all the world gone up thy pomp to see,
And glory dwelt within thy gates, and all thy sons been free!

3 "And who art thou that mournest me?" replied the ruin grey,
"And fear'st not rather that thyself may prove a castaway?
I am a dried and abject branch, my place is given to thee!
But woe to every barren graft of thy wild olive tree!

4 "Our day of grace is sunk in night, our time of mercy spent,
For heavy was my children's crime, and strange their punishment.
Yet gaze not idly on our fall, but, sinner, warnèd be,
Who sparèd not His chosen race may send His wrath on thee!

5 "Our day of grace is sunk in night, thy noon is in its prime;
Oh, turn and seek thy Saviour's face in this accepted time!
So, Gentile, may Jerusalem a lesson prove to thee,
And in the New Jerusalem thy home for ever be!"

Bishop Heber, 1811.

---

484 Prov. xiv. 10. "*A stranger doth not intermeddle with his joy.*" Tune Siloam. 7 7, 7 7. Or Pleyel.

1 SINNER, what hast thou to show,
Like the joys believers know?
Is thy path of fading flowers
Half so bright, so sweet, as ours?

2 Doth a skilful, healing Friend
On thy daily path attend,
And where thorns and stings abound,
Shed a balm on every wound?

3 When the tempest roars on high,
Hast thou still a refuge nigh?
Can, oh! can thy dying breath
Summon One more strong than death?

4 Canst thou, in that awful day,
Fearless tread the gloomy way,
Plead a glorious ransom given,
Burst from earth and soar to heaven?

Charlotte E. Tonna, 1829. (a.)

485 Rev. xx. 11. "*I saw a great white throne.*"

Tune Kedron. 886. D.

KEDRON (Brook). [H. P. 213.]

1 THOU God of glorious majesty,
To Thee, against myself, to Thee,
A worm of earth, I cry;
A half-awakened child of man,
An heir of endless bliss or pain,
A sinner born to die.

2 Lo! on a narrow neck of land,
'Twixt two unbounded seas, I stand
Secure, insensible:
A point of time, a moment's space,
Removes me to that heavenly place,
Or shuts me up in hell.

3 O God, my inmost soul convert,
And deeply on my thoughtful heart
Eternal things impress;
Give me to feel their solemn weight,
And, trembling on the brink of fate,
Wake me to righteousness.

4 Before me place, in dread array,
The pomp of that tremendous day,
When Thou with clouds shalt come
To judge the nations at Thy bar;
And tell me, Lord, shall I be there,
To meet a joyful doom?

5 Be this my one great business here,
With holy diligence and fear,
To make my calling sure;
Thine utmost counsel to fulfil,
And suffer all Thy righteous will,
And to the end endure.

6 Then, Saviour, then, my soul receive,
Transported from this vale to live
And reign with Thee above:
Where faith is sweetly lost in sight,
And hope in full supreme delight
And everlasting love!

Charles Wesley, 1742. (*a.*)

See Hymns 1026—1042.

THEME III.—The Gospel Welcomed and Embraced.

THE LIFE AND HISTORY OF A TRUE BELIEVER.

I. His Character Portrayed.

SALISBURY. [H. P. 62.]

(1) GRACE GIVEN TO BELIEVE.

486 Cant. i. 4. "*Draw me, we will run after Thee.*" Tune Salisbury. C. M.

1 DRAW me, oh draw me, gracious Lord!
Thy love is all Divine:
All hearts obey Thy sovereign word;
Come, triumph over mine.

2 I've heard the thunders of Thy law;
I've felt Thy lifted rod:
But 'tis Thy dying love must draw
My wayward soul to God.

3 Amidst Thy thunders, Lord, I slept,
Against Thy rod rebelled:
I looked upon the cross, and wept
To see my sins revealed.

4 My melting heart its power confessed,
The stone to flesh was turned;
Repentance kindled in my breast:
I gazed, rejoiced, and mourned.

5 There I beheld a Saviour's love,
There saw my sins forgiven:
Thence sprang my soul to hopes above,
By faith laid up in heaven.

6 Now, Saviour, now I come to Thee,
Constrained by grace Divine:
I yield me to Thy will, to be
For ever, ever Thine!

Professor Scholefield, D.D., 1836.

(2) SALVATION BY GRACE.

487 Rom. iv. 25. "*Who was delivered for our offences, and was raised again for our justification.*"

Tune Eden. C. M.

1 ALL that I was, my sin, my guilt,
My death, was all my own:
All that I am I owe to Thee,
My gracious God, alone.

2 The evil of my former state
Was mine, and only mine;
The good in which I now rejoice
Is Thine, and only Thine.

3 The darkness of my former state,
The bondage—all was mine;
The light of life in which I walk,
The liberty—is Thine.

EDEN. [H. P. 38.]

4 Thy grace first made me feel my sin,
And taught me to believe;
Then, in believing, peace I found,
And now I live, I live!

5 All that I am while here on earth,
All that I hope to be—
When Jesus comes, and glory dawns,
I owe it, Lord, to Thee.

Horatius Bonar, D.D., 1845.

EVAN II. [H. P. 77.]

488

Matt. xi. 28. *"Come unto Me, all ye that labour and are heavy laden."* Tune EVAN II. C. M. D.

1 I HEARD the voice of Jesus say,
"Come unto Me, and rest;
Lay down, thou weary one, lay down
Thy head upon My breast."
I came to Jesus as I was,
Weary, and worn, and sad:
I found in Him a resting-place,
And He has made me glad.

2 I heard the voice of Jesus say,
"Behold, I freely give
The living water—thirsty one,
Stoop down, and drink, and live."
I came to Jesus, and I drank
Of that life-giving stream;
My thirst was quenched, my soul revived,
And now I live in Him.

3 I heard the voice of Jesus say,
"I am this dark world's Light;
Look unto Me, thy morn shall rise,
And all thy day be bright."
I looked to Jesus, and I found
In Him my Star, my Sun;
And in that Light of Life I'll walk
Till travelling days are done!

Horatius Bonar, D.D., 1850.

IONA. [H. P. 37.]

489

Col. iii. 11. *"Christ is All, and in all."* Tune IONA. C. M.

1 I 'VE found the Pearl of greatest price,
My heart doth sing for joy;
And sing I must, a Christ I have—
Oh what a Christ have I!

2 Christ is a Prophet, Priest, and King;
A Prophet full of light,
A Priest that stands 'twixt God and man,
A King that rules with might.

3 My Christ, He is the Lord of lords,
He is the King of kings;
He is the Sun of righteousness,
With healing in His wings.

4 My Christ, He is the Tree of life,
Who in God's garden grows,
Whose fruit does feed, whose leaves do heal;
My Christ is Sharon's Rose.

5 Christ is my meat, Christ is my drink,
My medicine, and my health,
My peace, my strength, my joy, my crown,
My glory, and my wealth.

6 Christ is my father, and my friend,
My brother, and my love,
My head, my hope, my counsellor,
My advocate above.

7 My Christ, He is the heaven of heavens,
My Christ what shall I call!
My Christ is first, my Christ is last,
My Christ is All in all!

John Mason, 1683.

MAHANAIM. [H. P. 129.]

490 Isa. liii. 6. "*The Lord hath laid on Him the iniquity of us all.*"
Tune MAHANAIM. 76, 76. D. Or MUNICH.

1 I LAY my sins on Jesus,
  The spotless Lamb of God;
He bears them all, and frees us
  From the accursèd load.
I bring my guilt to Jesus,
  To wash my crimson stains
White in His blood most precious,
  Till not a spot remains.

2 I lay my wants on Jesus,
  All fulness dwells in Him;
He healeth my diseases,
  He doth my soul redeem.
I lay my griefs on Jesus,
  My burdens and my cares;
He from them all releases,
  He all my sorrows shares.

3 I rest my soul on Jesus,
  This weary soul of mine;
His right hand me embraces,
  I on His breast recline.
I love the name of Jesus—
  Emmanuel, Christ, the Lord;
Like fragrance on the breezes,
  His name abroad is poured.

4 I long to be like Jesus,
  Meek, loving, lowly, mild;
I long to be like Jesus,
  The Father's Holy Child;
I long to be with Jesus,
  Amid the heavenly throng;
To sing with saints His praises,
  To learn the angels' song!

Horatius Bonar, D.D., 1845.

PATMOS. [H. P. 147.]

491 Luke xv. 24. "*He was lost, and is found.*" Tune PATMOS. 77, 77.

1 WE were lost, but we are found;
  Dead, but now alive are we;
We were sore in bondage bound,
  But our Jesus sets us free.

2 Strangers, and He takes us in;
  Naked, He becomes our dress;
Sick, and He from stain of sin
  Cleanses with His righteousness.

3 Therefore will we sing His praise,
  Who His lost ones has restored,
Hearts and voices both shall raise
  Hallelujahs to the Lord!

John S. B. Monsell, LL.D., 1863.

BRIDEHEAD. [H. P. 310.]

492 John xv. 5. "*Without Me ye can do nothing.*" Tune BRIDEHEAD. 886. D.

1 CONTENT and glad I'll ever be,
    To have salvation, Lord, from Thee,
      Even as a sinner poor:
I nothing have, I nothing am,
My treasure's in the bleeding Lamb,
    Both now and evermore.

2 The more through grace myself I know,
  The more content I am to bow,
    And sink beneath Thy cross;
  To live by faith upon Thy blood,
  To wait on Thee for every good,
    And count my gain but loss!

William Batty, 1757.

LOIS. [H. P. 339.]

493 Ps. lvii. 7. "*My heart is fixed, O God.*"
Tune LOIS. 83, 83, 888, 33.

1 MY heart is fixed, eternal God,
Fixed on Thee;
And my immortal choice is made,
Christ for me;
He is my Prophet, Priest, and King,
Who did for me salvation bring,
And while I 've breath I mean to sing
Christ for me—Christ for me.

2 In Him I see the Godhead shine,
Christ for me,
He is the Majesty Divine,
Christ for me;
The Father's well-belovèd Son,
Co-partner of His royal throne,
Who did for human guilt atone,
Christ for me—Christ for me.

3 To-day as yesterday the same,
Christ for me;
How precious is His balmy name,
Christ for me;
Christ as mere man may answer you,
Who error's winding path pursue;
But I with part can never do;
Christ for me—Christ for me.

4 Let others boast of heaps of gold,
Christ for me;
His riches never can be told,
Christ for me;
Your gold will waste and wear away,
Your honours perish in a day;
My portion never can decay,
Christ for me—Christ for me.

5 In pining sickness, or in health,
Christ for me;
In deepest poverty or wealth,
Christ for me;
And in that all-important day
When I the summons must obey,
And pass from this dark world away,
Christ for me—Christ for me

Richard Jukes, 1862.

MAMRE (Plain of). [H. P. 226.]

(3) FAITH.

494 Ps. xl. 2. "*He . . . set my feet upon a rock.*" Tune MAMRE. 88, 88, 88.

1 MY hope is built on nothing less
Than Jesu's blood and righteousness:
I dare not trust the sweetest frame,
But wholly lean on Jesu's name:
On Christ, the solid Rock, I stand,
All other ground is sinking sand.

2 When darkness veils His glorious face,
I rest on His unchanging grace
In every high and stormy gale,
My anchor holds within the veil:
On Christ, etc.

3 His oath, His covenant, and His blood,
Support me in the sinking flood;
When all around my soul gives way,
He then is all my hope and stay:
On Christ, etc.

4 When the last awful trump shall sound,
Oh, may I then in Him be found,
Clothed in His righteousness alone,
Faultless to stand before the throne:
On Christ, etc.

Edward Mote, 1825. (*a.*)

LONDON NEW; or, NEWTON. [H. P. 55.]

495

Eph. ii. 8. "*Not of yourselves; it is the gift of God.*" Tune LONDON NEW. C. M.

1 'TIS not by works of righteousness
Which our own hands have done,
But we are saved by sovereign grace,
Abounding through the Son.

2 'Tis from the mercy of our God
That all our hopes begin;
'Tis by the water, and the blood,
Our souls are washed from sin.

3 'Tis through the purchase of His death
Who hung upon the tree,
The Spirit is sent down to breathe
On such dry bones as we.

4 Raised from the dead we live anew;
And, justified by grace,
We shall appear in glory too,
And see our Father's face!

Isaac Watts, D.D., 1709.

496

Heb. xii. 2. "*Looking unto Jesus.*" Tune STOBEL. 664, 6664.

STOBEL. [H. P. 110.]

1 MY faith looks up to Thee,
Thou Lamb of Calvary,
Saviour Divine:
Now hear me while I pray;
Take all my guilt away;
Oh! let me from this day
Be wholly Thine.

2 May Thy rich grace impart
Strength to my fainting heart,
My zeal inspire:
As Thou hast died for me,
Oh! may my love to Thee
Pure, warm, and changeless be,
A living fire.

3 While life's dark maze I tread,
And griefs around me spread,
Be Thou my Guide;
Bid darkness turn to day,
Wipe sorrow's tears away,
Nor let me ever stray
From Thee aside.

4 When ends life's transient dream,
When death's cold sullen stream
Shall o'er me roll,
Blest Saviour! then in love,
Fear and distrust remove;
Oh! bear me safe above,
A ransomed soul!

Ray Palmer, D.D., 1834.

FRANCONIA. [H. P. 87.]

497

Eph. ii. 8. "*It is the gift of God.*" Tune FRANCONIA. S. M.

1 FAITH is the gift of God,
By His own Spirit wrought;
The eye that sees, the hand that takes,
The blessings Christ hath bought.

2 Jesus it owns as King,
And all-atoning Priest;
It claims no merit of its own,
But looks for all in Christ.

3 To Him it leads the soul,
When filled with deep distress,
Flies to the fountain of His blood,
And trusts His righteousness.

4 All through the wilderness
It is our strength and stay;
Nor can we miss the heavenly road,
If faith direct our way.

5 Lord, 'tis Thy work alone,
And that divinely free;
Send down the Spirit of Thy Son,
To work this faith in me!

B. Beddome, 1769.—*ver.* 1, *F. R. H.*

See Hymns 1043—1062.

SOSTHENES. [H. P. 243.]

498 Ps. lxxxiv. 6. "*Passing through the valley of Baca make it a well.*" Tune SOSTHENES. 10 11 11 11, 12 11.

1 WEEP, pilgrim, weep! yet 'tis not for the sorrow
Which follows thy steps in this wilderness way;
Not as the hopeless who darken to-morrow
With cares which might well be enough for to-day:
The days of thy mourning an end soon shall see,
There are songs in the valley of Baca for thee!

2 Mourn, pilgrim, sadly and bitterly mourn!
For this is the valley of shadows and tears;
Yet not for past pleasures which may not return,
Nor childhood's decay with its young, happy years.
There are causes of sorrow, more sad and more true,
Yet songs in the valley of Baca for you!

3 Sigh, Christian pilgrim, for sins deeply sigh,
Which crucify Jesus again and again!
Let rivers of water flow down from your eye,
That He, the Beloved, is rejected of men:
Yet healing is found in the blood of the tree,
There are songs in the valley of Baca for thee!

4 Joy, pilgrim, joy! 'mid thy bosom's deep swelling,
Look up! there are fountains of life by the way:
Springs from the rock in the wilderness welling;
And comfort for thee, if that rock be thy stay—
A sinner forgiven! a bondsman made free!
Who should sing in the valley of Baca like thee?

5 Sing, pilgrim, sing! let the theme of thy singing
Be Jesus the Conqueror, Jesus the Lamb!
Let the wide earth with His glory be ringing;
Let praises for ever ascend to His name!
The journey is rough, but the way is not long;
Through the valley of Baca let Christ be thy song!

Horatius Bonar, D.D., 1844.

FARRANT. [H. P. 67.]

(4) REPENTANCE.

499 Acts xi. 18. "*God . . . granted repentance unto life.*" Tune FARRANT. C. M. Or ST. MARY.

1 COME, O Thou all-victorious Lord;
Thy power to us make known;
Come by Thy Spirit and Thy word,
And break these hearts of stone.

2 Oh that we all might now begin
Our foolishness to mourn,
And turn at once from every sin,
And to our Saviour turn!

3 Give us ourselves and Thee to know
In this our gracious day;
Repentance unto life bestow,
And take our sins away.

4 That solemn sense of guilt impart
Then, Lord, remove the load:
Comfort, and wash the troubled heart
In Thine atoning blood.

5 Our lost estate through sin declare,
But speak our sins forgiven:
In faith, in holiness, prepare,
And call us home to heaven!

Charles Wesley, 1746. (a.)

CARMEL (Mount). [H. P. 69.]

500

Exod. xv. 26. *"I am the Lord that healeth thee."* Tune CARMEL. C. M.

1 HEAL us, Emmanuel! here we are,
Waiting to feel Thy touch:
Deep-wounded souls to Thee repair,
And, Saviour, we are such.

2 Our faith is feeble, we confess,
We faintly trust Thy word;
But wilt Thou pity us the less?
Be that far from Thee, Lord!

3 Remember him who once applied
With trembling for relief;
"Lord, I believe," with tears he cried,
"Oh, help my unbelief!"

4 She, too, who touched Thee in the press,
And healing virtue stole,
Was answered, "Daughter, go in peace,
Thy faith hath made thee whole."

5 Concealed amid the gathering throng
She would have shunned Thy view,
And if her faith was firm and strong,
Had strong misgivings too.

6 Like her, with hopes and fears, we come
To touch Thee, if we may;
Oh! send us not despairing home,
Send none unhealed away!

William Cowper, 1779.

ST. BRIDE. [H. P. 95.]

501

Ps. li. 1. *"Have mercy upon me, O God."* Tune ST. BRIDE. S. M.

1 HAVE mercy, Lord, on me,
As Thou wert ever kind;
Let me, oppressed with loads of guilt,
Thy wonted mercy find.

2 Blot out, O Lord, my sins,
Nor me in anger view;
Create in me a heart that 's clean,
An upright mind renew.

3 Withdraw not Thou Thy help,
Nor cast me from Thy sight;
Nor let Thy Holy Spirit take
His everlasting flight.

4 The joy Thy favour gives
Let me again obtain,
And Thy free Spirit's firm support
My fainting soul maintain!

Tate and Brady, 1696.

GETHSEMANE. [H. P. 28.]

502

Ps. cxxx. 7. *"With the Lord there is mercy."* Tune GETHSEMANE. L. M.

1 HAVE mercy, Lord! O Lord, forgive;
Let the repenting sinner live;
Is not Thy mercy great and free?
May not the sinner trust in Thee?

2 Wash us from all our sins, O God,
In Thy dear Son's atoning blood;
Hear those who come before Thy throne,
Pleading His merits, not their own.

3 Though we have grieved Thy Spirit, Lord,
His gracious presence still afford;
And now salvation's joys impart,
To heal the broken, contrite heart.

4 A broken heart, O God our King,
Is all the sacrifice we bring;
Thou, God of grace, wilt not despise
A broken heart in sacrifice.

Isaac Watts, D.D., 1719.

503

Ps. cxxx. 2. *"Lord, hear my voice."* Tune ST. BRIDE. S. M.

1 IN sorrow and distress,
To Thee, O Lord, we fly;
In penitential lowliness
To Thee for mercy cry.

2 Mercy, oh mercy, Lord!
From Thee we have our breath:
We read it written in Thy word,
"God willeth not your death:

3 "God gave His only Son
Your sins to take away;
And God's dear Son to heaven is gone
On your behalf to pray."

4 By Thine own love we plead,
Oh hearken to our prayer;
By Him, who for our sins did bleed,
Spare us, O Father, spare.

5 Our drooping minds refresh
With showers of heavenly dew;
For hearts of stone give hearts of flesh—
Renew us, Lord, renew.

PART II.

6 Comfort and make us whole
With Thy free Spirit's grace;
Lift up, O Lord, upon our soul
The lustre of Thy face.

7 With Jesu's white robe hide
Our manifold offence;
And cleanse with blood from Jesu's side
Our tears of penitence.

8 Constrain us to abhor
The sins that made Him grieve;
And ne'er to tempt the Spirit more
Our thankless hearts to leave.

9 Make us, O Lord, to tread
The path which Jesus trod;
Which Him from earth in triumph led
To the right hand of God.

10 So with the saints in heaven
May we sing praise to Thee,
For peace restored, and sins forgiven—
To all eternity!

Bishop Christopher Wordsworth, 1862.

(5) RENUNCIATION OF THE WORLD.

504 Heb. xi. 13. "*Confessed that they were strangers and pilgrims on the earth.*"

Tune BEULAH. 64, 64, 6664.

BEULAH. [H. P. 102.]

1 I'M but a stranger here,
Heaven is my home;
Earth is a desert drear,
Heaven is my home.
Danger and sorrow stand
Round me on every hand;
Heaven is my fatherland,
Heaven is my home.

2 What though the tempest rage,
Heaven is my home;
Short is my pilgrimage,
Heaven is my home.
And time's wild wintry blast
Soon shall be overpast;
I shall reach home at last—
Heaven is my home.

3 There, at my Saviour's side,
Heaven is my home;
I shall be glorified,
Heaven is my home.
There are the good and blest,
Those I love most and best;
And there I too shall rest—
Heaven is my home.

4 Therefore I murmur not,
Heaven is my home;
Whate'er my earthly lot,
Heaven is my home.
And I shall surely stand
There at my Lord's right hand;
Heaven is my fatherland,
Heaven is my home!

Thomas Rawson Taylor, 1836.

FRENCH; *or,* DUNDEE. [H. P. 65.]

505 Jer. xxxi. 14. "*My people shall be satisfied with My goodness.*" Tune FRENCH. C. M.

1 LET worldly minds the world pursue,
It has no charms for me;
Once I admired its trifles too,
But grace has set me free.

2 Its pleasures now no longer please,
No more content afford;
Far from my heart be joys like these,
Now I have seen the Lord.

3 As by the light of opening day
The stars are all concealed,
So earthly pleasures fade away
When Jesus is revealed.

4 Creatures no more divide my choice,
I bid them all depart;
His name, and love, and gracious voice,
Have fixed my roving heart.

5 Now, Lord, I would be Thine alone,
And wholly live to Thee;
But may I hope that Thou wilt own
A worthless worm like me?

6 Yes! though of sinners I'm the worst,
I cannot doubt Thy will;
For if Thou hadst not loved me first,
I had refused Thee still!

John Newton, 1779.

LINUS. [H. P. 336.]

506

Gal. vi. 14. "*The cross of our Lord Jesus Christ.*"
Tune LINUS. 87, 87. D. Or ESDRAELON.

1 JESUS, I my cross have taken,
All to leave, and follow Thee;
Destitute, despised, forsaken,
Thou, from hence, my all shalt be.
Perish every fond ambition,
All I've sought, or hoped, or known;
Yet how rich is my condition!
God and heaven are still my own!

2 Let the world despise and leave me,
They have left my Saviour too;
Human hearts and looks deceive me;
Thou art not, like them, untrue:
And, while Thou shalt smile upon me,
God of wisdom, love, and might,
Foes may hate, and friends may shun me;
Show Thy face, and all is bright!

3 Go then, earthly fame and treasure!
Come, disaster, scorn, and pain!
In Thy service, pain is pleasure;
With Thy favour, loss is gain!
I have called Thee, Abba, Father!
I have stayed my heart on Thee!
Storms may howl, and clouds may gather,
All must work for good to me!

PART II.

4 Man may trouble and distress me,
'Twill but drive me to Thy breast:
Life with trials hard may press me,
Heaven will bring me sweeter rest:
Oh! 'tis not in grief to harm me,
While Thy love is left to me!
Oh! 'twere not in joy to charm me,
Were that joy unmixed with Thee!

5 Take, my soul, thy full salvation;
Rise o'er sin, and fear, and care;
Joy to find, in every station,
Something still to do or bear:
Think what Spirit dwells within thee!
What a Father's smile is thine!
What a Saviour died to win thee!
Child of heaven, shouldst thou repine?

6 Haste, then, on from grace to glory,
Armed by faith, and winged by prayer;
Heaven's eternal day's before thee,
God's own hand shall guide thee there!
Soon shall close thy earthly mission,
Swift shall pass thy pilgrim days;
Hope soon change to glad fruition,
Faith to sight, and prayer to praise!

Henry Francis Lyte, 1825.

FRENCH; *or*, DUNDEE. [H. P. 65.]

507

Col. iii. 2. "*Set your affection on things above.*" Tune FRENCH. C. M.

1 OH 'tis not what we fancied it—
This world, this world of ours;
We thought its skies were sunshine all,
And all its fields were flowers.

2 But soon o'erclouded are its skies,
Its flowers they fade away;
Our youthful hopes are vanishing,
Our early joys decay.

3 Another light is breaking bright,
Which beams from heaven on high;
And other flowers are blossoming,
Which cannot fade or die.

4 Above us is a brighter land,
To which we seek to come;
Our sure and quiet resting-place,
Our everlasting home.

5 Its fields are ever beautiful,
Its skies are ever fair,
Its day is always clear and bright,
For Christ, its Sun, is there.

6 O Sun of Righteousness, arise;
Thy light upon us beam;
For all this life is but a sleep,
And all this world a dream!

Horatius Bonar, D.D., 1844.

508

Num. x. 29. "*Come thou with us, and we will do thee good.*" Tune HONIDON. 77, 77. D. Or SAMARIA.

1 PEOPLE of the living God,
I have sought the world around,
Paths of sin and sorrow trod,
Peace and comfort nowhere found!
Now to you my spirit turns,
Turns, a fugitive unblest;
Brethren, where your altar burns,
Oh receive me into rest!

HONIDON. [H. P. 291.]

2 Lonely I no longer roam,
Like the cloud, the wind, the wave;
Where you dwell shall be my home,
Where you die shall be my grave;
Mine the God whom you adore,
Your Redeemer shall be mine;
Earth can fill my heart no more,
Every idol I resign.

3 Tell me not of gain or loss,
Ease, enjoyment, pomp, and power;
Welcome poverty and cross,
Shame, reproach, affliction's hour.

"Follow Me!" I know the voice;
Jesus, Lord, Thy steps I see;

Now I take Thy yoke by choice,
Light Thy burden now to me!

James Montgomery, 1819.

GILBOA (Mount). [H. P. 11.]

509

Heb. xi. 16. "*Now they desire a better country.*" Tune GILBOA. L. M.

1 THOU vain, deceitful world, farewell!
Thine idle joys no more we love;
By faith in brighter worlds we dwell,
In spirit find our home above.

2 Jesus, we go with Thee, to taste
Of joy supreme that never dies!
Our feet shall press the weary waste,
Our heart, our home, are in the skies.

3 And oh! while unto heaven's high hill
The toilsome path of life we tread,
Around us, loving Father, still
Thy circling wings of mercy spread.

4 From day to day, from hour to hour,
Oh, may our rising spirits prove
The strength of Thine almighty power,
The sweetness of Thy saving love!

Sir Edward Denny, 1838.

See Hymn 220.

HANOVER; *or*, MODERN 104TH. [H. P. 239.]

(6) CONFLICT.

510

1 Pet. i. 8. "*Believing, ye rejoice.*"
Tune HANOVER. 10 10, 11 11.

1 BEGONE, unbelief. My Saviour is near,
And for my relief Will surely appear;
By prayer let me wrestle, And He will perform,
With Christ in the vessel, I smile at the storm.

2 Though dark be my way, Since He is my guide,
'Tis mine to obey, 'Tis His to provide;
Though cisterns be broken, And creatures all fail,
The word He hath spoken Shall surely prevail.

3 His love in time past Forbids me to think
He'll leave me at last In trouble to sink;
Each sweet Ebenezer I have in review
Confirms His good pleasure To help me quite [through.

4 Determined to save, He watched o'er my path
When, Satan's blind slave, I sported with death:
And can He have taught me To trust in His name,
And thus far have brought me To put me to shame?

5 Why should I complain Of want or distress,
Temptation or pain? He told me no less;
The heirs of salvation, I know from His word,
Through much tribulation Must follow their Lord.

6 How bitter that cup No heart can conceive,
Which He drank quite up That sinners might live!
His way was much rougher And darker than mine:
Did Christ, my Lord, suffer, And shall I repine?

7 Since all that I meet Shall work for my good,
The bitter is sweet, The medicine is food;
Though painful at present, 'Twill cease before long,
And then, oh how pleasant The conqueror's song!

John Newton, 1779.

ARMAGEDDON (Valley of). [H. P. 90.]

511

1 Pet. ii. 25. "*Ye were as sheep going astray; but are now returned unto the Shepherd.*"
Tune ARMAGEDDON. S. M.

1 I WAS a wandering sheep,
I did not love the fold;
I did not love my Shepherd's voice,
I would not be controlled.
I was a wayward child,
I did not love my home;
I did not love my Father's voice,
I loved afar to roam.

2 The Shepherd sought His sheep,
The Father sought His child;
They followed me o'er vale and hill,
O'er deserts waste and wild.
They found me nigh to death,
Famished, and faint, and lone;
They bound me with the bands of love,
They saved the wandering one!

3 They spoke in tender love,
They raised my drooping head;
They gently closed my bleeding wounds,
My fainting soul they fed.
They washed my guilt away,
They made me clean and fair;
They brought me to my home in peace—
The long-sought wanderer!

4 Jesus my Shepherd is,
'Twas He that loved my soul,
'Twas He that washed me in His blood,
'Twas He that made me whole.
'Twas He that sought the lost,
That found the wandering sheep;
'Twas He that brought me to the fold,
'Tis He that still doth keep.

5 I was a wandering sheep,
I could not be controlled;
But now I love the Shepherd's voice,
I love, I love the fold!
I was a wayward child,
I once preferred to roam;
But now I love my Father's voice,
I love, I love His home!

Horatius Bonar, D.D., 1845.

ST. BRIDE. [H. P. 95.]

512

Ps. cxxxvii. 4. "*A strange land.*"
Tune ST. BRIDE. S. M.

1 FAR from my heavenly home,
Far from my Father's breast,
Fainting I cry, blest Spirit, come,
And speed me to my rest.

2 Upon the willows long
My harp has silent hung;
How should I sing a cheerful song
Till Thou inspire my tongue?

3 My spirit homeward turns,
And fain would thither flee:
My heart, O Zion, droops and mourns,
While I remember thee.

4 To thee, to thee I press,
A dark and toilsome road;
When shall I pass the wilderness,
And reach the saints' abode?

5 God of my life, be near,
On Thee my hopes I cast,
Oh guide me through the desert here,
And bring me home at last.

Henry Francis Lyte, 1847.

513

Ps. xlii. 2. "*My soul thirsteth for God.*"
Tune ST. CHRYSOSTOM. C. M.

ST. CHRYSOSTOM. [H. P. 53.]

1 AS pants the hart for cooling streams,
When heated in the chase,
So pants my soul, O God, for Thee
And Thy refreshing grace.

2 For Thee, my God—the living God—
My thirsty soul doth pine;
Oh! when shall I behold Thy face,
Thou Majesty Divine?

3 I sigh to think of happier days,
When Thou, O Lord, wert nigh;
When every heart was tuned to praise,
And none more blest than I.

4 Oh! why art thou cast down, my soul?
Hope still, and thou shalt sing
The praise of Him who is thy God,
Thy health's eternal spring!

Tate and Brady, 1696.

GETHSEMANE. [H. P. 28.]

514 Isa. xxx. 15. *"In quietness and in confidence shall be your strength."* Tune GETHSEMANE. L. M.

1 BE still, my heart! These anxious cares
To thee are burdens, thorns, and snares;
They cast dishonour on the Lord,
And contradict His gracious word.

2 Brought safely by His hand thus far,
Why wilt thou now give place to fear?
How canst thou want if He provide,
Or lose thy way with such a Guide?

3 When first before His mercy-seat
Thou didst to Him thine all commit,
He gave thee warrant, from that hour,
To trust His wisdom, love, and power.

4 Did ever trouble yet befall,
And He refuse to hear thy call?
And has He not His promise passed,
That thou shalt overcome at last?

5 He who has helped me hitherto
Will help me all my journey through;
And give me daily cause to raise
New Ebenezers to His praise.

6 Though rough and thorny be the road,
It leads thee home, apace, to God:
Then count thy present trials small,
For heaven will make amends for all!

John Newton, 1779.

FARRANT. [H. P. 67.]

515 Heb. iv. 16. *"Let us therefore come boldly unto the throne of grace."* Tune FARRANT. C. M.

1 APPROACH, my soul, the mercy-seat
Where Jesus answers prayer;
There humbly fall before His feet,
For none can perish there.

2 Thy promise is my only plea,
With this I venture nigh;
Thou callest burdened souls to Thee,
And such, O Lord, am I.

3 Bowed down beneath a load of sin,
By Satan sorely pressed,
By war without, and fears within,
I come to Thee for rest.

4 Be Thou my shield and hiding-place!
That, sheltered near Thy side,
I may my fierce accuser face,
And tell him Thou hast died.

5 O wondrous love, to bleed and die,
To bear the cross and shame,
That guilty sinners, such as I,
Might plead Thy gracious name!

6 "Poor tempest-tossèd soul, be still,
My promised grace receive:"
'Tis Jesus speaks—I must, I will,
I can, I do believe!

John Newton, 1779.

516 Ps. xxxviii. 15. *"In Thee, O Lord, do I hope.'* Tune GETHSEMANE. L. M.

1 GOD of my life, to Thee I call,
Afflicted at Thy feet I fall;
When the great water-floods prevail,
Leave not my trembling heart to fail.

2 Friend of the friendless and the faint,
Where should I lodge my deep complaint?
Where, but with Thee, whose open door
Invites the helpless and the poor?

3 Did ever mourner plead with Thee,
And Thou refuse the mourner's plea?
Does not Thy word still fixed remain,
That none shall seek Thy face in vain?

4 That were a grief I could not bear,
Didst Thou not hear and answer prayer;
But a prayer-hearing, answering God,
Supports me under every load.

5 Fair is the lot that's cast for me;
I have an Advocate with Thee:
They whom the world caresses most
Have no such privilege to boast.

6 Poor though I am, despised, forgot,
Yet God—my God—forgets me not;
And he is safe, and must succeed,
For whom the Lord vouchsafes to plead!

William Cowper, 1779.

517 Isa. xliv. 21. *"Thou shalt not be forgotten of Me."* Tune FARRANT. C. M.

1 O THOU, from whom all goodness flows!
I lift my soul to Thee:
In all my sorrows, conflicts, woes,
Good Lord! remember me.

2 When, on my groaning, burdened heart,
My sins lie heavily,
My pardon speak, new peace impart;
In love remember me.

3 When trials sore obstruct my way,
And ills I cannot flee,
Oh! give me strength, Lord, as my day:
For good remember me.

4 Distressed with pain, disease, and grief,
This feeble body see;
Grant patience, rest, and kind relief:
Hear and remember me.

5 If on my face for Thy dear name,
Shame and reproaches be
All hail reproach, and welcome shame,
If Thou remember me.

6 And oh! when in the hour of death
I own Thy just decree,
Be this the prayer of my last breath,
Dear Lord, remember me!

Thomas Haweis, LL.D., 1790.

SARDIS. (Hymn Chant.) [H. P. No. VI.]

518 Rom. v. 11. "*We also joy in God, through our Lord Jesus Christ.*"
Tune, Hymn Chant Sardis. 10 10, 10 10.

1 I THOUGHT upon my sins, and I was sad,
My soul was troubled sore, and filled with pain;
But then I thought on Jesus, and was glad;
My heavy grief was turned to joy again.

2 I thought upon the law, the fiery law—
Holy, and just, and good in its decree;
I looked to Jesus, and in Him I saw
That law fulfilled, its curse endured for me.

3 I thought I saw an angry, frowning God,
Sitting as Judge upon the great white throne;
My soul was overwhelmed; then Jesus showed
His gracious face, and all my dread was gone.

4 I saw my sad estate, condemned to die;
Then terror seized my heart, and dark despair;
But when to Calvary I turned my eye,
I saw the cross, and read forgiveness there.

5 I saw that I was lost, far gone astray,
No hope of safe return there seemed to be;
But then I heard that Jesus was the way,
A new and living way prepared for me.

6 Then in that way—so free, so safe, so sure—
Sprinkled all o'er with reconciling blood,
Will I abide, and never wander more,
Walking along in fellowship with God!

Horatius Bonar, D.D., 1843.

PURDAY. [H. P. 338.]

(7) ENCOURAGEMENT.

519 Heb. xii. 2. "*Looking unto Jesus.*"
Tune Purday. 87, 87, 77. Or Succoth.

1 YES! He knows the way is dreary,
Knows "the weakness of our frame,"
Knows that hand and heart are weary—
He "in all points" felt the same.
He is near to help and bless;
Be not weary, onward press.

2 Look to Him, who once was willing
All His glory to resign;
That, for thee the law fulfilling,
All His merit might be thine.
Strive to follow, day by day,
Where His footsteps mark the way.

3 Look to Him—the Lord of glory—
Tasting death to win thy life;
Gazing on that "wondrous story,"
Canst thou falter in the strife?
Is it not new life to know
That the Lord hath loved thee so?

4 Look to Him—who ever liveth,
Interceding for His own;
Seek, yea claim, the grace He giveth
Freely from His priestly throne:
Will He not thy strength renew,
With His Spirit's quickening dew?

5 Look to Him—and faith shall brighten,
Hope shall soar, and love shall burn,
Peace once more thy heart shall lighten;
Rise! He calleth thee: return!
Be not weary on thy way;
Jesus is thy strength and stay!

Frances Ridley Havergal, 1867.

520 2 Thess. iii. 13. "*Be not weary.*" Tune Linus. 15 15, 15 15.

1 "BE not weary," *toiling* Christian, good the Master thou dost serve;
Let no disappointment move thee, from thy service never swerve:
Sow in hope, nor cease thy sowing; lack not patience, faith, or prayer:
Seedtime passeth; harvest hasteneth; precious sheaves thou *then* shalt bear.

2 "Be not weary," *praying* Christian, open is thy Father's ear
To the fervent supplication and the agonising prayer;
Prayer the Holy Ghost begetteth—be it words, or groans, or tears—
Is the prayer that's always answered; banish then thy doubts and fears.

LINUS. [H. P. 336.]

3 "Be not weary," *suffering* Christian, scourged is each adopted child,
Else would grow in sad profusion nature's fruit, perverse and wild;
Chastening's needful for the spirit, though 'tis painful for the flesh;
God designs a blessing for thee: let this thought thy soul refresh.

4 "Be not weary," *tempted* Christian, sin can only lure on earth;
Faith is tried by sore temptation; 'tis the furnace proves its worth;
Bounds are set unto the tempter, which beyond he cannot go; [foe.
Battle on, on God relying, faith will overcome the

5 "Be not weary," *weeping* Christian, tears endure but for the night;
Joy, deep joy, thy spirit greeting, will return with morning light;
Every tear thou shedd'st is numbered in the register above!
Heaven is tearless; sweet the prospect—sighless, tearless land of love!

PART II.

6 "Be not weary," *hoping* Christian, though the vision tarry long;
Hope will bring the blessing nearer, change thy sorrow into song:
Nought shall press thy spirit downwards, if thy hopes all brightly shine;
Hold thy hope, whate'er thou loosest—living, precious hopes are thine!

7 "Be not weary," *troubled* Christian, rest remains for thee on high; [joy:
Dwell upon the untold glory of thy future home of
There nor sin nor sorrow entereth; there thy soul attuned to praise
Shall, in strains of heavenly fulness, songs of happy triumph raise.

8 "Be not weary," *loving* Christian, in this heavenly grace abound;
Jesus, well thou knowest, loved *thee,* though in mad rebellion found;
Drink, drink deeply of His Spirit—Jesu's love knows great nor small;
Nature loves but what is lovely—*grace* embraceth one and all.

9 Christian, thus in grace unwearied pass thy sojourn here below;
Spurn lukewarmness, let thy bosom ever with true fervour glow!
Look to Christ, thy bright Exemplar, copy Him in all His ways;
Let thy life and conversation tell to thy Redeemer's praise!

Albert Midlane, 1864.

VIENNA. [H. P. 149.]

521

2 Cor. iv. 1. *"As we have received mercy, we faint not."* Tune VIENNA. 77,77.

1 FAINT not, Christian! though the road
Leading to thy blest abode
Darksome be, and dangerous too—
Christ, thy Guide, will bring thee through.

2 Faint not, Christian! though in rage
Satan would thy soul engage;
Gird on faith's anointed shield,
Bear it to the battle-field.

3 Faint not, Christian! though the world
Hath its hostile flag unfurled;
Hold the cross of Jesus fast,
Thou shalt overcome at last.

4 Faint not, Christian! though within
There's a heart so prone to sin;
Christ the Lord is over all,
He'll not suffer thee to fall.

5 Faint not, Christian! though thy God
Smite thee with the chastening rod:
Smite He must with father's care,
That He may His love declare.

6 Faint not, Christian! Jesu's near;
Soon in glory He'll appear:
Then shall cease thy toil and strife,
Thou shalt wear the "crown of life!"

James Harington Evans, 1830.

NARENZA. [H. P. 80.]

522 Isa. xxxiii. 22. *"The Lord is our King; He will save us."* Tune NARENZA. S. M.

1 GIVE to the winds thy fears;
Hope, and be undismayed;
God hears thy sighs, and counts thy tears;
God shall lift up thy head.

2 Through waves, and clouds, and storms,
He gently clears thy way;
Wait thou His time: so shall the night
Soon end in joyous day.

3 He everywhere hath sway,
And all things serve His might;
His every act pure blessing is,
His path unsullied light.

4 When He makes bare His arm,
What shall His work withstand?
When He His people's cause defends,
Who, who shall stay His hand?

5 Leave to His sovereign sway
To choose and to command;
With wonder filled, thou then shalt own
How wise, how strong His hand.

6 Thou seest our weakness, Lord,
Our hearts are known to Thee:
Oh! lift Thou up the sinking hand,
Confirm the feeble knee!

7 Let us, in life and death,
Thy steadfast truth declare;
Proclaiming, with our latest breath,
Thy love and guardian care!

P. Gerhardt, 1659; *John Wesley* (*tr.*), 1739. (*a.*)

CRASSELIUS; *or*, WINCHESTER NEW. [H. P. 3.]

523 2 Tim. i. 12. *"I am not ashamed: for I know whom I have believed."* Tune CRASSELIUS. L. M.

1 JESUS! and shall it ever be?
A mortal man ashamed of Thee!
Ashamed of Thee, whom angels praise,
Whose glories shine through endless days.

2 Ashamed of Jesus! sooner far
Let evening blush to own a star;
He sheds the beams of Light Divine
O'er this benighted soul of mine.

3 Ashamed of Jesus! just as soon
Let midnight be ashamed of noon:
'Tis midnight with my soul, till He,
Bright Morning Star, bids darkness flee.

4 Ashamed of Jesus! that dear Friend
On whom my hopes of heaven depend?
No! when I blush, be this my shame,
That I no more revere His name.

5 Ashamed of Jesus! yes I may,
When I 've no guilt to wash away,
No tear to wipe, no good to crave,
No fears to quell, no soul to save.

6 Till then—nor is my boasting vain—
Till then I boast a Saviour slain:
And oh! may this my glory be,
That Christ is not ashamed of me!

J. Grigg, 1765; *B. Francis*, 1787.

GOSHEN. [H. P. 125.]

524 Heb. xii. 12. *"Lift up the hands which hang down, and the feeble knees."* Tune GOSHEN. 7 6, 7 6.

1 O FAINT and feeble hearted!
Why thus cast down with fear?
Fresh aid shall be imparted,
Thy God unseen is near.

2 His eye can never slumber,
He marks thy cruel foes;
Observes their strength, their number,
And all thy weakness knows.

3 Though heavy clouds of sorrow
Make dark thy path to-day,
There may shine forth to-morrow
Once more a cheering ray.

4 Doubts, griefs, and foes assailing,
Conceal heaven's fair abode;
Yet now faith's power prevailing
Should stay thy mind on God!

Charlotte Elliott, 1836.

TERTIUS. [H. P. 256.]

525

Matt. vi. 13. "*Thine is . . . the power.*"
Tune TERTIUS. 11 11, 11 11, 11 11, 5.

1 OUR Father, our Father! who dwellest in light,
We lean on Thy love, and we rest on Thy might;
In weakness and weariness joy shall abound,
For strength everlasting in Thee shall be found;
Our Refuge, our Helper, in conflict and woe,
Our mighty Defender, how blessèd to know
That Thine is the power!

That Thine is the Power, the Power, the Power, the Power!
That Thine, Thine, Thine is the Power, the Power, the Power!

2 Our Father! Thy promise we earnestly claim,
The sanctified heart that shall hallow Thy name.
In ourselves, in our dear ones, throughout the wide world,
Be Thy name as a banner of glory unfurled:
Let it triumph o'er evil and darkness and guilt;
We know Thou canst do it, we know that Thou wilt,
For Thine is the power!

3 Our Father, we long for the glorious day
When all shall adore Thee and all shall obey!
Oh hasten Thy kingdom, oh show fórth Thy might,
And wave o'er the nations Thy sceptre of right:
Oh make up Thy jewels, the crown of Thy love,
And reign in all hearts as Thou reignest above,
For Thine is the power!

4 Our Father, we pray that Thy will may be done;
For full acquiescence is heaven begun.
Both in us and by us Thy purpose be wrought,
In word and in action, in spirit and thought.
And Thou canst enable us thus to fulfil,
With holy rejoicing, Thy glorious will,
For Thine is the power!

5 Our Father, Thy children rejoice in Thy reign,
Rejoice in Thy highness, and praise Thee again!
Yea, Thine is the kingdom, and Thine is the might,
And Thine is the glory, transcendently bright.
For ever and ever that glory shall shine,
For ever and ever that kingdom be Thine,
For Thine is the power!

Frances Ridley Havergal, 1872.

NASSAU. [H. P. 155.]

526

Exod. xiv. 15. "*Speak unto the children of Israel, that they go forward.*"
Tune NASSAU. 7 7, 7 7, 8 8.

1 "FORWARD let the people go;"
Israel's God will have it so;
Though the path be through the sea,
Israel, what is that to thee?
He who bids thee pass the waters
Will be with His sons and daughters.

2 Deep and wide the sea appears,
Israel wonders, Israel fears;
Yet the word is "forward" still,
Israel, 'tis thy Master's will;
Though no way thou canst discover,
Not one plank to float thee over.

3 Israel, art thou sorely tried,
Art thou pressed on every side?
Does it seem as if no power
Could relieve thee in this hour?
Wherefore art thou thus disheartened?
Is the arm that saves thee shortened?

4 Forward go, and thou shalt see
Wonders wrought, and wrought for thee;
Safe thyself on yonder shore,
Thou shalt see thy foes no more;
Thine to see the Saviour's glory,
Thine to tell the wondrous story!

Thomas Kelly, 1815.

CARMEL (Mount). [H. P. 69.]

527 Ps. cxliii. 9. "*I flee unto Thee to hide me.*" Tune CARMEL. C. M.

1 DEAR Refuge of my weary soul,
On Thee when sorrows rise—
On Thee, when waves of trouble roll—
My fainting hope relies.

2 To Thee I tell each rising grief,
For Thou alone canst heal;
Thy word can bring a sweet relief
For every pain I feel.

3 But oh! when gloomy doubts prevail,
I fear to call Thee mine:
The springs of comfort seem to fail,
And all my hopes decline.

4 Yet, gracious God, where shall I flee?
Thou art mine only trust;
And still my soul would cleave to Thee,
Though prostrate in the dust.

5 Hast Thou not bid me seek Thy face?
And shall I seek in vain?
And can the ear of sovereign grace
Be deaf when I complain?

6 No! still the ear of sovereign grace
Attends the mourner's prayer:
Oh, may I ever find access,
To breathe my sorrows there.

7 Thy mercy-seat is open still;
There let my soul retreat;
With humble hope attend Thy will,
And wait beneath Thy feet!

Anne Steele, 1760.

See Hymns 436, 640.

(8) DECLINE AND RECOVERY.

528 Ps. cxix. 25. "*Quicken Thou me according to Thy word.*" Tune CARMEL. C. M.

1 LONG have we heard the joyful sound
Of Thy salvation, Lord;
But still how weak our faith is found,
And knowledge of Thy word!

2 Oft we frequent Thy holy place,
And hear almost in vain:
How small a portion of Thy grace
Do our false hearts retain!

3 How cold and feeble is our love!
How negligent our fear!
How low our hope of joys above!
How few affections there!

4 Great God! Thy sovereign power impart,
To give Thy word success:
Write Thy salvation on our heart,
And make us learn Thy grace.

5 Show our forgetful feet the way
That leads to joys on high;
Where knowledge grows without decay,
And love shall never die!

Isaac Watts, D.D., 1709.

529 Hos. xiv. 7. "*They that dwell under His shadow shall return.*"
Tune ST. CHRYSOSTOM. C. M. Or KENT.

1 OH for a closer walk with God,
A calm and heavenly frame;
A light to shine upon the road
That leads me to the Lamb!

2 Where is the blessedness I knew
When first I saw the Lord?
Where is the soul-refreshing view
Of Jesus and His word?

3 What peaceful hours I then enjoyed!
How sweet their memory still!
But now I find an aching void
The world can never fill.

4 Return, O holy Dove! return,
Sweet Messenger of rest!
I hate the sins that made Thee mourn,
And drove Thee from my breast.

5 The dearest idol I have known,
Whate'er that idol be,
Help me to tear it from Thy throne,
And worship only Thee.

ST. CHRYSOSTOM. [H. P. 53.]

6 So shall my walk be close with God,
Calm and serene my frame;
So purer light shall mark the road
That leads me to the Lamb!

William Cowper, 1779.

(9) DESIRES AFTER HOLINESS.

530 Heb. viii. 10. "*I will put My laws into their mind.*" Tune CARMEL. C. M.

1 I WANT a principle within
Of jealous, godly fear;
A sensibility of sin,
A pain to feel it near.

2 I want the first approach to feel
Of pride, or fond desire;
To catch the wandering of my will,
And quench the kindling fire.

3 That I from Thee no more may part,
No more Thy goodness grieve,
The filial awe, the fleshy heart,
The tender conscience, give.

4 Quick as the apple of an eye,
O God, my conscience make!
Awake my soul when sin is nigh,
And keep it still awake.

5 If to the right or left I stray,
That moment, Lord, reprove;
And let me weep my life away
For having grieved Thy love.

6 Oh, may the least omission pain
My ever watchful soul,
And drive me to the blood again
Which makes the wounded whole!

Charles Wesley, 1749. (*a.*)

531 Ps. xlv. 13. "*The King's daughter is all glorious within.*"

Tune Gershom. 8 8, 11 8.

GERSHOM. [H. P. 340.]

1 I WANT that adorning Divine
Thou only, my God, canst bestow;
I want in those beautiful garments to shine,
Which distinguish Thy household below.

2 I want every moment to feel
That Thy Spirit resides in my heart,
That His power is present to cleanse and to heal,
And newness of life to impart.

3 I want, oh! I want to attain
Some likeness, my Saviour, to Thee;
That longed-for resemblance once more to regain;
Thy comeliness put upon me.

4 I want to be marked for Thine own,
Thy seal on my forehead to wear;
To receive that "new name" on the mystic white stone,
Which none but Thyself can declare.

5 I want in Thee so to abide,
As to bring forth some fruit to Thy praise!
The branch which Thou prunest, though feeble and dried,
May languish, but never decays.

Part II.

6 I want Thine own hand to unbind
Each tie to terrestrial things,—
Too tenderly cherished, too closely entwined,
Where my heart too tenaciously clings.

7 I want by my aspect serene,
My actions and words, to declare
That my treasure is placed in a country unseen,—
That my heart's best affections are there.

8 I want, as a traveller, to haste
Straight onward, nor pause on my way,
Nor forethought, nor anxious contrivance, to waste
On the tent only pitched for a day.

9 I want—and this sums up my prayer—
To glorify Thee till I die;
Then calmly to yield up my soul to Thy care,—
And breathe out, in faith, my last sigh!

Charlotte Elliott, 1846.

OLD "TEN COMMANDMENTS' TUNE." [H. P. 15.]

532 Phil. i. 27. "*Let your conversation be as it becometh the gospel of Christ.*"

Tune Old Ten Commandments. L. M.

1 SO let our lips and lives express
The holy gospel we profess;
So let our works and virtues shine,
To prove the doctrine all Divine.

2 Thus shall we best proclaim abroad
The honours of our Saviour God,
When His salvation reigns within,
And grace subdues the power of sin.

3 Our flesh and sense must be denied,
Passion and envy, lust and pride;
While justice, temperance, truth, and love
Our inward piety approve.

4 The gospel bears our spirits up,
While we expect that blessèd hope,
The bright appearance of the Lord;
And faith stands leaning on His word!

Isaac Watts, D.D., 1709. (*a.*)

LINUS. [H. P. 336.]

533 John xiv. 23. *"We will come unto him, and make our abode with him."* Tune LINUS. 8 7, 8 7. D.

1 LOVE Divine, all love excelling,
Joy of heaven, to earth come down;
Fix in us Thy humble dwelling,
All Thy faithful mercies crown:
Jesus, Thou art all compassion;
Pure, unbounded love Thou art:
Visit us with Thy salvation;
Enter every waiting heart.

2 Come, almighty to deliver,
Let us all Thy grace receive;
Suddenly return, and never,
Never more, Thy temples leave;
Thee we would be always blessing;
Serve Thee as Thy hosts above;
Pray, and praise Thee, without ceasing,
Glory in Thy perfect love.

3 Finish then Thy new creation,
Pure and spotless let us be;
Let us see our great salvation
Perfectly secured in Thee:
Changed from glory into glory,
Till in heaven we take our place,
Till we cast our crowns before Thee,
Lost in wonder, love, and praise!

Charles Wesley, 1746. (*a.*)

See Hymns 216, 217, 425, 687.

OLD "TEN COMMANDMENTS' TUNE." [H. P. 15.]

(10) GROWTH IN GRACE.

534 Isa. xxxviii. 16. *"In all these things is the life of my spirit."* Tune OLD TEN COMMANDMENTS. L. M.

1 I ASKED the Lord that I might grow
In faith, and love, and every grace;
Might more of His salvation know,
And seek more earnestly His face.

2 I hoped that in some favoured hour
At once He'd answer my request;
And, by His love's constraining power,
Subdue my sins, and give me rest.

3 Instead of this, He made me feel
The hidden evils of my heart,
And let the angry powers of hell
Assault my soul in every part.

4 "Lord, why is this?" I trembling cried,
"Wilt Thou pursue Thy worm to death?"
"'Tis in this way," the Lord replied,
"I answer prayer for grace and faith.

5 "These inward trials I employ,
From self and pride to set thee free,
And break thy schemes of earthly joy,
That thou may'st seek thy all in Me!"

John Newton, 1774.

535 Isa. lx. 1. *"Arise, shine."* Tune MAGDALENE COLLEGE. 8 8 6. D.

1 CHILDREN of light, arise and shine!
Your birth, your hopes, are all Divine;
Your home is in the skies;
Oh! then, for heavenly glory born,
Look down on all with holy scorn
That earthly spirits prize.

2 With Christ, with glory full in view,
Oh! what is all the world to you?
What is it all but loss?
Come on, then; cleave no more to earth,
Nor wrong your high celestial birth,
Ye pilgrims of the cross.

3 The cross is ours; we bear it now;
But did not He beneath it bow,
And suffer there at last?
All that we feel can Jesus tell;
His gracious soul remembers well
The sorrows of the past.

MAGDALENE COLLEGE. [H. P. 210.]

4 O blessèd Lord, we yet shall reign,
Redeemed from sorrow, sin, and pain,
And walk with Thee in white.
We suffer now, but oh! at last
We'll bless Thee, Lord, for all the past,
And own our cross was light!

Sir Edward Denny, 1838.

536

Phil. iii. 13. "*Reaching forth unto those things which are before.*"

Tune St. Silas. 5 5 10. D.

ST. SILAS. [H. P. 98.]

1 UPWARD and onward,
Heavenward and sunward,
Rises the lark, as he joyously sings;
With music thrilling,
All the air filling,
Bearing a message of praise on his wings.

2 Like this sweet singer,
Let us not linger,
Clinging and cleaving to earth's weary sod;
But upward springing,
Our tribute bringing,
Strive to draw nearer and nearer to God.

3 Upward and onward,
Heavenward and sunward,
Soars the strong eagle, his flight speeding on;
With heart that quails not,
With eye that fails not,
Steadily fixing his gaze on the sun.

4 So our hearts raising,
Singing and praising,
Looking to Jesus, the Sun of the soul;
Our strength renewing,
Our way pursuing,
Let us press on till we reach the bright goal!

Richard Massie, 1864.

See Hymns 1063—1075.

VIENNA. [H. P. 149.]

(11) PRAYER.

537

Esther vii. 2. "*What is thy petition? . . . and it shall be granted thee.*" Tune Vienna. 7 7, 7 7.

1 COME, my soul, thy suit prepare,
Jesus loves to answer prayer;
He Himself has bid thee pray,
Therefore will not say thee nay.

2 Thou art coming to a King,
Large petitions with thee bring;
For His grace and power are such,
None can ever ask too much.

3 With my burden I begin,
Lord, remove this load of sin;
Let Thy blood, for sinners spilt,
Set my conscience free from guilt.

4 Lord, I come to Thee for rest,
Take possession of my breast;
There Thy blood-bought right maintain,
And without a rival reign.

5 While I am a pilgrim here,
Let Thy love my spirit cheer;
As my Guide, my Guard, my Friend,
Lead me to my journey's end!

John Newton, 1779.

EATON. [H. P. 313.]

538 Phil. iii. 10. "*That I may know Him.*"
Tune EATON. 88, 88, 88.

O JESUS, make Thyself to me
A living, bright reality;
More present to faith's vision keen
Than any outward object seen;
More dear, more intimately nigh,
Than e'en the sweetest earthly tie!

Charlotte Elliott, 1860.

539 Heb. x. 22. "*Let us draw near.*"
Tune FRANCONIA. S. M.

1 BEHOLD the throne of grace!
The promise calls me near;
There Jesus shows a smiling face,
And waits to answer prayer.

2 That rich atoning blood,
Which sprinkled round I see,
Provides for those who come to God
An all-prevailing plea.

3 My soul, ask what thou wilt,
Thou canst not be too bold;
Since His own blood for thee He spilt,
What else can He withhold?

FRANCONIA. [H. P. 87.]

4 Beyond thy utmost wants
His love and power can bless;
To praying souls He always grants
More than they can express.

5 Thine image, Lord, bestow,
Thy presence and Thy love;
I ask to serve Thee here below,
And reign with Thee above.

6 Teach me to live by faith,
Conform my will to Thine;
Let me victorious be in death,
And then in glory shine!

John Newton, 1779.

THYATIRA. (HYMN CHANT.) [H. P. No. V.]

540 Acts iii. 1. "*The hour of prayer.*"
Tune, Hymn Chant THYATIRA. 88, 84.

1 MY God! is any hour so sweet,
From blush of morn to evening star,
As that which calls me to Thy feet—
The hour of prayer?

2 Blest be that tranquil hour of morn,
And blest that hour of solemn eve,
When, on the wings of prayer upborne,
The world I leave.

3 For then a dayspring shines on me,
Brighter than morn's ethereal glow;
And richer dews descend from Thee
Than earth can know.

4 Then is my strength by Thee renewed;
Then are my sins by Thee forgiven;
Then dost Thou cheer my solitude
With hopes of heaven.

5 Words cannot tell what blest relief
Here for my every want I find;
What strength for warfare, balm for grief;
What peace of mind.

6 Hushed is each doubt, gone every fear;
My spirit seems in heaven to stay;
And e'en the penitential tear
Is wiped away.

7 Oh! till I reach yon peaceful shore,
No privilege so dear shall be,
As thus my inmost soul to pour
In prayer to Thee!

Charlotte Elliott, 1839.

EVAN I. [H. P. 54.]

541 Luke xi. 1. "*Lord, teach us to pray.*" Tune Evan I. C. M.

1 LORD, teach us how to pray aright,
With reverence and with fear;
Though dust and ashes in Thy sight,
We may, we must draw near.

2 We perish if we cease from prayer;
Oh, grant us power to pray;
And when to meet Thee we prepare,
Lord, meet us by the way!

James Montgomery, 1819.

HERMON. [H. P. 27.]

542 Matt. vii. 7. "*Ask, and it shall be given you.*" Tune Hermon. L. M.

1 PRAYER was appointed to convey
The blessings God designs to give:
Long as they live should Christians pray,
For only while they pray they live.

2 And shall we in dead silence lie,
When Christ stands waiting for our prayer?
My soul, thou hast a Friend on high;
Arise, and try thy interest there.

3 If pain afflict, or wrongs oppress;
If cares distract, or fears dismay;
If guilt deject, if sin distress;
The remedy's before thee: Pray!

4 Depend on Christ, thou canst not fail;
Make all thy wants and wishes known
Fear not; His merits must prevail;
Ask what thou wilt; it shall be done!

Joseph Hart, 1765.

543 Ps. lxii. 8. "*Pour out your heart before Him.*" Tune Evan I. C. M.

1 PRAYER is the soul's sincere desire,
Uttered, or unexpressed;
The motion of a hidden fire
That trembles in the breast.

2 Prayer is the burden of a sigh,
The falling of a tear,
The upward glancing of an eye
When none but God is near.

3 Prayer is the simplest form of speech
That infant lips can try;
Prayer the sublimest strains that reach
The Majesty on high.

4 Prayer is the Christian's vital breath,
The Christian's native air;
His watchword at the gates of death;
He enters heaven with prayer.

Part II.

5 Prayer is the contrite sinner's voice,
Returning from his ways;
While angels in their songs rejoice,
And cry, "Behold, he prays!"

6 The saints in prayer appear as one
In word, and deed, and mind;
While with the Father and the Son
Sweet fellowship they find.

7 Nor prayer is made on earth alone;
The Holy Spirit pleads;
And Jesus, on the' eternal throne,
For sinners intercedes.

8 O Thou by whom we come to God,
The Life, the Truth, the Way!
The path of prayer Thyself hast trod!
Lord, teach us how to pray!

James Montgomery, 1819.

544 1 Kings iii. 5. "*Ask what I shall give thee.*" Tune Hermon. L. M.

1 AND dost Thou say, "Ask what thou wilt"?
Lord, I would seize the golden hour;
I pray to be released from guilt,
And freed from sin and Satan's power.

2 More of Thy presence, Lord, impart,
More of Thine image let me bear;
Erect Thy throne within my heart,
And reign without a rival there.

3 Give me to read my pardon sealed,
And from Thy joy to draw my strength,
To have Thy boundless love revealed
In all its height, and breadth, and length.

4 Grant these requests, I ask no more,
But to Thy care the rest resign;
Living or dying, rich or poor,
All shall be well if Thou art mine.

John Newton, 1779.

SARDIS. (Hymn Chant.) [H. P. No. VI.]

545

Heb. iv. 16. "*The throne of grace.*" Tune, Hymn Chant Sardis. 10 10 10, 4.

1 THERE is a spot of consecrated ground,
Where brightest hopes and holiest joys are found;
'Tis named (and Christians love the well-known sound)
The throne of grace.

2 'Tis here a calm retreat is always found;
Perpetual sunshine gilds the sacred ground;
Pure airs and heavenly odours breathe around
The throne of grace.

3 While on this vantage-ground the Christian stands,
His quickened eye a boundless view commands;
Discovers fair abodes not made with hands—
Abodes of peace.

4 Terrestrial objects, disenchanted there,
Lose all their power to dazzle or ensnare;
One only object then seems worth our care,
To win the race!

Part II.

5 This is the mount where Christ's disciples see
The glory of the' incarnate Deity;
'Tis here they find it good indeed to be,
And view His face.

6 A new creation here begins to rise:
Fruits of the Spirit, flowers of paradise,
Watered from heaven, in full and sure supplies,
By streams of grace.

7 Towards this blest spot the Saviour bends His ear,
The fervent prayer, the contrite sigh to hear;
To bid the mourner banish every fear,
And go in peace.

8 Here may the comfortless and weary find
One who can cure the sickness of the mind,
One who delights the broken heart to bind—
The Prince of Peace.

9 Saviour! the sinner's Friend, our hope, our all!
Here teach us humbly at Thy feet to fall;
Here on Thy name, with love and faith, to call
For pardoning grace.

10 Ne'er let the glory from this spot remove,
Till numbered with Thy ransomed flock above,
We cease to want, but never cease to love,
The throne of grace!

Charlotte Elliott, 1839.

GETHSEMANE. [H. P. 28.]

546

Heb. iv. 16. "*Let us therefore come boldly unto the throne of grace.*" Tune Gethsemane. L. M.

1 WHAT various hindrances we meet
In coming to a mercy-seat!
Yet who that knows the worth of prayer,
But wishes to be often there?

2 Prayer makes the darkened cloud withdraw,
Prayer climbs the ladder Jacob saw,
Gives exercise to faith and love,
Brings every blessing from above.

3 Restraining prayer, we cease to fight;
Prayer makes the Christian's armour bright;
And Satan trembles when he sees
The weakest saint upon his knees.

4 While Moses stood with arms spread wide,
Success was found on Israel's side;
But when through weariness they failed,
That moment Amalek prevailed.

5 Have you no words? Ah; think again:
Words flow apace when you complain,
And fill your fellow-creature's ear
With the sad tale of all your care.

6 Were half the breath thus vainly spent
To heaven in supplication sent,
Your cheerful song would oftener be,
"Hear what the Lord has done for me!"

William Cowper, 1779.

CLAUDIA. [H. P. 104.]

547

Ps. lxi. 1. "*Hear my cry.*" Tune Claudia. 6 5, 6 5.

1 JESU, meek and gentle,
Son of God most high,
Pitying, loving Saviour,
Hear Thy children's cry.

2 Pardon our offences,
Loose our captive chains,
Break down every idol
Which our soul detains.

3 Give us holy freedom,
Fill our hearts with love;
Draw us, Holy Jesus,
To the realms above.

4 Lead us on our journey,
Be Thyself the way
Through terrestrial darkness
To celestial day.

5 Jesu, meek and gentle,
Son of God most high,
Pitying, loving Saviour,
Hear Thy children's cry!

George Rundle Prynne, 1856.

CARMEL (Mount). [H. P. 69.]

548

Ps. li. 17. "*A broken and a contrite heart, O God, Thou wilt not despise.*" Tune CARMEL. C. M.

1 LORD, when we bend before Thy throne,
And our confessions pour,
Teach us to feel the sins we own,
And hate what we deplore.

2 Our broken spirits pitying see,
True penitence impart;
And let a brightening ray from Thee
Beam peace upon the heart.

3 When we disclose our wants in prayer,
May we our wills resign;
And not a thought our bosom share
Which is not wholly Thine.

4 Let faith each meek petition fill,
And waft it to the skies;
And teach our hearts 'tis goodness still,
That grants it or denies!

Joseph Dacre Carlyle, 1805.

See Hymns 829–836.

(12) WATCHFULNESS.

549

Matt. xxvi. 41. "*Watch and pray.*"
Tune SAMOS. 77, 73.

SAMOS. [H. P. 135.]

1 "CHRISTIAN! seek not yet repose;"
Hear thy guardian angel say,
"Thou art in the midst of foes—
"Watch and pray!"

2 Principalities and powers,
Mustering their unseen array,
Wait for thy unguarded hours—
"Watch and pray!"

3 Gird thy heavenly armour on,
Wear it ever, night and day;
Ambushed lies the evil one—
"Watch and pray!"

4 Hear the victors who o'ercame,
Still they mark each warrior's way;
All, with one sweet voice, exclaim—
"Watch and pray!"

5 Hear, above all, hear thy Lord,
Him thou lovest to obey;
Hide within thy heart His word—
"Watch and pray!"

6 Watch as if on that alone
Hung the issue of the day;
Pray, that help may be sent down—
"Watch and pray!"

Charlotte Elliott, 1839.

MORAVIA. [H. P. 83.]

550

Luke xii. 37. "*Blessed are those servants, whom the Lord, when He cometh, shall find watching.*"
Tune MORAVIA. S. M.

1 YE servants of the Lord,
Each in his office wait,
Observant of His heavenly word,
And watchful at His gate.

2 Let all your lamps be bright,
And trim the golden flame:
Gird up your loins as in His sight,
For holy is His name.

3 Watch, 'tis your Lord's command:
And while we speak He's near:
Mark the first signal of His hand,
And ready all appear.

4 O happy servant he
In such a posture found!
He shall his Lord with rapture see,
And be with honour crowned.

5 Christ shall the banquet spread
With His own royal hand;
And raise that faithful servant's head
Amidst the' angelic band!

Philip Doddridge, D.D., 1755.

ST. MARY'S; *or*, HACKNEY. [H. P. 73.]

551 Prov. viii. 34. "*Watching daily.*" Tune St. Mary. C. M.

1 HOW vain are all things here below!
How false, and yet how fair!
Each pleasure hath its poison too,
And every sweet a snare.

2 The brightest things below the sky
Give but a flattering light;
We should suspect some danger nigh
Where we possess delight.

3 Our dearest joys, and nearest friends,
The partners of our blood,
How they divide our wavering minds,
And leave but half for God!

4 The fondness of a creature's love,
How strong it strikes the sense!
The warm affections thither move,
Nor can we call them thence.

5 Dear Saviour! let Thy beauties be
My soul's eternal food;
And grace command my heart away
From all created good!

Isaac Watts, D.D., 1709.

SARDIS. (Hymn Chant.) [H. P. No. VI.]

(13) FASTING.

552 Joel ii. 12. "*Turn ye even to Me with all your heart, and with fasting.*"
Tune, Hymn Chant Sardis. 10 10, 10 10.

1 MAN fell from grace by carnal appetite,
And forfeited the garden of delight;
To fast for us our Second Adam deigns,
These forty days, and paradise regains.

2 So Moses fasted, and received the law;
Elias fasted, and God's glory saw;
Moses, Elias, joined with Christ our Head,
Upon the mountain were transfigurèd.

3 Oh give us grace our appetites to tame,
To love Thy law, and glorify Thy name;
That we may, Lord, with all Thy saints and Thee,
Upon Thy heavenly hill transfigured be.

4 To Father, Son, and Holy Ghost be praise;
Blest Three in One, to Thee our hearts we raise;
On wings of prayer and fasting may we soar,
Through Christ to dwell with Thee for evermore!

Bishop Christopher Wordsworth, 1862.

SMYRNA. (Hymn Chant.) *Double Counterpoint.* [H. P. No. III.]

(14) SELF DISCIPLINE.

553 1 Kings xvii. 2. "*The word of the Lord came unto him.*" Tune, Hymn Chant Smyrna. C. M.

1 NOT gifts of prophecy can save,
Nor courage be our stay;
Lord, make us doers of Thy word,
Oh teach us to obey.

2 If God command thee to abstain
From royal Bethel's fare,
Taste not its food, though angel hands
Should spread a table there.

3 The' obedient seer from Jordan's stream
To trickling Cherith fled;
Him there the brook, in time of drought,
And hungry ravens fed.

4 Go to Zidonian Zarephath,
To Jezebel's domain;
Though Zidon's queen may seek thy life,
A widow shall sustain.

5 O widow, fear not, but God's seer
With thy last morsel feed;
Who in His prophets gives to God
Shall never suffer need.

6 Thy meal exhaustless is; to thee
Rivers of oil shall flow;
Obedience is thine olive yard,
Faith harvests can bestow.

7 By faith and by obedience
God's best rewards are won;
Thou dost a prophet feed, and he
Restores to thee a son.

8 Thy pious service is approved
And blessed by love Divine;
O Zarephath, thy widow's name
Shall in Christ's gospel shine.

9 To Father, Son, and Holy Ghost,
For faith and love we pray;
Thee ever may our voices praise,
And may our hearts obey!

Bishop Christopher Wordsworth, 1862.

LEIPSIC. [H. P. 19.]

554

Luke ix. 23. "*Let him deny himself, and take up his cross daily.*" Tune LEIPSIC. L. M.

1 TAKE up thy cross, the Saviour said,
If thou wouldst My disciple be;
Deny thyself, the world forsake,
And humbly, meekly, follow Me.

2 Take up thy cross; let not its weight
Fill thy weak spirit with alarm:
His strength shall bear thy spirit up,
And brace thy heart, and nerve thine arm.

3 Take up thy cross, nor heed the shame;
And let not carnal pride rebel:
Thy Lord for thee the cross endured,
To save thy soul from death and hell.

4 Take up thy cross in Jesu's strength,
And calmly every danger brave;
'Twill guide thee to a better home,
And lead to victory o'er the grave.

5 Take up thy cross and follow Christ,
Nor think till death to lay it down;
For only he, who bears the cross
On earth, will wear the heavenly crown.

6 To Thee, great Lord, the One in Three,
All praise for evermore ascend;
Oh grant us by Thy grace to see
The life above that knows no end.

Charles William Everest, 1833. (*a.*)

555

Phil. i. 27. "*Let your conversation be as it becometh the gospel of Christ.*" Tune LEIPSIC. L. M.

1 AND is the gospel peace and love?
Such let our conversation be;
The serpent blended with the dove,
Wisdom and meek simplicity.

2 Whene'er the angry passions rise,
And tempt our thoughts or tongues to strife,
To Jesus let us lift our eyes,
Bright Pattern of the Christian life.

3 Oh, how benevolent and kind!
How mild! how ready to forgive!
Be this the temper of our mind,
And these the rules by which we live.

4 But ah! how blind, how weak we are!
How frail! how apt to turn aside!
Lord, we depend upon Thy care,
And ask Thy Spirit for our Guide!

Anne Steele, 1760.

HARTS. [H. P. 284.]

556

Luke xxii. 61. "*The Lord turned, and looked upon Peter.*" Tune HARTS. 77, 77. Or OLDENBURG.

1 JESUS, cast a look on me:
Give me sweet simplicity,
Make me poor and keep me low,
Seeking only Thee to know.

2 Weanèd from my lordly self,
Weanèd from the miser's pelf,
Weanèd from the scorner's ways,
Weanèd from the lust of praise.

3 All that feeds my busy pride,
Cast it evermore aside;
Bid my will to Thine submit;
Lay me humbly at Thy feet.

4 Make me like a little child,
Of my strength and wisdom spoiled,
Seeing only in Thy light,
Walking only in Thy might.

5 Leaning on Thy loving breast,
Where a weary soul may rest;
Feeling well the peace of God
Flowing from Thy precious blood!

6 In this posture let me live,
And hosannas daily give;
In this temper let me die,
And hosannas ever cry!

C. Wesley, 1762; *John Berridge*, 1785. (*a.*)

See Hymn 532.

BADEN I.; *or*, NUREMBERG. [H. P. 188.]

(15) RESIGNATION.

557 Ps. cvii. 7. "*He led them forth by the right way.*" Tune BADEN I. 87, 87, 44, 88.

1 WHATE'ER my God ordains is right,
Holy His will abideth;
I will be still whate'er He doth,
And follow where He guideth.
He is my God,
Though dark my road;
He holds me that I shall not fall,
Wherefore to Him I leave it all.

2 Whate'er my God ordains is right,
He never will deceive me:
He leads me by the proper path,
I know He will not leave me,
And take content
What He hath sent:
His hand can turn my grief away,
And patiently I wait His day.

3 Whate'er my God ordains is right,
Though now this cup in drinking
May bitter seem to my faint heart,
I take it all unshrinking;
Tears pass away
With dawn of day:
Sweet comfort yet shall fill my heart,
And pain and sorrow shall depart.

4 Whate'er my God ordains is right,
Here shall my stand be taken:
Though sorrow, need, or death be mine,
Yet am I not forsaken:
My Father's care
Is round me there:
He holds me that I shall not fall,
And so to Him I leave it all

S. Rodigast, 1675; *C. Winkworth* (*tr.*), 1858.

SARDIS. (HYMN CHANT.) [H. P. No. VI.]

558 Matt. xxvi. 42. "*Thy will be done.*" Tune, Hymn Chant SARDIS. 888, 4.

MY God, my Father, while I stray,
Far from my home, on life's rough way,
Oh teach me from my heart to say,
"Thy will be done!"

2 Though dark my path, and sad my lot,
Let me be still and murmur not;
Or breathe the prayer divinely taught,
"Thy will be done!"

3 If Thou shouldst call me to resign
What most I prize—it ne'er was mine:
I only yield Thee what was Thine:
"Thy will be done!"

4 Let but my fainting heart be blest
With Thy sweet Spirit for its guest,
My God, to Thee I leave the rest:
"Thy will be done!"

5 Renew my will from day to day,
Blend it with Thine, and take away
All that now makes it hard to say,
"Thy will be done!"

6 Then, when on earth I breathe no more
The prayer, oft mixed with tears before,
I'll sing upon a happier shore,
"Thy will be done!"

Charlotte Elliott, 1836.

559 Matt. xxvi. 39. "*Not as I will, but as Thou wilt.*" Tune BESOR. C. M.

1 O LORD, my best desire fulfil,
And help me to resign
Life, health, and comfort to Thy will,
And make Thy pleasure mine.

2 Why should I shrink at Thy command,
Whose love forbids my fears?
Or tremble at the gracious hand
That wipes away my tears?

BESOR (Brook). [H. P. 51.]

3 No! let me rather freely yield
What most I prize to Thee;
Who never hast a good withheld,
Or wilt withhold, from me.

4 Thy favour, all my journey through,
Thou art engaged to grant;
What else I want, or think I do,
'Tis better still to want.

5 Wisdom and mercy guide my way,
Shall I resist them both?
A poor blind creature of a day,
And crushed before the moth!

6 But ah! my inward spirit cries,
Still bind me to Thy sway,
Else the next cloud that veils my skies
Drives all these thoughts away.

William Cowper, 1779.

560

Lam. iii. 24. "*The Lord is my portion, saith my soul.*"

Tune Besor. C. M. Or Farrant.

1 MY times of sorrow and of joy,
Great God, are in Thy hand;
My choicest comforts come from Thee,
And go at Thy command.

2 If Thou shouldst take them all away,
Yet would I not repine;
Before they were possessed by me,
They were entirely Thine.

3 Nor would I drop a murmuring word,
Though the whole world was gone,
But seek enduring happiness
In Thee, and Thee alone.

4 What is the world with all its store?
'Tis but a bitter sweet;
When I attempt to pluck the rose,
A pricking thorn I meet.

5 Here perfect bliss can ne'er be found,
The honey's mixed with gall;
'Midst changing scenes and dying friends,
Be Thou my All in all!

Benjamin Beddome, 1787. (*a.*)

OLD NUNC DIMITTIS. [H. P. 78.]

561

Luke xxii. 42. "*Not My will, but Thine, be done.*"

Tune Old Nunc Dimittis. C. M. D.

1 ONE prayer I have—all prayers in one,
When I am wholly Thine;
Thy will, my God, Thy will be done,
And let that will be mine,
All-wise, all-mighty, and all-good!
In Thee I firmly trust;
Thy ways, unknown or understood,
Are merciful and just.

2 Is life with many comforts crowned,
Upheld in peace and health,
With dear affections twined around?
Lord, in my time of wealth
May I remember that to Thee
Whate'er I have I owe;
And back, in gratitude to Thee,
May all Thy bounties flow.

3 Thy gifts are only then enjoyed,
When used as talents lent;
Those talents only well employed,
When in Thy service spent.
And though Thy wisdom takes away,
Shall I arraign Thy will?
No, let me bless Thy name, and say,
The Lord is gracious still.

4 A pilgrim through the earth I roam,
Of nothing long possest;
And all must fail when I go home,
For this is not my rest.
Is but my name upon the roll
Of Thy redeemed above?
Then heart, and mind, and strength, and soul
Shall love Thee for Thy love!

James Montgomery, 1825.

FRANCONIA. [H. P. 87.]

562

Ps. xxxi. 15. "*My times are in Thy hand.*" Tune FRANCONIA. S. M.

1 "MY times are in Thy hand,"
Their best and fittest place;
I would not have them at command
Without Thy guiding grace.

2 "My times," and yet not *mine*;
I cannot them ordain;
Not one e'er waits from me a sign,
Nor can I one detain.

3 "My times," O Lord, are Thine,
And Thine their oversight:
Thy wisdom, love, and power combine
To make them dark or bright.

4 I know not what shall be,
When passing times are fled;
But all events I leave with Thee,
And calmly bow my head.

5 Hence, Lord, in Thee I rest,
And wait Thy holy will;
I lean upon my Saviour's breast,
Or gladly go on still.

6 And when my "times" shall cease,
And life shall fade away,
Then bid me, Lord, depart in peace,
To realms of endless day!

William Henry Havergal, 1860.

LAODICEA. (HYMN CHANT.) [H. P. No. VIII.]

563

Eph. v. 17. "*Understanding what the will of the Lord is.*"
Tune, Hymn Chant LAODICEA. 86, 86, 88. Or LEBANON.

1 WITH quivering heart and trembling will
The word hath passed thy lips,
Within the shadow, cold and still,
Of some fair joy's eclipse,
"Thy will be done!" Thy God hath heard,
And He will crown that faith-framed word.

2 The prayer shall be fulfilled—but how?
His thoughts are not as thine;
While thou wouldst only weep and bow,
He saith, "Arise and shine!"
Thy thoughts were all of grief and night,
But His of boundless joy and light.

3 Thy Father reigns supreme above;
The glory of His name
Is grace and wisdom, truth and love—
His will must be the same,
And thou hast asked all joys in one,
In whispering forth, "Thy will be done."

4 His will—each soul to sanctify
Redeeming might hath won;
His will—that thou shouldst never die,
Believing on His Son;
His will—that thou, through earthly strife,
Shouldst rise to everlasting life.

5 That one unchanging song of praise
Should from our hearts arise;
That we should know His wondrous ways,
Though hidden from the wise;
That we, so sinful and so base,
Should show the glory of His grace.

6 His will—to grant the yearning prayer
For dear ones far away,
That they His peace and love may share,
And tread His pleasant way;
That in the Father and the Son
All perfect we may be in one.

7 His will—the little flock to bring
Into His royal fold,
To reign for ever with their King,
His beauty to behold;
Sin's fell dominion crushed for aye,
Sorrow and sighing fled away.

8 This thou hast asked! And shall the prayer
Float upward on a sigh?
No song were sweet enough to bear
Such glad desires on high.
But God thy Father shall fulfil,
In thee and for thee, all His will!

See Hymn 109.

Frances Ridley Havergal, 1866.

ST. CHRYSOSTOM. [H. P. 53.]

(16) PATIENCE.

564 Ps. lxii. 5. "*Wait thou only upon God.*"

Tune St. Chrysostom. C. M.

1 FATHER, whate'er of earthly bliss
Thy sovereign will denies,
Accepted at Thy throne of grace
Let this petition rise:

2 "Give me a calm, a thankful heart,
From every murmur free;
The blessings of Thy grace impart,
And make me live to Thee.

3 "Let the sweet hope that Thou art mine
My life and death attend:
Thy presence through my journey shine,
And crown my journey's end!"

Anne Steele, 1760.

EXPECTATION. [H. P. 342.]

565 Ps. xxxvii. 7. "*Wait patiently for Him.*"

Tune Expectation. S. M. D. Or Swabia.

1 GOD doth not bid thee wait,
To disappoint at last;
A golden promise, fair and great,
In precept-mould is cast.
Soon shall the morning gild
The dark horizon rim;
Thy heart's desire shall be fulfilled;
"*Wait* patiently for Him."

2 The weary waiting-times
Are but the muffled peals,
Low preluding celestial chimes
That hail His chariot-wheels.
Trust Him to tune thy voice
To blend with seraphim;
His "Wait" shall issue in "Rejoice!"
"Wait *patiently* for Him."

3 He doth not bid thee wait,
Like driftwood on the wave,
For fickle chance or fixèd fate
To ruin or to save.
Thine eyes shall surely see,
No distant hope or dim,
The Lord thy God arise for thee:
"Wait patiently *for Him!*"

Frances Ridley Havergal, 1868.

HARTS. [H. P. 284.]

566 Cant. viii. 5. "*Leaning upon her Beloved.*"

Tune Harts. 77, 77. Or Patmos.

1 LORD! a happy child of Thine,
Patient through the love of Thee,
In the light, the life Divine,
Lives and walks at liberty.

2 Leaning on Thy tender care,
Thou hast led my soul aright,
Fervent was my morning prayer,
Joyful is my song to-night.

3 O my Saviour, Guardian true,
All my life is Thine to keep:
At Thy feet my work I do,
In Thine arms I fall asleep!

Anna L. Waring, 1850.

ST. ETHELBURGA. (HYMN CHANT.) [H. P. 342.]

SILVANUS. [H. P. 176.]

(17) TRUST.

567

2 Sam. xxiii. 5. *"Ordered in all things."*
Tune, Hymn Chant ST. ETHELBURGA. 86, 86, 86. Or SILVANUS.

1 FATHER, I know that all my life
  Is portioned out for me,
And the changes that will surely come
  I do not fear to see;
But I ask Thee for a present mind,
  Intent on pleasing Thee.

2 I ask Thee for a thoughtful love,
  Through constant watching wise,
To meet the glad with joyful smiles,
  And wipe the weeping eyes;
And a heart at leisure from itself,
  To soothe and sympathise.

3 I would not have the restless will
  That hurries to and fro;
Seeking for some great thing to do,
  Or secret thing to know:
I would be treated as a child,
  And guided where I go.

4 Wherever in the world I am,
  In whatsoe'er estate,
I have a fellowship with hearts
  To keep and cultivate,
And a work of lowly love to do,
  For the Lord on whom I wait.

5 So I ask Thee for the daily strength
  To none that ask denied,
And a mind to blend with outward life
  While keeping at Thy side;
Content to fill a little space,
  If Thou be glorified.

6 And if some things I do not ask
  In my cup of blessing be,
I would have my spirit filled the more
  With grateful love to Thee;
More careful, not to serve Thee much,
  But to please Thee perfectly.

7 There are briers besetting every path,
  That call for patient care;
There is a cross in every lot,
  And an earnest need for prayer;
But a lowly heart that leans on Thee
  Is happy anywhere.

8 In a service which Thy will appoints
  There are no bonds for me;
For my inmost heart is taught the truth
  That makes Thy children free;
And a life of self-renouncing love
  Is a life of liberty! *Anna L. Waring*, 1850.

EVAN I. [H. P. 54.]

568

Phil. i. 22. *"What I shall choose I wot not."* Tune EVAN I. C. M.

1 LORD, it belongs not to my care,
  Whether I die or live;
To love and serve Thee is my share,
  And this Thy grace must give.

2 If life be long, I will be glad,
  That I may long obey:
If short—yet why should I be sad
  To soar to endless day?

3 Christ leads me through no darker rooms
  Than He went through before;
He that into God's kingdom comes
  Must enter by this door.

4 Come, Lord, when grace hath made me meet
  Thy blessed face to see;
For if Thy work on earth be sweet,
  What will Thy glory be?

5 Then I shall end my sad complaints,
  And weary, sinful days;
And join with the triumphant saints
  That sing Jehovah's praise.

6 My knowledge of that life is small,
  The eye of faith is dim;
But 'tis enough that Christ knows all,
  And I shall be with Him.
Richard Baxter, 1681. (a.)

569

Ps. lv. 23. *"I will trust in Thee."*
Tune Fides. 65, 65. D. Or Hermas.

1 JESUS, I will trust Thee, trust Thee with my soul;
Guilty, lost, and helpless, Thou canst make me whole.
There is none in heaven or on earth like Thee:
Thou hast died for sinners—therefore, Lord, for me.

2 Jesus, I may trust Thee, name of matchless worth
Spoken by the angel at Thy wondrous birth;
Written, and for ever, on Thy cross of shame,
Sinners read and worship, trusting in that name.

3 Jesus, I must trust Thee, pondering Thy ways,
Full of love and mercy all Thine earthly days:
Sinners gathered round Thee, lepers sought Thy face—
None too vile or loathsome for a Saviour's grace.

4 Jesus, I can trust Thee, trust Thy written word,
Though Thy voice of pity I have never heard.
When Thy Spirit teacheth, to my taste how sweet—
Only may I hearken, sitting at Thy feet.

5 Jesus, I do trust Thee, trust without a doubt:
"Whosoever cometh, Thou wilt not cast out,"
Faithful is Thy promise, precious is Thy blood—
These my soul's salvation, Thou my Saviour God!

Mary Jane Walker, 1864.

See Hymns 1076—1078.

* To this tune its composer, Frances Ridley Havergal, sang the first verse of this hymn ten minutes only before her death, Tuesday morning, June 3, 1879.

570

1 Pet. v. 7. *"He careth for you."*
Tune Sihor. 77, 77, 77.

1 QUIET, Lord, my froward heart,
Make me teachable and mild,
Upright, simple, free from art,
Make me as a weanèd child,
From distrust and envy free,
Pleased with all that pleases Thee.

2 What Thou shalt to-day provide
Let me as a child receive;
What to-morrow may betide,
Calmly to Thy wisdom leave:
'Tis enough that Thou wilt care;
Why should I the burden bear?

3 As a little child relies
On a care beyond his own,
Knows he's neither strong nor wise,
Fears to stir a step alone,
Let me thus with Thee abide,
As my Father, Guard, and Guide.

4 Thus preserved from Satan's wiles,
Safe from dangers, free from fears,
May I live upon Thy smiles
Till the promised hour appears,
When the sons of God shall prove
All their Father's boundless love!

John Newton, 1779.

See Hymns 99—103, 892.

BESOR (Brook). [H. P. 51.]

(18) HOPE.

571

Ps. lxxi. 5. "*Thou art my hope.*" Tune Besor. C. M.

1 MY God, my everlasting hope,
I live upon Thy truth;
Thy hands have held my childhood up,
And strengthened all my youth.

2 Still has my life new mercies seen
Repeated every year;
Behold my days that yet remain,
I trust them to Thy care.

3 Cast me not off when strength declines,
When hoary hairs arise;
And round me let Thy glory shine,
Whene'er Thy servant dies.

4 Then in the history of my age,
When men review my days,
They'll read Thy love in every page,
In every line Thy praise.

Isaac Watts, D.D., 1719.

CARPUS. [H. P. 219.]

572

Rom. xv. 13. "*Abound in hope.*" Tune Carpus. 888, 4.

1 HOPE, Christian soul; in every stage
Of this thine earthly pilgrimage
Let heavenly joy thy thoughts engage:
Abound in hope.

2 Hope! though thy lot be want and woe,
Though hate's rude storms against thee blow,
Thy Saviour's lot was such below:
Abound in hope.

3 Hope! for to all who meekly bear
His cross, He gives His crown to wear;
Abasement here is glory there:
Abound in hope.

4 Hope! though thy dear ones round thee die,
Behold with faith's illumined eye
Their blissful home beyond the sky:
Abound in hope.

5 Hope! for upon that happy shore
Sorrow and sighing will be o'er,
And saints shall meet to part no more:
Abound in hope.

6 Hope through the watches of the night;
Hope till the morrow bring the light;
Hope till thy faith be lost in sight:
Abound in hope.

Benjamin H. Kennedy, D.D., 1867.

THYATIRA. (Hymn Chant.) [H. P. No. V.]

573

Rom. xiii. 11. "*Now is our salvation nearer than when we believed.*"
Tune, Hymn Chant Thyatira. 66, 88.

1 ONE sweetly solemn thought
Comes to me o'er and o'er—
I am nearer my home to-day
Than I ever have been before.

2 Nearer the great white throne,
Nearer the crystal sea,
Nearer my Father's house,
Where the many mansions be.

3 Nearer the bound of life,
Where we lay our burdens down;
Nearer leaving the cross,
Nearer gaining the crown.

4 But lying darkly between,
Winding down through the night,
Is the deep and unknown stream,
To be crossed ere we reach the light.

5 Jesus, perfect my trust,
Strengthen the hand of my faith:
Let me feel Thee near when I stand
On the edge of the shore of death;

6 Feel Thee near when my feet
Are slipping over the brink;
For it may be I'm nearer home,
Nearer now than I think!

Phœbe Carey, 1854.

WINCHESTER. [H. P. 46.]

(19) FULL ASSURANCE.

574

1 John iv. 8. "*God is love.*"

Tune WINCHESTER. C. M.

1 SINCE my Redeemer's name is Love,
Why should I doubt His grace?
He will not let my soul remove,
Or start from His embrace.

2 Guided by Him, with strength Divine
I gladly urge my way,
And more and more my path shall shine
Unto the perfect day.

3 I cannot from the fold depart,
For Jesus is my guide;
His law is graven on my heart,
Nor shall my footsteps slide.

4 He loved me not for my desert;
(I merited His hate;)
Nor shall the love a period know,
Which never knew a date.

5 By grace a free partaker made
Of His immortal root,
I know my branch shall never fade,
Nor cease from yielding fruit.

6 Glory and grace to them He gives,
For whom He gave His Son;
And God must cease from being love,
Ere He can hate His own!

Augustus M. Toplady, 1777.

SWABIA. [H. P. 82.]

575

Jude 24. "*Able to keep you from falling and to present you faultless.*"

Tune SWABIA. S. M.

1 TO God the only wise,
Our Saviour and our King,
Let all the saints below the skies
Their humble praises bring.

2 His tried almighty love,
His counsel and His care,
Preserve us safe from sin and death,
And every hurtful snare.

3 He will present our souls
Unblemished and complete,
Before the glory of His face,
With joys divinely great.

4 Then all the chosen seed
Shall meet around the throne,
Shall bless the conduct of His grace,
And make His wonders known.

5 To our Redeemer God
Wisdom and power belong,
Immortal crowns of majesty,
And everlasting song!

Isaac Watts, D.D., 1709.

See Hymns 721, 723—729, 732, 734.

BEDFORD. [H. P. 66.]

(20) SUPPORT AND COMFORT.

576

Matt. xiv. 27. "*It is I; be not afraid.*"

Tune BEDFORD. C. M.

1 WHEN waves of trouble round me swell,
My soul is not dismayed:
I hear a voice I know full well—
"'Tis I; be not afraid."

2 When black the threatening skies appear,
And storms my path invade,
Those accents tranquillise each fear,
"'Tis I; be not afraid."

3 There is a gulf that must be crossed;
Saviour, be near to aid!
Whisper, when my frail bark is tossed,
"'Tis I; be not afraid."

4 There is a dark and fearful vale,
Death hides within its shade;
Oh say, when flesh and heart shall fail,
"'Tis I; be not afraid!"

Charlotte Elliott, 1834.

577 Heb. xii. 10. "*Chastened . . . for our profit.*"

Tune St. Hilda. 77,77. D. Or Seir.

1 'TIS my happiness below
Not to live without the cross,
But the Saviour's power to know,
Sanctifying every loss:
Trials must and will befall;
But with humble faith to see
Love inscribed upon them all—
This is happiness to me.

2 God in Israel sows the seeds
Of affliction, pain, and toil;
These spring up and choke the weeds
Which would else o'erspread the [soil:
Trials make the promise sweet;
Trials give new life to prayer;
Trials bring me to His feet,
Lay me low and keep me there.

3 Did I meet no trials here,
No correction by the way,
Might I not, with reason, fear
I should prove a castaway?
Others may escape the rod,
Sunk in earthly vain delight;
But the true-born child of God
Must not, would not, if he might!

William Cowper, 1774.

ST. HILDA. [H. P. 290.]

SMYRNA. (Hymn Chant.) *Double Counterpoint.* [H. P. No. III.]

578 Ps. xxvii. 9. "*Thou hast been my help.*"

Tune, Hymn Chant Smyrna. C. M. Or London New.

1 O GOD, our help in ages past,
Our hope for years to come,
Our shelter from the stormy blast,
And our eternal home:

2 Beneath the shadow of Thy throne
Thy saints have dwelt secure;
Sufficient is Thine arm alone,
And our defence is sure.

3 Before the hills in order stood,
Or earth received her frame,
From everlasting Thou art God,
To endless years the same.

4 O God, our help in ages past,
Our hope for years to come;
Be Thou our guard while life shall last,
And our eternal home!

Isaac Watts, D.D., 1719.

SARDIS. (Hymn Chant.) [H. P. No. VI.]

579 Mark iv. 39. "*Peace, be still.*"

Tune, Hymn Chant Sardis. 888, 3.

1 FIERCE raged the tempest o'er the deep;
Watch did Thine anxious servants keep,
But Thou wast wrapped in guileless sleep,
Calm and still.

2 "Save, Lord, we perish!" was their cry,
"Oh save us in our agony!"
Thy word above the storm rose high,
"Peace, be still!"

3 The wild winds hushed; the angry deep
Sank, like a little child, to sleep;
The sullen billows cease to leap,
At Thy will.

4 So when our life is clouded o'er,
And storm winds drift us from the shore,
Say, lest we sink to rise no more,
"Peace, be still!"

Godfrey Thring, 1858.

OLD "TEN COMMANDMENTS' TUNE." [H. P. 15.]

580 Ps. xlvi. 11. *"The God of Jacob is our refuge."* Tune Old Ten Commandments. L. M.

1 GOD is the refuge of His saints,
When storms of sharp distress invade;
Ere we can offer our complaints,
Behold Him present with His aid!

2 Let mountains from their seats be hurled
Down to the deep, and buried there;
Convulsions shake the solid world;
Our faith shall never yield to fear.

3 Loud let the troubled ocean roar,
In sacred peace our souls abide;
While every nation, every shore,
Trembles, and dreads the swelling tide!

Isaac Watts, D.D., 1719.

PARAN (Wilderness of). [H. P. 241.]

581 Ps. cvi. 9. *"He led them through the depths."* Tune Paran. 11 11, 11 11.

1 PRESS forward and fear not! the billows may roll,
The power of Jesus their rage will control;
Though waves rise in anger, their tumults shall cease,
One word of His bidding shall hush them to peace.

2 Press forward and fear not! though trial be near,
The Lord is our refuge; whom then shall we fear?
His staff is our comfort, our safeguard His rod;
Then let us be steadfast and trust in our God.

3 Press forward and fear not! be strong in the Lord,
The power of His promise, the truth of His word;
Through sea and through desert our pathway may tend,
But He who hath saved us will save to the end.

4 Then forward and fear not! we'll speed on our way;
Why should we e'er shrink from our path in dismay?
We tread but the road which our Leader hath trod;
Then let us press forward, and trust in our God!

Edward Wakefield, 1842.

582 Ps. civ. 34. *"My meditation of Him shall be sweet."* Tune, Hymn Chant Smyrna. C. M. Or Bedford.

1 WHEN languor and disease invade
This trembling house of clay,
'Tis sweet to look beyond the cage,
And long to fly away.

2 Sweet to look inward and attend
The whispers of His love;
Sweet to look upward to the place
Where Jesus pleads above.

3 Sweet to look back and see my name
In life's fair book set down;
Sweet to look forward and behold
Eternal joys my own.

4 Sweet to reflect how grace Divine
My sins on Jesus laid;
Sweet to remember that His blood
My debt of sufferings paid.

5 Sweet in His righteousness to stand,
Which saves from second death;
Sweet to experience, day by day,
His Spirit's quickening breath.

6 Sweet on His faithfulness to rest,
Whose love can never end;
Sweet on His covenant of grace
For all things to depend.

7 Sweet in the confidence of faith
To trust His firm decrees;
Sweet to lie passive in His hand,
And know no will but His.

8 Sweet to rejoice in lively hope,
That, when my change shall come,
Angels will hover round my bed,
And waft my spirit home.

9 There shall my disimprisoned soul
Behold Him and adore;
Be with His likeness satisfied,
And grieve and sin no more.

10 If such the sweetness of the stream,
What must the fountain be,
Where saints and angels draw their bliss
Immediately from Thee?

Augustus M. Toplady, 1778.

HANOVER; *or*, MODERN 104TH. [H. P. 239.]

583

Gen. xxii. 14. "*Jehovah-Jireh.*"
Tune HANOVER. 10 10, 11 11.

1 THOUGH troubles assail, And dangers affright,
Though friends should all fail, And foes all unite,
Yet one thing secures us, Whatever betide,
The Scripture assures us, "The Lord will provide."

2 The birds without barn Or storehouse are fed;
From them let us learn To trust for our bread;
His saints what is fitting Shall ne'er be denied,
So long as 'tis written, "The Lord will provide."

3 We may, like the ships, By tempest be tossed
On perilous deeps, But cannot be lost:
Though Satan enrages The wind and the tide,
The promise engages, "The Lord will provide."

4 His call we obey, Like Abra'm of old;
We know not the way, But faith makes us bold;
For, though we are strangers, We have a sure Guide,
And trust in all dangers, "The Lord will provide."

5 No strength of our own, No goodness we claim;
Our trust is all placed In Jesu's great name;
In this, our strong tower, For safety we hide;
The Lord is our power: "The Lord will provide."

6 When life sinks apace, And death is in view,
The word of His grace Shall comfort us through;
No fearing or doubting, With Christ on our side,
We hope to die shouting, "The Lord will provide."

John Newton, 1777.

BEDFORD. [H. P. 66.]

584

Matt. xv. 25. "*Lord, help me.*" Tune BEDFORD. C. M. Or DUNDEE.

1 OH help us, Lord! each hour of need
Thy heavenly succour give;
Help us in thought, and word, and deed,
Each hour on earth we live!

2 Oh help us when our spirits bleed
With contrite anguish sore;
And when our hearts are cold and dead,
Oh help us, Lord, the more!

3 Oh help us through the prayer of faith,
More firmly to believe;
For still, the more the servant hath
The more shall he receive.

4 Oh help us, Jesus, from on high!
We know no help but Thee;
Oh help us so to live and die,
As Thine in heaven to be!

Dean Henry Hart Milman, D.D., 1827.

HERMON. [H. P. 27.]

585

1 Sam. vii. 12. "*Hitherto hath the Lord helped us.*" Tune HERMON. L. M.

1 THUS far my God hath led me on,
And made His truth and mercy known;
My hopes and fears alternate rise,
And comforts mingle with my sighs.

2 Through this wide wilderness I roam,
Far distant from my blissful home;
Lord, let Thy presence be my stay,
And guard me in this dangerous way.

3 Temptations everywhere annoy,
And sins and snares my peace destroy:
My earthly joys are from me torn,
And oft an absent God I mourn.

4 Is this, dear Lord, that thorny road
Which leads us to the mount of God?
Are these the toils Thy people know,
While in the wilderness below?

5 'Tis even so, Thy faithful love
Doth thus Thy children's graces prove;
'Tis thus our pride and self must fall,
That Jesus may be All in all!

John Fawcett, 1782.

HUMILITY.

586 Ps. xxx. 5. "*Weeping may endure in the evening, but singing cometh in the morning.*" [Margin.]

Tune Godesberg. 8 7, 8 7.

GODESBERG. [H. P. 185.]

1 IN the evening there is weeping,
Lengthening shadows, failing sight;
Silent darkness, slowly creeping
Over all things dear and bright.

2 In the evening there is weeping,
Lasting all the twilight through;
Phantom shadows, never sleeping,
Wakening slumbers of the true.

3 In the morning cometh singing,
Cometh joy and cometh sight,
When the sun ariseth, bringing
Healing on his wings of light.

4 In the morning cometh singing,
Songs that ne'er in silence end,
Angel minstrels ever bringing
Praises new with thine to blend.

5 Are the twilight shadows casting
Heavy glooms upon thy heart?
Soon in radiance everlasting
Night for ever shall depart.

6 Art thou weeping, sad and lonely,
Through the evening of thy days?
All thy sighing shall be only
Prelude of more perfect praise.

7 Darkest hour is nearest dawning,
Solemn herald of the day;
Singing cometh in the morning,
God shall wipe thy tears away!

Frances Ridley Havergal, 1869.

See Hymns 360, 433.

GIBBONS. [H. P. 148.]

(21) HUMILITY.

587 1 Pet. v. 5. "*Be clothed with humility.*" Tune Gibbons. 7 7, 7 7.

1 LORD, if Thou Thy grace impart,
Poor in spirit, meek in heart,
I shall, as my Master, be
Clothèd with humility.

2 Simple, teachable, and mild,
Changed into a little child,
Pleased with all the Lord provides,
Weaned from all the world besides.

3 Father, fix my soul on Thee;
Every evil let me flee;
Nothing want, beneath, above,
Happy in Thy precious love.

4 Oh that all may seek and find
Every good in Christ combined!
Him let Israel still adore,
Trust Him, praise Him evermore!

Charles Wesley, 1741.

FARRANT. [H. P. 67.]

588 Phil. ii. 5. "*Let this mind be in you which was also in Christ Jesus.*" Tune Farrant. C. M.

1 JESUS! exalted far on high,
To whom a name is given,
A name surpassing every name,
That's known in earth or heaven.

2 Jesus! who in the form of God
Didst equal honour claim;
Yet, to redeem our guilty souls,
Didst stoop to death and shame.

3 Oh, may that mind in us be formed
Which shone so bright in Thee;
A humble, meek, and lowly mind,
From pride and envy free.

4 May we to others stoop, and learn
To emulate Thy love;
So shall we bear Thine image here,
And share Thy throne above!

Thomas Cotterill, 1812.

See Hymns 217, 555, 556, 570, 745.

SHENIR I. (Mount.) [H. P. 136.]

rall.

(22) LOVE.

589 1 Cor. xiii. 13. "*The greatest of these is charity.*" Tune SHENIR I. 777, 5.

1 GRACIOUS Spirit, Holy Ghost,
Taught by Thee, we covet most,
Of Thy gifts at Pentecost,
Holy, heavenly love.

2 Faith, that mountains could remove,
Tongues of earth or heaven above,
Knowledge—all things—empty prove,
Without heavenly love.

3 Though I as a martyr bleed,
Give my goods the poor to feed,
All is vain—if love I need;
Therefore, give me love.

4 Love is kind, and suffers long;
Love is meek, and thinks no wrong;
Love than death itself more strong;
Therefore, give us love.

5 Prophecy will fade away,
Melting in the light of day;
Love will ever with us stay;
Therefore, give us love.

6 Faith will vanish into sight;
Hope be emptied in delight;
Love in heaven will shine more bright;
Therefore, give us love.

7 Faith and hope and love we see
Joining hand in hand agree;
But the greatest of the three,
And the best, is love.

8 From the overshadowing
Of Thy gold and silver wing,
Shed on us, who to Thee sing,
Holy, heavenly love!

Bishop Christopher Wordsworth, 1862.

BESOR (Brock). [H. P. 51.]

590 John xxi. 16. "*Yea, Lord; Thou knowest that I love Thee.*" Tune BESOR. C. M.

1 DO not I love Thee, O my Lord?
Behold my heart and see;
And turn each earthly idol out
That dares to rival Thee.

2 Do not I love Thee from my soul?
Then let me nothing love:
Dead be my heart to every joy,
When Jesus cannot move.

3 Is not Thy name melodious still
To mine attentive ear?
Doth not each pulse with pleasure bound,
My Saviour's voice to hear?

4 Hast Thou a lamb in all Thy flock
I would disdain to feed?
Hast Thou a foe, before whose face
I fear Thy cause to plead?

5 Would not my ardent spirit vie
With angels round the throne,
To execute Thy sacred will,
And make Thy glory known?

6 Would not my heart pour forth its blood
In honour of Thy name,
And challenge the cold hand of death
To damp the' immortal flame?

7 Thou know'st I love Thee, dearest Lord;
But oh! I long to soar
Far from the sphere of mortal joys,
And learn to love Thee more!

Philip Doddridge, D.D., 1755.

BRIDEHEAD. [H P. 310.]

591 Eph. v. 2. "*Walk in love.*" Tune BRIDEHEAD. 886. D. Or KEDRON.

1 MAY we Thy precepts, Lord, fulfil,
To do on earth our Father's will
As angels do above;
To walk in Christ, the living Way,
With all Thy children, and obey
The law of Christian love.

2 Spirit of life, of love and peace,
Unite our hearts, our joy increase,
Thy gracious help supply;
To every soul the blessing give,
In Christian fellowship to live;
In joyful hope to die!

Edward Osler, 1833.

PATMOS. [H. P. 147.]

592 John xv. 12. "*Love one another, as I have loved you.*" Tune Patmos. 77, 77.

1 "LITTLE children, dwell in love
New begotten from above;
Ye by this your birth may know,
That ye dwell in love below.

2 "God your Father reigns on high,
Unbeheld by mortal eye;
Him ye see not; love Him then
In His types, your fellow-men.

3 "Not in semblance nor in word,
But in holy thoughts unheard
And in very truth and deed,
Share their joy, and help their need."

4 Thus the saint whom Jesus loved
Spoke in word, in action proved:
Lord, may Thy disciples be
Like to him, and like to Thee!

Dean Henry Alford, D.D., 1844.

SHENIR II. (Mount.) [H. P. 151.]

593 John xxi. 15. "*Lovest thou Me?*" Tune Shenir II. 77, 77. Or Luxemburg.

1 'TIS a point I long to know—
Oft it causes anxious thought—
Do I love the Lord, or no?
Am I His, or am I not?

2 Could my heart so hard remain,
Prayer a task and burden prove,
Every trifle give me pain,
If I knew a Saviour's love?

3 When I turn mine eyes within,
All is dark, and vain, and wild!
Filled with unbelief and sin,
Can I deem myself a child?

4 If I pray, or hear, or read,
Sin is mixed with all I do:
You that love the Lord indeed,
Tell me, is it thus with you?

5 Yet I mourn my stubborn will,
Find my sin a grief and thrall;
Should I grieve for what I feel,
If I did not love at all?

6 Could I joy His saints to meet,
Choose the ways I once abhorred,
Find, at times, the promise sweet,
If I did not love the Lord?

7 Lord, decide the doubtful case!
Thou who art Thy people's Sun,
Shine upon Thy work of grace,
If it be indeed begun.

8 Let me love Thee more and more,
If I love at all, I pray:
If I have not loved before,
Help me to begin to-day!

John Newton, 1779.

ST. ANN. [H. P. 52.]

594 1 John iv. 7. "*Love is of God.*" Tune St. Ann. C. M.

1 HAPPY the heart where graces reign,
Where love inspires the breast;
Love is the brightest of the train,
And strengthens all the rest.

2 Knowledge, alas! 'tis all in vain,
And all in vain our fear;
Our stubborn sins will fight and reign,
If love be absent there.

3 'Tis love that makes our cheerful feet
In swift obedience move;
The devils know and tremble too;
But Satan cannot love.

4 This is the grace that lives and sings
When faith and hope shall cease;
'Tis this shall strike our joyful strings
In the sweet realms of bliss.

Isaac Watts, D.D., 1707.

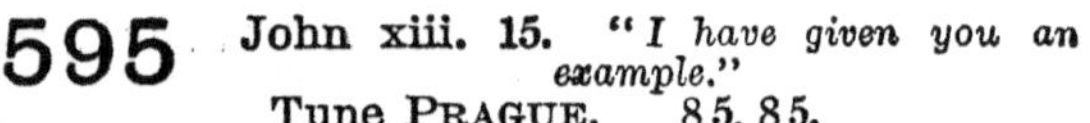

595 John xiii. 15. *"I have given you an example."*

Tune Prague. 8 5, 8 5.

PRAGUE. [H. P. 171.]

1 THOU who on that wondrous journey
Sett'st Thy face to die,
By Thy holy meek example
Teach us Charity!

2 Thou who that dread cup of suffering
Didst not put from Thee,
O most Loving of the loving,
Give us Charity!

3 Thou who reignest, bright in glory,
On God's throne on high,
Oh, that we may share Thy triumph,
Grant us Charity!

4 Send us Faith, that trusts Thy promise;
Hope, with upward eye;
But more blest than both, and greater,
Send us Charity!

Dean Henry Alford, D.D., 1867.

NAYLAND; *or*, ST. STEPHEN. [H. P. 47.]

596 1 John iii. 14. *"We know that we have passed from death unto life, because we love the brethren."*

Tune Nayland. C. M. Or St. Ann.

1 OUR God is love; and all His saints
His image bear below:
The heart, with love to God inspired,
With love to man will glow.

2 Oh may we love each other, Lord,
As we are loved of Thee:
For none are truly born of God
Who live in enmity.

3 Heirs of the same immortal bliss,
Our hopes and fears the same,
The cords of love our hearts should bind,
The law of love inflame.

4 So shall the vain contentious world
Our peaceful lives approve,
And wondering say, as they of old,
"See how these Christians love!"

Thomas Cotterill, 1819.

PERGAMOS. (Hymn Chant.) [H. P. No. IV.]

(23) ALMSGIVING.

597 1 Chron. xxix. 2. *"I have prepared with all my might."*

Tune, Hymn Chant Pergamos. 6 10, 10 10.

1 GIVE to the Lord thy heart!
Bring joyfully the silver and the gold:
The rich are they who keep not back a part;
The glad, the full, are those who ne'er withhold.

2 Give to the Lord thy heart!
Its morning fragrance and its noontide might,
And evening dews—all that thou hast and art,
Are but the Lord's by purchase and by right.

3 Give to the Lord thy heart!
Bring a whole offering, worthless though it be;
The love which took thy cross, and bore its smart,
Paid the full price, O ransomed one, for thee!

Jane Crewdson, 1860.

598 2 Cor. v. 14. *"The love of Christ constraineth us."*

Tune Nayland. C. M.

1 FOUNTAIN of good! to own Thy love
Our thankful hearts incline;
What can we render, Lord, to Thee,
When all the worlds are Thine?

2 But Thou hast needy brethren here,
Partakers of Thy grace,
Whose humble names Thou wilt confess
Before Thy Father's face.

3 In their sad accents of distress
Thy pleading voice is heard,
In them Thou may'st be clothed and fed
And visited and cheered.

4 Thy face, with reverence and with love,
We in Thy poor would see;
For while we minister to them,
We do it, Lord, to Thee!

Philip Doddridge, D.D., 1755. (a.)

See Hymns 589, 633, 691, 739.

(24) PRAISE.

599 Mark xi. 10. "*Hosanna in the highest.*"
Tune Baden II. 8 8, 8 8, 4 7.

1 HOSANNA to the living Lord!
Hosanna to the' Incarnate Word!
To Christ, Creator, Saviour, King,
Let earth, let heaven, Hosanna sing!
Hosanna, Lord! Hosanna in the highest.

2 Hosanna, Lord, Thine angels cry:
Hosanna, Lord, Thy saints reply:
Above, beneath us, and around,
The dead and living swell the sound;
Hosanna, Lord! Hosanna in the highest.

3 O Saviour, with protecting care,
Be with us in Thy house of prayer,
Assembled in Thy sacred name,
While we Thy parting promise claim:
Hosanna, Lord! Hosanna in the highest.

4 But chiefest in our cleansèd breast,
Eternal! bid Thy Spirit rest,
And make our secret soul to be
A temple pure, and worthy Thee!
Hosanna, Lord! Hosanna in the highest.

5 So in the last and dreadful day,
When earth and heaven shall melt away,
Thy flock, redeemed from sinful stain,
Shall swell the sound of praise again:
Hosanna, Lord! Hosanna in the highest.

Bishop Heber, 1811.

BADEN II.; *or*, NUREMBERG. [H. P. 225.]

ST. PAUL. [H. P. 253.]

600 Rev. v. 12. "*Worthy is the Lamb that was slain.*"

Tune St. Paul. 8 7, 8 8 7, 7 7, 7 7

1 "WORTHY of all adoration
Is the Lamb that once was slain,"
Cry, in raptured exultation,
His redeemed from every nation;
Angel myriads join the strain;
Sounding from their sinless strings
Glory to the King of kings;
Harping, with their harps of gold,
Praise which never can be told.

2 Hallelujahs full and swelling
Rise around His throne of might.
All our highest laud excelling,
Holy and Immortal, dwelling
In the unapproachèd light,
He is worthy to receive
All that heaven and earth can give.
Blessing, honour, glory, might,
All are His by glorious right.

3 As the sound of many waters
Let the full Amen arise!
Hallelujah! Ceasing never,
Sounding through the great For Ever,
Linking all its harmonies;
Through eternities of bliss,
Lord, our rapture shall be this;
And our endless life shall be
One Amen of praise to Thee!

Frances Ridley Havergal, 1867.

CHESALON (Mount). [H. P. 35.]

601 Ps. xcv. 1. *"O come, let us sing unto the Lord."*
Tune CHESALON. C. M.

1 COME, let us join our cheerful songs
With angels round the throne;
Ten thousand thousand are their tongues,
But all their joys are one.

2 "Worthy the Lamb that died," they cry,
"To be exalted thus";
"Worthy the Lamb," our lips reply,
"For He was slain for us."

3 Jesus is worthy to receive
Honour and power Divine;
And blessings more than we can give,
Be, Lord, for ever Thine.

4 Let all that dwell above the sky,
And air, and earth, and seas,
Conspire to lift Thy glories high,
And speak Thine endless praise.

5 The whole creation join in one,
To bless the sacred name
Of Him that sits upon the throne,
And to adore the Lamb!

Isaac Watts, D.D., 1709.

THE OLD 100th TUNE. [H. P. 1.]

602 Ps. cl. 6. *"Let every thing that hath breath praise the Lord."* Tune OLD HUNDREDTH. L. M.

1 FROM all that dwell below the skies
Let the Creator's praise arise;
Let the Redeemer's name be sung
Through every land, by every tongue.

2 Eternal are Thy mercies, Lord;
Eternal truth attends Thy word:
Thy praise shall sound from shore to shore,
Till suns shall rise and set no more!

Isaac Watts, D.D, 1719.

603 Ps. lxix. 16. *"The multitude of Thy tender mercies."*
Tune CHESALON. C. M. Or LONDON NEW.

1 FOR mercies countless as the sands,
Which daily I receive
From Jesus my Redeemer's hands,
My soul, what canst thou give?

2 Alas! from such a heart as mine
What can I bring Him forth?
My best is stained and dyed with sin;
My all is nothing worth.

3 Yet this acknowledgment I'll make
For all He has bestowed;
Salvation's sacred cup I'll take,
And call upon my God.

4 The best return for one like me,
So wretched and so poor,
Is from His gifts to draw a plea,
And ask Him still for more.

5 I cannot serve Him as I ought;
No works have I to boast;
Yet would I glory in the thought,
That I should owe Him most!

John Newton, 1779.

604 Ps. cxlv. 11. *"They shall speak of the glory of Thy kingdom, and talk of Thy power."*
Tune MAGDALENE COLLEGE. 8 8 6. D.

1 BEGIN, my soul, the' exalted lay;
Let each enraptured thought obey!
And praise the' Almighty's name:
Lo! heaven, and earth, and sea, and skies,
In one melodious concert rise,
To swell the' inspiring theme.

2 Ye angels, catch the thrilling sound;
While all the' adoring thrones around
His boundless mercy sing:
Let every listening saint above
Wake all the tuneful soul of love,
And touch the sweetest string.

3 Join, ye loud spheres, the vocal choir;
Thou glorious orb of liquid fire,
The mighty chorus aid:

MAGDALENE COLLEGE. [H. P. 210.]

Soon as grey evening gilds the plain,
Thou, moon, protract the melting strain,
And praise Him in the shade.

4 Whate'er a blooming world contains,
That wings the air or decks the plains,
United praise bestow:
Ye tempests, sound His awful name;
And widely roar your loud acclaim,
Ye swelling deeps below.

5 Let man, by nobler passions swayed,
The feeling heart, the judging head,
In heavenly praise employ;

Spread His tremendous name around,
Till heaven's broad arch rings back the sound,
The general burst of joy!

John Ogilvie, 1776.

ORIEL. [H. P. 302.]

605

Ps. cl. 1. "*Hallelujah! Praise God in His sanctuary.*" Tune ORIEL. 87, 87, 87. Or IDUMEA.

1 ALLELUIA! Song of gladness,
Voice of everlasting joy;
Alleluia! sound the sweetest
Heard among the choirs on high,
Hymning in God's blissful mansion
Day and night incessantly.

2 Alleluia! Church victorious,
Thou may'st lift the joyful strain.
Alleluia! songs of triumph
Well befit the ransomed train.
Faint and feeble are our praises
While in exile we remain.

3 Alleluia! songs of gladness
Suit not always souls forlorn.
Alleluia! sounds of sadness
'Midst our joyful strains are borne;
For in this dark world of sorrow
We with tears our sins must mourn.

4 Praises with our prayers uniting,
Hear us, blessèd Trinity;
Bring us to Thy blissful presence,
There the Paschal Lamb to see,
There to Thee our Alleluia
Singing everlastingly.

J. M. Neale, D.D. (*tr.*), 1851.

"NUN DANKET ALLE GOTT." [H. P. 251.]

606

Ps. xlviii. 14. "*This God is our God for ever and ever.*"
Tune, "NUN DANKET ALLE GOTT." 67, 67, 6666.

1 NOW thank we all our God,
With hearts, and hands, and voices;
Who wondrous things hath done,
In whom His world rejoices;
Who from our mother's arms
Hath blessed us on our way
With countless gifts of love,
And still is ours to-day.

2 Oh may this bounteous God
Through all our life be near us;
With ever joyful hearts
And blessèd peace to cheer us:
And help us in His grace,
And guide us when perplexed:
And free us from all ills
In this world and the next.

3 All praise and thanks to God
The Father now be given,
The Son, and Him who reigns
With Them in highest heaven:
The one eternal God
Whom heaven and earth adore;
For thus it was, is now,
And shall be evermore!

Martin Rinckart, 1586—1649; *C. Winkworth* (*tr.*), 1858.

ZAANAIM (Plain of.) [H. P. 191.]

607 Rev. iv. 11. *"Thou art worthy, O Lord, to receive glory."* Tune ZAANAIM. 87, 87, 47.

1 GLORY, glory everlasting
Be to Him who bore the cross!
Who redeemed our souls, by tasting
Death, the death deserved by us;
Spread His glory,
Who redeemed His people thus.

2 His is love, 'tis love unbounded,
Without measure, without end;
Human thought is here confounded,
'Tis too vast to comprehend:
Praise the Saviour!
Magnify the sinner's Friend.

3 While we hear the wondrous story
Of the Saviour's cross and shame,
Sing we "Everlasting glory
Be to God, and to the Lamb:"
Saints and angels,
Give ye glory to His name!

Thomas Kelly, 1809.

ESDRAELON. [H. P. 202.]

608 Eph. i. 6. *"To the praise of the glory of His grace."* Tune ESDRAELON. 87, 87. D.

1 COME, Thou Fount of every blessing,
Tune my heart to sing Thy grace,
Streams of mercy never ceasing
Call for songs of loudest praise.
Teach me some melodious measure,
Sung by flaming hosts above:
Fill my soul with sacred pleasure,
While I sing redeeming Love.

2 Here I raise my Ebenezer;
Hither by Thine help I'm come:
And I hope, by Thy good pleasure,
Safely to arrive at home.
Jesus sought me when a stranger,
Wandering from the fold of God;
He, to rescue me from danger,
Interposed His precious blood.

3 Oh! to grace how great a debtor
Daily I'm constrained to be!
Let that grace now, like a fetter,
Bind my wandering heart to Thee!
Prone to wander, Lord, I feel it;
Prone to leave the God I love—
Here's my heart, oh, take and seal it!
Seal it from Thy courts above!

Attributed to Robert Robinson, 1758; *also Selina, Countess of Huntingdon,* 1749; *and C. Wesley.*

HEATHLANDS. [H. P. 286.]

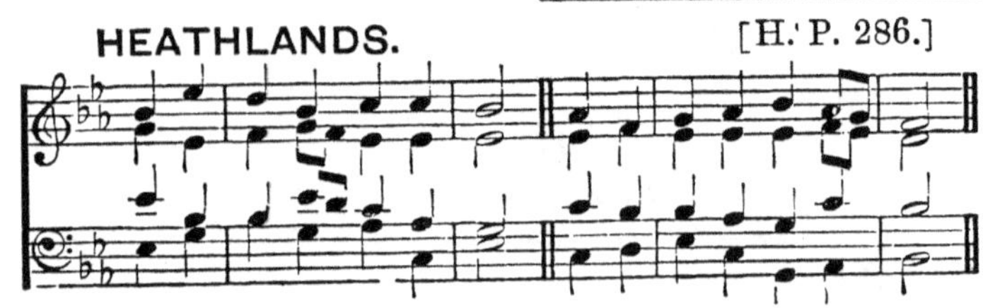

609 Ps. lxvii. 3. *"Let all the people praise Thee."*
Tune HEATHLANDS. 77, 77, 77.

1 GOD of mercy, God of grace,
Show the brightness of Thy face;
Shine upon us, Saviour, shine,
Fill Thy church with light Divine;

And Thy saving health extend
Unto earth's remotest end.

2 Let the people praise Thee, Lord;
Be by all that live adored;
Let the nations shout and sing
Glory to their Saviour King;
At Thy feet their tribute pay,
And Thy holy will obey.

3 Let the people praise Thee, Lord,
Earth shall then her fruits afford,
God to man His blessing give,
Man to God devoted live;
All below, and all above,
One in joy and light and love!

Henry Francis Lyte, 1834.

LUBECK. [H. P. 139.]

Hal - le - lu - jah, Hal - le - lu - jah!

610

Ps. ciii. 22. *"Bless the Lord, all His works, in all places of His dominion."*

Tune Lubeck. 77, 77.

1 PRAISE the Lord, His glories show,
Saints within His courts below,
Angels round His throne above,
All that see and share His love.

2 Earth to heaven, and heaven to earth,
Tell His wonders, sing His worth:
Age to age, and shore to shore,
Praise Him, praise Him, evermore.

3 Praise the Lord, His mercies trace!
Praise His providence and grace,
All that He for man hath done,
All He sends us through His Son:

4 Strings and voices, hands and hearts,
In the concert bear your parts;
All that breathe, your Lord adore,
Praise Him! praise Him, evermore!

Henry Francis Lyte, 1834.

611

Rom. xvi. 27. *"To God only wise, be glory through Jesu Christ for ever."*

Tune Darwell. 6666, 88.

DARWELL. [H. P. 274.]

1 WE give immortal praise
To God the Father's love,
For all our comforts here
And better hopes above;
He sent His own eternal Son
To die for sins that man had done.

2 To God the Son belongs
Immortal glory too,
Who bought us with His blood
From everlasting woe;
And now He lives, and now He reigns,
And sees the fruit of all His pains.

3 To God the Spirit's name
Immortal worship give,
Whose new-creating power
Makes the dead sinner live;
His work completes the great design,
And fills the soul with joy Divine.

4 Almighty God, to Thee
Be endless honours done;
The undivided Three,
And the mysterious One!
Where reason fails with all her powers,
There faith prevails, and love adores!

Isaac Watts, D.D., 1709.

612 Ps. ciii. 1. "*Bless the Lord, O my soul.*"

Tune CORFE MULLEN. 87, 87, 47.
OR ZAANAIM.

CORFE MULLEN. [H. P. 297.]

1 PRAISE, my soul, the King of heaven;
To His feet thy tribute bring!
Ransomed, healed, restored, forgiven,
Who like me His praise should sing?
Praise Him! praise Him!
Praise the everlasting King!

2 Praise Him for His grace and favour
To our fathers in distress!
Praise Him still the same for ever,
Slow to chide, and swift to bless!
Praise Him! praise Him!
Glorious in His faithfulness!

3 Father-like, He tends and spares us,
Well our feeble frame He knows;
In His hands He gently bears us,
Rescues us from all our foes.
Praise Him! praise Him!
Widely as His mercy flows!

4 Frail as summer's flower we flourish;
Blows the wind, and it is gone:
But while mortals rise and perish,
God endures unchanging on.
Praise Him! praise Him!
Praise the High Eternal One!

5 Angels, help us to adore Him;
Ye behold Him face to face:
Sun and moon, bow down before Him:
Dwellers all in time and space,
Praise Him! praise Him!
Praise with us the God of grace!

Henry Francis Lyte, 1834.

CULBACH. [H. P. 181.]

613 Ps. lxxxix. 1. "*I will make known Thy faithfulness.*" Tune CULBACH. 87, 87.

1 PRAISE the Lord! ye heavens, adore Him;
Praise Him, angels, in the height;
Sun and moon, rejoice before Him;
Praise Him, all ye stars of light.

2 Praise the Lord! for He hath spoken;
Worlds His mighty voice obeyed;
Laws which never shall be broken
For their guidance He hath made.

3 Praise the Lord! for He is glorious;
Never shall His promise fail:
God hath made His saints victorious,
Sin and death shall not prevail.

4 Praise the God of our salvation;
Hosts on high, His power proclaim;
Heaven and earth, and all creation,
Laud and magnify His name!

John Kempthorne, 1810.

GAIUS. [H. P. 319.]

614 Ps. cxlix. 1. "*Praise ye the Lord.*"

Tune GAIUS. 11 10, 11 10.

1 PRAISE ye Jehovah! praise the Lord most holy,
Who cheers the contrite, girds with strength the weak;
Praise Him who will, with glory, crown the lowly,
And, with salvation, beautify the meek.

2 Praise ye the Lord, for all His lovingkindness,
And all the tender mercies He hath shown;
Praise Him who pardons all our sin and blindness,
And calls us sons, and takes us for His own.

3 Praise ye Jehovah! Source of all our blessing;
Before His gifts earth's richest boons are dim;
Resting in Him, His peace and joy possessing,
All things are ours, for we have all in Him.

4 Praise ye the Father! God the Lord who gave us,
With full and perfect love, His only Son;
Praise ye the Son who died Himself to save us!
Praise ye the Spirit! praise the Three in One!

Lady M. C. Campbell, 1838.

CRASSELIUS; *or,* **WINCHESTER NEW.** [H. P. 3.]

615

Ps. cl. 1. *"Praise God in His sanctuary."* Tune CRASSELIUS. L. M.

1 OH praise the Lord in that blest place,
From whence His goodness largely flows!
Praise Him in heaven, where He His face
Unveiled in perfect glory shows!

2 Praise Him for all the mighty acts
Which He on our behalf has done!
His kindness this return exacts,
With which our praise should equal run.

3 Let all that vital breath enjoy,
The breath He does to them afford
In just returns of praise employ:
Let every creature praise the Lord!

Tate and Brady, 1696.

PEDAL TUNE. [H. P. 344.]

616

Dan. iv. 34, 35. *"Him that . . . doeth according to His will."*
Tune, PEDAL TUNE. 88, 88, 88.

1 PRAISE ye the Lord, the' eternal King,
Who reigns by right, and rules by love;
Let all the saints His glory sing,
The saints below and saints above.
To Him that lives, but once was slain,
Be honour, power, and praise. Amen.

2 Praise Him who sits upon His throne,
His throne of glory and of grace;
O'er heaven and earth He reigns alone,
Unlimited by time or place.
To Him that lives, etc.

3 No hand against His will can rise,
No heart against His love can stand;
No place is secret from His eyes,
Not heaven, nor hell, nor sea, nor land.
To Him that lives, etc.

4 What He desires to do is done:
The awful mandate of His will,
That moves the universe alone,
Can make the universe stand still.
To Him that lives, etc.

5 His smile is heaven, His frown is hell,
His dreadful vengeance breaks His foes;
His favour is the living well,
From which complete salvation flows.
To Him that lives, etc.

Joseph Swain, 1792.

617

Rev. i. 5, 6. *"Unto Him that loved us, and washed us from our sins, . . . be glory and dominion for ever."*
Tune ZION. 88, 88, 88.

ZION. [H. P. 312.]

1 PRAISE your Redeemer, praise His name,
Ye saints who live upon His grace;
Praise Him whose love remains the same,
Through every change of time and place.
Praise ye the Lord, the Saviour praise,
Hosanna to the God of grace.

2 Praise Him who came from heaven to bring
Glad tidings of salvation down;
Praise Him, for you have cause to sing,
Who hope for an immortal crown.
Praise ye the Lord, etc.

3 Praise Him who loved you on the cross,
Praise Him who loves you on His throne,
Praise Him who turns to gain your loss,
And makes your crosses prove your crown.
Praise ye the Lord, etc.

4 Praise Him who loved you long before
The wheels of time began to move;
Whose love, when time shall be no more,
Will still be everlasting love.
Praise ye the Lord, etc.

Joseph Swain, 1792.

PATMOS. [H. P. 147.]

618 Ps. cxxx. 7. "*Plenteous redemption.*"

Tune PATMOS. 77, 77.

1 NOW begin the heavenly theme,
Sing aloud in Jesu's name!
Ye, who His salvation prove,
Triumph in redeeming love.

2 Ye, who see the Father's grace
Beaming in the Saviour's face,
As to Canaan on ye move,
Praise and bless redeeming love.

3 Mourning souls, dry up your tears,
Banish all your guilty fears!
See your curse and guilt remove,
Cancelled by redeeming love.

4 Ye, alas! who long have been
Willing slaves to death and sin,
Now from bliss no longer rove;
Stop and taste redeeming love.

5 Welcome all by sin oppressed,
Welcome to His sacred rest,
Nothing brought Him from above,
Nothing but redeeming love.

6 When His Spirit leads us home,
When we to His glory come,
We shall all the fulness prove
Of our Lord's redeeming love!

Martin Madan's Collection, 1763.

WALDECK. [H. P. 4.]

619 Ps. cvi. 2. "*Who can show forth all His praise?*"

Tune WALDECK. L. M.

1 OH! render thanks to God above,
The Fountain of eternal love;
Whose mercy firm through ages past
Has stood, and shall for ever last.

2 Who can His mighty deeds express,
Not only vast, but numberless?
What mortal eloquence can raise
His tribute of immortal praise?

3 Extend to me that favour, Lord,
Thou to Thy chosen dost afford:
When Thou return'st to set them free,
Let Thy salvation visit me.

4 Oh! may I worthy prove to see
Thy saints in full prosperity!
That I the joyful choir may join,
And count Thy people's triumph mine!

Tate and Brady, 1696.

NOTTINGHAM; *or*, ST. MAGNUS. [H. P. 39.]

620 Ps. cv. 3. "*Glory ye in His holy Name.*"

Tune NOTTINGHAM. C. M.

1 OH! render thanks and bless the Lord,
Invoke His sacred name,
Acquaint the nations with His deeds,
His matchless deeds proclaim.

2 Sing to His praise in lofty hymns,
His wondrous works rehearse;
Make them the theme of your discourse,
And subject of your verse.

3 Rejoice in His almighty name,
Alone to be adored;
And let their hearts o'erflow with joy
That humbly seek the Lord!

Tate and Brady, 1696.

---

621 Zech. ix. 9. "*Rejoice greatly . . . thy King cometh.*"

Tune SOSTHENES. 10 11, 11 11, 12 11.

1 SHOUT the glad tidings, exultingly sing;
Jerusalem triumphs, Messiah is King!
Zion the marvellous story is telling,
The Son of the Highest, how lowly His birth!
The brightest archangel in glory excelling,
He stoops to redeem thee, He reigns upon earth.
Shout the glad tidings, etc.

SOSTHENES. [H. P. 243.]

FINE.

D. C. al fine ad lib.

2 Tell how He cometh, from nation to nation;
The heart-cheering news let the earth echo round;
How free to the faithful He offers salvation,
How His people with joy everlasting are crowned.
Shout the glad tidings, etc.

3 Mortals, your homage be gratefully bringing,
And sweet let the gladsome hosanna arise!
Ye angels, the full hallelujah be singing,
One chorus resound through the earth and the skies.
Shout the glad tidings, etc.

W. A. Muhlenberg, D.D., 1827.

ZOHELETH (Stone of). [H. P. 207.]

622

Ps. cvii. 21. "*Oh that men would praise the Lord for His goodness.*" Tune ZOHELETH. 87, 87, 887.

1 SING praise to God who reigns above,
The God of all creation,
The God of power, the God of love,
The God of our salvation;
With healing balm my soul He fills,
And every faithless murmur stills:
To God all praise and glory.

2 The angel-host, O King of kings,
Thy praise for ever telling,
In earth and sky all living things
Beneath Thy shadow dwelling,
Adore the wisdom which could span,
And power which formed creation's plan:
To God all praise and glory.

3 What God's almighty power hath made
His gracious mercy keepeth;
By morning glow or evening shade
His watchful eye ne'er sleepeth:
Within the kingdom of His might,
Lo! all is just and all is right:
To God all praise and glory.

PART II.

4 The Lord is never far away;
But, through all grief distressing,
An ever present help and stay,
Our peace and joy and blessing:
As with a mother's tender hand
He leads His own, His chosen band:
To God all praise and glory.

5 When every earthly hope has flown
From sorrow's sons and daughters,
Our Father from His heavenly throne
Beholds the troubled waters;
And at His word the storm is stayed
Which made His children's hearts afraid:
To God all praise and glory.

6 Thus all my toilsome way along
I sing aloud Thy praises,
That men may hear the grateful song
My voice unwearied raises:
Be joyful in the Lord, my heart;
Both soul and body, bear your part:
To God all praise and glory!

Johann Jacob Schütz, 1673; *F. E. Cox* (tr.), 1841.

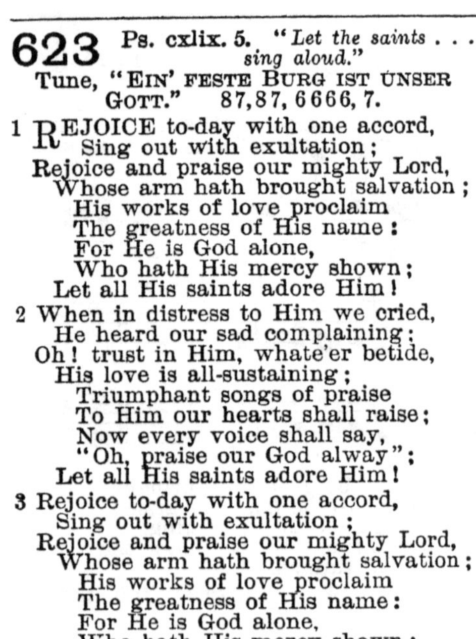

623 Ps. cxlix. 5. "*Let the saints . . . sing aloud.*"

Tune, "Ein' feste Burg ist unser Gott." 87,87, 6666, 7.

1 REJOICE to-day with one accord,
Sing out with exultation;
Rejoice and praise our mighty Lord,
Whose arm hath brought salvation;
His works of love proclaim
The greatness of His name:
For He is God alone,
Who hath His mercy shown;
Let all His saints adore Him!

2 When in distress to Him we cried,
He heard our sad complaining;
Oh! trust in Him, whate'er betide,
His love is all-sustaining;
Triumphant songs of praise
To Him our hearts shall raise;
Now every voice shall say,
"Oh, praise our God alway";
Let all His saints adore Him!

3 Rejoice to-day with one accord,
Sing out with exultation;
Rejoice and praise our mighty Lord,
Whose arm hath brought salvation;
His works of love proclaim
The greatness of His name:
For He is God alone,
Who hath His mercy shown;
Let all His saints adore Him!

Rev. Sir Henry W. Baker, Bart., 1860.

"EIN' FESTE BURG IST UNSER GOTT." [H. P. 252.]

THE OLD 100th TUNE. [H. P. 1.]

624 Ps. c. 2. "*Serve the Lord with gladness.*" Tune Old Hundredth. L. M.

1 ALL people that on earth do dwell,
Sing to the Lord with cheerful voice;
Him serve with mirth, His praise forth tell;
Come ye before Him and rejoice.

2 Know that the Lord is God indeed;
Without our aid He did us make;
We are His flock, He doth us feed;
And for His sheep He doth us take.

3 Oh, enter then His gates with praise,
Approach with joy His courts unto:
Praise, laud, and bless His name always,
For it is seemly so to do.

4 For why? the Lord our God is good,
His mercy is for ever sure;
His truth at all times firmly stood,
And shall from age to age endure!

William Kethe, 1562.

THE OLD 100th TUNE. [H. P. 1.]

625 Ps. c. 4. "*Enter into His . . . courts with praise.*" Tune Old Hundredth. L. M.

1 WITH one consent let all the earth
To God their cheerful voices raise;
Glad homage pay with awful mirth,
And sing before Him songs of praise:

2 Convinced that He is God alone,
From whom both we and all proceed;
We, whom He chooses for His own,
The flock that He vouchsafes to feed.

3 Oh, enter then His temple gate,
Thence to His courts devoutly press;
And still your grateful hymns repeat,
And still His name with praises bless.

4 For He's the Lord, supremely good,
His mercy is for ever sure;
His truth, which always firmly stood,
To endless ages shall endure!

Tate and Brady, 1696.

626 Job xxxviii. 7. "*The morning stars sang together, and all the sons of God shouted for joy.*"

Tune Pisgah. 77, 77.

1 SONGS of praise the angels sang,
Heaven with Hallelujahs rang,
When Jehovah's work begun,
When He spake, and it was done.

2 Songs of praise awoke the morn,
When the Prince of Peace was born:
Songs of praise arose, when He
Captive led captivity.

3 Heaven and earth must pass away;
Songs of praise shall crown that day:
God will make new heavens and earth;
Songs of praise shall hail their birth.

4 And shall man alone be dumb
Till that glorious kingdom come?
No! the church delights to raise
Psalms and hymns and songs of praise.

5 Saints below, with heart and voice,
Still in songs of praise rejoice;
Learning here, by faith and love,
Songs of praise to sing above.

6 Borne upon their latest breath,
Songs of praise shall conquer death;
Then, amidst eternal joy,
Songs of praise their powers employ!

James Montgomery, 1819.

PISGAH (Mount). [H. P. 137.]

Hal - le - lu - jah, Hal - le - lu - jah!

AVEN (Plain of). [H. P. 79.]

627 Rev. xv. 3. "*The song of the Lamb.*" Tune Aven. S. M.

1 AWAKE, and sing the song
Of Moses and the Lamb;
Tune every heart, and every tongue,
To praise the Saviour's name.

2 Sing of His dying love,
Sing of His rising power;
Sing how He intercedes above
For all whose sins He bore.

3 Sing till we feel our hearts
Ascending with our tongues;
Sing till the love of sin departs,
And grace inspires our songs.

4 Soon shall we hear Him say,
"Ye blessèd children, come";
Soon will He call us hence away,
To our eternal home.

5 There shall our joy be full,
And love a warmer flame,
And sweeter voices tune the song
Of Moses and the Lamb!

Isaac Watts, D.D., 1709; *William Hammond*, 1745.

RIPON. [H. P. 240.]

628 Rev. xix. 1. "*Salvation, and glory, and honour, and power, unto the Lord our God.*"

Tune Ripon. 10 10, 11 11. Or Hanover.

1 YE servants of God, Your Master proclaim,
And publish abroad His wonderful name;
The name all victorious Of Jesus extol;
His kingdom is glorious And reigns over all.

2 God ruleth on high, Almighty to save;
And still He is nigh, His presence we have;
The great congregation His triumph shall sing,
Ascribing salvation To Jesus our King.

3 Salvation to God, Who sits on the throne,
Let all cry aloud, And honour the Son;
The praises of Jesus The angels proclaim,
Fall down on their faces, And worship the Lamb.

4 Then let us adore, And give Him His right,
All glory and power, And wisdom and might;
All honour and blessing, With angels above,
And thanks never ceasing, For infinite love!

Charles Wesley, 1744. (a.)

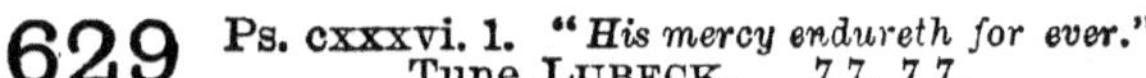

629 Ps. cxxxvi. 1. "*His mercy endureth for ever.*"
Tune LUBECK. 77, 77.

LUBECK. [H. P. 139.]

Hal - le - lu - jah, Hal - le - lu - jah!

1 LET us, with a gladsome mind,
Praise the Lord, for He is kind:
For His mercies shall endure,
Ever faithful, ever sure.

2 Let us sound His name abroad,
For of gods He is the God:
For His mercies shall endure,
Ever faithful, ever sure.

3 He, with all-commanding might,
Filled the new-made world with light:
For His mercies shall endure,
Ever faithful, ever sure.

4 All things living He doth feed;
His full hand supplies their need:
For His mercies shall endure,
Ever faithful, ever sure.

5 He His chosen race did bless
In the wasteful wilderness:
For His mercies shall endure,
Ever faithful, ever sure.

6 He hath, with a piteous eye,
Looked upon our misery:
For His mercies shall endure,
Ever faithful, ever sure.

7 Let us then, with gladsome mind,
Praise the Lord, for He is kind:
For His mercies shall endure,
Ever faithful, ever sure!

John Milton, 1628.

YORK. [H. P. 45.

630 Ps. ix. 1. "*I will praise Thee, O Lord, with my whole heart.*"
Tune YORK. C. M. Or GLOUCESTER.

1 TO celebrate Thy praise, O Lord,
I will my heart prepare;
To all the listening world Thy works,
Thy wondrous works, declare.

2 The thought of them shall to my soul
Exalted pleasure bring;
Whilst to Thy name, O Thou Most High,
Triumphant praise I sing.

3 All those who have His goodness proved
Will in His truth confide;
Whose mercy ne'er forsook the man
That on His help relied.

4 His suffering saints, when most distressed,
He ne'er forgets to aid;
Their expectations shall be crowned,
Though for a time delayed.

5 Sing praises, therefore, to the Lord
From Zion, His abode;
Proclaim His deeds, till all the world
Confess no other God!

Tate and Brady, 1696.

ARRAN. [H. P. 59.]

631 Ps. cxxxvii. 3. "*Sing us one of the songs of Zion.*" Tune ARRAN. C. M.

1 SING them, my children, sing them still,
Those sweet and holy songs!
Oh! let the psalms of Zion's hill
Be heard from youthful tongues.

2 Oh! sing them at the cheerful dawn,
The rising morn to cheer;
And sing them round the evening hearth,
When fires are blazing clear.

3 Sing them when Sabbath schools are met,
And your young voices raise
Their Sabbath evening melodies,
To their Redeemer's praise.

4 So shall each unforgotten word,
When distant far you roam,
Call back your hearts which once it stirred,
To childhood's blessèd home!

Horatius Bonar, D.D., 1844.

GOSHEN. [H. P. 125.]

632 Ps. xxviii. 7. "*With my song will I praise Him.*" Tune Goshen. 7 6, 7 6.

1 SING to the little children,
And they will listen well;
Sing grand and holy music,
For they can feel its spell.

2 Sing at the cottage bedside;
They have no music there,
And the voice of praise is silent,
After the voice of prayer.

3 Sing of the gentle Saviour
In the simplest hymns you know,
And the pain-dimmed eye will brighten
As the soothing verses flow.

4 When you long to bear the Message
Home to some troubled breast,
Then sing with loving fervour,
"Come unto Me, and rest."

5 Sing when His mighty mercies
And marvellous love you feel,
And the deep joy of gratitude
Springs freshly as you kneel.

6 Sing on in grateful gladness!
Rejoice in this good thing
Which the Lord thy God hath given thee:
The happy power to sing!

Frances Ridley Havergal, 1867.

See Hymns 1—16, 24—26, 30, 88—92, 133—136, 191, 192, 286, 368, 430, 432, 1022—1024.

(25) ZEAL.

633 1 Sam. xii. 24. "*Consider how great things He hath done for you.*"

Tune Baca. 6 6 6 6, 6 6.

BACA (Valley of). [H. P. 116.]

1 I GAVE My life for thee,
My precious blood I shed
That thou might'st ransomed be,
And quickened from the dead.
I gave My life for thee:
What hast thou given for Me?

2 I spent long years for thee,
In weariness and woe,
That an eternity
Of joy thou mightest know.
I spent long years for thee:
Hast thou spent one for Me?

3 My Father's home of light,
My rainbow-circled throne,
I left, for earthly night,
For wanderings sad and lone.
I left it all for thee:
Hast thou left aught for Me?

4 I suffered much for thee,
More than thy tongue may tell
Of bitterest agony,
To rescue thee from hell.
I suffered much for thee:
What canst thou bear for Me?

5 And I have brought to thee,
Down from My home above,
Salvation full and free,
My pardon and My love.
Great gifts I brought to thee:
What hast thou brought to Me?

6 Oh! let thy life be given,
Thy years for Him be spent,
World-fetters all be riven,
And joy with suffering blent.
Bring thou thy worthless all:
Follow thy Saviour's call!

Frances Ridley Havergal, 1859.

LONDON NEW; *or*, NEWTON. [H. P. 55.]

634 2 Tim. ii. 3. "*Endure hardness, as a good soldier of Jesus Christ.*" Tune London New. C. M.

1 ARE we the soldiers of the cross,
The followers of the Lamb?
And shall we fear to own His cause,
Or blush to speak His name?

2 Now we must fight, if we would reign:
Increase our courage, Lord;
We'll bear the toil, endure the pain,
Supported by Thy word.

3 Thy saints in all this glorious war
Shall conquer, though they're slain;
They see the triumph from afar,
And shall with Jesus reign.

4 When that illustrious day shall rise,
And all Thine armies shine
In robes of victory through the skies,
The glory shall be Thine!

Isaac Watts, D.D., 1721.

635 Phil. iii. 14. "*I press toward the mark.*"

Tune OLYMPAS. 76, 76, 77, 76.

1 RISE, my soul, and stretch thy wings,
Thy better portion trace ;
Rise from transitory things,
Towards heaven thy native place!
Sun, and moon, and stars decay,
Time shall soon this earth remove ;
Rise, my soul, and haste away
To seats prepared above!

2 Rivers to the ocean run,
Nor stay in all their course ;
Fire ascending seeks the sun :
Both speed them to their source:
So my soul, derived from God,
Pants to view His glorious face,
Upward tends to His abode,
To rest in His embrace.

3 Cease, ye pilgrims, cease to mourn,
Press onward to the prize ;
Soon your Saviour will return
Triumphant in the skies!
Yet a season, and you know
Happy entrance will be given,
All your sorrows left below,
And earth exchanged for heaven!

Robert Seagrave, 1742.

636 Deut. xxxii. 12. "*The Lord alone did lead him.*"

Tune EVERTON. 87, 87. D. Or ESDRAELON.

1 RISE, my soul, thy God directs thee,
Stranger hands no more impede ;
Pass thou on ; His hand protects thee,
Strength that has the captive freed.
Is the wilderness before thee,
Desert lands where drought abides?
Heavenly springs shall there restore thee,
Fresh from God's exhaustless tides.

2 Light Divine surrounds thy going,
God Himself shall mark thy way;
Secret blessings richly flowing
Lead to everlasting day.
In the desert God will teach thee
What the God that thou hast found,
Patient, gracious, powerful, holy,
All His grace shall there abound.

3 On to Canaan's rest still wending,
E'en thy wants and woes shall bring
Suited grace, from high descending ;
Thou shalt taste of mercy's spring.
Though thy way be long and dreary,
Eagle-strength He'll still renew :
Garments fresh and feet unweary
Tell how God hath brought thee through.

4 When to Canaan's long loved dwelling
Love Divine thy foot shall bring,
There with shouts of triumph swelling,
Zion's songs in rest to sing—
There no stranger-God shall meet thee,
Stranger thou in courts above,
He who to His rest shall greet thee
Greets thee with a well-known love!

J. N. Darby, 1837.

637 Heb. xii. 1. "*Let us run.*"

Tune IONA. C. M.

1 AWAKE, my soul, stretch every nerve,
And press with vigour on ;
A heavenly race demands thy zeal,
And an immortal crown.

2 A cloud of witnesses around
Hold thee in full survey ;
Forget the steps already trod,
And onward urge thy way.

3 'Tis God's all-animating voice
That calls thee from on high ;
'Tis His own hand presents the prize
To thine aspiring eye.

4 Blest Saviour, introduced by Thee,
Have I my race begun ;
And crowned with victory, at Thy feet
I'll lay my honours down!

Philip Doddridge, D.D., 1755.

IONA. [H. P. 37.]

NARENZA. [H. P. 80.]

638 Eph. vi. 11. *"Put on the whole armour of God."* Tune NARENZA. S. M.

1 SOLDIERS of Christ, arise,
And put your armour on,
Strong in the strength which God supplies
Through His eternal Son:

2 Strong in the Lord of Hosts,
And in His mighty power;
Who in the strength of Jesus trusts
Is more than conqueror.

3 Stand then in His great might,
With all His strength endued;
But take, to arm you for the fight,
The panoply of God.

4 To keep your armour bright,
Attend with constant care,
Still walking in your Captain's sight,
And watching unto prayer.

5 In fellowship alone,
To God with faith draw near:
Approach His courts, besiege His throne
With all the power of prayer:

6 From strength to strength go on,
Wrestle, and fight, and pray,
Tread all the powers of darkness down,
And win the well-fought day!

Charles Wesley, 1749.

LINUS. *Minor—verses* 1, 2, 3. [H. P. 336.]

639 John ix. 4. *"I must work the works of Him that sent Me, while it is day."* Tune LINUS. 87, 87.

1 SHALL this life of mine be wasted?
Shall this vineyard lie untilled?
Shall true joy pass by untasted,
And this soul remain unfilled?

2 Shall the God-given hours be scattered,
Like the leaves upon the plain?
Shall the blossoms die unwatered
By the drops of heavenly rain?

3 Shall this heart still spend its treasures
On the things that fade and die?
Shall it court the hollow pleasures
Of bewildering vanity?

Major.

4 No, I was not born to trifle
Life away in dreams or sin!
No, I must not, dare not, stifle
Longings such as these within!

5 Swiftly moving, upward, onward,
Let my soul in faith be borne,
Calmly gazing—skyward, sunward,
Let my eye unshrinking turn!

6 Where the cross, God's love revealing,
Sets the fettered spirit free;
Where it sheds its wondrous healing,
There, my soul, thy rest shall be.

7 Then no longer, idly dreaming,
Shall I fling my years away;
But each precious hour redeeming,
Wait for the eternal day!

Horatius Bonar, D.D., 1857.

PATMOS. [H. P. 147.]

640 2 Tim. ii. 3. "*A good soldier of Jesus Christ.*"

Tune PATMOS. 7 7, 7 7.

1 OFT in sorrow, oft in woe;
Onward, Christians, onward go;
Fight the fight, maintain the strife,
Strengthened by the Bread of Life.

2 Onward, Christians, onward go;
Join the war, and face the foe;
Faint not! much doth yet remain;
Dreary is the long campaign.

3 Shrink not, Christians! will ye yield?
Will ye quit the battle-field?
Will ye flee in danger's hour?
Know ye not your Captain's power?

4 Let your drooping hearts be glad;
March, in heavenly armour clad;
Fight, nor think the battle long;
Victory soon shall tune your song.

5 Let not sorrow dim your eye,
Soon shall every tear be dry;
Let not fears your course impede;
Great your strength, if great your need.

6 Onward then to glory move;
More than conquerors ye shall prove;
Though opposed by many a foe,
Christian soldiers, onward go!

H. Kirke White, 1806; *F. F. Maitland*, 1827.

SARDIS. (HYMN CHANT.) [H. P. No. VI.]

641 Gal. ii. 20. "*I live by the faith of the Son of God.*"

Tune, Hymn Chant SARDIS. 10 10, 10 10.

1 TEACH me to live! 'tis easier far to die—
Gently and silently to pass away—
On earth's long night to close the heavy eye,
And waken in the realms of glorious day.

2 Teach me that harder lesson—how to live,
To serve Thee in the darkest paths of life!
Arm me for conflict now—fresh vigour give,
And make me more than conqueror in the strife.

3 Teach me to live!—Thy purpose to fulfil;
Bright for Thy glory let my taper shine!
Each day renew, remould my stubborn will:
Closer round Thee my heart's affections twine.

4 Teach me to live for self and sin no more;
But use the time remaining to me yet,
Not mine own pleasure seeking as before—
Wasting no precious hours in vain regret.

5 Teach me to live! no idler let me be.
But in Thy service hand and heart employ;
Prepared to do Thy bidding cheerfully—
Be this my highest and my holiest joy.

6 Teach me to live!—my daily cross to bear;
Nor murmur though I bend beneath its load.
Only be with me; let me feel Thee near:
Thy smile sheds gladness on the darkest road.

7 Teach me to live!—and find my life in Thee—
Looking from earth and earthly things away;
Let me not falter, but untiringly
Press on; and gain new strength and power each day.

8 Teach me to live!—with kindly words for all—
Wearing no cold, repulsive brow of gloom;
Waiting, with cheerful patience, till Thy call
Summons my spirit to her heavenly home!

Ellen Elizabeth Burman, 1860.

See Hymns 765—773, 956, 970.

(26) COURAGE.

642 Ps. lxxi. 16. "*I will go in the strength of the Lord God.*"

Tune AQUILA. 9 9 9 8, 8 8 8 8.

AQUILA. [H. P. 232.]

1 I WILL go in the strength of the Lord,
In the path He hath marked for my feet;
I will follow the light of His word,
Nor shrink from the dangers I meet.
His presence my steps shall attend;
His fulness my wants shall supply;
On Him, till my journey shall end,
My hope shall securely rely.

COURAGE. 249

2 I will go in the strength of the Lord
To the work He appoints me to do;
In the joy which His smile shall afford,
My soul shall her vigour renew.
His wisdom will guard me from harm,
His power my sufficiency prove:
I trust His omnipotent arm;
I rest in His covenant love.

3 I will go in the strength of the Lord
To each conflict which faith may require;
And His grace, as my shield and reward,
My courage and zeal shall inspire.
If He give the word of command
To meet and encounter the foe,
With sling and with stone in my hand,
In the strength of the Lord I will go!

Church Missionary Gleaner, January, 1861.

FRANCONIA. [H. P. 87.]

643 Josh. i. 9. "*Be strong and of a good courage.*"

Tune FRANCONIA. S. M.

1 YOUR harps, ye trembling saints,
Down from the willows take:
Loud to the praise of love Divine,
Bid every string awake.

2 Though in a foreign land,
We are not far from home;
And nearer to our house above
We every moment come.

3 His grace will to the end
Stronger and brighter shine;
Nor present things, nor things to come,
Shall quench the spark Divine.

4 The people of His choice
He will not cast away;
Yet do not always here expect
On Tabor's mount to stay.

5 When we in darkness walk
Nor feel the heavenly flame,
Then is the time to trust our God,
And rest upon His name.

6 Soon shall our doubts and fears
Subside at His control;
His loving-kindness shall break through
The midnight of the soul.

7 Wait till the shadows flee;
Wait thy appointed hour,
Wait till the Bridegroom of thy soul
Reveals His sovereign power.

8 Tarry His leisure then,
Although He seem to stay,
A moment's intercourse with Him
Thy grief will overpay.

9 Blest is the man, O God,
That stays himself on Thee!
Who waits for Thy salvation, Lord,
Shall Thy salvation see!

Augustus M. Toplady, 1772.

644 1 Tim. vi. 12. "*Fight the good fight of faith.*"

Tune ST. SILAS. 10 10, 11 11.

ST. SILAS. [H. P. 98.]

* For verse 3 omit first note.

1 BREAST the wave, Christian, when it is strongest;
Watch for day, Christian, when the night's longest;
Onward, and onward still, be thine endeavour;
The rest that remaineth will be for ever.

2 Fight the fight, Christian—Jesus is o'er thee;
Run the race, Christian—heaven is before thee:
He who hath promisèd faltereth never;
The love of eternity flows on for ever.

3 Lift the eye, Christian, just as it closeth;
Raise the heart, Christian, ere it reposeth;
Thee from the love of Christ nothing shall sever:
Mount when thy work is done—praise Him for ever.

Joseph Stammers, 1830.

645 Eph. vi. 10. "*Be strong in the Lord.*"

Tune St. John's. 6666, 88.

ST. JOHN. [H. P. 272.]

1 HARK, 'tis a martial sound!
To arms, ye saints, to arms!
Your foes are gathering round,
And peace has lost its charms:
Prepare the helmet, sword, and shield;
The trumpet calls you to the field.

2 No common foes appear
To dare you to the fight,
But such as own no fear,
And glory in their might:
The powers of darkness are at hand;
Resist, or bow to their command.

3 An arm of flesh must fail
In such a strife as this;
He only can prevail
Whose arm immortal is:
'Tis Heaven itself the strength must yield,
And weapons fit for such a field.

4 And Heaven supplies them too!
The Lord, who never faints,
Is greater than the foe,
And He is with His saints:
Thus armed, they venture to the fight;
Thus armed, they put their foes to flight.

5 And, when the conflict's past,
On yonder peaceful shore
They shall repose at last,
And see their foes no more;
The fruits of victory enjoy,
And never more their arms employ!

Thomas Kelly, 1809.

FRANKFORT. [H. P. 183.]

646 Heb. xii. 11. "*Nevertheless, afterward.*"

Tune Frankfort. 87, 87.

1 NOW, the sowing and the weeping,
Working hard and waiting long;
Afterward, the golden reaping,
Harvest home and grateful song.

2 Now, the pruning, sharp, unsparing;
Scattered blossom, bleeding shoot;
Afterward, the plenteous bearing
Of the Master's pleasant fruit.

3 Now, the plunge, the briny burden,
Blind faint gropings in the sea;
Afterward, the pearly guerdon
That shall make the diver free.

4 Now, the long and toilsome duty
Stone by stone to carve and bring;
Afterward, the perfect beauty
Of the palace of the King.

5 Now, the tuning and the tension,
Wailing minors, discord strong;
Afterward, the grand ascension
Of the Alleluia song.

6 Now, the spirit conflict-riven,
Wounded heart, unequal strife;
Afterward, the triumph given,
And the victor's crown of life.

7 Now, the training, strange and lowly,
Unexplained and tedious now;
Afterward, the service holy,
And the Master's "Enter thou!"

Frances Ridley Havergal, 1870.

See Hymn 149.

EVAN I. [H. P. 54.]

(27) PEACE AND JOY.

647 Isa. xxvi. 3. "*Perfect peace.*" Tune Evan I. C. M. Or Kent.

1 A MIND at "perfect peace" with God!
Oh, what a word is this!
A sinner reconciled through blood—
This, this indeed is peace.

2 By nature and by practice far—
How very far, from God!
Yet now by grace brought nigh to Him,
Through faith in Jesu's blood.

3 So nigh, so very nigh to God,
I cannot nearer be;
For in the person of His Son
I am as near as He.

4 So dear, so very dear to God,
More dear I cannot be;
The love wherewith He loves His Son,
Such is His love for me.

5 Why should I ever careful be,
Since such a God is mine?
He watches o'er me night and day,
And tells me, "Mine is thine!"

Catesby Paget, 1855.

EIRENE. [H. P. 246.]

648 John xiv. 27. *"Peace I leave with you, My peace I give unto you."* Tune Eirene. 11 10, 11 10.

1 CHILD of My love; ere from the cross uplifted,
The heavens receive Me to My kingly throne,
My peace I leave thee—not as earth bestoweth
Her fading gifts, I give unto Mine own.

2 Child of My purchase! heir of fadeless glory,
In tribulation great thou shalt be tried;
Yet in My peace, which passeth understanding,
Thy steadfast soul for ever shall abide.

3 My peace I give thee—though to thy dim vision
The narrow path in darkness fade away;
Strengthen thy faltering faith, the morn shall show thee
My bleeding footprints on the rugged way.

4 Peace shall be thine—though bitter memories thronging,
Of countless sins, across thy spirit roll,
Although the' accuser of the holy brethren
With darkest doubts assail thy weary soul.

5 Peace, in the lonely hours of weary waiting,
In valley twilight, cold, and sad, and grey;
Behold the mountain tops already rosy
With the bright flush of the long looked-for day!

6 Peace, in the day when death's cold waters swelling
Around thy feet thy trembling soul affright;
The Hand that in the wilderness hath led thee
By the right way shall guide thee into light.

7 Peace, when the strange new sound of angel hymnings
Breaks in wild music on thy wondering ear;
Peace, when thy human soul, unclothed and lonely,
Before My throne in judgment shall appear.

8 Peace perfected, when from the din of battle
The everlasting doors shall close thee in:
When thou shalt know, upon My throne beside Me,
Victorious calm, freedom from strife and sin!

Isabella I. Bird, 1860.

649 John xvi. 27. *"The Father Himself loveth you."* Tune Eirene. 10 10, 10 10, 10 12. Or Laodicea.

1 BE still, my soul, Jehovah loveth thee!
Fret not, nor murmur at thy weary lot;
Though dark and lone thy journey seems to be,
Be sure that thou art ne'er by Him forgot.
He ever loves; then trust Him, trust Him still:
Let all thy care be this—the doing of His will.

2 Thy hand in His, like fondest, happiest child,
Place thou, nor draw it for a moment thence;
Walk thou with Him, a Father reconciled,
Till in His own good time He calls thee hence.
Walk with Him now; so shall thy way be bright,
And all thy soul be filled with His most glorious light.

3 Take courage, faint not, though the foe be strong,
Christ is thy strength! He fighteth on thy side;
Swift be thy race; remember 'tis not long,
The goal is near; the prize He will provide.
And then from earthly toil thou restest ever;
Never again to toil, or fight, or fear—Oh! never.

4 He comes, with His reward; 'tis just at hand;
He comes in glory to His promised throne;
My soul, rejoice! ere long thy feet shall stand
Within the city of the Blessèd One.
Thy perils past, thy heritage secure,
Thy tears all wiped away, thy joy for ever sure!

Horatius Bonar, D.D., 1867.

650

Ps. xvi. 11. *"In Thy presence is fulness of joy; at Thy right hand there are pleasures for evermore."*

Tune IDUMEA. 87, 87, 47.

1 FAITHFUL pilgrim, homeward wending,
Toward the city sure and fair;
Hopeful pilgrim, heavenward tending,
Knowest thou what awaits thee there?
Joy in fulness,
Pleasures bright for evermore.

2 Here—the fierceness of temptation,
Frequent tears for frequent sin,
Strife of secret tribulation:
But when once thou 'rt entered in,
Joy in fulness,
Pleasures bright for evermore.

3 Here—the broken voice of weeping
For thine own or others' care;
Wave of stormy sorrow sweeping
O'er thy troubled heart: but there,
Joy in fulness,
Pleasures bright for evermore.

4 Here—the shade of death's dark portal,
Widowed grief and orphan cries,
Dust to dust, as vile and mortal:
But when thou hast gained the prize,
Joy in fulness,
Pleasures bright for evermore.

5 Keep my soul, O loving Saviour,
From the world and Satan's snare;
Guard me by Thy gracious favour:
Make me meet with Thee to share
Joy in fulness,
Pleasures bright for evermore!

Ebenezer Hewlett, 1860.

651

Mark vi. 31. *"Come ye yourselves apart."* Tune KENT. C. M.

1 FAR from the world, O Lord, I flee,
From strife and tumult far;
From scenes where Satan wages still
His most successful war.

2 The calm retreat, the silent shade,
With prayer and praise agree,
And seem by Thy sweet bounty made
For those who follow Thee.

3 There, if Thy Spirit touch the soul,
And grace her mean abode,
Oh! with what peace, and joy, and love,
She communes with her God!

4 There, like the nightingale, she pours
Her solitary lays,
Nor asks a witness of her song,
Nor thirsts for human praise.

5 Author and Guardian of my life;
Sweet Source of light Divine;
And, all harmonious names in one,
My Saviour! Thou art mine!

6 What thanks I owe Thee, and what love,
A boundless, endless store,
Shall echo through the realms above
When time shall be no more!

William Cowper, 1765.

652

Col. i. 13. *"He hath translated us into the kingdom of His dear Son."* Tune KENT. C. M. Or EDEN.

1 HAPPY the souls to Jesus joined,
And saved by grace alone:
Walking in all His ways, they find
Their heaven on earth begun.

2 The church triumphant in Thy love,
Their mighty joys we know:
They sing the Lamb in hymns above,
And we in hymns below.

3 Thee in Thy glorious realms they praise,
And bow before Thy throne;
We in the kingdom of Thy grace:
The kingdoms are but one.

4 The holy to the holiest leads;
From thence our spirits rise;
And he that in Thy statutes treads
Shall meet Thee in the skies!

Charles Wesley, 1745.

653

Phil. iv. 4. *"Rejoice in the Lord alway."* Tune HOBAH. 12 11, 12 11.

1 REJOICE in the Lord! there is light in the dwelling,
And peace in the spirit, where Christ is the Guest;
And surely the chorus might always be swelling
Around the glad threshold which Jesus has blessed.

2 Rejoice in the Lord! He will scatter the sadness
That broods o'er the sanctified home of His friends;
And days as they pass will be radiant with gladness,
Where prayer from the family altar ascends.

HOBAH. [H. P. 248.]

3 Rejoice in the Lord! the fresh flowerets are springing
In fragrance and beauty to gladden thy way:
The Father of mercies His largess is flinging—
New tokens of love for each newly born day.

4 Rejoice in the Lord! He is tenderly leading
Each step that His wisdom requires thee to take;
And He will supply all the strength thou art needing,
Who loveth for ever, and will not forsake.

5 Rejoice in the Lord! there is joy for thee ever,
If thou in thy lifetime belongest to Him;
A bond—all of love—which no change can e'er sever
A sun o'er thy head which no storm-cloud can dim

6 Rejoice in the Lord! He awaits thee in heaven,
With myriads who make His light service thei' choice;
And shortly the robe and the crown will be given
To thee! Then, believer, oh! always rejoice!

Marianne Farningham Hearn, 1860.

---

654 Ps. xci. 4. "*Under His wings shalt thou trust.*"
Tune IDUMEA. 87, 87, 47.

1 HAPPY they who trust in Jesus,
Sweet their portion is and sure:
When the foe on others seizes,
He will keep His own secure;
Happy people!
Happy, though despised and poor.

2 Ye whom God has saved from error,
Ye "who know the joyful sound,"
Fear ye not the nightly terror;
Arms of mercy close you round:
Dread no evil;
God will all your foes confound.

3 Since His love and mercy found you,
Ye are precious in His sight;
Thousands now may fall around you,
Thousands more be put to flight;
But His presence
Keeps you safe, by day and night.

4 Lo! your Saviour never slumbers,
Ever watchful is His care;
Though ye cannot boast of numbers,
In His strength secure ye are;
Sweet their portion,
Who our Saviour's kindness share.

5 As a bird beneath her feathers
Guards the objects of her care,
So the Lord His children gathers,
Spreads His wings and hides them there;
Thus protected,
All their foes they boldly dare!

Thomas Kelly, 1806.

WINCHESTER. [H. P. 46.]

655 Rom. xv. 13. "*Joy and peace in believing.*"
Tune WINCHESTER. C. M.

1 JOY is a fruit that will not grow
In nature's barren soil;
All we can boast, till Christ we know,
Is vanity and toil.

2 But where the Lord has planted grace,
And made His glories known,
There fruits of heavenly joy and peace
Are found, and there alone.

3 A bleeding Saviour seen by faith,
A sense of pardoning love,
A hope that triumphs over death,
Give joys like those above.

4 To take a glimpse within the veil,
To know that God is mine,
Are springs of joy that never fail—
Unspeakable, Divine!

5 These are the joys which satisfy
And sanctify the mind;
Which make the spirit mount on high,
And leave the world behind!

John Newton, 1779.

GIBBONS. [H. P. 148.]

656 Deut. xxxiii. 29. "*Happy art thou.*"
Tune GIBBONS. 77, 77. Or PATMOS.

1 HAPPY Christian! God's own child,
Chosen, called, and reconciled;
Once a rebel far from God,
Now brought nigh by Jesu's blood.

2 Happy Christian! look on high,
See thy portion in the sky:
Fixed by everlasting love,
Who that portion can remove?

3 Happy Christian! though the earth
Knows not now thy heavenly birth,
Yet thy God shall soon proclaim,
Through all worlds, thy favoured name.

4 Happy Christian! hear Him say,
"Turn thy heart from earth away,
Leave the world and all its woes,
Seek in Me thy full repose."

5 Happy Christian! look on high,
Christ, thy Lord, thy life, is nigh!
Soon thou shalt His glory see—
Learn His wondrous love to thee!

John Harington Evans' Collection, 1838.

THYATIRA. (HYMN CHANT.) [H. P. No. V.]

657 Job xxii. 21. "*Acquaint now thyself with Him, and be at peace.*"
Tune, Hymn Chant THYATIRA. L. M. Or HERMON.

1 ART thou acquainted, O my soul!
With such a Saviour, such a Friend?
Whose power can all events control,
And from all evils can defend?

2 Why art thou then oppressed with fears?
Knowledge of Him should give thee peace,
Should check these often-flowing tears,
And bid these sad misgivings cease.

3 Is it the past that gives thee pain?
Transgressions, falls, dost thou deplore?
The' atoning blood pleads not in vain,
Thy God remembers them no more.

4 Do present troubles vex thy mind?
Sufferings of body, mental care?
In God a refuge thou wilt find;
And oh! what sweet relief in prayer.

5 Dost thou o'er friends much valued weep,
Who seem in hopeless fetters bound?
Christ will seek out His wandering sheep,
Those who seem lost will then be found.

6 Dost thou the unknown future dread?
Thy passage through death's awful vale?
E'en there shall light around be shed;
Thy God's sure promise cannot fail.

7 Dost thou with dread still greater shrink
From pain for those on earth most dear?
And oft with sickening anguish think
On all they yet may suffer here?

8 O faithless, unbelieving heart,
So slow to trust that tenderest Friend:
Who then will needful strength impart,
Who "loving, loves unto the end!"

9 No longer doubt, nor fear, nor grieve,
Nor on uncertain evils dwell:
Past, present, future calmly leave
To Him who will do all things well!

Charlotte Elliott, 1830.

EVAN I. [H. P. 54.]

658 Ps. xxiii. 5. "*My cup runneth over.*"
Tune EVAN I. C. M.

1 O THOU whose bounty fills my cup
With every blessing meet,
I give Thee thanks for every drop,
The bitter and the sweet.

2 I praise Thee for the desert road,
And for the river side;
For all Thy goodness hath bestowed,
And all Thy grace denied.

3 I thank Thee both for smile and frown,
And for the gain and loss;
I praise Thee for the future crown,
And for the present cross.

4 I thank Thee for the wing of love,
Which stirred my worldly nest,
And for the stormy clouds that drove
The flutterer to Thy breast.

5 I bless Thee for the glad increase,
And for the waning joy;
And for this strange, this settled peace,
Which nothing can destroy!

Jane Crewdson, 1860.

LAODICEA. (HYMN CHANT.) [H. P. No. VIII.]

659

Cant. ii. 16. "*My Beloved is mine, and I am His.*" Tune, Hymn Chant LAODICEA. 10 10, 10 10, 10 10.

1 LONG did I toil, and knew no earthly rest;
Far did I rove, and found no certain home;
At last I sought them in His sheltering breast,
Who opes His arms, and bids the weary come:
With Him I found a home, a rest Divine;
And I, since then, am His, and He is mine.

2 Yes! He is mine! and nought of earthly things,
Not all the charms of pleasure, wealth, or power,
The fame of heroes or the pomp of kings,
Could tempt me to forego His love an hour.
Go, worthless world, I cry, with all that's thine!
Go! I my Saviour's am, and He is mine.

3 The good I have is from His stores supplied;
The ill is only what He deems the best;
He for my friend, I'm rich with nought beside;
And poor without Him, though of all possessed:
Changes may come; I take, or I resign;
Content while I am His, while He is mine.

4 Whate'er may change, in Him no change is seen;
A glorious Sun, that wanes not nor declines:
Above the clouds and storms He walks serene,
And sweetly on His people's darkness shines:
All may depart; I fret not, nor repine,
While I my Saviour's am, while He is mine.

5 He stays me falling, lifts me up when down,
Reclaims me wandering, guards from every foe;
Plants on my worthless brow the victor's crown,
Which, in return, before His feet I throw,
Grieved that I cannot better grace His shrine,
Who deigns to own me His, as He is mine.

6 While here, alas! I know but half His love,
But half discern Him, and but half adore;
But when I meet Him in the realms above,
I hope to love Him better, praise Him more,
And feel, and tell, amid the choir Divine,
How fully I am His, and He is mine!

Henry Francis Lyte, 1833.

ST. ASAPH. [H. P. 307.]

660

John xiv. 27. "*My peace I give unto you.*" Tune ST. ASAPH. 87, 87. D.

1 PEACE in Jesus! blessèd promise,
Covenant word of changeless love,
Sealed in blood, and daily witnessed
By Thy grace, Eternal Dove.
Peace in Jesus! oh what blessing,
Calm and pure, our spirits know;
When, the ties of earth forgotten,
All our joys from Jesus flow.

2 Softly glides Siloah's fountain
Through this wide and howling waste;
Surest, sweetest peace affording
All, its hallowed streams who taste.
From the conflict, faint and thirsty,
Deep we drain the cup of love;
Oh that deeper still our spirits
Might its endless blessings prove.

3 Peace in Jesus! though around us
Rage the tempest's angry strife;
Though the deep her fountains open,
O'er them floats the ark of life.
There the weary dove, returning
From that dark and trackless sea,
Folds in peace her drooping pinions,
Sheltered from the storm in Thee.

4 Though on earth we've scorn and trouble,
In ourselves but shame and sin;
All without, the reign of darkness,
Fearful conflict oft within;
He who died, and lives for ever,
Saves and guards from every ill;
Jesus walks upon the waters,
And commandeth, "Peace, be still!"

Hymns of the Household of Faith, 1861.

ST. CHRYSOSTOM. [H. P. 53.]

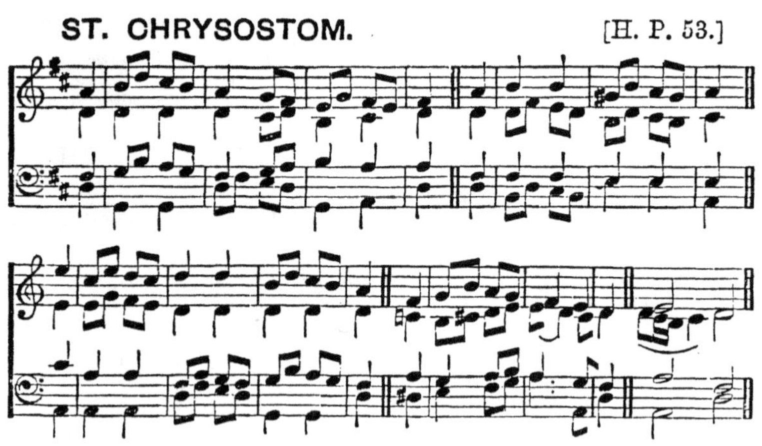

661 Ps. iv. 6. *"Lift Thou up the light of Thy countenance."*

Tune St. Chrysostom. C. M. Or Nayland.

1 ETERNAL Sun of Righteousness,
Display Thy beams Divine,
And cause the glory of Thy face
Upon my heart to shine.

2 Light, in Thy light, oh may I see,
Thy grace and mercy prove;
Revived and comforted by Thee,
The God of pardoning love.

3 Lift up Thy countenance serene,
And let Thy happy child
Behold, without a cloud between,
The Godhead reconciled.

4 Thy peace, with holiness, bestow
On me through grace forgiven;
My wish, to serve Thee here below,
Then reign with Thee in heaven!

Charles Wesley, 1741. (a.)

662 Luke x. 5. *"Peace be to thi house!"*

Tune Godesberg. 87, 87. D.

1 PEACE be to this habitation;
Peace to all that dwell therein;
Peace, the earnest of salvation;
Peace, the fruit of pardoned sin;
Peace that speaks the heavenly Giver;
Peace to worldly minds unknown;
Peace Divine, that lasts for ever;
Peace that comes from God alone.

2 Jesus, Prince of Peace, be near us,
Fix in all our hearts Thy home;
With Thy gracious presence cheer us,
Let Thy sacred kingdom come;
Raise to heaven our expectation;
Give our ransomed souls to prove
Glorious and complete salvation
In the realms of bliss above!

Charles Wesley, 1749.

GODESBERG. [H. P. 185.]

BOSTON. [H. P. 278.]

663 Ps. cxii. 4. *"There ariseth light in the darkness."*

Tune Boston. 76, 76. D. Or Mahanaim.

1 SOMETIMES a light surprises
The Christian while he sings;
It is the Lord who rises
With healing in His wings.
When comforts are declining,
He grants the soul again
A season of clear shining,
To cheer it, after rain.

2 In holy contemplation
We sweetly then pursue
The theme of God's salvation,
And find it ever new.
Set free from present sorrow,
We cheerfully can say,
E'en let the unknown morrow
Bring with it what it may.

3 It can bring with it nothing
But He will bear us through:
Who gives the lilies clothing
Will clothe His people too:
Beneath the spreading heavens
No creature but is fed;
And He who feeds the ravens
Will give His children bread.

4 Though vine nor fig-tree neither
Their wonted fruit should bear,
Though all the field should wither,
Nor flocks nor herds be there;
Yet God the same abiding,
His praise shall tune my voice;
For while in Him confiding,
I cannot but rejoice!

William Cowper, 1779.

664 Isa. xxxv. 10. "*Come to Zion with songs.*"
Tune DURHAM. 77, 77. Or VIENNA.

1 CHILDREN of the heavenly King,
As ye journey, sweetly sing;
Sing your Saviour's worthy praise,
Glorious in His works and ways.

2 We are travelling home to God,
In the way the fathers trod;
They are happy now, and ye
Soon their happiness shall see.

3 Shout, ye little flock and blest!
You on Jesu's throne shall rest;
There your seat is now prepared,
There your kingdom and reward.

4 Fear not, brethren; joyful stand
On the borders of your land;
Jesus Christ, your Father's Son,
Bids you undismayed go on.

5 Lord, obediently we go,
Gladly leaving all below;
Only Thou our Leader be,
And we still will follow Thee!

John Cennick, 1742.

665 John xvi. 22. "*Your joy no man taketh from you.*"
Tune AVEN. S. M.

1 COME, ye that love the Lord,
And let your joys be known;
Join in a song with sweet accord,
And thus surround the throne.

2 The sorrows of the mind
Be banished from the place:
Religion never was designed
To make our pleasures less.

3 The sons of grace have found
Glory begun below;
Celestial fruits on earthly ground
From faith and hope may grow.

4 The hill of Zion yields
A thousand sacred sweets
Before we reach the heavenly fields,
Or walk the golden streets.

5 Then let our songs abound,
And every tear be dry:
We're marching through Emmanuel's ground,
To fairer worlds on high!

Isaac Watts, D.D., 1709.

666 1 Pet. i. 8. "*Believing, ye rejoice.*"
Tune STERNBERG. 10 10, 10 10. D.

1 JOYFULLY, joyfully, onward we move,
Bound to the land of bright spirits above;
Jesus, our Saviour, in mercy says—"Come,
Joyfully, joyfully haste to your home."
Soon will our pilgrimage end here below,
Home to the land of delight will we go;
Pilgrims and strangers no more shall we roam,
Joyfully, joyfully resting at home.

2 Friends fondly cherished have passed on before;
Waiting, they watch us approaching the shore;
Singing to cheer us through death's chilling gloom,
"Joyfully, joyfully haste to your home."
Sounds of sweet melody fall on the ear,
Harps of the blessèd, your strains we shall hear,
Filling with harmony heaven's high dome;
Joyfully, joyfully, Jesus, we come.

3 Death with his arrow may soon lay us low;
Safe in our Saviour, we fear not the blow:
Jesus hath broken the bars of the tomb;
Joyfully, joyfully will we go home.
Bright will the morn of eternity dawn,
Death shall be banished, his sceptre be gone;
Joyfully then shall we witness his doom,
Joyfully, joyfully, safely at home!

William Hunter, D.D., 1851. (*a.*)

CHESALON (Mount). [H. P. 35.]

667 Luke i. 47. "*My spirit hath rejoiced in God my Saviour.*" Tune CHESALON. C. M.

1 OH for a thousand tongues to sing
My great Redeemer's praise!
The glories of my God and King,
The triumphs of His grace.

2 My gracious Master, and my God,
Assist me to proclaim,
And spread through all the earth abroad,
The honours of Thy name.

3 Jesus, the name that charms our fears,
That bids our sorrows cease;
'Tis music in the sinner's ears,
'Tis life, and health, and peace.

4 He breaks the power of cancelled sin,
He sets the prisoner free:
His blood can make the foulest clean,
His blood availed for me!

Charles Wesley, 1740.

See Hymns 38, 39, 63, 134, 281, 697, 701, 730.

VIENNA. [H. P. 149.]

II.—Privileges Enjoyed.

(1) UNION WITH CHRIST.

668 John vi. 56. "*He . . . dwelleth in Me, and I in him.*" Tune VIENNA. 7 7, 7 7.

1 ONE with Christ! O blissful thought!
We are by His Spirit taught;
On His fulness now we live,
Grace for grace we thence receive.

2 One with Christ! ye saints, rejoice,
As the objects of His choice;
He will every want supply,
While He lives we cannot die.

3 One with Christ! for ever one!
Debts are paid, and work is done:
Grace and glory both are given,
We are on our way to heaven!

Joseph Irons, 1825.

BESOR (Brook). [H. P. 51.]

669 1 John v. 20. "*We are in Him.*" Tune BESOR. C. M.

1 AND is my soul with Jesus one?
Is He my covenant Head?
Was it for me He left His throne,
Obeyed the law, and bled?

2 And is my soul with Jesus one
In everlasting ties?
Oh! matchless mercy—grace unknown,
And love that never dies!

3 And is my soul with Jesus one!
Betrothed to Him in love?
Will He so vile a sinner own,
And faithful to me prove?

4 And is my soul with Jesus one?
Does He possess my heart?
Then He will take me to His throne,
For we can never part!

Joseph Irons, 1825.

670 Col. i. 27. "*Christ in you, the hope of glory.*" Tune LONDON NEW. C. M.

1 LORD JESUS, are we one with Thee?
O height! O depth of love!
With Thee we died upon the tree,
In Thee we live above.

2 Such was Thy grace, that for our sake
Thou didst from heaven come down;
Thou didst of flesh and blood partake,
In all our sorrows one.

3 Our sins, our guilt, in love Divine,
Confessed and borne by Thee;
The gall, the curse, the wrath were Thine,
To set Thy members free.

4 Ascended now, in glory bright,
Still one with us Thou art,
Nor life, nor death, nor depth, nor height,
Thy saints and Thee can part.

LONDON NEW; *or*, NEWTON. [H. P. 55.]

5 Oh! teach us, Lord, to know and own
This wondrous mystery,
That Thou with us art truly one,
And we are one with Thee!

6 Soon, soon shall come that glorious day,
When, seated on Thy throne,
Thou shalt to wondering worlds display
That Thou with us art one!

James George Deck, 1837.

CIVITAS REGIS MAGNI. [H. P. 301.]

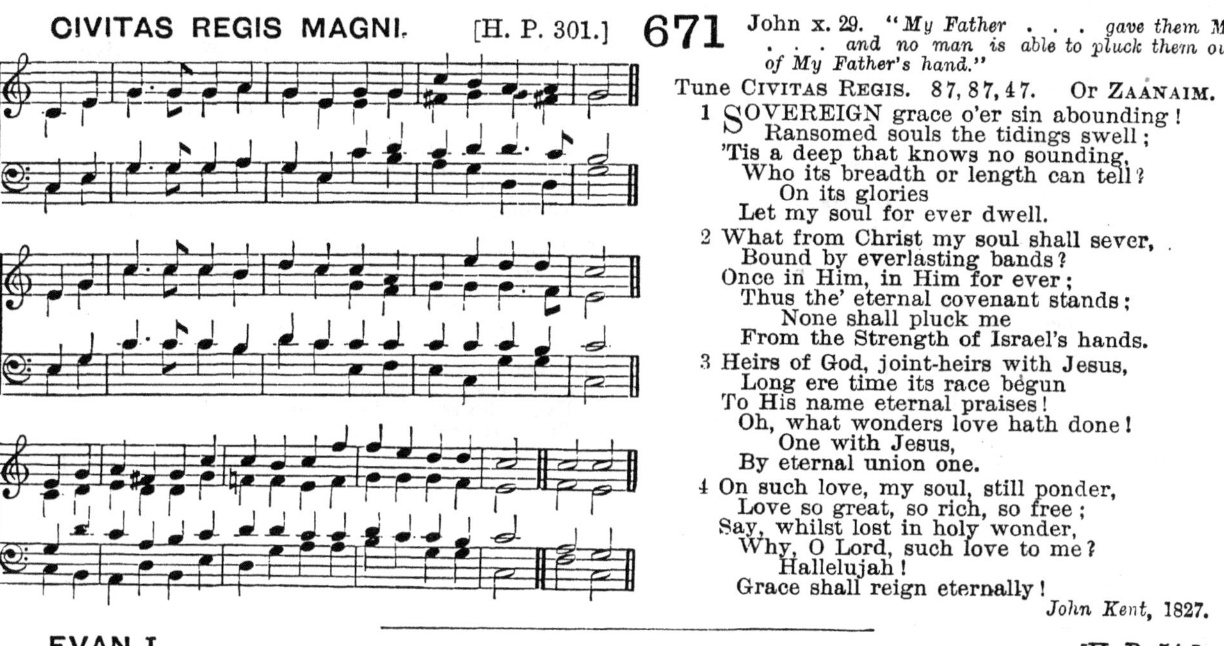

671

John x. 29. "*My Father . . . gave them Me . . . and no man is able to pluck them out of My Father's hand.*"

Tune CIVITAS REGIS. 87, 87, 47. Or ZAANAIM.

1 SOVEREIGN grace o'er sin abounding!
Ransomed souls the tidings swell;
'Tis a deep that knows no sounding,
Who its breadth or length can tell?
On its glories
Let my soul for ever dwell.

2 What from Christ my soul shall sever,
Bound by everlasting bands?
Once in Him, in Him for ever;
Thus the' eternal covenant stands;
None shall pluck me
From the Strength of Israel's hands.

3 Heirs of God, joint-heirs with Jesus,
Long ere time its race begun
To His name eternal praises!
Oh, what wonders love hath done!
One with Jesus,
By eternal union one.

4 On such love, my soul, still ponder,
Love so great, so rich, so free;
Say, whilst lost in holy wonder,
Why, O Lord, such love to me?
Hallelujah!
Grace shall reign eternally!

John Kent, 1827.

EVAN I. [H. P. 54.]

672

Gal. ii. 20. "*Christ liveth in me.*"

Tune EVAN I. C. M.

1 OH, what a happy lot is mine,
Since God my portion is!
How blest am I, whate'er betide,
Since He has made me His!

2 Here in the gloomiest, darkest hour,
Is cause for ceaseless joy;
Well may my heart enraptured sing,
And praise my tongue employ!

3 By Him my cup is daily filled
With mercies rich and free;
Whate'er I want in Him I find,
He's all in all to me.

4 He watches o'er me day by day,
In Him I rest each night;
And soft and sweet the sleep He gives
Until the morning light.

5 Or, if He bids my sleep depart,
'Tis but to let me hear,
While all around is still and calm,
His voice, like music clear,

6 Inviting my poor weary soul
To find upon His breast
Repose more tranquillising e'en
Than nature's sweetest rest.

7 Upon His arm of faithful love
My soul doth lean each hour;
His hand upholds me lest I fall;
He shields me by His power.

8 His word of covenant truth is pledged
To keep me to the end,
And through eternity He'll be
My never failing Friend!

Christina Forsyth, 1853.

THYATIRA. (Hymn Chant.) [H. P. No. V.]

673

John xv. 4. "*Abide in Me, and I in you.*"
Tune, Hymn Chant Thyatira. 10 10, 10 10.
Or Deptford.

1 "ABIDE in Me!" Most loving counsel this,
Nearest approach on earth to heavenly bliss;
With the command, O Saviour, give me power
To live by faith on Thee, from hour to hour.

2 "Abide in Me!" For I have strength to give
The grace to make thee henceforth heavenward live;
Eternal things My Spirit can reveal,
And thy heart's earthly dark diseases heal.

3 "Abide in Me!" All else must pass away,—
This earth so fair, these idols formed of clay;
Its riches, pleasures, friendships, pomp and fame,—
All evanescent are—all but a name!

4 "Abide in Me!" For changeless is My love;
Its depth unmeasured, as its height above:
Not all thy feelings can its power repel:
Wilt thou not trust the love that loves so well?

5 "Abide in Me!" No ill can hurt thee there;
In Me thou 'rt safe e'en from the tempter's snare:
Before his fiery darts o'er thee prevail
My life must end, My faithfulness must fail!

Part II.

6 "Abide in Me!" if thou wouldst fruitful be:
The branch bears not when severed from the tree;
Without My Spirit's power, the sapless bough
No fruit can bear, for it can nothing do.

7 "Abide in Me!" All grace is Mine to give:
My voice the dead shall hear, and hearing live!
My Spirit can thy strongest sins subdue,
Soften thine heart, and all thy thoughts renew.

8 "Abide in Me!" Live only on My love,
And thou shalt taste the bliss of saints above;
In Me thou shalt have peace; in Me find rest,
Though storms should rage around, or cares molest.

9 "Abide in Me!" Then safe within the veil,
Death cannot hurt, though heart and flesh may fail;
One with Myself, who vanquished death and hell,
It only breaks the bondage of thy cell!

10 "Abide in Me!" Then thou may'st calmly smile
On ruined hopes, or ruined worlds the while:
Even the trumpet's awful sound shall be
The sweetest music ever heard by thee!

Charlotte H. Inglis, 1860.

FRANKFORT. [H. P. 183.]

674

Gen. xxii. 17. "*In blessing I will bless thee.*"
Tune Frankfort. 87, 87.

1 MAY the Lord of glory bless thee
With His deepest, sweetest love
May His Spirit's breath caress thee
With a glimpse of joys above.

2 May the God of grace protect thee
Wheresoe'er 'tis thine to go;
Angel-hosts befriend, direct thee,
While a pilgrim here below.

3 May the Lord who died to save thee,
Turning crimson sins to wool—
Quench the fears that still enslave thee,
Whispering pardon free and full.

4 May the blood of Christ restore thee,
When thou feel'st the weight of guilt;
May His Spirit then empower thee
To believe for thee 'twas spilt.

5 May the God of love, who chose thee
Ere this lower world began,
Prove He seeks, and loves, and knows thee,
Saved in Christ the glory-man.

6 May thy Sire reveal His glory,
Christ the Lamb—O matchless sight!—
Scattering mists and clouds before thee
With a blaze of heavenly light!

Part II.

7 May'st thou find, when griefs oppress thee,
Sweet relief from Jesu's smile;
May the Bridegroom haste to bless thee,
Weary days and nights beguile.

8 If, without a kinsman near thee,
Lone, unfriended, thou shouldst stand,
May His Spirit kindly cheer thee,
Whispering comfort, soft and bland.

9 Yea—thou 'lt find, when He doth lure thee
To some desert drear and lone,
'Tis that He may more assure thee
Thou art more and more His own.

10 E'en when fiery serpents sting thee
This shall prove a cause of weal,
Christ His blood will fondly bring thee—
Balm of life, thy wounds to heal.

11 Thus to glory's clime He'll lead thee,
Intertwining joy and woe—
Cloud, by day, shall still precede thee,
Fire, by night, before thee go.

12 Bright the spousal that awaits thee,
When the school of time is o'er,—
To His Son Jehovah gives thee,
Bride of Christ for evermore!

William Mushett, 1850.

See Hymns 419, 420, 445, 446.

---

(2) ADOPTION.

675 Isa. lxi. 9. "*The seed which the Lord hath blessed.*"

Tune Ratisbon. 77,77,77. Or Sihor.

1 BLESSED are the sons of God;
They are bought with Jesu's blood,
They are ransomed from the grave,
Life eternal they shall have.
With them numbered may we be,
Now, and through eternity.

2 God did love them in His Son,
Long before the world begun;
They the seal of this receive,
When on Jesus they believe.
With, etc.

3 They are justified by grace,
They enjoy a solid peace;
All their sins are washed away,
They shall stand in God's great day.
With, etc.

4 They produce the fruits of grace
In the works of righteousness!
Born of God, they hate all sin,
God's pure word remains within.
With, etc.

5 They have fellowship with God,
Through the Mediator's blood;
One with God, through Jesus one,
Glory is in them begun!
With, etc.

Joseph Humphreys, 1743.

RATISBON. [H. P. 157.]

CYRENE. [H. P. 92.]

676 1 John iii. 1. "*Behold, what manner of love.*"

Tune Cyrene. S. M.

1 BEHOLD what wondrous grace
The Father hath bestowed
On sinners of a mortal race,
To call them sons of God!

2 It doth not yet appear
How great we must be made;
But when we see our Saviour here
We shall be like our Head.

3 A hope so much Divine
May trials well endure,
May purge our souls from sense and sin,
As Christ the Lord is pure.

4 If in my Father's love
I share a filial part,
Send down Thy Spirit like a dove,
To rest upon my heart.

5 We would no longer lie
Like slaves beneath the throne;
My faith shall Abba Father cry,
And Thou the kindred own!

Isaac Watts, D.D., 1709.

ZAANAIM (Plain of.) [H. P. 191.]

677 Eph. i. 5. *"Having predestinated us unto the adoption of children by Jesus Christ."* Tune ZAANAIM. [87, 87, 47.

1 SONS we are through God's election,
Who in Jesus Christ believe;
By His own predestination,
Sovereign grace we here receive:
Lord, Thy mercy
Does both grace and glory give.

2 Every fallen soul, by sinning,
Merits everlasting pain;
But Thy love, without beginning,
Has restored Thy sons again:
Countless millions
Shall in life, through Jesus, reign.

3 Pause, my soul! adore, and wonder!
Ask, "Oh! why such love to me?"
Grace has put me in the number
Of the Saviour's family;
Hallelujah!
Thanks, eternal thanks, to Thee.

4 Since that love had no beginning,
And shall never, never cease;
Keep, oh! keep me, Lord, from sinning!
Guide me in the way of peace!
Safely treading
All the paths of holiness!

PART II.

5 When I quit this earthly mansion,
And my soul returns to Thee,
Let the power of Thy ascension
Manifest itself in me:
Through Thy Spirit
Give the final victory!

6 When the angel sounds the trumpet,
When my soul and body join,
When my Saviour comes to judgment
Bright in majesty Divine;
Let me triumph
In Thy righteousness as mine.

7 When in that blest habitation
Which my God has foreordained;
When in glory's full possession,
I with saints and angels stand;
Free grace only
Shall resound through Canaan's land!

S. P. R., 1777.

WINCHESTER. [H. P. 46.]

678 Eph. i. 11. *"Being predestinated."* Tune WINCHESTER. C. M. Or BESOR.

1 AMAZING love, transcendent grace,
Redemption's scheme displays,
In God's predestinated race;
To His eternal praise.

2 His sons, by Him, were all foreknown,
And registered above;
Predestinated to a crown,
By everlasting love.

3 On this eternal, fixed decree,
All things in time depend;
Salvation, perfect, full and free,
And glory without end.

4 'Tis God's predestinating love
Transforms the chosen race;
Prepares the church for joys above,
And crowns triumphant grace!

Joseph Irons, 1825.

679 Rom. viii. 17. *"If children, then heirs; heirs of God, and joint-heirs with Christ."*

Tune GODESBERG. 87, 87. Or FRANKFORT.

1 HEIR of glory, art thou weeping?
Why should tears bedim thine eyes?
Is there not a time of reaping
Endless joys beyond the skies?

2 Are not all thy sins forgiven?
Hast thou not the Spirit's seal?
Is not thine a home in heaven?
Dost thou not the earnest feel?

3 What now passing, heir of glory,
Should thy blissful hopes obscure?
When the clouds of earth come o'er thee,
Look to Jesus! and endure.

4 See Him there—for thee He's pleading;
See thy name upon His breast:
He the grace that thou art needing
Will supply, and give thee rest.

5 Heir of glory, rise o'er sadness;
What of earth is worth thy care?
Think upon the songs of gladness
Thou shalt soon with angels share!

6 Jesus says, He'll never leave thee,
Heavenward He will safely guide;
Let not passing shadows grieve thee:
Thou art safe when by His side.

7 Fix thine eyes on coming glory—
Short the space that lies between;
For the joy that's set before thee,
Slight the things that now are seen!

Charlotte H. Inglis, 1858.

See Hymns 20, 21.

GODESBERG. [H. P. 185.]

GILBOA (Mount). [H. P. 11.]

(3) PARDON.

680 Col. i. 20. "*Peace through the blood of His cross.*"

Tune Gilboa. L. M.

1 In types and shadows, we are told,
Jesus was seen in days of old,
Before the gospel dawn came in,
A glorious Sacrifice for sin.

2 The Paschal Lamb which Israel slew,
Ye seed of Jacob, speaks to you;
Sets Jesus forth, from blemish free,
His blood the sign of peace to thee.

3 If sprinkled o'er thy conscience now,
How greatly loved and blest art thou;
Thousands there are, who never see
His sign of peace made known to thee.

4 Art thou a son for sin distrest?
Doth guilt lie heavy on thy breast?
In Christ the Lamb deliverance see;
His blood the sign of peace to thee.

5 Once Jesus as thy Surety bled,
Was crowned with thorns, to Calvary led,
From Sinai's curse to set thee free;
His blood the sign of peace to thee.

6 Then why, my soul, shouldst thou despair,
And doubt thy Saviour's constant care?
Torn from Himself thou canst not be;
His blood the sign of peace to thee.

7 And when thy God shall bid thee rise
To join the chorus of the skies,
This thy support in death shall be,
His blood the sign of peace to thee!

John Kent, 1803.

STUTTGARD. [H. P. 182.]

681 Col. ii. 13. "*Having forgiven you all trespasses.*"

Tune Stuttgard. 8 7, 8 7. Or Culbach.

1 Now, O joy! my sins are pardoned,
Now I can and do believe;
All I have, and am, and shall be,
To my precious Lord I give;
He aroused my deathly slumbers,
He dispersed my soul's dark night;
Whispered peace, and drew me to Him—
Made Himself my chief delight.

2 Let the babe forget its mother,
Let the bridegroom slight his bride;
True to Him, I'll love none other,
Cleaving closely to His side.
Jesus, hear my soul's confession:
Weak am I, but strength is Thine;
On Thine arms for strength and succour,
Calmly may my soul recline!

Albert Midlane, 1865.

MAHANAIM. [H. P. 129.]

682

Rom. viii. 1. "*No condemnation.*" Tune MAHANAIM. 7 6, 7 6. D.

1 THERE is no condemnation,
But peace and joy unpriced,
And full and free salvation
To all that are in Christ;
The sinner broken-hearted,
In penitential tears,
Has joy and peace imparted
As soon as Christ appears.

2 The law of life in Jesus,
The Spirit's power within
This only can release us,
And break and cancel sin;
The Saviour and the Spirit
Received by simple faith:
And then we rise renewed,
And conquer sin and death.

3 Made free from condemnation,
And Jesus all our own,
In Him we have salvation,
We trust in Him alone;
And walking in the Spirit,
Into new life we rise,
And, heirs with Christ, inherit
A mansion in the skies!

Benjamin Gough, 1865.

JORDAN. [H. P. 211.]

683

1 John i. 7. "*The blood of Jesus Christ His Son cleanseth us from all sin.*" Tune JORDAN. 8 8 6. D.

1 LET Zion in her songs record
The honours of her dying Lord,
Triumphant over sin;
How sweet the song there's none can say,
But those whose sins are washed away,
Who feel the same within.

2 We claim no merit of our own,
But self-condemned, before Thy throne,
Our hopes on Jesus place;
Though once in heart and life depraved,
We now can sing as sinners saved,
And praise redeeming grace.

3 We'll sing the same while life shall last;
And when, at the archangel's blast,
Our sleeping dust shall rise,
Then in a song for ever new
The glorious theme we'll still pursue
Throughout the azure skies.

4 Prepared of old, at God's right hand
Bright everlasting mansions stand
For all the blood-bought race;
And till we reach those seats of bliss,
We'll sing no sweeter song than this—
Salvation all of grace!

John Kent, 1803. (*a.*)

684

Mark ii. 5. "*Thy sins be forgiven thee.*" Tune MAON. 8 8, 8 8, 8 8.

1 WHEN first, o'erwhelmed with sin and shame,
To Jesu's cross I trembling came,
Burdened with guilt and full of fear,
Yet drawn by love I ventured near,
I pardon found, and peace with God,
In Jesu's rich atoning blood.

2 My sin is gone, my fears are o'er,
I shun His presence now no more;
He sits upon the throne of grace,
He bids me boldly seek His face;
For sprinkled on the throne of God
I see that rich atoning blood.

MAON (Wilderness of). [H. P. 229.]

3 Before His face my Priest appears,
My Advocate the Father hears;
That precious blood before His eyes,
Both day and night, for mercy cries;
It speaks, it ever speaks, to God—
The voice of that atoning blood.

4 By faith that voice I also hear:
It answers doubt, it stills each fear;
The' accuser seeks in vain to move
The wrath of Him whose name is love;
Each charge against the sons of God
Is silenced by the' atoning blood.

5 Here I can rest without a fear;
By this to God I now draw near;
By this, I triumph over sin,
For this has made and keeps me clean;
And when I reach the throne of God,
I'll praise that rich atoning blood!

James George Deck, 1847.

See Hymn 58.

MELCOMBE. [H. P. 24.]

(4) JUSTIFICATION.

685 Isa. lxi. 10. *"He hath covered me with the robe of righteousness."*

Tune MELCOMBE. L. M.

1 JESUS, Thy blood and righteousness
My beauty are, my glorious dress;
'Midst flaming worlds, in these arrayed,
With joy shall I lift up my head.

2 When from the dust of death I rise,
To take my mansion in the skies,
E'en then shall this be all my plea,
"Jesus hath lived and died for me."

3 Bold shall I stand in that great day,
For who aught to my charge shall lay?
While through Thy blood absolved I am
From sin's tremendous curse and shame.

4 This spotless robe the same appears
When ruined nature sinks in years;
No age can change its glorious hue,
The robe of Christ is ever new.

5 Oh! let the dead now hear Thy voice;
Bid, Lord, Thy banished ones rejoice:
Their beauty this, their glorious dress,
Jesus, the Lord, our Righteousness!

Count Zinzendorf, 1739; *J. Wesley* (*tr.*), 1740. (*a.*)

686 Gal. vi. 14. *"God forbid that I should glory, save in the cross of our Lord Jesus Christ."*

Tune MELCOMBE. L. M.

1 NO more, my God, I boast no more
Of all the duties I have done;
I quit the hopes I held before,
To trust the merits of Thy Son.

2 Now for the love I bear His name,
What was my gain I count my loss;
My former pride I call my shame,
And only glory in His cross.

3 Yes, and I must and will esteem
All things but loss for Jesu's sake:
Oh! may my soul be found in Him,
And of His righteousness partake!

4 The best obedience of my hands
Dares not appear before Thy throne,
But faith can answer Thy demands,
By pleading what my Lord has done!

Isaac Watts, D.D., 1709.

See Hymns 173, 416, 417.

(5) SANCTIFICATION.

ST. CHRYSOSTOM. [H. P. 53.]

687 Deut. xxx. 6. *"The Lord thy God will circumcise thine heart . . . to love the Lord thy God."*

Tune St. Chrysostom. C. M.
Or Bedford.

1 OH for a heart to praise my God,
A heart from sin set free!
A heart that always feels Thy blood,
So freely shed for me.

2 A heart resigned, submissive, meek,
My dear Redeemer's throne;
Where only Christ is heard to speak,
Where Jesus reigns alone:

3 A humble, lowly, contrite heart—
Believing, true, and clean—
Which neither life nor death can part
From Him that dwells within:

4 A heart in every thought renewed,
And full of love Divine;
Perfect, and right, and pure, and good,
A copy, Lord, of Thine!

5 Thy nature, gracious Lord, impart;
Come quickly from above;
Write Thy new name upon my heart,
Thy new, best name of Love!

Charles Wesley, 1742.

See Hymns 346—378, 529—535.

FRENCH; *or*, DUNDEE. [H. P. 65.]

(6) FELLOWSHIP WITH THE FATHER AND WITH THE SON.

688 Gen. v. 24. *"Enoch walked with God."*

Tune French. C. M.

1 WALK with thy God—a sinner walk
With the almighty God!
Yes, this may be my happy state,
Brought nigh by Jesu's blood.

2 Walk then with God—in Christ He 's mine,
And I His own dear child;
By faith I see the Father near,
Holy, yet reconciled.

3 Walk then with God—be this each hour
My privileged employ;
O Holy Ghost, within me dwell,
And ever give this joy.

4 Walk then with God, and patient wait,
Till faith be changed for sight;
Then shall I see God face to face,
My portion, praise, delight!

Edward Bickersteth, 1833.

PERSIS. [H. P. 187.]

689 1 John i. 3. *"Truly our fellowship is with the Father, and with His Son Jesus Christ."*

Tune Persis. 8 7, 8 7. Or Frankfort.

1 ALL unseen the Master walketh
By the toiling servant's side;
Comfortable words He speaketh,
While His hands uphold and guide.

2 Grief, nor pain, nor any sorrow
Rends thy heart, to Him unknown;
He to-day, and He to-morrow,
Grace sufficient gives His own.

3 Holy strivings nerve and strengthen,
Long endurance wins the crown:
When the evening shadows lengthen,
Thou shalt lay thy burden down!

Thomas Mackellar, 1853.

690 Cant. i. 4. *"Draw me, we will run after Thee."*

Tune Eaton. 88, 88, 88.

EATON. [H. P. 313.]

1 OH draw me, Saviour, after Thee,
So shall I run and never tire;
With gracious words still comfort me;
Be Thou my hope, my sole desire;
Free me from every weight; nor fear
Nor sin shall come, if Thou art near.

2 In suffering be Thy love my peace,
In weakness be Thy love my power;
And when the storms of life shall cease,
Jesus, in that important hour,
In death, as life, be Thou my guide,
And save me, who for me hast died!

P. Gerhardt, 1666; *J. Wesley (tr.)*, 1739.

---

691 Col. iii. 2. *"Set your affection on things above."*

Tune Bashan. 66, 66.

1 GO up, go up, my heart,
Dwell with thy God above;
For here thou canst not rest,
Nor here give out thy love.

BASHAN (Hill of). [H. P. 112.]

2 Go up, go up, my heart,
Be not a trifler here;
Ascend above these clouds,
Dwell in a higher sphere.

3 Let not thy love flow out
To things so soiled and dim;
Go up to heaven and God,
Take up thy love to Him.

4 Waste not thy precious stores
On creature-love below;
To God that wealth belongs,
On Him that wealth bestow!

Horatius Bonar, D.D., 1856.

LAODICEA. (Hymn Chant.) [H. P. No. VIII.]

692 John vi. 68. *"Lord, to whom shall we go?"*

Tune, Hymn Chant Laodicea. 6666, 88.

1 I BRING my sins to Thee,
The sins I cannot count,
That all may cleansèd be
In Thy once opened Fount.
I bring them, Saviour, all to Thee,
The burden is too great for me.

2 My heart to Thee I bring,
The heart I cannot read;
A faithless, wandering thing,
An evil heart indeed.
I bring it, Saviour, now to Thee,
That fixed and faithful it may be.

3 To Thee I bring my care,
The care I cannot flee,
Thou wilt not only share,
But bear it all for me.
O loving Saviour, now to Thee
I bring the load that wearies me.

Part II.

4 I bring my grief to Thee,
The grief I cannot tell;
No words shall needed be,
Thou knowest all so well.
I bring the sorrow laid on me,
O suffering Saviour, now to Thee.

5 My joys to Thee I bring,
The joys Thy love hath given,
That each may be a wing
To lift me nearer heaven.
I bring them, Saviour, all to Thee,
For Thou hast purchased all for me.

6 My life I bring to Thee,
I would not be my own;
O Saviour, let me be
Thine ever, Thine alone.
My heart, my life, my all I bring
To Thee, my Saviour, and my King!

Frances Ridley Havergal, 1870.

693 1 Sam. iii. 9. "*Speak, Lord; for Thy servant heareth.*"
Tune CASSEL. 87, 87, 77.

1 MASTER, speak! Thy servant heareth,
Longing for Thy gracious word,
Longing for Thy voice that cheereth;
Master, let it now be heard.
I am listening, Lord, for Thee;
What hast Thou to say to me?

2 Often through my heart is pealing
Many another voice than Thine,
Many an unwilled echo stealing
From the walls of this Thy shrine.
Let Thy longed for accents fall;
Master, speak! and silence all.

3 Master, speak! I do not doubt Thee,
Though so tearfully I plead;
Saviour, Shepherd! oh, without Thee
Life would be a blank indeed.
But I long for fuller light,
Deeper love and clearer sight.

4 Master, speak! I kneel before Thee,
Listening, longing, waiting still;
Oh! how long shall I implore Thee
This petition to fulfil!
Hast Thou not one word for me?
Must my prayer unanswered be?

5 Speak to me by name, O Master,
Let me know it is to me;
Speak, that I may follow faster,
With a step more firm and free,
Where the Shepherd leads the flock,
In the shadow of the rock!

Frances Ridley Havergal, 1867.

CASSEL. [H. P. 190.]

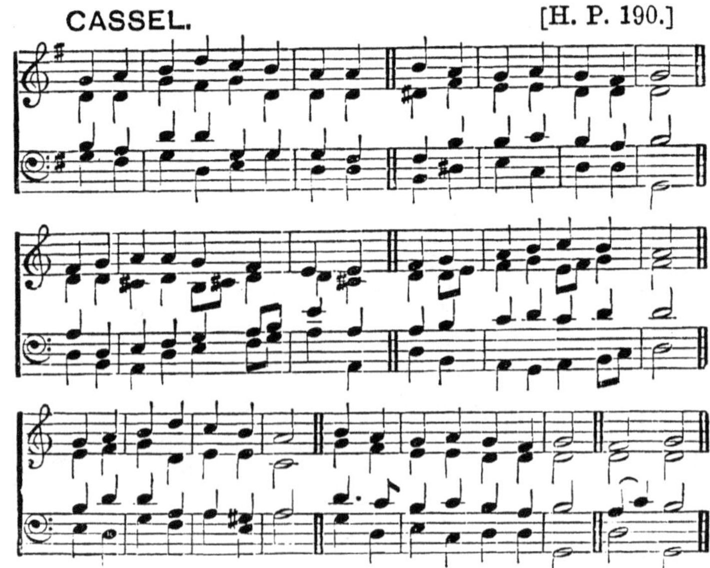

694 Matt. xvii. 8. "*Jesus only.*"
Tune CASSEL. 87, 87, 77. Or SUCCOTH.

1 "JESUS only!" In the shadow
Of the cloud so chill and dim,
We are clinging, loving, trusting,
He with us, and we with Him;
All unseen, though ever nigh,
"Jesus only!"—all our cry.

2 "Jesus only!" In the glory,
When the shadows all are flown,
Seeing Him in all His beauty,
Satisfied with Him alone;
May we join His ransomed throng,
"Jesus only!"—all our song!

Frances Ridley Havergal, 1870.

ONESIMUS. [H. P. 257.]

695 Phil. i. 21. "*To me to live is Christ.*"
Tune ONESIMUS. 74, 74. D.

1 PRECIOUS Saviour, may I live
Only for Thee!
Spend the powers Thou dost give
Only for Thee!
Be my spirit's deep desire
Only for Thee!
May my intellect aspire
Only for Thee!

2 In my joys may I rejoice
Only for Thee!
In my choices make my choice
Only for Thee!
Meekly may I suffer grief
Only for Thee!
Gratefully accept relief
Only for Thee!

3 Be my smiles and be my tears
Only for Thee!
Be my young and riper years
Only for Thee!
Be my peace and be my strife
Only for Thee!
Be my love and be my life
Only for Thee!

4 Be my singing and my sighing
Only for Thee!
Be my sickness and my dying
Only for Thee!
Be my rising, be my glory
Only for Thee!
Be my whole eternity
Only for Thee!

Eliza Ann Walker, 1864.

696 Acts xi. 23. "*Exhorted them all, that . . . they would cleave unto the Lord.*"
Tune PYRMONT. 64, 64. D. Or STERNBERG.

1 CLING to the Mighty One,
Cling in thy grief;
Cling to the Holy One,
He gives relief;
Cling to the Gracious One,
Cling in thy pain;
Cling to the Faithful One,
He will sustain.

PYRMONT. [H. P. 316.]

2 Cling to the Living One,
Cling in thy woe;
Cling to the Loving One,
Through all below;
Cling to the Pardoning One,
He speaketh peace;
Cling to the Healing One,
Anguish shall cease.

3 Cling to the Bleeding One,
Cling to His side;
Cling to the Risen One,
In Him abide;
Cling to the Coming One,
Hope shall arise;
Cling to the Reigning One,
Joy lights thine eyes!

Henry Bennett, 1864.

697

Ps. civ. 34. "*My meditation of Him shall be sweet.*"

Tune Ebronah. 10 10, 10 10.

EBRONAH. [H. P. 236.]

1 I JOURNEY through a desert drear and wild,
Yet is my heart by such sweet thoughts beguiled
Of Him on whom I lean, my Strength, my Stay,
I can forget the sorrows of the way.

2 Thoughts of His love—the root of every grace
Which finds in this poor heart a dwelling-place;
The sunshine of my soul, than day more bright,
And my calm pillow of repose by night.

3 Thoughts of His sojourn in this vale of tears—
The tale of love unfolded in those years
Of sinless suffering and patient grace,
I love again, and yet again, to trace.

4 Thoughts of His glory—on the cross I gaze,
And there behold its sad yet healing rays;
Beacon of hope, which, lifted up on high,
Illumes with heavenly light the tear-dimmed eye.

5 Thoughts of His coming; for that joyful day
In patient hope I watch, and wait, and pray;
The dawn draws nigh, the midnight shadows flee;
Oh, what a sunrise will that Advent be!

6 Thus while I journey on, my Lord to meet,
My thoughts and meditations are so sweet
Of Him on whom I lean, my Strength, my Stay,
I can forget the sorrows of the way!

Mary Jane Deck, 1846.

PARAN (Wilderness of). [H. P. 241.]

698

John xxi. 17. "*Lord, Thou knowest all things; Thou knowest that I love Thee.*" Tune Paran. 11 11, 11 11.

1 MY Saviour, I love Thee, I know Thou art mine!
For Thee all the follies of sin I resign:
My gracious Redeemer, my Saviour art Thou:
If ever I loved Thee, my Saviour, 'tis now!

2 I love Thee because Thou hast first lovèd me,
And purchased my pardon on Calvary's tree;
I love Thee for wearing the thorns on Thy brow;
If ever I loved Thee, my Saviour, 'tis now!

3 I will love Thee in life, I will love Thee in death,
And praise Thee as long as Thou lendest me breath;
And say, when the death dew lies cold on my brow,
If ever I loved Thee, my Saviour, 'tis now.

4 In mansions of glory and endless delight,
I'll ever adore Thee in heaven so bright;
I'll sing, with the glittering crown on my brow,
If ever I loved Thee, my Saviour, 'tis now!

London Hymn Book, 1864.

CYPRUS. [H. P. 26.]

699 John vi. 68. "*Lord, to whom shall we go?*"

Tune CYPRUS. L. M. Or MELCOMBE.

1 JESUS, Thou joy of loving hearts!
Thou Fount of life! Thou Light of men!
From the best bliss that earth imparts,
We turn unfilled to Thee again.

2 Thy truth unchanged hath ever stood:
Thou savest those that on Thee call:
To them that seek Thee Thou art good,
To them that find Thee, All in all!

3 We taste Thee, O Thou living Bread,
And long to feast upon Thee still;
We drink of Thee, the Fountain Head,
And thirst our souls from Thee to fill.

4 Our restless spirits yearn for Thee,
Where'er our changeful lot is cast;
Glad, when Thy gracious smile we see;
Blest, when our faith can hold Thee fast.

5 O Jesus, ever with us stay:
Make all our moments calm and bright;
Chase the dark night of sin away;
Shed o'er the world Thy holy light!

St. Bernard of Clairvaux, 1140; *Ray Palmer, D.D.* (*tr.*), 1834.

PENIEL. [H. P. 23.]

700 John xvii. 24. "*With Me, where I am.*" Tune PENIEL. L. M.

1 LET me be with Thee, where Thou art,
My Saviour, my eternal Rest!
Then only will this longing heart
Be fully and for ever blest.

2 Let me be with Thee, where Thou art,
Thy unveiled glory to behold;
Then surely will this wandering heart
Cease to be faithless, treacherous, cold!

3 Let me be with Thee, where Thou art,
Where spotless saints Thy name adore;
Then only will this sinful heart
Be evil and defiled no more.

4 Let me be with Thee, where Thou art,—
Where none can die,—where none remove;
Where life nor death my soul can part,
From Thy blest presence and Thy love

Charlotte Elliott, 1841.

GOLDBACH. (PART I.) [H. P. 130.]

701 Luke i. 47. "*My spirit hath rejoiced in God my Saviour.*"

Tune GOLDBACH. (Part I.) 7 6, 7 6.

1 TO Thee, O dear, dear Saviour,
My spirit turns for rest;
My peace is in Thy favour,
My pillow on Thy breast.

2 Though all the world deceive me,
I know that I am Thine,
And Thou wilt never leave me,
O blessèd Saviour mine!

3 O Thou whose mercy found me,
From bondage set me free,
And then for ever bound me
With threefold cords to Thee,

4 Oh for a heart to love Thee
More truly as I ought,
And nothing place above Thee,
In deed, or word, or thought.

5 Oh for that choicest blessing
Of living in Thy love,
And thus on earth possessing
The peace of heaven above!

John S. B. Monsell, LL.D., 1863.

HONIDON. [H. P. 291.]

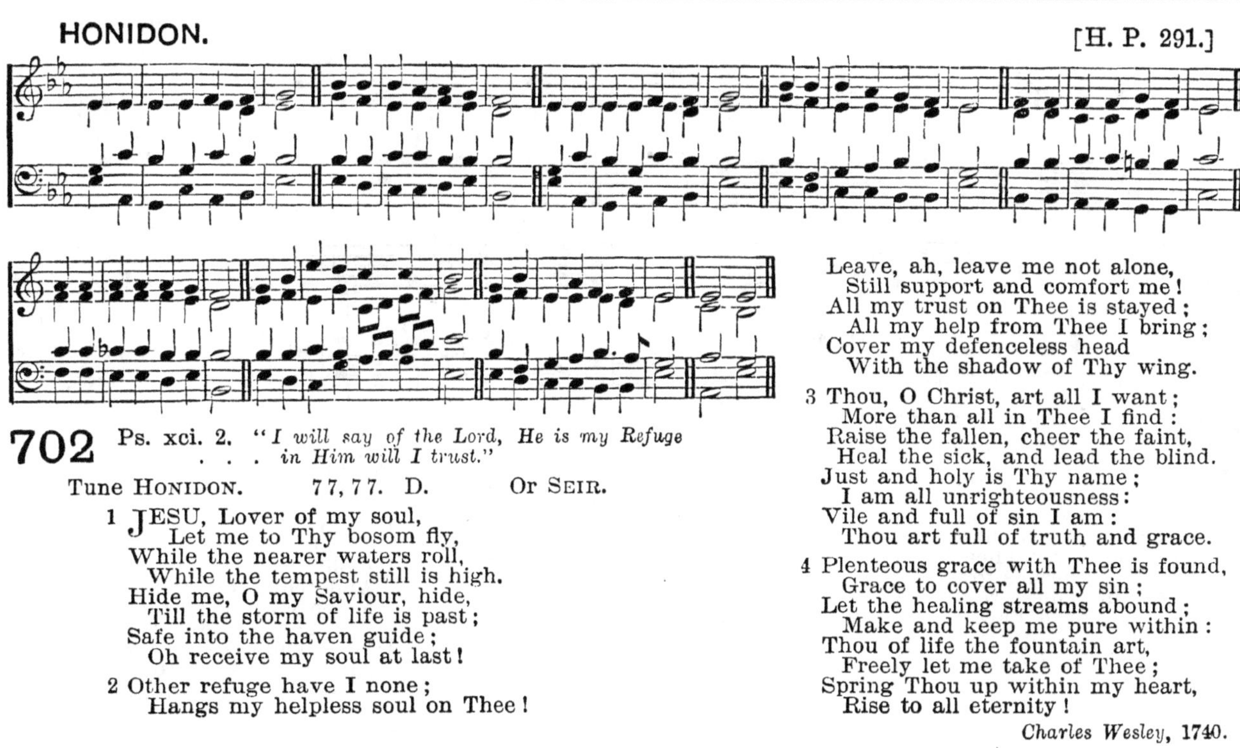

702 Ps. xci. 2. *"I will say of the Lord, He is my Refuge . . . in Him will I trust."*

Tune HONIDON. 77, 77. D. Or SEIR.

1 JESU, Lover of my soul,
Let me to Thy bosom fly,
While the nearer waters roll,
While the tempest still is high.
Hide me, O my Saviour, hide,
Till the storm of life is past;
Safe into the haven guide;
Oh receive my soul at last!

2 Other refuge have I none;
Hangs my helpless soul on Thee!
Leave, ah, leave me not alone,
Still support and comfort me!
All my trust on Thee is stayed;
All my help from Thee I bring;
Cover my defenceless head
With the shadow of Thy wing.

3 Thou, O Christ, art all I want;
More than all in Thee I find:
Raise the fallen, cheer the faint,
Heal the sick, and lead the blind.
Just and holy is Thy name;
I am all unrighteousness:
Vile and full of sin I am:
Thou art full of truth and grace.

4 Plenteous grace with Thee is found,
Grace to cover all my sin;
Let the healing streams abound;
Make and keep me pure within:
Thou of life the fountain art,
Freely let me take of Thee;
Spring Thou up within my heart,
Rise to all eternity!

Charles Wesley, 1740.

MAHANAIM. [H. P. 129.]

703 John xv. 5. *"Without Me ye can do nothing."* Tune MAHANAIM. 76, 76. D. Or GOLDBACH.

1 I NEED Thee, precious Jesus!
For I am full of sin;
My soul is dark and guilty,
My heart is dead within;
I need the cleansing fountain,
Where I can always flee,
The blood of Christ most precious,
The sinner's perfect plea.

2 I need Thee, blessèd Jesus!
For I am very poor;
A stranger and a pilgrim,
I have no earthly store;
I need the love of Jesus
To cheer me on my way,
To guide my doubting footsteps,
To be my strength and stay.

3 I need Thee, blessèd Jesus!
I need a friend like Thee;
A friend to soothe and pity,
A friend to care for me.
I need the heart of Jesus
To feel each anxious care,
To tell my every trial,
And all my sorrows share.

4 I need Thee, blessèd Jesus!
And hope to see Thee soon,
Encircled with the rainbow,
And seated on Thy throne:
There, with Thy blood-bought children,
My joy shall ever be
To sing Thy praise, Lord Jesus,
To gaze, my Lord, on Thee!

Frederick Whitfield, 1861.

GOLDBACH. [H. P. 130.]

704

Cant. i. 7. "*O Thou whom my soul loveth.*"
Tune GOLDBACH. 76, 76. D.

1 IS it for me, dear Saviour,
Thy glory and Thy rest?
For me, so weak and sinful,
Oh shall *I* thus be blessed?
Is it for me to see Thee
In all Thy glorious grace,
And gaze in endless rapture
On Thy belovèd Face?

2 Is it for me to listen
To Thy belovèd voice,
And hear its sweetest music
Bid even me rejoice?
Is it for me, Thy welcome,
Thy gracious "Enter in"?
For me, Thy "Come, ye blessèd!"
For me, so full of sin?

3 O Saviour, precious Saviour,
My heart is at Thy feet,
I bless Thee and I love Thee,
And Thee I long to meet.
A thrill of solemn gladness
Has hushed my very heart,
To think that I shall really
Behold Thee as Thou art;

4 Behold Thee in Thy beauty,
Behold Thee face to face;
Behold Thee in Thy glory,
And reap Thy smile of grace,
And be with Thee for ever,
And never grieve Thee more!
Dear Saviour, I *must* praise Thee,
And lovingly adore.

Frances Ridley Havergal, 1871.

SARDIS. (HYMN CHANT.) [H. P. No. VI.]

705

Phil. iii. 10. "*That I may know Him.*"
Tune, Hymn Chant SARDIS. 10 10, 10 10.

1 ONE fervent wish, my God! it speaks the whole,
And every longing of my weary soul;
To know my Saviour is my one desire—
The great high prize to which I most aspire.

2 To know Him in His depth of love to me,
The poorest, weakest, vilest though I be,
His lost one, whom He came to seek and save,
His loved one, for whose life Himself He gave.

3 To know Him as my chiefest, dearest friend,
Who loveth, and will love me to the end;
Who feels my every pain, my griefs, my fears,
Who tasted oft the bitterness of tears.

4 To know Him as my wise and skilful guide;
A pilgrim I, yet safe with Him beside;
The path to me untrodden heretofore,
He knoweth well, who traced each step before.

5 To know Him as the "All in all" to me,
All mine for time, all for eternity;
And in each gift of providence and grace
Himself in all His loveliness to trace.

6 To know Him as He sits at God's right hand,
All things in heaven and earth at His command;
All, all are His, and what are His are mine;
Oh, what shall ever such rich grace outshine!

7 To know Him as earth's rightful King and Lord,
Who soon shall claim His great and full reward;
The travail of His soul He then shall see,
And at His feet creation bow the knee!

Mary Shekleton, 1867.

706

Ps. cxlviii. 14. "*A people near unto Him.*" Tune NIMRIM. 64, 64, 664.

1 NEARER, my God, to Thee,
Nearer to Thee!
E'en though it be a cross
That raiseth me;
Still all my song shall be,
"Nearer, my God, to Thee—
Nearer to Thee!"

2 Though like the wanderer,
The sun gone down,
Darkness be over me,
My rest a stone;
Yet in my dreams I'd be
Nearer, my God, to Thee—
Nearer to Thee!

3 Then with my waking thoughts
Bright with Thy praise,
Out of my stony griefs
Beth-El I'll raise:
So through my woes to be
Nearer, my God, to Thee—
Nearer to Thee!

NIMRIM. [H. P. 100.]

4 Or if on joyful wing
Cleaving the sky,
Sun, moon, and stars forgot,
Upwards I fly:
Still all my song shall be,
Nearer, my God, to Thee—
Nearer to Thee!

5 Christ alone beareth me
Where Thou dost shine;
Joint-heir He maketh me
Of the Divine:
In Christ my soul shall be
Nearest, my God, to Thee—
Nearest to Thee!

Sarah Fuller Adams, 1841; last verse by A. T. Russell, 1856.

EVAN I. [H. P. 54.]

707

Cant. i. 3. "*Thy name is as ointment poured forth.*"

Tune Evan I. C. M.

1 JESU, the very thought of Thee
With sweetness fills my breast!
But sweeter far Thy face to see,
And in Thy presence rest.

2 No voice can sing, no heart can frame,
Nor can the memory find
A sweeter sound than Thy blest name,
O Saviour of mankind!

3 O hope of every contrite heart!
O joy of all the meek!
To those who fall, how kind Thou art!
How good to those who seek!

4 But what to those who find? Ah! this
Nor tongue nor pen can show;
The love of Jesus—what it is,
None but His loved ones know.

5 Jesu! our only joy be Thou,
As Thou our prize wilt be;
Jesu! be Thou our glory now,
And through eternity!

St. Bernard of Clairvaux, 1141.

EIRENE. [H. P. 246.]

708

John xv. 10. "*Ye shall abide in My love.*"

Tune Eirene. 11 10, 11 10.

1 FATHER, abide with us! the storm-clouds gather
In gloomy vengeance o'er the sinking head;
Go with us through our pilgrimage, dear Father,
Cheer with Thy smile the stormy path we tread.

2 Shepherd, abide with us! our souls are thirsting
For life's pure waters that around Thee flow;
Pity the spirits that with woe are bursting;
Oh! lead us where the heavenly pastures grow.

3 Saviour, abide with us! we have been clinging
To fragile reeds that droop and pass away!
But now our souls, their clasping tendrils flinging
Around Thy strength, ask Thee to be their stay.

4 Jesus, abide with us! our hearts are weary,
And those who blessed us with their love are gone;
Thou, always kind to the distressed and weary,
Love us, O Jesus, as we journey on!

E. Clay's Collection, 1864.

FRANKFORT. [H. P. 183.]

709 Matt. x. 27. *"What I tell you in darkness, that speak ye in light."* Tune FRANKFORT. 87, 87.

1 HE hath spoken in the darkness,
In the silence of the night,
Spoken sweetly of the Father,
Words of life and love and light.
Floating through the sombre stillness
Came the loved and loving Voice,
Speaking peace and solemn gladness,
That His children might rejoice.
What He tells thee in the darkness,
Songs He giveth in the night—
Rise and speak it in the morning,
Rise and sing them in the light!

2 He hath spoken in the darkness,
In the silence of thy grief,
Sympathy so deep and tender,
Mighty for thy heart relief.
Speaking in thy night of sorrow
Words of comfort and of calm,
Gently on thy wounded spirit
Pouring true and healing balm.
What He tells thee in the darkness,
Weary watcher for the day,
Grateful lip and life should utter
When the shadows flee away.

3 He is speaking in the darkness,
Though thou canst not see His face,
More than angels ever needed,
Mercy, pardon, love, and grace.
Speaking of the many mansions,
Where, in safe and holy rest,
Thou shalt be with Him for ever,
Perfectly and always blest.
What He tells thee in the darkness,
Whispers through Time's lonely night,
Thou shalt speak in glorious praises,
In the everlasting light!

Frances Ridley Havergal, 1869.

BEULAH. [H. P. 102.]

710 Cant. ii. 16. *"My Beloved is mine."*

Tune BEULAH. 64, 64, 6664.

1 PASS away earthly joy,
Jesus is mine!
Break every mortal tie,
Jesus is mine!
Dark is the wilderness;
Distant the resting-place;
Jesus alone can bless—
Jesus is mine!

2 Tempt not my soul away—
Jesus is mine!
Here would I ever stay,
Jesus is mine!
Perishing things of clay,
Born but for one brief day,
Pass from my heart away—
Jesus is mine!

3 Fare ye well, dreams of night,
Jesus is mine!
Mine is a dawning bright,
Jesus is mine!
All that my soul has tried
Left but a dismal void,
Jesus has satisfied—
Jesus is mine!

4 Farewell mortality,
Jesus is mine!
Welcome eternity,
Jesus is mine!
Welcome ye scenes of rest,
Welcome ye mansions blest,
Welcome a Saviour's breast,
Jesus is mine!

Jane Bonar, 1844.

MAGDEBURG. [H. P. 300.]

(7) DIRECTION AND GUIDANCE.

711 Ps. lxxiii. 24. *"Thou shalt guide me with Thy counsel, and afterward receive me to glory."*
Tune MAGDEBURG. 87, 87, 87. Or LUSATIA.

1 GUIDE me, O Thou great Jehovah,
Pilgrim through this barren land;
I am weak, but Thou art mighty,
Hold me with Thy powerful hand;
Bread of heaven, Bread of heaven,
Feed me now and evermore.

2 Open now the crystal fountain,
Whence the healing stream doth flow,
Let the fire and cloudy pillar
Lead me all my journey through:
Strong Deliverer, strong Deliverer,
Be Thou still my strength and shield.

3 When I tread the verge of Jordan
Bid my anxious fears subside;
Death of deaths, and hell's destruction,
Land me safe on Canaan's side:
Songs of praises, songs of praises,
I will ever give to Thee.

4 Musing on my habitation,
Musing on my heavenly home,
Fills my soul with holy longings:
Come, my Jesus, quickly come.
Vanity is all I see;
Lord, I long to be with Thee!
William Williams, 1773.

MUNICH. [H. P. 279.]

712

Ps. cxix. 105. *"Thy word is a lamp unto my feet, and a light unto my path."*

Tune Munich. 76, 76. D.

1 O WORD of God Incarnate,
O Wisdom from on high,
O Truth unchanged, unchanging,
O Light of our dark sky;
We praise Thee for the radiance
That from the hallowed page,
A lantern to our footsteps,
Shines on from age to age.

2 The Church from her dear Master
Received the gift Divine,
And still that light she lifteth
O'er all the earth to shine.
It is the golden casket
Where gems of truth are stored;
It is the heaven-drawn picture
Of Christ, the living Word.

3 It floateth like a banner
Before God's host unfurled,
It shineth like a beacon
Above the darkling world;
It is the chart and compass,
That o'er life's surging sea,
'Mid mists, and rocks, and quicksands,
Still guide, O Christ, to Thee.

4 Oh make Thy Church, dear Saviour,
A lamp of burnished gold,
To bear before the nations
Thy true light as of old;
Oh teach Thy wandering pilgrims
By this their path to trace,
Till, clouds and darkness ended,
They see Thee face to face.
Bishop Wm. Walsham How, 1867.

ZAANAIM (Plain of.) [H. P. 191.]

713

Ps. xlviii. 14. *"This God is our God for ever and ever; He will be our guide even unto death."*

Tune Zaanaim. 87, 87, 47.

1 WHY those fears? behold 'tis Jesus
Holds the helm and guides the ship:
Spread the sails, and catch the breezes
Sent to waft us through the deep
To the regions
Where the mourners cease to weep.

2 Led by Christ, we brave the ocean;
Led by Him, the storm defy;
Calm amidst tumultuous motion,
Knowing that our Lord is nigh:
Waves obey Him,
And the storms before Him fly.

3 Rendered safe by His protection,
We shall pass the watery waste;
Trusting to His wise direction,
We shall gain the port at last!
And with wonder,
Think on toils and dangers past.

4 Oh! what pleasures there await us,
There the tempests cease to roar:
There it is that those who hate us
Can molest our peace no more:
Trouble ceases
On that tranquil, happy shore!
Thomas Kelly, 1809

DIMON (Waters of). [H. P. 64.]

714 Matt. xxviii. 20. "*Lo, I am with you alway.*"

Tune DIMON. C. M.

1 OH! what a lonely path were ours,
Could we, O Father, see
No home of rest beyond it all,
No guide or help in Thee.

2 But Thou art near and with us still,
To keep us on the way
That leads along this vale of tears
To the bright world of day.

3 There shall Thy glory, O our God!
Break fully on our view;
And we, Thy saints, rejoice to find
That all Thy word was true.

4 There Jesus, on His heavenly throne,
Our wondering eyes shall see;
While we the blest associates there
Of all His joy shall be.

5 Sweet hope! we leave without a sigh
A blighted world like this;
To bear the cross, despise the shame,
For all that weight of bliss!

Sir Edward Denny, 1838.

See Hymns 27, 733.

(8) EVERLASTING LOVE.

KEDRON (Brook). [H. P. 213.]

715 Rom. v. 5. "*The love of God is shed abroad in our hearts by the Holy Ghost.*"

Tune KEDRON. 886. D.

1 O LOVE Divine, how sweet Thou art!
When shall I find my willing heart
All taken up by Thee?
I thirst, I faint, I die to prove
The greatness of redeeming love,
The love of Christ to me!

2 Stronger His love than death or hell;
Its riches are unsearchable:
The first-born sons of light
Desire in vain its depths to see;
They cannot reach the mystery,
The length, and breadth, and height.

3 God only knows the love of God:
Oh that it now were shed abroad
In this poor stony heart!
For love I sigh, for love I pine:
This only portion, Lord, be mine,
Be mine this better part!

4 Oh that I could for ever sit
With Mary at the Master's feet;
Be this my happy choice:
My only care, delight, and bliss,
My joy, my heaven on earth, be this,
To hear the Bridegroom's voice!

Charles Wesley, 1746.

PHILADELPHIA. (HYMN CHANT.) [H. P. VII.]

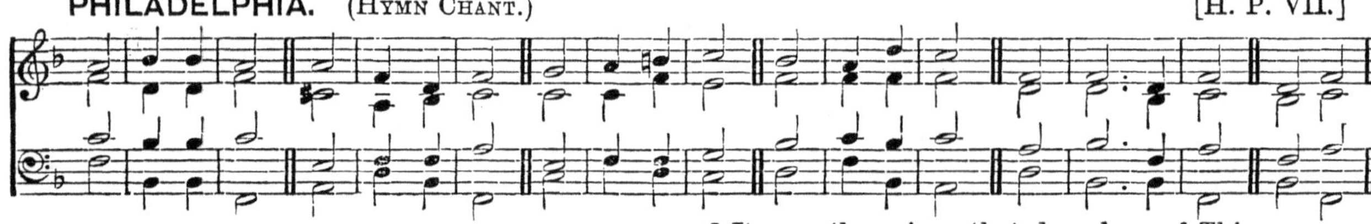

716 Eph. iii. 19. "*The love of Christ, which passeth knowledge.*"

Tune, Hymn Chant PHILADELPHIA. 10 10, 10 10, 4.

1 IT passeth knowledge, that dear love of Thine,
My Jesus, Saviour; yet this soul of mine
Would of Thy love, in all its breadth and length,
Its height and depth, its everlasting strength,
Know more and more.

2 It passeth telling, that dear love of Thine,
My Jesus, Saviour; yet these lips of mine
Would fain proclaim to sinners, far and near,
A love which can remove all guilty fear,
And love beget.

3 It passeth praises, that dear love of Thine,
My Jesus, Saviour; yet this heart of mine
Would sing that love, so full, so rich, so free,
Which brings a rebel sinner, such as me,
Nigh unto God.

4 But though I cannot sing, or tell, or know
The fulness of Thy love while here below,
My empty vessel I may freely bring:
O Thou, who art of love the living spring,
My vessel fill.

5 I am an empty vessel—not one thought,
Or look of love, I ever to Thee brought;
Yet I may come, and come again to Thee,
With this, the empty sinner's only plea,
Thou lovest me.

EVERLASTING LOVE. 277

6 O fill me, Jesus, Saviour, with Thy love!
Lead, lead me to the living Fount above;
Thither may I, in simple faith, draw nigh,
And never to another fountain fly,
But unto Thee.

7 And when my Jesus face to face I see,
When at His lofty throne I bow the knee;
Then of His love, in all its breadth and length,
Its height and depth, its everlasting strength,
My soul shall sing!

Mary Shekleton, 1833.

PATMOS. [H. P. 147.]

717 John xv. 9. *"As the Father hath loved Me, so have I loved you."* Tune PATMOS. 77, 77.

1 SWEET the theme of Jesu's love!
Sweet the theme all themes above;
Love unmerited and free
Our triumphant song shall be.

2 Love so vast that nought can bound;
Love too deep for thought to sound;
Love which made the Lord of all
Drink the wormwood and the gall.

3 Love which led Him to the cross,
Bearing there unuttered loss;
Love which brought Him to the gloom
Of the cold and darksome tomb.

4 Love which made Him hence arise
Far above the starry skies;
There with tender, loving care,
All His people's griefs to share.

5 Love which will not let Him rest
Till His chosen all are blest;
Till they all for whom He died
Live rejoicing by His side!

Albert Midlane, 1864. (a.)

EATON. [H. P. 313.]

718 1 John iv. 16. *"God is love."*
Tune EATON. 88, 88, 88.

1 THOU hidden love of God, whose height,
Whose depth unfathomed, no man knows;
I see from far Thy beauteous light,
And inly sigh for Thy repose:
My heart is pained, nor can it be
At rest, till it find rest in Thee.

2 Is there a thing beneath the sun
That strives with Thee my heart to share?
Ah! tear it thence, and reign alone,
The Lord of every motion there!
Then shall my heart from earth be free,
When it hath found repose in Thee.

3 Each moment draw from earth away
My heart, that lowly waits Thy call;
Speak to my inmost soul, and say,
"I am thy Love, thy God, thy All!"
To feel Thy power, to hear Thy voice,
To taste Thy love, be all my choice!

G. Tersteegen, 1731; *J. Wesley* (*tr.*), 1739.

GOLDBACH. (PART I.) [H. P. 130.]

719 John xv. 16. *"I have chosen you."* Tune GOLDBACH. (Part I.) 76, 76.

1 'TIS not that I did choose Thee;
For, Lord, that could not be,
This heart would still refuse Thee;
But Thou hast chosen me:

2 Thou from the sin that stained me
Washed me and made me free,
And to this end ordained me,
That I should live to Thee.

3 'Twas sovereign mercy called me,
And taught my opening mind;
The world had else enthralled me,
To heavenly glories blind.

4 My heart owns none above Thee;
For Thy rich grace I thirst;
This knowing, if I love Thee,
Thou must have loved me first!

Josiah Conder, 1856.

A-men.

720 Heb. xiii. 5. "*I will never leave thee, nor forsake thee.*"

Tune EATON. 88, 88, 88.

EATON. [H. P. 313.]

1 STILL nigh me, O my Saviour, stand!
And guard in fierce temptation's hour,
Hide in the hollow of Thy hand,
Show forth in me Thy saving power;
Still be Thy arms my sure defence,
Nor earth nor hell shall pluck me thence.

2 What in Thy love possess I not?
My star by night, my sun by day;
My spring of life, when parched with drought,
My wine to cheer, my bread to stay,
My strength, my shield, my safe abode,
My robe before the throne of God!

3 From all eternity, with love
Unchangeable Thou hast me viewed;
Ere knew this beating heart to move,
Thy tender mercies me pursued—
Ever with me may they abide,
And close me in on every side.

4 In suffering be Thy love my peace,
In weakness be Thy love my power;
And when the storms of life shall cease,
Jesus, in that important hour,
In death as life be Thou my guide,
And save me, who for me hast died!

P. Gerhardt, after J. Arndt, 1666; *J. Wesley* (*tr.*), 1739—*ver.* 1, *C. Wesley*, 1739.

PERSIS. [H. P. 187.]

721 1 Pet. v. 7. "*He careth for you.*" Tune PERSIS. 87, 87. Or SOREK.

1 YES, for me, for me He careth
With a brother's tender care:
Yes, with me, with me He shareth
Every burden, every fear.

2 Yes, o'er me, o'er me He watcheth—
Ceaseless watcheth, night and day:
Yes, e'en me, e'en me He snatcheth
From the perils of the way.

3 Yes, for me He standeth pleading,
At the mercy-seat above;
Ever for me interceding,
Constant in untiring love.

4 Yes, in me abroad He sheddeth
Joys unearthly—love and light;
And to cover me He spreadeth
His paternal wing of might.

5 Yes, in me, in me He dwelleth—
I in Him, and He in me!
And my empty soul He filleth,
Here and through eternity.

6 Thus I wait for His returning,
Singing all the way to heaven;
Such the joyful song of morning,
Such the tranquil song of even!

Horatius Bonar, D.D., 1844.

SHENIR II. (Mount.) [H. P. 151.]

722 Mal. i. 2. "*I have loved you, saith the Lord.*" Tune SHENIR II. 77, 77. Or VIENNA.

1 HARK, my soul! it is the Lord;
'Tis thy Saviour—hear His word;
Jesus speaks, and speaks to thee:
"Say, poor sinner, lov'st thou Me?"

2 "I delivered thee when bound,
And, when bleeding, healed thy wound;
Sought thee wandering, set thee right,
Turned thy darkness into light.

3 "Can a woman's tender care
Cease toward the child she bare?
Yes, she may forgetful be,
Yet will I remember thee.

4 "Mine is an unchanging love,
Higher than the heights above;
Deeper than the depths beneath,
Free and faithful, strong as death.

5 "Thou shalt see My glory soon,
When the work of grace is done;
Partner of My throne shalt be:
Say, poor sinner, lov'st thou Me?"

6 Lord, it is my chief complaint,
That my love is weak and faint:
Yet I love Thee and adore—
Oh for grace to love Thee more!

See Hymns 14, 17, 23, 117, 121—127, 189—194, 404, 407.

William Cowper, 1771.

GOLDBACH. (PART I.) [H. P 130.]

(9) SECURITY IN CHRIST.

723

1 John ii. 25. "*The promise that He hath promised us, even eternal life.*" Tune GOLDBACH, Part I. 76, 76.

1 LORD JESUS! we believing
In Thee have peace with God;
Eternal life receiving,
The purchase of Thy blood.

2 Our curse and condemnation
Thou barest in our stead;
Secure is our salvation
In Thee, our risen Head.

3 The Holy Ghost, revealing
Thy grace, hath given us rest,
Thy stripes have been our healing,
Thy love doth make us blest.

4 In Thee the Father sees us
Accepted and complete;
The blood from sin which frees us
For glory makes us meet!

Samuel Prideaux Tregelles, D.D., 1861.

ARISTARCHUS. [H. P. 224.]

724

Isa. xlv. 17. "*Saved in the Lord with an everlasting salvation.*" Tune ARISTARCHUS. 88, 88.

1 A DEBTOR to mercy alone,
Of covenant mercy I sing;
Nor fear, with Thy righteousness on,
My person and offering to bring:
The terrors of law, and of God,
With me can have nothing to do:
My Saviour's obedience and blood
Hide all my transgressions from view.

2 The work which His goodness began,
The arm of His strength will complete;
His promise is Yea and Amen,
And never was forfeited yet:
Things future nor things that are now,
Not all things below nor above,
Can make Him His purpose forego,
Or sever my soul from His love.

3 My name from the palms of His hands
Eternity will not erase;
Impressed on His heart it remains
In marks of indelible grace:
Yes, I to the end shall endure,
As sure as the earnest is given;
More happy, but not more secure,
The glorified spirits in heaven!

Augustus M. Toplady, 1771.

TRYPHENA. [H. P. 217.]

725

Eph. i. 6. "*Accepted in the Beloved.*"
Col. i. 28. "*Perfect in Christ Jesus.*"
Col. ii. 10. "*Complete in Him.*"

Tune TRYPHENA. 888.

1 ACCEPTED, Perfect, and Complete,
For God's inheritance made meet!
How true, how glorious, and how sweet!

2 In the Belovèd—by the King
Accepted, though not anything
But forfeit lives had we to bring.

3 And Perfect in Christ Jesus made,
On Him our great transgressions laid,
We in His righteousness arrayed.

4 Complete in Him, our glorious Head,
With Jesus raisèd from the dead,
And by His mighty Spirit led!

5 O blessèd Lord, is this for me?
Then let my whole life henceforth be
One Alleluia-song to Thee!

Frances Ridley Havergal, 1870.

TROPHIMUS. [H. P. 123.]

726 1 Pet. i. 5. "*Kept by the power of God.*"

Tune Trophimus. 669.

1 SPARED a little longer,
May our souls grow stronger,
To maintain the arduous fight of faith.

2 Many foes surround us,
Hoping to confound us,
But the Lord Himself is our defence.

3 We have hearts deceitful,
And of truth forgetful,
Yet our gracious Lord His people spares.

4 Pilgrims here, and strangers,
Who can tell our dangers?
But our Lord will save us from them all.

5 He has dearly bought us,
Hitherto has brought us,
And will lead us to Himself at last.

6 By His eye directed,
By His arm protected,
We shall gain the presence of our God!

Thomas Kelly, 1804.

---

727 Phil. i. 6. "*He which hath begun . . . will perform.*"

Tune Mizpeh. 6666, 88.

MIZPEH (Valley of). [H. P. 120.]

1 O MY distrustful heart,
How small thy faith appears!
But greater, Lord, Thou art
Than all my doubts and fears:
Did Jesus once upon me shine?
Then Jesus is for ever mine.

2 Unchangeable His will,
Whatever be my frame;
His loving heart is still
Eternally the same:
My soul through many changes goes,
His love no variation knows.

3 Thou, Lord, wilt carry on,
And perfectly perform,
The work Thou hast begun
In me, a sinful worm:
'Midst all my fears, and sin, and woe,
Thy Spirit will not let me go.

4 Thy rich and sovereign grace
At first did freely move:
I still shall see Thy face,
And feel that God is love:
My soul into Thine arms I cast,
I know I shall be saved at last!

William Hammond, 1745; *Augustus M. Toplady*, 1776.

ST. CHRYSOSTOM. [H. P. 53.]

See Hymns 11, 12, 410, 411, 419—423.

728 Ps. xci. 1. "*The secret place of the Most High.*"

St. Chrysostom. C. M. Or Gloucester.

1 THERE is a safe and secret place
Beneath the wings Divine,
Reserved for all the heirs of grace:
Oh, be that refuge mine!

2 The least, the feeblest there may hide
Uninjured and unawed!
While thousands fall on every side,
He rests secure in God.

3 The angels watch him on his way,
And aid with friendly arm;
And Satan, roaring for his prey,
May hate, but cannot harm.

4 He feeds in pastures large and fair,
Of love and truth Divine:
O child of God, O glory's heir,
How rich a lot is thine!

5 A hand almighty to defend,
An ear for every call,
An honoured life, a peaceful end,
And heaven to crown it all!

Henry Francis Lyte, 1834.

---

(10) FINAL PERSEVERANCE.

729 John xiii. 1. "*He loved them unto the end.*" Tune Maon. 88, 88, 88.

1 IF ever it could come to pass
That sheep of Christ might fall away,
My fickle, feeble soul, alas!
Would fall a thousand times a day;
Were not Thy love as firm as free,
Thou soon wouldst take it, Lord, from me.

2 I on Thy promises depend
(At least I to depend desire)
That Thou wilt love me to the end,
Be with me in temptation's fire.
Wilt for me work, and in me too,
And guide me right, and bring me through.

3 No other stay have I beside;
If these can alter, I must fall:
I look to Thee to be supplied
With life, with will, with power, with all:
Rich souls may glory in their store,
But Jesus will relieve the *poor!*

Joseph Hart, 1759.

MAON (Wilderness of). [H. P. 229.]

730 Rom. viii. 37. "*More than conquerors through Him that loved us.*"

Tune NOTTINGHAM. C. M. Or WINTON.

1 REJOICE, believer, in the Lord,
Who makes your cause His own;
The hope that's built upon His word
Can ne'er be overthrown.

2 Though many foes beset your road,
And feeble is your arm,
Your life is hid with Christ in God,
Beyond the reach of harm.

3 Weak as you are, you shall not faint;
Or fainting shall not die;
Jesus, the strength of every saint,
Will aid you from on high.

NOTTINGHAM; *or,* ST. MAGNUS. [H. P. 39.]

4 Though sometimes unperceived by sense,
Faith sees Him always near,
A guide, a glory, a defence;
Then what have you to fear?

5 As surely as He overcame,
And triumphed once for you;
So surely you that love His name
Shall triumph in Him too!

John Newton, 1779.

731 Josh. i. 5. "*I will not fail thee, nor forsake thee.*"

Tune STERNBERG. 11 10, 11 10.

1 PILGRIM of earth, who art journeying to heaven!
Heir of eternal life! child of the day!
Cared for, watched over, beloved and forgiven,
Art thou discouraged because of the way?

2 Cared for, watched over, though often thou seemest
Justly forsaken, nor counted "a child"—
Loved and forgiven, though rightly thou deemest
Thyself all unlovely, impure, and defiled.

3 Weary and thirsty, no waterbrook near thee,
Press on, nor faint at the length of the way;
God in His grace will assuredly hear thee;
He will provide thee with strength for the day.

4 Break through the brambles and briers that obstruct thee;
Dread not the gloom or the blackness of night;
Lean on the Hand that will safely conduct thee;
Trust to His eye to whom darkness is light!

5 Trustful, and steadfast, whatever betide thee,
"One" thing alone do thou ask of the Lord—
"Grace" to go forward, wherever He guide thee,
Simply believing the truth of His word!

6 Still on thy spirit deep anguish is pressing—
Not for the yoke that His wisdom bestows;
A heavier burden thy soul is distressing,
A heart that is slow in His love to repose.

7 Earthliness, coldness, unthankful behaviour;
Oh! thou may'st sorrow, but do not despair:
Even this grief thou may'st bring to thy Saviour,
Cast upon Him e'en this burden and care.

STERNBERG. [H. P. 245.]

8 Bring all thy hardness; His power can subdue it;
Full is the promise! the blessing how free!
"All that ye ask in My name, I will do it;"
"Rest in My love, and be joyful in Me!"

Ryle's "Hymns for the Church on Earth," 1860. (*a.*)

ZOAN I. (Field of). [H. P. 127.]

732 Ps. lvi. 3. "*What time I am afraid, I will trust in Thee.*" Tune ZOAN I. 7 6, 7 6. D.

1 IS God for me? I fear not, though all against me rise;
I call on Christ my Saviour, the host of evil flies;
My Friend—the Lord Almighty, and He who loves me—God,
What enemy shall harm me, though coming as a flood?
I know it, I believe it, I say it fearlessly,
That God, the Highest, Mightiest, for ever loveth me!
At all times, in all places, He standeth at my side!
He rules the battle fury, the tempest, and the tide.

2 There is no condemnation, there is no hell for me,
The torment and the fire my eyes shall never see;
For me there is no sentence, for me has death no sting,
Because the Lord who loves me shall shield me with His wing!
Above my soul's dark waters His Spirit hovers still
He guards me from all sorrow, from terror and from ill:
In me He works, and blesses the life seed He has sown;
From Him I learn the "Abba," that prayer of faith alone.

3 No angel and no heaven, no throne nor power nor might,
No love, no tribulation, no danger, fear nor fight,
No height, no depth, no creature that has been or can be,
Can drive me from Thy bosom, can sever me from Thee.
My heart in joy upleapeth, grief cannot linger there,
While singing high in glory amidst the sunshine fair;
The sun that shines upon me is Jesus and His love;
The fountain of my singing is deep in heaven above!

Paul Gerhardt, 1659; Frances Shuttleworth (tr.), 1854.

733 Ps. lxxviii. 53. "*He led them on safely.*"
Tune ST. WERBERGH. 8 7, 8 7, 4 7.
Or HAVILAH.

1 SAVIOUR! through the desert lead us;
Without Thee we cannot go:
Thou from cruel chains hast freed us,
Thou hast laid the tyrant low:
Let Thy presence
Cheer us all our journey through.

2 With a price Thy love has bought us;
Saviour! what a love is Thine!
Hitherto Thy power has brought us—
Power and love in Thee combine!
Lord of glory!
Ever on Thy household shine.

3 Through a desert waste and cheerless
Though our destined journey lie,
Rendered by Thy presence fearless,
We may every foe defy:
Nought shall move us,
While we see our Saviour nigh.

4 When we halt (no track discovering),
Fearful lest we go astray,
O'er our path Thy pillar hovering,
Fire by night and cloud by day,
Shall direct us:
Then we shall not miss our way.

5 When we hunger, Thou wilt feed us,
Manna shall our camp surround;
Faint and thirsty, Thou wilt heed us,
Streams shall from the rock abound:
Happy Israel!
What a Saviour thou hast found!

ST. WERBERGH. [H. P. 304.]

Thomas Kelly, 1804.

LINUS. [H. P. 336.]

(11) EVERLASTING SALVATION.

734 Isa. xlv. 17. "*Saved in the Lord with an everlasting salvation.*" Tune LINUS. 1515, 1515. Or ESDRAELON.

1 OH what everlasting blessings God outpoureth on His own!
Ours by promise true and faithful, spoken from the' eternal throne;
Ours by His eternal purpose ere the universe had place;
Ours by everlasting covenant, ours by free and royal grace.

2 With salvation everlasting He shall save us, He shall bless
With the largess of Messiah, everlasting righteousness;
Ours the everlasting mercy all His wondrous dealings prove;
Ours His everlasting kindness, fruit of everlasting love.

3 In the Lord Jehovah trusting, everlasting strength have we;
He Himself, our Sun, our Glory, Everlasting Light shall be;
Everlasting life is ours, purchased by The Life laid down;
And our heads, oft bowed and weary, everlasting joy shall crown.

4 We shall dwell with Christ for ever, when the shadows flee away,
In the everlasting glory of the everlasting day.
Unto Thee, belovèd Saviour, everlasting thanks belong,
Everlasting adoration, everlasting laud and song!

Frances Ridley Havergal, 1871.

PHILADELPHIA. (HYMN CHANT.) [H. P. VII.]

III.—Talents Improved.

(1) TIME.

735 Eccles. ix. 10. "*There is no work . . . in the grave, whither thou goest.*"

Tune, Hymn Chant PHILADELPHIA. 66, 86, 6.

1 MAKE haste, O man, to live,
For thou so soon must die;
Time hurries past thee like the breeze—
How swift its moments fly!
Make haste, O man, to live

2 Make haste, O man, to do
Whatever must be done!
Thou hast no time to lose in sloth,
Thy day will soon be gone:
Make haste, O man, to live.

3 Up then, with speed, and work;
Fling ease and self away;
This is no time for thee to sleep,
Up, watch, and work, and pray!
Make haste, O man, to live.

4 The useful, not the great,
The thing that never dies,
The silent toil that is not lost:
Set these before thine eyes:
Make haste, O man, to live.

5 Make haste, O man, to live,
Thy time is almost o'er;
Oh sleep not, dream not, but arise,
The Judge is at the door:
Make haste, O man, to live!

Horatius Bonar, D.D., 1857.

GENNESARET. [H. P. 17.]

(2) TONGUE.

736 Ps. cxli. 3. "*Keep the door of my lips.*" Tune GENNESARET. L. M. Or HERMON.

1 GUARD well thy lips; none, none can know
What evil from the tongue may flow;
What guilt, what grief may be incurred,
By one incautious, hasty word.

2 Be "slow to speak"; look well within,
To check what there may lead to sin;
And pray unceasingly for aid,
Lest unawares thou be betrayed.

3 "Condemn not, judge not"—not to man
Is given his brother's faults to scan;
One task is thine, and one alone—
To search out and subdue thine own.

4 Indulge no murmurings; oh, restrain
Those lips so ready to complain;
And, if they can be numbered, count
Of one day's mercies the amount.

5 Shun vain discussions, trifling themes;
Dwell not on earthly hopes or schemes;
Let words of wisdom, meekness, love,
Thy heart's true renovation prove.

6 Set God before thee; every word
Thy lips pronounce by Him is heard;
Oh! couldst thou realize this thought,
What care, what caution would be taught!

7 Think on thy parting hour: ere long
The' approach of death may chain thy tongue,
And powerless all attempts be found
To' articulate one meaning sound.

8 "The time is short"—this day may be
The very last assigned to thee:
So speak, that shouldst thou ne'er speak more,
Thou may'st not this day's words deplore!

Charlotte Elliott, 1839.

EVAN I. [H. P. 54.]

737 2 Cor. x. 1. "*I beseech you by the meekness and gentleness of Christ.*"

Tune EVAN I. C. M.

1 SPEAK gently, it is better far
To rule by love than fear;
Speak gently, let not harsh word mar
The good we might do here.

2 Speak gently, love should whisper low
To friends when faults we find;
Gently let truthful accents flow:
Affection's voice is kind.

3 Speak gently to the young, for they
Will have enough to bear;
Pass through this life as best they may,
'Tis full of anxious care.

4 Speak gently to the aged one,
Grieve not the careworn heart;
The sands of life are nearly run,
Let such in peace depart.

5 Speak gently, kindly, to the poor,
Let no harsh tones be heard;
They have enough they must endure,
Without an unkind word.

6 Speak gently to the erring, know
That thou thyself art vain;
Perchance unkindness made them so,
Oh, win them back again.

7 Speak gently, for 'tis like the Lord,
Whose accents, meek and mild,
Bespoke Him as the Son of God,
The gracious Holy Child!

George Washington Hangford, 1847.

See Hymns 547, 556, 587, 970.

(3) INFLUENCE.

738 Rom. xiv. 7. "*None of us liveth to himself.*"

Tune, Hymn Chant EPHESUS. C. M.
Or BRISTOL.

1 THE glorious universe around,
The heavens with all their train,
Sun, moon, and stars, are firmly bound,
In one mysterious chain.

2 God, in creation, thus displays
His wisdom and His might!
While all His works with all His ways
Harmoniously unite.

3 In one fraternal bond of love,
One fellowship of mind,
The saints below and saints above
Their bliss and glory find.

EPHESUS. (Hymn Chant.) (*Unison.*) [H. P. No. II.]

4 Here, in their house of pilgrimage,
Thy statutes are their song:
There, through one bright eternal age,
Thy praises they prolong.

5 Lord, may our union form a part
Of that thrice happy whole;
Derive its pulse from Thee the heart,
Its life from Thee the soul!

James Montgomery, 1825.

See Hymn 970.

CULBACH. [H. P. 181.]

(4) WEALTH.

739

1 Chron. xxix. 14. "*All things come of Thee, and of Thine own have we given Thee.*"

Tune Culbach. 87, 87.

1 WITH my substance I will honour
My Redeemer and my Lord;
Were ten thousand worlds my manor
All were nothing to His word.

2 While the heralds of salvation
His abounding grace proclaim,
Let His friends of every station
Gladly join to spread His fame.

3 Be His kingdom now promoted,
Let the earth her Monarch know;
Be my all to Him devoted,
To my Lord my all I owe.

4 Praise the Saviour, all ye nations;
Praise Him, all ye hosts above;
Shout, with joyful acclamations,
His Divine, victorious love!

Benjamin Francis, 1787.

ST. BARNABAS II. [H. P. 345.]

See Hymns 597, 598; *also "Missions."*

740

Luke vi. 40. "*The disciple is not above his Master.*"

Tune St. Barnabas II. 86, 86, 88. Or Lebanon.

1 AS much have I of worldly good
As e'er my Master had;
I diet on as dainty food,
And am as richly clad,
Though plain my garb, though scant my board,
As Mary's Son and nature's Lord.

2 The manger was His infant bed,
His home the mountain cave;
He had not where to lay His head,
He borrowed e'en His grave;
Earth yielded Him no resting spot—
Her Maker! but she knew Him not.

3 As much the world's good-will I share,
Its favour and applause,
As He whose blessèd name I bear,
Hated without a cause,
Despised, rejected, mocked by pride,
Betrayed, forsaken, crucified.

4 Why should I court my Master's foe?
Why should I fear its frown?
Why should I seek for rest below,
Or sigh for brief renown?
A pilgrim to a better land,
An heir of joy at God's right hand!

Josiah Conder, 1824.

ST. ANN. [H. P. 52.]

IV.—Duties Fulfilled.

(1) SOCIAL AND RELATIVE.

741 Ps. cxxxiii. 1. *"How good and how pleasant it is for brethren to dwell together in unity."*

Tune St. Ann. C. M.

1 HOW sweet, how heavenly is the sight,
When those that love the Lord
In one another's peace delight,
And so fulfil His word!

2 When each can feel his brother's sigh,
And with him bear a part;
When sorrow flows from eye to eye,
And joy from heart to heart;

3 When free from envy, scorn, and pride,
Our wishes all above,
Each can his brother's failings hide,
And show a brother's love;

4 When love, in one delightful stream,
Through every bosom flows,
When union sweet and kind esteem
In every action glows.

5 Love is the golden chain that binds
The happy souls above;
And he's an heir of heaven that finds
His bosom glow with love!

Joseph Swain, 1792.

742 Rom. xiii. 7. *"Render therefore to all their dues."*

Tune Merom. 8 8 7. D.

MEROM (Waters of). [H. P. 215.]

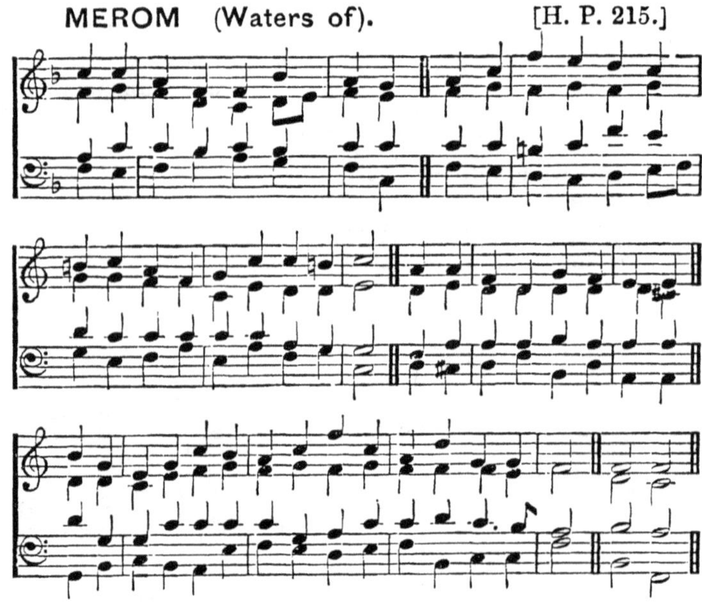

1 CHRISTIANS, in your several stations,
Dutiful to all relations,
Give to each his proper due;
Let not their unkind behaviour
Make you disobey your Saviour;
Be His word the rule for you!

2 Parents, be to children tender;
Children, full obedience render
To your parents in the Lord;
Never slight nor disrespect them;
Nor, through pride, when old, reject them;
'Tis the precept of His word.

3 Wives, to husbands yield subjection;
Husbands, with a kind affection
Cherish as yourselves your wives;
Masters, rule with moderation,
Swayed by justice, not by passion:
By the Scriptures guide your lives.

4 Servants, serve your masters truly,
Not unfaithful nor unruly,
To the good, nor to the bad;
Not replying when corrected,
Nor refusing aught suggested;
'Tis the ordinance of God.

5 Thus you solve the' important question,
"Am I now indeed a Christian?"
Better far than fancy's dream;
Better far than lip expression,
Lofty words, and great profession:
Thus you prove your love to Him!

Joseph Hart, 1759. (a.)

See Hymns 589, 592.

(2) CHRISTIAN FELLOWSHIP.

743 Luke xxiv. 15. *"While they communed together and reasoned, Jesus Himself drew near."*

Tune Cyprus. L. M. D.

1 IT is a practice greatly blessed
To speak, Lord Jesu Christ, of Thee;
Thou art amongst us as a guest,
We feel it, though we cannot see:
We seem to breathe, in glad surprise,
An atmosphere of love and bliss,
And read, within each other's eyes,
To whom it is we owe all this.

2 How quickly strife and envy end,
How soon all idle griefs depart,
When friend takes counsel thus with friend,
When soul meets soul and heart meets heart:
We have so many things to say,
So many failings to confess,
Time flies, alas! so soon away,
We cannot half we would express.

CYPRUS. [H. P. 26.]

3 How fain would we repeat again
The touching tale of God's dear Son,
His faithfulness and love to men,
And the great things which He hath done;
How He first touched our heart and feelings
By joy and grief's alternate sway,
And led us by His gracious dealings
In safety to this very day.

4 Oh let us then, dear Lord, be blest
With Thy sweet presence every day,
Be with us as our daily guest,
And our companion on the way;
Fan our devotion's feeble flame,
Let us press on to things before,
Bring us together in Thy name,
Until we meet to part no more!

C. J. P. Spitta, 1833; *R. Massie (tr.)*, 1860.

TALLIS'S ORDINAL. [H. P. 44.]

(3) MUTUAL FORBEARANCE.

744 Rom. xii. 5. *"One body in Christ, and every one members one of another."* Tune TALLIS. C. M. Or WINCHESTER.

1 LET party names no more be known
Among the ransomed throng;
For Jesus claims them for His own,
To Him they all belong.

2 One in their covenant Head and King,
They should be one in heart;
Of one salvation all should sing,
Each claiming his own part.

3 One bread, one family, one rock,
One building, formed by love,
One fold, one Shepherd, yea, one flock,
They shall be one above.

4 One city, ruled by laws Divine,
"Peace be within her walls";
Zion shall in full glory shine,
When Satan's empire falls!

Joseph Irons, 1825.

745 1 John iv. 7. *"Beloved, let us love one another."*

Tune CASSEL. 8 7, 8 7, 7 7.

CASSEL. [H. P. 190.]

1 BRETHREN, called by one vocation,
Members of one family,
Heirs through Christ of one salvation,
Let us live in harmony;
Nor by strife Embitter life,
Journeying to eternity.

2 In a land where all are strangers
And our sojourning so short,
In the midst of common dangers,
Concord is our best support:
Heart with heart Divides the smart,
Lightens grief of every sort.

3 Let us shun all vain contention
Touching words and outward things,
Whence, alas! so much dissension
And such bitter rancour springs;
Troubles cease, Where Christ brings peace
And sweet healing on His wings.

4 Judge not hastily of others,
But thine own salvation mind;
Nor be lynx-eyed to thy brother's,
To thine own offences blind;
God alone Discerns thine own,
And the hearts of all mankind.

5 Let it be our chief endeavour,
That we may the Lord obey,
Then shall envy cease for ever,
And all hate be done away;
Free from strife Shall be his life
Who serves God both night and day.

See Hymn 214.

C. J. P. Spitta, 1833; *R. Massie (tr.)*, 1860.

HERMON. [H. P. 27.]

(4) SAINTS AND MARTYRS—THEIR HOLY EXAMPLE.

THE BLESSED VIRGIN MARY.

746 Luke xi. 28. "*Yea rather, blessed are they that hear the word of God, and keep it.*"

Tune Hermon. L. M.

1 AGE after age has called thee blessed,
Yet none have fathomed all thy bliss;
Mothers, who read the secret best,
Or angels—yet its depths must miss.

2 To dwell at home with Him for years,
And prove His filial love thine own;
In all a mother's tender cares
To serve thy Saviour in thy Son:

3 To see before thee day by day
That perfect light expand and shine,
And learn by sight, as angels may,
All that is holy and Divine:

4 The measure of a blessedness,
Yet by that measure unexpressed:
Sealing the mother's joy with "Yes,"
The Christian's with His "rather blessed."

Elizabeth Charles, 1860.

GOLDBACH. [H. P. 130.]

SAINTS.

747 Rev. xv. 3. "*Just and true are Thy ways, Thou King of saints.*" Tune Goldbach. 76, 76. D.

1 FROM all Thy saints in warfare, for all Thy saints at rest,
To Thee, O blessèd Jesus, all praises be addressed.
Thou, Lord, didst win the battle that they might conquerors be;
Their crowns of living glory are lit with rays from Thee.

(*Insert here the stanza for the special Saint's Day to be celebrated.*)

SAINT ANDREW.

2 Praise, Lord, for Thine apostle, the first to welcome Thee,
The first to lead his brother the very Christ to see.
With hearts for Thee made ready, watch we throughout the year,
Forward to lead our brethren to own Thine Advent near.

SAINT THOMAS.

3 All praise for Thine apostle, whose short-lived doubtings prove
Thy perfect two-fold nature, the fulness of Thy love.
On all who wait Thy coming shed forth Thy peace, O Lord,
And grant us faith to know Thee, true Man, true God, adored.

SAINT STEPHEN.

4 Praise for the first of martyrs, who saw Thee ready stand,
To aid in midst of torment, to plead at God's right hand.
Share we with him, if summoned by death our Lord to own,
On earth the faithful witness, in heaven the martyr-crown.

Saint John the Evangelist.

5 Praise for the loved disciple, exile on Patmos' shore;
Praise for the faithful record he to Thy Godhead bore;
Praise for the mystic vision, through him to us revealed:
May we, in patience waiting, with Thine elect be sealed.

The Innocents' Day.

6 Praise for Thine infant martyrs, by Thee with tenderest love
Called early from the warfare to share the rest above.
O Rachel, cease thy weeping; they rest from pains and cares;
Lord, grant us hearts as guileless, and crowns as bright as theirs.

The Conversion of Saint Paul.

7 Praise for the light from heaven, praise for the voice of awe,
Praise for the glorious vision the persecutor saw:
Thee, Lord, for his conversion we glorify to-day;
So lighten all our darkness with Thy true Spirit's ray.

Saint Matthias.

8 Lord, Thine abiding presence directs the wondrous choice;
For one in place of Judas the faithful now rejoice.
Thy church from false apostles for evermore defend,
And by Thy parting promise be with her to the end.

Saint Mark.

9 For him, O Lord, we praise Thee, the weak by grace made strong,
Whose labours and whose Gospel enrich our triumph-song.
May we in all our weakness find strength from Thee supplied,
And all, as fruitful branches, in Thee, the Vine, abide.

Saint Philip and Saint James.

10 All praise for Thine apostle, blessed guide to Greek and Jew,
And him surnamed Thy brother: keep us Thy brethren true;
And grant the grace to know Thee, the Way, the Truth, the Life;
To wrestle with temptations till victors in the strife.

Saint Barnabas.

11 The son of consolation, moved by Thy law of love,
Forsaking earthly treasures, sought riches from above.
As earth now teems with increase, let gifts of grace descend,
That Thy true consolations may through the world extend.

Saint John Baptist.

12 We praise Thee for the Baptist, forerunner of the Word,
Our true Elias, making a highway for the Lord.
Of prophets last and greatest, he saw Thy dawning ray,
Make us the rather blessèd, who love Thy glorious day.

Saint Peter.

13 Praise for Thy great apostle, the eager and the bold;
Thrice falling, yet repentant, thrice charged to feed Thy fold.
Lord, make Thy pastors faithful, to guard their flocks from ill;
And grant them dauntless courage, with humble earnest will.

Saint James.

14 For him, O Lord, we praise Thee, who, slain by Herod's sword,
Drank of Thy cup of suffering, fulfilling thus Thy word.
Curb we all vain impatience to read Thy veiled decree!
And count it joy to suffer, if so brought nearer Thee.

Saint Bartholomew.

15 All praise for Thine apostle, the faithful, pure, and true,
Whom, underneath the fig-tree, Thine eye all-seeing knew.
Like him may we be guileless, true Israelites indeed;
That Thine abiding presence our longing souls may feed.

Saint Matthew.

16 Praise, Lord, for him whose Gospel Thy human life declared,
Who, worldly gains forsaking, Thy path of suffering shared.
From all unrighteous mammon, oh! give us hearts set free,
That we, whate'er our calling, may rise and follow Thee.

Saint Luke.

17 For that beloved physician, all praise, whose Gospel shows
The Healer of the nations, the Sharer of our woes.
Thy wine and oil, O Saviour, on bruised hearts deign to pour,
And with true balm of Gilead anoint us evermore.

Saint Simon and Saint Jude.

18 Praise, Lord, for Thine apostles, who sealed their faith to-day;
One love, one zeal impelled them to tread the sacred way.
May we with zeal as earnest the faith of Christ maintain,
And, bound in love as brethren, at length Thy rest attain.

General Ending.

19 Apostles, Prophets, Martyrs, and all the sacred throng,
Who wear the spotless raiment, who raise the ceaseless song!
For these passed on before us, Saviour, we Thee adore,
And, walking in their footsteps, would serve Thee more and more.

20 Then praise we God the Father, and praise we God the Son,
And God the Holy Spirit, eternal Three in One;
Till all the ransomed number fall down before the throne,
And honour, power, and glory ascribe to God alone! Amen.

Earl Nelson, 1867.

CRASSELIUS; *or*, WINCHESTER NEW. [H. P. 3.]

748

Eph. iii. 15. "*The whole family in heaven and earth.*" Tune CRASSELIUS. L. M.

1 FOR all Thy saints in heaven and earth,
One hallowed day is set apart
For deep communion, holy mirth,
And mystic unity of heart:
One brotherhood of love unites,
Which neither time nor death can sever;
One song is sung, one joy delights
The family of God for ever.

2 What shining ranks around God's throne!
Confessors, martyrs, patriarchs, seers,
Gathered from every clime and zone,
Since the world's infancy of years:
Blood-bought, and clothed in robes of white,
Victors who sing the victor's song;
For ever with the saints in light,
Their bliss ineffable prolong.

3 Earth's myriads join their songs to-day,
And earth and heaven in concert meet;
O grand and universal lay!
O heavenly song of songs complete!
Salvation, honour, glory, praise,
From saints below and saints on high:
The Alleluia chorus raise
To Christ through all eternity.

4 One throbbing heart, one burning love,
Cements Christ's lovers to each other;
All have their common home above,
And all in Christ an elder Brother:
And soon—no more to weep or roam,
No wanderer lost—with palm and crown,
God's family shall meet at home,
And in their Father's house sit down!

Benjamin Gough, 1865.

SARDIS. (HYMN CHANT.) [H. P. No. VI.]

749

Heb. xii. 1. "*So great a cloud of witnesses.*" Tune, Hymn Chant SARDIS. 10 10 10, 4.

1 FOR all Thy saints, who from their labours rest,
Who Thee by faith before the world confessed,
Thy name, O Jesu, be for ever blessed. Alleluia!

2 Thou wast their rock, their fortress, and their might;
Thou, Lord, their Captain in the well-fought fight;
Thou in the darkness drear their one true light. Alleluia!

3 O may Thy soldiers, faithful, true, and bold,
Fight as the saints who nobly fought of old,
And win with them the victor's crown of gold. Alleluia!

4 O pure communion, fellowship Divine!
We feebly struggle, they in glory shine;
Yet all are one in Thee, for all are Thine. Alleluia!

5 And when the strife is fierce, the warfare long,
Steals on the ear the distant triumph-song,
And hearts are brave again, and arms are strong. Alleluia!

6 The golden evening brightens in the west:
Soon, soon to faithful warriors cometh rest;
Sweet is the calm of Paradise the blest. Alleluia!

7 But lo, there breaks a yet more glorious day:
The saints triumphant rise in bright array:
The King of glory passes on His way. Alleluia!

8 From earth's wide bounds, from ocean's farthest coast,
Through gates of pearl streams in the countless host,
Singing to Father, Son, and Holy Ghost. Alleluia!

Bishop William Walsham How, 1867.

See *Hymns* 437—440.

SAMARIA (Hill of). [H. P. 162.]

THE NOBLE ARMY OF MARTYRS.

750

Rev. xiv. 4. "*The first-fruits unto God and to the Lamb.*"

Tune SAMARIA. 77, 77. D. Or KADESH.

1 HOLY Jesus, mighty Lord,
Light of light, incarnate Word,
Who didst take our fleshly dress
In an infant's helplessness,
And didst pass to manhood's stage,
Consecrating every age;
Thou from whom all graces fall;
Be Thou worshipped, Lord, by all.

2 Planets, as their race they run,
Drink their radiance from the sun;
Saints derive their holiness
From the Sun of Righteousness:
He lit up Saint Stephen's face,
Crowned Saint John's old age with grace,
Gilded life's first lineaments
In the Holy Innocents.

3 At Thy birth, incarnate Lord,
They were slain by Herod's sword;
But they, Lord, who for Thee died,
By Thy birth were glorified;
Thou, an infant born, didst give
Life by which they dying live;
Thou didst love them as Thine own,
Thou didst set them near Thy throne.

4 Some, like Stephen, for Thee bleed,
Martyrs both in will and deed!
Some, like John, Thy law fulfil
By the martyrdom of will;
Others yield their life-blood's price
An unconscious sacrifice!
Thou, the Fountain of all lights,
Shinest in all Thy satellites.

5 Thou, who givest infants breath,
Didst them beautify by death;
Thou hast woven in Thy crown
These sweet flowers of spring unblown:
Mortify in us and kill
Whatsoe'er resists Thy will;
Make us, blessèd Lord, to be
Infants in simplicity!

Bp. Christ. Wordsworth, 1862.

FRANCONIA. [H. P. 87.]

751

Rev. xiv. 5. "*They are without fault before the throne of God.*"
Tune Franconia. S. M.

1 GLORY to Thee, O Lord!
Who from this world of sin,
By the fierce Herod's ruthless sword,
Those precious ones didst win!

2 Glory to Thee, O Lord!
For now, all grief unknown,
They wait in patience their reward,
The martyr's heavenly crown!

3 Baptized in their own blood,
Earth's untried perils o'er,
They passed unconsciously the flood,
And safely gained the shore.

4 Glory to Thee for all
The ransomed infant band
Who since that hour have heard Thy call
And reached the quiet land!

5 Oh that our hearts within
Were innocent and bright:
Oh that, as free from wilful sin,
We shrunk not from Thy sight!

6 Lord, help us every hour
Thy cleansing grace to share;
In life to glorify Thy power,
In death Thy praise declare.

7 All praise, while ages run,
To Father ever blest,
To Spirit, and eternal Son,
In flesh made manifest!

Emma Toke, 1853.

OLD 81st. [H. P. 75.]

752

Rev. xii. 11. "*They loved not their lives unto the death.*" Tune Old Eighty-first. C. M. D.

1 THE Son of God goes forth to war,
A kingly crown to gain;
His blood-red banner streams afar:
Who follows in His train?
Who best can drink his cup of woe,
Triumphant over pain,
Who patient bears his cross below,
He follows in His train.

2 The martyr first, whose eagle eye
Could pierce beyond the grave;
Who saw his Master in the sky,
And called on Him to save.
Like Him, with pardon on his tongue,
In midst of mortal pain,
He prayed for them that did the wrong:
Who follows in his train?

3 A glorious band, the chosen few,
On whom the Spirit came;
Twelve valiant saints, their hope they knew,
And mocked the cross and flame.
They met the tyrant's brandished steel,
The lion's gory mane;
They bowed their necks the death to feel:
Who follows in their train?

4 A noble army, men and boys,
The matron and the maid,
Around the Saviour's throne rejoice,
In robes of light arrayed.
They climbed the steep ascent of heaven,
Through peril, toil, and pain:
O God! to us may grace be given
To follow in their train!

Bishop Heber, 1827.

(5) ANGELS—MINISTERING SPIRITS.

753 Heb. i. 14. *"Are they not all ministering spirits?"* Tune LINUS. 87, 87. Or EVERTON.

1 THEY are evermore around us,
Though unseen to mortal sight,
In the golden hour of sunshine,
And in sorrow's starless night.
Deepening earth's most sacred pleasures
With the peace of sin forgiven,
Whispering to the lonely mourner
Of the painless joys of heaven.

2 Lovingly they come to help us
When our faith is cold and weak,
Guiding us along the pathway
To the blessèd home we seek.
In our hearts we hear their voices,
Breathing sympathy and love:
Echoes of the spirit language
In the sinless world above.

3 They are with us in the conflict,
With their words of hope and cheer,
When the foe of our salvation
And his armèd hosts draw near.
And a greater One is with us,
And we shrink not from the strife,
While the Lord of angels leads us
On the battle-field of life!

James Drummond Burns, 1858.

754 Ps. xci. 11. *"He shall give His angels charge over thee."* Tune SALISBURY. C. M.

1 INCARNATE God, the soul that knows
Thy name's mysterious power
Shall dwell in undisturbed repose,
Nor fear the trying hour.

2 Angels, unseen, attend the saints,
And bear them in their arms,
To cheer the spirit when it faints,
And guard the life from harms.

3 The angels' Lord Himself is nigh
To them that love His name;
Ready to save them when they cry,
And put their foes to shame.

4 Crosses and changes are their lot,
Long as they sojourn here;
But since their Saviour changes not,
What have the saints to fear?

John Newton, 1779.

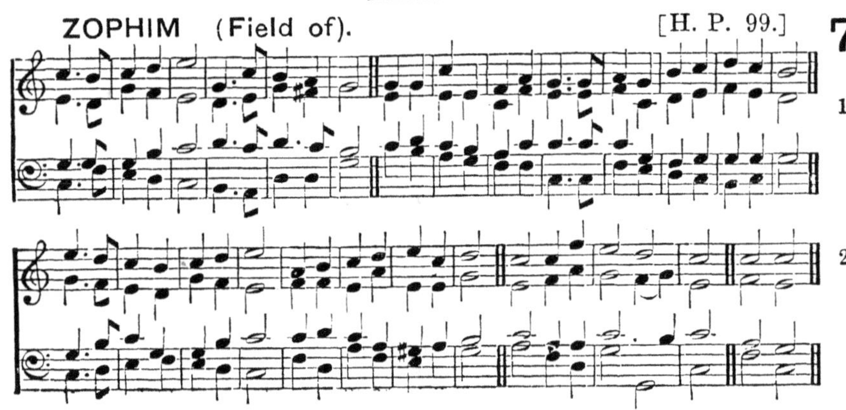

755 Luke xv. 10. *"Joy in the presence of the angels of God."*

Tune ZOPHIM. 5 5, 7 7, 7 7 6.

1 THERE was joy in heaven!
There was joy in heaven!
When this goodly world to frame
The Lord of might and mercy came:
Shouts of joy were heard on high,
And the stars sang from the sky—
"Glory to God in heaven!"

2 There was joy in heaven!
There was joy in heaven!
When the billows, heaving dark,
Sank around the stranded ark,
And the rainbow's watery span
Spake of mercy, hope to man,
And peace with God in heaven!

3 There was joy in heaven!
There was joy in heaven!
When of love the midnight beam
Dawned on the towers of Bethlehem;
And along the echoing hill
Angels sang, "On earth good will,
And glory in the heaven!"

4 There is joy in heaven!
There is joy in heaven!
When the sheep that went astray
Turns again to virtue's way;
When the soul, by grace subdued,
Sobs its prayer of gratitude,
Then is there joy in heaven!

5 There is joy in heaven!
There is joy in heaven!
When the worn and panting soul
Outstrips death and gains the goal:
When he views, with rapturous eyes,
Christ, his own eternal prize,
Then is all joy in heaven!

Bishop Heber, 1827; *last verse by W. H. Havergal*, 1853.

See Hymns 223, 224.

THEME IV.—Ambassadors for Christ.

CRETE (WITH DOXOLOGY). [H. P. 22.]

(1) CONSECRATION AND ORDINATION.

756 John xx. 22. "*He breathed on them, and saith unto them, Receive ye the Holy Ghost.*"

Tune CRETE. L. M. Or DORTMUND.

1 COME, Holy Ghost, our souls inspire,
And lighten with celestial fire.
Thou the anointing Spirit art,
Who dost Thy sevenfold gifts impart.

2 Thy blessèd unction from above
Is comfort, life, and fire of love.
Enable with perpetual light
The dulness of our blinded sight.

3 Anoint and cheer our soilèd face
With the abundance of Thy grace.
Keep far our foes, give peace at home:
Where Thou art guide no ill can come.

4 Teach us to know the Father, Son,
And Thee of both to be but One,
That, through the ages all along,
This may be our endless song;
Praise to Thy eternal merit,
Father, Son, and Holy Spirit!

From Latin Hymn of Fourth Century;
Bishop John Cosin (tr.), 1627.

DORTMUND (WITH DOXOLOGY). [H. P. 21.]

GILBOA (Mount). [H. P. 11.]

757 Acts i. 8. "*Ye shall receive power, after that the Holy Ghost is come upon you.*"

Tune GILBOA. L. M. Or WALDECK.

1 POUR out Thy Spirit from on high,
Lord, Thine ordainèd servants bless:
Graces and gifts to each supply,
And clothe Thy priests with righteousness.

2 Within Thy temple as they stand,
To teach the truth as taught by Thee,
Saviour, like stars in Thy right hand,
Let all Thy church's pastors be.

3 Wisdom and zeal and love impart,
Firmness with meekness from above,
To bear Thy people in their heart,
And love the souls whom Thou dost love:

4 To love and pray and never faint,
By day and night strict guard to keep,
To warn the sinner, cheer the saint,
Nourish Thy lambs, and feed Thy sheep.

5 Then when their work is finished here,
May they in hope their charge resign:
When the Chief Shepherd shall appear,
May they, O God, in glory shine!

James Montgomery, 1835.

See Hymns 346, 363, 366.

(2) MINISTERS OF CHRIST AND STEWARDS OF THE MYSTERIES OF GOD.

KEDRON (Brook). [H. P. 213.]

758 2 Thess. iii. 1. "*Brethren, pray for us.*"

Tune KEDRON. 8 8 6. D.

1 LORD of the church, we humbly pray
For those who guide us in Thy way,
And speak Thy holy word:
With love Divine their hearts inspire,
And touch their lips with hallowed fire,
And needful grace impart.

2 Help them to preach the truth of God,
Redemption through the Saviour's blood;
Nor let Thy Spirit cease
On all the church His gifts to shower;
To them, a messenger of power,
To us, of life and peace.

3 So may they live to Thee alone;
Then hear the welcome word—"Well done,"
And take their crown above;
Enter into their Master's joy,
And all eternity employ
In praise and bliss and love!

Edward Osler, 1836.

See Hymns 120, 431, 837-841, 867, 868, 970, 1025, 1041, 1062, 1069, 1084, 1093.

ANGELS' SONG. [H. P. 227.]

759 Col. iv. 7. "*A faithful minister . . . in the Lord.*"

Tune ANGELS' SONG. 8 8, 8 8, 8 8.

1 O THOU, who didst at Pentecost
Send down from heaven the Holy Ghost,
That He might with Thy church abide
For ever to defend and guide;
Illuminate and strengthen, Lord,
The preachers of Thy holy word.

2 Oh, may Thy pastors faithful be,
Not labouring for themselves, but Thee;
And may they feed with wholesome food
The sheep and lambs bought by Thy blood;
And tending Thy dear flock, may prove
How dearly they the Shepherd love!

3 That which the Holy Scriptures teach,
That, and that only, may they preach;
May they the true foundation lay,
Build gold thereon, not wood or hay;
And meekly preach, in days of strife,
The sermon of a holy life.

4 As ever in Thy holy eyes,
And stewards of Thy mysteries,
May they the people teach to see
Not, Lord, Thy ministers, but Thee;
To see a loving Saviour's face
Revealed in all Thy means of grace.

5 May they Thy word with boldness speak,
And bear with tenderness the weak;
Not seeking their own things as best,
But what may edify the rest;
With wisdom and simplicity,
And most of all with charity.

6 Oh, may Thy people faithful be,
And in Thy pastors honour Thee,
And, labouring with them, for them pray,
And gladly Thee in them obey;
And love the prophet of the Lord,
And gain the prophet's own reward!

Bishop Christopher Wordsworth, 1862.

760 Rom. x. 15. "*How beautiful are the feet of them that preach the gospel of peace.*"

Tune FUGAL. S. M. Or NARENZA.

1 HOW beauteous are their feet
Who stand on Zion's hill,
Who bring salvation on their tongues,
And words of peace reveal!

2 How charming is their voice!
How sweet the tidings are!
"Zion, behold thy Saviour King;
He reigns and triumphs here."

3 How happy are our ears,
That hear this joyful sound,
Which kings and prophets waited for,
And sought but never found.

FUGAL. [H. P. 346.]

4 How blessèd are our eyes,
That see this heavenly light;
Prophets and kings desired it long,
But died without the sight!

5 The Lord makes bare His arm
Through all the earth abroad;
Let every nation now behold
Their Saviour and their God!

Isaac Watts, D.D., 1709.

BESOR (Brook). [H. P. 51.]

761

Rev. ii. 10. "*Be thou faithful unto death.*"

Tune Besor. C. M.

1 LET Zion's watchmen all awake,
And take the' alarm they give;
Now let them from the mouth of God
Their solemn charge receive.

2 'Tis not a cause of small import
The pastor's care demands;
But what might fill an angel's heart,
And filled a Saviour's hands.

3 They watch for souls, for which the Lord
Did heavenly bliss forego;
For souls which must for ever live
In raptures or in woe.

4 All to the great tribunal haste,
The' account to render there;
And shouldst Thou strictly mark our faults,
Lord, how should we appear?

5 May they that Jesus, whom they preach,
Their own Redeemer see;
And watch Thou daily o'er their souls,
That they may watch for Thee!

Philip Doddridge, D.D., 1755.

SAXONY. [H. P. 32.]

ILLNESS OF MINISTERS.

762

2 Cor. i. 10. "*We trust that He will yet deliver.*" Tune Saxony. L. M.

1 O THOU, before whose gracious throne
We bow our suppliant spirits down!
Thou know'st the anxious cares we feel,
And all our trembling lips would tell.

2 With power benign, Thy servant spare;
Nor turn aside Thy people's prayer;
Avert Thy swift descending stroke,
Nor smite the shepherd of the flock!

3 Restore him, sinking to the grave,
Stretch out Thine arm, make haste to save;
Back to our hopes and wishes give,
And bid our friend and father live.

4 Yet, if our supplications fail,
And prayers and tears can nought prevail,
Be Thou his strength, be Thou his stay,
And guide him safe to endless day!

J. K., 1787.

DEATH OF MINISTERS.

763

Rev. xiv. 13. "*Rest from their labours.*" Tune Fugal. S. M. Or Cyrene.

1 REST from thy labour, rest,
Soul of the just, set free!
Blest be thy memory, and blest
Thy bright example be.

2 Faith, perseverance, zeal,
Language of light and power,
Love, prompt to act and quick to feel,
Marked thee till life's last hour.

3 Now, toil and conflict o'er,
Go, take with saints thy place;
But go as each has gone before,
A sinner saved by grace.

4 Saviour, into Thy hands
Our pastor we resign;
And now we wait Thine own commands—
We were not his, but Thine.

5 Thou art Thy church's Head;
And, when the members die,
Thou raisest others in their stead:
To Thee we lift our eye;

6 On Thee our hopes depend,
We gather round our Rock;
Send whom Thou wilt, but condescend
Thyself to feed Thy flock!

James Montgomery, 1851.

See Hymns 973, 980.

FRANCONIA. [H. P. 87.]

764 Matt. xxv. 23. "*Well done, good and faithful servant.*" Tune FRANCONIA. S. M.

1 SERVANT of God, well done!
Rest from thy loved employ;
The battle fought, the victory won,
Enter thy Master's joy.

2 The pains of death are past;
Labour and sorrow cease;
And, life's long warfare closed at last,
His soul is found in peace.

3 Soldier of Christ, well done!
Praise be thy new employ;
And, while eternal ages run,
Rest in thy Saviour's joy!

James Montgomery, 1816.

PHILADELPHIA. (HYMN CHANT.) [H. P. VII.]

(3) FELLOW HELPERS.

765 Matt. xxi. 28. "*Go, work to-day in My vineyard.*" Tune, Hymn Chant PHILADELPHIA. 4, 10 10, 10 4.

1 COME, labour on!
Who dares stand idle on the harvest plain?
While all around him waves the golden grain,
And to each servant does the Master say,
"Go work to-day!"

2 Come, labour on!
Claim the high calling angels cannot share—
To young and old the gospel-gladness bear:
Redeem the time; its hours too swiftly fly,
The night draws nigh.

3 Come, labour on!
The labourers are few, the field is wide,
New stations must be filled, and blanks supplied;
From voices distant far, or near at home,
The call is "Come!"

4 Come, labour on!
Away with gloomy doubts and faithless fear!
No arm so weak but may do service here;
By feeblest agents can our God fulfil
His righteous will.

5 Come, labour on!
No time for rest, till glows the western sky,
While the long shadows o'er our pathway lie,
And a glad sound comes with the setting sun—
"Servants, well done!"

6 Come, labour on!
The toil is pleasant, the reward is sure,
Blessèd are those who to the end endure;
How full their joy, how deep their rest shall be,
O Lord, with Thee!

See *Hymn* 689.

Jane Borthwick, 1859.

EPHESUS. (HYMN CHANT.) (*Unison.*) [H. P. No. II.]

766 2 Cor. xii. 15. "*I will very gladly spend and be spent.*" Tune, Hymn Chant EPHESUS. L. M. Or GILBOA.

1 GO labour on! spend and be spent—
Thy joy to do thy Father's will;
It is the way the Master went,
Should not the servant tread it still?

2 Go labour on! 'tis not for nought,
All earthly loss is heavenly gain!
Men heed thee not, men praise thee not;
The Master praises! what are men?

3 Go labour on! enough, enough,
If Jesus praise thee, if He deign
To notice e'en thy willing mind,
No toil for Him shall be in vain.

4 Go labour on! thy hands are weak,
Thy knees are faint, thy soul cast down;
Yet falter not—the prize is near,
The throne, the kingdom, and the crown!

5 Go labour on—while it is day,
The long dark night is hastening on;
Speed, speed thy work—up from thy sloth—
It is not thus that souls are won!

6 See thousands dying at your side,
Your brethren, kindred, friends of home.
See millions perishing afar,
Haste, brethren, to the rescue come!

7 Toil on, toil on; rebuke, exhort,
Be wise the souls of men to win;
Go forth into the world's highway,
Intreat, compel them to come in.

8 Toil on, toil on: thou soon shalt find
For labour rest, for exile home;
Soon shalt thou hear the Bridegroom's voice,
The midnight peal, "Behold I come!"

Horatius Bonar, D.D., 1843.

SWABIA. [H. P. 82.]

767 Luke x. 2. "*The harvest truly is great.*"

Tune SWABIA. S. M.

1 HOW vast the field of souls,
Of souls that cannot die!
Where earth expands or ocean rolls,
That field invites our eye.

2 The harvest of that field
How ready for our hand!
But they who well the sickle wield
Are still a little band.

3 Then let us earnest be
In faith for souls to care:
The Master of the field is He,
Who bids us join in prayer.

4 Thy Spirit, Lord, forth send,
More labourers to provide;
Throughout the field be Thou their Friend,
Their Keeper and their Guide.

5 Then, when their toils are past,
And all Thy garner stored,
Be Thou the First, and Thou the Last,
Unceasingly adored!

William Henry Havergal, 1858.

---

768 Rev. xxii. 17. "*Let him that heareth say, Come.*"

Tune SIHOR. 77, 77, 77. Or RATISBON.

1 YE who hear the blessèd call
Of the Spirit and the Bride:
Hear the Master's word to all,
Your commission and your guide—
"And let him that heareth say,
Come," to all yet far away.

2 "Come!" alike to age and youth,
Tell them of our Friend above,
Of His beauty and His truth,
Preciousness and grace and love.
Tell them what you know is true,
Tell them what He is to you.

3 "Come!" to those who do not care
For the Saviour's precious death,
Having not a thought to spare
For the gracious words He saith.
Ere the shadows gather deep,
Rouse them from their fatal sleep.

4 "Come!" to those who, while they hear,
Linger, hardly knowing why;
Tell them that the Lord is near,
Tell them Jesus passes by.
Call them *now*; oh! do not wait,
Lest to-morrow be too late.

5 Brothers, sisters, do not wait,
Speak for Him who speaks to you!
Wherefore should you hesitate?
This is no great thing to do.
Jesus only bids you say,
"Come!" and will you not obey?

SIHOR (River). [H. P. 158.]

6 Lord! to Thy command we bow,
Touch our lips with altar fire;
Let Thy Spirit kindle now
Faith, and zeal, and strong desire;
So that henceforth we may be
Fellow workers, Lord, with Thee!

Frances Ridley Havergal, 1839.

MELCOMBE. [H. P. 24.]

(4) SUNDAY SCHOOL TEACHERS.

769 John xxi. 15. "*Feed My lambs.*"
Tune MELCOMBE. L. M.

1 O LORD, with thankful hearts we meet
Once more before Thy mercy-seat,
To offer Thee our humble prayer
For all the children of our care.

2 'Tis Thine, O Lord, alone to bless
Our feeble efforts with success;
And while we teach, oh grant that we
May every one be taught of Thee.

3 Oft as we speak of Jesu's love,
Send down Thy blessing from above;
That all who thus Thy day employ,
And sow in tears, may reap in joy!

Sunday School Hymn Book, 1810.

---

770 2 Tim. ii. 25. "*In meekness instructing.*" Tune MELCOMBE. L. M. Or GILBOA.

1 SPIRIT of wisdom from above,
Dispenser of the Father's love,
True Witness of adopting grace,
Great Sanctifier of our race;

2 Oh, give us knowledge, give us zeal,
Teach us to think, and make us feel;
Hallow our spirit, conduct, tongue,
And bless, oh, bless us to the young.

3 May we be gentle, patient, kind,
Possessors of the Saviour's mind;
In purpose firm, and motive pure,
Fitted to labour and endure.

4 Accept our praise, our prayer inspire;
Baptize us now with sacred fire;
And may our lives reflect the same,
And prove from whence the ardour came!

Sunday School Hymns, 1857.

---

771 1 Cor. xv. 58. "*Your labour is not in vain in the Lord.*"
Tune PURDAY. 87, 87, 77.

PURDAY. [H. P. 338.]

1 "ALL the night and nothing taken"—
How shall we let down the net?
All our steadfast hopes are shaken,
Every scheme with failure met:
Though we speak the message clear,
Yet the sinner will not hear.

2 "All the night and nothing taken"—
And the hours be speeding by;
Is the chosen flock forsaken?
Is no Master standing nigh?
Nought is found among the band
But faint heart and weary hand.

3 Still, though night may pass in sorrow,
And no guiding star appear,
Sounds the promise for the morrow
From the Master standing near:
"Ye shall find": then hopeful yet
At His word we loose the net!

Dean Alford, D.D., 1867.

---

(5) DISTRICT VISITORS.

772 Ps. c. 2. "*Serve the Lord with gladness.*" Tune BOSTON. 76, 86. D. Or GOLDBACH.

1 'TIS sweet to work for Jesus;
In this life's little day,
To spread around "The joyful sound,"
As those forgiven may;
To tell His lovingkindness,
His promises so true;
To urge the young That they may come,
And trust this Saviour too.

2 'Tis sweet to work for Jesus,
For Him who loved, and gave
Himself for us, An offering thus
Our ruined souls to save.
Glad service we would render
For grace so rich and free;
Yet, Lord, we mourn, That we have borne
So little fruit to Thee.

BOSTON. [H. P. 278.]

3 'Tis sweet to work for Jesus:
Be this our one desire,
Our purpose still To do His will,
Whatever He require.
No action is too lowly,
No work of love too small;
If Christ but lead, We may indeed
Well follow such a call.

4 'Tis sweet to work for Jesus,
While our weak spirits rest
In His own care, Safe sheltered there,
And with His presence blest.
In such calm, happy moments,
No greater joy we know;
Redeemed from sin, We live for Him
To whom our all we owe.

5 'Tis sweet to work for Jesus—
Oh! weary not of this,
But onward press With cheerfulness,
Though rough the pathway is.
Hold on unmoved and patient,
Till He shall call thee home,
With joy to stand At God's right hand,
To serve before the throne!

Elizabeth Lydia Starling, 1862.

---

773 Rom. xiv. 7. "*None of us liveth to himself.*"
Tune Melcombe. L. M. Or Gilboa.

1 LORD, speak to me, that I may speak
In living echoes of Thy tone:
As Thou hast sought, so let me seek
Thy erring children, lost and lone.

2 Oh, lead me, Lord, that I may lead
The wandering and the wavering feet;
Oh, feed me, Lord, that I may feed
Thy hungering ones with manna sweet.

3 Oh, strengthen me, that while I stand
Firm on the Rock, and strong in Thee,
I may stretch out a loving hand
To wrestlers with the troubled sea.

4 Oh, teach me, Lord, that I may teach
The precious things Thou dost impart;
And wing my words, that they may reach
The hidden depths of many a heart.

5 Oh, give Thine own sweet rest to me,
That I may speak with soothing power
A word in season, as from Thee,
To weary ones in needful hour.

6 Oh, fill me with Thy fulness, Lord,
Until my very heart o'erflow
In kindling thought and glowing word,
Thy love to tell, Thy praise to show.

7 Oh, use me, Lord, use even me,
Just *as* Thou wilt, and *when*, and *where*;
Until Thy blessèd Face I see,
Thy rest, Thy joy, Thy glory share.

Frances Ridley Havergal, 1872.

See Hymns 689, 867, 868.

Theme V.—The Two Sacraments.

(1) BAPTISM.

ST. CHRYSOSTOM. [H. P. 53.]

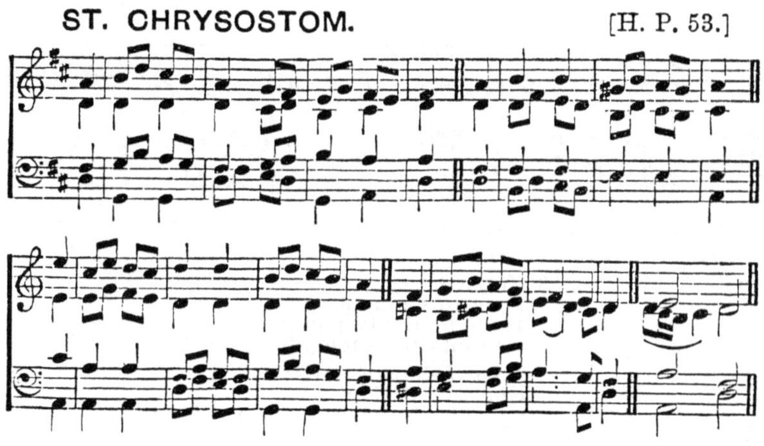

774 Mark x. 16. "*He took them up in His arms.*"
Tune St. Chrysostom. C. M.

1 SEE Israel's gentle Shepherd stand
With all-engaging charms;
Hark, how He calls the tender lambs,
And folds them in His arms!

2 "Permit them to approach," He cries,
"Nor scorn their humble name;
For 'twas to bless such souls as these
The Lord of angels came."

3 We bring them, Lord, in thankful hands,
And yield them up to Thee:
Joyful that we ourselves are Thine,
Thine let our offspring be.

4 Ye little flock, with pleasure hear:
Ye children, seek His face;
And fly with transport to receive
The blessings of His grace!

Philip Doddridge, D.D., 1755.

EATON. [H. P. 313.]

775 Rom. vi. 3. "*Baptized into Jesus Christ.*"
Tune EATON. 88, 88, 88. Or MAON.

1 LORD! may the inward grace abound
Through Thine appointed outward sign;
A milder seal than Abraham found,
Of covenant blessings more Divine:
Which opens glory to our view
Beyond the brightest hope he knew!

2 Type of the Spirit's living flow,
In faith we pour the hallowed stream;
We sign the cross upon the brow,
The solemn pledge of truth to Him,
Who shed for us His precious blood
To seal the covenant of God.

3 Baptized into the Trinity,
Adopted children of Thy grace,
Oh, help us, Lord, to live to Thee,
A humble, pure, and faithful race!
Instruct us, sanctify, defend,
And crown with heavenly life our end!

Edward Osler, 1836.

BEDFORD. [H. P. 66.]

776 Mark x. 13. "*They brought young children to Him.*" Tune BEDFORD. C. M.

1 OUR children, Lord, in faith and prayer
We now present to Thee;
Let them Thy covenant mercies share,
And Thy salvation see.

2 Such helpless babes Thou didst embrace,
While dwelling here below;
To us and ours, O God of grace,
The same compassion show.

3 In early days their hearts secure
From worldly snares, we pray;
And may they to the end endure
In every righteous way.

4 Before them let their parents live
In godly faith and fear;
Then first to heaven their souls receive,
Next bring their children there!

Marianne Nunn, 1830.

SHENIR II. (Mount.) [H. P. 151.]

777 Matt. xxviii. 19. "*Baptizing . . . in the name of the Father, and of the Son, and of the Holy Ghost.*"
Tune SHENIR II. 77, 77. Or VIENNA.

1 HEAVENLY Father! may Thy love
Beam upon us from above;
Let this infant find a place
In Thy covenant of grace.

2 Son of God, be with us here,
Listen to our humble prayer:
Let Thy blood on Calvary spilt
Cleanse this child from nature's guilt.

3 Holy Ghost, to Thee we cry,
Thou this infant sanctify;
Thine almighty power display,
Seal him to redemption's day.

4 Great Jehovah, Father, Son,
Holy Spirit, Three in One,
Let the blessing come from Thee,
Thine shall all the glory be!

Benjamin Guest, 1813.

[H. P. 44.]

778 2 Tim. ii. 4. "*Chosen . . . to be a soldier.*"

Tune TALLIS. C. M.

1 IN token that thou shalt not fear
Christ crucified to own,
We print the cross upon thee here,
And stamp thee His alone.

2 In token that thou shalt not blush
To glory in His name,
We blazon here upon thy front
His glory and His shame.

3 In token that thou shalt not flinch
Christ's quarrel to maintain,
But 'neath His banner manfully
Firm at thy post remain;

4 In token that thou too shalt tread
The path He travelled by,
Endure the cross, despise the shame,
And sit thee down on high;

5 Thus, outwardly and visibly,
We seal thee for His own:
And may the brow that wears His cross
Hereafter share His crown!

Dean Alford, D.D., 1832.

MELCOMBE. [H. P. 24.]

(2) THE LORD'S SUPPER.

779 Luke xiv. 17. "*Come, for all things are now ready.*" Tune MELCOMBE. L. M.

1 MY God, and is Thy table spread?
And doth Thy cup with love o'erflow?
Thither be all Thy children led,
And let them all its sweetness know.

2 Hail, sacred feast, which Jesus makes,
Rich banquet of His flesh and blood!
Thrice happy he who here partakes
That sacred stream, that heavenly food!

3 Why are its dainties all in vain
Before unwilling hearts displayed?
Was not for you the Victim slain?
Are you forbid the children's bread?

4 Oh, let Thy table honoured be,
And furnished well with joyful guests:
And may each soul salvation see
That here its sacred pledges tastes!

Philip Doddridge, D.D., 1755.

FRENCH; *or*, DUNDEE. [H. P. 65.]

780 Luke xxii. 19. "*This do in remembrance of Me.*" Tune FRENCH. C. M.

1 ACCORDING to Thy gracious word,
In deep humility,
This will I do, my dying Lord,
I will remember Thee.

2 Thy body, broken for my sake,
My bread from heaven shall be;
The sacramental cup I'll take,
And thus remember Thee.

3 Can I Gethsemane forget,
Or there Thy conflict see,
Thine agony and bloody sweat,
And not remember Thee?

4 When to the cross I turn mine eyes,
And gaze on Calvary,
O Lamb of God, my Sacrifice,
I must remember Thee.

5 Remember Thee, and all Thy pains,
And all Thy love to me?
Yes, while a breath, a pulse remains,
Will I remember Thee.

6 And when these failing lips grow dumb,
And mind and memory flee,
When Thou shalt in Thy kingdom come,
Jesus, remember me!

James Montgomery, 1825.

GOLDBACH. [H. P. 130.]

781 Cant. ii. 3. "*I sat down under His shadow with great delight.*" Tune GOLDBACH, Part I. 76, 76.

1 SIT down beneath His shadow,
And rest with great delight;
The faith that now beholds Him
Is pledge of future sight.

2 Our Master's love remember,
Exceeding great and free;
Lift up thy heart in gladness,
For He remembers thee.

3 Bring every weary burden,
Thy sin, thy fear, thy grief;
He calls the heavy laden
And gives them kind relief.

4 His righteousness "all glorious"
Thy festal robe shall be;
And love that passeth knowledge
His banner over thee.

5 A little while, though parted,
Remember, wait, and love,
Until He comes in glory,
Until we meet above.

6 Till in the Father's kingdom
The heavenly feast is spread,
And we behold His beauty,
Whose blood for us was shed!

Frances Ridley Havergal, 1870.

CYRENE. [H. P. 92.]

782 Cant. ii. 3. "*His fruit was sweet to my taste.*"
Tune CYRENE. S. M. Or ARMAGEDDON.

1 SWEET feast of love Divine!
'Tis grace that makes us free
To feed upon this bread and wine,
In memory, Lord, of Thee.

2 Here every welcome guest
Waits, Lord, from Thee to learn
The secrets of Thy Father's breast,
And all Thy grace discern.

3 The blood that flowed for sin,
In symbol here we see;
And feel the blessèd pledge within,
That we are loved of Thee.

4 Oh, if this glimpse of love
Is so divinely sweet,
What will it be, O Lord, above,
Thy gladdening smile to meet?

5 To see Thee face to face,
Thy perfect likeness wear,
And all Thy ways of wondrous grace
Through endless years declare?

Sir Edward Denny, 1839.

MELCOMBE. [H. P. 24.]

783 Cant. ii. 4. "*He brought me to the banqueting house.*"
Tune MELCOMBE. L. M.

1 OURS is a rich and royal feast,
Provided by the King of heaven:
How privileged are they, and blest,
To whom the bread of life is given!

2 In sacred fellowship we meet,
To celebrate our Saviour's death:
His blood we drink, His flesh we eat;
And feed on Him by living faith.

3 We worship Him who bore the cross;
We glory in His death alone:
The world itself appears but loss
To those to whom His name is known.

4 The blood He sheds supplies a stream
That washes all our guilt away;
How precious, then, the Lord should seem,
Whose death we celebrate to-day!

5 On earth His dying love shall be
Our spring of hope, our theme of joy;
And, when in heaven our Lord we see,
His praise shall all our powers employ!

Thomas Kelly, 1809. (a.)

GOTHA. [H. P. 296.]

784 Col. i. 20. "*Peace through the blood of His cross.*" Tune GOTHA. 87, 87. D. Or SALZBURG.

1 SWEET the moments, rich in blessing,
Which before the cross I spend,
Life, and health, and peace possessing,
From the sinner's dying Friend.
Here I'll sit for ever viewing
Mercy's streams, in streams of blood:
Precious drops! my soul bedewing,
Plead and claim my peace with God.

2 Truly blessèd is this station,
Low before His cross to lie;
While I see Divine compassion
Floating in His languid eye.
Here it is I find my heaven,
While upon the cross I gaze;
Love I much? I've more forgiven;
I'm a miracle of grace.

3 Love and grief my heart dividing,
With my tears His feet I'll bathe,
Constant still in faith abiding,
Life deriving from His death.
May I still enjoy this feeling,
In all need to Jesus go;
Prove His wounds each day more healing,
And Himself more fully know!

J. Allen, 1757; *W. Shirley*, 1774.

FRANKFORT. [H. P. 183.]

785 Ps. xxiii. 5. "*Thou preparest a table before me.*" Tune FRANKFORT. 87, 87.

1 ISRAEL'S Shepherd! guide me, feed me,
Through my pilgrimage below;
And beside the waters lead me,
Where Thy flock rejoicing go.

2 Jesus! Heavenly Shepherd! ever
Guard and keep me in Thy way;
I have found Thee, and would never,
Never from Thy presence stray.

3 Oh! how sweet, how comfortable,
In the wilderness to see
Rich provisions, and a table
Spread for sinners, spread for me.

4 Here Thy bounty still partaking,
Consecrated bread and wine,
Freely all things else forsaking,
I behold the Saviour mine.

5 In His bruisèd body broken,
In the shedding of His blood,
See, my soul, a gracious token,
Sure and full for every good.

6 Cleansed, and washed, and freely pardoned
By His matchless love and power;
Hear Him say (no longer hardened),
"Go in peace, and sin no more!"

John Bickersteth, 1819.

HAVERGAL. (PART I.) [H. P. 163.]

786 Ezek. xxxiv. 14. "*I will feed them.*"
Tune HAVERGAL, Part I. 777.

1 JESU, to Thy table led,
Now let every heart be fed
With the true and living Bread.

2 While in penitence we kneel,
Thy sweet presence let us feel,
All Thy wondrous love reveal!

3 While on Thy dear cross we gaze,
Mourning o'er our sinful ways,
Turn our sadness into praise!

4 When we taste the mystic wine,
Of Thine outpoured blood the sign,
Fill our hearts with love Divine!

5 Draw us to Thy wounded side,
Whence there flowed the healing tide;
There our sins and sorrows hide!

6 From the bonds of sin release,
Cold and wavering faith increase,
Lamb of God, grant us Thy peace!

7 Lead us by Thy piercèd hand,
Till around Thy throne we stand,
In the bright and better land!

Robert Hall Baynes, 1873.

BASHAN (Hill of). [H. P. 112.]

787 John vi. 51. "*The bread that I will give is My flesh.*"

Tune BASHAN. 66, 66.

1 I HUNGER and I thirst:
Jesus! my manna be;
Ye living waters, burst
Out of the Rock for me.

2 Thou bruised and broken Bread!
My lifelong wants supply;
As living souls are fed,
Oh, feed me, or I die.

3 Thou true life-giving Vine!
Let me Thy sweetness prove,
Renew my life with Thine,
Refresh my soul with love.

4 Rough paths my feet have trod
Since first their course began;
Feed me, Thou Bread of God;
Help me, Thou Son of man!

5 For still the desert lies
My thirsting soul before;
O living waters, rise
Within me evermore.

J. S. B. Monsell, LL.D., 1861.

788 1 Cor. xi. 26. "*Till He come.*"

Tune SIHOR. 77, 77, 77.

SIHOR (River). [H. P. 158.]

1 TILL He come! Oh, let the words
Linger on the trembling chords;
Let the little while between
In their golden light be seen;
Let us think how heaven and home
Lie beyond that "Till He come."

2 When the weary ones we love
Enter on their rest above,
Seems the earth so poor and vast,
All our life-joy overcast?
Hush! be every murmur dumb,—
It is only "Till He come."

3 Clouds and conflicts round us press;
Would we have one sorrow less?
All the sharpness of the cross,
All that tells the world is loss,
Death, and darkness, and the tomb,
Only whisper, "Till He come."

4 See, the feast of love is spread:
Drink the wine and break the bread;
Sweet memorials,—till the Lord
Call us round His heavenly board;
Some from earth, from glory some,
Severed only "Till He come."

Edward Henry Bickersteth, 1869.

CORPUS CHRISTI. [H. P. 347.]

789 John vi. 51. "*I am the living Bread*"

Tune CORPUS CHRISTI. 98, 98.

1 BREAD of the world, in mercy broken,
Wine of the soul, in mercy shed,
By whom the words of life were spoken,
And in whose death our sins are dead;

2 Look on the heart by sorrow broken,
Look on the tears by sinners shed;
And be Thy feast to us the token
That by Thy grace our souls are fed

Bishop Heber, 1827.

790 Cant. i. 12. "*The King sitteth at His table.*"

Tune GODESBERG. 87, 87. D. Or SALZBURG.

GODESBERG. [H. P. 185.]

1 WHILE in sweet communion feeding
On this earthly bread and wine,
Saviour, may we see Thee bleeding
On the cross, to make us Thine!
Now our eyes for ever closing
To this fleeting world below,
On Thy gentle breast reposing,
Teach us, Lord, Thy grace to know.

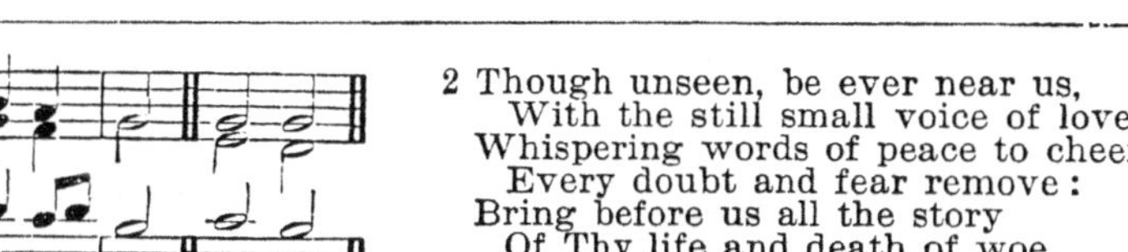

2 Though unseen, be ever near us,
With the still small voice of love,
Whispering words of peace to cheer us,
Every doubt and fear remove:
Bring before us all the story
Of Thy life and death of woe,
And with hopes of endless glory
Wean our hearts from all below!

Sir Edward Denny, 1813.

See Hymns 21, 168, 603, 1086—1089.

EVAN I. [H. P. 54.]

COMMUNION OF THE SICK.

791 Isa. xli. 10. "*Fear thou not, for I am with thee.*"

Tune Evan I. C. M. Or French.

1 OH, fear not, though before thee lies
A dark and narrow way,
For at thy side thy Saviour walks,
Thy Comforter and Stay.

2 Hold fast His hand, and lean in faith
Upon that mighty arm;
His love and power will guide thy steps,
And shelter thee from harm.

3 Thou Son of God, eternal Lord,
Who wearest human flesh,
And dost Thy blood and body give
To cleanse us and refresh:

4 Oh, make our sinful bodies clean
With this most holy food
Of Thine own flesh, and wash our souls
With Thy most precious blood.

5 The Resurrection and the Life
Be Thou to us, O Lord,
Fulfil to us the gracious pledge
Of Thy most holy word.

6 "Who eats My flesh, and drinks My blood,
Dwells evermore in Me,
And shall by Me at the last day
Upraised in glory be."

7 Therefore we fear not, though we tread
A dark and narrow way;
For Thou art walking at our side,
Our Comforter and Stay.

8 We clasp Thy hand, and lean in faith
On Thy most mighty arm;
Thy love and power support our steps,
And shelter us from harm.

9 Oh, lead us through the gate of death
Forth to that blessèd place,
Where we may evermore behold
The brightness of Thy face;

10 And praise the Father and the Son,
By whom we ever live,
And praise to God the Holy Ghost
Through endless ages give!

Bishop Christopher Wordsworth, 1863.

Theme VI.—The Lord's Day.

(1) OPENING OF THE LORD'S DAY.

792 Num. x. 2. "*Trumpets of silver . . . for the calling of the assembly.*"

Tune Zion. 88, 88, 88. Or Mamre.

1 THE day of rest once more comes round,
A day to all believers dear;
The silver trumpets seem to sound,
That call the tribes of Israel near;
Ye people all Obey the call,
And in Jehovah's courts appear.

2 Obedient to Thy summons, Lord,
We to Thy sanctuary come;
Thy gracious presence here afford,
And send Thy people joyful home.
Of Thee, our King, Oh may we sing,
And none with such a theme be dumb!

3 Oh, hasten, Lord, the day when those
Who know Thee here shall see Thy face;
When suffering shall for ever close,
And they shall reach their destined place;
Then shall they rest Supremely blest,
Eternal debtors to Thy grace!

Thomas Kelly, 1806.

ZION. [H. P. 312.]

X

SWABIA. [H. P. 82.]

793 Ps. lxxxiv. 10. *"A day in Thy courts."* Tune SWABIA. S. M.

1 WELCOME, sweet day of rest,
That saw the Lord arise;
Welcome to this reviving breast,
And these rejoicing eyes!

2 The King Himself comes near,
And feasts His saints to-day;
Here we may sit, and see Him here,
And love, and praise, and pray!

Isaac Watts, D.D., 1709.

EDEN. [H. P. 38.]

794 Rev. i. 10. *"I was in the Spirit on the Lord's day."* Tune EDEN. C. M. Or GLOUCESTER.

1 BLEST day of God, most calm, most bright,
The first and best of days:
The labourer's rest, the saint's delight,
A day of mirth and praise.

2 My Saviour's face did make thee shine,
His rising did thee raise:
This made thee heavenly and Divine
Beyond the common days.

3 The firstfruits do a blessing prove
To all the sheaves behind;
And they that do the Sabbath love
A happy week shall find.

4 This holy day doth saints enrich,
And smiles upon them all;
It is their Pentecost, on which
The Holy Ghost doth fall!

John Mason, 1683.

GOLDBACH. [H. P. 130.]

795 Ps. cxviii. 24. *"We will rejoice and be glad in it."* Tune GOLDBACH. 76, 76. D. Or MAHANAIM.

1 O DAY of rest and gladness,
O day of joy and light,
O balm of care and sadness,
Most beautiful, most bright;
On thee, the high and lowly,
Through ages joined in tune,
Sing, holy, holy, holy,
To the great God Triune.

2 On thee, at the creation,
The light first had its birth;
On thee for our salvation
Christ rose from depths of earth;
On thee our Lord victorious
The Spirit sent from heaven;
And thus on thee most glorious
A triple light was given.

3 Thou art a port protected
From storms that round us rise;
A garden intersected
With streams of Paradise;
Thou art a cooling fountain
In life's dry dreary sand;
From thee, like Pisgah's mountain,
We view our promised land.

PART II.

4 Thou art a holy ladder,
Where angels go and come;
Each Sunday finds us gladder,
Nearer to heaven our home.
A day of sweet refection
Thou art, a day of love;
A day of resurrection
From earth to things above.

5 To-day on weary nations
The heavenly manna falls;
To holy convocations
The silver trumpet calls,
Where gospel light is glowing
With pure and radiant beams,
And living water flowing
With soul-refreshing streams.

6 New graces ever gaining
From this our day of rest,
We reach the rest remaining
To spirits of the blest.
To Holy Ghost be praises,
To Father and to Son;
The church her voice upraises
To Thee, blest Three in One.

Bishop Christopher Wordsworth, 1862.

MELCOMBE. [H. P. 24.]

796 Isa. lviii. 13. *"Call the sabbath a delight."*

Tune MELCOMBE. L. M.

1 DEAR is to me the sabbath morn;
The village bells, the pastor's voice;
These oft have found my heart forlorn,
And these have bid that heart rejoice.

2 And dear to me the wingèd hour
Spent in Thy hallowed courts, O Lord!
To feel devotion's soothing power,
And catch the manna of Thy word.

3 And dear to me the loud Amen,
Which echoes through the blessed abode,
Which swells and sinks, and swells again,
Dies on the walls, but lives to God.

4 Oh! when the world, with iron hand,
Would bind me in its six days' chain,
Thus burst, O Lord! the strong man's band,
And let my spirit loose again!

John William Cunningham, 1822.

IONA. [H. P. 37.]

797 Ps. cxviii. 24. *"This is the day which the Lord hath made."*

Tune IONA. C. M. Or Hymn Chant EPHESUS.

1 THIS is the day the Lord hath made,
He calls the hours His own
Let heaven rejoice, let earth be glad,
And praise surround Thy throne.

2 To-day He rose and left the dead,
And Satan's empire fell;
To-day the saints His triumph spread,
And all His wonders tell.

3 Hosanna to the' anointed King,
To David's holy Son:
Help us, O Lord; descend and bring
Salvation from Thy throne.

4 Blest be the Lord, who comes to men
With messages of grace;
Who comes in God His Father's name,
To save our sinful race.

5 Hosanna in the highest strains
The church on earth can raise;
The highest heavens, in which He reigns,
Shall give Him nobler praise!

Isaac Watts, D.D., 1719.

798 Mal. iv. 2. *"Unto you that fear My name shall the Sun of Righteousness arise."*

Tune MELCOMBE. L. M. Or Hymn Chant WORCESTER.

1 THOU glorious Sun of Righteousness,
On this day risen to set no more,
Shine on me now to heal, to bless,
With brighter beams than e'er before.

2 Shine on Thy work of grace within,
On each celestial blossom there;
Destroy each bitter root of sin,
And make Thy garden fresh and fair.

3 Shine on Thy pure eternal word,
Its mysteries to my soul reveal;
And whether read, remembered, heard,
Oh, let it quicken, strengthen, heal.

4 Shine on the temples of Thy grace;
In spotless robes Thy priests be clad;
There show the brightness of Thy face,
And make Thy chosen people glad.

5 Shine on those unseen things, displayed
To faith's far penetrating eye;
And let their splendour cast a shade
On every earthly vanity.

PART II.

6 Shine in the hearts of those most dear,
Disperse each cloud 'twixt them and Thee;
Their glorious heavenward prospects clear;
"Light in Thy light," oh, let them see.

7 Shine on those friends for whom we mourn,
Who know not yet Thy healing ray;
Quicken their souls, and bid them turn
To Thee, "the Life, the Truth, the Way."

8 Shine on those tribes no country owns,
On Judah, once Thy dwelling place;
"Thy servants think upon her stones,"
And long to see her day of grace.

9 Shine on the missionary's home,
Give him his heart's desire to see;
Collect Thy scattered ones who roam;
One fold, one Shepherd, let there be.

10 Shine, till Thy glorious beams shall chase
The blinding film from every eye;
Till every earthly dwelling place
Shall hail the Dayspring from on high.

11 Shine on, shine on, Eternal Sun!
Pour richer floods of life and light,
Till that bright sabbath be begun,
That glorious day which knows no night!

Charlotte Elliott, 1839.

AVEN (Plain of). [H. P. 79.]

(2) OPENING OF PUBLIC WORSHIP.

799 Ps. cxxxii. 14. *"Here will I dwell."* Tune Aven. S. M. Or Amana.

1 COME to Thy temple, Lord,
Thy waiting church to bless:
Let here Thy glory be adored,
Give here Thy word success.

2 Our inmost hearts refine,
And for Thyself prepare:
Cast out all thoughts but thoughts Divine,
And reign triumphant there.

3 Thy servants, Lord, we are,
Baptized into Thy name:
All hurtful things put from us far,
All works of sin and shame.

4 Come to Thy temple, Lord,
Thine own assembly bless:
That all may offer with accord
Offerings of righteousness!

Dean Alford, D.D., 1844.

LONDON NEW; *or*, NEWTON. [H. P. 55.]

800 1 Kings viii. 29. *"That Thine eyes may be open toward this house night and day."*
Tune London New. C. M.

1 GREAT Shepherd of Thy people, hear,
Thy presence now display;
As Thou hast given a place for prayer,
So give us hearts to pray.

2 Show us some token of Thy love,
Our fainting hope to raise;
And pour Thy blessings from above,
That we may render praise.

3 Within these walls let holy peace
And love and concord dwell;
Here give the troubled conscience ease,
The wounded spirit heal.

4 The feeling heart, the melting eye,
The humble mind bestow;
And shine upon us from on high,
To make our graces grow.

5 May we in faith receive Thy word,
In faith present our prayers:
And in the presence of our Lord
Unbosom all our cares.

6 And may the gospel's joyful sound,
Enforced by mighty grace,
Awaken many sinners round,
To come and fill the place!

John Newton, 1779.

MELCOMBE. [H. P. 24.]

801 Matt. xviii. 20. *"Where two or three are gathered together in My name, there am I in the midst."*
Tune Melcombe. L. M.

1 JESUS, where'er Thy people meet,
There they behold Thy mercy-seat;
Where'er they seek Thee, Thou art found,
And every place is hallowed ground.

2 For Thou, within no walls confined,
Inhabitest the humble mind;
Such ever bring Thee where they come,
And going, take Thee to their home.

3 Great Shepherd of Thy chosen few,
Thy former mercies here renew;
Here to our waiting hearts proclaim
The sweetness of Thy saving name.

4 Here may we prove the power of prayer
To strengthen faith, and sweeten care;
To teach our faint desires to rise,
And bring all heaven before our eyes.

5 Lord, we are weak, but Thou art near,
Nor short Thine arm, nor deaf Thine ear:
Oh, rend the heavens, come quickly down,
And make the sinner's heart Thine own!

William Cowper, 1779.

ARMAGEDDON (Valley of). [H. P. 90.]

802 Luke i. 78. "*The Dayspring from on high.*" Tune ARMAGEDDON. S. M.

1 NO dawn of holy light,
No day of sacred rest,
E'er breaks upon the heathen's sight,
To soothe his troubled breast.

2 But lo! with healing ray,
The Dayspring meets our eye:
And Christians on their Master's day
Rejoice to feel Him nigh.

3 To Him let praise be given,
The noblest, sweetest, best;
For He has brought us light from heaven,
And hope of endless rest.

4 Lord, let Thy saving light,
Thy day of glorious rest,
Soon chase from earth the toilsome night,
And soothe each wearied breast!

William Henry Havergal, 1825.

STUTTGARD. [H. P. 182.]

803 Luke vi. 5. "*Lord also of the Sabbath.*"
Tune STUTTGARD. 87, 87.

1 HALLELUJAH! Lord, our voices
Rise in choral strains to Thee:
Son of Man, Thy church rejoices
In her weekly jubilee.

2 Hallelujah! praise ascending
Calls on prayer to wing her way:
Lord, before Thy gospel bending
Let the heathen hail Thy day.

3 Let the nations sad and weary,
Idol-bound and sin-opprest,
Soon rejoice in drawing near Thee,
On Thy day of hallowed rest!

4 Hallelujah! mercy beaming
Lights the path that leads to God;
Herald lips, divinely teeming,
Publish blessings bought with blood.

5 Hallelujah! Saviour, hear us;
Downward send Thy quickening Dove;
May His silver pinions bear us
To the realms of rest and love!

William Henry Havergal, 1828.

PSALM 148th. [H. P. 114.]

804 Ps. lxxxiv. 4. "*Blessed are they that dwell in Thy house.*"
Tune PSALM 148TH, O. V. 6666, 4444.
Or DARWELL.

1 LORD of the worlds above,
How pleasant and how fair
The dwellings of Thy love,
Thy earthly temples are!
To Thine abode Our hearts aspire,
With warm desire To see our God.

2 O happy souls that pray,
Where God appoints to hear!
O happy men that pay
Their constant service there!
They praise Thee still: Thrice happy they
That love the way To Zion's hill.

3 They go from strength to strength
Through this dark vale of tears;
Till each arrives at length,
Till each in heaven appears;
O glorious seat, When God, our King,
Shall thither bring Our willing feet!

Isaac Watts, D.D., 1719.

MEDIA. [H. P. 195.]

805 Ps. lxiii. 2. "*To see Thy power and Thy glory, so as I have seen Thee in the sanctuary.*"

Tune Media. 87, 87, 47. Or Idumea.

1 IN Thy name, O Lord, assembling,
We, Thy people, now draw near;
Teach us to rejoice with trembling;
Speak and let Thy servants hear—
Hear with meekness,
Hear Thy word with godly fear.

2 While our days on earth are lengthened,
May we give them, Lord, to Thee;
Cheered by hope, and daily strengthened,
May we run, nor weary be,
Till Thy glory
Without clouds in heaven we see.

3 Then in worship, purer, sweeter,
Thee Thy people shall adore;
Tasting of enjoyment greater
Far than thought conceived before;
Full enjoyment,
Full, unmixed, and evermore!

Thomas Kelly, 1815.

MUNICH. [H. P. 279.]

806 Heb. x. 19. "*Boldness to enter into the holiest.*" Tune Munich. 76, 76. D. Or Goldbach.

1 THE holiest we enter
In perfect peace with God:
Our thoughts are made to centre
In Jesus and His blood;
And while we mourn our dulness,
In thought, and word, and deed,
We glory in His fulness,
Which meets our every need.

2 Much incense is ascending
Before our Father's throne,
His gracious ear is bending
To hear our feeblest groan;
To all our prayers and praises
Christ adds His sweet perfume;
And love the altar raises
These odours to consume.

3 O God, we come with singing,
Because our great High Priest
Our names to Thee is bringing,
And ne'er forgets the least:
For us He wears the mitre,
Where holiness shines bright;
For us His robes are whiter
Than heaven's unclouded light.

Mary Bowly, 1847.

ST. ANN. [H. P. 52.]

807 Isa. li. 9. "*Awake, awake, put on strength, O arm of the Lord.*" Tune St. Ann. C. M.

1 NOW, gracious Lord, Thine arm reveal,
And make Thy glory known;
Now let us all Thy presence feel,
And soften hearts of stone!

2 Help us to venture near Thy throne,
And plead a Saviour's name;
For all that we can call our own
Is vanity and shame.

3 From all the guilt of former sin
May mercy set us free;
And let the week we now begin
Begin and end with Thee.

4 Send down Thy Spirit from above,
That saints may love Thee more
And sinners now may learn to love,
Who never loved before.

John Newton, 1779.

NARENZA. [H. P. 80.]

808 Neh. ix. 5. "*Stand up and bless the Lord your God.*"

Tune Narenza. S. M.

1 STAND up, and bless the Lord,
Ye people of His choice;
Stand up, and bless the Lord your God
With heart and soul and voice.

2 Though high above all praise,
Above all blessing high,
Who would not fear His holy name,
And laud and magnify!

3 Oh for the living flame,
From His own altar brought,
To touch our lips, our mind inspire,
And wing to heaven our thought!

4 God is our strength and song,
And His salvation ours;
Then be His love in Christ proclaimed,
With all our ransomed powers.

5 Stand up, and bless the Lord,
The Lord your God adore;
Stand up, and bless His glorious name
Henceforth for evermore!

James Montgomery, 1825.

(3) BEFORE THE SERMON.

809 1 Cor. iii. 7. "*God that giveth the increase.*"

Tune Havilah. 87, 87, 47.

1 COME, Thou soul-transforming Spirit,
Bless the sower and the seed;
Let each heart Thy grace inherit,
Raise the weak, the hungry feed:
From the gospel,
Now supply Thy people's need.

2 Oh may all enjoy the blessing
Which Thy holy word can give:
Let us all, Thy love possessing,
Joyfully the truth receive;
And for ever
To Thy praise and glory live.

Jonathan Evans, 1784.

810 1 Cor. iii. 11. "*Other foundation can no man lay.*"

Tune Havilah. 87, 87, 47. Or Civitas Regis.

1 CHRIST is made the sure Foundation,
Christ the Head and Corner Stone!
Chosen of the Lord, and precious,
Binding all the church in one;
Holy Zion's help for ever,
And her confidence alone.

2 All that dedicated city,
Dearly loved of God on high,
In exultant jubilation
Pours perpetual melody:
God, the One in Three, adoring
In glad hymns eternally.

3 To this temple, where we call Thee,
Come, O Lord of Hosts, to-day:
With Thy wonted loving-kindness,
Hear Thy servants as they pray;
And Thy fullest benediction
Shed within its walls alway.

HAVILAH. [H. P. 192.]

4 Here vouchsafe to all Thy servants,
What they ask of Thee to gain,
What they gain from Thee, for ever
With the blessèd to retain;
And hereafter in Thy glory
Evermore with Thee to reign.

5 Praise and honour to the Father,
Praise and honour to the Son,
Praise and honour to the Spirit,
Ever Three and ever One:
One in might, and One in glory,
While eternal ages run!

Ninth Century; John M. Neale, D.D. (tr.), 1851.

811

Isa. xi. 2. "*The Spirit of the Lord shall rest upon Him.*" Tune JORDAN. 8 8 6. D.

1 SPIRIT Jehovah! glorious Lord!
Vouchsafe Thy presence with Thy word,
To all Thy church around:
Lord! give to each of Thine now here,
The seeing eye, the hearing ear,
To know the joyful sound.

2 O Spirit! on Christ's garden blow,
And cause the spices all to flow,
As grace for grace each suits:
For then will our Belovèd come
Into this garden of His own,
And eat His pleasant fruits.

3 'Tis Thine, O Lord, in blessing thus,
To take of Christ's and show to us,
Of Him, and His, impart:
And Thine no less the same to prove,
And shed abroad the Father's love,
In each renewèd heart.

4 Almighty Lord! let all around
In sweet communion now abound,
With God, and God's dear Son:
If Thou wilt open to our view
The love of each, and draw us too,
Then will our hearts be won.

5 Then will loud praises through our host,
To Father, Son, and Holy Ghost,
By every tongue be given:
And each will say in godly fear,
"This is God's house, the Lord is here;
And this the gate of heaven!"

Robert Hawker, D.D., 1827.

SEIR (Mount). [H. P. 161.]

812

Jer. i. 9 "*The Lord put forth His hand, and touched my mouth.*" Tune SEIR. 77, 77. D.

1 SOURCE of light and power Divine,
Deign upon Thy truth to shine:
Lord, behold Thy servant stands;
Lo! to Thee we lift our hands:
Satisfy our soul's desire,
Touch his lips with holy fire;
Source of light and power Divine,
Deign upon Thy truth to shine.

2 Breathe Thy Spirit! so shall fall
Unction sweet upon us all;
Till, by odours scattered round,
Christ Himself be traced and found:
Then shall every raptured heart,
Rich in peace and joy, depart:
Source of light and power Divine,
Deign upon Thy truth to shine!

Walter Shirley, 1774.

813 Hos. xiv. 5. "*I will be as the dew.*"
Tune GODESBERG. 87, 87. Or SALZBURG.

1 AS the dew from heaven distilling
Gently on the grass descends,
Richly unto all fulfilling
What Thy providence intends:
So may truth, Divine and gracious,
To our waiting spirits prove;
Bless and make it efficacious
In the children of Thy love.

2 Lord, behold this congregation,
All Thy promises fulfil;
From Thy holy habitation
Let the dew of life distil:
Let our cry come up before Thee,
Sweetest influence shed around;
So Thy people shall adore Thee,
And confess the joyful sound.

Thomas Kelly, 1804; *and John Bulmer*, 1835.

814 Matt. xiii. 3. "*Behold, a sower went forth to sow.*"
Tune NAYLAND. C. M.

1 YE sons of earth, prepare the plough,
Break up your fallow ground;
The sower is gone forth to sow,
And scatter blessings round.

2 The seed that finds a stony soil
Shoots forth a hasty blade;
But ill repays the sower's toil,
Soon withered, scorched, and dead.

3 The thorny ground is sure to baulk
All hopes of harvest there:
We find a tall and sickly stalk,
But not the fruitful ear.

4 The beaten path and highway side
Receive the trust in vain;
The watchful birds the spoil divide,
And pick up all the grain.

5 But where the Lord of grace and power
Has blessed the happy field,
How plenteous is the golden store
The deep-wrought furrows yield!

6 Father of mercies! we have need
Of Thy preparing grace:
Let the same Hand that gives the seed
Provide a fruitful place!

William Cowper, 1779.

(4) CLOSE OF PUBLIC WORSHIP.

815 Acts xx. 32. "*I commend you to God, and to the word of His grace.*"
Tune PATMOS. 77, 77.

1 CHRISTIAN brethren, ere we part,
Let us each with grateful heart
Once more to our Father raise
Our united hymns of praise.

2 Here perhaps we meet no more;
But we seek a brighter shore,
Where, above all sin and pain,
Brethren, we shall meet again.

3 To the Triune God of heaven
Love and praise be ever given,
Here, and by His hosts above,
Endless praise, adoring love!

Henry Kirke White, 1806. (*a.*)

816 Ps. iii. 8. "*Thy blessing is upon Thy people.*"
Tune GODESBERG. 87, 87, 77, 87.

OF Thy love some gracious token
Grant us, Lord, before we go;
Bless Thy word which has been spoken;
Life and peace on all bestow;
When we join the world again,
Let our hearts with Thee remain:
Oh, direct us,
And protect us,
Till the heavenly shore we gain!

Thomas Kelly, 1804.

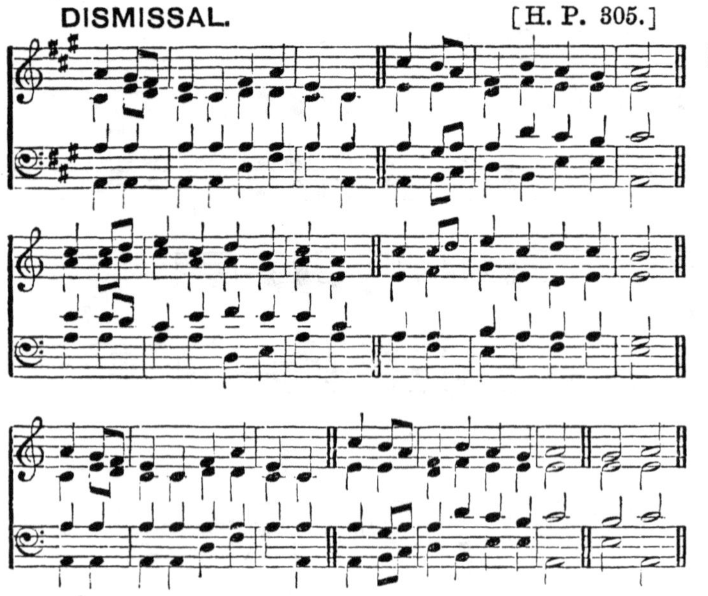

817 1 Sam. i. 17. "*Go in peace: and the God of Israel grant thee thy petition.*"

Tune DISMISSAL. 87, 87, 47.

1 LORD, dismiss us with Thy blessing,
Fill our hearts with joy and peace;
Let us each, Thy love possessing,
Triumph in redeeming grace:
Oh, refresh us!
Travelling through this wilderness.

2 Thanks we give, and adoration,
For Thy gospel's joyful sound:
May the fruits of Thy salvation
In our hearts and lives abound;
May Thy presence
With us evermore be found!

3 So whene'er the signal's given,
Us from earth to call away,
Borne on angels' wings to heaven,
Glad the summons to obey,
We shall surely
Reign with Christ in endless day!

Walter Shirley, 1774.

818 2 Cor. xiii. 14. "*The grace of the Lord Jesus Christ.*"

Tune DISMISSAL (repeating last two strains). 87, 87. D. Or SALZBURG.

1 MAY the grace of Christ our Saviour,
And the Father's boundless love,
With the Holy Spirit's favour,
Rest upon us from above:

Thus may we abide in union
With each other and the Lord;
And possess, in sweet communion,
Joys which earth cannot afford!

John Newton, 1779.

(5) THE CLOSE OF THE LORD'S DAY.

819 Ps. lxv. 8. "*Thou makest . . . the evening to rejoice.*" Tune DURHAM. 77, 77. Or VIENNA.

1 ERE another sabbath's close,
Ere again we seek repose,
Lord, our song ascends to Thee;
At Thy feet we bow the knee.

2 Cold our services have been,
Mingled every prayer with sin;
But Thou canst and wilt forgive;
By Thy grace alone we live.

3 Whilst this thorny path we tread,
May Thy love our footsteps lead;
When our journey here is past,
May we rest with Thee at last.

4 Let these earthly sabbaths prove
Foretastes of our joys above;
While their steps Thy pilgrims bend
To the rest that knows no end!

B. W. Noel's Selection, 1832.

820 Ps. xxii. 27. "*All the kindreds of the nations shall worship before Thee.*"

Tune ST. GREGORY. L. M. Or TALLIS'S CANON.

1 MILLIONS within Thy courts have met,
Millions this day before Thee bowed;
Their faces Zionward were set,
Vows with their lips to Thee they vowed.

2 But Thou, soul-searching God! hast known
The hearts of all that bent the knee,
And hast accepted those alone,
In spirit and truth that worshipped Thee.

3 People of many a tribe and tongue,
Men of strange colours, climates, lands,
Have heard Thy truth, Thy glory sung,
And offered prayer with holy hands.

4 Still, as the light of morning broke
O'er island, continent, or deep,
Thy far-spread family awoke,
Sabbath all round the world to keep.

ST. GREGORY. [H. P. 259.]

5 From east to west the sun surveyed,
From north to south, adoring throngs;
And still, when evening stretched her shade,
The stars came out to hear their songs.

6 Yet one prayer more!—and be it one,
In which both heaven and earth accord,—
Fulfil Thy promise to Thy Son,
Let all that breathe call Jesus Lord!

James Montgomery, 1853.

821 Cant. iv. 16. "*Blow upon My garden, that the spices thereof may flow out.*"

Tune St. Gregory. L. M. Or Dalmatia.

1 NOW let our heavenly plants and flowers
Diffuse a fragrance more Divine;
Refreshed by the sweet Sabbath showers,
With richer beauty they should shine.

2 We have been wafted for a while
Far, far away from this low scene;
Been cheered by our Redeemer's smile,
Been suffered on His breast to lean.

3 What has He taught us? what should be
The fruit of intercourse so blest?
Oh, should not all around us see
His image on our souls imprest?

4 Within this ivory palace fair
We entered, a much favoured train;
Myrrh, aloes, cassia, filled the air,
Our garments should the scent retain.

5 And we should pass along the earth,
Like birds that live upon the wing;
Rise to the country of our birth,
And on our way its anthems sing!

Charlotte Elliott, 1839.

THYATIRA. (Hymn Chant.) [H. P. No. V.]

822 Luke xxiv. 29. "*Abide with us, for it is toward evening.*"

Tune, Hymn Chant Thyatira. 888, 6.

1 THE Sabbath day has reached its close!
Yet, Saviour, ere I seek repose,
Grant me the peace Thy love bestows,
Smile on my evening hour!

2 O heavenly Comforter, sweet Guest!
Hallow and calm my troubled breast,
Weary I come to Thee for rest,
Smile on my evening hour!

3 If ever I have found it sweet
To worship at my Saviour's feet,
Now to my soul that bliss repeat.
Smile on my evening hour!

4 Let not the gospel seed remain
Unfruitful, or be lost again;
Let heavenly dews descend like rain.
Smile on my evening hour!

5 Oh! ever present, ever nigh,
Jesus, on Thee I fix mine eye:
Thou hear'st the contrite spirit's sigh.
Smile on my evening hour!

6 My only Intercessor Thou,
Mingle Thy fragrant incense now
With every prayer and every vow.
Smile on my evening hour!

7 And oh! when life's short course shall end,
And death's dark shades around impend,
My God, my everlasting Friend,
Smile on my evening hour!

Charlotte Elliott, 1839.

(6) DEPRIVED OF PUBLIC WORSHIP FOR A SEASON.

823 Luke xxiv. 15. "*Jesus Himself drew near, and went with them.*"

Tune, Hymn Chant Thyatira. 88, 84. Or Jezreel.

1 I WANT a sabbath talk with Thee;
I ask Thee for one little word;
Alone, alone! draw near to me,
Dear risen Lord!

2 Oh, join Thyself to me, and deign
To commune as in days foregone;
As once Thou talkedst with the twain,
So with the one.

3 Their sabbath journey, e'en like mine,
Without a present Lord, was sad;
Like them, I want the voice Divine,
To make me glad.

4 Draw near; and make my heart to burn,
And open Thou the living word,
And talk of sweet things that concern
Thyself, my Lord.

5 Unfold the wonders of Thy grace;
Make hidden meanings clear and plain;
And through each glowing scripture trace
Love's golden chain.

6 Mine eyes are holden! draw Thou near;
And break the bread, and pour the wine;
The strength, the sweetness, and the cheer,
All, all are Thine!

Jane Crewdson, 1860.

KADESH. [H. P. 159.]

824 Ps. lxxxiv. 4. "*Blessed are they that dwell in Thy house.*" Tune KADESH. 77, 77. D.

1 PLEASANT are Thy courts above,
In the land of light and love;
Pleasant are Thy courts below,
In this land of sin and woe.
Oh! my spirit longs and faints
For the fellowship of saints;
For the brightness of Thy face,
King of glory, God of grace.

2 Happy birds that sing and fly
Round Thine altars, O Most High;
Happier souls that find a rest
In their heavenly Father's breast:
Like the wandering dove that found
No repose on earth around,
They can to Thine ark repair,
And enjoy it ever there.

3 Happy souls! their praises flow,
Even in this vale of woe:
Waters in the desert rise,
Manna feeds them from the skies:
On they go from strength to strength,
Till they see Thy face at length,
At Thy feet adoring fall
Who hast led them safe through all.

4 Lord, be mine this prize to win:
Guide me through a world of sin;
Keep me by Thy saving grace;
Give me at Thy side a place:
Sun and Shield alike Thou art,
Guide and guard my erring heart;
Grace and glory flow from Thee,
Shower, oh shower them, Lord, on me!

Henry Francis Lyte, 1834.

YORK. [H. P. 45.]

(7) RESTORED TO PUBLIC WORSHIP.

825 Ps. cxvi. 14. "*I will pay my vows unto the Lord.*"
Tune YORK. C. M. Or BESOR.

1 WHAT shall I render to my God
For all His kindness shown?
My feet shall visit Thine abode,
My songs address Thy throne.

2 Among the saints that fill Thy house
My offerings shall be paid;
There shall my zeal perform the vows
My soul in anguish made.

3 How happy all Thy servants are!
How great Thy grace to me!
My life which Thou hast made Thy care,
Lord, I devote to Thee!

Isaac Watts, D.D., 1719.

THEME VII.—Special Services.

(1) FOUNDATION, DEDICATION, OR CONSECRATION OF A CHURCH.

826 2 Chron. vi. 18. "*But will God in very deed dwell with men on the earth?*"
Tune OLD HUNDREDTH. L. M.

1 THIS stone to Thee in faith we lay;
We build the temple, Lord, to Thee;
Thine eye be open night and day,
To guard this house and sanctuary.

2 Here, when Thy people seek Thy face,
And dying sinners pray to live,
Hear Thou, in heaven, Thy dwelling-place,
And when Thou hearest, oh, forgive!

3 Here, when Thy messengers proclaim
The blessed gospel of Thy Son,
Still, by the power of His great name
Be mighty signs and wonders done.

THE OLD 100th TUNE. [H. P. 1.]

4 But will indeed Jehovah deign
Here to abide, no transient guest?
Here will the world's Redeemer reign,
And here the Holy Spirit rest?

5 That glory never hence depart!
Yet choose not, Lord, this house alone:
Thy kingdom come to every heart,
In every bosom fix Thy throne.

James Montgomery, 1819.

827 Eph. ii. 20. "*Christ Himself being the chief Corner Stone.*"

Tune Darwell. 6666, 88. Or Moriah.

DARWELL. [H. P. 274.]

1 Christ is our Corner Stone,
On Him alone we build;
With His true saints alone
The courts of heaven are filled;
On His great love Our hopes we place
Of present grace And joys above.

2 Oh, then with hymns of praise
These hallowed courts shall ring;
Our voices we will raise
The Three in One to sing;
And thus proclaim In joyful song
Both loud and long That glorious Name.

3 Here, gracious God, do Thou
For evermore draw nigh;
Accept each faithful vow,
And mark each suppliant sigh:
In copious shower On all who pray
Each holy day Thy blessings pour.

4 Here may we gain from heaven
The grace which we implore;
And may that grace, once given,
Be with us evermore,
Until that day When all the blest
To endless rest Are called away!

See Hymns 799, 800, 810.

Latin Hymn, circa 8th Century; J. Chandler (tr.), 1837.

(2) CHOIR MEETINGS.

828 2 Chron. v. 13. "*The singers were as one . . to be heard in praising and thanking the Lord.*"

Tune Zared II. 85, 85, 843.

ZARED II. (Valley of). [H. P. 173.]

1 Angel voices ever singing
Round Thy throne of light,
Angel harps for ever ringing,
Rest not day nor night;
We would join with them to bless Thee,
And confess Thee, Lord of might!

2 Thou, who art beyond the farthest
Mortal eye can scan,
Can it be that Thou regardest
Songs of sinful man?
Can we feel that Thou art near us,
And wilt hear us? Yea! we can.

3 Lord, we know that Thou rejoicest
O'er each work of Thine;
Thou didst ears, and hands, and voices,
For Thy praise combine;
Craftsman's art and music's measure
For Thy pleasure Didst design.

4 In Thy house, great God, we offer
Of Thine own to Thee,
And for Thine acceptance proffer,
All unworthily,
Hearts, and minds, and hands, and voices,
In our choicest Melody.

5 Honour, glory, might, and merit,
Thine shall ever be,
Father, Son, and Holy Spirit,
Blessèd Trinity!
Of the best that Thou hast given,
Earth and heaven Render Thee!

Francis Pott, 1861. (a.)

SHENIR II. (Mount.) [H. P. 151.]

(3) PRAYER MEETINGS.

829 Isa. xlv. 19. *"I said not, . . . Seek ye Me in vain."*

Tune SHENIR II. 77, 77. Or LUXEMBURG.

1 LORD, we come before Thee now,
At Thy feet we humbly bow;
Oh, do not our suit disdain:
Shall we seek Thee, Lord, in vain?

2 In Thy own appointed way
Now we seek Thee, here we stay;
Lord, from hence we would not go,
Till a blessing Thou bestow.

3 Send some message from Thy word,
That may joy and peace afford;
Let Thy Spirit now impart
Full salvation to each heart.

4 Grant that those who seek may find
Thee a God supremely kind;
Heal the sick, the captive free;
Let us all rejoice in Thee!

William Hammond, 1745. (*a*.)

830 Matt. xviii. 20. *"Where two or three are gathered together in My name, there am I in the midst."*

Tune SHENIR II. 77, 77. Or VIENNA.

1 JESUS, we Thy promise claim,
We are gathered in Thy name;
In the midst do Thou appear;
Manifest Thy presence here.

2 Sanctify us, Lord, and bless;
Breathe Thy Spirit, give Thy peace;
Come, and dwell within each heart,
Light, and life, and joy impart.

3 Make us all in Thee complete,
Make us all for glory meet;
Meet to' appear before Thy sight,
Partners with the saints in light!

Charles Wesley, 1740.

831 Acts vi. 4. *"We will give ourselves continually to prayer."*

Tune GODESBERG. 87, 87.

1 LET us pray! the Lord is willing,
Ever waiting, prayer to hear;
Ready, His kind words fulfilling,
Loving hearts to help and cheer.

2 Let us pray! our God with blessing
Satisfies the praying soul!
Bends to hear the heart's confessing,
Moulding it to His control.

3 Let us pray! though foes surrounding
Vex and trouble, and dismay;
Precious grace, through Christ abounding,
Still shall cheer us on our way.

4 Let us pray! our life is praying;
Prayer with time alone may cease;
Then in heaven, God's will obeying,
Life is praise and perfect peace!

Henry Bateman, 1862.

GODESBERG. [H. P. 185.]

MELCOMBE. [H. P. 24.]

832 Ps. cxxxiii. 3. *"The Lord commanded the blessing."*

Tune MELCOMBE. L. M. Or WALDECK.

1 COMMAND Thy blessing from above,
O God, on all assembled here;
Behold us with a Father's love,
While we look up with filial fear.

2 Command Thy blessing, Jesus, Lord;
May we Thy true disciples be;
Speak to each heart the mighty word;
Say to the weakest, "Follow Me."

3 Command Thy blessing in this hour,
Spirit of Truth, and fill this place
With humbling and exalting power,
With quickening and confirming grace.

4 O Thou, our Maker, Saviour, Guide!
One true eternal God confessed;
May nought in life or death divide
The saints in Thy communion blessed.

5 With Thee, and these, for ever bound,
May all, who here in prayer unite,
With harps and songs Thy throne surround,
Rest in Thy love, and reign in light!

James Montgomery, 1816.

833

Heb. x. 22. *"Let us draw near."*

Tune LEBANON. 86, 86, 88.

1 LORD, when before Thy throne we meet,
Thy goodness to adore,
From heaven, the' eternal mercy-seat,
On us Thy blessing pour;
And make our inmost souls to be
A habitation meet for Thee.

2 Be Thou, O Holy Spirit, nigh;
Accept the humble prayer,
The contrite soul's repentant sigh,
The sinner's heartfelt tear;
And let our adoration rise,
As fragrant incense, to the skies!

T. G. Nicholas, 1838.

834

Exod. xxv. 22. *"I will commune with thee from above the mercy-seat."* Tune MELCOMBE. L. M.

1 FROM every stormy wind that blows,
From every swelling tide of woes,
There is a calm, a safe retreat;
'Tis found beneath the mercy-seat.

2 There is a place where Jesus sheds
The oil of gladness o'er our heads;
A place than all beside more sweet;
It is the blood-stained mercy-seat.

3 There is a spot where spirits blend,
Where friend holds fellowship with friend:
Though sundered far, by faith we meet
Around our common mercy-seat.

4 Ah! whither could we flee for aid,
When tempted, desolate, dismayed;
Or how the hosts of hell defeat,
Had suffering saints no mercy-seat?

5 There, there, on eagle wings we soar,
And time and sense seem all no more,
And heaven comes down our souls to greet,
And glory crowns the mercy-seat.

6 Oh! let my hands forget their skill,
My tongue be silent, cold, and still,
This bounding heart forget to beat,
If I forget the mercy-seat!

Hugh Stowell, 1832. (*a*.)

835

Ps. civ. 34. *"My meditation of Him shall be sweet."*

Tune PATMOS. 77, 77.

1 SWEET the time, exceeding sweet,
When the saints together meet,
When the Saviour is the theme,
When they join to sing of Him.

2 Sing we then eternal love,
Such as did the Father move;
When He saw the world undone,
Loved the world, and gave His Son.

3 Sing the Son's amazing love,
How He left the realms above,
Took our nature and our place,
Lived and died to save our race.

4 Sing we too the Spirit's love;
With our wretched hearts He strove;
Turned our feet from ways of shame,
Made us trust in Jesu's name.

5 Sweet the place, exceeding sweet,
Where the saints in glory meet;
Where the Saviour is the theme,
Where they see, and sing of Him!

George Burder, 1784. (*a*.)

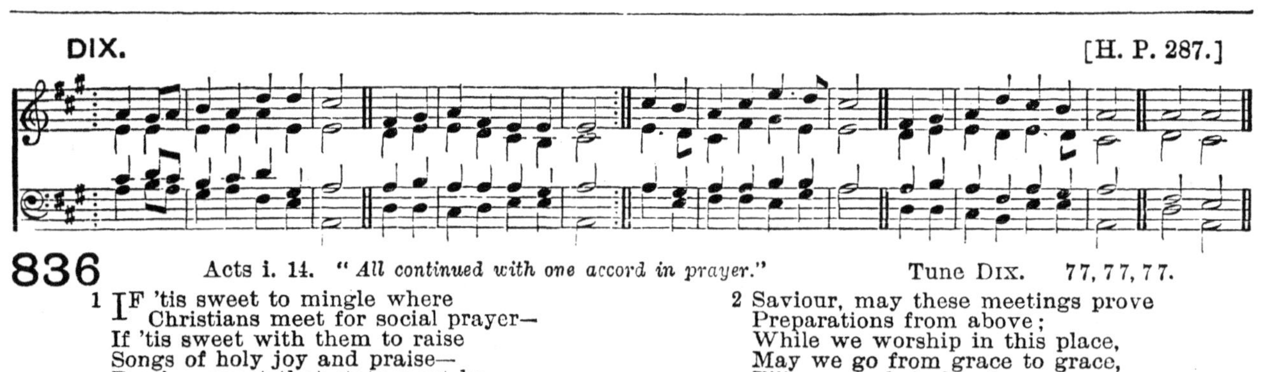

836 Acts i. 14. *"All continued with one accord in prayer."* Tune DIX. 77, 77, 77.

1 IF 'tis sweet to mingle where
Christians meet for social prayer—
If 'tis sweet with them to raise
Songs of holy joy and praise—
Passing sweet that state must be
Where they meet eternally.

2 Saviour, may these meetings prove
Preparations from above;
While we worship in this place,
May we go from grace to grace,
Till we, each in his degree,
Meet for endless glory be!

Ingram Cobbin, 1828.

(4) TIMES OF REFRESHING.

837 Ezek. xxxiv. 26. *"There shall be showers of blessing."*

Tune HAVILAH. 87, 87, 87. Or IDUMEA.

1 "SHOWERS of blessing!" gracious promise,
From the God who rules on high:
From the everlasting Father,
He who will not, cannot lie.
Showers of blessing
He has promised from the sky.

2 "Showers of blessing!" joyful showers,
Making every heart rejoice.
Come, ye saints, and plead the promise,
Raise in faith the suppliant voice;
Showers of blessing,
Oh! let nothing less suffice!

Albert Midlane, 1865.

838 Ezek. xxxiv. 26. *"I will cause the shower to come down in his season."* Tune STUTTGARD. 87, 87.

1 FATHER, for Thy promised blessing
Still we plead before Thy throne;
For the times of sweet refreshing,
Which can come from Thee alone.

2 Blessèd earnests Thou hast given;
But in these we would not rest,
Blessings still with Thee are hidden:
Pour them forth, and make us blest.

3 Prayer ascendeth to Thee ever;
Answer, Father! answer prayer:
Bless, oh, bless each weak endeavour,
Blood-bought pardon to declare!

4 Wake Thy slumbering children, wake them,
Bid them to Thy harvest go;
Blessings, O our Father, make them:
Round their steps let blessings flow.

5 Give reviving, give refreshing,
Give the looked-for jubilee;
To Thyself may crowds be pressing,
Bringing glory unto Thee.

6 Let no hamlet be forgotten,
Let Thy showers on all descend;
That in one loud blessèd anthem
Myriads may in triumph blend!

Albert Midlane, 1865.

TIMES OF REFRESHING.

PERSIS. [H. P. 187.]

839 Gen. xxvii. 38. "*Bless me, even me also, O my Father.*"

Tune PERSIS. 87, 87, 3.

1 LORD, I hear of showers of blessing
 Thou art scattering full and free;
Showers the thirsty land refreshing:
 Let some droppings fall on me,
 Even me.

2 Pass me not, O gracious Father!
 Sinful though my heart may be;
Thou might'st curse me, but the rather
 Let Thy mercy light on me,
 Even me.

3 Pass me not, O tender Saviour!
 Let me love and cling to Thee;
I am longing for Thy favour;
 When Thou comest, call for me,
 Even me.

4 Pass me not, O mighty Spirit!
 Thou canst make the blind to see;
Witnesser of Jesu's merit,
 Speak the word of power to me,
 Even me.

5 Have I long in sin been sleeping,
 Long been slighting, grieving Thee?
Has the world my heart been keeping?
 Oh, forgive and rescue me,
 Even me.

6 Love of God, so pure and changeless,
 Blood of God, so rich and free,
Grace of God, so strong and boundless,
 Magnify them all in me,
 Even me.

7 Pass me not, this lost one bringing;
 Satan's slave Thy child shall be;
All my heart to Thee is springing;
 Blessing others, oh, bless me,
 Even me!

Elizabeth Codner, 1860.

NARENZA. [H. P. 80.]

840 Hab. iii. 2. "*O Lord, revive Thy work.*"

Tune NARENZA. S. M.

1 REVIVE Thy work, O Lord,
 Thy mighty arm make bare;
Speak with the voice that wakes the dead,
 And make Thy people hear.

2 Revive Thy work, O Lord,
 Disturb this sleep of death;
Quicken the smouldering embers now
 By Thine almighty breath.

3 Revive Thy work, O Lord,
 Create soul-thirst for Thee:
And hungering for the bread of life
 O may our spirits be!

4 Revive Thy work, O Lord,
 Exalt Thy precious name;
And, by the Holy Ghost, our love
 For Thee and Thine inflame.

5 Revive Thy work, O Lord,
 And give refreshing showers;
The glory shall be all Thine own,
 The blessing, Lord, be ours!

Albert Midlane, 1865.

MELCOMBE. [H. P. 24.]

841 Ps. lxxxv. 6. "*Wilt Thou not revive us again?*"

Tune MELCOMBE. L. M.

1 OH for that flame of living fire
 Which shone so bright in saints of old!
Which bade their souls to heaven aspire,
 Calm in distress, in danger bold!

2 Where is that spirit, Lord, which dwelt
 In Abraham's breast, and sealed him Thine?
Which made Paul's heart with sorrow melt,
 And glow with energy Divine?

3 Is not Thy grace as mighty now
 As when Elijah felt its power?
When glory beamed from Moses' brow,
 Or Job endured the trying hour?

4 Remember, Lord, the ancient days;
 Renew Thy work, Thy grace restore;
Warm our cold hearts to prayer and praise,
 And teach us how to love Thee more!

William Hiley Bathurst, 1831.

See Hymns 867—869, 1041, 1048, 1056, 1057, 1064, 1084, 1093.

PATMOS. [H. P. 147.]

(5) MOTHERS' MEETINGS.

842 Luke ii. 51. *"His mother kept all these sayings in her heart."*

Tune PATMOS. 7 7, 7 7. Or VIENNA.

1 JESUS, Thou wast once a child,
Meek, obedient, pure, and mild;
Such may our dear children be!
Teach them, Lord, to follow Thee.

2 Thou didst grow in grace and truth
Up from infancy to youth;
May we, Lord, our children see
Striving thus to copy Thee.

3 Subject to Thy parents' word,
When their least command was heard,
May we, Lord, our children see
Thus obedient unto Thee!

4 At Thy heavenly Father's voice,
Thou in duty didst rejoice;
Changed by grace, O Lord, would we
See our children follow Thee!

James Gabb, 1864. (*a.*)

843 Mark x. 13. *"They brought young children to Him."*

Tune PATMOS. 7 7, 7 7.

1 GOD of mercy, hear our prayer
For the children Thou hast given;
Let them all Thy blessings share,
Grace on earth, and bliss in heaven!

2 In the morning of their days
May their hearts be drawn to Thee;
Let them learn to lisp Thy praise
In their earliest infancy.

3 Cleanse their souls from every stain,
Through the Saviour's precious blood;
Let them all be born again,
And be reconciled to God.

4 For this mercy, Lord, we cry;
Bend Thine ever-gracious ear;
While on Thee our souls rely,
Hear our prayer, in mercy hear!

Thomas Hastings, 1834.

THEME VIII.—National Occasions.

CRASSELIUS; *or*, WINCHESTER NEW. [H. P. 3.]

(1) NATIONAL HYMNS.

844 Prov. viii. 15. *"By Me kings reign."*

Tune CRASSELIUS. L. M.

1 O KING of Kings, Thy blessing shed
On our anointed sovereign's head;
And, looking from Thy throne in heaven,
Protect the crown Thyself hast given.

2 Her, for Thy sake, may we obey;
Uphold her right, and love her sway;
Remembering, all the powers that be
Are ministers ordained by Thee.

3 By her this favoured nation bless;
To her wise counsels give success;
In peace, in war, Thine aid be seen;
Confirm her strength; oh, save our Queen!

4 And when all earthly thrones decay,
And earthly glories fade away,
Give her a nobler crown on high,
A crown of immortality.

Thomas Cotterill, 1819. (*a.*)

NATIONAL ANTHEM. [H. P. 271.]

845 1 Sam. x. 24. *"God save the king."*

Tune NATIONAL ANTHEM. 6 6 4, 6 6 6 4.

1 GOD save our gracious Queen,
Long live our noble Queen!
God save the Queen:
Send her victorious,
Happy and glorious,
Long to reign over us;
God save the Queen.

2 O Lord our God, arise;
Scatter her enemies,
And make them fall:

Confound their politics,
Frustrate their knavish tricks;
On Thee our hopes we fix;
God save us all.

3 Thy choicest gifts in store
On her be pleased to pour;
Long may she reign:
May she defend our laws,
And ever give us cause
To sing with heart and voice,
God save the Queen!

Circa 1606. (*a.*)

HOBAH. [H. P. 248.]

846

Eph. v. 25. "*Christ also loved the Church.*"

Tune Hobah. 11 11, 11 11.

1 THE Church of our fathers! so dear to our souls;
Ay, dear as the life-blood within us that rolls!
We'll rally around her, by dangers unawed:
The Church of our fathers! the Church of our God!

2 Built on the apostles and prophets alone,
On Jesus, the Saviour and Chief Corner Stone:
The winds may arise, and her prospects deform;
She fears not the tempest, she dreads not the storm.

3 Her Cranmers, her Ridleys, for truth nobly stood;
Her rights and her charters they signed with their blood;
Asserted her freedom, and sent forth abroad
The light and the truth of the pure word of God.

4 The people may rage, and the Papists assail;
No weapon against her shall ever prevail.
The Church of our fathers for ages hath stood,
Cemented and sealed by our ancestors' blood.

5 From the Church of our fathers we'll never depart;
She's entwined round each fibre, each nerve of our heart:
The Church of our fathers! our glory and crown,
We will, unimpaired, to our children hand down!

Felicia D. Hemans, 1834.

847

Ps. lxxix. 9. "*Help us, O God of our salvation, for the glory of Thy name.*"

Tune Lillingston. 11 11 11, 5.

LILLINGSTON. [H. P. 348.]

1 LORD of our life, and God of our salvation,
Star of our night, and Hope of every nation,
Hear and receive Thy church's supplication,
Lord God Almighty.

2 See round Thine ark the angry billows curling,
See how Thy foes their banners are unfurling;
Lord, while their darts envenomed they are hurling,
Thou canst preserve us.

3 Lord, Thou canst help when earthly armour faileth,
Lord, Thou canst save when deadly sin assaileth,
Lord, o'er Thy Rock nor death nor hell prevaileth;
Grant us Thy peace, Lord.

4 Grant us Thy help till foes are backward driven,
Grant them Thy truth, that they may be forgiven,
Grant peace on earth, and, after we have striven,
Peace in Thy heaven!

Eighth Century (*tr.* 1856).

IONA. [H. P. 37.]

848 Ps. lxxxv. 9. "*That glory may dwell in our land.*" Tune IONA. C. M.

1 SHINE, mighty God, on Britain shine,
With beams of heavenly grace;
Reveal Thy power through all our coasts,
And show Thy smiling face.

2 Amidst our isle, exalted high,
Do Thou, our glory, stand,
And, like a wall of guardian fire,
Surround this favoured land.

3 When shall Thy name, from shore to shore,
Sound all the earth abroad;
And distant nations know and love
Their Saviour and their God?

4 Sing to the Lord, ye distant lands,
Sing loud, with solemn voice;
While British tongues exalt His praise,
And British hearts rejoice.

5 Earth shall obey her Maker's will,
And yield a full increase;
Our God will crown His chosen isle
With fruitfulness and peace.

6 God, the Redeemer, scatters round
His choicest favours here;
While the creation's utmost bound
Shall see, adore, and fear!

Isaac Watts, D.D., 1719.

NOTTINGHAM; *or*, ST. MAGNUS. [H. P. 39.]

849 Deut. xi. 12. "*A land which the Lord thy God careth for.*"

Tune NOTTINGHAM. C. M.

1 LORD, while for all mankind we pray,
Of every clime and coast,
Oh hear us for our native land—
The land we love the most.

2 Our fathers' sepulchres are here,
And here our kindred dwell:
Our children too—how should we love
Another land so well!

3 Oh guard our shores from every foe,
With peace our borders bless;
With prosperous times our cities crown,
Our fields with plenteousness.

4 Unite us in the sacred love
Of knowledge, truth, and Thee;
And let our hills and valleys shout
The songs of liberty.

5 Lord of the nations! thus to Thee
Our country we commend;
Be Thou her refuge and her trust,
Her everlasting Friend!

John Reynell Wreford, D.D., 1840.

See Hymn 863.

KADESH. [H. P. 159.]

(2) HARVEST.

850 Lev. xxiii. 39. "*When ye have gathered in the fruit of the land, ye shall keep a feast unto the Lord.*"

Tune KADESH. 77, 77. D. Or HESHBON.

1 COME, ye thankful people, come,
Raise the song of harvest-home!
All is safely gathered in,
Ere the winter storms begin:
God our Maker doth provide
For our wants to be supplied:
Come to God's own temple, come,
Raise the song of harvest-home!

2 All the world is God's own field,
Fruit unto His praise to yield;
Wheat and tares together sown,
Unto joy or sorrow grown:
First the blade, and then the ear,
Then the full corn shall appear:
Lord of harvest, grant that we
Wholesome grain and pure may be.

3 For the Lord our God shall come
And shall take His harvest home:
From His field shall in that day
All offences purge away:
Give His angels charge at last
In the fire the tares to cast;
But the fruitful ears to store
In His garner evermore.

4 Even so, Lord, quickly come,
To Thy final harvest-home;
Gather Thou Thy people in,
Free from sorrow, free from sin;
There for ever purified,
In Thy presence to abide:
Come, with all Thine angels, come,
Raise the glorious Harvest-home!

See *Hymn* 646.

Dean Alford, D.D., 1844; *revised*, 1864.

HERMAS. [H. P. 105.]

851

Isa. ix. 3. "*The joy in harvest.*"

Tune HERMAS. 65, 65. D. and Chorus.

1 EARTH below is teeming, Heaven is bright above;
Every brow is beaming In the light of love:
Every eye rejoices, Every thought is praise;
Happy hearts and voices Gladden nights and days:
O Almighty Giver, bountiful and free!
As the joy in harvest, joy we before Thee.

2 Every youth and maiden On the harvest plain,
Round the wagons laden With their golden grain,
Swell the happy chorus On the evening air,
Unto Him who o'er us Bends with constant care:
O Almighty Giver, etc.

3 For the sun and showers, For the rain and dew,
For the happy hours Spring and summer knew;
For the golden autumn And its precious stores,
For the love that brought them Teeming to our doors:
O Almighty Giver, etc.

4 Earth's broad harvest whitens In a brighter Sun
Than the orb that lightens All we tread upon:
Send out labourers, Father! Where fields ripening wave;
And the nations gather, Gather in and save.
O Almighty Giver, Bountiful and free!
Then as joy in harvest, we shall joy in Thee!

J. S. B. Monsell, LL.D., 1863.

852

Ps. lxv. 13. "*The valleys are covered over with corn; they shout for joy, they also sing.*"

Tune MOSCOW. 664, 6664.

MOSCOW. [H. P. 107.]

1 THE God of harvest praise:
In loud thanksgiving raise
Hand, heart, and voice:
The valleys laugh and sing;
Forests and mountains ring;
The plains their tribute bring;
The streams rejoice.

2 Yea, bless His holy name,
And joyous thanks proclaim
Through all the earth:
To glory in your lot
Is comely; but be not
God's benefits forgot
Amid your mirth!

3 The God of harvest praise;
Hands, hearts, and voices raise
With sweet accord:
From field to garner throng,
Bearing your sheaves along,
And in your harvest song
Bless ye the Lord.

James Montgomery, 1838.

853

Ps. lxv. 11. "*Thou crownest the year with Thy goodness.*"

Tune ABILENE. 77,77. Or LUBECK.

ABILENE. [H. P. 138.]

Hal-le-lu-jah, Hal-le-lu-jah!

1 PRAISE to God, immortal praise,
For the love that crowns our days!
Bounteous Source of every joy,
Let Thy praise our tongues employ.

2 For the blessings of the field,
For the stores the gardens yield,
For the joy which harvests bring,
Grateful praises now we sing.

3 Clouds that drop refreshing dews;
Suns that genial heat diffuse;
Flocks that whiten all the plain;
Yellow sheaves of ripened grain.

4 All that Spring with bounteous hand
Scatters o'er the smiling land;
All that liberal Autumn pours
From her overflowing stores:

5 These, great God, to Thee we owe,
Source whence all our blessings flow;
And for these our souls shall raise
Grateful vows and solemn praise.

Anna L. Barbauld, 1773.

GOSHEN. [H. P. 125.]

854

Matt. iii. 12. "*He will gather His wheat into the garner.*"

Tune GOSHEN. 76, 76.

1 OUR faithful God hath sent us
A fruitful harvest tide;
He summer boons hath lent us,
And winter wants supplied.

2 The fields, at His ordaining,
Stand thick with golden sheaves;
And man, full oft complaining,
New bounty now receives.

3 Though Mercy largely giveth,
Is Justice pacified?
We live through Him who liveth,
The "Corn of Wheat" that died.

4 Then full be our thanksgiving,
And clear each note of joy;
While faith and holy living
Our earnest thoughts employ.

5 And at the last great reaping,
When Christ His sheaves will [own,
May we, no longer weeping,
Be garnered near His throne.

6 Praise we the Godhead-Union,
The' Eternal Three in One:
With Them may our communion
For ever be begun!

William Henry Havergal, 1863.

ZOAN I. (Field of). [H. P. 127.]

855

Ps. cxlv. 16. "*Thou openest Thine hand.*"

Tune ZOAN I. 76, 76. D.

1 O NATION, Christian nation,
Lift high the hymn of praise!
The God of our salvation
Is love in all His ways!
He blesseth us, and feedeth
Each creature of His hand;
He succours him that needeth,
And gladdens all the land.

2 Rejoice, ye happy people,
And peal the changing chime
From every belfried steeple,
In symphony sublime;
Let cottage and let palace
Be thankful and rejoice,
And woods, and hills, and valleys,
Re-echo the glad voice!

3 Oh! praise the Hand that giveth,
And giveth evermore,
To every soul that liveth,
Abundance flowing o'er!
For every soul He filleth
With manna from above,
And over all distilleth
The unction of His love.

4 To God the loving Father,
Who biddeth us rejoice,
Let all within His temple
Lift high their thankful voice:
To Jesus, our Redeemer,
On His bright throne in heaven,
And Holy Ghost the Comforter,
All praise and might be given!

Martin F. Tupper, 1846.

856 Hab. iii. 17, 18. "*Although the fields shall yield no meat, yet I will rejoice in the Lord.*"

Tune Sihor. 77, 77, 77.

[To be used when there is deficiency in the crops.]

1 WHAT our Father does is well;
  Blessèd truth His children tell!
Though He send, for plenty, want,
Though the harvest store be scant,
Yet we rest upon His love,
Seeking better things above.

2 What our Father does is well;
Shall the wilful heart rebel?
If a blessing He withhold
In the field, or in the fold,
Is it not Himself to be
All our store eternally?

3 What our Father does is well;
Though He sadden hill and dell,
Upward yet our praises rise
For the strength His word supplies.
He has called us sons of God,
Can we murmur at His rod?

4 What our Father does is well;
May the thought within us dwell;
Though nor milk nor honey flow
In our barren Canaan now,
God can save us in our need,
God can bless us, God can feed.

5 Therefore unto Him we raise
Hymns of glory, songs of praise;
To the Father, and the Son,
And the Spirit, Three in One,
Honour, might, and glory be,
Now, and through eternity!

Benj. Schmolke, 1704; *Rev. Sir H. W. Baker* (*tr.*), 1861.

SIHOR (River). [H. P. 158.]

TEKOA (Wilderness of). [H. P. 200.]

(3) WAR AND PEACE

857 Isa. ii. 4. "*He shall rebuke many people.*"

Tune Tekoa. 87, 87, 87.

1 ART Thou, Lord, rebuking nations?
  Hast Thou bared Thy glittering sword?
War, commotions, tribulations,
  Are they marching at Thy word?
    Shield us, Saviour, With Thy favour,
  When Thy vials are outpoured!

2 If Thy judgments now are waking,
  Let not Thy compassion sleep:
But, while earthly powers are shaking,
  Firm and free Thy kingdom keep.
    Jesu, hear us, Be Thou near us,
  When the storm shall round us sweep

3 Courage, saints, your fears assuaging,
  Chant a bold and blissful strain!
Holy seers, of peace presaging,
  Bid us hail Messiah's reign.
    Strife, sedition, Superstition,
  Then no votaries shall gain.

4 Warrior hosts, no longer mustering,
  Cease the gleaming lance to wield:
Now they watch the fruitage clustering;
  Now they crop the sunny field.
    Thus shall sadness Change to gladness,
  When Messiah is revealed.

5 Prince of Peace, let every nation
  Soon Thy Spirit's empire own;
Bow the world in supplication:
  Bring the heathen to Thy throne!
    Earth possessing Boundless blessing
  Then shall honour Thee alone!

William Henry Havergal, 1831.

HERMON. [H. P. 27.]

858

Ps. cxlvii. 14. "*He maketh peace.*" Tune HERMON. L. M.

1 GIVE peace in these our days, O Lord!
 Times of great peril are at hand;
Thine enemies, with one accord,
 Christ's name blaspheme in every land.

2 Give us that peace that we do lack
 Through unbelief and evil life;
Thy word to give Thou dost not slack,
 Which we unkindly use for strife.

3 Give peace, O Lord! Thy Spirit send;
 With grief, and with repentance true,
Pierce Thou our hearts, our lives amend,
 And by true faith in Christ renew.

4 Give peace, and grant that fear and dread—
 Through Thy sweet mercy, Lord, and grace—
May fly, and truth lift up her head,
 And dwell and shine in every place!

Sternhold and Hopkins' Psalms, 1562.

KEDAR. [H. P. 42.]

859

Ps. xlvi. 9. "*He maketh wars to cease.*"
Tune KEDAR. C. M. Or GLOUCESTER.

1 HELP us, O Lord! with grateful minds
 To bow before Thy throne,
And, with united thanks to Thee,
 Thy tender mercies own.

2 May we, from feared destruction saved,
 Our Ebenezer raise;
And with our hearts, and lives, and tongues,
 Proclaim Thy wondrous praise.

3 Oh, haste the glowing time, foretold
 In Thine unerring word;
When, from the greatest to the least,
 All men shall serve the Lord.

4 No more let nations, learning war,
 In hostile rage appear,
But into ploughshares beat the sword,
 To pruning-hooks the spear.

5 From Satan's long usurped domain,
 A sinful world release:
Then with each other all shall dwell
 In universal peace!

Thomas Cotterill, 1810.

See Hymn 49.

ST. MARY'S; *or*, HACKNEY. [H. P. 73.]

(4) NATIONAL FAST AND HUMILIATION.

860

Neh. ix. 33. "*Thou hast done right, but we have done wickedly.*" Tune ST. MARY. C. M.

1 ALMIGHTY God, before Thy throne
 Thy mourning people bend,
'Tis on Thy pardoning grace alone
 Our prostrate hopes depend.

2 Dire judgments from Thy heavy hand
 Thy dreadful power display;
Yet mercy spares our guilty land,
 And still we live to pray.

3 Oh, turn us, turn us, mighty Lord,
 By Thy subduing grace:
So shall our hearts obey Thy word,
 And we shall see Thy face.

4 If famine, plague, or foes invade,
 We shall not sink or fear,
Secure of all-sufficient aid
 When God, our God, is near!

Anne Steele, 1760. (a.)

BREMEN. [H. P. 186.]

861 Dan. ix. 19. *"O Lord, hear; O Lord, forgive."* Tune Bremen. 8 7, 8 7. Or Augsburg.

1 DREAD Jehovah, God of nations,
From Thy temple in the skies,
Hear Thy people's supplications,
Now for their deliverance rise.

2 Lo! with deep contrition turning,
Humbly at Thy feet we bend;
Hear us fasting, praying, mourning;
Hear us, spare us, and defend.

3 Though our sins, our hearts confounding,
Long and loud for vengeance call,
Thou hast mercy more abounding,
Jesu's blood can cleanse them all.

4 Let that love veil our transgression;
Let that blood our guilt efface;
Save Thy people from oppression;
Save from spoil Thy holy place!

C. F., 1804.

DUNDEE; *or*, WINDSOR. [H. P. 72.]

862 Joel i. 14. *"Sanctify ye a fast, call a solemn assembly."*

Tune Dundee. C. M.

1 THE solemn season calls us now
A holy fast to keep;
And see within the temple how
Both priest and people weep.

2 But come not thou with tears alone,
Or outward form of prayer;
But let it in thy heart be known,
That penitence is there.

3 Oh, let us then, with heartfelt grief,
Draw near unto our God,
And pray to Him to grant relief,
And stay the' uplifted rod.

4 O righteous Judge, if Thou wilt deign
To grant us all we need,
We pray for time to turn again,
And grace to turn indeed.

5 Blest Three in One, with grief sincere,
To Thee we humbly pray,
That fruits of mercy may appear,
To bless this fasting day!

John Chandler (tr.), 1837.

See Hymn 552.

CANTERBURY. [H. P. 294.]

(5) NATIONAL THANKSGIVING AND REJOICING.

863 Ps. lxvii. 5. *"Let the people praise Thee, O God."* Tune Canterbury. 8 7, 8 7. Or Culbach.

1 LORD of heaven, and earth, and ocean,
Hear us from Thy bright abode:
While our hearts, with deep devotion,
Own their great and gracious God.

2 Now with joy we come before Thee;
Countless have Thy mercies been;
Lord of life, and strength, and glory,
Guard Thy Church, and guide our Queen.

3 Thee, with humble adoration,
Lord, we praise for mercies past;
Strength of this most favoured nation,
May those mercies ever last:

4 May our sons appear before Thee,
In Thy Church Thy praise be seen;
Lord of life, and light, and glory,
Bless Thy people—bless our Queen!

John Cross, 1812. (*a.*)

See Hymns 844—849.

SALZBURG. [H. P. 203.]

3 Spread Thy golden pinions o'er them,
Holy Spirit, heavenly Dove;
Guide them, lead them, go before them,
Give them peace, and joy, and love.
Temples of the Holy Spirit,
May they with Thy glory shine,
And immortal bliss inherit,
And for evermore be Thine!

Bishop Christopher Wordsworth, 1863.

See Hymns 923—948.

(2) MISSION SERVICES.

867

Luke xiv. 13. "*Call the poor.*" Tune SALZBURG. 87, 87. D. Or ESDRAELON.

1 "CALL them in!"—the poor, the wretched,
Sin-stained wanderers from the fold;
Peace and pardon freely offer,—
Can you weigh their worth with gold?
"Call them in!"—the weak, the weary,
Laden with the doom of sin;
Bid them come and rest in Jesus;
He is waiting;—"call them in!"

2 "Call them in!"—the Jew, the Gentile;
Bid the stranger to the feast;
"Call them in!"—the rich, the noble,
From the highest to the least.
Forth the Father runs to meet them,
He hath all their sorrows seen;
Robe and ring and royal sandals
Wait the lost ones;—"call them in!"

3 "Call them in!"—the broken-hearted,
Cowering 'neath the brand of shame;
Speak love's message, low and tender,—
"'Twas for sinners Jesus came."
See! the shadows lengthen round us,
Soon the day-dawn will begin;
Can you leave them lost and lonely?
Christ is coming;—"call them in!"

Anna Shipton, 1868.

EVAN II. [H. P. 77.]

868

Isa. xxvii. 12. "*Ye shall be gathered one by one.*" Tune EVAN II. C. M. D. Or OLD EIGHTY-FIRST.

1 ANOTHER called, another brought, dear Master, to Thy feet!
Oh, where are words to tell the joy so wonderful and sweet?
Oh, where are words to give Thee thanks that Thou indeed hast heard—
That Thou hast proved and sealed anew Thy faithful promise-word?

2 Yes, conquering Thy word goes forth on all-triumphant way!
"Ye shall be gathered one by one,"—'tis true afresh to-day!
And so we hush the yearning cry, "How long, O Lord, how long?"
A sweet new token Thou hast given to change it into song.

3 So once again we bless Thee with Thy holy ones above,
Because another heart has seen Thy great and mighty love;
Another heart will own Thee Lord, and worship Thee as King,
And grateful love, and glowing praise, and willing service bring.

4 Another voice to "tell it out," what great things Thou hast done;
Another life to live for Thee, another witness won;
Another faithful soldier on our Master's side enrolled;
Another heart to read aright Thy heart of love untold!

Frances Ridley Havergal, 1872.

EATON. [H. P. 313.]

(6) PRAYER FOR THOSE AT SEA.

864 Ps. cvii. 24. *"These see the works of the Lord, and His wonders in the deep."*

Tune EATON. 88, 88, 88. Or MAON.

1 ETERNAL Father, strong to save,
Whose arm hath bound the restless wave,
Who bidd'st the mighty ocean deep
Its own appointed limits keep;
Oh, hear us when we cry to Thee
For those in peril on the sea.

2 O Christ, whose voice the waters heard,
And hushed their raging at Thy word,
Who walkedst on the foaming deep,
And calm amidst its rage didst sleep;
Oh, hear us when we cry to Thee
For those in peril on the sea.

3 Most Holy Spirit, who didst brood
Upon the chaos dark and rude,
And bid its angry tumult cease,
And give, for wild confusion, peace;
Oh, hear us when we cry to Thee
For those in peril on the sea.

4 O Trinity of love and power,
Our brethren shield in danger's hour;
From rock and tempest, fire and foe,
Protect them wheresoe'er they go:
Thus evermore shall rise to Thee
Glad hymns of praise from land and sea!

William Whiting, 1860. (*a.*)

THEME IX.—Missions. I.—At Home.*

(1) SCHOOLS.

865 Luke ii. 51. *"He was subject unto them."*

Tune PURDAY. 87, 87, 77. Or SUCCOTH.

1 BLESSED Jesus, Lord and Brother!
Once Thou wast a lowly child,
Subject to Thy Virgin-mother,
"Holy, harmless, undefiled;"
Wisdom, favour, grace, and truth,
Graced, like morning stars, Thy youth.

2 Great Redeemer, Mediator!
Now Thou art enthroned in light;
But Thou wearest still our nature,
And all heaven admires the sight.
Lord, to tender years impart
Mercy's boon, the tender heart.

3 Jesu, by Thy childhood's favour,
By Thy manhood's agony,
Fill us with Thy Spirit's savour,
Train us for eternity;
With the glittering hosts above,
May we sing Thy boundless love!

William Henry Havergal, 1833.

PURDAY. [H. P. 338.]

866 Isa. liv. 13. *"All thy children shall be taught of the Lord."* Tune SALZBURG. 87, 87. D.

1 HEAVENLY Father, send Thy blessing
On Thy children gathered here;
May they all, Thy name confessing,
Be to Thee for ever dear.
May they be, like Joseph, loving,
Dutiful, and chaste, and pure,
And their faith, like David, proving,
Steadfast unto death endure.

2 Holy Saviour, who in meekness
Didst vouchsafe a child to be,
Guide their steps, and help their weakness;
Bless, and make them like to Thee;
Bear Thy lambs, when they are weary,
In Thine arms, and at Thy breast;
Through life's desert, dry and dreary,
Bring them to Thy heavenly rest.

* Also, for MISSION SERVICES, Hymns 103, 353 to 356, 363, 372, 431, 465 to 493, 569, 600 to 603, 633, 690 to 717, 730, 830 to 840, 14, 1024, 428, 1041 to 1075, 817.

SWABIA. [H. P. 82.]

869 Cant. i. 4. "*The King hath brought me into His chambers.*"
Tune SWABIA. S. M. Or FRANCONIA.

1 AND may I really tread
The palace of my King,
Gaze on the glory of His face,
And of His beauty sing?

2 I am not worthy, Lord!
Not worthy to draw near;
My feet are dusty with the way,
I hesitate—I fear!

3 "But wherefore tremble thus?
I washed thee clean and white;
I decked thee with salvation's robe,
Fairer than morning light!

4 "I hold thy hand in Mine,
And as I walk beside,
The pearly gates lift up their heads,
And for us open wide.

5 "They opened long ago,
Opened to let *Me* in,
When I, returning from the fight,
Had conquered death and sin.

6 "And they stand open still,
Open, My child, for thee!
Then enter in with joyfulness,
And use thy liberty."

7 Jesus! I *will* draw nigh,
And in the "secret place"
Behold the beauty of my Lord,
And banquet on His grace.
William Pennefather, 1871.

(3) HOSPITAL SUNDAY.

870 Matt. xiv. 35. "*They brought unto Him all that were diseased.*"
Tune SUCCOTH. 87, 87, 77. Or CASSEL.

SUCCOTH (Valley of). [H. P. 189.]

1 THOU to whom the sick and dying
Ever came, nor came in vain,
Still with healing word replying
To the weary cry of pain;
Hear us, Jesu, as we meet,
Suppliants at Thy mercy-seat.

2 Every care and every sorrow,
Be it great, or be it small;
Yesterday, to-day, to-morrow,
When, where'er, it may befall;
Lay we humbly at Thy feet,
Suppliants round Thy mercy-seat.

3 Still the weary, sick, and dying
Need a brother's, sister's care;
On Thy higher help relying,
May we now their burden share:
Bringing all our offerings meet,
Suppliants at Thy mercy-seat.

4 May each child of Thine be willing,
Willing both in hand and heart,
Every law of love fulfilling,
Every comfort to impart:
Ever bringing offerings meet,
Suppliants at Thy mercy-seat.

5 Then shall sickness, sin, and sadness
To Thy healing power yield;
Till the sick and sad in gladness,
Rescued, ransomed, cleansèd, healed,
Shall the saints together meet,
Pardoned at Thy judgment seat!
Godfrey Thring, 1866.

See Hymns 597, 598, 1085.

II.—Missions Abroad.

ORIEL. [H. P. 302.]

(1) JEWS.

871 Isa. lii. 8. "*The Lord shall bring again Zion.*" Tune ORIEL. 87, 87, 47. Or IDUMEA.

1 ON the mountain's top appearing,
Lo! the sacred herald stands;
Welcome news to Zion bearing,
Zion long in hostile lands;
Mourning captive!
God Himself will loose thy bands.

2 Has thy night been long and mournful?
Have thy friends unfaithful proved?
Have thy foes been proud and scornful,
By thy sighs and tears unmoved?
Cease thy mourning,
Zion still is well beloved.

3 God, thy God, will now restore thee:
He Himself appears thy friend:
All thy foes shall flee before thee,
Here their boasts and triumphs end;
Great deliverance
Zion's King vouchsafes to send.

4 Enemies no more shall trouble,
All thy wrongs shall be redressed;
For thy shame thou shalt have double,
In thy Maker's favour blessed;
All thy conflicts
End in everlasting rest! *Thomas Kelly*, 1804.

ST. MICHAEL. [H. P. 85.]

872

Ps. lxvii. 2. "*That Thy way may be known upon earth.*" Tune St. Michael. S. M.

1 TO bless Thy chosen race,
In mercy, Lord, incline:
And cause the brightness of Thy face
On all Thy saints to shine;

2 That so Thy wondrous way
May through the world be known,
While distant lands their tribute pay,
And Thy salvation own.

3 Let differing nations join
To celebrate Thy fame;
Let all the world, O Lord, combine
To praise Thy glorious name.

4 Oh let them shout and sing,
With joy and pious mirth;
For Thou, the righteous Judge and King,
Shalt govern all the earth!
Tate and Brady, 1696.

KEDAR. [H. P. 42.]

873

Isa. lx. 15. "*I will make thee an eternal excellency.*" Tune Kedar. C. M. Or Nottingham.

1 O ZION, when thy Saviour came
In grace and love to thee,
No beauty in thy royal Lord
Thy faithless eye could see.

2 Yet, onward in His path of grace,
The holy Sufferer went,
To feel, at last, that love on thee
Had all in vain been spent.

3 Yet not in vain: o'er Israel's land
The glory yet will shine;
And He, thy once rejected King,
Messiah, shall be thine.

4 Then thou, beneath the peaceful reign
Of Jesus and His bride,
Shalt sound His grace and glory forth
To all the earth beside.

5 The nations to thy glorious light,
O Zion! yet shall throng;
And all the listening islands wait
To catch the joyful song.

6 The name of Jesus yet shall ring
Through earth and heaven above,
And all His ransomed people know
The sabbath of His love.
Sir Edward Denny, 1838.

HERMON. [H. P. 27.]

874

Ps. lxxiv. 2. "*Remember . . . Thine inheritance which Thou hast redeemed.*"
Tune Hermon. L. M.

1 GREAT God of Abraham! hear our prayer;
Let Abraham's seed Thy mercy share:
Oh, may they now at length return,
And look on Him they pierced, and mourn!

2 Remember Jacob's flock of old;
Bring home the wanderers to Thy fold;
Remember too Thy promised word,
"Israel at last shall seek the Lord."

3 Though outcasts still, estranged from Thee,
Cut off from their own olive-tree;
Why should they longer such remain?
For Thou canst graft them in again.

4 Lord, put Thy law within their hearts,
And write it in their inward parts;
The veil of darkness rend in two,
Which hides Messiah from their view.

5 Oh! haste the day, foretold so long,
When Jew and Greek, a glorious throng,
One house shall seek, one prayer shall pour,
And one Redeemer shall adore!
Thomas Cotterill, 1819.

See Hymns 129, 226, 929, 302, 322—330, 334, 483.

CRASSELIUS; *or*, WINCHESTER NEW. [H. P. 3.]

(2) GENTILES.

875 Joel ii. 28. *"I will pour out My Spirit upon all flesh."*

Tune CRASSELIUS. L. M.

1 O SPIRIT of the living God,
In all Thy plenitude of grace,
Where'er the foot of man hath trod,
Descend on our apostate race.

2 Give tongues of fire and hearts of love,
To preach the reconciling word;
Give power and unction from above,
Whene'er the joyful sound is heard.

3 Be darkness, at Thy coming, light,
Confusion order in Thy path;
Souls without strength inspire with might,
Bid mercy triumph over wrath.

4 O Spirit of the Lord, prepare
All the round earth her God to meet;
Breathe Thou abroad like morning air,
Till hearts of stone begin to beat.

5 Baptize the nations far and nigh;
The triumphs of the cross record;
The name of Jesus glorify,
Till every kindred call Him Lord!

James Montgomery, 1825.

ZOAN I. (Field of). [H. P. 127.]

876 Acts xvi. 9. *"Come over . . . and help us."*

Tune ZOAN I. 76, 76. D.

1 FROM Greenland's icy mountains,
From India's coral strand,
Where Afric's sunny fountains
Roll down their golden sand;
From many an ancient river,
From many a palmy plain,
They call us to deliver
Their land from error's chain.

2 What though the spicy breezes
Blow soft o'er Ceylon's isle;
Though every prospect pleases,
And only man is vile:
In vain with lavish kindness
The gifts of God are strewn;
The heathen, in his blindness,
Bows down to wood and stone.

3 Can we, whose souls are lighted
With wisdom from on high,
Can we, to men benighted,
The lamp of life deny?
Salvation, oh! salvation,
The joyful sound proclaim;
Till each remotest nation
Has learned Messiah's name.

4 Waft, waft, ye winds, His story!
And you, ye waters, roll,
Till, like a sea of glory,
It spreads from pole to pole;
Till o'er our ransomed nature,
The Lamb for sinners slain,
Redeemer, King, Creator,
In bliss returns to reign!

Bishop Heber, 1819.

877 Gen. i. 3. *"God said, Let there be light."*

Tune MOSCOW. 664, 6664.

1 THOU, whose almighty word
Chaos and darkness heard,
And took their flight:
Hear us, we humbly pray,
And where the gospel's day
Sheds not its glorious ray,
"Let there be light."

2 Thou, who didst come to bring,
On Thy redeeming wing,
Healing and sight,
Health to the sick in mind,
Sight to the inly blind:
Oh! now to all mankind
"Let there be light."

3 Spirit of truth and love,
Life-giving, holy Dove,
Speed forth Thy flight:
Move o'er the waters' face,
Bearing the lamp of grace,
And in earth's darkest place
"Let there be light."

4 Blessèd and holy Three,
Glorious Trinity,
Wisdom, Love, Might!
Boundless as ocean's tide
Rolling in fullest pride,
Through the world, far and wide,
"Let there be light."

John Marriott, 1813.

MOSCOW. [H. P. 107.]

ZAANAIM (Plain of). [H. P. 191.]

878

Ps. lxxii. 19. *"Let the whole earth be filled with His glory."*

Tune Zaanaim. 8 7, 8 7, 4 7. Or Regent Square.

1 O'ER the gloomy hills of darkness,
Look, my soul, be still and gaze;
All the promises do travail
With a glorious day of grace:
Blessed jubilee,
Let thy glorious morning dawn!

2 Let the Indian, let the Negro,
Let the rude Barbarian see
That Divine and glorious conquest
Once obtained on Calvary;
Let the gospel
Loud resound from pole to pole

3 Kingdoms wide that sit in darkness,
Grant them, Lord, the saving light;
And from eastern coast to western
May the morning chase the night,
And redemption,
Freely purchased, win the day.

4 Fly abroad, thou mighty gospel,
Win and conquer, never cease;
May Thy lasting, wide dominions,
Multiply, and still increase,
Sway Thy sceptre,
Saviour, all the world around.

William Williams, 1772.

GILBOA (Mount). [H. P. 11.]

879

Ps. xlv. 3. *"Gird Thy sword upon Thy thigh, O Most Mighty."*

Tune Gilboa. L. M.

1 CAPTAIN of Thine enlisted host,
Display Thy glorious banner high;
The summons send from coast to coast,
And call a numerous army nigh.

2 Bid, bid Thy heralds publish loud
The peaceful blessings of Thy reign;
And when they speak of sprinkling blood,
The mystery to the heart explain.

3 Fight for Thyself, O Jesus, fight,
The travail of Thy soul regain;
Before the blind make darkness light,
The crooked paths do Thou make plain!

Christopher Batty, 1867. (a.)

880 Mark xvi. 15. "*Preach the gospel to every creature.*"

Tune Stobel. 664, 6664. Or Moscow.

STOBEL. [H. P. 110.]

1 SOUND, sound the truth abroad,
Bear ye the word of God
Through the wide world:
Tell what our Lord has done;
Tell how the day is won,
And from his lofty throne
Satan is hurled.

2 Speed on the wings of love;
Jesus, who reigns above,
Bids us to fly:
They who His message bear
Should neither doubt nor fear;
He will their Friend appear,
He will be nigh.

3 When on the mighty deep,
He will their spirits keep
Stayed on His word;
When in a foreign land,
No other friend at hand,
Jesus will by them stand,
Jesus their Lord.

4 Ye who, forsaking all,
At your loved Master's call,
Comforts resign;
Soon will your work be done,
Soon will the prize be won,
Brighter than yonder sun
Then shall ye shine!

Thomas Kelly, 1820.

881 Ps. xcvi. 10. "*Say among the heathen that the Lord reigneth.*"

Tune All Saints. 87, 87, 77.

ALL SAINTS. [H. P. 298.]

1 HERALDS of the Lord of glory!
Lift your voices, lift them high:
Tell the gospel's wondrous story,
Tell it fully, faithfully;
Tell the heathen 'midst their woe,
Jesus reigns, above, below.

2 Haste the day, the bright, the glorious!
When the sad and sin-bound slave
High shall laud, in pealing chorus,
Him who reigns, and reigns to save.
Tempter, tremble! Idols, fall!
Jesus reigns, the Lord of all!

3 Christians! send to joyless regions
Heralds of the gladdening word;
Let them, voiced like trumpet legions,
Preach the kingdom of the Lord:
Tell the heathen, Jesus died!
Reigns He now, though crucified.

4 Saviour, let Thy quickening Spirit
Touch each herald lip with fire:
Nations then shall own Thy merit,
Hearts shall glow with Thy desire:
Earth in jubilee shall sing,
Jesus reigns, the' eternal King!

William Henry Havergal, 1827.

SHARON. [H. P. 295.]

882 Jer. li. 27. "*Blow the trumpet among the nations.*"

Tune Sharon. 87, 87.

1 SOON the trumpet of salvation
Loudly, sweetly shall be blown;
And each kindred, tongue, and nation
Shall the thrilling mandate own.

2 Myriads, verging on perdition,
Roused by its persuasive sound,
Shall with ardour and contrition
Come from earth's remotest bound.

3 All shall haste and come believing
To the refuge of the cross;
And the Saviour's grace receiving,
Joyous count all else but loss.

4 Great Immanuel! send Thy Spirit!
Let Thy gospel trumpet sound;
May the heathen know Thy merit,
Make Thy glorious grace abound!

William Henry Havergal, 1826.

ZOAN I. (Field of). [H. P. 127.]

883

Ps. xlv. 4. "*In Thy majesty ride prosperously.*"

Tune ZOAN I. 76, 76. D.

1 WITH hearts in love abounding,
Prepare we now to sing
A lofty theme, resounding
Thy praise, Almighty King:
Whose love, rich gifts bestowing,
Redeemed the human race;
Whose lips, with zeal o'erflowing,
Breathe words of truth and grace.

2 In majesty transcendent,
Gird on Thy conquering sword;
In righteousness resplendent,
Ride on, Incarnate Word!
Ride on, O King Messiah,
To glory and renown;
Pierced by Thy darts of fire,
Be every foe o'erthrown!

3 So reign, O God, in heaven
Eternally the same;
And endless praise be given
To Thy eternal name!
Clothed in Thy dazzling brightness,
Thy church on earth behold,
In robe of purest whiteness,
In raiment wrought of gold.

4 And let each Gentile nation
Come gladly in her train,
To share Thy great salvation,
And join her grateful strain:
Then ne'er shall note of sadness
Awake the trembling string;
One song of joy and gladness
The ransomed world shall sing!

Harriet Auber, 1829.

884

Acts xiv. 26. "*Recommended to the grace of God for the work which they fulfilled.*"

Tune IDUMEA. 87, 87, 47.

IDUMEA. [H. P. 193.]

1 SPEED Thy servants, Saviour, speed them,
Thou art Lord of winds and waves;
They were bound, but Thou hast freed them;
Now they go to free the slaves;
Be Thou with them:
'Tis Thine arm alone that saves.

2 Friends, and home, and all forsaking,
Lord, they go at Thy command;
As their stay Thy promise taking
While they traverse sea and land:
Oh, be with them!
Lead them safely by the hand.

3 When they reach the land of strangers,
And the prospect dark appears,
Nothing seen but toils and dangers,
Nothing felt but doubts and fears,
Be Thou with them;
Hear their sighs, and count their tears.

4 When they think of home, now dearer
Than it ever seemed before,
Bring the promised glory nearer;
Let them see that peaceful shore,
Where Thy people
Rest from toil, and weep no more.

5 When no fruit appears to cheer them,
And they seem to toil in vain;
Then in mercy, Lord, draw near them,
Then their sinking hopes sustain:
Thus supported,
Let their zeal revive again.

6 In the midst of opposition,
Let them trust, O Lord, in Thee;
When success attends their mission,
Let Thy servants humbler be;
Never leave them,
Till Thy face in heaven they see:

7 There to reap in joy, for ever,
Fruit that grows from seed here sown;
There to be with Him who never
Ceases to preserve His own;
And with gladness
Give the praise to Him alone!

Thomas Kelly, 1826.

See Hymns 165, 209—211, 323, 330, 332, 333, 338, 342, 414, 461, 767.

Theme X.—Times and Seasons.

I.—Seasons of the Day.

MELCOMBE. [H. P. 24.]

(1) MORNING.

885 Lam. iii. 23. "*They are new every morning.*"
Tune Melcombe. L. M.

1 NEW every morning is the love
Our wakening and uprising prove;
Through sleep and darkness safely brought,
Restored to life, and power, and thought.

2 New mercies, each returning day,
Hover around us while we pray;
New perils past, new sins forgiven,
New thoughts of God, new hopes of heaven.

3 If on our daily course our mind
Be set to hallow all we find,
New treasures still, of countless price,
God will provide for sacrifice.

4 Old friends, old scenes will lovelier be,
As more of heaven in each we see:
Some softening gleam of love and prayer
Shall dawn on every cross and care.

5 Only, O Lord, in Thy dear love
Fit us for perfect rest above;
And help us, this and every day,
To live more nearly as we pray!

John Keble, 1827.

TALLIS'S CANON. [H. P. 13.]

886 Ps. lvii. 8. "*Awake up, my glory.*" Tune Tallis's Canon. L. M. Or Crasselius.

1 AWAKE, my soul, and with the sun
Thy daily stage of duty run;
Shake off dull sloth, and joyful rise,
To pay thy morning sacrifice.

2 Thy precious time misspent, redeem,
Each present day thy last esteem;
Improve thy talent with due care,
For the great day thyself prepare.

3 Let all thy converse be sincere,
Thy conscience as the noonday clear:
Think how the' all-seeing God thy ways
And all thy secret thoughts surveys.

4 Wake, and lift up thyself, my heart,
And with the angels bear thy part;
Who all night long unwearied sing
High praise to the Eternal King.

5 I wake, I wake, ye heavenly choir,
May your devotion me inspire;
That I, like you, my age may spend,
Like you, may on my God attend!

Part II.

6 All praise to Thee, who safe hast kept,
And hast refreshed me whilst I slept;
Grant, Lord, when I from death shall wake,
I may of endless light partake.

7 Lord, I my vows to Thee renew,
Disperse my sins as morning dew,
Guard my first springs of thought and will,
And with Thyself my spirit fill.

8 Direct, control, suggest, this day,
All I design, or do, or say;
That all my powers, with all their might,
In Thy sole glory may unite.

9 Praise God from whom all blessings flow,
Praise Him, all creatures here below;
Praise Him above, ye heavenly host,
Praise Father, Son, and Holy Ghost!

Bishop Ken, 1697; *revised* 1709.

887 John i. 4. "*The Life was the Light of men.*"
Tune Lubeck. 77, 77. Or Chios.

1 SON of God, Eternal Word,
Glorious Dayspring, Christ the Lord!
Shine upon us with Thy rays,
While we celebrate Thy praise.

2 When Thou madest heaven and earth,
Angels shouted at their birth;
Morning stars in chorus sang
When the world from darkness sprang.

LUBECK. [H. P. 139.]

3 When in sin and death we lay,
Thou didst wake us into day;
Thou, in human nature born,
Wert to us a glorious morn.

4 When Thou didst arise from death,
We were quickened by Thy breath;
We arose with Thee our Head,
First-begotten from the dead.

5 Look on all with pitying eye
Who in heathen darkness lie;
Scatter, Lord, their shades of night,
Dawn upon them with Thy light.

PART II.

6 Send to us the Holy Ghost,
Give the light of Pentecost;
That we may for ever bless
Thee, the Sun of Righteousness.

Hal - le - lu - jah, Hal - le - lu - jah!

7 Keep us safe from harm and sin,
Foes around us, and within;
May we see Thee ever nigh,
Ever walk as in Thine eye.

8 Lead us onward, Lord, we pray,
To the pure and perfect day,
Where we may the glory see
Of the blessèd Trinity.

9 Glory to the Father be,
Glory, Light of Light, to Thee;
With the Father and the Son,
Praise the Spirit, Three in One!

Bishop Christopher Wordsworth, 1867.

ST. GREGORY. [H. P. 259.]

888

Ps. xvi. 8. "*I have set the Lord always before me.*"
Tune ST. GREGORY. L. M. Or CRASSELIUS.

1 FORTH in Thy name, O Lord, I go,
My daily labour to pursue;
Thee, only Thee, resolved to know,
In all I think, or speak, or do.

2 The task Thy wisdom hath assigned,
Oh let me cheerfully fulfil;
In all my works Thy presence find,
And prove Thy good and perfect will.

See Hymns 105, 286.

3 Thee may I set at my right hand,
Whose eyes my inmost substance see;
And labour on at Thy command,
And offer all my works to Thee.

4 Give me to bear Thy easy yoke,
And every moment watch and pray;
And still to things eternal look,
And hasten to Thy glorious day

5 For Thee delightfully employ
Whate'er Thy bounteous grace hath given;
And run my course with even joy,
And closely walk with Thee to heaven!

Charles Wesley, 1749. (a.)

SMYRNA. (HYMN CHANT.) *Double Counterpoint.* [H. P. No. III.]

Saturday Morning.

889

Prov. xvi. 1. "*The preparations of the heart . . . from the Lord.*"
Tune, Hymn Chant SMYRNA. C. M. Or ST. ANN.

1 THIS is the day to tune with care
Each unseen chord within:
Would we for Sabbaths well prepare,
To-day we should begin.

2 Before the majesty of Heaven
To-morrow we appear;
No honour half so great is given,
Throughout man's sojourn here.

3 Yet if his heart be not prepared,
His soul not meetly dressed,
In vain that honour will be shared,
No smile will greet the guest.

4 We must beforehand lay aside
Our own polluted dress,
And wear the robe of Jesu's bride,
His spotless righteousness.

5 We must forsake this world below,
Forget all earthly things;
Strive with a seraph's love to glow,
And soar on angel wings.

6 The altar must be cleansed to-day,
Meet for the offered Lamb:
The wood in order we must lay,
And wait to-morrow's flame.

7 Lord of the sacrifice we bring,
To Thee our hopes aspire:
Our Prophet, our High Priest, and King,
Send down the sacred fire!

Charlotte Elliott, 1839.

SOUTHGATE. [H. P. 349.]

(2) EVENING.

890

Ps. cxxxix. 3. "*Thou compassest . . . my lying down.*"

Tune SOUTHGATE. 84, 84, 88 84.

1 GOD, who madest earth and heaven,
Darkness and light;
Who the day for toil hast given,
For rest the night;
May Thine angel guards defend us,
Slumber sweet Thy mercy send us,
Holy dreams and hopes attend us,
This livelong night.

2 Guard us waking, guard us sleeping:
And when we die
May we, in Thy mighty keeping,
All peaceful lie:
When the last dread call shall wake us,
Do not Thou, our God, forsake us,
But to reign in glory take us
With Thee on high.

Bishop Heber, 1827—*ver.* 2, *Archbishop Whately.*

HYMN CHANT (Troyte's). [H. P. 311.]

891

Luke xxiv. 29. "*Abide with us.*"

Tune, TROYTE'S HYMN CHANT. 10 10, 10 10.

1 ABIDE with me: fast falls the eventide;
The darkness deepens; Lord, with me abide:
When other helpers fail, and comforts flee,
Help of the helpless, oh, abide with me.

2 Swift to its close ebbs out life's little day;
Earth's joys grow dim, its glories pass away!
Change and decay in all around I see;
O Thou who changest not, abide with me.

3 Come not in terrors, as the king of kings;
But kind and good, with healing in Thy wings:
Tears for all woes, a heart for every plea;
Come, Friend of sinners, thus abide with me.

4 I need Thy presence every passing hour:
What but Thy grace can foil the tempter's power?
Who like Thyself my guide and stay can be?
Through cloud and sunshine, oh, abide with me.

5 I fear no foe, with Thee at hand to bless:
Ills have no weight, and tears no bitterness:
Where is death's sting? where, grave, thy victory?
I triumph still, if Thou abide with me.

6 Hold Thou Thy cross before my closing eyes,
Shine through the gloom, and point me to the skies;
Heaven's morning breaks, and earth's vain shadows flee;
In life, in death, O Lord, abide with me!

Henry Francis Lyte, 1847.

PHILEMON. [H. P. 223.]

892

Ps. xxx. 5. "*But joy cometh in the morning.*"

Tune PHILEMON. 87, 87.

1 LORD! in love and mercy save us,
For our trust is all in Thee;
In that cleansing fountain lave us,
Which alone can make us free!

2 Weary, life's rough billows breasting,
Through the long lone dismal night,
Grant that calmly, on Thee resting,
We may wait for morning light:

3 When the Sun shall shine forth, bringing
Peace with healing on His wings;
And, all sadness changed to singing,
Thirst be slaked in living springs.

4 Lord! we pray, and know Thou hearest,
For Thy promises are true:
Grant the heart-wish that is dearest;
He who knows can also do!

5 What though night-black storms of sorrow,
Chafing, blind our eyes with tears?
Joy, we know, comes with the morrow,
For our Heavenly Father hears;

6 Hears, and shall not, more or longer,
Try us, than our strength can bear—
Lift the cross, or make us stronger:—
Trust all to His loving care!

7 Change, O Lord!—we pray in meekness—
Israel's wail to Miriam's song:
Feeling our own utter weakness,
Let us in Thy strength be strong!

Andrew J. Symington, 1869.

893

Ps. xxxix. 7. "*And now, Lord, what wait I for? My hope is in Thee.*"
Tune PHILEMON. 87, 87. Or FRANKFORT. Or GODESBERG.

1 GRACIOUS Saviour, thus before Thee
With our varied want and care,
For a blessing we implore Thee;
Listen to our evening prayer!

2 By Thy favour safely living,
With a grateful heart we raise
Songs of jubilant thanksgiving;
Listen to our evening praise.

3 Through the day, Lord, Thou hast given
Strength sufficient for our need;
Cheered us with sweet hopes of heaven,
Helped and comforted indeed.

4 Lord, we thank Thee, and adore Thee,
For the solace of Thy love;
And rejoicing thus before Thee,
Wait Thy blessing from above!

Henry Bateman, 1862.

LAODICEA. (HYMN CHANT.) [H. P. No. VIII.]

894

Zech. xiv. 7. "*At evening time it shall be light.*"
Tune, Hymn Chant LAODICEA. 10 10, 10 10, 10 10.

1 THE day is gently sinking to a close,
Fainter and yet more faint the sunlight grows;
O Brightness of Thy Father's glory, Thou
Eternal Light of Light, be with us now:
Where Thou art present, darkness cannot be,
Midnight is glorious noon, O Lord, with Thee.

2 Our changeful lives are ebbing to an end,
Onward to darkness and to death we tend;
O Conqueror of the grave, be Thou our Guide,
Be Thou our Light in death's dark eventide;
Then in our mortal hour will be no gloom,
No sting in death, no terror in the tomb.

3 Thou who in darkness walking didst appear
Upon the waves, and Thy disciples cheer,
Come, Lord, in lonesome days, when storms assail,
And earthly hopes and human succours fail,
When all is dark, may we behold Thee nigh,
And hear Thy voice, "Fear not, for it is I."

4 The weary world is mouldering to decay,
Its glories wane, its pageants fade away:
In that last sunset, when the stars shall fall,
May we arise, awakened by Thy call,
With Thee, O Lord, for ever to abide
In that blest day which has no eventide!

Bishop Christopher Wordsworth, 1865.

DISMISSAL. [H. P. 305.]

895

Ps. cxxvii. 2. "*So He giveth His beloved sleep.*"
Tune DISMISSAL. 87, 87, 77. Or SUCCOTH.

1 THROUGH the day Thy love has spared us,
Now we lay us down to rest,
Through the silent watches guard us,
Let no foe our peace molest;
Jesus, Thou our guardian be,
Sweet it is to trust in Thee.

2 Pilgrims here on earth, and strangers,
Dwelling in the midst of foes,
Us and ours preserve from dangers,
In Thine arms may we repose!
And when life's sad day is past,
Rest with Thee in heaven at last.

Thomas Kelly, 1806.

SHENIR II. (Mount.) [H. P. 151.]

896 Matt. xiv. 23. "*He went up into a mountain apart to pray.*" Tune SHENIR II. 77, 77.

1 SOFTLY now the light of day
Fades upon my sight away;
Free from care, from labour free,
Lord, I would commune with Thee!

2 Thou whose all-pervading eye
Nought escapes, without, within,
Pardon each infirmity,
Open fault and secret sin.

3 Soon for me the light of day
Shall for ever pass away:
Then, from sin and sorrow free,
Take me, Lord, to dwell with Thee!

4 Thou who, sinless, yet hast known
All of man's infirmity;
Then, from Thine eternal throne,
Jesus, look with pitying eye!

Bp. G. W. Doane, D.D., 1826.

LAODICEA. (HYMN CHANT.) [H. P. No. VIII.]

897 Deut. xxxi. 6. "*He will not fail thee, nor forsake thee.*"
Tune, Hymn Chant LAODICEA. 88, 88, 88. Or MAON.

1 AS every day Thy mercy spares
Will bring its trials and its cares:
O Saviour, till my life shall end,
Be Thou my Counsellor and Friend;
Teach me Thy precepts, all Divine,
And be Thy great example mine.

2 When each day's scenes and labours close,
And wearied nature seeks repose,
With pardoning mercy richly blest,
Guard me, my Saviour, while I rest;
And as each morning sun shall rise,
Still lead me onward to the skies.

3 And at my life's last setting sun,
My conflicts o'er, my labours done,
Jesus, Thine heavenly radiance shed,
To cheer and bless my dying bed;
And from death's gloom my spirit raise,
To see Thy face and sing Thy praise!

William Shrubsole, jun., 1813.

AMPLIAS. [H. P. 103.]

898 Ps. cxli. 2. "*The lifting up of my hands as the evening sacrifice.*"
Tune AMPLIAS. 64, 66.

1 THE sun is sinking fast,
The daylight dies;
Let love awake, and pay
Her evening sacrifice.

2 As Christ upon the cross
His head inclined,
And to His Father's hands
His parting soul resigned,—

3 So now herself my soul
Would wholly give
Into His sacred charge,
In whom all spirits live.

4 So now beneath His eye
Would calmly rest,
Without a wish or thought
Abiding in the breast;

5 Save that His will be done,
Whate'er betide;
Dead to herself, and dead
In Him to all beside.

6 Thus would I live; yet now
Not I, but He,
In all His power and love
Henceforth alive in me.

7 One sacred Trinity,
One Lord Divine;
May I be ever His,
And He for ever mine!

Latin Hymn, Eighteenth Century; tr. 1858.

TALLIS'S CANON. [H. P. 13.]

899 Ps. xci. 4. "*Under His wings shalt thou trust.*" Tune TALLIS'S CANON. L. M.

1 ALL praise to Thee, my God, this night,
For all the blessings of the light!
Keep me, oh, keep me, King of kings,
Beneath Thy own almighty wings.

2 Forgive me, Lord, for Thy dear Son,
The ill that I this day have done
That with the world, myself, and Thee,
I, ere I sleep, at peace may be.

3 Teach me to live, that I may dread
The grave as little as my bed
Teach me to die, that so I may
Rise glorious at the awful day.

4 Oh! may my soul on Thee repose,
And may sweet sleep my eyelids close;
Sleep, that may me more vigorous make,
To serve my God when I awake.

5 When in the night I sleepless lie,
My soul with heavenly thoughts supply
Let no ill dreams disturb my rest,
No powers of darkness me molest.

Praise God from whom all blessings flow, etc.

Bishop Ken, 1697; *revised*, 1709.

SHENIR I. (Mount.) [H. P. 136.]

900

Ps. lxv. 8. "*Thou makest the outgoings of the morning and evening to rejoice.*" Tune Shenir I. 777, 5.

1 THREE in One, and One in Three,
Ruler of the earth and sea,
Hear us, while we lift to Thee
Holy chant and psalm.

2 Light of lights! with morning shine;
Lift on us Thy light Divine;
And let charity benign
Breathe on us her balm.

3 Light of lights! when falls the even,
Let it close on sins forgiven;
Fold us in the peace of heaven,
Shed a holy calm.

4 Three in One, and One in Three;
Dimly here we worship Thee;
With the saints hereafter we
Hope to bear the palm!

Gilbert Rorison, LL.D., 1850. (*a.*)

PENIEL. [H. P. 23.]

901

Ps. iv. 8. "*I will both lay me down in peace and sleep.*" Tune Peniel. L. M. Or Hursley.

1 SUN of my soul, Thou Saviour dear,
It is not night if Thou be near:
Oh, may no earth-born cloud arise
To hide Thee from Thy servant's eyes.

2 When the soft dews of kindly sleep
My wearied eyelids gently steep,
Be my last thought, how sweet to rest
For ever on my Saviour's breast.

3 Abide with me from morn till eve,
For without Thee I cannot live;
Abide with me when night is nigh,
For without Thee I dare not die.

4 If some poor wandering child of Thine
Have spurned to-day the voice Divine,
Now, Lord, the gracious work begin:
Let him no more lie down in sin.

5 Watch by the sick; enrich the poor
With blessings from Thy boundless store;
Be every mourner's sleep to-night,
Like infant's slumbers, pure and light.

6 Come near and bless us when we wake,
Ere through the world our way we take;
Till in the ocean of Thy love
We lose ourselves in heaven above!

John Keble, 1827.

902

Ps. lxxiv. 16. "*The night also is Thine.*"
Tune Godesberg. 87, 87.

1 SAVIOUR, breathe an evening blessing,
Ere repose our spirits seal;
Sin and want we come confessing;
Thou canst save, and Thou canst heal.

2 Though destruction walk around us,
Though the arrow past us fly,
Angel-guards from Thee surround us,
We are safe if Thou art nigh.

3 Though the night be dark and dreary,
Darkness cannot hide from Thee;
Thou art He, who, never weary,
Watchest where Thy people be.

4 Should swift death this night o'ertake us,
And our couch become our tomb,
May the morn in heaven awake us,
Clad in light and deathless bloom!

James Edmeston, 1820.

GODESBERG. [H. P. 185.]

903 2 Cor. iv. 18. "*The things which are not seen are eternal.*" Tune BETHAVEN. C. M. D.

1 THE roseate hues of early dawn,
The brightness of the day,
The crimson of the sunset sky,
How fast they fade away.
Oh for the pearly gates of heaven!
Oh for the golden floor!
Oh for the Sun of Righteousness,
That setteth never more!

2 The highest hopes we cherish here,
How fast they tire and faint;
How many a spot defiles the robe
That wraps an earthly saint.
Oh for a heart that never sins!
Oh for a soul washed white!
Oh for a voice to praise our King,
Nor weary day or night!

3 Here faith is ours, and heavenly hope,
And grace to lead us higher;
But there are perfectness and peace
Beyond our best desire:
Oh by Thy love and anguish, Lord,
Oh by Thy life laid down;
Oh that we fall not from Thy grace,
Nor cast away our crown!

Cecil Frances Alexander, 1853.

See Hymns 525, 566.

Saturday Evening.

904 Exod. xix. 10, 11. "*Sanctify them to-day and to-morrow, . . . and be ready.*"
Tune SIHOR. 77, 77, 77.

1 SAFELY through another week
God has brought us on our way;
Let us now a blessing seek
On the' approaching Sabbath-day:
Day of all the week the best,
Emblem of eternal rest.

2 Mercies multiplied each hour,
Through the week, our praise demand:
Guarded by Almighty power,
Fed and guided by His hand:
From our worldly care set free,
May we rest this night with Thee.

3 When the morn shall bid us rise,
May we feel Thy presence near:
May Thy glory meet our eyes
When we in Thy house appear;
Thus may all our Sabbaths prove
Till we join the church above!

John Newton, 1774.

905 Ps. iv. 4. "*Commune with your own heart.*" Tune KEDRON. 886. D.

1 ANOTHER portion of the span,
Assigned to transitory man,
Has now for ever flown;
And ere I taste the sweet repose
My heavenly Guardian's care bestows,
I kneel before His throne.

2 God of my life! to Thee I pray;
The passing pilgrim of a day,
Soon, soon to sleep in death—
Let me not spend unthinkingly
These moments that so quickly fly,
Shortened by every breath.

3 Ere yet that hallowed morn appear,
Given to recruit the soul and cheer,
Pour down Thy light Divine;
That while my progress I retrace,
Since last I hailed the day of grace,
Its beams within may shine.

4 Oh, has that rapid ceaseless tide,
Of which the waves so noiseless glide,
Borne me towards heaven, my home:
As surely as each day, each hour,
Has borne me with resistless power
On to the silent tomb?

5 Have my affections soared above?
And has my Saviour's wondrous love
Constrained me, day by day,
For Him to act, to think, to speak,
His glory as my end to seek,
His Spirit to obey?

6 Have I His constant influence felt?
And has His holy word so "dwelt
Richly" my heart within,
That outward faults have been subdued,
And inward hidden thoughts renewed,
Cleansed from the taint of sin?

7 Lord! if my only answer now
Must be these silent tears that flow,
For days not given to Thee;
Still let a holier life begin,
A life not thus defaced by sin,
If I to-morrow see.

8 Then let Thy word its power exert,
To quicken, cleanse, transform my heart,
Within Thy house of prayer;
Or, if that boon be still denied,
With me in solitude abide,
And make my wants Thy care.

KEDRON (Brook). [H. P. 213.]

9 Now let me peacefully lie down,
Cleansed, pardoned, numbered with Thine own,
While strengthening sleep is given;
Then let the' auspicious Sabbath bring
Peace, gladness, healing on its wing,
And rest, like that of heaven!

Charlotte Elliott, 1839.

ARISTARCHUS. [H. P. 224.]

(3) MIDNIGHT.

906

Ps. cxxi. 3. "*He that keepeth thee will not slumber.*"

Tune ARISTARCHUS. 88, 88.

1 INSPIRER and Hearer of prayer,
Thou Shepherd and Guardian of Thine;
My all to Thy covenant care
I, sleeping and waking, resign.

2 If Thou art my Shield and my Sun,
The night is no darkness to me;
And, fast as my moments roll on,
They bring me but nearer to Thee.

3 Thy ministering spirits descend
To watch while Thy saints are asleep;
By day and by night they attend
The heirs of salvation to keep.

4 Thy worship no interval knows,
Their fervour is still on the wing;
And, while they protect my repose,
They chant to the praise of my King.

5 I too, at the season ordained,
Their chorus for ever shall join;
And love, and adore, without end,
Their faithful Creator and mine!

Augustus M. Toplady, 1776.

PHILEMON. [H. P. 223.]

907

Ps. cxix. 151. "*Thou art near, O Lord.*"

Tune PHILEMON. 88, 88.

1 LORD! of life the Guard and Giver,
Blessèd be Thy name for ever!
Thou who slumberest not nor sleepest,
Safe are those Thou kindly keepest.

2 Through night's curtains, round us closing,
Seen of Thee is our reposing;
Let Thine angels, without number,
Watch around our beds of slumber.

3 Grant to those, in pain that languish,
Sleep to lull the sense of anguish;
Give to those, in sorrow waking,
Sleep to soothe the heart's sore aching.

4 Thou that, ever wakeful, livest,
Sleep to Thy belovèd givest,
Night by night, oh send, to ease us,
Sleep—until we sleep in Jesus!

James Hogg, 1807. *(a.)*

THYATIRA. (HYMN CHANT.) [H. P. No. V.]

908 Job xxxv. 10. "*Who giveth songs in the night.*" Tune, Hymn Chant THYATIRA. 11 10, 11 10, 10 10, 10 12.

1 MY God, my God, I know that Thou dost hear me,
Though midnight darkness be around me spread;
I know Thy presence is for ever near me,
Around my dwelling, and about my bed;
My rock, my shield, the tower of my defence;
The songs of angels echo round Thy throne,
And yet Thou lov'st the trembling confidence
Of the poor sinful heart that trusts in Thee alone.

2 Creator: Father, Son, and Holy Spirit!
My soul would praise Thee in the silent night,
I dwell beneath Thy love, Thy power, Thy merit,
Thou my salvation, my eternal light:
And when my feet shall tread the dreary vale
Of death's dark shadow; in that dreadful hour,
When all is dark, and flesh and blood must fail,
Oh! then, my God, as now, uphold me with Thy power.

3 Be with me then, now make my heart an altar
Fragrant with incense of perpetual praise:
Let not my weak soul shrink, nor spirit falter,
Nor my frail heart mistrust those darksome ways:
But Thou, O Sun of Righteousness, arise,
Bright as a morning from a gloomy night;
Till my rapt soul spring upward to the skies,
And know and own Thee there, her strength, her joy, her light!

From Rev. E. Garbett, circa 1860.

II.—The Year.

ST. GREGORY. [H. P. 259.]

(1) OPENING OF THE YEAR.

909 1 Cor. ix. 24. "*So run, that ye may obtain.*" Tune ST. GREGORY. L. M. Or OLD TEN COMMANDMENTS.

1 ANOTHER year has now begun
With silent pace its course to run;
Our hearts and voices let us raise
To God in prayer and songs of praise.

2 Father, Thy bounteous love we bless,
For gifts and mercies numberless;
For life and health, for grace and peace,
For hope of joys that never cease.

3 O Son of God, in faith and fear
Teach us to walk as strangers here,
With hearts in heaven, that we may come
To where Thou art, our Father's home.

4 Grant us, O Comforter, Thy grace,
And speed us on our earthly race,
In body, spirit, and in soul,
Right onward to the heavenly goal.

5 Thou, Lord, who makest all things new,
Oh, give us hearts both pure and true;
That we, as jewels, ever Thine,
In New Jerusalem may shine.

6 Blest Three in One, to Thee we pray,
Defend and guide us on our way;
That we at last with joy may see
The new year of eternity!

Bishop Christopher Wordsworth, 1862.

PATMOS. [H. P. 147.]

910 Ps. xxxi. 3. "*For Thy name's sake, lead me and guide me.*" Tune PATMOS. 7 7, 7 7. Or VIENNA.

1 BLESS, O Lord, the opening year
To each soul assembled here;
Clothe Thy word with power Divine,
Make us willing to be Thine.

2 Shepherd of Thy blood-bought sheep,
Teach the stony heart to weep;
Let the blind have eyes to see,
See themselves, and look to Thee.

3 Where Thou hast Thy work begun,
Give new strength the race to run;
Scatter darkness, doubts, and fears,
Wipe away the mourner's tears.

4 Bless us all, both old and young;
Call forth praise from every tongue;
Let this whole assembly prove
All Thy power and all Thy love!

John Newton, 1797.

HERMAS. [H. P. 105.]

911 Isa. xli. 10. "*Fear thou not, for I am with thee.*"

Tune Hermas. 6 5, 6 5. D. and Chorus.

1 STANDING at the portal Of the opening year,
Words of comfort meet us, Hushing every fear;
Spoken through the silence By our Father's voice,
Tender, strong, and faithful, Making us rejoice.

Chorus.—Onward then, and fear not, Children of the day!
For His word shall never, Never pass away.

2 "I the Lord am with thee, Be thou not afraid!
I will help and strengthen, Be thou not dismayed!
Yea, I will uphold thee With My own right hand!
Thou art called and chosen In My sight to stand."

Chorus.—Onward then, etc.

3 For the year before us, Oh what rich supplies!
For the poor and needy Living streams shall rise;
For the sad and sinful Shall His grace abound;
For the faint and feeble Perfect strength be found!

Chorus.—Onward then, etc.

4 He will never fail us, He will not forsake,
His eternal covenant He will never break,
Resting on His promise What have we to fear?
God is All-Sufficient For the coming year!

Chorus.—Onward then, etc.

Frances Ridley Havergal, 1873.

See Hymns 920, 921, 932, 1076—1079.

FRANCONIA. [H. P. 87.]

912 Ps. xxxi. 15. "*My times are in Thy hand.*"

Tune Franconia. S. M.

1 MY times are in Thy hand:
My God, I wish them there;
My life, my friends, my soul I leave
Entirely to Thy care.

2 My times are in Thy hand,
Whatever they may be;
Pleasing or painful, dark or bright,
As best may seem to Thee.

3 My times are in Thy hand,
Why should I doubt or fear?
A Father's hand will never cause
His child a needless tear.

4 My times are in Thy hand,
Jesus, the Crucified;
The Hand my cruel sins had pierced
Is now my guard and guide.

5 My times are in Thy hand;
I'll always trust in Thee;
And after death at Thy right hand
I shall for ever be!

William Freeman Lloyd, 1835.

ZOAN I. (Field of.) [H. P. 127.]

913

Ps. xxiii. 6. "*Surely goodness and mercy shall follow me all the days of my life.*"

Tune ZOAN I. 7 6, 7 6. D.

1 TO Thee, O gracious Father,
My New Year's hymn I raise;
A song of exultation,
A psalm of soul-felt praise!
For Thou hast been my Keeper,
My every want supplied;
The Lord Jehovah-Jireh,
He ever doth provide.

2 To Thee, O blessèd Saviour,
Who died that I might live,
A heart's best adoration
Of gratitude I give:
In Thy sweet grace confiding,
I rest this bright new year;
Beneath Thy wings abiding,
Oh, what have I to fear?

3 To Thee, O Holy Spirit,
O gentle heavenly Dove,
I raise my Ebenezer,
And sing of all Thy love:
Thy strength in perfect weakness,
Thy strivings with my soul;
Till, in my Lord's completeness,
Thy help hath made me whole.

4 I bring my countless treasures,
Thy new year's gifts to me;
To hide in Thy pavilion,
O Triune Deity!
And o'er Thy feet, dear Master,
While tears of gladness fall,
I break my alabaster,
For Thou hast purchased all.

L. H. R., 1866.

See Hymns 726, 920, 921, 1076—1078.

OLD 124th. [H. P. 237.]

(2) CLOSE OF THE YEAR.

914

Ps. xliii. 3. "*O send out Thy light and Thy truth.*"

Tune OLD 124TH. 10 10 10, 10 10.

1 OUR year of grace is wearing to its close,
Its autumn storms are louring from the sky;
Shine on us with Thy light, O God Most High:
Abide with us where'er our pathway goes,
Our Guide in toil, our Guardian in repose.

2 All through the months hath beamed Thy cheering light,
From Bethlehem's day-star waxing ever on:
Through every cloud Thy blessèd Sun hath shone.
Earth may be dark to them that walk by sight,
But for Thy church the day is always bright.

3 Light us in life, that we may see Thy will,
The track Thine hand hath ordered for our way;
Light us, when shadows gather o'er our day:
Shine on us in that passage lone and chill,
And then our darkness with Thy glory fill.

4 Praise be to God from earth's remotest coast,
From lands and seas, and each created race:
Praise from the worlds His hand hath launched in space:
Praise from the church, and from the heavenly host:
Praise to the Father, Son, and Holy Ghost.

Dean Alford, D.D., 1867.

VIENNA. [H. P. 149.]

915 2 Cor. i. 10. "*Who delivered us, . . . and doth deliver; in whom we trust that He will yet deliver.*"

Tune VIENNA. 7 7, 7 7.

1 FOR Thy mercy and Thy grace,
Faithful through another year,
Hear our song of thankfulness,
Father, and Redeemer, hear.

2 In our weakness and distress,
Rock of strength, be Thou our stay:
In the pathless wilderness
Be our true and living Way.

3 Who of us death's awful road
In the coming year shall tread;
With Thy rod and staff, O God,
Comfort Thou his dying head.

4 Keep us faithful, keep us pure,
Keep us evermore Thine own;
Help, oh, help us to endure:
Fit us for the promised crown.

5 So within Thy palace gate
We shall praise on golden strings,
Thee, the only Potentate,
Lord of lords, and King of kings.

Henry Downton, 1851.

PLEYEL. [H. P. 285.]

916 Ps. xc. 9. "*We spend our years as a tale that is told.*" Tune PLEYEL. 7 7, 7 7. Or SILOAM.

1 WHILE with ceaseless course the sun
Hasted through the passing year,
Many souls their race have run,
Never more to meet us here:

2 Fixed in an eternal state,
They have done with all below:
We a little longer wait,
But how little none can know.

3 Swiftly thus our fleeting days
Bear us down life's rapid stream;
Upwards, Lord, our spirits raise,
All below is but a dream.

4 Bless Thy word to young and old:
Fill us with a Saviour's love;
And when life's short tale is told,
May we dwell with Thee above!

John Newton, 1779.

SHENIR II. (Mount.) [H. P. 151.]

917 Ps. xc. 12. "*So teach us to number our days.*" Tune SHENIR II. 7 7, 7 7. Or LUXEMBURG.

1 TIME by moments steals away,
First the hour, and then the day;
Thus another year is flown,
Now it is no more our own.

2 But each year, let none forget,
Finds and leaves us deep in debt:
Favours from the Lord received,
Sins that have the Spirit grieved.

3 We have nothing, Lord, to pay:
Take, oh, take our guilt away:
Self condemned, on Thee we call,
Freely, Lord, forgive us all.

4 If we see another year,
May we spend it in Thy fear;
All its days devote to Thee,
Living for eternity.

John Newton, 1779. (a.)

See Hymns 104, 456, 571, 573, 578, 1020, 1021.

(3) YEAR OF JUBILEE.

918 Lev. xxv. 9. "*Cause the trumpet of the Jubilee to sound.*"

Tune Bevan. 6 6 6 6, 8 8.

1 BLOW ye the trumpet, blow,
The gladly solemn sound;
Let all the nations know,
To earth's remotest bound,
The year of Jubilee is come;
Return, ye ransomed sinners, home.

2 Jesus, our great High Priest,
Hath full atonement made;
Ye weary spirits, rest;
Ye mournful souls, be glad;
The year of Jubilee is come;
Return, ye ransomed sinners, home.

3 Extol the Lamb of God,
The all-atoning Lamb;
Redemption by His blood
Throughout the world proclaim;
The year of Jubilee is come;
Return, ye ransomed sinners, home.

4 Ye who have sold for nought
Your heritage above,
Receive it back unbought,
The gift of Jesus' love:
The year of Jubilee is come;
Return, ye ransomed sinners, home.

Charles Wesley, 1750.

919 Ps. lxxii. 17. "*And men shall be blessed in Him; all nations shall call Him blessed.*"

Tune Zaanaim. 8 7, 8 7, 7 7. Or Succoth.

1 SHOUT, O earth! from silence waking,
Tune with joy thy varied tongue;
Shout! as when from chaos breaking
Sweetly flowed thy natal song:
Shout! for thy Creator's love
Sends redemption from above.

2 Downward from His star-paved dwelling
Comes the' incarnate Son of God;
Countless voices, thrilling, swelling,
Tell the triumphs of His blood;
Shout! He comes thy tribes to bless
With His spotless righteousness.

3 See His glowing hand uplifted!
Clustering bounties drop around;
Rebels e'en are richly gifted,
Pardon, peace, and joy abound!
Shout, O earth! and let thy song
Ring the vaulted heavens along.

4 Call Him blessèd! on thy mountains,
In thy wilds and citied plains;
Call Him blessèd! where thy fountains
Speak in softly murmuring strains.
Let thy captives, let thy kings
Join thy lyre of thousand strings.

5 Blessèd Lord, and Lord of blessing!
Pour Thy quickening gifts abroad;
Raptured tongues, Thy love confessing,
Shall extol the living God.
Blessèd, Blessèd, Blessèd Lord!
Heaven shall chant no other word.

William Henry Havergal, 1841.

III.—Seasons of Life.

(1) BIRTHDAYS.

920 Rom. xiii. 12. "*The night is far spent, the day is at hand.*" Tune Bethaven. C. M. D.

1 REJOICE, my fellow-pilgrim! for another stage is o'er
Of the weary homeward journey, to be travelled through no more;
No more *these* clouds and shadow-veils shall darken all our sky:
No more these snares and stumbling-blocks across our path shall lie.

2 Rejoice, my fellow-soldier! for another long campaign
Is ended, and its dangers have not all been met in vain:
Some enemies are driven back, some ramparts overthrown;
Some earnests given that victory at length shall be our own!

BETHAVEN (Wilderness of). [H. P. 76.]

3 Rejoice, my fellow-servant! for another year is past;
The heat and burden of the day will not for ever last;
And yet the work is pleasant now, and sweet the Master's smile;
And well may we be diligent through all our "little while."

4 Rejoice, my Christian brother! for the race is nearer run,
And home is drawing nearer still with each revolving sun;
And if some ties are breaking here, of earthly hope and love,
More sweet the fair attractions of the better land above.

5 The light that shone through all the past will still our steps attend,
The Guide who led us hitherto will lead us to the end;
The distant view is brightening fast, with fewer clouds between,
The golden streets are gleaming now, the pearly gates are seen.

6 Oh for the joyous greetings *there*, to meet and part no more!
For ever with the Lord, and all His loved ones gone before!
New mercies from our Father's hand with each new year may come;
But that will be the best of all, a blissful welcome *home.*

Jane Borthwick, 1859.

SALZBURG. [H. P. 203.]

921

Exod. iii. 12. "*Certainly I will be with thee.*" Tune SALZBURG. 15 15, 15 15.

1 "CERTAINLY I will be with thee!" Father, I have found it true:
To Thy faithfulness and mercy I would set my seal anew,
All the year Thy grace hath kept me, Thou my help indeed hast been,
Marvellous the loving-kindness every day and hour hath seen.

2 "Certainly I will be with thee!" Let me feel it, Saviour dear,
Let me know that Thou art with me, very precious, very near.
On this day of solemn pausing, with Thyself all longing still,
Let Thy pardon, let Thy presence, let Thy peace my spirit fill.

3 "Certainly I will be with thee!" Blessèd Spirit, come to me,
Rest upon me, dwell within me, let my heart Thy temple be;
Through the trackless year before me, Holy One, with me abide!
Teach me, comfort me, and calm me, be my ever-present Guide.

4 "Certainly I will be with thee!" Starry promise in the night!
All uncertainties, like shadows, flee away before its light.
"Certainly I will be with thee!" He hath spoken: I have heard!
True of old, and true this moment, I will trust Jehovah's word.

Frances Ridley Havergal, 1871.

922 Num. xxviii. 11. *"In the beginnings of your months ye shall offer a burnt offering."*

Tune Kedron. 886. D.

1 As the new moons of old were given
A sacred offering to Heaven,
Enjoined by laws Divine,
So, Lord, as each new month is lent,
Its primal day would I present,
Time's first-fruits, at Thy shrine.

2 And chiefly, while I dwell on earth,
Should this, the month which gave me birth,
Be given to Thee, my God;
Oh deign to bless each hour's employ,
And fill with peace, and hope, and joy,
This heart, Thy mean abode.

3 Let me pursue my heavenly way
With growing strength, from day to day,
Advancing more and more;
And on the day my life commenced
May showers of blessing be dispensed,
Where drops were given before!

4 Let me be Thine, and Thine alone:
Make every faculty Thine own,
My Saviour and my King!
Each bounteous gift by Thee bestowed,
Laid on Thine altar, O my God,
To Thee shall glory bring.

Charlotte Elliott, 1863.

See Hymns 104, 105, 571, 585, 726.

(2) CHILDHOOD AND YOUTH.

923 Matt. xviii. 2. *"Jesus called a little child unto Him."*

Tune Carol III. 886. D. Or Kedron.

1 And is it true what I am told,
That there are lambs within the fold
Of God's belovèd Son?
That Jesus Christ, with tender care,
Will in His arms most gently bear
The helpless little one?

2 And I, a little straying lamb,
May come to Jesus as I am,
Though goodness I have none:
May now be folded on His breast,
As birds within the parent nest,
And be His little one.

3 And He can do all this for me,
Because, in sorrow, on the tree
He once for sinners hung;
And, having washed their sin away,
He now rejoices, day by day,
To cleanse the little one.

4 Others there are who love me too;
But who, with all their love, can do,
What Jesus Christ has done?
Then, if He teaches me to pray,
I'll surely go to Him, and say,
Lord, keep Thy little one.

5 Thus, by this gracious Shepherd fed,
And by His mercy gently led
Where living waters run,
My greatest pleasure will be this,
That I'm a little lamb of His,
Who loves the little one.

Amelia Matilda Hull, 1860.

924 Ps. li. 7. *"Whiter than snow."*

Tune Evan I., with refrain from Abilene. C. M.

1 Around the throne of God in heaven
Thousands of children stand;
Children whose sins are all forgiven,
A holy, happy band,
Singing, Glory, glory, glory.

2 In flowing robes of spotless white
See every one arrayed:
Dwelling in everlasting light,
And joys that never fade,
Singing, Glory, glory, glory.

3 What brought them to that world above,
That heaven so bright and fair,
Where all is peace, and joy, and love:
How came those children there,
Singing, Glory, glory, glory?

4 Because the Saviour shed His blood
To wash away their sin,
Bathed in that precious, purple flood,
Behold them white and clean,
Singing, Glory, glory, glory.

5 On earth they sought the Saviour's grace,
On earth they loved His name;
So now they see His blessèd face,
And stand before the Lamb:
Singing, Glory, glory, glory.

6 And is that fountain flowing yet?
Blest Saviour, lead us there:
That we those happy ones may meet,
And in their praises share,
Singing, Glory, glory, glory.

Anne Houlditch, 1847.

925

Rev. xxi. 18. "*The city was pure gold, like unto clear glass.*"

Tune Patmos. 77, 77.

1 BEAUTIFUL Zion, built above!
Beautiful city that I love!
Beautiful gates of pearly white!
Beautiful temple, God its light!

2 Beautiful trees, for ever there!
Beautiful fruits they always bear!
Beautiful rivers gliding by!
Beautiful fountains, never dry!

3 Beautiful light, without the sun!
Beautiful day revolving on!
Beautiful worlds on worlds untold!
Beautiful streets of shining gold!

4 Beautiful heaven where all is light!
Beautiful angels clothed in white!
Beautiful songs that never tire!
Beautiful harps through all the choir!

5 Beautiful crowns on every brow!
Beautiful palms the conquerors show!
Beautiful robes the ransomed wear!
Beautiful all who enter there!

George Gill, 1859.

926

Ps. xciv. 9. "*He that planted the ear, shall He not hear?*"

Tune Eden. C. M. Or Evan I.

1 GOD is in heaven. Can He hear
A little prayer like mine?
Yes, that He can; I need not fear;
He'll listen unto mine.

2 God is in heaven. Can He see
When I am doing wrong?
Yes, that He can; He looks at me
All day and all night long.

3 God is in heaven. Would He know
If I should tell a lie?
Yes; though I said it very low,
He'd hear it in the sky.

4 God is in heaven. Does He care,
Or is He good to me?
Yes; all I have to eat or wear,
'Tis God that gives it me.

5 God is in heaven. May I go
To thank Him for His care?
Not yet; but love Him here below,
And He will see it there.

6 God is in heaven. May I pray
To go there when I die?
Yes; love Him, seek Him, and one day
He'll call me to the sky.

Ann Taylor, 1827. (a.)

A A

STUTTGARD. [H. P. 182.]

927 Matt. vi. 10. "*Thy kingdom come.*" Tune STUTTGARD. 87, 87.

1 GOD of heaven, hear our singing!
Only little ones are we,
Yet a great petition bringing,
Father, now we come to Thee.

2 Let Thy kingdom come, we pray Thee,
Let the world in Thee find rest;
Let all know Thee and obey Thee,
Loving, praising, blessing, blessed!

3 Let the sweet and joyful story
Of the Saviour's wondrous love
Wake on earth a song of glory,
Like the angels' song above.

4 Father, send the glorious hour;
Every heart be Thine alone;
For the kingdom and the power
And the glory are Thine own.

Frances Ridley Havergal, 1869.

"OH THAT WILL BE JOYFUL." [H. P. 350.]

928 Rev. vii. 17. "*God shall wipe away all tears.*" Tune, "OH THAT WILL BE JOYFUL." 776, 67.

1 HERE we suffer grief and pain,
Here we meet to part again;
In heaven we part no more.
Oh! that will be joyful
When we meet to part no more!

2 All who love the Lord below
When they die to heaven will go,
And sing with saints above.
Oh! that, etc.

3 Little children will be there,
Who have sought the Lord by prayer,
From every Sunday school.
Oh! that, etc.

4 Teachers too shall meet above,
Pastors, parents, whom we love,
Shall meet to part no more.
Oh! that, etc.

5 Oh, how happy we shall be,
For our Saviour we shall see,
Exalted on His throne.
Oh! that, etc.

6 There we all shall sing with joy,
And eternity employ,
In praising Christ the Lord.
Oh! that, etc.

Thomas Bilby, 1832.

929 Matt. xxi. 15. "*The children crying . . . Hosanna.*" Tune ST. THEODULPH. 76, 76. D.

1 HOSANNA! loud hosanna!
The little children sang:
Through pillared court and temple
The lovely anthem rang:
To Jesus, who had blessed them,
Close folded to His breast,
The children sang their praises,
The simplest and the best.
Hosanna, loud Hosanna!
Hosanna, Lord, we sing.

2 From Olivet they followed,
'Mid that exultant crowd,
The victor palm-branch waving,
And shouting clear and loud:
Bright angels joined the chorus,
Beyond the cloudless sky—
"Hosanna in the highest:
Glory to God on high!"
Hosanna, loud Hosanna!
Hosanna, Lord, we sing.

ST. THEODULPH. [H. P. 277.]

3 Fair leaves of silvery olive
They strewed upon the ground,
Whilst Salem's circling mountains
Echoed the joyful sound:
The Lord of men and angels
Rode on in lowly state,
Nor scorned that little children
Should on His bidding wait.
Hosanna, loud Hosanna!
Hosanna, Lord, we sing.

4 "Hosanna in the highest!"
That ancient song *we* sing;
For Christ is our Redeemer,
The Lord of heaven our King.
Oh! may we ever praise Him,
With heart, and life, and voice,
And in His blissful presence
Eternally rejoice!
Hosanna, loud Hosanna!
Hosanna, Lord, we sing.

Jennette Threlfall, 1868.

GOLDBACH. [H. P. 130.]

930 John xiii. 15. "*I have given you an example.*" Tune GOLDBACH. 76, 76. D. Or ZOAN I.

1 I LOVE to hear the story,
Which angel voices tell,
How once the King of glory
Came down on earth to dwell.
I am both weak and sinful,
But this I surely know,
The Lord came down to save me,
Because He loved me so.

2 I 'm glad my blessèd Saviour
Was once a child like me,
To show how pure and holy
His little ones might be.
And if I try to follow
His footsteps here below,
He never will forget me,
Because He loves me so.

3 To sing His love and mercy,
My sweetest songs I'll raise,
And though I cannot see Him
I know He hears my praise:
For He has kindly promised,
That even I may go
To sing among His angels,
Because He loves me so.

E. H. Miller.

ZOAN II. (Field of.) [H. P. 166.]

931 Ps. lxxxiv. 11. "*The Lord will give grace and glory.*" Tune ZOAN II. 87, 87. D.

1 I'M glad I ever saw the day,
Sing glory, glory, glory,
When first I learned to sing and pray
Of glory, glory, glory.
'Tis glory's foretaste makes me sing
Of glory, glory, glory,
And praise my Saviour and my King,
Like those who dwell in glory.

2 I hope to praise Him when I die,
In glory, glory, glory,
And shout salvation as I fly
To glory, glory, glory.
I'll sing while mounting through the air
To glory, glory, glory,
Then meet my Father's children there
In glory, glory, glory.

3 A few more rising suns at most,
(Sing glory, glory, glory,)
And we shall join the ransomed host
In glory, glory, glory.
Upon Mount Zion we shall meet
In glory, glory, glory;
Then cast our crowns beneath His feet
In glory, glory, glory.

4 Come, sinners, come, and seek the grace
That leads to glory, glory;
There's room enough in that blest place
Where Jesus dwells in glory.
Believe, repent, seek holiness,
And glory, glory, glory;
For God doth freely give His grace,
And glory, glory, glory.

Anon., 1821.

HERMAS. [H. P. 105.]

New Year's, or Birthday, Hymn.

932 Heb. xii. 2. "*Looking unto Jesus.*" Tune HERMAS. 65, 65. D. and Chorus.

1 JESUS, blessèd Saviour, Help us now to raise
Songs of glad thanksgiving, Songs of holy praise.
Oh, how kind and gracious Thou hast always been!
Oh, how many blessings Every day has seen!
Chorus.—Jesus, blessèd Saviour, Now our praises hear,
For Thy grace and favour, Crowning all the year.

2 Jesus, holy Saviour, Only Thou canst tell
How we often stumbled, How we often fell!
All our sins, (so many!) Saviour, Thou dost know;
In Thy blood most precious, Wash us white as snow.
Chorus.—Jesus, blessèd Saviour, Keep us in Thy fear,
Let Thy grace and favour Pardon all the year.

3 Jesus, loving Saviour, Only Thou dost know
All that may befall us, As we onward go.
So we humbly pray Thee, Take us by the hand,
Lead us ever upward To the Better Land.
Chorus.—Jesus, blessèd Saviour, Keep us ever near,
Let Thy grace and favour Shield us all the year.

4 Jesus, precious Saviour, Make us all Thine own,
Make us Thine for ever, Make us Thine alone.
Let each day, each moment, Of this glad New-Year,
Be for Jesus only, Jesus, Saviour dear.
Chorus.—Then, O blessèd Saviour, Never need we fear,
For Thy grace and favour Crown our bright New-Year!

Frances Ridley Havergal, 1872.

GOLDBACH. (Part I.) [H. P. 130.]

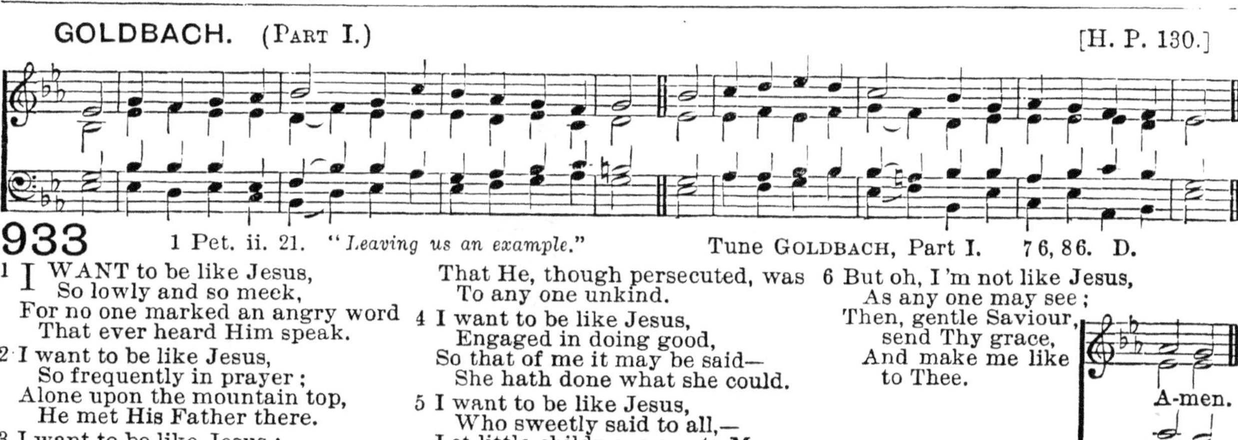

933 1 Pet. ii. 21. "*Leaving us an example.*" Tune Goldbach, Part I. 76, 86. D.

1 I WANT to be like Jesus,
So lowly and so meek,
For no one marked an angry word
That ever heard Him speak.

2 I want to be like Jesus,
So frequently in prayer;
Alone upon the mountain top,
He met His Father there.

3 I want to be like Jesus:
I never, never find
That He, though persecuted, was
To any one unkind.

4 I want to be like Jesus,
Engaged in doing good,
So that of me it may be said—
She hath done what she could.

5 I want to be like Jesus,
Who sweetly said to all,—
Let little children come to Me:
I would obey the call.

6 But oh, I'm not like Jesus,
As any one may see;
Then, gentle Saviour, send Thy grace,
And make me like to Thee.

A-men.

William Meynell Whittemore, D.D., 1841.

934 John x. 11. "*I am the good Shepherd.*"
Tune Rabenlei. 65, 65. D. Or Hermas.

RABENLEI. [H. P. 267.]

1 JESUS is our Shepherd,
Wiping every tear;
Folded in His bosom
What have we to fear?
Only let us follow
Whither He doth lead,
To the thirsty desert,
Or the dewy mead.

2 Jesus is our Shepherd:
Well we know His voice,
How its gentlest whisper
Makes our heart rejoice;
Even when He chideth,
Tender is its tone:
None but He shall guide us:
We are His alone.

3 Jesus is our Shepherd;
For the sheep He bled;
Every lamb is sprinkled
With the blood He shed;
Then on each He setteth
His own secret sign,—
"They that have My Spirit,
These," saith He, "are Mine."

4 Jesus is our Shepherd:
Guarded by His arm,
Though the wolves may ravin,
None can do us harm;
When we tread death's valley,
Dark with fearful gloom,
We will fear no evil,
Victors o'er the tomb.

5 Jesus is our Shepherd;
With His goodness now,
And His tender mercy,
He doth us endow:
Let us sing His praises
With a gladsome heart,
Till in heaven we meet Him,
Never more to part.

Canon H. Stowell, D.D., 1831.

PATMOS. [H. P. 147.]

935 Matt. xix. 14. "*Suffer little children to come unto Me.*"
Tune Patmos. 77, 77. Or Vienna.

1 JESUS loves me! this I know,
For the Bible tells me so;
Little ones to Him belong,
They are weak, but He is strong.

2 Jesus loves me! He who died
Heaven's gate to open wide;
He will wash away my sin,
Let His little child come in.

3 Jesus loves me! loves me still,
Though I'm very weak and ill;
From His shining throne on high,
Comes to watch me when I lie.

4 Jesus loves me! He will stay
Close beside me all the way:
If I love Him, when I die
He will take me home on high.

From "Happy Voices," 1865.

936 Luke xxiv. 29. "*Abide with us, for it is toward evening.*"
Tune Patmos. 77, 77. Or Shenir II.

1 NOW the daylight goes away,
Saviour, listen while I pray,
Asking Thee to watch and keep,
And to send me quiet sleep.

2 Jesus, Saviour, wash away
All that has been wrong to-day;
Help me every day to be
Good and gentle, more like Thee.

3 Let my near and dear ones be
Always near and dear to Thee;
Oh! bring me and all I love
To Thy happy home above.

4 Now my evening praise I give;
Thou didst die that I might live;
All my blessings come from Thee;
Oh, how good Thou art to me!

5 Thou, my best and kindest Friend,
Thou wilt love me to the end;
Let me love Thee more and more,
Always better than before.

Frances Ridley Havergal, 1839.

BOSTON. [H. P. 278.]

937 Isa. lviii. 13. "*Call the Sabbath a delight.*"

Tune BOSTON. 76, 76. D. Or ZOAN I.

1 O HAPPY, happy Sunday!
Thou day of peace and heaven,
'Tis fit we should give one day
To God who gives us seven.
Though other days bring sadness,
Thou bidd'st us cease to mourn;
Then hail, thou day of gladness,
I welcome thy return.

2 O happy, happy Sunday!
We will not toil to-day,
But leave to busy Monday
Our work, and toil, and play.
Thy face is ever smiling,
Thou fairest of the seven;
They only speak of toiling,
But thou of rest and heaven.

3 O happy, happy Sunday!
Thy holy hours I prize,
Thou art indeed heaven's own day,
The emblem of the skies.
May I, O Lord, inherit
That rest when life is o'er,
And with each perfect spirit
Adore Thee evermore.

Leeds Sunday School Hymn-book, 1833.

STERNBERG. [H. P. 245.]

938 Rev. v. 9. "*They sung a new song.*"

Tune STERNBERG. 11 10, 11 10.

1 SINGING for Jesus, oh, singing for Jesus,
Trying to serve Him wherever I go;
Pointing the lost to the way of salvation—
This be my mission, a pilgrim below.

2 Singing for Jesus glad hymns of devotion,
Lifting the soul on her pinions of love;
Dropping a word or a thought by the wayside,
Telling of rest in the mansions above.

3 Singing for Jesus, my blessèd Redeemer,
God of the pilgrims, for Thee I will sing,
When o'er the billows of time I am wafted,
Still with Thy praise shall eternity ring.

4 Glory to God for the prospect before me,
Soon shall my spirit transported ascend;
Singing for Jesus, oh, blissful employment,
Loud Hallelujahs that never will end.

Fanny Crosby, 1866.

939 Ps. cl. 6. "*Let everything that hath breath praise the Lord.*" Tune STERNBERG. 11 10, 11 10.

1 SWEET Hallelujahs! the birds and the blossoms
Chant forth in harmony, Praise to the Lord.
Sweet Hallelujahs from penitent bosoms:
Angels in rapture re-echo the word.

2 Sweet Hallelujahs! the works of creation
Praise Him who only may e'er be adored;
Sweeter the thrill of a new animation,
When sinners, new pardoned, sing, Praise to the Lord.

3 Sweet Hallelujahs to Jesus their Saviour:
All the bright seraphim join in the song;
Nations shall start from their evil behaviour,
And sweet Hallelujahs to Jesus prolong.

4 Sweet Hallelujahs! the great congregation
Round the white throne shall re-echo the word.
Pass with their palms through the gates of salvation,
With sweet Hallelujahs in praise to the Lord.

Paxton Hood, 1862.

ARRAN. [H. P. 59.]

940 Ps. v. 3. "*In the morning will I direct my prayer unto Thee.*" Tune ARRAN. C. M.

1 THE morning bright with rosy light
Has waked me up from sleep;
Father, I own Thy love alone
Thy little one doth keep.

2 All through the day I humbly pray,
Be Thou my guard and guide;
My sins forgive, and let me live,
Lord Jesus, near Thy side.

3 Oh, make Thy rest within my breast,
Great Spirit of all grace;
Make me like Thee, then I shall be
Prepared to see Thy face.

Thomas O. Summers, 1851.

MUNICH. [H. P. 279.]

941 1 Cor. ii. 9. "*The things which God hath prepared for them that love Him.*" Tune MUNICH. 76, 76. D.
Or ZOAN I.

1 THERE'S a Friend for little children
Above the bright blue sky;
A Friend who never changeth,
Whose love can never die.
Unlike our friends by nature
Who change with changing years,
This Friend is always worthy
The precious name He bears.

2 There's a rest for little children
Above the bright blue sky;
For those who love the Saviour,
And Abba Father cry.
A rest from every trouble,
From sin and danger free,
Where every little pilgrim
Shall rest eternally.

3 There's a home for little children
Above the bright blue sky,
Where Jesus reigns in glory—
A home of peace and joy;
No home on earth is like it,
Nor can with it compare,
For every one is happy,
Nor can be happier, there.

4 There's a crown for little children
Above the bright blue sky,
And all who look to Jesus
Shall wear it by-and-by.
A crown of brightest glory,
Which He will then bestow
On those who found His favour,
And loved Him here below.

5 There's a song for little children
Above the bright blue sky,
A song that will not weary
Though sung continually;
A song which even angels
Can never, never sing,
They know not Christ as Saviour,
But worship Him as King.

6 There's a robe for little children
Above the bright blue sky,
A harp of sweetest music,
A palm of victory.
All, all above is treasured,
And found in Christ alone:
Oh, come, dear little children,
That all may be your own.

Albert Midlane, 1861.

ZOAN I. (Field of.) [H. P. 127.]

Ho-san-na! Ho-san-na! Ho-san-na! A - men, A - men.

942 Matt. xxi. 9. *"Blessed is He that cometh in the name of the Lord"*

ZOAN I., with Hosanna from EUPHRATES. 76, 76. D.

1 WHEN His salvation bringing,
To Zion Jesus came,
The children all stood singing
"Hosanna" to His name.
Nor did their zeal offend Him,
But as He rode along
He let them still attend Him,
And smiled to hear their song.
Hosanna! Hosanna! Hosanna! Amen.

2 And since the Lord retaineth
His love for children still;
Though now as King He reigneth
On Zion's heavenly hill,
We'll flock around His banner
Who sits upon the throne,
And raise a loud Hosanna
To David's royal Son.
Hosanna! Hosanna! Hosanna! Amen.

3 For should we fail proclaiming
Our great Redeemer's praise,
The stones, our silence shaming,
Would their Hosannas raise.
But shall we only render
The tribute of our words?
No; while our hearts are tender,
They too shall be the Lord's.
Hosanna! Hosanna! Hosanna! Amen.

Joshua King, 1830.

See Hymns 95, 129, 153, 179, 226, 286, 386, 390, 397, 456, 547, 631, 664, 666, 865, 866.

CAROL I. [H. P. CAROL No. I.]

CHRISTMAS CAROLS FOR CHILDREN.

943 Luke ii. 18. *"Those things which were told them by the shepherds."* Tune, CAROL No. I.

1 SO happy all the day
Had I been without play;
And such good thoughts had come o'er my mind:
That I wondered what it meant,
Or for why it was sent;
As I ne'er had felt aught of the kind.

2 And the birds, all day long,
Had kept trilling their song;
And the sun had gone down, oh, so red!
We had folded the sheep,
And were talking of sleep,
But, somehow, we cared not for bed.

3 The stars were all drest
In their brightest and best;
And the moon showed a streak of her gold:
'Twas a glorious night;
And we thought of the sight
Of which David our father has told.

4 A sound struck our ear,
Sweet, joyous, and clear,
It seemed like a musical breeze:
But, ere we could gaze,
We were all in a blaze,
And found ourselves down on our knees.

5 A bright one then said,
('Twas like life from the dead,)
"Good tidings, good tidings I bring!
Messiah 's come down;
In your own little town
You will find Him a Babe and a King!"

6 And then the whole choir,
Rising higher and higher,
Sang of "glory, sweet peace and good-will."
The sheep seemed to dance,
And the mountains to prance,
And the stars could no longer stand still.

7 Then onward we sped,
To find out the bed,
Where the Saviour in lowliness lay:
Near Bethlehem's inn,
(Oh shame on their sin!)
We found Him 'midst cattle and hay.

8 But we saw the blest sight;
'Twas our Judah's delight;
And Mary and Joseph were there:
And soon we made known
To all in the town
What we heard the good angel declare.

9 And now, every day,
I sing and I pray
To the Babe who is Saviour and all:
May His wonderful birth
Be known through the earth,
And cheer both the great and the small!

William Henry Havergal, circa 1834.

A - men.

CAROL II. [H. P. CAROL NO. II.]

How grand and how bright, That won-der-ful night, When an - gels to Beth - le - hem came! They

rall.
burst forth like fires, They struck their gold lyres, And min - gled their sound with the flame!

944

Luke ii. 9. "*The glory of the Lord shone round about them.*" Tune, CAROL NO. II.

1 HOW grand and how bright
That wonderful night,
When angels to Bethlehem came!
They burst forth like fires,
They struck their gold lyres,
And mingled their sound with the flame.

2 The shepherds were 'mazed,
The pretty lambs gazed
At darkness thus turned into light:
No voice was there heard
From man, beast, or bird,
So sudden and solemn the sight.

3 And then, when the sound
Re-echoed around,
The hills and the dales all awoke;
The moon and the stars
Stopped their fiery cars,
And listened while Gabriel spoke:

4 "I bring you," said he,
"From the glorious Three,
Good tidings to gladden mankind;
The Saviour is born,
But He lies all forlorn
In a manger, as soon you will find."

5 At mention of this,
(The source of all bliss,)
The angels sang loudly and long;
They soared to the sky,
Beyond mortal eye,
But left us the words of their song:

6 "All glory to God,"
Who laid by His rod,
To smile on the world through His Son;
"And peace be on earth,"
For this wonderful birth
Most wonderful conquests has won;

7 "And good-will to man,"
Though his life 's but a span,
And his thoughts all evil and wrong:
Then pray, Christians, pray;
But let Christmas-Day
Have your sweetest and holiest song.

William Henry Havergal, circa 1827.

CAROL III. [H. P. Carol No. III.]

945 Ps. cv. 2. "*Talk ye of all His wondrous works.*" Tune, Carol No. III.

1 COME, shepherds, come, 'tis just a year
Since sweetest music woke our ear,
And angels blessed our sight.
Come, lift your heart and tune your voice,
And bid the hills and vales rejoice,
As on that glorious night.

2 'Tis just a year ago, we say,
When night shone out as clear as day,
And heaven came down to earth.
How did we fear, how did we gaze,
Surrounded by the sudden blaze,
And thrilled with sounds of mirth!

3 Ah! see you not that angel choir?
And hear you not that mighty lyre
Which hushed our bleating sheep?
And, oh, that voice of sweetest awe,
Which told us all we after saw!
Who now would silence keep?

4 Come, shepherds, come, with prayer and song,
This night to be remembered long
Rejoice to celebrate.
With reedy pipe, chant forth who can
To God all glory, love to man,
And peace in every gate!

5 'Tis just a year ago to-night,
From heaven came down the Prince of Light,
Our guilty world to bless;
Let Gentiles now with Israel sing
Our Saviour, Brother, Friend, and King,
Our promised Righteousness!

William Henry Havergal, 1860.

A - men.

KADESH. [H. P. 159.]

946 Ps. xx. 5. "*We will rejoice in Thy salvation.*" Tune Kadesh. 77, 77. D.

1 WELCOME Christmas! welcome here!
Happiest season of the year!
Fires are blazing, thee to greet,
Families together meet,
Brothers, sisters circle round,
Loud the joyous, happy sound;
For old England loves to see
All her children welcome thee.

2 Welcome Christmas! for thy voice
Calls upon us to rejoice;
Not with foolish, idle mirth,
Born and perishing on earth.
Far be such ungrateful thought,
Ours are blessings dearly bought;
Dearly bought, but freely given,
By the Lord of earth and heaven.

3 Fix we then on Christ our eye;
May we feel the Saviour nigh;
May we meet around the board,
All rejoicing in the Lord.
Be the Babe of Bethlehem near!
May His love the season cheer,
And each gladdened heart and tongue
Join the angels' Christmas song.

Mary Ann Stodart, 1840.

FIDES. [H. P. 343.]

947 Ps. cxlviii. 12, 13. "*Children, . . praise the name of the Lord.*"
Tune Fides. 6 5, 6 5. D. and Chorus. Or Hermas.

1 WAKEN, Christian children!
  Up! and let us sing
With glad voice the praises
  Of our new-born King.
Up! 'tis meet to welcome
  With a joyous lay
Christ the King of Glory,
  Born for us to-day.
    Waken, etc.

2 Up! nor fear to seek Him,
  Children though we be!
Once He said of children,
  "Let them come to Me."
Fear not then to enter,
  Though we cannot bring
Gold, or myrrh, or perfume,
  Fitting for a King.
    Waken, etc.

3 Gifts He asketh richer,
  Offerings costlier still,
Yet may Christian children
  Bring them if they will.
Brighter than all jewels
  Shines the modest eye;
Best of gifts, He loveth
  Infant purity. Waken, etc.

Samuel Collingwood Hamerton, 1860.

948 John xiv. 3. "*I will come again.*"
Tune Regent Square. 15, 15, 15.
Or Idumea.

REGENT SQUARE. [H. P. 299.]

1 JESUS came (the heavens adoring), came with peace from realms on high:
Jesus came for man's redemption, lowly came on earth to die.
Hallelujah, Hallelujah! Came in deep humility.

2 Jesus comes again in mercy, when our hearts are bowed with care;
Jesus comes again in answer to an earnest heartfelt prayer.
Hallelujah, Hallelujah! Comes to save us from despair.

3 Jesus comes to hearts rejoicing, bringing news of sin forgiven;
Jesus comes in sounds of gladness, leading souls redeemed to heaven.
Hallelujah, Hallelujah! Now the gate of death is riven.

4 Jesus comes in joy and sorrow, shares alike our hopes and fears;
Jesus comes, whate'er befalls us, glads our hearts and dries our tears.
Hallelujah, Hallelujah! Cheering e'en our failing years.

5 Jesus comes on clouds triumphant, when the heavens shall pass away;
Jesus comes again in glory,—let us then our homage pay;
Hallelujah! ever singing, till the dawning of the day.

Godfrey Thring, 1866.

GODESBERG. [H. P. 185.]

(3) CONFIRMATION.

949 Mark i. 17. "*Jesus said unto them, Come ye after Me.*"
Tune Godesberg. 8 7, 8 7.

1 JESUS calls us—o'er the tumult
  Of our life's wild, restless sea;
Day by day His sweet voice soundeth,
  Saying, "Christian, follow Me."

2 Jesus calls us from the worship
  Of the vain world's golden store,
From each idol that would keep us:
  Saying, "Christian, love Me more."

3 In our joys, and in our sorrows,
  Days of toil and hours of ease,
Still He calls, in cares and pleasures,
  "Christian, love Me more than these."

4 Jesus calls us! by Thy mercies,
  Saviour, may we hear Thy call,
Give our hearts to Thy obedience,
  Serve and love Thee best of all.

Cecil Frances Alexander, 1853.

BEDFORD. [H. P. 66.]

950 Jer. l. 5. *"Come and let us join ourselves to the Lord in a perpetual covenant."*

Tune BEDFORD. C. M.

1 COME, let us seek the grace of God,
And all with one accord
In a perpetual covenant join
Ourselves to Christ the Lord.

2 Come, let us join ourselves to Him
Who died our souls to save,
Who died that sinners, such as we,
Eternal life might have.

3 And may we ever, through His grace,
This covenant bear in mind;
No more forsake the Lord our God,
Nor cast His word behind.

4 Oh! let the days already past
Suffice to have spent in vain;
Let Satan's power no more prevail,
Nor in our members reign.

5 Thee, Father, Son, and Holy Ghost,
May we by faith receive;
And henceforth die to all below,
And to Thee only live.

C. Wesley, 1762; *E. Bickersteth*, 1833.

GILBOA (Mount). [H. P. 11.]

951 Ps. x. 17. *"Thou wilt prepare their heart."*

Tune GILBOA. L. M.

1 LOOK down, O Lord! and on our youth
Bestow Thy gifts of heavenly grace,
And let the seed of sacred truth
Find in each mind a fruitful place.

2 Soon to appear before Thy sight,
Their vow and promise to renew,
Prepare them for the solemn rite,
Bid each his heart and life review.

3 The cross that marked their infant brow,
May it a faithful emblem prove
That they shall keep that sacred vow,
And walk as children of Thy love.

4 Now in the strength of power Divine,
Oh! may they all, with glad accord,
In holy covenant combine,
And join themselves to Christ the Lord.

5 Thy sons and daughters may they be,
Confirmed and strengthened by Thy grace;
And, safe through life preserved by Thee,
In heaven behold Thee face to face.

Thomas Cotterill, 1821.

AVEN (Plain of). [H. P. 79.]

952 Lev. xxiii. 17. *"The first-fruits unto the Lord."*

Tune AVEN. S. M. Or MORAVIA.

1 FAIR waved the golden corn
In Canaan's pleasant land,
When full of joy, some shining morn,
Went forth the reaper-band.

2 To God, so good and great,
Their cheerful thanks they pour,
Then carry to His temple gate
The choicest of their store.

3 For thus the holy word,
Spoken by Moses, ran:
"The first ripe ears are for the Lord,
The rest He gives to man."

4 Like Israel, Lord, we give
Our earliest fruits to Thee,
And pray that long as we shall live
We may Thy children be.

5 Thine is our youthful prime,
And life and all its powers;
Be with us in our morning time,
And bless our evening hours.

6 In wisdom let us grow,
As years and strength are given,
That we may serve Thy church below,
And join Thy saints in heaven.

John Hampden Gurney, 1851.

PATMOS. [H. P. 147.]

953

Ps. cxix. 94. "*I am Thine.*"
Tune PATMOS. 7 7, 7 7.

1 THINE for ever:—God of love,
Hear us from Thy throne above;
Thine for ever may we be,
Here and in eternity.

2 Thine for ever:—Lord of life,
Shield us through our earthly strife;
Thou the Life, the Truth, the Way,
Guide us to the realms of day.

3 Thine for ever:—oh how blessed
They who find in Thee their rest!
Saviour, Guardian, Heavenly Friend,
Oh defend us to the end.

4 Thine for ever:—Saviour, keep
These Thy frail and trembling sheep;
Safe alone beneath Thy care,
Let us all Thy goodness share.

5 Thine for ever:—Thou our Guide,
All our wants by Thee supplied,
All our sins by Thee forgiven,
Lead us, Lord, from earth to heaven.

Mary Fawler Maude, 1818.

MELCOMBE. [H. P. 24.]

954

Ps. cviii. 1. "*O God, my heart is fixed, I will sing and give praise.*" Tune MELCOMBE. L. M.

1 OH happy day, that fixed my choice
On Thee, my Saviour, and my God;
Well may this glowing heart rejoice,
And tell its raptures all abroad.

2 'Tis done, the great transaction 's done;
I am my Lord's, and He is mine;
He drew me, and I followed on,
Charmed to confess the voice Divine.

3 Now rest, my long divided heart;
Fixed on this blissful centre, rest:
With ashes who would grudge to part,
When called on angels' bread to feast?

4 Our God, who heard the solemn vow,
That vow renewed shall daily hear,
Till in life's latest hour I bow,
And bless in death a bond so dear.

Philip Doddridge, D.D., 1755.

GROSVENOR. [H. P. 269.]

955

Phil. iii. 14. "*I press toward the mark.*"
Tune GROSVENOR. 6 5, 6 5. D.

1 ONWARD, holy champion! Run the Christian race;
Leave the world behind thee, heavenward set thy face;
Fresh from cleansing water, bright with oil Divine,
Trained with wholesome nurture, heavenly bread and wine.

2 Onward, holy champion! Throw all weight aside,
All distracting pleasure, all encumbering pride;
Shun the subtle pitfalls laid by Satan's spite;
Let not smiles betray thee, let not frowns affright.

3 Onward, holy champion! Angels, bending down,
Watch thy brave endeavour, guard thy future crown;
Christ, thy gracious Saviour, cheers thy striving soul,
And thy prize awaits thee at the heavenly goal.

Benjamin H. Kennedy, D.D., 1867.

956

2 Tim. iv. 8. *"Henceforth there is laid up for me a crown of righteousness."*
Tune Hermas. 6 5, 6 5. D. and Chorus.

1 "ONWARD, upward, homeward!" hastily I flee,
From this world of sorrow, with my Lord to be;
Onward to the glory, upward to the prize,
Homeward to the mansions far above the skies.
Onward to the glory, etc.

2 "Onward, upward, homeward!" Here I find no rest;
Treading o'er the desert which my Saviour pressed;
"Onward, upward, homeward!" I shall soon be there,
Soon its joys and pleasures, I, through grace, shall share.
Onward to the glory, etc.

3 "Onward, upward, homeward!" Come along with me:
Ye who love the Saviour, bear me company;
"Onward, upward, homeward!" press with vigour on,
Yet a little moment, and the race is won!
Onward to the glory, etc.

Albert Midlane, 1864.

957

Luke ix. 57. *"I will follow Thee whithersoever Thou goest."* Tune Mahanaim. 7 6, 7 6. D. Or Goldbach.

1 O JESUS, I have promised
To serve Thee to the end;
Be Thou for ever near me,
My Master and my Friend!
I shall not fear the battle
If Thou art by my side,
Nor wander from the pathway
If Thou wilt be my Guide.

2 Oh let me feel Thee near me:
The world is ever near;
I see the sights that dazzle,
The tempting sounds I hear:
My foes are ever near me,
Around me and within;
But, Jesus, draw Thou nearer,
And shield my soul from sin.

3 Oh let me hear Thee speaking
In accents clear and still,
Above the storms of passion,
The murmurs of self will.
Oh speak! to reassure me,
To hasten or control;
Oh speak! to make me listen,
Thou Guardian of my soul.

4 Oh! let me see Thy features,
The look that once could make
So many a true disciple
Leave all things for Thy sake;
The look that beamed on Peter,
When he Thy name denied;
The look that draws Thy lovers
Close to Thy piercèd side.

5 O Jesus! Thou hast promised
To all who follow Thee,
That where Thou art in glory
There shall Thy servant be;
And, Jesus, I have promised
To serve Thee to the end;
Oh give me grace to follow
My Master and my Friend!

6 Oh! let me see Thy footmarks,
And in them plant mine own;
My hope to follow duly
Is in Thy strength alone.
Oh! guide me, call me, draw me,
Uphold me to the end;
And then in heaven receive me,
My Saviour and my Friend!

John Ernest Bode, 1860.

See Hymns 32—40, 633—641, 695, 698.

ST. ALPHEGE. [H. P. 275.]

(4) HOLY MATRIMONY.

958 Gen. i. 28. "*And God blessed them.*" Tune ST. ALPHEGE. 76, 76. Or GOLDBACH, Part I.

1 THE voice that breathed o'er Eden,
That earliest wedding day,
The primal marriage blessing,
It hath not passed away.

2 Still in the pure espousal
Of Christian man and maid,
The Holy Three are with us,
The threefold grace is said.

3 For dower of blessèd children,
For love and faith's sweet sake,
For high, mysterious union
Which naught on earth may break.

4 Be present, heavenly Father,
To give away this bride,
As Eve Thou gav'st to Adam,
Out of his own pierced side.

5 Be present, gracious Saviour,
To join their loving hands,
As Thou didst bind two natures
In Thine eternal bands.

6 Be present, Holiest Spirit,
To bless them as they kneel;
As Thou, for Christ the Bridegroom,
The heavenly spouse dost seal.

7 Oh spread Thy pure wing o'er them,
Let no ill power find place,
When onward to Thy presence
The hallowed path they trace,

8 To cast their crowns before Thee,
In perfect sacrifice,
Till to the home of gladness
With Christ's own bride they rise.

John Keble, 1856.

KEDRON (Brook). [H. P. 213.]

959 Eph. v. 32. "*This is a great mystery.*" Tune KEDRON. 886. D.

1 HOW blest are hearts which Christ the Lord
Couples, as with a silver cord,
In nuptial unity:
That animated are with love
And aspirations from above,
O Holy Ghost, by Thee!

2 Anthems angelical were heard,
When Christ, the everlasting Word,
To wed His bride did come,
And take that consecrated bride,
Cleansed by the life-blood from His side,
Unto her heavenly home.

3 Mirrored in nuptial purity,
The marriage of the church we see
And Christ the Bridegroom's love.
Angels look down, and anthems sing;
The Holy Dove, with golden wing,
Sheds blessings from above.

4 Bless these Thy servants, gracious Lord,
Whom Thou dost join in sweet accord,
The bridegroom and the bride;
In sorrow, sickness, and in health,
In tribulation and in wealth,
Be Thou their Help and Guide.

5 Be with them, Lord, as day by day
They with one heart together pray,
Thy word together read;
Together at Thy table kneel,
And with Thy blood their union seal,
On Thee together feed.

Bishop Christopher Wordsworth, 1862.

MAMRE (Plain of). [H. P. 226.]

960 1 Pet. iii. 7. "*Heirs together of the grace of life.*" Tune MAMRE. 98, 98, 88.

1 RAISE high the note of exultation
To God's bright throne with voices clear;
The mighty Lord of all creation
Lends to our songs a Father's ear.
Eternal Lord of heaven above,
Look down and bless their plighted love.

2 O'er each event of life presiding,
May God rich gifts on both bestow;
With heavenly light your footsteps guiding,
As through the world's dark wild ye go.
Eternal Lord of heaven above, etc.

3 By God's own word each action measure,
Let Christ your great Exemplar be;
Still fix your hearts on heavenly treasure,
We hasten towards eternity.
Eternal Lord of heaven above, etc.

4 With cheerful faith in God confide ye,
The pilgrim's staff with courage take;
And, till the silent grave divide ye,
God and each other ne'er forsake.
Eternal Lord of heaven above, etc.

5 May peace and love, your lives adorning,
Attend you all your course along;
Your Christian walk, each night and morning,
Oh strengthen still with prayer and song.
Eternal Lord of heaven above, etc.

6 Together now your voices raising,
Vow truth to God, hand joined in hand:
Till, on His glories ever gazing,
Ye meet in heaven's own happy land.
Eternal Lord of heaven above, etc.

From the German; F. E. Cox (tr.), 1864.

KENT. [H. P. 63.]

961 (5) THANKSGIVING AFTER CHILDBIRTH.

Ps. cxvi. 1. "*I love the Lord, because He hath heard my voice.*" Tune KENT. C. M.

1 ON every new-born babe of earth
A heavenly light is shed,
Incarnate Saviour, by Thy Birth,
And from Thy lowly bed.

2 And in Thy Resurrection's morn
Another birth we have;
Since Thou our nature, Lord, hast borne
In triumph through the grave.

3 And Thou hast made us heirs of heaven,
And sons of God to be;
And glorious life to us is given
Regenerate in Thee.

4 Bright angels of the King of kings
His countenance behold,
And, sheltering with their silver wings,
Christ's little ones enfold.

5 Therefore in childbirth throes, which Eve
In sorrow bore and pain,
Are gleams to all who Thee receive,
Of joy and endless gain.

6 Then praise the Giver of our breath,
Who helps us in distress,
And guides us through the pangs of death
To life and joyfulness.

7 Oh, praise be to the loving Lord,
Who heard His handmaid's prayer,
And has her to His house restored,
To bless His goodness there.

8 Preserve her, Lord, and with her bring
Us to Thy courts above,
That we together there may sing
Praise to Thy boundless love.

Bishop Christopher Wordsworth, 1865.

962 (6) SICKNESS.

Luke x. 5. "*Say, Peace be to this house.*" PART I., Tune JEZREEL. 888, 4.

1 PEACE to this house! O Thou whose way
Was on the waves, whose voice did stay
The wild wind's rage, Come, Lord, and say,
Peace to this house!

2 Thou who in pity for the weak
Didst leave Thy heavenly throne to seek
And save the lost, Come, Lord, and speak
Peace to this house!

JEZREEL (Valley of). [H. P. 220.]

3 Thou, who dost all our sorrows know,
And when our tears of anguish flow,
Dost feel compassion, Come, bestow
Peace on this house!

4 Thou, who in agony didst pray
"Take, Father, take this cup away,"
And then wast strengthened, Come and say,
Peace to this house!

5 Thou, by whose precious death we live,
From which we all our hope derive,
Thou Lord and Saviour! Come and give
Peace to this house!

6 Thou who didst hang upon the tree,
Uniting God and man in Thee,
And wert our peace, Come, Lord, and be
Peace to this house!

7 O Conqueror by suffering!
O mighty Victor, glorious King!
From out of pain and sorrow bring
Peace to this house!

8 Thou who triumphant from the dead
Thine hands didst o'er the' apostles spread,
And say, "Peace to you," Come, and shed
Peace on this house!

THYATIRA. (Hymn Chant.) [H. P. No. V.]

Part II. Tune, Hymn Chant Thyatira.

9 Thou who didst on the clouds ascend,
And then the Holy Spirit send,
Send Him to comfort and defend
All in this house.

10 Save, save us sinking in the deep,
Give ease from pain, and quiet sleep,
And under Thy wing's shelter keep
All in this house.

11 Oh, make our doubts and terrors cease,
And from the bands of sin release,
In soul and body give us peace,
Peace to this house!

12 "Peace to this house," come, Lord, and say;
Come to us, Lord, and with us stay;
Oh give, and never take away,
Peace from this house.

13 And when at last our fainting breath
On trembling lips scarce quivereth,
Oh, bring us through the gate of Death,
Lord, to Thine house;

14 To Thine own house in paradise,
To Thine own house above the skies,
To live the life that never dies,
Lord, in Thine house.

Bishop Christopher Wordsworth, 1865.

GOLDBACH. (Part I.) [H. P. 130.]

963

Ps. civ. 34. "*My meditation of Him shall be sweet.*"
Tune Goldbach, Part I. 76, 76.

1 I THINK of Thee, O Saviour!
And count affliction gain,
If aught of suffering aid me
To realize Thy pain.

2 I think of Thee, O Saviour!
And bless the chastening rod,
Conforming to Thine image,
Thou chastened Son of God.

3 My sufferings no atonement
For sin could make to God:
Alone, of all the people,
Thou hast the winepress trod.

4 So there is naught of anger
In this, my Father's stroke;
He is but gently teaching
My neck to bear Thy yoke.

5 Oh! 'tis well-nigh presumption,
In sufferings light as mine,
To speak, my stricken Saviour,
Of fellowship with Thine!

6 I would press closer to Thee,
A heavier cross would bear,
So I might better know Thee
And more Thy spirit share.

7 It was Thy cloud which led me
All through the joyous day;
But now the fiery pillar
Is shining on my way.

8 And I shall better praise Thee,
Seeing Thee thus by night,
Than if the desert pathway
Had all been tracked in light.

9 I had been lost for ever,
Hadst Thou not thought on me:
Cold is my heart and selfish,
Yet, Lord, I think of Thee.

Jennette Threlfall, 1853.

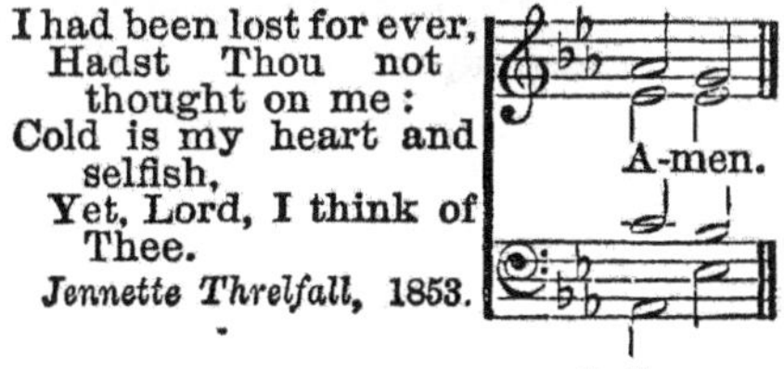

B B

BOHEMIA. [H. P. 268.]

964 Luke xxii. 32. "*I have prayed for thee.*"
Tune BOHEMIA. Or ST. BARNABAS.
65, 65. D.

1 IN the hour of trial, Jesu, pray for me;
Lest by base denial I depart from Thee:
When Thou seest me waver, With a look recall,
Nor for fear or favour Suffer me to fall.

2 With its witching pleasures Would this vain world charm,
Or its sordid treasures Spread to work me harm?
Bring to my remembrance Sad Gethsemane,
Or, in darker semblance, Cross-crowned Calvary.

3 If with sore affliction Thou in love chastise,
Pour Thy benediction On the sacrifice:
Then, upon Thine altar Freely offered up,
Though the flesh may falter, Faith shall drink the cup.

4 When in dust and ashes To the grave I sink,
While heaven's glory flashes O'er the shelving brink,
On Thy truth relying Through that mortal strife,
Lord, receive me dying To eternal life.

James Montgomery, 1825.

ST. BARNABAS. [H. P. 106.]

LUXEMBURG. [H. P. 152.]

965 1 Pet. ii. 21. "*Christ also suffered for us.*"
Tune LUXEMBURG. 77, 77.

1 SEE the destined day arise,
See a willing Sacrifice;
Jesus, to redeem our loss,
Hangs upon the shameful cross.

2 Jesu, who but Thou had borne,
Lifted on that tree of scorn,
Every pang and bitter throe,
Finishing Thy life of woe?

3 Who but Thou had dared to drain,
Steeped in gall, the cup of pain;
And with tender body bear
Thorns, and nails, and piercing spear?

4 Thence the cleansing water flowed,
Mingled from Thy side with blood:
Sign to all attesting eyes
Of the finished Sacrifice.

5 Holy Jesu, grant us grace
In that Sacrifice to place
All our trust for life renewed,
Pardoned sin, and promised good.

Bishop Mant (tr.), 1837.

URBANE. [H. P. 171A.]

966

John xii. 26. "*Let him follow Me.*"

Tune URBANE. 8 5, 8 3. Or PRAGUE.

1 ART thou weary, art thou languid,
Art thou sore distressed?
"Come to Me," saith One, "and coming,
Be at rest."

2 Hath He marks to lead me to Him,
If He be my Guide?
"In His feet and hands are wound prints,
And His side."

3 Is there diadem, as Monarch,
That His brow adorns?
"Yea, a crown, in very surety,
But of thorns."

4 If I find Him, if I follow,
What His guerdon here?
"Many a sorrow, many a labour,
Many a tear."

5 If I still hold closely to Him,
What hath He at last?
"Sorrow vanquished, labour ended,
Jordan passed."

6 If I ask Him to receive me,
Will He say me nay?
"Not till earth and not till heaven
Pass away."

7 Finding, following, keeping, struggling,
Is He sure to bless?
"Saints, apostles, prophets, martyrs,
Answer, Yes."

See Hymn 1079.

Greek Hymn, Eighth Century; J. M. Neale, D.D. (tr.), 1862.

967

1 Cor. iii. 22. "*Life or death . . . all are yours.*"

Tune STERNBERG. 11 11, 11 11.

STERNBERG. [H. P. 245.]

1 ALL things are ours; how abundant the treasure,
All riches which heaven or earth can afford!
Oh, may our thanks, like His grace, without measure,
Abound to the glory and praise of our Lord!

2 All things are ours; be it sickness or healing,
'Tis ordered alike for our infinite good;
Determined by grace, and for ever revealing
This truth, that we love and are loved of our God.

3 All things are ours; though the body may perish,
We faint not to feel it fast wasting away;
The soul its bright visions of glory will cherish,
And strengthen in holiness day after day.

4 All things are ours; yea, the present affliction,
Though now through the gloom of mortality viewed;
For soon shall we join in the blissful conviction,
That thus it was good to be tried and subdued.

5 All things are ours; through the Saviour's merit,
The shame of His cross, which must needs be our own,
Will brighten the glory that circles the spirit
And sparkles like gems in our heavenly crown.

James Holme, 1861.

LINUS.—*Minor.*

968

1 Cor. xv. 3, 4. "*Christ died . . . and was buried.*"

Tune LINUS. 8 7, 8 7.

(*Verse 1 minor; verse 2 major.*)

1 SHALL I fear, O earth, thy bosom,
Shrink and faint to lay me there,
Whence the fragrant, lovely blossom
Springs to gladden earth and air?
Whence the tree, the brook, the river,
Soft clouds floating in the sky,
All fair things, come whispering ever
Of the love Divine on high?

LINUS.—*Major.* [H. P. 336.]

2 Yea, whence One arose victorious
O'er the darkness of the grave;
His strong arm revealing, glorious
In its might Divine to save.

No, fair earth! a tender mother
Thou hast been, and yet canst be;
And through Him, my Lord and Brother,
Sweet shall be my rest in thee.

Thomas Davis, 1860.

See Hymns 517, 582, 791.

FIDES. [H. P. 343.]

D.C. al fine.

(7) MORE FRUIT.

969

John xv. 8. "*Herein is My Father glorified, that ye bear much fruit.*"

Tune Fides. 65, 65. D. Or Hermas.

1 SAVIOUR, blessèd Saviour,
Listen whilst we sing,
Hearts and voices raising
Praises to our King.
All we have to offer;
All we hope to be,
Body, soul, and spirit,
All we yield to Thee.

2 Nearer, ever nearer,
Christ, we draw to Thee,
Deep in adoration
Bending low the knee:
Thou for our redemption
Camest on earth to die;
Thou, that we might follow,
Hast gone up on high.

3 Great and ever greater
Are Thy mercies here,
True and everlasting
Are the glories there,
Where no pain or sorrow,
Toil or care, is known,
Where the angel legions
Circle round Thy throne.

4 Dark and ever darker
Was the wintry past,
Now a ray of gladness
O'er our path is cast;
Every day that passeth,
Every hour that flies,
Tells of love unfeignèd,
Love that never dies.

PART II.

5 Clearer still and clearer
Dawns the light from heaven,
In our sadness bringing
News of sin forgiven;
Life has lost its shadows,
Pure the light within;
Thou hast shed Thy radiance
On a world of sin.

6 Brighter still and brighter
Glows the western sun,
Shedding all its gladness
O'er our work that's done;
Time will soon be over,
Toil and sorrow past;
May we, blessèd Saviour,
Find a rest at last.

7 Onward, ever onward,
Journeying o'er the road
Worn by saints before us,
Journeying on to God;
Leaving all behind us,
May we hasten on,
Backward never looking
Till the prize is won.

8 Bliss, all bliss excelling,
When the ransomed soul
Earthly toils forgetting
Finds its promised goal;
Where, in joys unheard of,
Saints with angels sing,
Never weary raising
Praises to their King. Amen.

Godfrey Thring, 1866.

970 Heb. xiii. 15. "*The fruit of our lips.*" Tune LINUS (*Major*). 15 15, 15 15. Or SALZBURG.

1 HAVE you not a word for Jesus? not a word to say for Him?
He is listening through the chorus of the burning seraphim.
He is listening: does He hear you speaking of the things of earth,
Only of its passing pleasure, selfish sorrow, empty mirth?
He has spoken words of blessing, pardon, peace, and love to you,
Glorious hopes and gracious comfort, strong and tender, sweet and true;
Does He hear you telling others something of His love untold,
Overflowings of thanksgiving for His mercies manifold?

2 Have you not a word for Jesus? Will the world His praise proclaim?
Who shall speak if ye are silent, ye who know and love His name?
You, whom He hath called and chosen His own witnesses to be,
Will you tell your gracious Master, "Lord, we cannot speak for Thee!"
"Cannot!" though He suffered for you, died because He loved you so!
"Cannot!" though He has forgiven, making scarlet white as snow!
"Cannot!" though His grace abounding is your freely promised aid!
"Cannot!" though He stands beside you, though He says "Be not afraid!"

3 What shall be our word for Jesus? Master, give it day by day,
Ever as the need arises, teach Thy children what to say.
Give us holy love and patience, grant us deep humility,
That of self we may be emptied, and our hearts be full of Thee.
Give us zeal and faith and fervour, make us winning, make us wise,
Single-hearted, strong and fearless: Thou hast called us, we will rise!
Let the might of Thy good Spirit go with every loving word,
And by hearts prepared and opened be our message always heard.

4 Yes, we have a word for Jesus! Living echoes we will be
Of Thine own sweet words of blessing, of Thy gracious "Come to Me!"
Jesus, Master! yes, we love Thee! and to prove our love would lay
Fruit of lips which Thou wilt open, at Thy blessèd feet to-day.
Give us grace to follow fully, vanquishing our faithless shame,
Feebly it may be, but truly, witnessing for Thy dear name.
Ours shall be the joy and honour Thy redeemèd ones to bring,
Jewels for the coronation of our coming Lord and King.

5 Yes, we have a word for Jesus! We will bravely speak for Thee;
And Thy bold and faithful soldiers, Saviour, we would henceforth be;
In Thy name set up our banners, while Thine own shall wave above,
With Thy crimson name of Mercy, and Thy golden name of Love.
Help us lovingly to labour, looking for Thy present smile,
Looking for Thy promised blessing, through the brightening "little while."
Words for Thee in weakness spoken Thou wilt here accept and own,
And confess them in Thy glory, when we see Thee on Thy throne.

Frances Ridley Havergal, 1871.

EIRENE. [H. P. 246.]

(8) OLD AGE.

971 John xii. 21. "*We would see Jesus.*"
Tune EIRENE. 11 10, 11 10.

1 WE would see Jesus—for the shadows lengthen
Across the little landscape of our life;
We would see Jesus, our weak faith to strengthen
For the last weariness, the final strife.

2 We would see Jesus—for life's hand hath rested,
With its dark touch, upon both heart and brow;
And though our souls have many a billow breasted,
Others are rising in the distance now.

3 We would see Jesus—the great rock foundation
Whereon our feet were set by sovereign grace;
Not life, nor death, with all their agitation,
Can thence remove us if we see His face.

4 We would see Jesus—though the spirit lingers
Round the dear objects it has loved so long,
And earth from earth can scarce unclose its fingers,
Our love to Thee makes not this love less strong.

5 We would see Jesus—this is all we're needing,
Strength, joy, and willingness come with the sight;
We would see Jesus, dying, risen, pleading—
Then welcome day, and farewell mortal night.

Leaflet, Taylor, Edinburgh, 1864.

GOLDBACH. [H. P. 130.]

972 Isa. xlvi. 4. "*To hoar hairs will I carry you.*" Tune GOLDBACH. 7 6, 7 6. D.

1 I'M kneeling at the threshold, aweary, faint, and sore;
I'm waiting for the dawning, for the opening of the door:
I'm waiting till the Master shall bid me rise and come
To the glory of His presence, the gladness of His home.

2 A weary path I've travelled, 'mid darkness, storm, and strife,
Bearing many a burden, contending for my life;
But now the morn is breaking, my toil will soon be o'er,
I'm kneeling at the threshold, my hand is at the door.

3 Methinks I hear the voices of the blessèd, as they stand,
Sweet singing in the sunshine of the unclouded land:
Oh! would that I were with them, amid the shining throng!
Uniting in their worship, rejoicing in their song!

4 The friends that started with me have entered long ago;
Ah! one by one they left me to struggle with the foe;
Their pilgrimage was shorter, their triumph sooner won:
How lovingly they'll hail me, when my work too is done!

5 With them the blessèd angels that know no grief or sin,
I see them at the portals, prepared to let me in:
O Lord, I wait Thy pleasure, Thy time and way are best;
But I'm wasted, worn, and weary; my Father, bid me rest!

W. L. Alexander, D.D., 1860.

See Hymns 571, 582.

CYPRUS. [H. P. 26.]

(9) DEATH.

973 1 Thess. iv. 14. "*Them which sleep in Jesus.*" Tune CYPRUS. L. M.

1 ASLEEP in Jesus! blessèd sleep,
From which none ever wakes to weep,
A calm and undisturbed repose,
Unbroken by the last of foes.

2 Asleep in Jesus! oh, how sweet
To be for such a slumber meet!
With holy confidence to sing
That death has lost his venomed sting.

3 Asleep in Jesus! peaceful rest,
Whose waking is supremely blest;
No fear, no foe, shall dim that hour
That manifests the Saviour's power.

4 Asleep in Jesus! oh, for me
May such a blissful refuge be;
Securely shall my ashes lie,
Waiting the summons from on high!

Margaret Mackay, 1832.

974 Ps. xxiii. 4. "*Thou art with me.*" Tune GOLDBACH. 7 6, 7 6. D.

1 BE with me in the valley,
When heart and flesh shall fail,
And softly, safely lead me on
Until within the veil;
Then faith shall turn to gladness,
To find myself with Thee,
And trembling hope shall realize
Her full felicity.

2 Angels shall gather round me,
And joyous greeting give,
A sinner brought from sinful earth,
With them in bliss to live.
But angels shall be silent,
While dearer spirits press,
To mingle with my gushing joy
Their calmer happiness.

3 And gently shall they bear me,
Through that bright company,
Towards the brighter throne of Him
Who died to ransom me;
No further guidance needing,
Together shall we bend,
And bless the grace that loving once
Hath loved me to the end.

4 Be with me in the valley,
When heart and flesh shall fail,
And softly, safely lead me on
Until within the veil.
And, Saviour, deal as gently
With those I leave behind,
Till each shall in our heavenly home
As sweet a welcome find.

Elizabeth Glyde, 1840.

SEIR (Mount). [H. P. 161.]

975 1 Cor. xv. 57. *"Thanks be to God which giveth us the victory."*

Tune SEIR. 77, 77. D.

1 DEATHLESS principle, arise;
Soar, thou native of the skies;
Pearl of price, by Jesus bought,
To His glorious likeness wrought,
Go, to shine before His throne;
Deck His mediatorial crown;
Go, His triumphs to adorn;
Made for God, to God return.

2 Lo, He beckons from on high!
Fearless to His presence fly;
Thine the merit of His blood,
Thine the righteousness of God.
Angels, joyful to attend,
Hovering round thy pillow bend;
Wait to catch the signal given,
And escort thee quick to heaven.

3 Is thy earthly house distressed,
Willing to retain her guest?
'Tis not thou, but she must die:
Fly, celestial tenant, fly.
Burst thy shackles, drop thy clay,
Sweetly breathe thyself away,
Singing to thy crown remove;
Swift of wing, and fired with love.

PART II.

4 Shudder not to pass the stream;
Venture all thy care on Him;
Him, whose dying love and power
Stilled its tossing, hushed its roar.
Safe is the expanded wave,
Gentle as a summer's eve;
Not one object of His care
Ever suffered shipwreck there.

5 See the haven full in view!
Love Divine shall bear thee through.
Trust to that propitious gale,
Weigh thy anchor, spread thy sail.
Saints in glory, perfect made,
Wait thy passage through the shade;
Ardent for thy coming o'er,
See they throng the blissful shore.

6 Mount, their transports to improve;
Join the longing choir above;
Swiftly to their wish be given;
Kindle higher joy in heaven.
Such the prospects that arise
To the dying Christian's eyes!
Such the glorious vista faith
Opens through the shades of death!

Augustus M. Toplady, 1778.

976 1 Thess. iv. 18. *"Comfort . . . with these words."*

Tune PEOR. 10 10, 11 10. D.

1 OH! call it not death—it is life begun,
For the waters are passed, the home is won;
The ransomed spirit hath reached the shore
Where they weep, and suffer, and sin no more.
She is safe in her Father's house above,
In the place prepared by her Saviour's love;
To depart from a world of sin and strife,
And to be with Jesus—yes, this is life.

2 Oh! call it not death—'tis a holy sleep,
And the precious dust the Lord doth keep;
She shall wake again, and how satisfied!
With the likeness of Him for her who died.
As He rose again she shall also rise,
From the quiet bed where now safe she lies;
Then cheer ye, fond mourners, who sadly weep,
For happy are they who in Jesus sleep.

3 Oh! call it not death—'tis a glorious rest,
"Yea, saith the Spirit," for all such are blest:
"They rest from their labours," their work is done,
The goal is attained, the weary race run,
The battle is fought, the struggle is o'er,
The crown now replaces the cross they bore,
The pilgrimage path shall no more be trod,
A rest remains to the people of God.

E. E. H., 1834.

PEOR (Mount). [H. P. 242.]

KENT. [H. P. 63.]

977 Titus ii. 13. "*Looking for that blessed hope.*" Tune KENT. C. M. Or FARRANT.

1 'TIS sweet to think of those at rest,
Who sleep in Christ the Lord;
Whose spirits now with Him are blest,
According to His word.

2 They once were pilgrims here with us,
In Jesus now they sleep;
And we for them, while resting thus,
As hopeless cannot weep.

3 The Lord who died in triumph rose
Victorious o'er the tomb;
E'en so we know that, with Him, those
Who sleep in Him will come.

4 How bright the resurrection morn
On all the saints will break!
The Lord Himself will then return
His ransomed church to take.

5 The raised and living saints will meet,
All grief and care removed;
What joy 'twill be to us to greet
Each saint whom here we loved!

6 Our Lord Himself we then shall see,
Whose blood for us was shed;
With Him for ever we shall be,
Made like our glorious Head.

Samuel P. Tregelles, LL.D., 1846.

SAXONY. [H. P. 32.]

978 2 Cor. v. 10. "*We must all appear before the judgment-seat of Christ.*" Tune SAXONY. L. M.

1 OFT as the bell with solemn toll
Speaks the departure of a soul;
Let each one ask himself,—"Am I
Prepared, should I be called to die?"

2 Only this frail and fleeting breath
Preserves me from the jaws of death;
Soon as it fails, at once I'm gone,
And plunged into a world unknown.

3 Then, leaving all I love below,
To God's tribunal I must go;
Must hear the Judge pronounce my fate,
And fix my everlasting state.

4 Lord Jesus, help me now to flee,
And seek my hope alone in Thee;
Apply Thy blood, Thy Spirit give,
Subdue my sin, and let me live.

5 Then when the solemn bell I hear,
If saved from guilt, I need not fear;
Nor would the thought distressing be,—
"Perhaps it next may toll for me!"

6 My spirit rather would rejoice,
And long, and wish, to hear Thy voice;
Glad when it bids me earth resign,
Secure of heaven, if Thou art mine.

John Newton, 1774.

See Hymns 455--457.

CARMEL (Mount). [H. P. 69.]

(10) BURIAL.

979 Rev. xiv. 13. "*Blessed are the dead which die in the Lord.*"
Tune CARMEL. C. M.

1 HEAR what the voice from heaven proclaims,
For all the pious dead;
Sweet is the savour of their names,
And soft their sleeping bed.

2 They die in Jesus, and are blessed;
How kind their slumbers are!
From sufferings and from sins released,
And freed from every snare.

3 Far from this world of toil and strife,
They're present with the Lord;
The labours of their mortal life
End in a large reward.

Isaac Watts, D.D., 1709.

980 Ps. cxvi. 15. "*Precious in the sight of the Lord is the death of His saints.*"
Tune ST. BARNABAS. 6 5, 6 5. D.

1 LAY the precious body
In the quiet grave;
'Tis the Lord hath taken,
'Twas the Lord that gave:
Till the resurrection,
Lay the treasure by;
It will then awaken,
And go up on high!

2 Farewell, blessèd body,
Till the morn arise:
Welcome, happy spirit,
Into paradise!
No more work or weeping,
Gone for ever home;
In Christ's holy keeping
Rest until He come.

3 Here the casket lieth
  Waiting for repair;
There doth Christ the jewel
  In His bosom wear:
Wait a little season,
  And in Him shall be
Both again united
  Through eternity!

J. S. B. Monsell, LL.D., 1863.

981

1 Cor. xv. 42. "*Sown in corruption . . . raised in incorruption.*"

Tune MANNHEIM. 8 7, 8 7. D.

1 SONS of God by blest adoption!
  View the dead with faithful eyes:
What is sown thus in corruption
  Shall in incorruption rise.
What is sown in death's dishonour
  Shall revive to glory's light;
What is sown in this weak manner
  Shall be raised in matchless might.

2 Earthly cavern, to thy keeping
  We commit our brother's dust:
Keep it safely, softly sleeping,
  Till our Lord demand thy trust.
Sweetly sleep, dear saint, in Jesus;
  Thou, with us, shalt wake from death;
Hold he cannot, though he seize us,
  We his power defy by faith.

3 Jesus, Thy rich consolations
  To Thy mourning people send;
May we all, with faith and patience,
  Wait for our approaching end;
Keep from courage vain or vaunted;
  For our change our hearts prepare;
Give us confidence undaunted,
  Cheerful hope and godly fear!

Joseph Hart, 1762.

982

1 Thess. iv. 13. "*Ye sorrow not even as others which have no hope.*"

Tune EPAPHRODITUS. 13 11, 12 12.

1 THOU art gone to the grave! but we will not deplore thee,
  Though sorrows and darkness encompass the tomb:
Thy Saviour has passed through its portal before thee,
  And the lamp of His love is thy guide through the gloom!

2 Thou art gone to the grave! we no longer behold thee,
  Nor tread the rough paths of the world by thy side;
But the wide arms of mercy are spread to enfold thee,
  And sinners may die, for the Sinless has died!

3 Thou art gone to the grave! and, its mansion forsaking,
  Perchance thy weak spirit in fear lingered long;
But the mild rays of paradise beamed on thy waking,
  And the sound which thou heard'st was the seraphim's song!

4 Thou art gone to the grave! but we will not deplore thee,
  Whose God was thy Ransom, thy Guardian, and [Guide;
He gave thee, He took thee, and He will restore thee,
  And death has no sting, for the Saviour has died!

Bishop Heber, 1827.

ST. BRIDE. [H. P. 95.]

983 John xi. 25. "*Jesus said, I am the Resurrection, and the Life.*" Tune St. Bride. S. M.

1 We hear the tolling bell,
We see the bier and pall;
Bearers and mourners clothed in black;
The solemn funeral.

2 We see the open grave,
We hear the sobbing moan,
When earth to earth and dust to dust
Falls on the coffin thrown.

3 We hear the holy prayers,
We see the closèd ground,
Where naught appears to human eye,
Except a heaving mound.

4 But bearers robed in white
Appear not to our eyes;
The angels, wafting on their wings
The soul to paradise.

5 We do not see the souls
Which there enjoy repose,
And taste such bliss as here on earth
No heart of mortal knows.

6 We see not yet the joys,
Joys that the just await,
When they will stand with bodies raised,
Lord, at Thy palace gate.

7 Lift from our hearts the veil,
And help us by Thy light
To see the world unseen, and walk
By faith, and not by sight.

8 O gracious Lord, to Thee
We praise and glory give!
For Thou didst die and rise again,
That we might ever live.

9 O Death, where is thy sting?
Grave, where thy victory?
Death and the grave are now the path
To life that cannot die.

10 The Way, the Truth, the Life,
O mighty Lord, art Thou,
The Resurrection from the dead,
To Thee shall all things bow.

11 Then wherefore mourn for those
Who fall asleep in Thee?
They have begun to live the life
Of immortality.

12 Then praise we, praise the Lord,
The Father, and the Son,
And Holy Ghost, whose breath is Life,
Eternal Three in One.

Bishop Christopher Wordsworth, 1862.

See Hymns 245—247, 250, 259.

IV.—The Life to Come.

(1) THE FIRST RESURRECTION.

984 1 John iii. 2. "*We shall be like Him; for we shall see Him as He is.*"
Tune Havilah. 87, 87, 47.

HAVILAH. [H. P. 192.]

1 'Mid the splendours of the glory
Which we hope ere long to share;
Christ our Head, and we His members,
Shall appear, divinely fair.
Oh how glorious!
When we meet Him in the air.

2 From the dateless, timeless periods,
He has loved us without cause;
And for all His blood-bought myriads
His is love that knows no pause.
Matchless Lover!
Changeless as the' eternal laws.

3 Oh what gifts shall yet be granted,
Palms, and crowns, and robes of white,
When the hope for which we panted
Bursts upon our gladdened sight,
And our Saviour
Makes us glorious through His might.

4 Bright the prospect, soon that greets us,
Of that longed for nuptial day,
When our heavenly Bridegroom meets us
On His kingly conquering way;
In the glory,
Bride and Bridegroom reign for aye!

William Reid, D.D., 1863.

CHESALON (Mount). [H. P. 35.]

985

1 Cor. xv. 52. "*The trumpet shall sound.*"

Tune CHESALON. C. M.

1 HARK to the trump! behold it breaks
The sleep of ages now;
And lo! the light of glory shines
On many an aching brow.

2 Changed in a moment, raised to life,
The quick, the dead arise,
Responsive to the angel's voice,
That calls us to the skies.

3 Ascending through the crowded air,
On eagles' wings we soar,
To dwell in the full joy of love,
And sorrow there no more.

4 Undazzled by the glorious light
Of that belovèd Brow,
We see, without a single cloud,
We see the Saviour now.

5 O Lord! the bright and blessèd hope
That cheered us through the past,
Of full eternal rest in Thee,
Is all fulfilled at last.

6 The cry of sorrow here is hushed,
The voice of prayer is o'er;
'Tis needless now; for, Lord, we crave
Thy gracious help no more.

7 Praise, endless praise, alone becomes
This bright and blessèd place,
Where every eye beholds unveiled
The mysteries of grace.

8 Past conflict here, O Lord, 'tis ours,
Through everlasting days,
To sing our song of victory now,
And only live to praise.

Sir Edward Denny, 1846.

EASTHAM. [H. P. 351.]

986

Rom. viii. 18. "*The glory which shall be revealed in us.*"

Tune EASTHAM. 76, 86. D.

1 TEN thousand times ten thousand,
In sparkling raiment bright,
The armies of the ransomed saints
Throng up the steeps of light:
'Tis finished—all is finished,
Their fight with death and sin;
Fling open wide the golden gates,
And let the victors in.

2 What rush of Hallelujahs
Fills all the earth and sky!
What ringing of a thousand harps
Bespeaks the triumph nigh!
O day! for which creation
And all its tribes were made:
O joy! for all its former woes
A thousandfold repaid.

3 Oh then what raptured greetings
On Canaan's happy shore!
What knitting severed friendships up,
Where partings are no more.
Then eyes with joy shall sparkle,
That brimmed with tears of late:
No longer orphans fatherless,
Nor widows desolate.

[*Repeat verse* 1.]

Dean Alford, D.D., 1867.

MAMRE (Plain of). [H. P. 226.]

987 1 Cor. xv. 54. "*Death is swallowed up in victory.*"

Tune MAMRE. 88, 88, 88.

1 WE sing His love, who once was slain,
Who soon o'er death revived again,
That all His saints through Him might have
Eternal conquest o'er the grave.
Soon shall the trumpet sound, and we
Shall rise to immortality.

2 The saints who now in Jesus sleep
His own almighty power shall keep,
Till dawns the bright illustrious day,
When death itself shall die away.
Soon shall, etc.

3 How loud shall our glad voices sing,
When Christ His risen saints shall bring
From beds of dust and silent clay,
To realms of everlasting day!
Soon shall, etc.

4 When Jesus we in glory meet,
Our utmost joys shall be complete;
When landed on that heavenly shore,
Death and the curse will be no more!
Soon shall, etc.

Rowland Hill, 1796.

See Hymns 253, 254, 259.

(2) THE GENERAL RESURRECTION.

988 Rev. xi. 18. "*The time of the dead is come, that they should be judged.*"

Tune ALTORF. 87, 87, 887.

ALTORF; *or*, LUTHER'S HYMN. [H. P. 208.]

1 GREAT God, what do I see and hear,
The end of things created!
The Judge of mankind doth appear,
On clouds of glory seated.
The trumpet sounds, the graves restore
The dead which they contained before:
Prepare, my soul, to meet Him.

2 The dead in Christ shall first arise,
At the last trumpet's sounding,
Caught up to meet Him in the skies,
With joy their Lord surrounding.
No gloomy fears their souls dismay,
His presence sheds eternal day
On those prepared to meet Him.

3 But sinners, filled with guilty fears,
Behold His wrath prevailing;
For they shall rise, and find their tears
And sighs are unavailing:
The day of grace is past and gone,
Trembling, they stand before the throne,
All unprepared to meet Him.

4 Great God, what do I see and hear,
The end of things created!
The Judge of mankind doth appear,
On clouds of glory seated.
Beneath His cross I view the day
When heaven and earth shall pass away,
And thus prepare to meet Him.

B. Ringwaldt, 1550; *W. B. Collyer, D.D.,* 1812.

989 2 Thess. i. 8. "*In flaming fire taking vengeance.*"

Tune TEKOA. 87, 87, 47.

1 DAY of vengeance! loud resounding,
Hark! the thrilling trumpet's swell,
Peal on peal o'er earth rebounding,
Nature's universal knell,
Deeply echoing,
Bursts the bands of death and hell.

2 O'er the ruins of creation
See on high the Crucified,
'Mid the widening devastation,
On the wings of whirlwinds ride.
Man before Him
Bows the spirit of his pride.

TEKOA (Wilderness of). [H. P. 200.]

3 Lo! the dead in thronging numbers,
Awestruck at His stern command,
Springing from their iron slumbers,
Round the dread tribunal stand,
View with trembling
Judgment in His red right hand.

4 O Immanuel! spirit broken,
At Thy piercèd feet I lie:
What my hope? Behold that token!
See that blood-stained cross on high!
Glorious symbol,
Brightly beaming on my eye.

5 By Thy griefs on wild or mountain,
By Thine agonising groan,
By Thy life-spring's purple fountain,
By Thy dark sepulchral stone,
O Immanuel,
Save me, prostrate at Thy throne!

John A. Latrobe, 1825.

MOSCOW.—*Minor: ver.* 1, 2, 3. [H. P. 107.]

990

John v. 28, 29. "*All that are in the graves shall hear His voice, and shall come forth.*"

Tune Moscow. 664, 6664.

Ver. 1, 2, 3, *minor; ver.* 4 *to* 8 *major.*

1 HARK! 'tis the trump of God
Sounds through the realms abroad,
Time is no more.
Horrors invest the skies;
Graves burst, and myriads rise:
Nature, in agonies,
Yields up her store.

2 Changed in a moment's space,
Lo the affrighted race
Shriek and despair;
Now they attempt to flee,
Curse immortality,
And eye their misery
Dreadfully near.

3 Quick reels the bursting earth,
Rocked by a storm of wrath,
Hurled from her sphere.
Heartrending thunders roll,
Demons tormented howl:
Great God, support my soul,
Yielding to fear.

PART II.

4 O my Redeemer, come!
And through the fearful gloom
Brighten Thy way;
How would our souls arise,
Soar through the flaming skies,
Join the solemnities
Of this great day!

5 See! see! the' incarnate God
Swiftly emits abroad
Glories benign;
Lo! lo! He comes, He's here;
Angels and saints appear,
Fled is my every fear,
Jesus is mine.

Major: ver. 4 *to* 8.

6 High on a flaming throne
Rides the eternal Son,
Sovereign august!
Worlds from His presence fly,
Shrink at His majesty:
Stars, dashed along the sky,
Awfully burst.

7 Thousands of thousands wait
Round the judicial seat,
Glorified there;
Prostrate the elders fall,
Winged is my raptured soul,
High to the Judge of all,
Lo! I draw near.

8 O my approving God!
Washed in Thy precious blood,
Bold I advance;
Fearless we range along,
Join the triumphant throng,
Shout an ecstatic song
Through the expanse.

Admiral Kempenfelt, 1777.

991

Dan. xii. 13. "*Thou shalt rest, and stand in thy lot at the end of the days.*"

Tune Sihor. 77, 77, 77.

SIHOR (River). [H. P. 158.]

1 WHEN this passing world is done,
When has sunk yon glaring sun,
When we stand with Christ in glory,
Looking o'er life's finished story,
Then, Lord, shall I fully know,—
Not till then,—how much I owe.

2 When I hear the wicked call
On the rocks and hills to fall;
When I see them start and shrink,
On the fiery deluge brink;
Then, Lord, shall I fully know,—
Not till then,—how much I owe.

3 When I stand before the throne,
Dressed in beauty not my own;
When I see Thee as Thou art,
Love Thee with unsinning heart;
Then, Lord, shall I fully know,—
Not till then,—how much I owe.

4 When the praise of heaven I hear,
Loud as thunders to the ear,
Loud as many waters' noise,
Sweet as harp's melodious voice;
Then, Lord, shall I fully know,—
Not till then,—how much I owe.

5 Even on earth, as through a glass,
Darkly, let Thy glory pass;
Make forgiveness feel so sweet,
Make Thy Spirit's help so meet;
Even on earth, Lord, make me know
Something of how much I owe.

6 Chosen not for good in me,
Wakened up from wrath to flee,
Hidden in the Saviour's side,
By the Spirit sanctified!
Teach me, Lord, on earth to show,
By my love, how much I owe.

Robert Murray McCheyne, 1837.

See Hymns 301, 314.

PARAN (Wilderness of). [H. P. 241.]

(3) THE GREAT DAY OF JUDGMENT.

992

Luke xxi. 27. "*Then shall they see the Son of man coming in a cloud with power and great glory.*"

Tune Paran. 11 11, 11 11. Or Peor.

1 THE chariot! the chariot! its wheels roll on fire,
As the Lord cometh down in the pomp of His ire;
Self-moving, it drives on its pathway of cloud,
And the heavens with the burden of Godhead are bowed.

2 The glory! the glory! By myriads are poured
The hosts of the angels to wait on their Lord;
And the glorified saints, and the martyrs, are there,
And all who the palm wreath of victory wear.

3 The trumpet! the trumpet! The dead have all heard;
Lo! the depths of the stone-covered charnels are stirred;
From the sea, from the land, from the south and the north,
The vast generations of man are come forth.

4 The judgment! the judgment! the thrones are all set,
Where the Lamb and the white-vested elders are met;
All flesh is at once in the sight of the Lord,
And the doom of eternity hangs on His word.

5 O Saviour, Redeemer, look down from above,
O Father! on us, Thy own children, with love;
When beneath to their darkness the wicked are driven,
May our purified souls find a mansion in heaven.

Dean Henry Hart Milman, D.D., 1827.

993 Matt. xxv. 31. *"Then shall He sit upon the throne of His glory."*

Tune Paran. 11 11, 11 11. Or Peor.

1 THE throne of His glory! As snow it is white,
Upborne in the air by the legions of light;
And startled to life by the trumpet's last sound,
The hosts of the nations stand waiting around.

The throne of His glory! There lieth unsealed
The life roll, the death roll, of names ne'er revealed,
Now secret no longer; the millions divide,
To the right and the left, on the throne's either side.

3 The throne of His glory! And glorious there stand
The' elect of His love, and the sheep of His hand;
While dark on His left, shrunk away from His face,
The lost ones that sought not the throne of His grace.

4 The throne of His glory! My poor trembling soul,
Oh what, when arraigned there, thy dread shall control,
Of that doom of the exiled, "Ye cursèd, depart!"
For ever and ever to toll on the heart.

5 From thy Father an exile? Thy home never see?
No, child of His mercy, unchanging and free,
Ere creation begun, in the councils of love
He wrote thee an heir of His kingdom above.

W. A. Muhlenberg, D.D., 1839.

---

994 2 Tim. i. 18. *"The Lord grant unto him that he may find mercy of the Lord in that day."*

Tune Dies Iræ. 888.

DIES IRÆ. Part I. [H. P. 218.]

1 DAY of wrath, O day of mourning!
See the Crucified returning,
Heaven and earth in ashes burning!
Oh, what fear man's bosom rendeth,
When from heaven the Judge descendeth
On whose sentence all dependeth!

2 Wondrous sound the trumpet flingeth;
Through earth's sepulchres it ringeth;
All before the throne it bringeth.
Death is struck, and nature quaking:
All creation is awaking,
To its Judge an answer making.

3 Lo, the book exactly worded,
Wherein all hath been recorded:
Thence shall judgment be awarded.
When the Judge His seat attaineth,
And each hidden deed arraigneth,
Nothing unavenged remaineth.

4 What shall I, frail man, be pleading;
Who for me be interceding,
When the just are mercy needing?
King of Majesty tremendous,
Who dost free salvation send us,
Fount of pity, then befriend us.

Part II.

Part II.

5 Think, kind Jesu, my salvation
Caused Thy wondrous incarnation:
Leave me not to desolation:
Faint and weary, Thou hast sought me,
On the cross of suffering bought me;
Shall such grace be vainly brought me?

6 Righteous Judge, for sin's pollution
Grant Thy gift of absolution,
Ere that day of retribution.
Guilty, now I pour my moaning,
All my shame with anguish owning:
Spare, O God, Thy suppliant groaning.

7 Thou the sinful woman savedst;
Thou the dying thief forgavest;
And to me a hope vouchsafest.
Worthless are my prayers and sighing;
Yet, good Lord, in grace complying,
Rescue me from fires undying.

8 With Thy favoured sheep oh place me;
Nor among the goats abase me;
But to Thy right hand upraise me.
Low I kneel with heart submission:
See, like ashes, my contrition:
Save, oh! save me from perdition.

Part III.

9 Ah, that day of tears and mourning!
From the dust of earth returning,
Man for judgment must prepare him;
Spare, O God, in mercy spare him,
Lord, all pitying, Jesu blest,
Grant us Thine eternal rest. Amen.

Thomas of Celano, 1230; *William J. Irons, D.D. (tr.)*, 1848.

ZOHELETH (Stone of). [H. P. 207.]

995

John xiv. 3. "*I will come again.*"
Tune ZOHELETH. 87, 87, 887.

1 THE Lord of might, from Sinai's brow,
Gave forth His voice of thunder;
And Israel lay on earth below,
Outstretched in fear and wonder.
Beneath His feet was pitchy night,
And, at His left hand and His right,
The rocks were rent asunder.

2 The Lord of love, on Calvary,
A meek and suffering Stranger,
Upraised to heaven His languid eye,
In nature's hour of danger.
For us He bore the weight of woe,
For us He gave His blood to flow,
And met His Father's anger.

3 The Lord of love and Lord of might,
The King of all created,
Shall back return to claim His right,
On clouds of glory seated:
With trumpet sound and angel song,
And Hallelujahs loud and long
O'er death and hell defeated.

Bishop Heber, 1827.

996

Jude 6. "*The judgment of the great day.*"
Tune CIVITAS REGIS. 87, 87, 47. Or TEKOA.

CIVITAS REGIS MAGNI. [H. P. 301.]

1 DAY of judgment, day of wonders!
Hark! the trumpet's awful sound,
Louder than a thousand thunders,
Shakes the vast creation round:
How the summons
Will the sinner's heart confound!

2 See the Judge, our nature wearing,
Clothed in majesty Divine!
Ye who long for His appearing
Then shall say, "This God is mine!"
Gracious Saviour,
Own me in that day for Thine.

3 At His call the dead awaken,
Rise to life from earth and sea;
All the powers of nature, shaken
By His looks, prepare to flee:
Careless sinner!
What will then become of thee?

4 But to those who have confessèd,
Loved and served the Lord below,
He will say, "Come near, ye blessèd!
See the kingdom I bestow:
You for ever
Shall My love and glory know."

John Newton, 1774.

SAXONY. [H. P. 32.]

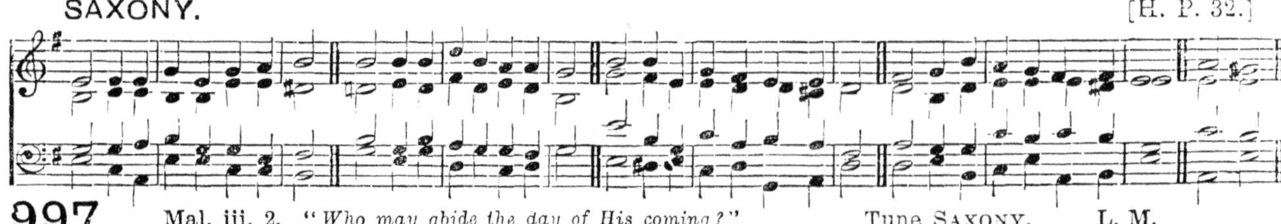

997

Mal. iii. 2. "*Who may abide the day of His coming?*" Tune SAXONY. L. M.

1 THAT day of wrath, that dreadful day,
When heaven and earth shall pass away;
What power shall be the sinner's stay?
How shall he meet that dreadful day?

2 When, shivering like a parchèd scroll,
The flaming heavens together roll;
When, louder yet, and yet more dread,
Swells the high trump that wakes the dead!

3 Oh, on that day, that wrathful day,
When man to judgment wakes from clay,
Be Thou the trembling sinner's stay,
Though heaven and earth shall pass away.

Sir Walter Scott, 1805.

SILOAM (Pool of). [H. P. 153.]

998 Luke xxi. 25. "*There shall be signs.*" Tune SILOAM. 77, 77.

1 IN the sun, and moon, and stars,
Signs and wonders there shall be:
Earth shall quake with inward wars,
Nations with perplexity.

2 Soon shall ocean's hoary deep
Tossed with stronger tempests rise;
Darker storms the mountains sweep,
Fiercer lightnings rend the skies.

3 Evil thoughts shall shake the proud,
Racking doubt, and restless fear;
And amid the thunder cloud
Shall the Judge of men appear.

4 But, though from that awful face
Heaven shall fade and earth shall fly,
Fear not ye, His chosen race,
Your redemption draweth nigh.

Bishop Heber, 1811.

ST. BRIDE. [H. P. 95.]

999 Joel ii. 1. "*The day of the Lord cometh.*" Tune ST. BRIDE. S. M.

1 AND will the Judge descend?
And must the dead arise?
And not a single soul escape
His all-discerning eyes?

2 How will my heart endure
The terrors of that day,
When earth and heaven before His face
Astonished shrink away?

3 But ere the trumpet shake
The mansions of the dead;
Hark! from the gospel's cheering sound,
What joyful tidings spread.

4 Ye sinners, seek His grace,
Whose wrath ye cannot bear;
Fly to the shelter of His cross,
And find salvation there.

Philip Doddridge, D.D., 1755.

See Hymns 296, 301, 314, 316, 318.

(4) THE STATE OF THE LOST—HELL. THE SECOND DEATH.

1000 Rev. xx. 14. "*This is the second death.*" Tune ST. BRIDE. S. M. Or ARMAGEDDON.

1 OH, where shall rest be found?
Rest for the weary soul?
'Twere vain the ocean's depths to sound,
Or pierce to either pole.

2 Beyond this vale of tears
There is a life above,
Unmeasured by the flight of years;
And all that life is love.

3 There is a death whose pang
Outlasts the fleeting breath;
Oh, what eternal horrors hang
Around "the second death!"

4 Lord God of truth and grace,
Teach us that death to shun;
Lest we be banished from Thy face,
And evermore undone.

5 Here would we end our quest;
Alone are found in Thee,
The life of perfect love,—the rest
Of immortality.

James Montgomery, 1819.

See Hymns 1020, 1021.

GOLDBACH. (PART I.) [H. P. 130.]

(5) THE NEW JERUSALEM.

1001 Rev. xxi. 10. "*That great city, the holy Jerusalem.*"

PART I. (*Introductory.*) Tune GOLDBACH. 76, 76. D. Or GOLDSTERN.

1 THE world is very evil;
The times are waxing late:
Be sober and keep vigil;
The Judge is at the gate:
The Judge that comes in mercy,
The Judge that comes with might,
To terminate the evil,
To diadem the right.

2 Arise, arise, good Christian,
Let right to wrong succeed;
Let penitential sorrow
To heavenly gladness lead;
To light that hath no evening,
That knows nor moon nor sun,
The light so new and golden,
The light that is but one.

3 And when the Sole-Begotten
Shall render up once more
The kingdom to the Father
Whose own it was before,—
Then glory yet unheard of
Shall shed abroad its ray,
Resolving all enigmas,
An endless Sabbath day.

386 SONGS OF GRACE AND GLORY.

Part II.—ST. ALPHEGE. [H. P. 275.]

Part II.

4 Brief life is *here* our portion,
Brief sorrow, short-lived care;
The life that knows no ending,
The tearless life, is *there*.
O happy retribution!
Short toil, eternal rest;
For mortals and for sinners
A mansion with the blest!

5 And now we fight the battle,
But then shall wear the crown
Of full and everlasting
And passionless renown:
And now we watch and struggle,
And now we live in hope,
And Zion, in her anguish,
With Babylon must cope:

6 For He whom now we trust in
Shall then be seen and known,
And they that know and see Him
Shall have Him for their own.
With light that hath no evening,
And health that hath no sore,
And life that hath no ending,
But lasteth evermore.

7 The morning shall awaken,
The shadows shall decay,
And each true-hearted servant
Shall shine as doth the day:
Yes! God our King and portion,
In fulness of His grace,
We then shall see for ever,
And worship face to face.

Part III.—MAHANAIM. [H. P. 129.]

Part III.

8 For thee, O dear, dear country,
Mine eyes their vigils keep;
For very love, beholding
Thy happy name, they weep:
The mention of thy glory
Is unction to the breast,
And medicine in sickness,
And love, and life, and rest.

9 O one, O only mansion!
O paradise of joy!
Where tears are ever banished,
And smiles have no alloy.
Upon the Rock of Ages
They raise thy holy tower:
Thine is the victor's laurel,
And thine the golden dower.

10 Thine ageless walls are bonded
With amethyst unpriced:
Thy saints build up its fabric,
And the corner-stone is Christ.
The cross is all thy splendour,
The Crucified thy praise:
His laud and benediction
Thy ransomed people raise:

11 Jesus, the Gem of Beauty,
True God and man, they sing:
The never-failing Garden,
The ever-golden Ring: [band,
The Door, the Pledge, the Hus-
The Guardian of His court:
The Day-star of Salvation,
The Porter and the Port.

Part IV.—ZOAN I. (Field of.) [H. P. 127.]

Part IV.

12 Jerusalem the golden,
With milk and honey blest,
Beneath thy contemplation
Sink heart and voice oppressed:
I know not, oh I know not
What joys await us there;
What radiancy of glory,
What light beyond compare!

13 They stand, those halls of Zion,
All jubilant with song,

And bright with many an angel,
And all the martyr throng:
And they who, with their Leader,
Have conquered in the fight
For ever and for ever
Are clad in robes of white!

14 Jerusalem the glorious!
The home of God's elect!
O dear and future vision
That eager hearts expect:
Even now by faith I see thee:
Even here thy walls discern:
To thee my thoughts are kindled,
And strive and pant and yearn.

15 Jerusalem exulting
On that securest shore,—
I hope thee, wish thee, sing thee,
And love thee evermore!
Exult, O dust and ashes!
The Lord shall be thy part:
His only, His for ever,
Thou shalt be, and thou art!

Bernard de Morlaix, 1140; *J. M. Neale, D.D.* (tr.), 1851.

1002 Heb. xii. 22. "*The heavenly Jerusalem.*"

Tune St. Chrysostom. C. M. Or Nayland.

ST. CHRYSOSTOM. [H. P. 53.]

1 JERUSALEM! my happy home!
Name ever dear to me;
When shall my labours have an end,
In joy, and peace, and thee?

2 When shall these eyes thy heaven-built walls
And pearly gates behold?
Thy bulwarks with salvation strong,
And streets of shining gold?

3 Oh when, thou city of my God,
Shall I thy courts ascend,
Where congregations ne'er break up,
And sabbaths have no end?

4 Apostles, martyrs, prophets there
Around my Saviour stand;
And soon my friends in Christ below
Will join the glorious band.

5 Jesus, my Saviour, dwells therein
In glorious majesty;
And Him, through every stormy scene,
I onward press to see.

6 Jerusalem, my happy home!
My soul still pants for thee;
Then shall my labours have an end,
When I thy joys shall see.

Francis Baker, 1576; *D. Dickson*, 1660; *W. Burkitt*, 1693.

KADESH. [H. P. 159.]

(6) THE NEW HEAVENS AND NEW EARTH.

1003 2 Pet. iii. 13. "*We, according to His promise, look for new heavens and a new earth.*"

Tune Kadesh. 77, 77. D.

1 THEN it burst, the glorious view,
In the Spirit as I lay;
Heavens and earth created new,
For the first were passed away:
Sea was none, with billowy roar
Severing shore from kindred shore:
But, refulgent as a bride
For her husband beautified,

2 Forth from heaven and God descending,
Lo! the Holy City came,
Glories past expression blending,
New Jerusalem her name;
Hark! a voice from heaven,—"Our God
Plants with men His blest abode;
They His hallowed people; He,
He their present God shall be.

3 "God's own hand from all their eyes
Wipes for ever every tear;
Death is dead—no more to rise;
Pain and sorrow disappear."
Hark! He speaks—the First, the Last!
See! the whole creation past!
A new universe begun!
Write the changeless truth—'tis done.

Thomas Grinfield, 1836.

WINCHESTER. [H. P. 46.]

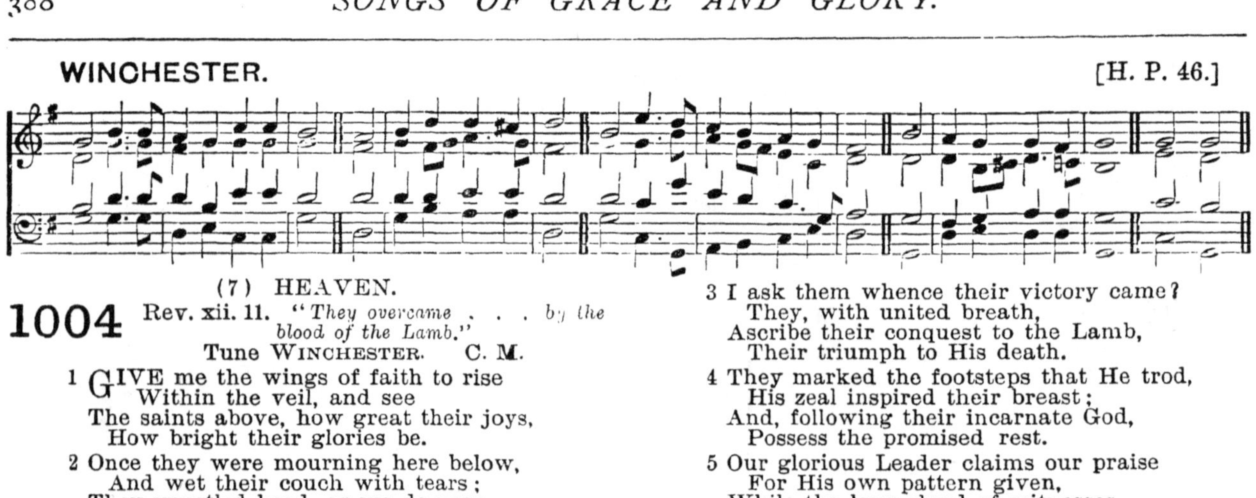

(7) HEAVEN.

1004 Rev. xii. 11. "*They overcame . . . by the blood of the Lamb.*"
Tune WINCHESTER. C. M.

1 GIVE me the wings of faith to rise
Within the veil, and see
The saints above, how great their joys,
How bright their glories be.

2 Once they were mourning here below,
And wet their couch with tears;
They wrestled hard, as we do now,
With sins and doubts and fears.

3 I ask them whence their victory came?
They, with united breath,
Ascribe their conquest to the Lamb,
Their triumph to His death.

4 They marked the footsteps that He trod,
His zeal inspired their breast;
And, following their incarnate God,
Possess the promised rest.

5 Our glorious Leader claims our praise
For His own pattern given,
While the long cloud of witnesses
Show the same path to heaven.

Isaac Watts, D.D., 1709.

PHILEMON. [H. P. 223.]

1005 Rev. v. 11. "*I heard the voice of many angels.*" Tune PHILEMON. 8 8 8, 7.

1 ANGEL voices sweetly singing,
Echoes through the blue dome ringing,
News of wondrous gladness bringing;
Ah, 'tis heaven! 'tis heaven at last!

2 Sin for ever left behind us,
Earthly visions cease to blind us,
Fleshly fetters cease to bind us;
Ah, 'tis heaven at last!

3 On the jasper threshold standing,
Like a pilgrim safely landing,
See the strange bright scene expanding!
Ah, 'tis heaven at last!

4 What a city! what a glory!
Far beyond the brightest story
Of the ages old and hoary;
Ah, 'tis heaven at last!

5 Softest voices, silver pealing,
Freshest fragrance, spirit healing,
Happy hymns around us stealing;
Ah, 'tis heaven at last!

6 Not a broken blossom yonder,
Not a link can snap asunder,
Stayed the tempest, sheathed the thunder;
Ah, 'tis heaven at last!

7 Not a tear-drop ever falleth,
Not a pleasure ever palleth,
Song to song for ever calleth;
Ah, 'tis heaven at last!

8 Christ Himself the living Splendour,
Christ the Sunlight mild and tender;
Praises to the Lamb we render,
Ah, 'tis heaven at last!

9 Now at length the veil is rended,
Now the pilgrimage is ended,
And the saints their thrones ascended;
Ah, 'tis heaven at last!

10 Broken death's dread bands that bound us,
Life and victory around us;
Christ, the King, Himself hath crowned us;
Ah, 'tis heaven at last!

Horatius Bonar, D.D., 1861.

KENT. [H. P. 63.]

1006 John xiv. 1, 2. "*Let not your heart be troubled, . . . in My Father's house are many mansions.*"
Tune KENT. C. M.

1 WHEN I can read my title clear
To mansions in the skies,
I bid farewell to every fear,
And wipe my weeping eyes.

2 Should earth against my soul engage,
And hellish darts be hurled,
Then I can smile at Satan's rage,
And face a frowning world.

3 Let cares like a wild deluge come,
And storms of sorrow fall,
May I but safely reach my home,
My God, my heaven, my all!

4 Then shall I bathe my weary soul
In seas of heavenly rest,
And not a wave of trouble roll
Across my peaceful breast.

Isaac Watts, D.D., 1709.

CRASSELIUS; *or*, WINCHESTER NEW. [H. P. 3.]

1007

Heb. xiii. 14. *"Here have we no continuing city."*

Tune CRASSELIUS. L. M.

1 "WE 've no abiding city here,"
This may distress the worldling's mind;
But should not cost the saint a tear,
Who hopes a better rest to find.

2 "We 've no abiding city here,"
Then let us live as pilgrims do;
Let not the world our rest appear,
But let us haste from all below.

3 "We 've no abiding city here,"
We seek a city out of sight,
Zion its name, the Lord is there,
It shines with everlasting light.

4 O sweet abode of peace and love,
Where pilgrims freed from toil are blest!
Had I the pinions of the dove,
I 'd fly to thee and be at rest.

5 But hush, my soul, nor dare repine;
The time my God appoints is best:
While here, to do His will be mine;
And His to fix my time of rest.

Thomas Kelly, 1804.

SWABIA. [H. P. 82.]

1008

1 Thess. iv. 17. *"So shall we ever be with the Lord."*

Tune SWABIA. S. M.

1 "FOR ever with the Lord,"
Amen, so let it be!
Life from the dead is in that word;
'Tis immortality!

2 Here in the body pent,
Absent from Him I roam;
Yet nightly pitch my moving tent
A day's march nearer home.

3 My Father's house on high,
Home of my soul! how near,
At times, to faith's foreseeing eye,
Thy golden gates appear!

4 Ah! then my spirit faints
To reach the land I love,
The bright inheritance of saints,
Jerusalem above!

5 "For ever with the Lord!"
Father, if 'tis Thy will,
The promise of that faithful word
Even here to me fulfil.

6 Be Thou at my right hand,
Then can I never fail;
Uphold Thou me, and I shall stand,
Fight, and I must prevail.

7 That resurrection word,
That shout of victory;
Once more, "For ever with the Lord!"
Amen, so let it be!

James Montgomery, 1835.

1009

Heb. xi. 16. *"They desire a better country."*

Tune SWABIA, repeating the last line, with Hallelujah from LUBECK. S. M.

1 FROM Egypt lately come,
Where death and darkness reign,
We seek our new, our better home,
Where we our rest shall gain.
Hallelujah!
We are on our way to God.

2 To Canaan's sacred bound
We haste with songs of joy;
Where peace and liberty are found,
And sweets that never cloy.
Hallelujah, etc.

3 Our toils and conflicts cease
On Canaan's happy shore;
We there shall dwell in endless peace,
And never hunger more.
Hallelujah, etc.

4 But hark! those distant sounds
That strike our listening ears;
They come from Canaan's happy bounds,
Where God our King appears.
Hallelujah, etc.

5 There, in celestial strains,
Enraptured myriads sing;
There, love in every bosom reigns,
For God Himself is King.
Hallelujah, etc.

6 We soon shall join the throng;
Their pleasures we shall share,
And sing the everlasting song,
With all the ransomed there.
Hallelujah, etc.

Thomas Kelly, 1812.

Hal - le - lu - jah, Hal - le - lu - jah! We are on our way to God.

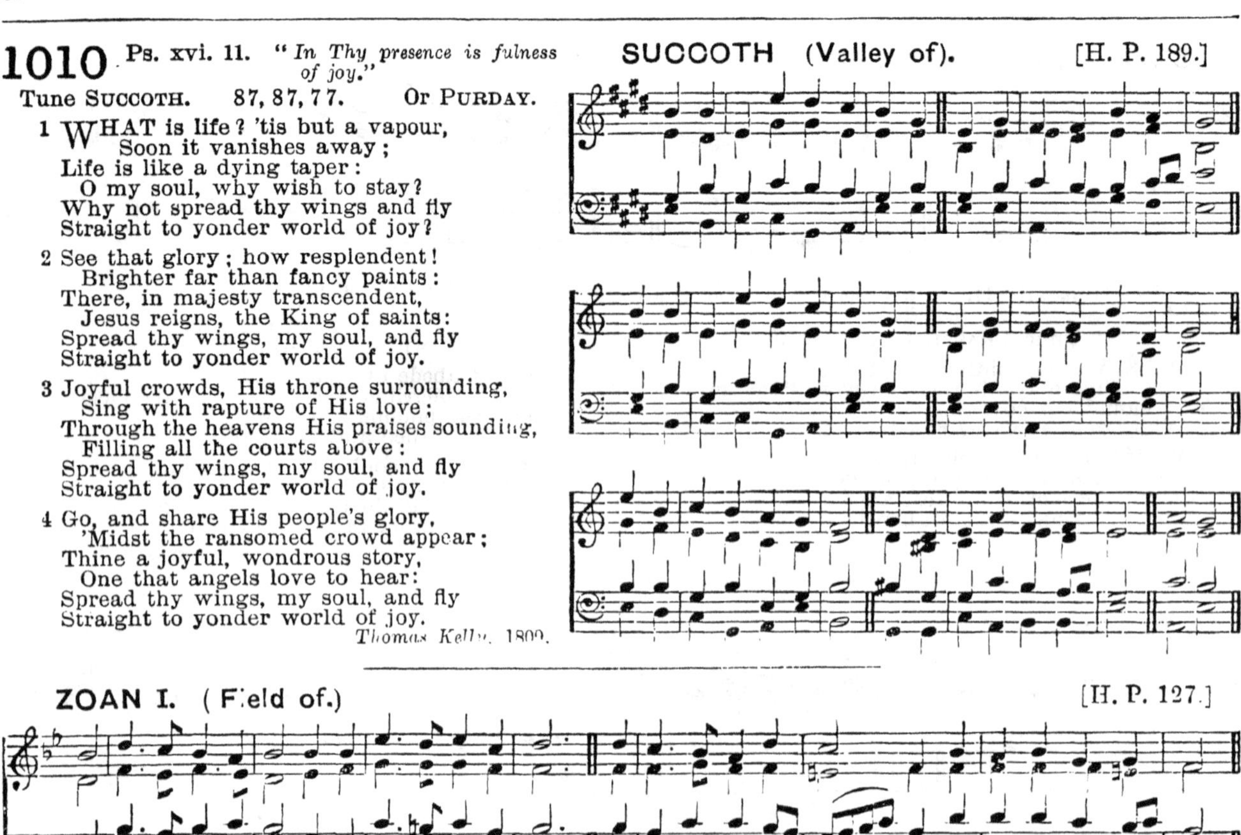

1010 Ps. xvi. 11. *"In Thy presence is fulness of joy."*

Tune SUCCOTH. 87, 87, 77. Or PURDAY.

1 WHAT is life? 'tis but a vapour,
Soon it vanishes away;
Life is like a dying taper:
O my soul, why wish to stay?
Why not spread thy wings and fly
Straight to yonder world of joy?

2 See that glory; how resplendent!
Brighter far than fancy paints:
There, in majesty transcendent,
Jesus reigns, the King of saints:
Spread thy wings, my soul, and fly
Straight to yonder world of joy.

3 Joyful crowds, His throne surrounding,
Sing with rapture of His love;
Through the heavens His praises sounding,
Filling all the courts above:
Spread thy wings, my soul, and fly
Straight to yonder world of joy.

4 Go, and share His people's glory,
'Midst the ransomed crowd appear;
Thine a joyful, wondrous story,
One that angels love to hear:
Spread thy wings, my soul, and fly
Straight to yonder world of joy.

Thomas Kelly, 1809.

ZOAN I. (Field of.) [H. P. 127.]

1011 Heb. ii. 10. *"Bringing many sons unto glory."*

Tune ZOAN I. 76, 76. D. Or GOSHEN.

1 I GO from grief and sighing, the valley and the clod,
To join the chosen people, in the palace-halls of God;
There sounds no cry of battle amid the shadowing palms,
But mighty songs of victory and glorious golden psalms.

2 The army of the conquerors, a palm in every hand,
In robes of state and splendour, in rest eternal stand:
Those marriage robes of glory, the righteousness of God,
He bought them for His people with His most precious blood.

3 The Lamb of God has led them from hell's deep sea of fire,
The Lamb of God adorns them in spotless white attire:
The Lamb of God presents them as kings in crowns of light,
As priests in God's own temple, to serve Him day and night.

4 Salvation, strength, and wisdom, to Him whose works and ways
Are wonderful and glorious, eternal in His praise:
The Lamb who died and liveth, alive for evermore,
The Saviour who redeemed us, for ever we adore.

John Heerman, 1647; (tr.) Frances Bevan, 1854.

1012 Ps. xvii. 15. *"I shall be satisfied."*

Tune ARMAGEDDON. S. M.

1 I HAVE a home above,
From sin and sorrow free;
A mansion which eternal love
Designed and formed for me:
My Father's gracious hand
Has built this sweet abode;
From everlasting it was planned,
My dwelling-place with God.

2 My Saviour's precious blood
Has made my title sure;
He passed through death's dark raging flood,
To make my rest secure.
The Comforter is come,
The earnest has been given;
He leads me onward to the home
Reserved for me in heaven.

ARMAGEDDON (Valley of). [H. P. 90.]

3 Bright angels guard my way;
His ministers of power,
Encamping round me night and day,
Preserve in danger's hour.
Loved ones are gone before,
Whose pilgrim days are done;
I soon shall greet them on that shore,
Where partings are unknown.

4 But more than all, I long
His glories to behold,
Whose smile fills all that radiant throng
With ecstasy untold:
That bright, yet tender smile,
My sweetest welcome there,
Shall cheer me through the "little while"
I tarry for Him here.

5 Thy love, Thou precious Lord,
My joy and strength shall be;
Till Thou shalt speak the gladdening word
That bids me rise to Thee;
And then, through endless days,
Where all Thy glories shine,
In happier, holier strains I 'll praise
The grace that made me Thine.

Henry Bennett, 1851.

MAHANAIM. [H. P. 129.]

1013

Isa. xxxiii. 17. "*Thine eyes shall see the King in His beauty: they shall behold the land that is very far off.*"

Tune MAHANAIM. 76, 76. D. Or GOLDBACH.

1 THE sands of time are sinking,
The dawn of heaven breaks,
The summer morn I've sighed for,
The fair sweet morn awakes.
Dark, dark hath been the midnight,
But dayspring is at hand,
And glory, glory dwelleth
In Immanuel's land.

2 There the red Rose of Sharon
Unfolds its heartsome bloom,
And fills the air of heaven
With ravishing perfume.
Oh to behold it blossom,
While by its fragrance fanned,
Where glory, glory dwelleth
In Immanuel's land.

3 The King there in His beauty
Without a veil is seen:
It were a well-spent journey
Though seven deaths lay between.
The Lamb, with His fair army,
Doth on mount Zion stand,
And glory, glory dwelleth
In Immanuel's land.

PART II.

4 Oh! Christ He is the fountain,
The deep sweet well of love!
The streams on earth I 've tasted,
More deep I 'll drink above;
There, to an ocean fulness,
His mercy doth expand,
And glory, glory dwelleth
In Immanuel's land.

5 Oh! I am my Belovèd's,
And my Beloved is mine!
He brings a poor vile sinner
Into His "house of wine";
I stand upon His merit,
I know no safer stand,
Not e'en where glory dwelleth
In Immanuel's land.

6 I shall sleep sound in Jesus,
Filled with His likeness rise
To live and to adore Him,
To see Him with these eyes.
My kingly King, at His white throne,
My presence doth command,
Where glory, glory dwelleth
In Immanuel's land.

7 The bride eyes not her garment,
But her dear bridegroom's face;
I will not gaze at glory,
But on my King of Grace;
Not at the crown He gifteth,
But on His piercèd hand;—
The Lamb is all the glory
Of Immanuel's land.

Ann Ross Cousins, 1857.

MAGDEBURG. [H. P. 300.]

1014

Rev. v. 12. "*Worthy is the Lamb that was slain.*" Tune MAGDEBURG. 87, 87, 47.

1 SAINTS, exalted high in glory,
Round the throne a sacred throng,
Make redemption's wondrous story
Still the burden of their song:
Ever praising Him who was for sinners slain.

2 Rebels, now received to favour,
Robed in merit not their own,
There, as priests, present a savour
Of sweet incense at the throne:
Ever praising Him who was for sinners slain.

3 Kings do service at the altar,
Never ceasing night nor day,
From redemption's wondrous psalter
Choosing their melodious lay:
Ever praising Him who was for sinners slain.

4 Pilgrims there no longer tarry,
Waiting for the morning light:
They have ceased the cross to carry:
They have ceased to toil and fight:
Ever praising Him who was for sinners slain.

James Gabb, 1870.

GOSHEN. [H. P. 125.]

1015

Isa. xxxiii. 17. "*Thine eyes shall see the King in His beauty.*" Tune GOSHEN. 76, 76.

1 OH, for the robes of whiteness!
Oh, for the tearless eyes!
Oh, for the glorious brightness
Of the unclouded skies!

2 Oh, for the no more weeping
Within that land of love,
The endless joy of keeping
The bridal feast above!

3 Oh, for the bliss of flying,
My risen Lord to meet!
Oh, for the rest of lying
For ever at His feet!

4 Oh, for the hour of seeing
My Saviour face to face!
The hope of ever being
In that sweet meeting-place!

5 Jesus! Thou King of Glory,
I soon shall dwell with Thee;
I soon shall sing the story
Of Thy great love to me.

6 Meanwhile, my thoughts shall enter
E'en now before Thy throne,
That all my love may centre
In Thee, and Thee alone.

Charitie Lees Smith, 1860.

LUBECK. [H. P. 139.]

1016

Rev. vii. 9. "*White robes, and palms in their hands.*" Tune LUBECK. 77, 77. Or PISGAH.

1 PALMS of glory, raiment bright,
Crowns that never fade away,
Gird and deck the saints in light;
Priests, and kings, and conquerors they.

2 Yet the conquerors bring their palms
To the Lamb amidst the throne,
And proclaim in joyful psalms
Victory through His cross alone.

3 Kings for harps their crowns resign,
Crying, as they strike the chords,
"Take the kingdom, it is Thine,
King of kings, and Lord of lords!"

4 Round the altar priests confess,
If their robes are white as snow,
'Twas the Saviour's righteousness
And His blood that made them so.

5 Who were these? on earth they dwelt;
Sinners once of Adam's race;
Guilt and fear and suffering felt;
But were saved by sovereign grace.

6 They were mortal, too, like us:
Ah! when we, like them, must die,
May our souls, translated thus,
Triumph, reign, and shine on high!

James Montgomery, 1829.

1017

Isa. xxxv. 9. "*The redeemed shall walk there.*" Tune ARISTARCHUS. 88, 88.

1 WE speak of the realms of the blest,
That country so bright and so fair;
And oft are its glories confessed;
But what must it be to be there?

2 We speak of its pathways of gold,
Its walls decked with jewels most rare,
Its wonders and pleasures untold;
But what must it be to be there?

ARISTARCHUS. [H. P. 224.]

3 We speak of its freedom from sin,
From sorrow, temptation, and care,
From trials without and within;
But what must it be to be there?

4 We speak of its anthems of praise,
With which we can never compare
The sweetest on earth we can raise;
But what must it be to be there?

5 We speak of its service of love,
The robes which the glorified wear,
The church of the first-born above;
But what must it be to be there?

6 Do Thou, Lord, 'midst pleasure or woe,
For heaven our spirits prepare;
And shortly we also shall know
And feel what it is to be there.

Elizabeth Mills, 1829.

1018 Rev. xxi. 23. "*The Lamb is the light thereof.*"

Tune SHEBA. 66, 66. D.

SHEBA. [H. P. 117.]

1 THERE is a blessèd home
Beyond this land of woe,
Where trials never come,
Nor tears of sorrow flow;
Where faith is lost in sight,
And patient hope is crowned,
And everlasting light
Its glory throws around.

2 There is a land of peace,
Good angels know it well;
Glad songs that never cease
Within its portals swell;
Around its glorious throne
Ten thousand saints adore
Christ, with the Father One,
And Spirit, evermore.

3 Oh, joy all joys beyond,
To see the Lamb who died
And count each sacred wound
In hands, and feet, and side;
To give to Him the praise
Of every triumph won,
And sing through endless days
The great things He hath done!

4 Look up, ye saints of God,
Nor fear to tread below
The path your Saviour trod
Of daily toil and woe;
Wait but a little while
In uncomplaining love,
His own most gracious smile
Shall welcome you above.

Rev. Sir H. W. Baker, 1861.

See Hymns 437—440, 1094.

THEME XI. — Eternity.

(1) THE MEDIATORIAL KINGDOM DELIVERED UP TO THE FATHER.

1019 Rev. xix. 6. "*Alleluia . . the Lord God reigneth.*"

Tune PISGAH. 77, 77.

PISGAH (Mount). [H. P. 137.]

1 HARK! the song of Jubilee,
Loud as mighty thunders roar,
Or the fulness of the sea,
When it breaks upon the shore.

2 Hallelujah! for the Lord
God omnipotent shall reign;
Hallelujah! let the word
Echo round the earth and main.

3 Hallelujah! Hark! the sound,
From the centre to the skies,
Wakes above, beneath, around,
All creation's harmonies.

4 See Jehovah's banner furled,
Sheathed His sword: He speaks—'tis done,
And the kingdoms of this world
Are the kingdoms of His Son.

5 He shall reign from pole to pole,
With illimitable sway;
He shall reign when like a scroll
Yonder heavens have passed away:

6 Then the end; beneath His rod
Man's last enemy shall fall;
Hallelujah! Christ in God,
God in Christ, is all in all.

Hal-le-lu-jah, Hal-le-lu-jah!

James Montgomery, 1819. (*a.*)

SAXONY. [H. P. 32.]

(2) THE SOLEMNITIES OF ETERNITY.

1020 Matt. xxv. 46. "*Everlasting punishment . . . life eternal.*" Tune SAXONY. L. M.

1 ETERNITY! eternity!
That boundless, soundless, tideless sea,
Of mysteries the mystery;
What is eternity to me?

2 Infinite bliss or misery,
Woe past, woe present, woe to be,
Or fulness of felicity;
These are eternity to me.

3 Two voices from eternity!
A voice from heaven comes down to me,
A voice from hell breaks dolefully,
"Life, Death, O man! are offered thee."

4 The' abyss is moved; even Wrath cries "Flee!"
The height expands, and Love cries "See,
What God hath here prepared for thee:
Choose thou thine own eternity!"

James Montgomery, 1853.

1021 Isa. lvii. 15. "*The high and lofty One that inhabiteth eternity.*"

Tune ALTORF. 88, 88, 888.

ALTORF; *or*, LUTHER'S HYMN. [H. P. 208.]

1 ETERNITY, eternity!
How vast, how near eternity!
The haven where the soul hath rest,
In God Himself for ever blest,
Unbroken rest, unfading day;
O wondrous world without decay!
Now ponder well eternity.

2 Eternity, eternity!
O drear and dark eternity
To all who God's great mercy scorn!
Ah, better had they ne'er been born,
Who live to spurn the saving Name
By which our great redemption came,
Nor ponder well eternity.

3 Eternity, eternity!
O bright, O blest eternity,
Which Jesus has obtained for those
Who seek in Him their sure repose!
A little while they suffer here,
But rest, eternal rest, is near.
Oh, ponder well eternity.

4 Eternity, eternity!
Strange glories of eternity!
Lord, let us now the world despise,
And upward raise our thankful eyes
To joy that ever shall abide,
From sin and sorrow purified,
And ponder well eternity.

5 Eternity, eternity!
Prepare us for eternity.
Grant us, great Lord, the humble mind,
To all the Father's will resigned:
Give faith and hope to look above,
And fill us with Thy perfect love
In time and through eternity.

Daniel Wülffer, 1660; *F. E. Cox (tr).*, 1841.

---

(3) THE PRAISES OF ETERNITY.

1022 Ps. cxlv. 2. "*I will praise Thy name for ever and ever.*"

Tune, Hymn Chant ST. BOTOLPH. Or ST. DUNSTAN. 10 10, 7.

ST. BOTOLPH. [H. P. 352.]
For Verses 1, 2, 3.

1 SING Alleluia forth in | duteous praise,
O citizens of heaven, and | sweetly raise
An endless Alleluia!

2 Ye next, who stand before the' | Eternal Light,
In hymning choirs re-echo | to the height
An endless Alleluia!

3 The Holy City shall take | up your strain,
And with glad songs resounding | wake again
An endless Alleluia!

For Verses 4, 5.

4 Ye who have gained your palms at | length in bliss,
Victorious ones, your | chant shall still be this,
An endless Alleluia!

5 There, in one grand acclaim, for | ever ring
The strains which tell the | honour of your King,
An endless Alleluia!

For Verse 6.

6 This is the rest for weary | ones brought back,
This is the food and drink which | none shall lack,
An endless Alleluia!

For Verses 7, 8.

7 While Thee, by whom were all things | made, we praise
For ever, and tell out in | sweetest lays
An endless Alleluia!

8 To Thee, Almighty Christ, our | voices sing
Glory for evermore; to | Thee we bring
An endless Alleluia!

John Ellerton, 1867.

ST. DUNSTAN. [H. P. 353.]

CHURCH TRIUMPHANT. [H. P. 258.]

1023

Rev. v. 13. "*Blessing, and honour, and glory, and power, be unto Him that sitteth upon the throne, and unto the Lamb for ever and ever.*"

Tune Church Triumphant. L. M.

1 THE countless multitude on high,
Who tune their songs to Jesus' name,
All merit of their own deny,
And Jesus' worth alone proclaim.

2 Firm on the ground of sovereign grace
They stand before Jehovah's throne;
The new song in that blessèd place
Is, "Thou art worthy, Thou alone!"

3 With spotless robes of purest white,
And branches of triumphal palm,
They shout, with transports of delight,
Heaven's ceaseless, universal psalm:

4 "Salvation's glory all be paid
To Him who sits upon the throne,
And to the Lamb whose blood was shed;
Thou, Thou art worthy, Thou alone;

5 For Thou wast slain, and in Thy blood
These robes were washed so spotless pure!
Thou mad'st us kings and priests to God:
For ever let Thy praise endure!"

6 While thus the ransomed myriads shout,
"Amen!" the holy angels cry—
Amen! Amen! resounds throughout
The boundless regions of the sky.

R. Sandeman, 1775.

1024 1 Tim. i. 17. "*Glory for ever and ever. Amen.*"

Tune Zaanaim. 87, 87, 47.

1 GLORY be to God the Father!
Glory be to God the Son!
Glory be to God the Spirit!
Great Jehovah, Three in One!
Glory, glory,
While eternal ages run!

See Hymn 600.

2 Glory be to Him who loved us,
Washed us from each spot and stain!
Glory be to Him who bought us,
Made us kings with Him to [reign!
Glory, glory,
To the Lamb that once was slain!

3 Glory to the King of angels!
Glory to the church's King!
Glory to the King of nations!
Heaven and earth, your praises [bring—
Glory, glory,
To the King of glory bring!

4 Glory, blessing, praise eternal!
Thus the choir of angels sings;
Honour, riches, power, dominion!
Thus its praise creation brings;
Glory, glory,
Glory to the King of kings!

Horatius Bonar, D.D., 1868.

CONCLUSION. GRACE CONSUMMATED IN GLORY.

1025 1 Pet. v. 10, 11. "*The God of all Grace, who hath called us unto His eternal Glory, by Christ Jesus.*"

Tune St. Paul. 87, 887, 77, 77.

1 SOVEREIGN Lord and gracious Master,
Thou didst freely choose Thine own,
Thou hast called with mighty calling,
Thou wilt save, and keep from falling;—
Thine the glory, Thine alone!
Yet Thy hand shall crown in heaven
All the grace Thy love hath given;
Just, though undeserved, reward
From our glorious, gracious Lord.

2 From the martyr and apostle
To the sainted baby boy,
Every consecrated chalice
In the King of Glory's palace
Overflows with holy joy.
Sovereign choice of gift and dower,
Differing honour, differing power,—
Yet are all alike in this,
Perfect love and perfect bliss.

3 In those heavenly constellations
Lo! what differing glories meet;
Stars of radiance soft and tender,
Stars of full and dazzling splendour,
All in God's own light complete;
Brightest they whose holy feet,
Faithful to His service sweet,
Nearest to their Master trod,
Winning wandering souls to God.

4 Oh the rapture of that vision!
(Every earthly passion o'er,)
Our Redeemer's coronation,
And the blissful exaltation
Of the dear ones gone before.
Grace that shone for Christ below,
Changed to glory we shall know;
And before His unveiled face
Sing the glory of His grace.

Frances Ridley Havergal, Oct. 22, 1871.

APPENDIX,

FOR

MISSION SERVICES AND OTHER SPECIAL OCCASIONS.

PATROBAS. [H. P. 354.]

Gospel Echoes.

1026

2 Cor. x. 5. "*Casting down imaginations.*"

Tune Patrobas. 77, 77. D. Or Seir.

1 CAST thyself on Jesus *now*,
  Self relinquish wholly;
Low before His footstool bow,
  Trust in Jesus solely:
Look away from all to Him,
  Nothing here can aid thee:
Jesus is the Good Supreme—
  Go! He'll not upbraid thee.

2 Cast thyself on Jesus *now*,
  Self relinquish wholly;
Peace and joy thou then shalt know,
  Saved in Jesus fully:
He is waiting now to bless,
  Waiting now to save thee;
To His loving bosom press,
  Gladly He'll receive thee.

Albert Midlane, 1865.

1027

Luke xiv. 17. "*Come, for all things are now ready.*"

Tune Beulah. 64, 64, 6664.

BEULAH. [H. P. 102.]

1 COME to the royal feast,
  Come, sinners, come;
Come, and salvation taste,
  Come, sinners, come.
There is a full supply,
Haste, ere in want you die,
Now to the Saviour fly;
  Come, sinners, come.

2 Jesus will bless you all,
  Come, sinners, come;
Heed ye His gracious call,
  Come, sinners, come.
None are too bad for Him,
Worthless though you may seem,
He doth the *lost* redeem;
  Come, sinners, come.

3 Welcome you all shall be,
  Come, sinners, come;
Now to the Saviour flee;
  Come, sinners, come.
Make Him your happy choice,
List to His gracious voice,
Then shall your hearts rejoice
  Come, sinners, come.

4 Glory shall then be yours,
  Come, sinners, come;
Peace that for aye endures;
  Come, sinners, come.
Jesus will ne'er deceive
Those who in Him believe;
Come then, and life receive,
  Come, sinners, come.

Albert Midlane, 1865.

1028 Gal. iv. 4. "*When the fulness of the time was come.*"

Tune SIHOR. 77, 77, 77.

1 EIGHTEEN hundred years ago
Jesus died upon the tree,
And a full atonement made,
Sinner, there, for thee and me:
There He died, that He might prove
God the very God of love.

2 Eighteen hundred years ago,
All was finished, all was done;
And the Father proved it so,
When He raised up His Son;
When in glory He sat down
High upon His heavenly throne.

3 Eighteen hundred years ago,
Works were proved of no avail;
In salvation's glorious plan
Works of every sort must fail;
And the grace of God so free
All the sinner's hope must be.

4 Sinner, come at once, and prove
Rich the mercy God bestows;
Come and taste of Jesus' love,
And the joy that from it flows;
Thine shall then a glory be,
Lasting as eternity.

Albert Midlane, 1865.

SIHOR (River). [H. P. 158.]

SALZBURG. [H. P. 203.]

1029 Luke xviii. 13. "*God be merciful to me a sinner.*" Tune SALZBURG. 87, 87. D.

1 GOD be gracious to a sinner,
God be merciful to me,
Long a daring, hardened rebel—
Can e'en I forgiven be?
Can my dreadful guilt be pardoned?
Can I yet Thy mercies prove?
Can I view a Father's smiles?
Can I taste a Saviour's love?

2 Yes! the voice from heaven declareth,
"Come, ye wretched, needy, vile,
Come and take a free salvation,
Precious fruit of Jesus' toil;"
Mercy calleth not the righteous,
Only sinners mercy need,
They alone can claim the blessing
Of salvation, sweet indeed!

Albert Midlane, 1865.

1030 Eph. i. 11. "*The counsel of His own will.*"

Tune St. John. 6 6 6 6, 8 8.
Or Moriah.

1 HE saves because He will:
Man's will was to be lost;
But Jesus interposed,
And paid the fearful cost;
His precious blood He freely gave,
That He the guilty ones might save.

2 He saves because He will:
For this He came to die;
No mortal claimed His aid,
Love brought Him from on high,
Pure, sovereign, unrequested love,
Brought Jesus from the realms above.

ST. JOHN. [H. P. 272.]

3 He saves because He will:
Delighting still to bless,
He loves to clothe the soul
In His own righteousness;
A righteousness which God can own,
Wrought out by His belovèd Son.

Albert Midlane, 1865.

WINCHESTER. [H. P. 46.]

1031 Rev. i. 5. "*Jesus Christ, the faithful Witness.*" Tune Winchester. C. M. Or Evan I.

1 IF Jesus came to seek and save
The wretched and the lost,
I know He came to rescue *me*,
By sin and misery tossed.

2 If Jesus died upon the cross,
That sinners might be free,
I am a sinner, and I know
That Jesus died for *me*.

3 If Jesus bids the weary "Come,
And I will give you rest,"
I, a poor weary one, will go,
And in His love be blessed.

4 I know that what He says is true,
He never can deceive;
He says, "Believing, life is thine,"
And I His word believe.

Albert Midlane, 1865.

FRANKFORT. [H. P. 183.]

1032 Heb. xii. 2. "*Looking unto Jesus.*"

Tune Frankfort. 87, 87.

1 JESUS *lived*,—He lived for sinners,
Outcast, in the world He made;
Lived, that in His blessèd person
God's full grace might be displayed.

2 Jesus *died*,—He died for sinners,
On the cross He cried, "Forgive";
Died, that lost and ruined rebels
Through His precious blood might live.

3 Jesus *rose*,—He rose for sinners,
Proving that the work was done;
Sweet assurance that the Father
Was well pleasèd with His Son.

4 Jesus *lives*,—He lives for sinners,
High upon the Father's throne;
Liveth, evermore to succour
Those who make His love their own.

5 Jesus *loves*,—He loveth sinners,
Loveth more than tongue can say;
Prove Him now, accept His mercy,
Turn not from such love away.

Albert Midlane, 1865.

IDUMEA. [H. P. 193.]

1033 Hos. xiv. 4. "*I will love them freely.*"
Tune IDUMEA. 87, 87, 87.

1 LOVE us *freely*, blessèd Jesus,
For we have not aught to pay;
Saviour Thou, but we poor sinners,
Is alone what we can say;
Love us freely, blessèd Jesus,
For we have not aught to pay.

2 Love us *ever*, blessèd Jesus,
We are changing as the wind;
If Thy love on us depended,
We should ne'er salvation find;
Love us ever, blessèd Jesus,
We are changing as the wind.

3 Love and *help* us, blessèd Jesus;
Help us to be wholly Thine,
Every idol and enchantment
For Thy glory to resign;
Love and help us, blessèd Jesus,
Help us to be wholly Thine.

4 Love and *keep* us, blessèd Jesus,
Keep us from denying Thee;
Keep our wayward feet from straying
Into paths of vanity;
Love and keep us, blessèd Jesus,
Keep us from denying Thee.

Albert Midlane, 1865.

1034 2 Cor. v. 18. "*All things are of God.*"
Tune ST. CHRYSOSTOM. C. M.
Or LONDON NEW.

ST. CHRYSOSTOM. [H. P. 53.]

1 NOUGHT but the *voice of God* can speak
Deliverance to the slave;
Nought but His blessèd voice can break
The fetters of the grave.

2 Nought but the *power of God* can set
The captive sinner free,
And give him to possess the joy
Of perfect liberty.

3 Nought but the *love of God* can melt
The hard, hard heart of stone;
The law but hardens, love subdues,
And precious love alone.

4 Nought but the *grace of God* can give
A pardon full and free,
And make the rebel sinner meet
His face in peace to see.

5 Nought but the *blood of Christ* can cleanse
The sinner from his guilt,
Nought but that precious blood, upon
The cross of Calvary spilt.

Albert Midlane, 1865.

STUTTGARD. [H. P. 182.]

1035 2 Cor. xiii. 5. "*Examine yourselves.*"
Tune STUTTGARD. 87, 87. Or FRANKFORT.

1 OH, art thou an heir of glory?
Art thou sheltered by the blood?
Hast thou heavenly bliss before thee?
Hast thou present peace with God?

2 Or does Satan still deceive thee
With his subtilties and lies,
Hoping that he might receive thee
Where the torment never dies?

3 Oh awake! nor longer slumber;
Do not trifle with thy soul;
Its exceeding worth remember—
Worth unknown, unspeakable.

4 Oh, be wise, thou unforgiven,
Flee to Christ, and flee to-day:
Jesus beckons thee to heaven,
Jesus bids thee not delay.

5 Oh receive Him; oh believe Him,
Faith in Him will make thee whole:
Then thou shalt, for ever near Him,
Live where endless pleasures roll.

Albert Midlane, 1865.

PERSIS. [H. P. 187.]

1036

Luke i. 79. *"Guide our feet into the way of peace."* Tune PERSIS. 87, 87, 3.

1 PEACE with God! how great a treasure;
Peace with God! how true a joy;
Peace with God! how high a pleasure;
Peace with God! heaven's full supply.
Peace with God!

2 Peace with God! 'tis sins forgiven:
Peace with God! 'tis guilt removed;
Peace with God! 'tis gleams of heaven;
Peace with God! 'tis mercy proved.
Peace with God!

3 Peace with God! it comes through Jesus,
He for man the boon has won;
Now 'tis God's delight to give us
Peace with Him, through His dear Son.
Peace with God!

4 Sinner, be no longer straying,
Look to Him who bore sin's load;
So, His gracious call obeying,
Thou shalt have sweet peace with God.
Peace with God!

Albert Midlane, 1865.

1037

Rom. v. 20. *"Where sin abounded, grace did much more abound."* Tune IDUMEA. 87, 87, 47.

1 SCRIPTURE says, "Where sin abounded,
There did grace much more abound;"
Thus has Satan been confounded,
And his own discomfit found.
Christ has triumphed!
Spread the glorious news around.

2 Sin is strong; but grace is stronger,
Christ than Satan more supreme;
Yield, oh, yield to sin no longer,
Turn to Jesus, yield to Him;
He has triumphed!
Sinners, henceforth Him esteem.

Albert Midlane, 1865.

ZOAN I. (Field of.) [H. P. 127.]

1038

Lev. xxv. 9. *"The trumpet of the jubilee."* Tune ZOAN I. 76, 76. D.

1 THE silver trumpet's sounding
The year of jubilee;
And grace is all abounding,
To set the bondmen free.
Return, return, ye captives,
Return unto your home,
The silver trumpet's sounding,
"The jubilee is come."

2 Forsake your wretched service,
Your master's claims are o'er;
Avail yourselves of freedom,
Be Satan's slaves no more.
Return, return, etc.

3 A better Master's calling,
In accents true and kind:
He asks a loving service,
And claims a willing mind.
Return, return, etc.

4 He tells you of salvation,
And points to joys above;
And, longing, waits to show you
His purposes of love.
Return, return, etc.

5 In living faith accept Him,
And give up all beside:
While grace is loudly calling,
Look to the Crucified.
Return, return, etc.

Albert Midlane, 1865.

"JESUS OF NAZARETH." [H. P. 322.]

1039 Luke xviii. 37. "*Jesus of Nazareth passeth by.*"

Tune, "JESUS OF NAZARETH." 88, 88, 89.

1 WHAT means this eager anxious throng,
Which moves with busy haste along,
These wondrous gatherings day by day?
What means this strange commotion, say?
In accents hushed the throng reply,
"Jesus of Nazareth passeth by!"

2 E'en children feel the potent spell,
And haste their new-found joy to tell;
In crowds they to the place repair,
Where Christians daily bow in prayer;
Hosannas mingle with the cry,
"Jesus of Nazareth passeth by!"

3 Who is this Jesus? Why should He
The city move so mightily?
A passing stranger, has He skill
To move the multitude at will?
Again the stirring tones reply,
"Jesus of Nazareth passeth by!"

4 Jesus! 'Tis He who once below
Man's pathway trod, 'mid pain and woe;
And burdened ones, where'er He came,
Brought out their sick, and deaf, and lame,
The blind rejoiced to hear the cry,
"Jesus of Nazareth passeth by!"

5 Again He comes; from place to place
His holy footprints we can trace;
He pauses at our threshold—nay,
He enters, condescends to stay!
Shall we not gladly raise the cry,
"Jesus of Nazareth passeth by"?

6 Ho, all ye heavy-laden, come!
Here 's pardon, comfort, rest, a home:
Lost wanderers from a Father's face,
Return, accept His proffered grace;
Ye tempted, there 's a refuge nigh,
"Jesus of Nazareth passeth by!"

7 But if you still this call refuse,
And dare such wondrous love abuse,
Soon will He sadly from you turn,
Your bitter prayer in justice spurn:
"Too late, too late!" will be the cry,
"Jesus of Nazareth *has* passed by!"

Miss Campbell, 1869.

CULBACH. [H. P. 181.]

1040 Phil. iii. 8. "*The excellency of the knowledge of Christ.*" Tune CULBACH. 77, 77.

1 WHO can tell the *worth* of Jesus?
Gold compared with Him is mean;
Rising far beyond, in value,
All that is or e'er has been.

2 Who can tell the *grace* of Jesus?
Grace displayed in matchless ways,
Soaring o'er all opposition,
Grace demanding endless praise.

3 Who can tell the *power* of Jesus?
That by which the worlds were made;
Power which has since then in action
Every moment been displayed.

4 Who can tell the *love* of Jesus?
Perfect, pure, ineffable;
Love which tunes the rapturous anthems
Which eternity shall swell.

5 Ah! the *worth* and *grace* of Jesus,
And His matchless *power* and *love*,
By no saint has e'er been sounded,
Here or in the realms above.

6 Never told, yet ever telling,
Are the attributes Divine
Of the One who, in His mercy,
Says, "Poor sinner, I am thine."

Albert Midlane, 1865.

LUCIUS. [H. P. 293.]

1041 Matt. xi. 28. "*Come unto Me.*"
Tune Lucius. 86, 889, 8869.

1 WILL ye not come to Him for *life*?
Why will ye die, oh why?
He gave His life for you, for you!
The gift is free, the word is true!
Will ye not come? oh, why will ye die?
Will ye not come? Will ye not come?
Will ye not come to Him, to Him?
Oh, come, come, come to Him!
Come unto Jesus, oh, come for *life*.

2 Will ye not come to Him for *peace*,
Peace through His cross alone?
He shed His precious blood for you;
The gift is free, the word is true!
He is our Peace, oh is He your own?
Will ye not come, etc. . . . for *peace*?

3 Will ye not come to Him for *rest*?
All that are weary, come:
The rest He gives is deep and true,
'Tis offered now, 'tis offered you;
Rest in His love, and rest in His home.
Will ye not come, etc. . . . for *rest*?

Part II.

4 Will ye not come to Him for *joy*?
Will ye not come for this?
He laid His joys aside for you,
To give you joy, so sweet, so true!
Sorrowing heart, oh drink of the bliss!
Will ye not come, etc. . . . for *joy*?

5 Will ye not come to Him for *love*,
Love that can fill the heart?
Exceeding great, exceeding free!
He loveth you, He loveth me!
Will you not come? why stand ye apart?
Will ye not come, etc. . . . for *love*?

6 Will ye not come to Him for ALL?
Will ye not "taste and see"?
He waits to give it all to you,
The gifts are free, the words are true!
Jesus hath said it, "Come unto Me."
Will ye not come, etc. . . . to Him.

Frances Ridley Havergal, 1873.

"YET THERE IS ROOM." [H. P. 355.]

1042 Luke xiv. 22. "*Yet there is room.*"
Tune, "Yet there is Room."
Or Conway (repeating last line of verses).

1 YET there is room! The Lamb's bright hall of song,
With its fair glory, beckons thee along:
Room, room, still room! oh enter, enter now!

2 Day is declining, and the sun is low;
The shadows lengthen, light makes haste to go:
Room, room, still room! oh enter, enter now!

3 The bridal hall is filling for the feast:
Pass in, pass in, and be the Bridegroom's guest:
Room, room, still room! oh enter, enter now!

4 It fills, it fills, that hall of jubilee!
Make haste, make haste; 'tis not too full for thee:
Room, room, still room! oh enter, enter now!

See Hymns 458–485.

5 Yet there is room! Still open stands the gate,
The gate of love; it is not yet too late:
Room, room, still room! oh enter, enter now!

6 Pass in, pass in! That banquet is for thee,
That cup of everlasting love is free:
Room, room, still room! oh enter, enter now!

7 All heaven is there, all joy! Go in, go in;
The angels beckon thee the prize to win:
Room, room, still room! oh enter, enter now!

8 Louder and sweeter sounds the loving call;
Come, lingerer, come; enter that festal hall:
Room, room, still room! oh enter, enter now!

9 Ere night that gate may close, and seal thy doom;
Then the last, low, long cry:—"No room, no room!"
No room, no room!—oh, woeful cry, "No room!"

Horatius Bonar, D.D., 1873.

Faith Hymns.

1043 Acts xxvi. 18. "*Sanctified by faith that is in Me.*" Tune LINUS. 87, 87. D. Or ESDRAELON.

1 CHURCH of God, beloved and chosen, Church of Christ, for whom He died,
Claim thy gifts and praise thy Giver!—"*Ye are washed and sanctified.*"
Sanctified by God the Father, and by Jesus Christ His Son,
And by God the Holy Spirit, Holy, Holy, Three in One.

2 By His will He sanctifieth, by the Spirit's power within;
By the loving hand that chasteneth, fruits of righteousness to win;
By His truth and by His promise; by the Word, His gift unpriced;
By His own blood, and by union with the risen life of Christ.

3 Holiness by faith in Jesus, not by effort of thine own,—
Sin's dominion crushed and broken by the power of grace alone,—
God's own holiness within thee, His own beauty on thy brow,—
This shall be thy pilgrim brightness, this thy blessèd portion now.

4 He will sanctify thee wholly; body, spirit, soul shall be
Blameless till thy Saviour's coming in His glorious majesty!
He hath perfected for ever those whom He hath sanctified;
Spotless, glorious, and holy is the Church, His chosen bride.

Frances Ridley Havergal, 1873.

1044 1 Cor. iii. 11. "*Other foundation can no man lay.*"
Tune, PEDAL TUNE. 88, 88, 88. Or MAMRE.

1 CHRIST is the one Foundation laid,
In the deep counsels of the Lord,
In promises to sinners made,
In the inspired, prophetic word,
In welcome news of peace Divine,
In all His people's hearts and mine!

2 Him Prophet, Priest, and King we own,
Essential God and real man;
The Church is built on Christ alone,
Its doctrines, discipline, and plan;
Its duties and its blessings rise
On Him, the Lord of earth and skies.

3 Rock of eternity, He stood
Immovable in steadfast grace,
Beneath the utmost wrath of God,
Beneath the sin of Adam's race;
And still my faith's support remains,
And still He all my load sustains.

4 Sole Basis of our faith and hope,
We on His life and death rely,
His death from hell shall lift us up,
His life shall bear us to the sky,
Entitled, fitted for the place,
By Jesus' blood and righteousness.

Charles Wesley, 1786.

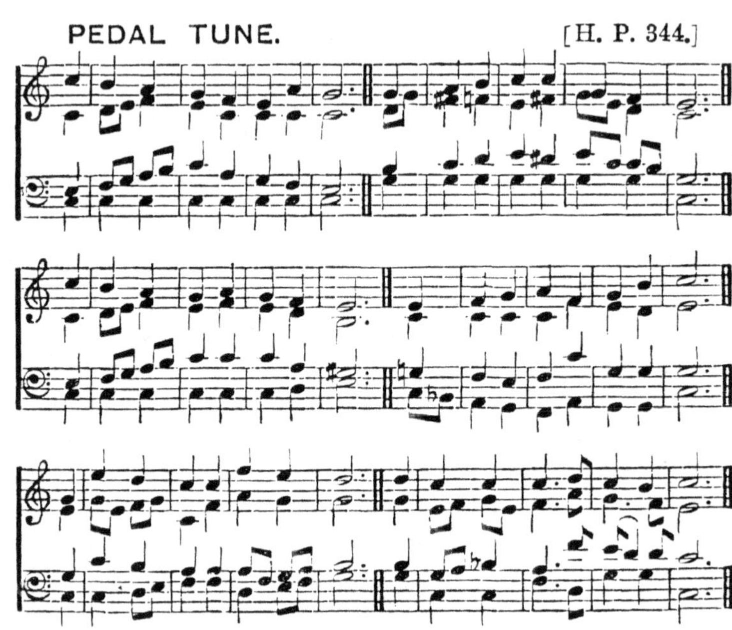

HOBAH. [H. P. 248.]

1045 Ps. li. 7. "*Whiter than snow.*"
Tune HOBAH, repeating last half for chorus. 11 11, 11 11, 11 11.

1 DEAR Jesus, I long to be perfectly whole,
I want Thee for ever to dwell in my soul;
Break down every idol, cast out every foe,
Now wash me, and I shall be whiter than snow.
Yes, whiter than snow, yes, whiter than snow.
Now wash me, and I shall be whiter than snow.

2 Dear Jesus, let nothing unholy remain,
Apply Thine own blood, and extract every stain:
To have this blest washing I all things forego,
Now wash me, and I shall be whiter than snow.
Yes, whiter than snow, etc.

3 Dear Jesus, come down from Thy throne in the skies,
And help me to make a complete sacrifice;
I give up myself—and whatever I know,
Now wash me, and I shall be whiter than snow.
Yes, whiter than snow, etc.

4 Dear Jesus, Thou seest I patiently wait;
Come now, and within me a new heart create;
To those who have sought Thee Thou never saidst no,
Now wash me, and I shall be whiter than snow.
Yes, whiter than snow, etc.

5 The blessing by faith I receive from above,
And praise Him who maketh me perfect in love;
My prayer has prevailed, and this moment I know,
The blood is applied, I am whiter than snow.
Yes, whiter than snow, yes, whiter than snow;
Dear Jesus, Thy blood makes me whiter than snow.

James Nicholson, 1872.

MAHANAIM. [H. P. 129.]

1046 Ps. xxxvii. 4. "*Delight thyself also in the Lord.*" Tune MAHANAIM. 76, 76. D.

1 DELIGHT thyself in Jesus,
In whom true pleasures meet,
To all thy heart's desirings
He'll be the answer sweet.
Think what the bridegroom's joy is
Over his precious bride;
Think of His holy anguish
When He was crucified.

2 Commit thy way to Jesus,
He knows thy utmost need,
He feels the secret sorrows
Which make thy lone heart bleed.
To smooth thy rugged journey
He will with thee abide;
Then cast thou all upon Him,
On Him the Crucified!

3 Commit thy way to Jesus,
Lean on His loving arm;
And though the world despise thee,
What is each threat or charm?
If darkness shroud thy pathway,
Light *must* with Him abide;
Still trust the One who loves thee,
Jesus, the Crucified!

H. R. King. 1873.

PATMOS. [H. P. 147.]

1047 1 Pet. ii. 4. *"To whom coming"*
Tune Patmos. 77, 77. D.
Or "Coming to the Cross."

1 I AM coming to the cross;
I am poor, and weak, and blind;
I am counting all but dross,
I shall full salvation find.
I am trusting, Lord, in Thee,
Holy Lamb of Calvary;
Humbly at Thy cross I bow:
Save me, Jesus, save me now.

2 Long my heart has sighed for Thee,
Long has evil reigned within:
Jesus sweetly speaks to me,
I will cleanse you from all sin.
I am trusting, Lord, in Thee, etc.

3 Here I give my all to Thee,
Friends and time and earthly store;
Soul and body Thine to be,—
Wholly Thine for evermore.
I am trusting, Lord, in Thee, etc.

4 In the promises I trust,
Now I feel the blood applied;
I am prostrate in the dust,
I with Christ am crucified.
I am trusting, Lord, in Thee, etc.

"COMING TO THE CROSS." [H. P. 356.]

5 Jesus comes! He fills my soul,
Perfected in love I am;
I am every whit made whole,
Glory, glory to the Lamb!
I am trusting, Lord, in Thee, etc.

William McDonald, 1872.

URBANE. (Part II.) [H. P. 292.]

1048 Isa. xii. 2. *"I will trust, and not be afraid."* Tune, Urbane, Part II. 7 5, 8 3.

1 I AM trusting Thee, Lord Jesus,
Trusting only Thee!
Trusting Thee for full salvation,
Great and free!

2 I am trusting Thee for pardon,
At Thy feet I bow;
For Thy grace and tender mercy
Trusting now.

3 I am trusting Thee for cleansing,
In the crimson flood;
Trusting Thee to make me holy,
By Thy blood.

4 I am trusting Thee to guide me;
Thou alone shalt lead,
Every day and hour supplying
All my need.

5 I am trusting Thee for power;
Thine can never fail:
Words which Thou Thyself shalt give me
Must prevail.

6 I am trusting Thee, Lord Jesus!
Never let me fall!
I am trusting Thee for ever,
And for all!

Frances Ridley Havergal, 1874.

GOLDBACH. [H. P. 130.]

1049

John vi. 68. *"Lord, to whom shall we go?"* Tune GOLDBACH. 76,76. D.

1 I COULD not do without Thee,
O Saviour of the lost!
Whose wondrous love redeemed me
At such tremendous cost.
Thy righteousness, Thy pardon,
Thy precious blood, must be
My only hope and comfort,
My glory and my plea!

2 I could not do without Thee,
I cannot stand alone,
I have no strength or goodness,
No wisdom of my own.
But Thou, belovèd Saviour,
Art all-in-all to me,
And weakness will be power
If leaning hard on Thee!

3 I could not do without Thee,
For oh! the way is long,
And I am often weary,
And sigh replaces song.
How could I do without Thee?
I do not know the way!
Thou knowest, and Thou leadest,
And wilt not let me stray.

PART II.

4 I could not do without Thee,
O Jesus, Saviour dear!
E'en when my eyes are holden
I know that Thou art near.
How dreary and how lonely
This changeful life would be,
Without the sweet communion,
The secret rest with Thee.

5 I could not do without Thee!
No other friend could read
The spirit's strange deep longings,
Interpreting its need.
No human heart could enter
Each dim recess of mine,
And soothe and hush and calm it,
O blessèd Lord, but Thine!

6 I could not do without Thee!
For life is fleeting fast,
And then, in solemn loneliness,
The river must be passed.
But Thou wilt never leave me,
And, though the waves roll high,
I know Thou wilt be with me,
And whisper "It is I."

Frances Ridley Havergal, 1873.

PARAN (Wilderness of). [H. P. 241.]

1050

Phil. iv. 19. *"My God shall supply all your need."* Tune PARAN. 11 12, 11 11.

1 IN some way or other the Lord will provide:
It may not be *my* way, It may not be *thy* way;
And yet in His own way "the Lord will provide."
Then trust in the Lord—He will surely provide.

2 At some time or other the Lord will provide:
It may not be *my* time, It may not be *thy* time;
And yet in His own time "the Lord will provide."
Then trust in the Lord, etc.

3 Despond then no longer; the Lord will provide;
And this be the token, No word He hath spoken
Was ever yet broken; "the Lord will provide."
Then trust in the Lord, etc.

4 March on then right boldly, the sea shall divide;
The pathway made glorious, With shoutings victorious,
We'll join in the chorus, "the Lord will provide."
Then trust in the Lord, etc.

Mrs. M. A. W. Cook, 1873.

1051 John vi. 37. "*Him that cometh to Me I will in no wise cast out.*"

Tune Godesberg. 8 7, 8 7.

GODESBERG. [H. P. 185.]

1 JESUS, Lord, I come before Thee,
With my sin and guilt and care;
Though Thou art enthroned in glory,
Cast not out my feeble prayer!

2 I am vile, but Thou art holy;
Thou art strong, though I am weak;
Trusting in Thy mercy solely,
Let me find the grace I seek!

3 All my promises are broken,
Often have I gone astray,
Words of sin have freely spoken,
Holy thoughts have cast away.

4 Life with its vain fleeting pleasures
I have loved, without a thought
Of the never failing treasures
Which Thy blood for me hath bought.

5 But the long delusion's ended,
From my dreaming I awake,
To behold myself BEFRIENDED
For Thy tender mercy's sake.

6 In my heart I hear Thee saying,
"Come poor sinner unto Me!
All thy fear and guilt allaying,
Peace and joy I'll give to thee!"

Robert Gardner Smith, 1869.

PATMOS. [H. P. 147.]

1052 Matt. i. 21. "*He shall save His people from their sins.*"

Tune Patmos, repeating first and last strains.
7 7, 7 7. With Chorus.

1 JESUS saves me every day,
Jesus saves me every night;
Jesus saves me all the way,
Through the darkness, through the light.
Jesus saves, oh bliss sublime!
Jesus saves me all the time.

2 Jesus saves when I repine,
Jesus saves when I rejoice,
Jesus saves when hopes decline,
Faith can always hear His voice.
Jesus saves, etc.

3 Jesus saves when sorrows come;
Jesus saves when death appears;
Jesus saves and leads me home,
Where shall end my doubts and fears.
Jesus saves, etc.

4 Jesus saves me, He is mine;
Jesus saves me, I am His;
Jesus saves while I recline
On His precious promises.
Jesus saves, etc.

5 Jesus saves, He saves from sin;
Jesus saves, I feel Him nigh;
Jesus saves, He dwells within,
Gladly do I testify.
Jesus saves, etc.

Leaflet, 1873.

1053 Rev. iii. 20. "*I stand at the door, and knock.*"

Tune, "Knocking, Knocking." 77, 87, 87.

1 KNOCKING, knocking, who is there?
Waiting, waiting, oh, how fair!
'Tis a Pilgrim, strange and kingly,
Never such was seen before.
Ah! my soul, for such a wonder,
Wilt thou not undo the door?

2 Knocking, knocking, still He's there,
Waiting, waiting, wondrous fair;
But the door is hard to open,
For the weeds and ivy-vine,
With their dark and clinging tendrils,
Ever round the hinges twine.

3 Knocking, knocking; what, still there?
Waiting, waiting, grand and fair;
Yes, the piercèd hand still knocketh,
And beneath the crownèd hair
Beam the patient eyes, so tender,
Of thy Saviour, waiting there.

Mrs. Stowe and G. F. Root, 1870.

"KNOCKING." *With feeling.* [H. P. 321.]

1054

Heb. iv. 3. *"We which have believed do enter into rest."*

Tune St. Chrysostom. C. M.

1 Lord, I believe a rest remains,
To all Thy people known,
A rest where pure enjoyment reigns,
And Thou art loved alone;

2 A rest where all our soul's desire
Is fixed on things above;
Where fear, and sin, and grief expire,
Cast out by perfect love.

3 Oh that I now the rest might know,
Believe, and enter in!
Now, Saviour, now the power bestow,
And let me cease from sin.

4 Remove this hardness from my heart,
This unbelief remove;
To me the rest of faith impart,
The sabbath of Thy love.

5 Thy name to me, Thy nature grant;
This, only this, be given;
Nothing beside, my God, I want;
Nothing in earth or heaven.

Charles Wesley, 1739.

ST. CHRYSOSTOM. [H. P. 53.]

EVAN I. [H. P. 54.]

1055

Cant. ii. 4. *"He brought me to the banqueting house."* Tune Evan I. C. M.

1 My heart is resting, O my God,—
I will give thanks and sing;
My heart is at the secret source
Of every precious thing.

2 Now the frail vessel Thou hast made
No hand but Thine shall fill;
For the waters of the earth have failed,
And I am thirsty still.

3 I thirst for springs of heavenly life,
And here all day they rise;
I seek the treasure of Thy love,
And close at hand it lies.

4 And a new song is in my mouth,
To long-loved music set—
Glory to Thee for all the grace
I have not tasted yet.

5 My heart is resting, O my God,
My heart is in Thy care;
I hear the voice of joy and health
Resounding everywhere.

6 "Thou art my portion," saith my soul,
Ten thousand voices say,—
The music of their glad Amen
Will never die away.

Anna Lætitia Waring, 1850.

"IT IS BETTER FARTHER ON." [H. P. 327.]

1056 Rom. xv. 13. *"Ye may abound in hope."*
Tune, "IT IS BETTER FARTHER ON."

1 METHINKS I hear hope sweetly singing,
Singing in an undertone;
Singing, as though God had taught her,
"It is better farther on."
Night and day she sings this same song,
Sings it when I sit alone,
Sings it till my heart can hear her—
It is better farther on!

Chorus.—It is better farther on, farther on!
It is better farther on, farther on!
Hope is ever sweetly singing, It is better farther on.

2 When first, by faith, I viewed my Saviour,
Light Divine within me shone;
And I knew, from that glad hour,
It is better farther on.
Daily coming to the fountain,
Flowing free for thirsty ones,
I am saved, and hope is singing,
It is better farther on. *Chorus.*—It is, etc.

3 Within my soul hope sings most sweetly,
When I absent friends bemoan,
(Oh, sweet words, they cheer my spirit!)
"It is better farther on."
Sitting on the grave hope sings it,
Sings it when my heart doth groan,
Sings it when the clouds are darkest,
It is better farther on. *Chorus.*—It is, etc.

CHORUS.

4 Farther on! but how much farther?
Count the milestones one by one.
No! not counting, only trusting
It is better farther on.
Hope, my soul, hope on for ever,
All thy doubts and fears be gone!
Jesus will forsake thee never,
It is better farther on. *Chorus.*—It is, etc.

Faith Hymns, 1874.

URBANE. [H. P. 292.]

1057 1 Pet. i.19. *"The precious blood."*
Tune URBANE. 7 5, 8 3.

1 PRECIOUS, precious blood of Jesus,
Shed on Calvary,
Shed for rebels, shed for sinners,
Shed for thee!
Precious, precious blood of Jesus,
Ever flowing free!
Oh believe it, oh receive it, 'Tis for thee!

2 Precious, precious blood of Jesus,
Let it make thee whole!
Let it flow in mighty cleansing
O'er thy soul.
Precious, precious blood of Jesus, etc.

3 Though thy sins are red like crimson,
Deep in scarlet glow,
Jesu's precious blood shall wash thee
White as snow.
Precious, precious blood of Jesus, etc.

4 Precious blood that hath redeemed us!
All the price is paid!
Perfect pardon now is offered,
Peace is made.
Precious, precious blood of Jesus, etc.

5 Now the holiest with boldness
We may enter in,
For the opened fountain cleanseth
From all sin.
Precious, precious blood of Jesus, etc.

6 Precious blood! by this we conquer
In the fiercest fight,
Sin and Satan overcoming
By its might.
Precious, precious blood of Jesus, etc.

7 Precious blood, whose full atonement
Makes us nigh to God!
Precious blood! our song of glory,
Praise and laud!
Precious, precious blood of Jesus, etc.
Frances Ridley Havergal, 1874.

HOBAH. [H. P. 248.]

1058 Ps. lix. 16. *"I will sing aloud of Thy mercy."* 11 11, 11 11, 11 11.
Tune HOBAH, repeating last half for chorus.

1 OH, bliss of the purified! bliss of the free!
I plunge in the crimson tide opened for me!
O'er sin and uncleanness exulting I stand,
And point to the print of the nails in His hand.
Oh, sing of His mighty love, mighty to save.

2 Oh, bliss of the purified! Jesus is mine,
No longer in dread condemnation I pine;
In conscious salvation I sing of His grace,
Who lifteth upon me the smiles of His face.
Oh, sing, etc.

3 Oh, bliss of the purified! bliss of the pure!
No wound hath the soul that His blood cannot cure;
No sorrow-bowed head but may sweetly find rest;
No tears, but may dry them on Jesus's breast.
Oh, sing, etc.

4 O Jesus the crucified! Thee will I sing,
My blessèd Redeemer, my God and my King;
My soul, filled with rapture, shall shout o'er the grave,
And triumph at death in the "Mighty to save!"
Oh, sing, etc. *Dr. F. Bottome*, 1873.

"THE GREAT PHYSICIAN." [H. P. 324.]

1059 Cant. i. 3. *"Thy name is as ointment poured forth."*

Tune, "THE GREAT PHYSICIAN."

1 THE great Physician now is near,
The sympathising Jesus,
He speaks the drooping heart to cheer;
Oh, hear the voice of Jesus.
Chorus.—Sweetest note in seraph song,
Sweetest name on mortal tongue,
Sweetest carol ever sung,
Jesus, Jesus, Jesus!

2 Your many sins are all forgiven;
Oh, hear the voice of Jesus;
Go on your way in peace to heaven,
And wear a crown with Jesus.
Sweetest note, etc.

3 All glory to the dying Lamb!
I now believe in Jesus;
I love the blessèd Saviour's name,
I love the name of Jesus.
Sweetest note, etc.

4 His name dispels my guilt and fear,
No other name but Jesus;
Oh how my soul delights to hear
The precious name of Jesus.
Sweetest note, etc.

5 The children too, both great and small,
Who love the name of Jesus,
May now accept the glorious call
To work and live for Jesus.
Sweetest note, etc.

6 And when to the bright world above
We rise, to see our Jesus,
We'll sing, around the throne of love,
His name—the name of JESUS.
Sweetest note, etc. *Leaflet*, 1873.

EVERTON. [H. P. 308.]

1060 Prov. xviii. 24. *"A Friend that sticketh closer than a brother."* Tune EVERTON. 8 7, 8 7. D.

1 WHAT a friend we have in Jesus,
All our sins and griefs to bear;
What a privilege to carry
Everything to God in prayer!
Oh what peace we often forfeit,
Oh what endless pain we bear;
All because we do not carry
Everything to God in prayer.

2 Have we trials and temptations?
Is there trouble anywhere?
We should never be discouraged,
Take it to the Lord in prayer.
Can we find a friend so faithful,
Who will all our sorrows share?
Jesus knows our every weakness,
Take it to the Lord in prayer.

3 Are we weak and heavy laden,
Cumbered with a load of care?
Precious Saviour, still our refuge,
Take it to the Lord in prayer.
Do thy friends despise, forsake thee?
Take it to the Lord in prayer;
In His arm He'll take and shield thee,
Thou wilt find a solace there.

Faith Hymns, 1874.

"MORE TO FOLLOW." [H. P. 326.]

1061 James iv. 6. *"He giveth more grace."*
Tune, "MORE TO FOLLOW."

1 HAVE you on the Lord believed?
Still there's more to follow;
Of His grace have you received?
Still there's more to follow;
Oh, the grace the Father shows!
Still there's more to follow;
Freely He His grace bestows,
Still there's more to follow.

Chorus.—More and more, more and more,
Always more to follow,
Oh, His matchless boundless love!
Still there's more to follow.

2 Have you felt the Saviour near?
Still there's more to follow;
Does His blessèd presence cheer?
Still there's more to follow;
Oh, the love that Jesus shows!
Still there's more to follow;
Freely He His love bestows,
Still there's more to follow.
More and more, etc.

3 Have you felt the Spirit's power?
Still there's more to follow;
Falling like the gentle shower?
Still there's more to follow;
Oh, the power the Spirit shows!
Still there's more to follow;
Freely He His power bestows,
Still there's more to follow.
More and more, etc.

P. P. Bliss, 1873.

"HOLD THE FORT." [H. P. 323.]

1062 Rev. ii. 25. *"Hold fast till I come."*
Tune, "Hold the Fort."

1 HO! my comrades, see the signal
Waving in the sky!
Reinforcements now appearing,
Victory is nigh!
Chorus.—"Hold the fort, for I am coming,"
Jesus signals still;
Wave the answer back to heaven,
"By Thy grace we will."

2 See the mighty host advancing,
Satan leading on;
Mighty men around us falling,
Courage almost gone!
"Hold the fort," etc.

3 See the glorious banner waving,
Hear the trumpet blow;
In our Leader's name we'll triumph
Over every foe.
"Hold the fort," etc.

See Hymns 494—498.

Chorus.

4 Fierce and long the battle rages;
But our help is near;
Onward comes our great Commander,
Cheer, my comrades, cheer!
"Hold the fort," etc.

P. P. Bliss, 1871.

THYATIRA. (Hymn Chant.) [H. P. No. V.]

Consecration Hymns.

1063 Ps. cxix. 94. *"I am Thine, save me."* Tune, Hymn Chant Thyatira. 6664.

1 I AM Thine own, O Christ,
Henceforth entirely Thine;
And life, from this glad hour,
New life, is mine!

2 No earthly joy shall lure
My quiet soul from Thee;
This deep delight, so pure,
Is heaven to me.

3 My little song of praise
In sweet content I sing;
To Thee the note I raise,
My King! my King!

4 I cannot tell the art
By which such bliss is given;
I know Thou hast my heart,
And I—have heaven.

5 O peace! O holy rest!
O balmy breath of love!
A heart divinest, best,
Thy depth I prove.

6 I ask this gift of Thee—
A life, all lily fair,
And fragrant as the place
Where seraphs are.

Mrs. Helen Bradley, 1873.

1064 Rom. xiv. 17. "*Peace and joy in the Holy Ghost.*"

Tune, "I have Entered the Valley."
11 8, 11 8. Or Crescens.

1 I HAVE entered the valley of blessing so sweet,
And Jesus abides with me there;
And His Spirit and blood make my cleansing complete,
And His perfect love casteth out fear.
Chorus.—Oh, come to this valley of blessing so sweet!
Where Jesus will fulness bestow;
And believe, and receive, and confess Him,
That all His salvation may know.

2 There is peace in the valley of blessing so sweet,
And plenty the land doth impart;
And there's rest for the weary, worn traveller's feet,
And joy for the sorrowing heart.
Oh, come to the valley, etc.

"I HAVE ENTERED THE VALLEY." [H. P. 357.]

3 There is love in the valley of blessing so sweet,
Such as none but the blood-washed may feel,
When heaven comes down redeemed spirits to greet,
And Christ sets His covenant seal.
Oh, come to the valley, etc.

4 There's a song in the valley of blessing so sweet
And angels would fain join the strain,
As with rapturous praises we bow at His feet,
Crying, "Worthy the Lamb that was slain."
Oh, come to the valley, etc.

Annie Wittenmeyer, 1872.

GOLDBACH. [H. P. 130.]

1065 1 Thess. v. 23. "*The God of peace sanctify you wholly.*" Tune Goldbach. 7 6, 7 6. D.

1 MY body, soul, and spirit,
Jesus, I give to Thee;
A consecrated offering,
Thine evermore to be.
My all is on the altar, I'm waiting for the fire,
Yes, waiting, waiting, waiting, I'm waiting for the fire.

2 O Jesus, mighty Saviour,
I trust in Thy great name;
I look for Thy salvation,
Thy promise now I claim.
My all, etc.

3 Oh, let the fire, descending,
My heart set now on flame:
I look for Thy salvation,
Thy prŏmise now I claim.
My all, etc.

4 I'm Thine, O blessèd Jesus,
Washed by Thy precious blood;
Now seal me by Thy Spirit,
A sacrifice to God.
My all, etc.

Mary D. James, 1873.

PARAN (Wilderness of). [H. P. 241.]

1066

2 Cor. vii. 1. "*Perfecting holiness.*" Tune PARAN. 11, 11, 11, 11.

1 MORE holiness give me,
More sweetness within,
More patience in suffering,
More sorrow for sin,
More faith in my Saviour,
More sense of His care,
More joy in His service,
More purpose in prayer.

2 More gratitude give me,
More trust in the Lord,
More pride in His glory,
More hope in His word,
More tears for His sorrows,
More pain at His grief,
More meekness in trial,
More praise for relief.

3 More victory give me,
More strength to o'ercome,
More freedom from earth stains,
More longings for home;
More fit for the kingdom,
More useful, I'd be,
More blessèd and holy,
More, Saviour, like Thee.

P. P. Bliss, 1873.

HOBAH. [H. P. 248.]

1067

Rev. xxi. 5. "*Behold I make all things new.*" Tune HOBAH. 11 11, 11 11.

1 NEW mercies, new blessings, new light on thy way;
New courage, new hope, and new strength for each day;
New notes of thanksgiving, new chords of delight;
New praise in the morning, new songs in the night;

2 New wine in thy chalice, new altars to raise;
New fruit for thy Master, new garments of praise;
New gifts from His treasures, new smiles from His face;
New streams from the Fountain of infinite grace;

3 New stars for thy crown, and new tokens of love;
New gleams of the glory that waits thee above;
New light of His countenance, clear and unpriced!
All this be the joy of thy new life in Christ!

Frances Ridley Havergal, 1874.

PHEBE. [H. P. 282.]

1068

Matt. xvii. 8. *"Jesus only."* Tune PHEBE. 77, 76. D.

1 OH to be nothing,—nothing!
Only to lie at His feet,
A broken—emptied—vessel,
Thus for His use made meet;
Emptied—that He may fill me,
As to His service I go;
Broken,—so that unhindered
Through me His life may flow.

2 Oh to be nothing,—nothing!
Though painful the humbling be,
Though it lay me low in the sight of those
Who are now perhaps praising me.
I would rather be nothing,—nothing,
That to Him—be their voices raised,
Who alone—is the Fountain of blessing,
Who alone—is meet to be praised.

Georgiana M. Taylor, 1869.

"ONE MORE DAY'S WORK." [H. P. 325.]

CHORUS.

1069

John ix. 4. *"I must work the works of Him that sent Me."*

Tune, "ONE MORE DAY'S WORK." 76, 556. 46.

1 ONE more day's work for Jesus;
One less of life for me!
But heaven is nearer,
And Christ is dearer,
Than yesterday, to me;
His love and light
Fill all my soul to-night.
Chorus.—One more day's work for Jesus,
One more day's work for Jesus,
One more day's work for Jesus,
One less of life for me.

2 One more day's work for Jesus;
How glorious is my King!
'Tis joy, not duty,
To speak His beauty;
My soul mounts on the wing
At the mere thought
How Christ my life has bought.
One more, etc.

3 One more day's work for Jesus;
How sweet the work has been,
To tell the story,
To show the glory,
When Christ's flock enter in!
How it did shine
In this poor heart of mine!
One more, etc.

4 One more day's work for Jesus—
Oh, yes, a weary day;
But heaven shines clearer,
And rest comes nearer,
At each step of the way;
And Christ in all,—
Before His face I fall!
One more, etc.

5 Oh, blessèd work for Jesus!
Oh, rest at Jesus' feet!
There toil seems pleasure,
My wants are treasure,
And pain for Him is sweet.
Lord, if I may,
I'll serve another day.
One more, etc.

Anna Warner, 1869.

1070

Deut. xxxiii. 27. *"Underneath are the everlasting arms."* Tune, "SAFE IN THE ARMS." 76, 76. D.

1 SAFE in the arms of Jesus,
Safe on His gentle breast,
There, by His love o'ershadowed,
Sweetly my soul shall rest.
Hark, 'tis the voice of angels,
Borne in a song to me,
Over the fields of glory,
Over the jasper sea.
Safe in the arms, etc.

2 Safe in the arms of Jesus,
Safe from corroding care,
Safe from the world's temptations,
Sin cannot harm me there.
Free from the blight of sorrow,
Free from my doubts and fears,
Only a few more trials,
Only a few more tears.
Safe in the arms, etc.

"SAFE IN THE ARMS OF JESUS." [H. P. 320.]

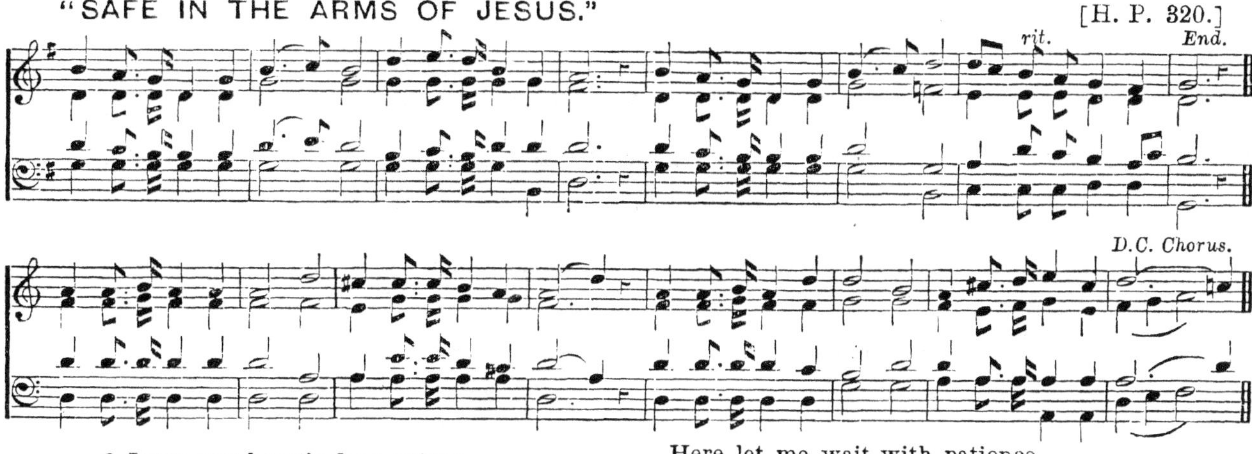

3 Jesus, my heart's dear refuge,
Jesus has died for me;
Firm on the Rock of Ages
Ever my trust shall be.
Here let me wait with patience,
Wait till the night is o'er;
Wait till I see the morning
Break on the golden shore.
Safe in the arms, etc.

Fanny Crosby, 1870.

"SWEET HOUR OF PRAYER." [H. P. 358.]

1071

Acts iii. 1. *"The hour of prayer."*
Tune, "SWEET HOUR OF PRAYER."
L. M. D. Or MELCOMBE.

D.S.

1 SWEET hour of prayer! sweet hour of prayer!
That calls me from a world of care,
And bids me at my Father's throne
Make all my wants and wishes known.
In seasons of distress and grief
My soul has often found relief,
And oft escaped the tempter's snare,
By thy return, sweet hour of prayer!

2 Sweet hour of prayer! sweet hour of prayer!
Thy wings shall my petition bear
To Him whose truth and faithfulness
Engage the waiting soul to bless:
And since He bids me seek His face,
Believe His word, and trust His grace,
I'll cast on Him my every care,
And wait for thee, sweet hour of prayer!

3 Sweet hour of prayer! sweet hour of prayer!
May I thy consolation share;
Till from mount Pisgah's lofty height
I view my home, and take my flight.
This robe of flesh I'll drop, and rise
To seize the everlasting prize;
And shout, while passing through the air,
"Farewell, farewell, sweet hour of prayer!"

Walford, 1849.

PATMOS. [H. P. 147.]

1072

2 Sam. xix. 30. *"Yea, let him take all."* Tune PATMOS. 77, 77.

[The two last lines of the hymn may be sung as Chorus after each verse to first and fourth strains of the tune.]

1 TAKE my life, and let it be
Consecrated, Lord, to Thee.
Take my moments and my days,
Let them flow in ceaseless praise.

2 Take my hands, and let them move
With the impulse of Thy love.
Take my feet, and let them be
Swift and "beautiful" for Thee.

3 Take my voice, and let me sing
Always, only, for my King.
Take my lips, and let them be
Filled with messages from Thee.

4 Take my silver and my gold,
Not a mite would I withhold.
Take my intellect, and use
Every power as Thou dost choose.

5 Take my will, and make it Thine!
It shall be no longer mine.
Take my heart, it is Thine own;
It shall be Thy royal throne.

6 Take my love, my Lord, I pour
At Thy feet its treasure store.
Take myself, and I will be
Ever, only, all, for Thee!

Frances Ridley Havergal, 1873.

See Hymn 695.

MELCOMBE. [H. P. 24.]

1073 Acts xv. 14. "*Take out of them a people.*"
Tune MELCOMBE. L. M. Or PENIEL.

1 TAKE my poor heart, and let it be
  For ever closed to all but Thee!
Seal Thou my breast, and let me wear
That pledge of love for ever there!

2 How blest are they who still abide
Close sheltered by Thy bleeding side!
Who life and strength from Thee derive,
And by Thee move, and in Thee live.

3 O Lord! enlarge our scanty thought,
To know the wonders Thou hast wrought;
Unloose our stammering tongues, to tell
Thy love immense, unsearchable.

J. Wesley, from Count Zinzendorf, 1738—1740.

FRENCH; *or*, DUNDEE. [H. P. 65.]

1074 1 John i. 7. "*Walk in the light.*"
Tune FRENCH. C. M.

1 WALK in the light, and thou shalt know
  That fellowship of love
His Spirit only can bestow
  Who reigns in light above.

2 Walk in the light, and thou shalt find
  The heart made truly His
Who dwells in cloudless light enshrined,
  In whom no darkness is.

3 Walk in the light, and sin abhorred
  Shall ne'er defile again;
The blood of Jesus Christ the Lord
  Shall cleanse from every stain.

4 Walk in the light, and e'en the tomb
  No fearful shade shall wear;
Glory shall chase away its gloom,
  For Christ hath conquered there.

5 Walk in the light, and thine shall be
  A path, though thorny, bright;
For God, by grace, shall dwell in thee,
  And God Himself is light.

Bernard Barton, 1826.

ZAANAIM (Plain of). [H. P. 191.]

1075 Ps. lvii. 7. "*My heart is fixed.*"
Tune ZAANAIM. 87, 87, 47.

1 WELCOME, welcome, dear Redeemer,
  Welcome to this heart of mine;
Lord, I make a full surrender,
  Every power and thought be Thine;
    Thine entirely,
  Through eternal ages Thine.

2 Known to all to be Thy mansion,
  Earth and hell shall disappear;
Or in vain attempt possession,
  When they find the Lord is there.
    Shout, ye angels,
  Shout, O saints, the Lord is here.

William Mason, 1794.

See Hymns 32—40, 530—536, 735—745, 1093.

FRANCONIA. [H. P. 87.]

Birthday, New Year, and Anniversaries.

1076 Luke xxi. 28. *"Your redemption draweth nigh."* Tune FRANCONIA. S. M.

1 A FEW more years shall roll,
A few more seasons come,
And we shall be with those that rest,
Asleep within the tomb.

2 A few more suns shall set
O'er these dark hills of time,
And we shall be where suns are not,
A far serener clime.

3 A few more storms shall beat
On this wild, rocky shore,
And we shall be where tempests cease,
And surges swell no more.

4 A few more struggles here,
A few more partings o'er,
A few more toils, a few more tears,
And we shall weep no more.

5 A few more Sabbaths here
Shall cheer us on our way,
And we shall reach the endless rest,
The' eternal Sabbath-day.

6 Then, O my Lord, prepare
My soul for that great day;
Oh wash me in Thy precious blood,
And take my sins away.

Horatius Bonar, D.D., 1844.

HOBAH. [H. P. 248.]

1077 Mark vi. 50. *"Be of good cheer."* Tune HOBAH. 11 11, 11 11.

1 A HAPPY New Year! Even such may it be,
Right joyously, surely, and fully for thee!
Then fear not and faint not, but "be of good cheer!"
And trustfully enter this Happy New Year!

2 So happy—so happy! Thy Father shall guide,
Protect thee, preserve thee, and always provide!
Then onward and upward, along "the right way,"
He lovingly leading thee day after day.

3 So happy—so happy! Thy Saviour shall be
Still ever more precious, and present with thee!
So happy—so happy! His Spirit thy Guest,
And filling with glory the place of His rest.

4 So happy—so happy! Though shadows around
May gather and darken,—they flee at the sound—
His loving voice bidding thee "Be of good cheer!"
Then joyously enter thy Happy New Year!

Frances Ridley Havergal, 1874.

GOLDBACH. (PART I.) [H. P. 130.]

1078 Ps. lxv. 11. *"Thou crownest the year with Thy goodness."* Tune GOLDBACH, Part I. 76, 76.

1 ANOTHER year is dawning!
Dear Master, let it be,
In working or in waiting,
Another year with Thee.

2 Another year of leaning
Upon Thy loving breast;
Of ever deepening trustfulness,
Of quiet, happy rest.

3 Another year of mercies,
Of faithfulness and grace,
Another year of gladness
In the shining of Thy face.

4 Another year of progress,
Another year of praise,
Another year of proving
Thy presence "all the days."

5 Another year of service,
Of witness for Thy love,
Another year of training
For holier work above.

6 Another year is dawning!
Dear Master, let it be,
On earth, or else in heaven,
Another year with Thee!

Frances Ridley Havergal, 1874.

PHILADELPHIA. (Hymn Chant.) [H. P. VII.]

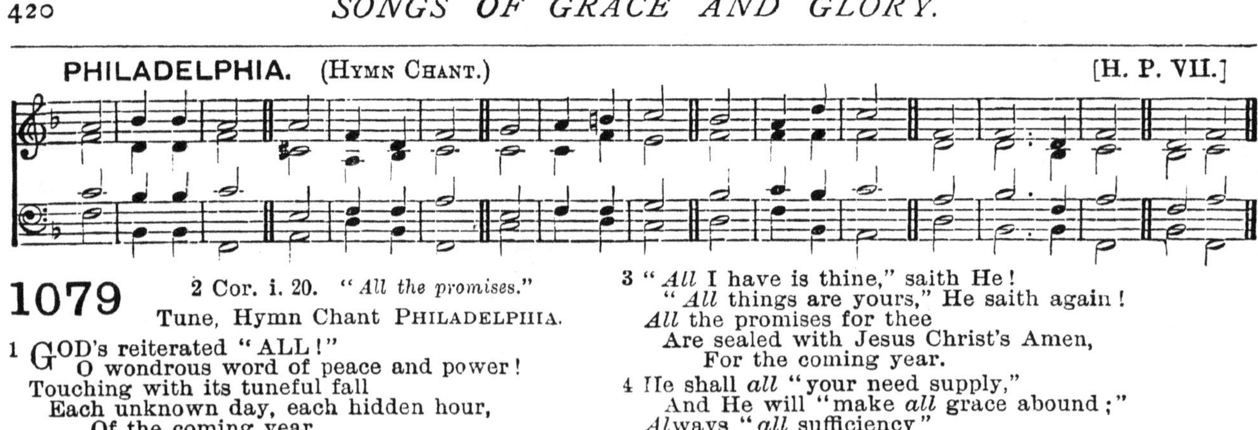

1079

2 Cor. i. 20. "*All the promises.*"
Tune, Hymn Chant PHILADELPHIA.

1 GOD's reiterated "ALL!"
O wondrous word of peace and power!
Touching with its tuneful fall
Each unknown day, each hidden hour,
Of the coming year.

2 Only *all* His word believe!
All peace and joy your heart shall fill,
All things asked ye shall receive;
This is thy Father's word and will,
For the coming year.

3 "*All* I have is thine," saith He!
"*All* things are yours," He saith again!
All the promises for thee
Are sealed with Jesus Christ's Amen,
For the coming year.

4 He shall *all* "your need supply,"
And He will "make *all* grace abound;"
*Al*ways "*all* sufficiency"
In Him for *all* things shall be found,
Through the coming year.

5 *All* "His work He shall fulfil,"
All "the good pleasure of His will,"
Keeping thee in "*all* thy ways,"
And "with thee *always*," *all* the days
Of the coming year.

Frances Ridley Havergal, 1871.

See Hymns 909—913.

ZAANAIM (Plain of). [H. P. 191.]

"Preserved in Christ."

1080

Heb. xiii. 5. "*I will never leave thee, nor forsake thee.*"
Tune ZAANAIM, repeat last two strains. 87, 87, 47.

1 I WILL never, never leave thee,
I will never thee forsake;
I will guard, and save, and keep thee,
For My name and mercy's sake.
Fear no evil!
Only all My counsel take;
For I'll never, never leave thee,
I will never thee forsake.

2 When the storm is raging round thee,
Call on Me in humble prayer;
I will fold My arms about thee,
Guard thee with the tenderest care;
In the trial
I will make thy pathway clear:
For I'll never, etc.

3 When the sky above is glowing,
And around thee all is bright,
Pleasure like a river flowing,
All things tending to delight,
I'll be with thee,
I will guide thy steps aright:
For I'll never, etc.

PART II.

4 When thy soul is dark and clouded,
Filled with doubt, and grief, and care,
Through the mist by which 'tis shrouded
I will make a light appear;
And the banner
Of My love I will uprear:
For I'll never, etc.

5 If thou leave My care and keeping,
Thou may'st wander far from Me;
Sorrow then, and woe, and weeping,
Mercy must mete out to thee.
To the righteous,
My rich blessings all are free:
For I'll never, etc.

6 When thy feeble flame is dying,
And thy soul about to soar
To that land where pain and sighing
Shall be heard and known no more,
I will teach thee
To rejoice that life is o'er:
For I'll never, etc.

Weaver's Hymn Book, 1869.

1081

Jude 1. "*Preserved in Jesus Christ.*"
Tune GOSHEN. 76, 76.

1 PART sunbeams from their centre,
Part saltness from the sea,
No height, no depth, shall ever
Part My redeemed from Me!

2 I'll shake the earth and heavens,
I'll build this world anew;
But as My word remaineth,
I still will shelter you.

E. Clay's Collection, 1866.

GOSHEN. [H. P. 125.]

SMYRNA. (Hymn Chant.) *Double Counterpoint.* [H. P. No. III.]

1082

Matt. xiv. 27. "*Be of good cheer; it is I!*" Tune, Hymn Chant Smyrna. 888, 6.

1 TOSSED with rough winds, and faint with fear,
Above the tempest, soft and clear,
What still soft accents greet thine ear?
"'Tis I, be not afraid!"

2 'Tis I, who washed thy spirit white;
'Tis I, who gave thy blind eyes sight;
'Tis I, thy Lord, thy Life, thy Light;
"'Tis I, be not afraid!"

3 These raging winds, this surging sea,
Bear not a breath of wrath to thee;
That storm has all been spent on Me;
"'Tis I, be not afraid!"

4 The bitter cup, I drank it first;
For thee it is no draught accurst:
The hand that gives it thee is pierced;
"'Tis I, be not afraid!"

5 Mine eyes are watching by thy bed,
Mine arms are underneath thy head,
My blessing is around thee shed;
"'Tis I, be not afraid!"

6 When, on the other side, thy feet
Shall rest 'mid thousand welcomes sweet,
One well known voice thy heart shall greet,
"'Tis I, be not afraid!"

Mrs. Elizabeth Charles, 1865.

KEDRON (Brook). [H. P. 213.]

1083

Ps. xxx. 5. "*Weeping may endure for a night, but joy cometh in the morning.*" Tune Kedron. 884. D.

1 WHAT care the saints of God, if they
'Mid pain and wounds are called away
To their reward?
What matters one short day of tears
Which ushers in the countless years
With their dear Lord?

2 To all the saints of God saith He,
Take up your cross and follow Me,
I lead Mine own.
I go your mansions to prepare,
And you in bliss shall meet Me there
Before the throne.

3 The lot of God's elect below
Was ever thus, and must be so
While earth shall last:
Trials must lie about our feet,
Till in the courts of God we meet,
All troubles past.

4 But there the Lord in that bright day
For His own saints shall wipe away
Tears from all eyes;
And no more sorrow shall be there,
No tears, no weeping, no more care
Beyond the skies.

5 'Midst trembling here we joyful find
The path to bliss, nor look behind
In doubt and fear;
While sometimes faint, and sometimes loud,
The murmur of the tempest cloud
Falls on our ear.

6 But all the saints of Jesus know
That when the storms of trouble blow,
They see in faith
Their Saviour walking on the wave,
And He is ever strong to save
Their souls from death.

Gerard Moultrie, 1870.

See Hymns 668—734.

EIRENE. [H. P. 246.]

To Refresh the Missioner.

1084 Luke viii. 39. "*Show how great things God hath done unto thee.*"

Tune Eirene. 11 10, 11 10.

1 NOT now, my child,—a little more rough tossing,
A little longer on the billows' foam,—
A few more journeyings in the desert darkness,
And then the sunshine of thy Father's home!

2 Not now,—for I have wanderers in the distance,
And thou must call them in with patient love;
Not now,—for I have sheep upon the mountains,
And thou must follow them where'er they rove.

3 Not now,—for I have loved ones sad and weary;
Wilt thou not cheer them with a kindly smile?
Sick ones, who need thee in their lonely sorrow;
Wilt thou not tend them yet a little while?

4 Not now,—for wounded hearts are sorely bleeding,
And thou must teach those widowed hearts to sing.
Not now,—for orphans' tears are thickly falling;
They must be gathered 'neath some sheltering wing.

5 Not now,—for many a hungry one is pining;
Thy willing hand must be outstretched and free;
Thy Father hears the mighty cry of anguish,
And gives His answering messages to thee.

6 Go with the name of Jesus to the dying,
And speak that name in all its living power;
Why should thy fainting heart grow chill and weary?
Canst thou not watch with Me one little hour?

7 One little hour!—and then the glorious crowning—
The golden harp-strings and the victor's palm.
One little hour! and then the Hallelujah!
Eternity's long, deep, thanksgiving psalm!

Mrs. Catherine Pennefather, 1863.

See Hymns 565—569, 765—773.

DALMATIA. [H. P. 20.]

Sickness, or Hospital Sundays.

1085 Mark i. 32. "*And at even, when the sun did set, they brought unto Him all that were diseased.*"

Tune Dalmatia. L. M.

1 AT even, when the sun was set,
The sick, O Lord, around Thee lay;
Oh, in what divers pains they met!
Oh, with what joy they went away!

2 Once more 'tis eventide, and we
Oppressed with various ills draw near:
What if Thy form we cannot see?
We know and feel that Thou art here.

3 O Saviour Christ, our woes dispel;
For some are sick, and some are sad,
And some have never loved Thee well,
And some have lost the love they had;

4 And some are pressed with worldly care;
And some are tried with sinful doubt;
And some such grievous passions tear
That only Thou canst cast them out;

5 And some have found the world is vain,
Yet from the world they break not free
And some have friends who give them pain,
Yet have not sought a Friend in Thee.

6 O Saviour Christ, Thou too art man;
Thou hast been troubled, tempted, tried;
Thy kind but searching glance can scan
The very wounds that shame would hide;

7 Thy touch has still its ancient power;
No word from Thee can fruitless fall:
Hear, in this solemn evening hour,
And in Thy mercy heal us all.

Henry Twells, 1866.

See Hymns 870, 962—967.

The Lord's Supper.

1086 Mark xiv. 26. "*When they had sung an hymn.*" Tune Magdeburg. 87, 87, 47. Or Zaanaim.

1 COME, ye saints, and raise an anthem,
Cleave the skies with shouts of praise;
Sing to Him who found a ransom,
The' Ancient of eternal days:
In your nature,
Born to suffer in your place.

2 Lo, He comes! and on mount Calvary
Pours His blood, resigns His breath,
Finishes the great salvation,
Kills the killing power of Death;
Then arises,
Lives, and reigns for evermore.

MAGDEBURG. [H. P. 300.]

3 High on yon celestial mountains
Stands His gem-built throne, all bright
Midst incessant acclamations,
Bursting from the sons of light:
Zion's praises
Are His chosen dwelling-place.

4 Bring your harps, and bring your odours,
Sweep the string and pour the lay;
View His works! behold His wonders,
Let Hosannas crown the day!
He is worthy
Of eternal, boundless praise.

PART II.

5 Hungry souls, that faint and languish,
By His bounteous hand are fed;
Yes, He gives them food immortal,
Gives Himself, the living Bread;
This revives them;
Life, and health, and strength it gives.

6 See His guardian wing extended,
To secure His own from harm;
See the gates of hell confounded
By His high, imperial arm;
Devils tremble
At His word, or at His nod.

7 Trust Him then, ye fearful pilgrims:
Who shall pluck you from His hand?
Pledged He stands for your salvation,
Soon you'll see the promised land;
Soon He'll crown you,
And exalt you to His throne!

8 There amazed you'll view His glories
Brighter than ten thousand suns;
There you'll drink the living pleasure,
Which from endless fountains runs,
And with angels
Swell the everlasting song.

Job Hupton, 1805.

LINUS. [H. P. 336.]

1087

Isa. lxii. 5. *"So shall thy God rejoice over thee."* Tune LINUS. 8888, 7777.

1 DECK thyself, my soul, with gladness,
Leave the gloomy haunts of sadness,
Come into the daylight's splendour,
There with joy thy praises render
Unto Him whose boundless grace
Grants thee at His feast a place;
He whom all the heavens obey
Deigns to dwell in thee to-day.

2 Hasten, as a bride, to meet Him,
And with loving reverence greet Him
Who, with words of life immortal,
Now is knocking at thy portal.
Haste to make for Him a way,
Cast thee at His feet, and say—
"Since, O Lord! Thou com'st to me,
Never will I turn from Thee."

3 Ah, how hungers all my spirit
For the love I do not merit!
Ah, how oft with sighs fast thronging
For this food have I been longing,
How have thirsted in the strife
For this draught, O Prince of Life!
Pined, O Friend of man! to be
Ever one with God through Thee!

PART II.

4 Here I sink before Thee lowly,
Filled with joy most deep and holy,
As with trembling awe and wonder
On Thy mighty works I ponder,
On this banquet's mystery,
On the depths we cannot see;
Far beyond all mortal sight
Lie the secrets of Thy might.

5 Sun, who all my life dost brighten!
Light, who dost my soul enlighten!
Joy, the sweetest man e'er knoweth!
Fount whence all my being floweth!
Here I fall before Thy feet:
Grant me worthily to eat
Of this blessèd heavenly food,
To Thy praise, and to my good!

Catherine Winkworth, 1858.

CYPRUS. [H. P. 26.]

1088 John iii. 29. *"Rejoiceth greatly because of the Bridegroom's voice."* Tune CYPRUS. L. M.

1 HE cometh as the bridegroom comes,
Unto the feast Himself hath spread,
His flesh and blood the heavenly food
With which true wedding-guests are fed.

2 He cometh gently as the dew,
And sweet as drops of honey clear,
And good as God's own manna-shower,
To longing souls that wait Him here.

3 He cometh as He came of old,
Suddenly to His Father's shrine,
Into the hearts He died to make
Meet temples for His grace Divine.

4 He cometh—praises in the Church,
And hymns of praise in heaven above,
And in our hearts repentant faith,
And love that springs to meet His love.

Cecil Frances Alexander, 1859.

SWABIA. [H. P. 82.]

1089 Isa. xxv. 6. *"A feast of fat things."* Tune SWABIA. S. M.

1 NO gospel like this feast,
Spread for Thy Church by Thee,
Nor prophet nor evangelist
Preach the glad news so free.

2 All our redemption cost,
All our redemption won,
All it has won for us, the lost,
All it cost Thee, the Son.

3 Thine was the bitter price,
Ours is the free gift given;
Thine was the blood of sacrifice,
Ours is the wine of heaven.

4 For Thee the burning thirst,
The shame, the mortal strife,
The broken heart, the side transpierced;
To us the bread of life.

5 Here we would rest midway,
As on a sacred height,
That darkest and that brightest day
Meeting before our sight.

6 From that dark depth of woes
Thy love for us hath trod,
Up to the heights of blest repose
Thy love prepares with God.

7 Till, from self's chains released,
One sight alone we see,
Still at the cross, as at the feast,
Behold Thee, only Thee!

Mrs. Elizabeth Charles, 1870.

See Hymns 779—791.

The Second Advent.

1090 Titus ii. 13. *"Looking for that blessed hope."*

Tune ST. PAUL. 87, 887, 77, 77.

1 THOU art coming, O my Saviour!
Thou art coming, O my King!
In Thy beauty all-resplendent,
In Thy glory all-transcendent;
Well may we rejoice and sing!
Coming! In the opening east
Herald brightness slowly swells;
Coming! O my glorious Priest,
Hear we not Thy golden bells?

2 Thou art coming, Thou art coming!
We shall meet Thee on Thy way,
We shall see Thee, we shall know Thee,
We shall bless Thee, we shall show Thee
All our hearts could never say!
What an anthem that will be,
Ringing out our love to Thee,
Pouring out our rapture sweet
At Thine own all-glorious feet!

3 Not a cloud and not a shadow,
Not a mist and not a tear,
Not a sin and not a sorrow,
Not a dim and veiled to-morrow,
For that sunrise grand and clear!
Jesus, Saviour, once with Thee,
Nothing else seems worth a thought!
Oh how marvellous will be
All the bliss Thy pain hath bought!

ST. PAUL. [H. P. 253.]

PART II.

4 Thou art coming! At Thy table
We are witnesses for this,
While remembering hearts Thou meetest,
In communion clearest, sweetest,
Earnest of our coming bliss.
Showing not Thy death alone,
And Thy love exceeding great,
But Thy coming and Thy throne,
All for which we long and wait.

5 Thou art coming! We are waiting
With a hope that cannot fail;
Asking not the day or hour,
Resting on Thy word of power,
Anchored safe within the veil.
Time appointed may be long,
But the vision must be sure:
Certainty shall make us strong,
Joyful patience shall endure!

6 Oh the joy to see Thee reigning,
Thee, my own belovèd Lord!
Every tongue Thy name confessing,
Worship, honour, glory, blessing,
Brought to Thee with glad accord!
Thee, my Master and my Friend,
Vindicated and enthroned!
Unto earth's remotest end
Glorified, adored, and owned!

Frances Ridley Havergal, 1873.

STERNBERG. [H. P. 245.]

1091

1 Cor. i. 7. *"Waiting for the coming of our Lord Jesus Christ."*

Tune STERNBERG. 11 10, 11 10.

1 WAITING for Jesus, and *loving* while waiting,
Loving to speak for His honour and praise,
Loving to sit at His feet and adore Him,
Loving to ponder His words and His ways.

2 Waiting for Jesus, and *praying* while waiting,
E'er in communion with Him whom I love;
E'er at the footstool of mercy imploring
Showers of blessing on all from above.

3 Waiting for Jesus, and *serving* while waiting,
Serving, and oh! what a Master to serve;
Helping, rewarding, and cheering in labour;
Oh that my heart from Him never may swerve!

4 Waiting for Jesus, and *praising* while waiting,
Praising in action, in word, and in song.
Oh! it is sweet to be ever rehearsing
Strains which eternity will but prolong.

5 Waiting for Jesus, and daily expecting;
Gazing to catch the first beams in the sky;
Oh! what a moment; 'tis quickly approaching,
Moment of triumph, of rapture, and joy.

Albert Midlane, 1874.

See Hymns 291—341.

Farewell.

1092

John xiv. 3. *"I will come again."*
DISMISSAL. 87, 87, 47. Or TEMAN.

1 YES, we part, but not for ever;
Joyful hopes our bosoms swell;
They who love the Saviour never
Know a long, a last farewell.
Blissful unions
Lie beyond this parting vale.

2 Sweet this hour of benediction,
When such unions come to mind,
When each holy heart-conviction,
With the promises combined,
Tell of meetings
By the Lord for us designed.

3 Oh what meetings are before us,
Brighter far than tongue can tell,
Glorious meetings to restore us
Him, with whom we long to dwell.
With what raptures
Will the sight our bosoms swell!

4 Thus we part, but not for ever;
Joyful hopes our bosoms swell;
They who love the Saviour never
Know a last, a long farewell.
Blissful unions
Lie beyond this parting vale.

See Hymns 1007—1025. *Joseph Denham Smith, 1860.*

DISMISSAL. [H. P. 305.]

ZOAN I. (Field of). [H. P. 127.]

Glory: Present.

1093 2 Cor. iii. 18. "*From glory to glory.*"

Tune ZOAN I. 76, 76. D. Or EASTHAM.

1 "FROM glory unto glory!" Our faith hath seen the King!
We own His matchless beauty, as adoringly we sing;
But He hath more to show us! Oh thought of untold bliss!
And we press on exultingly in certain hope of this.

2 Our own belovèd Master "hath many things to say";
Look forward to His teaching, unfolding day by day;
To whispers of His Spirit, while resting at His feet,
To glowing revelation, to insight clear and sweet;

3 To marvellous outpourings of His "treasures new and old,"
To largess of His bounty, paid in the King's own gold,
To glorious expansion of His mysteries of grace,
To radiant unveilings of the brightness of His face.

4 And "greater things," far greater, our longing eyes shall see!
We can but wait and wonder what "greater things" shall be;
But glorious fulfilments rejoicingly we claim,
While pleading in the power of the All-Prevailing Name.

5 The fulness of His blessing encompasseth our way;
The fulness of His promises crowns every brightening day;
The fulness of His glory is beaming from above,
While more and more we realise the fulness of His love.

6 "From glory unto glory!" without a shade of care,
Because the Lord who loves us will every burden bear;
Because we trust Him fully, and know that He will guide,
And know that He will keep us at His belovèd side.

PART II.

7 Abiding in His presence, and walking in the light,
And seeking to "do always what is pleasing in His sight,"
We look to Him to keep us "all-glorious within,"
Because "the blood of Jesus Christ is cleansing from all sin."

8 "From glory unto glory!" Our fellow-travellers still
Are gathering on the journey; the bright electric thrill
Of quick, instinctive union, more frequent and more sweet,
Shall swiftly pass from heart to heart, in true and tender beat.

9 And closer yet, and closer the golden bonds shall be,
Enlinking all who love our Lord in pure sincerity;
And wider yet, and wider, shall the circling glory glow,
As more and more are taught, of God, that mighty love to know.

10 O ye who seek the Saviour, look up in faith and love,
Come up into the sunshine, so bright and warm above!
No longer tread the valley, but clinging to His hand,
Ascend the shining summits, and view the glorious land.

11 Our harp-notes should be sweeter, our trumpet-tones more clear,
Our anthems ring so grandly that all the world must hear!
Oh, royal be our music, for who hath cause to sing
Like the chorus of redeemed ones, the children of the King!

12 In full and glad surrender we give ourselves to Thee,
Thine utterly, and only, and evermore to be!
O Son of God, who lovest us, we will be Thine alone,
And all we are, and all we have, shall henceforth be Thine own.

Frances Ridley Havergal, 1873.

See Hymns 439—448, 1011—1025, 1043, 1056, 1058, 1066.

Glory: Future.

1094 Rev. iv. 3. *"There was a rainbow round about the throne."*

Tune AQUILA. 8988, 8888.

1 AROUND that magnificent throne,
Where the Lamb all His glory displays,
United for ever in one,
His people are singing His praise.
How holy, how happy are they!
No tongue can express their delight:
My soul, now unwilling to stay,
Prepares for her heavenly flight.

2 But why do I wish to be gone?
Do I want from the danger to flee?
And shall I do nothing for One
Who was such a Suff'rer for me?
Ah, Lord, let me think of the day
When Thou wast "rejected of men,"
And put the base wish far away;
And never be fearful again.

Thomas Kelly, 1809.

See Hymns 1011—1025.

TUNES AND HYMNS

IN

"SONGS OF GRACE AND GLORY FOR THE YOUNG,"

WHICH ARE NOT FOUND IN THE ADULT EDITION.

EUNICE. [H. P. 333.]

54 Heb. xiii. 5. *"He hath said, I will never leave thee, nor forsake thee."*

Tune EUNICE. 10 10, 10 10.

1 "WHO will take care of me?" darling, you say!
Lovingly, tenderly, watched as you are!
Listen! I give you the answer to-day,
ONE who is never forgetful or far!

2 He will take care of you! All through the day
Jesus is near you, to keep you from ill;
Walking or resting, at lessons or play,
Jesus is with you and watching you still.

3 He will take care of you! All through the night
Jesus, the Shepherd, His little one keeps;
Darkness to Him is the same as the light;
He never slumbers, and He never sleeps.

4 He will take care of you! All through the year
Crowning each day with His kindness and love,
Sending you blessings, and shielding from fear,
Leading you on to the bright home above.

5 He will take care of you! Yes, to the end!
Nothing can alter His love to His own.
Darling, be glad that you have such a Friend;
He will not leave you one moment alone!

Frances Ridley Havergal, 1873.

KÖCKER. [H. P. 329.]

55 Zech. xiii. 7. *"I will turn Mine hand upon the little ones."*

Tune KÖCKER. 7 6, 7 6.

1 THE little ones, the weak ones,
The lambs of Jesus' care,
Are folded in His bosom,
And find their shelter there.

2 The little ones, the weak ones,
The tremblers of the flock,
Are rooted like the oak trees,
Are grounded on the Rock.

3 The little ones, the weak ones,
That Satan loves to try,
Are just the kind of Christians
That Satan's arts defy.

4 The little ones, the weak ones,
That cry "What shall we do?"
Are answered by Emmanuel,
"My grace sufficeth you."

5 The little ones, the weak ones,
Are yet the great and strong,
Because it is to Jesus
The small and weak belong.

6 And, knowing they are weak ones
And also very small,
They trust alone in Jesus,
And not in self at all.

S. A. Walker, 1870.

87 Acts ix. 6. *"Lord, what wilt Thou have me to do?"*

Tune Apphia. 98, 98. D.

1 OH what can I do for Friend so true,
Oh what can I do for Jesus?
I'll give Him all, and myself give too,
Oh, that will I give to Jesus.

Chorus—Oh what can I do for Friend so true,
Oh what can I do for Jesus?
I'll give Him all, and myself give too,
Oh, that will I do for Jesus.

2 Through the long dark night I have slumbered sweet,
'Neath His loving smile so tender;
Never will I fear, for I know He's near,
Ever near, my great Defender.
Oh what can I do, etc.

3 The meadow and grove rejoice in love,
Resounding the praise of Jesus.
Shall we not join in that song Divine,
"Hosanna to Him—to Jesus!"
Oh what can I do, etc.

APPHIA. [H. P. 332.]

4 Far above we hear voices sweet and clear,
'Tis the angels' song ascending:
And with them we'll sing of our Saviour King,
Of His love, His love unending.
Oh what can I do, etc.

George S. Weeks, 1870.

"BRIGHT JEWELS." [H. P. 334.]

97 Ps. xcv. 1. *"O come, let us sing unto the Lord."*

Tune Bright Jewels. 11 11, 11 11.

1 BRIGHT jewels of song to the Saviour we bring,
Glad anthems of praise to our glorified King;
With seraphs and angels before Thee we raise,
In humbler devotion, our chorus of praise.
Bright jewels of song,
Bright jewels of song,
Bright jewels to Jesus, to Jesus belong.

2 Our grateful hosannas we offer to Thee,
Proclaiming salvation so boundless and free,
Till o'er the wide earth the sweet story we send
Of Jesus, the sinner's Redeemer and Friend.
Bright jewels, etc.

3 Accept Thou our offering; oh, make it sincere.
These songs of rejoicing life's pathway shall cheer;
And when with the ransomed in glory we sing,
Bright jewels we'll shine in the crown of our King.
Bright jewels, etc.

W. F. Sherwin, 1869.

FORTUNATUS. [H. P. 331.]

116 Isa. lviii. 13. "*Call the Sabbath a delight.*"

Tune FORTUNATUS. 8888, 68, 88, 68.

1 I LOVE the blessèd Sabbath-day,
"The first and best of all the seven,"
I love to sing, to read, and pray,
To hear of God, and Christ, and heaven.
Happy day! happy day!
I love the holy Sabbath-day,
The day my God in love has given,
That I might find the path to heaven.
Happy day! happy day!
I love the holy Sabbath-day.

2 'Tis sweet from earthly toils to rest,
To worship at our Father's throne;
To welcome Christ, the heavenly Guest,
And thank Him for His mercy shown.
Happy day! etc.

3 'Tis sweet the Spirit's power to prove,
With lowly heart His grace to seek;
'Tis sweet to think of joys above,
And thus with God commence the week.
Happy day! etc.

J. Lees, "Sacred Songs," 1858.

JUNIA. [H. P. 328.]

131 Matt. xxv. 22. "*Behold I have gained two other talents.*" Tune JUNIA. 56, 56.

1 GOD entrusts to all
Talents few or many;
None so young or small
That they have not any.

2 Though the great and wise
Have a greater number,
Yet my one I prize,
And it must not slumber.

3 God will surely ask,
Ere I enter heaven,
Have I done the task
Which to me was given?

4 Little drops of rain
Bring the springing flowers;
And I may attain
Much by little powers.

5 Every little mite,
Every little measure,
Helps to spread the light,
Helps to swell the treasure.

6 God entrusts to all
Talents few or many;
None so young or small
That they have not any.

James Edmeston, 1846.

"'TIS A LESSON." [H. P. 359.]

133 Phil. iv. 13. *"I can do all things through Christ which strengtheneth me."*

Tune, "'Tis a Lesson." 7 5, 7 5, 7 7 7 5.

1 'TIS a lesson you should heed,
Try, try, try again.
If at first you don't succeed,
Try, try, try again.
Then your courage should appear;
For if you will persevere,
You will conquer, never fear:
Try, try, try again.

2 Once or twice though you may fail,
Try, try, try again.
If at last you would prevail,
Try, try, try again.
If we strive, 'tis no disgrace,
Though at first we miss the race.
What to do in such a case,
Try, try, try again.

3 If you find your task is hard,
Try, try, try again.
Prayer will bring you your reward,
Try, try, try again.
All that other people do,
Why, with patience, should not you?
Only keep this rule in view,
Try, try, try again.

"Hymns for Infant Schools," 1845.

(The preceding Seven Hymns and Tunes from "Songs of Grace and Glory for the Young" have been added in this edition, that ALL *the tunes might here be found complete for adults and children.)*

Doxologies.
THE OLD 100th TUNE.
[H. P. 1.]
I.
Tune OLD HUNDREDTH. L. M.
PRAISE God from whom all blessings flow;
Praise Him, all creatures here below;
Praise Him above, ye heavenly host;
Praise Father, Son, and Holy Ghost. Amen.
Bishop Ken, 1697.
II.
Tune TALLIS'S ORDINAL. C. M.
TO Father, Son, and Holy Ghost,
The God whom we adore,
Be glory, as it was, is now,
And shall be evermore. Amen.
Tate and Brady, 1696.
TALLIS'S ORDINAL.
[H. P. 44.]
SWABIA.
[H. P. 82.]
III.
Tune SWABIA. S. M.
GIVE to the Father praise,
Give glory to the Son,
And to the Spirit of His grace
Be equal honour done. Amen.
Isaac Watts, D.D., 1709.
IV.
Tune ZOAN I. 76,76. D.
O FATHER, ever glorious,
O everlasting Son,
O Spirit all victorious,
Thrice holy Three in One:
Great God of our salvation,
Whom earth and heaven adore,
Praise, glory, adoration,
Be Thine for evermore. Amen.
E. H. Bickersteth, 1869.
V.
Tune LUBECK. 77,77.
SING we to our God above
Praise eternal as His love:
Praise Him, all ye heavenly host,
Father, Son, and Holy Ghost.
Amen.
Charles Wesley, 1739.
ZOAN I. (Field of.)
[H. P. 127.]
LUBECK.
[H. P. 139.]

NASSAU. [H. P. 155.]

VI.

Tune NASSAU. 77, 77, 77.

GOD of everlasting love,
One in co-eternal Three,
All the shining hosts above
Give unceasing praise to Thee.
So we worship Thee and cry
Glory be to God most high! Amen.

VII.

Tune KADESH. 77, 77. D.

HOLY Father, Fount of light,
God of wisdom, goodness, might;
Holy Son, who cam'st to dwell,
God with us, Emmanuel;
Holy Spirit, heavenly Dove,
God of comfort, peace, and love;
Evermore be Thou adored,
Holy, holy, holy Lord. Amen.

E. H. Bickersteth, 1869.

[For 10 lines 7's, prefix to these the last two lines.]

KADESH. [H. P. 159.]

VIII.

Tune ZAANAIM. 87, 87, 87.

NOW to Him who loved us, gave us
Every pledge that love could give,
Freely shed His blood to save us,
Gave His life that we might live:
Be the kingdom and dominion,
And the glory, evermore! Amen.

Samuel M. Waring, 1827. (*a.*)

IX.

Tune ZAANAIM. 87, 87, 47.

FATHER, God, we bow before Thee;
Thee we worship, God the Son;
God the Spirit, we adore Thee;
Praise the glorious Three in One.
Hallelujah!
Praise Jehovah, God Triune. Amen.

ZAANAIM (Plain of). [H. P. 191.]

F F

LINUS. [H. P. 336.]

X.

Tune Linus. 87, 87. D.

PRAISE the God of all creation!
  Praise the Father's boundless love!
Praise the Lamb, our Expiation,
  Priest and King, enthroned above!
Praise the Fountain of salvation,
  Him by whom our spirits live!
Undivided adoration
  To the One Jehovah give. Amen.

Josiah Conder, 1837.

XI.

Tune Shen. 87, 87. D.

FOR Thy free electing favour,
  Thee, O Father, we adore;
Jesus, our redeeming Saviour,
  Thee we worship evermore:
Holy Ghost, from both proceeding,
  Let Thy praise the church employ:
Earnest of our future heaven,
  Source of holiness and joy. Amen.

Augustus M. Toplady, 1776.

SHEN (The Rock). [H. P. 201.]

HANOVER, *or*, MODERN 104th. [H. P. 239.]

XII.

Tune Hanover. 10 10, 11 11.

BY angels in heaven of every degree,
  And saints upon earth, all praise be addressed
To God in Three Persons, one God ever blessed,
As it has been, now is, and always shall be.
Amen.

Tate and Brady, 1696.

INDEX OF FIRST LINES.

INDEX OF FIRST LINES.

INDEX OF FIRST LINES.

INDEX OF FIRST LINES.

INDEX OF FIRST LINES.

INDEX OF FIRST LINES.

Butler & Tanner,
The Selwood Printing Works,
Frome, and London.

NOTE.

"*It is with very sincere gratification I here record my warm thanks to Messrs. Butler & Tanner and the intelligent members of their staff for their efficient and ready help in carrying out this important work, and I have great pleasure in testifying to the value and excellence of their labour.*"

Signed, C. B. SNEPP.

Tell it out!
Words and Music by
FRANCES RIDLEY HAVERGAL.
Tell it out among the heathen that the Lord is King! Tell it out! . . Tell it
Tell it out! . . .
Tell it out! Tell it out! that the Lord is King! Tell it out! . . .
out! . . . Tell it out among the nations, bid them shout and sing! Tell it
. Tell it out! Tell it out! Tell it out! bid them shout and sing! Tell it
out! . . . Tell it out! Tell it out with a-do-ra-tion that He shall increase; That the
FINE.
out! . . . Tell it out! Tell it out! . . . . that He shall increase; That the
Tell it out! Tell it out! Tell it out with a-do-ra-tion that He shall increase; That the
out! Tell . . . it out! Tell it out! . . . . that He shall increase; That the
mighty King of Glory is the King of Peace; Tell it out with ju-bi-lation though the
D.S.
waves may roar, That He sitteth on the water-floods, our King for ev-er-more! Tell it
Tell it out among the heathen that the Saviour reigns!
Tell it out! Tell it out!
Tell it out among the nations, bid them burst their
Tell it out! Tell it out! [chains.
Tell it out among the weeping ones that Jesus lives;
Tell it out among the weary ones what rest He gives;
Tell it out among the sinners that He came to save;
Tell it out among the dying that He triumphed o'er
the grave.
Tell it out among the heathen Jesus reigns above!
Tell it out! Tell it out!
Tell it out among the nations that His reign is love!
Tell it out! Tell it out!
Tell it out among the highways and the lanes at home;
Let it ring across the mountains and the ocean foam!
Like the sound of many waters let our glad shout be,
Till it echo and re-echo from the islands of the sea!

Frances wrote to James Parlane in a letter in 1876:[1]

. . . I must tell you a wonderful bit of Ministry of Song, through "Whom having not seen, ye love." I was taken on speculation to call on a clever young gentleman, just an infidel, knowing the Bible and disbelieving it, and believing that nobody else really believes, but that religion is all humbug and mere profession. I was not primed at all, only knew that he was "not a religious man." In the first place, I had no end of fun with him, and got on thoroughly good terms—then was asked to sing. I prayed the whole time I was singing, and felt God very near and helping me. After a Handel song or two which greatly delighted him, I sang "Tell it out!" felt the glorious truth that He is King, and couldn't help breaking off in the very middle and saying so, right out!

Then I sang, "Whom having not seen, ye love," and felt as if could sing out all the love of my heart in it. Well, this young infidel, who had seemed extremely surprised and subdued by "tell it out," completely broke down, and went away to hide his tears in a bay window. And afterwards we sat down together, and he let me "tell it out" as I pleased, and it was not hard to speak of Him of whom I had sung. He seemed altogether struck and subdued, and listened like a child. He said, "Well there is faith then, you have it anyhow—I saw it when you sang, and could not stand it, and that's the fact!" He was anxious for me to come again.

When I came away, his sister, who had introduced me, wept for joy, saying she had persuaded me to come with a vague hope that he "might find he could tolerate a religious person," but never dared to hope such an effect as this, and that she thought I had been most marvellously guided in drawing the bow at a venture, for every word and even action had been just right. I tell you this just because you are publishing both "Tell it out" and other leaflets for me. Will you sometimes pray that God's especial blessing will go with them? I should add that it was almost a miracle in another way, for I had such a wretched cold that I doubted being able to sing at all, and yet I believe I never sang clearer and better and stronger. How good *God is!*

[1] *Letters by the Late Frances Ridley Havergal* edited by her sister Maria V. G. Havergal (London: James Nisbet & Co., 1886), pages 265–266. See pages 221–222 of Volume IV of the Havergal edition. See also pages 450–451, 622–623, and 1279–1281 of Volume V of the Havergal edition.

This next set of hymns copied from *Songs of Grace and Glory* is the set of the hymn scores composed by Frances Ridley Havergal, here gathered in one place for the convenience of the reader. These hymn scores and also all the other extant scores composed by F.R.H. (hymn scores, art songs, and *Loyal Responses* with music) have been newly typeset by Dr. Glen Wegge and are presented in his sterling volume *The Music of Frances Ridley Havergal.* That is a Companion Volume to the Havergal edition, containing first the same dissertation that is given in the first 122 pages of Volume V of the Havergal edition, and then all of F.R.H.'s extant compositions that were found, presented in newly typeset scores by Dr. Wegge. David Chalkley

EIRENE. [H. P. 246.]

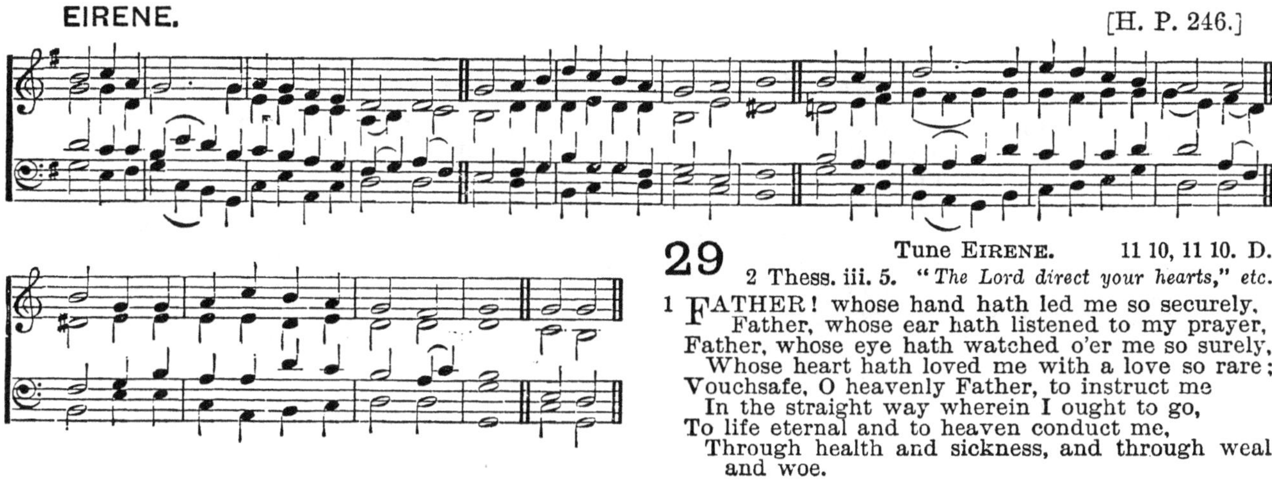

29 Tune EIRENE. 11 10, 11 10. D.

2 Thess. iii. 5. "*The Lord direct your hearts,*" etc.

1 FATHER! whose hand hath led me so securely,
  Father, whose ear hath listened to my prayer,
Father, whose eye hath watched o'er me so surely,
  Whose heart hath loved me with a love so rare;
Vouchsafe, O heavenly Father, to instruct me
  In the straight way wherein I ought to go,
To life eternal and to heaven conduct me,
  Through health and sickness, and through weal and woe.

2 O my Redeemer! who hast my redemption
  Purchased, and paid for, by Thy precious blood;
Thereby procuring an entire exemption
  From the dread wrath and punishment of God:
Thou who hast saved my soul from condemnation,
  Redeem it also from the power of sin,
Be Thou the Captain still of my salvation,
  Through whom alone I can the victory win.

3 O Holy Ghost! who from the Father flowest—
  And from the Son, oh teach me how to pray!
Thou, who the love and peace of God bestowest,
  With faith and hope inspire and cheer my way;
Direct, control, and sanctify each motion
  Within my soul, and make it thus to be
Prayerful, and still, and full of deep devotion,
  A holy temple, worthy, Lord, of Thee!

C. J. P. Spitta, 1833; *R. Massie (tr.),* 1860.

PHILADELPHIA. (HYMN CHANT.) [H. P. VII.]

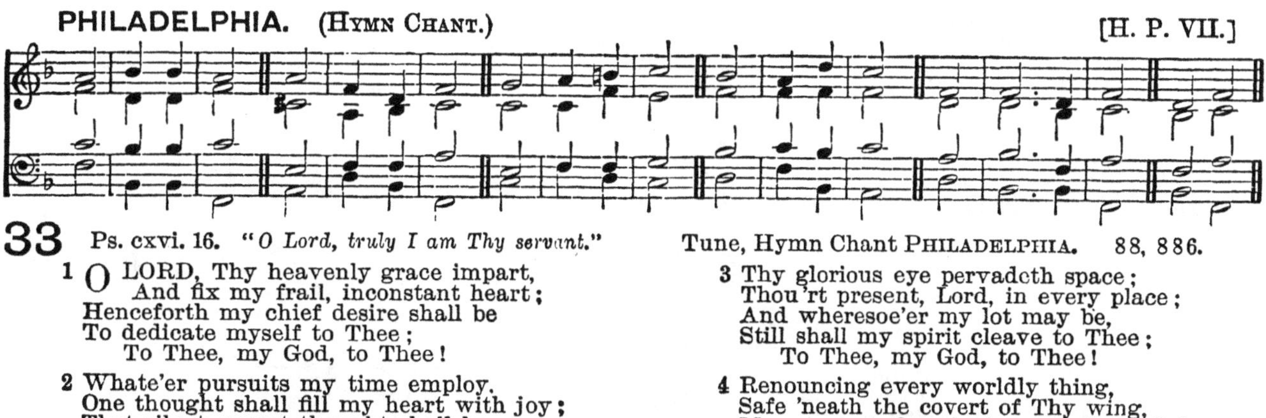

33 Ps. cxvi. 16. "*O Lord, truly I am Thy servant.*"

Tune, Hymn Chant PHILADELPHIA. 88, 886.

1 O LORD, Thy heavenly grace impart,
  And fix my frail, inconstant heart;
Henceforth my chief desire shall be
To dedicate myself to Thee;
  To Thee, my God, to Thee!

2 Whate'er pursuits my time employ,
One thought shall fill my heart with joy;
That silent, secret thought shall be,
That all my hopes are fixed on Thee;
  On Thee, my God, on Thee!

3 Thy glorious eye pervadeth space;
Thou'rt present, Lord, in every place;
And wheresoe'er my lot may be,
Still shall my spirit cleave to Thee;
  To Thee, my God, to Thee!

4 Renouncing every worldly thing,
Safe 'neath the covert of Thy wing,
My sweetest thought henceforth shall be,
That all I want I find in Thee;
  In Thee, my God, in Thee!

J. F. Oberlin, 1820; *Caroline Wilson (tr.),* 1829.

SARDIS. (Hymn Chant.) [H. P. VI.]

35 Heb. xiii. 5. *"He hath said, I will never leave thee."* Tune, Hymn Chant Sardis.

1 BY Thee, Jesu, will I stay,
Evermore Thy servant stand;
From Thee, my feet shall never stray,
But I will go where points Thy hand.

2 Thou! life of all the life that's mine,
My soul's core-sap and vital power,
As to its branch from out the vine
Flows sap of life from hour to hour.

3 Stay near me through this heat and glow;
Stay near, too, when my day sinks down,
And long the evening shadows grow,
And the dark night comes stealing on.

4 Lay in blessing, then, Thy hand
On my weary, weakly head;
Saying, "Rest, child! to the land
Thy faith hath sought thou shalt be led."

5 Stay near me; in Thine arms enfold,
When most the chill of death I dread;
Chill, like the sharp and bitter cold,
Ere dawns in heaven the morning red.

6 When darkness shall mine eyes o'ertake,
Light Thou my spirit through the gloom,
That unto me the morn may break
As breaks to him the exile's home.

C. J. P. Spitta; John B. Walter (tr.), 1868.

THE ETERNITY OF GOD.

44 Tune St. Paul. 87, 887, 77, 77.
1 Tim. i. 17. *"The King, eternal, immortal, invisible."*

1 KING, Eternal and Immortal!
We, the children of an hour,
Bend in lowly adoration,
Rise in raptured admiration,
At the whisper of Thy power.
Myriad ages in Thy sight
Are but as the fleeting day;
Like a vision of the night,
Worlds may rise and pass away.

2 All Thy glories are eternal,
None shall ever pass away;
Truth and mercy all-victorious,
Righteousness and love all-glorious,
Shine with everlasting ray:
All-resplendent, ere the light
Bade primeval darkness flee;
All-transcendent, through the flight
Of eternities to be.

3 Thou art God from everlasting,
And to everlasting art!
Ere the dawn of shadowy ages,
Dimly guesssed by angel sages,
Ere the beat of seraph-heart;
Thou, Jehovah, art the same,
And Thy years shall have no end;
Changeless nature, changeless name,
Ever Father, God, and Friend.

Frances Ridley Havergal, 1872.

ST. PAUL. [H. P. 253.]

PERGAMOS. (Hymn Chant.) [H. P. No. IV.]

70 Ps. lxxxix. 1. "*I will sing of the mercies of the Lord for ever.*" Hymn Chant Pergamos. 66, 84. D. Or Arnon.

1 THE God of Abraham praise,
Who reigns enthroned above,
Ancient of everlasting days,
And God of love!
Jehovah, great I AM!
By earth and heaven confessed;
I bow and bless the sacred Name,
For ever blest!

2 The God of Abraham praise,
At whose supreme command
From earth I rise and seek the joys
At His right hand:
I all on earth forsake,
Its wisdom, fame, and power;
And Him my only portion make,
My shield and tower.

3 The God of Abraham praise,
Whose all-sufficient grace
Shall guide me all my happy days
In all His ways:
He calls a worm His friend,
He calls Himself my God!
And He shall save me to the end,
Through Jesu's blood.

4 He by Himself hath sworn,
I on His oath depend:
I shall, on eagles' wings upborne,
To heaven ascend:
I shall behold His face,
I shall His power adore,
And sing the wonders of His grace
For evermore!

Part II.

5 Though nature's strength decay,
And earth and hell withstand,
To Canaan's bounds I urge my way
At His command:
The watery deep I pass
With Jesus in my view,
And through the howling wilder- [ness
My way pursue.

6 The goodly land I see,
With peace and plenty blest;
A land of sacred liberty,
And endless rest:
There milk and honey flow;
And oil and wine abound;
And trees of life for ever grow,
With mercy crowned.

7 There dwells the Lord our King,
The Lord our Righteousness!
Triumphant o'er the world and sin,
The Prince of Peace!
On Zion's sacred height
His kingdom still maintains;
And glorious with His saints in [light
For ever reigns!

8 He keeps His own secure,
He guards them by His side,
Arrays in garments white and pure
His spotless bride;
With streams of sacred bliss,
With groves of living joys,
With all the fruits of paradise,
He still supplies.

Part III.

9 Before the Great Three-One
They all exulting stand,
And tell the wonders He hath done
Through all their land:
The listening spheres attend,
And swell the growing fame;
And sing, in songs which never end,
The wondrous Name.

10 The God who reigns on high
The great archangels sing;
And "Holy, holy, holy," cry,
"Almighty King!
Who was and is the same,
And evermore shall be;
Jehovah, Father, great I AM,
We worship Thee."

11 Before the Saviour's face
The ransomed nations bow,
O'erwhelmed at His almighty grace,
For ever new:
He shows His prints of love;
They kindle to a flame, [above,
And sound, through all the world
The slaughtered Lamb.

12 The whole triumphant host
Give thanks to God on high,
"Hail Father, Son, and Holy
They ever cry: [Ghost!"
Hail, Abraham's God, and mine!
(I join the heavenly lays;)
All might and majesty are Thine,
And endless praise!

Thomas Olivers, 1772.

79 Tune Crescens. 118, 118.

Eph. i. 3. "*Blessed be the God and Father of our Lord Jesus Christ.*"

CRESCENS. [H. P. 244.]

1 IN songs of sublime adoration and praise,
Ye pilgrims to Zion above,
Break forth, and extol the great Ancient of Days,
His rich and distinguishing love.

2 His love, from eternity fixed upon you,
Broke forth and discovered its flame,
When each with the cords of His kindness He drew,
And brought you to love His great name.

3 Oh, had He not pitied the state you were in,
Your bosoms His love had ne'er felt;
You all would have lived, would have died too, in sin,
And sunk with the load of your guilt.

4 What was there in you that could merit esteem,
Or give the Creator delight?
"'Twas even so, Father," Thy love did redeem,
"Because it seemed good in Thy sight."

5 'Twas all of Thy grace we were brought to obey,
While others were suffered to go;
The road which, by nature, we chose as our way,
Leads only to regions of woe.

6 Then give Him the glory all due to His name,
To Him all the glory belongs;
Be yours the high joy still to sound forth His fame,
And crown Him with jubilant songs!

George Keith, 1787. (a.)

JULIUS. [H. P. 266.]

89 Tune JULIUS. 87, 887.

Ps. cxlviii. 13. *"Let them praise the name of the Lord."*

1 ANGELS holy,
High and lowly,
Sing the praises of the Lord!
Earth and sky, all living nature,
Man, the stamp of thy Creator,
Praise ye, praise ye, God the Lord!

2 Sun and moon bright,
Night and noonlight,
Starry temples azure-floored;
Cloud and rain, and wild winds' madness,
Sons of God that shout for gladness,
Praise ye, praise ye, God the Lord!

3 Ocean hoary,
Tell His glory,
Cliffs, where tumbling seas have roared!
Pulse of waters, blithely beating,
Wave advancing, wave retreating,
Praise ye, praise ye, God the Lord!

4 Rock and high land,
Wood and island,
Crag, where eagle's pride hath soared;
Mighty mountains, purple-breasted,
Peaks cloud-cleaving, snowy-crested,
Praise ye, praise ye, God the Lord!

5 Rolling river,
Praise Him ever,
From the mountain's deep vein poured;
Silver fountain, clearly gushing,
Troubled torrent, madly rushing,
Praise ye, praise ye, God the Lord!

6 Praise Him ever,
Bounteous Giver;
Praise Him, Father, Friend, and Lord!
Each glad soul, its free course winging,
Each glad voice, its free song singing,
Praise the great and mighty Lord!

John Stuart Blackie, 1857.

EUODIAS. [H. P. 255.]

101 2 Kings iv. 26. *"It is well."*

Tune EUODIAS. 84, 84, 8884.

1 THROUGH the love of God our Saviour,
All will be well;
Free and changeless is His favour,
All, all is well!
Precious is the blood that healed us;
Perfect is the grace that sealed us;
Strong the hand stretched out to shield us;
All must be well!

2 Though we pass through tribulation,
All will be well;
Ours is such a full salvation,
All, all is well!
Happy, still in God confiding;
Fruitful, if in Christ abiding;
Holy, through the Spirit's guiding:
All must be well!

3 We expect a bright to-morrow,
All will be well;
Faith can sing through days of sorrow,
All, all is well!
On our Father's love relying,
Jesus every need supplying,
Both in living and in dying,
All must be well!

Mary Bowly, 1847.

PERSIS. [H. P. 187.]

(4) THE PROMISE BY THE FATHER, OF THE HOLY GHOST, THROUGH THE SON.

120 Ps. lxxxvii. 7. "*All my springs are in Thee.*" Tune PERSIS. 87, 87.

1 HEAR the Father's ancient promise!
Listen, thirsty, weary one!
"I will pour My Holy Spirit
On Thy chosen seed, O Son."
Promise to the Lord's Anointed,
Gift of God to Him for thee!
Now, by covenant appointed,
All thy springs in Him shall be.

2 Springs of life in desert places
Shall thy God unseal for thee;
Quickening and reviving graces,
Dew-like, healing, sweet and free.
Springs of sweet refreshment flowing,
When thy work is hard or long,
Courage, hope, and power bestowing,
Lightening labour with a song.

3 Springs of peace, when conflict heightens,
Thine uplifted eye shall see;
Peace that strengthens, calms, and brightens,
Peace, itself a victory.
Springs of comfort, strangely springing
Through the bitter wells of woe;
Founts of hidden gladness, bringing
Joy that earth can ne'er bestow.

4 Thine, O Christian, is this treasure,
To thy risen Head assured!
Thine in full and gracious measure,
Thine by covenant secured!
Now arise! His word possessing,
Claim the promise of the Lord;
Plead through Christ for showers of blessing,
Till the Spirit be outpoured!

Frances Ridley Havergal, 1870.

LAODICEA. (HYMN CHANT.) [H. P. No. VIII.]

ALL IN ALL.

141 Col. ii. 9. "*In Him dwelleth all the fulness.*" Tune, Hymn Chant LAODICEA. 66, 86, 88.

1 I NEED no other plea
With which to' approach my God,
Than His own mercy, boundless, free,
Through Christ on man bestowed,
A Father's love, a Father's care
Receives and answers every prayer.

2 I need no other priest
Than One High Priest above;
His intercession ne'er has ceased
Since first I knew His love:
Through that my faith shall never fail,
E'en when I pass through death's dark vale.

3 I need no human ear
In which to pour my prayer;
My great High Priest is ever near,
On Him I cast my care:
To Him, Him only, I confess,
Who can alone absolve and bless.

4 I need no works by me
Wrought with laborious care,
To form a meritorious plea
The bliss of heaven to share:
Christ's finished work, through boundless grace,
Has there secured my dwelling-place!

PART II.

5 I need no prayers to saints,
Beads, relics, martyrs' shrines;
Hardships 'neath which the spirit faints,
Yet still, sore burdened, pines:
Christ's service yields my soul delight,
Easy His yoke, His burden light.

6 I need no other book
To guide my steps to heaven,
Than that on which I daily look,
By God's own Spirit given;
For this, when He illumes our eyes,
Unto salvation makes us wise.

7 I need no holy oil
To' anoint my lips in death;
No priestly power my guilt to' assoil,
And ease my parting breath;
Long since, those words bade fear to cease,
"Thy faith hath saved thee; go in peace."

8 I need no priestly mass,
No purgatorial fires,
My soul to' anneal, my guilt to' efface,
When this brief life expires.
Christ died my endless life to win,
His blood has cleansed me from all sin.

9 I need no other dress,
I urge no other claim,
Than His imputed righteousness;
In Him complete I am.
Heaven's portals at that word fly wide,
No passport do I need beside!

Charlotte Elliott, 1863.

EPENETUS.
[H. P. 254.]
Tell it
Tell it out a-mong the hea-then that the Lord is King ! Tell it out ! Tell it out ! out ! . . . Tell it out a-mong the na-tions, bid them
Tell it out ! Tell it out ! that the Lord is King ! Tell it out ! . . . . Tell it out ! Tell it out ! Tell it out ! bid them
Fine. Tell it out with a-do-ra-tion that He shall in-crease ;
shout and sing ! Tell it out ! Tell it out ! Tell it out !
Tell it out ! . . . . . . that He shall in-crease ;
Tell it out with a-do-ra-tion that He shall in-crease ;
That the migh-ty King of Glo-ry is the
shout and sing ! Tell it out ! Tell . . . it out ! Tell it out ! . . . . . . that He shall in-crease ;
D.S.
King of Peace ; Tell it out with ju-bi-la-tion though the waves may roar, That He sit-teth on the wa-ter-floods, our King for e-ver-more. Tell it

KING.

165

Ps. xcvi. 10. (P.B.V.) "*Tell it out among the heathen that the Lord is King.*"

Tune Epenetus. 13 6, 13 6, 13 13, 13 15.

[1 Tell it out among the heathen that the Lord is King!
Tell it out! Tell it out!
Tell it out among the nations, bid them shout and sing!
Tell it out! Tell it out!]
Tell it out with adoration that He shall increase;
That the mighty King of Glory is the King of Peace;
Tell it out with jubilation, though the waves may roar,
That He sitteth on the water-floods, our King for evermore!
[Tell it out among the heathen that the Lord is King, etc.]

2 Tell it out among the heathen that the Saviour reigns!
Tell it out! Tell it out!
Tell it out among the nations, bid them burst their chains!
Tell it out! Tell it out!
Tell it out among the weeping ones that Jesus lives;
Tell it out among the weary ones what rest He gives:
Tell it out among the sinners that He came to save;
Tell it out among the dying that He triumphed o'er the grave.
[Tell it out among the heathen that the Lord is King, etc.]

3 Tell it out among the heathen Jesus reigns above!
Tell it out! Tell it out!
Tell it out among the nations that His reign is love!
Tell it out! Tell it out!
Tell it out among the highways and the lanes at home;
Tell it out across the mountains and the ocean foam!
Like the sound of many waters let our glad shout be,
Till it echo and re-echo from the islands of the sea!
[Tell it out among the heathen that the Lord is King, etc.]

Frances Ridley Havergal, 1872.

PHILEMON. [H. P. 223.]

197 Luke ii. 11. *"A Saviour, which is Christ the Lord."* Tune PHILEMON. 8 8 8, 7.

1 BRING to Christ your best oblation,
Grateful hearts and adoration,
Join in songs of gratulation,
Christian people, on this day.

2 Sin and hell may look astounded,
Death and devil be confounded;
We, in whom grace hath abounded,
Cast all griefs and fears away.

3 See the precious Gift God giveth!
His own Son, who ever liveth:
He who in His name believeth
Shall be savèd through His grace.

4 Oh how great was His compassion,
Thus to come in human fashion,
And to visit with salvation
Our poor sin-polluted race!

5 Jacob's Star, desired for ages,
Guides from far the Eastern sages;
The old dragon fumes and rages,
When he sees the woman's Seed.

6 Long we sat in bitter anguish,
In a dungeon left to languish;
Jesus comes our foe to vanquish,
Bursts our bonds, and we are freed!

7 Blessèd hour! when full confession
First we made of our transgression,
And obtained a free remission,
Jesus, through Thy precious blood!

8 Smile upon us, heavenly Stranger,
Cradled in a lowly manger,
Bring us from this world of danger,
To Thyself, our Lord and God!

Paul Gerhardt, 1659; *R. Massie (tr.)*, 1864.

239 1 Thess. iv. 14. *"We believe that Jesus died."*
Tune STEPHANAS. 8 3, 8 3, 8 8 8, 3 3.

STEPHANAS. [H. P. 168.]

1 THERE is a word I fain would speak:
Jesus died.
O eyes that weep, and hearts that break:
Jesus died.
No music from the quivering string
Could such sweet sounds of rapture bring,
Oh! may I always love to sing,
Jesus died, Jesus died.

2 Though Satan seeks my soul to have:
Jesus died.
Yes, Jesus died my soul to save,
Jesus died.
The holy Lord, the bleeding Lamb,
The Crucified, the Great I Am:
There's life in every lovely name.
Jesus died, Jesus died.

3 And now I need not fear to pray:
Jesus died.
He washes all my sins away:
Jesus died.
He washes all my sins away,
He is the Life, the Truth, the Way;
And now to all men I can say,
Jesus died, Jesus died.

4 'Twill soothe my heart with death in view—
Jesus died.
And bear me that cold river through:
Jesus died.
That word will heaven's bright gate unclose,
Release me from my mortal woes,
And bear me where Thy glory glows:
Jesus died, Jesus died.

Paxton Hood, 1862.

TRYPHOSA. [H. P. 209.]

286

Rev. v. 9. *"Thou hast redeemed us to God by Thy blood."* Tune Tryphosa. 8 8 6.

1 TO Him who for our sins was slain,
To Him, for all His dying pain,
Sing we Alleluia!

2 To Him, the Lamb, our Sacrifice,
Who gave His life our ransom-price,
Sing we Alleluia!

3 To Him who died, that we might die
To sin, and live with Him on high,
Sing we Alleluia!

4 To Him who rose, that we might rise,
And reign with Him beyond the skies,
Sing we Alleluia!

5 To Him who now for us doth plead,
And helpeth us in all our need,
Sing we Alleluia!

6 To Him who doth prepare on high
Our home in immortality,
Sing we Alleluia!

7 To Him be glory evermore!
Ye heavenly hosts, your Lord adore!
Sing we Alleluia!

8 To Father, Son, and Holy Ghost,
One God most great, our joy and boast,
Sing we Alleluia! Amen.

Arthur T. Russell, 1851.

ARCHIPPUS. [H. P. 34a.]

And crown Him Lord, And crown Him Lord, And crown Him Lord of all! A - men.

324

Rev. xix. 16. *"King of kings, and Lord of lords."*

Tune Archippus. C.M. Or Miles' Lane.

1 ALL hail the power of Jesu's name!
Let angels prostrate fall:
Bring forth the royal diadem,
To crown Him Lord of all.

2 Let high-born seraphs tune the lyre,
And as they tune it, fall
Before His face, who tunes their choir,
And crown Him Lord of all.

3 Crown Him, ye morning stars of light,
Who fixed this floating ball;
Now hail the Strength of Israel's might,
And crown Him Lord of all.

4 Crown Him, ye martyrs of your God,
Who from His altar call;
Extol the stem of Jesse's rod,
And crown Him Lord of all.

DAMARIS.

396

Ps. cxix. 89. *"For ever, O Lord, Thy word is settled in heaven."* Tune Damaris. 6 6, 6 6.

1 LORD, Thy Word abideth,
And our footsteps guideth;
Who its truth believeth
Light and joy receiveth.

2 When our foes are near us,
Then Thy Word doth cheer us,
Word of consolation,
Message of salvation.

3 When the storms are o'er us,
And dark clouds before us,
Then its light directeth,
And our way protecteth.

4 Who can tell the pleasure,
Who recount the treasure,
By Thy Word imparted
To the simple-hearted?

5 Word of mercy, giving
Succour to the living;
Word of life, supplying
Comfort to the dying!

6 Oh, that we discerning
Its most holy learning,
Lord, may love and fear Thee,
Evermore be near Thee!

The Rev. Sir Henry Williams Baker, 1861.

(1) CALLED.

415 Heb. iii. 1. "*Partakers of the heavenly calling.*"
Tune ESDRAELON. 15 15, 15 15.

1 HOLY brethren, called and chosen by the Sovereign
Voice of might, [light!
See your high and holy calling, out of darkness into
Called according to His purpose, and the riches of
His love, [Dove.
Won to listen by the leading of the gentle heavenly

2 Called to suffer with our Master, patiently to run
His race; [grace;
Called a blessing to inherit, called to holiness and
Called to fellowship with Jesus, by the Ever-faithful
One; [Son.
Called to His eternal glory, to the kingdom of His

3 Whom He calleth He preserveth, and His glory they
shall see; [not ye!
He is faithful that hath called you; He will do it, fear
Therefore, holy brethren, onward! make your
heavenly calling sure;
For the prize of this high calling, bravely to the end
endure.

Frances Ridley Havergal, 1872.

(2) JUSTIFIED.

416 Jer. xxxiii. 16. "*She shall be called, The Lord our Righteousness.*"
Tune ESDRAELON. 15 15, 15 15.

1 ISRAEL of God, awaken! Church of Christ, arise
and shine! [longer thine!
Mourning garb and soilèd raiment henceforth be no
For the Lord thy God hath clothed thee with a new
and glorious dress, [righteousness.
With the garments of salvation, with the robe of

2 By the grace of God the Father, thou art freely
justified,
Through the great redemption purchased by the
blood of Him who died;
By His life, for thee fulfilling God's command exceeding broad, [God.
By His glorious resurrection, seal and signet of thy

3 Therefore justified for ever by the faith which He
hath given, [path to heaven:
Peace, and joy, and hope abounding, smooth thy trial
Unto Him betrothed for ever, who thy life shall
crown and bless, [our Righteousness!"
By His name thou shalt be callèd, Christ, "The Lord

Frances Ridley Havergal, 1871.

424 Exod. xv. 4. "*Pharaoh's chariots and his host hath He cast into the sea.*" Tune SOSTHENES. 10 11, 11 11, 12 11.

1 SOUND the loud timbrel o'er Egypt's dark sea,
Jehovah hath triumphed, His people are free!
Sing, for the pride of the tyrant is broken:
His chariots and horsemen, all splendid and brave,
How vain was their boasting! The Lord hath but
spoken,
And chariots and horsemen are sunk in the wave.
Sound, etc.

2 Praise to the Conqueror, praise to the Lord;
His word was our arrow—His breath was our sword:
Who shall return to tell Egypt the story
Of those she sent forth in the hour of her pride?
The Lord hath looked out from His pillar of glory,
And all her brave thousands are dashed in the tide!
Sound, etc.

Thomas Moore, 1816.

See Hymns 728—734.

THYATIRA. (Hymn Chant.) [H. P. No. V.]

466

Jer. iii. 22. "*Behold, we come unto Thee.*"

Tune, Hymn Chant Thyatira. Or Bethabara.

1 JUST as I am—without one plea,
But that Thy blood was shed for me,
And that Thou bidd'st me come to Thee,
O Lamb of God, I come.

2 Just as I am—and waiting not
To rid my soul of one dark blot,
To Thee, whose blood can cleanse each spot,
O Lamb of God, I come.

3 Just as I am—though tossed about
With many a conflict, many a doubt,
Fightings within, and fears without,
O Lamb of God, I come.

4 Just as I am—poor, wretched, blind,
Sight, riches, healing of the mind,
Yea, all I need, in Thee to find,
O Lamb of God, I come.

5 Just as I am—Thou wilt receive,
Wilt welcome, pardon, cleanse, relieve;
Because Thy promise I believe,
O Lamb of God, I come.

6 Just as I am—(Thy love unknown
Has broken every barrier down)
Now, to be Thine, yea, Thine alone,
O Lamb of God, I come.

7 Just as I am—of that free love
The breadth, length, depth, and height to prove,
Here for a season, then above,
O Lamb of God, I come!

Charlotte Elliott, 1841.

LOIS. [H. P. 339.]

493

Ps. lvii. 7. "*My heart is fixed, O God.*"

Tune Lois. 83, 83, 888, 33.

1 MY heart is fixed, eternal God,
Fixed on Thee;
And my immortal choice is made,
Christ for me;
He is my Prophet, Priest, and King,
Who did for me salvation bring,
And while I've breath I mean to sing
Christ for me—Christ for me.

2 In Him I see the Godhead shine,
Christ for me,
He is the Majesty Divine,
Christ for me;
The Father's well-belovèd Son,
Co-partner of His royal throne,
Who did for human guilt atone,
Christ for me—Christ for me.

3 To-day as yesterday the same,
Christ for me;
How precious is His balmy name,
Christ for me;
Christ as mere man may answer you,
Who error's winding path pursue;
But I with part can never do;
Christ for me—Christ for me.

4 Let others boast of heaps of gold,
Christ for me;
His riches never can be told,
Christ for me;
Your gold will waste and wear away,
Your honours perish in a day;
My portion never can decay,
Christ for me—Christ for me.

5 In pining sickness, or in health,
Christ for me;
In deepest poverty or wealth,
Christ for me;
And in that all-important day
When I the summons must obey,
And pass from this dark world away,
Christ for me—Christ for me

Richard Jukes, 1862.

TERTIUS. [H. P. 256.]

525 Matt. vi. 13. "*Thine is . . . the power.*"
Tune TERTIUS. 11 11, 11 11, 11 11, 5.

That Thine is the Power, the Power, the Power, the Power !
That Thine, Thine, Thine is the Power, the Power, the Power !

1 OUR Father, our Father! who dwellest in light,
We lean on Thy love, and we rest on Thy might;
In weakness and weariness joy shall abound,
For strength everlasting in Thee shall be found;
Our Refuge, our Helper, in conflict and woe,
Our mighty Defender, how blessèd to know
That Thine is the power!

2 Our Father! Thy promise we earnestly claim,
The sanctified heart that shall hallow Thy name.
In ourselves, in our dear ones, throughout the wide world,
Be Thy name as a banner of glory unfurled:
Let it triumph o'er evil and darkness and guilt;
We know Thou canst do it, we know that Thou wilt,
For Thine is the power!

3 Our Father, we long for the glorious day
When all shall adore Thee and all shall obey!
Oh hasten Thy kingdom, oh show forth Thy might,
And wave o'er the nations Thy sceptre of right:
Oh make up Thy jewels, the crown of Thy love,
And reign in all hearts as Thou reignest above,
For Thine is the power!

4 Our Father, we pray that Thy will may be done;
For full acquiescence is heaven begun.
Both in us and by us Thy purpose be wrought,
In word and in action, in spirit and thought.
And Thou canst enable us thus to fulfil,
With holy rejoicing, Thy glorious will,
For Thine is the power!

5 Our Father, Thy children rejoice in Thy reign,
Rejoice in Thy highness, and praise Thee again!
Yea, Thine is the kingdom, and Thine is the might,
And Thine is the glory, transcendently bright.
For ever and ever that glory shall shine,
For ever and ever that kingdom be Thine,
For Thine is the power!

Frances Ridley Havergal, 1872.

536 Phil. iii. 13. "*Reaching forth unto those things which are before.*"
Tune ST. SILAS. 5 5 10. D.

ST. SILAS. [H. P. 98.]

1 UPWARD and onward,
Heavenward and sunward,
Rises the lark, as he joyously sings;
With music thrilling,
All the air filling,
Bearing a message of praise on his wings.

2 Like this sweet singer,
Let us not linger,
Clinging and cleaving to earth's weary sod;
But upward springing,
Our tribute bringing,
Strive to draw nearer and nearer to God.

3 Upward and onward,
Heavenward and sunward,
Soars the strong eagle, his flight speeding on;
With heart that quails not,
With eye that fails not,
Steadily fixing his gaze on the sun.

4 So our hearts raising,
Singing and praising,
Looking to Jesus, the Sun of the soul;
Our strength renewing,
Our way pursuing,
Let us press on till we reach the bright goal!

Richard Massie, 1864.

644 1 Tim. vi. 12. "*Fight the good fight of faith.*"

Tune St. Silas. 10 10, 11 11.

1 BREAST the wave, Christian,
when it is strongest;
Watch for day, Christian, when
the night's longest;
Onward, and onward still, be thine
endeavour;
The rest that remaineth will be for
ever.

2 Fight the fight, Christian—Jesus is
o'er thee;
Run the race, Christian—heaven is
before thee:
He who hath promisèd faltereth
never;
The love of eternity flows on for
ever.

3 Lift the eye, Christian, just as it closeth;
Raise the heart, Christian, ere it reposeth;
Thee from the love of Christ nothing shall sever:
Mount when thy work is done—praise Him for ever.

Joseph Stammers, 1830.

547 Ps. lxi. 1. "*Hear my cry.*"

Tune Claudia. 6 5, 6 5.

1 JESU, meek and gentle,
Son of God most high,
Pitying, loving Saviour,
Hear Thy children's cry.

2 Pardon our offences,
Loose our captive chains,
Break down every idol
Which our soul detains.

3 Give us holy freedom,
Fill our hearts with love;
Draw us, Holy Jesus,
To the realms above.

4 Lead us on our journey,
Be Thyself the way
Through terrestrial darkness
To celestial day.

5 Jesu, meek and gentle,
Son of God most high,
Pitying, loving Saviour,
Hear Thy children's cry!

George Rundle Prynne, 1856.

(17) TRUST.

567 2 Sam. xxiii. 5. "*Ordered in all things.*"
Tune, Hymn Chant St. Ethelburga.
86, 86, 86. Or Silvanus.

1 FATHER, I know that all my life
Is portioned out for me,
And the changes that will surely come
I do not fear to see;
But I ask Thee for a present mind,
Intent on pleasing Thee.

2 I ask Thee for a thoughtful love,
Through constant watching wise,
To meet the glad with joyful smiles,
And wipe the weeping eyes;
And a heart at leisure from itself,
To soothe and sympathise.

3 I would not have the restless will
That hurries to and fro;
Seeking for some great thing to do,
Or secret thing to know:
I would be treated as a child,
And guided where I go.

4 Wherever in the world I am,
In whatsoe'er estate,
I have a fellowship with hearts
To keep and cultivate,
And a work of lowly love to do,
For the Lord on whom I wait.

5 So I ask Thee for the daily strength
To none that ask denied,
And a mind to blend with outward life
While keeping at Thy side;
Content to fill a little space,
If Thou be glorified.

6 And if some things I do not ask
In my cup of blessing be,
I would have my spirit filled the more
With grateful love to Thee;
More careful, not to serve Thee much,
But to please Thee perfectly.

SILVANUS. [H. P. 176.]

7 There are briers besetting every path,
That call for patient care;
There is a cross in every lot,
And an earnest need for prayer;
But a lowly heart that leans on Thee
Is happy anywhere.

8 In a service which Thy will appoints
There are no bonds for me;
For my inmost heart is taught the truth
That makes Thy children free;
And a life of self-renouncing love
Is a life of liberty! *Anna L. Waring*, 1850.

HERMAS.* [H. P. 105.]

569 Ps. lv. 23. "*I will trust in Thee.*"
Tune Fides. 65, 65. D. Or Hermas.

1 JESUS, I will trust Thee, trust Thee with my soul;
Guilty, lost, and helpless, Thou canst make me whole.
There is none in heaven or on earth like Thee:
Thou hast died for sinners—therefore, Lord, for me.

2 Jesus, I may trust Thee, name of matchless worth
Spoken by the angel at Thy wondrous birth;
Written, and for ever, on Thy cross of shame,
Sinners read and worship, trusting in that name.

3 Jesus, I must trust Thee, pondering Thy ways,
Full of love and mercy all Thine earthly days:
Sinners gathered round Thee, lepers sought Thy face—
None too vile or loathsome for a Saviour's grace.

4 Jesus, I can trust Thee, trust Thy written word,
Though Thy voice of pity I have never heard.
When Thy Spirit teacheth, to my taste how sweet—
Only may I hearken, sitting at Thy feet.

5 Jesus, I do trust Thee, trust without a doubt:
"Whosoever cometh, Thou wilt not cast out,"
Faithful is Thy promise, precious is Thy blood—
These my soul's salvation, Thou my Saviour God!

Mary Jane Walker, 1864.

See Hymns 1076—1078.

* To this tune its composer, Frances Ridley Havergal, sang the first verse of this hymn ten minutes only before her death, Tuesday morning, June 3, 1879.

CARPUS. [H. P. 219.]

572

Rom. xv. 13. "*Abound in hope.*" Tune CARPUS. 888, 4.

1 HOPE, Christian soul; in every stage
Of this thine earthly pilgrimage
Let heavenly joy thy thoughts engage:
Abound in hope.

2 Hope! though thy lot be want and woe,
Though hate's rude storms against thee blow,
Thy Saviour's lot was such below:
Abound in hope.

3 Hope! for to all who meekly bear
His cross, He gives His crown to wear;
Abasement here is glory there:
Abound in hope.

4 Hope! though thy dear ones round thee die,
Behold with faith's illumined eye
Their blissful home beyond the sky:
Abound in hope.

5 Hope! for upon that happy shore
Sorrow and sighing will be o'er,
And saints shall meet to part no more:
Abound in hope.

6 Hope through the watches of the night;
Hope till the morrow bring the light;
Hope till thy faith be lost in sight:
Abound in hope.

Benjamin H. Kennedy, D.D., 1867.

GAIUS. [H. P. 319.]

614

Ps. cxlix. 1. "*Praise ye the Lord.*"
Tune GAIUS. 11 10, 11 10.

1 PRAISE ye Jehovah! praise the Lord most holy,
Who cheers the contrite, girds with strength the weak;
Praise Him who will, with glory, crown the lowly,
And, with salvation, beautify the meek.

2 Praise ye the Lord, for all His lovingkindness,
And all the tender mercies He hath shown;
Praise Him who pardons all our sin and blindness,
And calls us sons, and takes us for His own.

3 Praise ye Jehovah! Source of all our blessing:
Before His gifts earth's richest boons are dim;
Resting in Him, His peace and joy possessing,
All things are ours, for we have all in Him.

4 Praise ye the Father! God the Lord who gave us,
With full and perfect love, His only Son;
Praise ye the Son who died Himself to save us!
Praise ye the Spirit! praise the Three in One!

Lady M. C. Campbell, 1838.

635 Phil. iii. 14. "*I press toward the mark.*"

Tune OLYMPAS. 76, 76, 77, 76.

1 RISE, my soul, and stretch thy wings,
Thy better portion trace;
Rise from transitory things,
Towards heaven thy native place!
Sun, and moon, and stars decay,
Time shall soon this earth remove:
Rise, my soul, and haste away
To seats prepared above!

2 Rivers to the ocean run,
Nor stay in all their course;
Fire ascending seeks the sun:
Both speed them to their source:
So my soul, derived from God,
Pants to view His glorious face,
Upward tends to His abode,
To rest in His embrace.

3 Cease, ye pilgrims, cease to mourn,
Press onward to the prize;
Soon your Saviour will return
Triumphant in the skies!
Yet a season, and you know
Happy entrance will be given,
All your sorrows left below,
And earth exchanged for heaven!

Robert Seagrave, 1742.

OLYMPAS. [H. P. 281.]

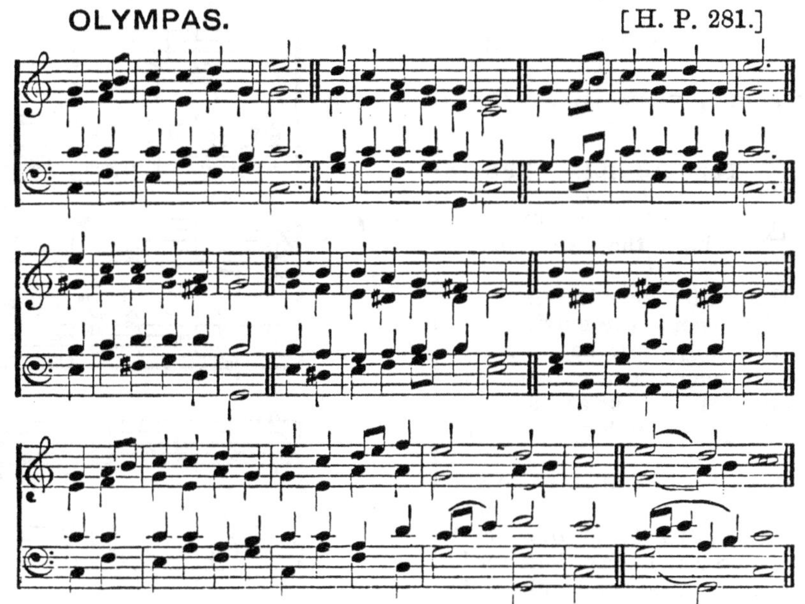

(26) COURAGE.

642 Ps. lxxi. 16. "*I will go in the strength of the Lord God.*"

Tune AQUILA. 9998, 8888.

1 I WILL go in the strength of the Lord,
In the path He hath marked for my feet;
I will follow the light of His word,
Nor shrink from the dangers I meet.
His presence my steps shall attend;
His fulness my wants shall supply;
On Him, till my journey shall end,
My hope shall securely rely.

2 I will go in the strength of the Lord
To the work He appoints me to do;
In the joy which His smile shall afford,
My soul shall her vigour renew.
His wisdom will guard me from harm,
His power my sufficiency prove:
I trust His omnipotent arm;
I rest in His covenant love.

3 I will go in the strength of the Lord
To each conflict which faith may require;
And His grace, as my shield and reward,
My courage and zeal shall inspire.
If He give the word of command
To meet and encounter the foe,
With sling and with stone in my hand,
In the strength of the Lord I will go!

Church Missionary Gleaner, January, 1861.

AQUILA. [H. P. 232.]

Glory: Future.

1094 Rev. iv. 3. *"There was a rainbow round about the throne."*

Tune AQUILA. 8 9 8 8, 8 8 8 8.

1 AROUND that magnificent throne,
Where the Lamb all His glory displays,
United for ever in one,
His people are singing His praise.
How holy, how happy are they!
No tongue can express their delight:
My soul, now unwilling to stay,
Prepares for her heavenly flight.

2 But why do I wish to be gone?
Do I want from the danger to flee?
And shall I do nothing for One
Who was such a Suff'rer for me?
Ah, Lord, let me think of the day
When Thou wast "rejected of men,"
And put the base wish far away;
And never be fearful again.

Thomas Kelly, 1809.

See Hymns 1011—1025.

695 Phil. i. 21. *"To me to live is Christ."*
Tune ONESIMUS. 7 4, 7 4. D.

1 PRECIOUS Saviour, may I live
Only for Thee!
Spend the powers Thou dost give
Only for Thee!
Be my spirit's deep desire
Only for Thee!
May my intellect aspire
Only for Thee!

2 In my joys may I rejoice
Only for Thee!
In my choices make my choice
Only for Thee!
Meekly may I suffer grief
Only for Thee!
Gratefully accept relief
Only for Thee!

3 Be my smiles and be my tears
Only for Thee!
Be my young and riper years
Only for Thee!
Be my peace and be my strife
Only for Thee!
Be my love and be my life
Only for Thee!

4 Be my singing and my sighing
Only for Thee!
Be my sickness and my dying
Only for Thee!
Be my rising, be my glory
Only for Thee!
Be my whole eternity
Only for Thee!

Eliza Ann Walker, 1864.

ARISTARCHUS. [H. P. 224.]

724 Isa. xlv. 17. "*Saved in the Lord with an everlasting salvation.*" Tune ARISTARCHUS. 88, 88.

1 A DEBTOR to mercy alone,
Of covenant mercy I sing;
Nor fear, with Thy righteousness on,
My person and offering to bring:
The terrors of law, and of God,
With me can have nothing to do:
My Saviour's obedience and blood
Hide all my transgressions from view.

2 The work which His goodness began,
The arm of His strength will complete;
His promise is Yea and Amen,
And never was forfeited yet:
Things future nor things that are now,
Not all things below nor above,
Can make Him His purpose forego,
Or sever my soul from His love.

3 My name from the palms of His hands
Eternity will not erase;
Impressed on His heart it remains
In marks of indelible grace:
Yes, I to the end shall endure,
As sure as the earnest is given;
More happy, but not more secure,
The glorified spirits in heaven!

Augustus M. Toplady, 1771.

TRYPHENA. [H. P. 217.]

725 Eph. i. 6. "*Accepted in the Beloved.*"
Col. i. 28. "*Perfect in Christ Jesus.*"
Col. ii. 10. "*Complete in Him.*"
Tune TRYPHENA. 888.

1 ACCEPTED, Perfect, and Complete,
For God's inheritance made meet!
How true, how glorious, and how sweet!

2 In the Belovèd—by the King
Accepted, though not anything
But forfeit lives had we to bring.

3 And Perfect in Christ Jesus made,
On Him our great transgressions laid,
We in His righteousness arrayed.

4 Complete in Him, our glorious Head,
With Jesus raisèd from the dead,
And by His mighty Spirit led!

5 O blessèd Lord, is this for me?
Then let my whole life henceforth be
One Alleluia-song to Thee!

Frances Ridley Havergal, 1870.

TROPHIMUS. [H. P. 123.]

726 1 Pet. i. 5. "*Kept by the power of God.*"
Tune TROPHIMUS. 669.

1 SPARED a little longer,
May our souls grow stronger,
To maintain the arduous fight of faith.

2 Many foes surround us,
Hoping to confound us,
But the Lord Himself is our defence.

3 We have hearts deceitful,
And of truth forgetful,
Yet our gracious Lord His people spares.

4 Pilgrims here, and strangers,
Who can tell our dangers?
But our Lord will save us from them all.

5 He has dearly bought us,
Hitherto has brought us,
And will lead us to Himself at last.

6 By His eye directed,
By His arm protected,
We shall gain the presence of our God!

Thomas Kelly, 1804.

898

Ps. cxli. 2. "*The lifting up of my hands as the evening sacrifice.*"

Tune Amplias. 64, 66.

AMPLIAS. [H. P. 103.]

1 THE sun is sinking fast,
The daylight dies;
Let love awake, and pay
Her evening sacrifice.

2 As Christ upon the cross
His head inclined,
And to His Father's hands
His parting soul resigned,—

3 So now herself my soul
Would wholly give
Into His sacred charge,
In whom all spirits live.

4 So now beneath His eye
Would calmly rest,
Without a wish or thought
Abiding in the breast;

5 Save that His will be done,
Whate'er betide;
Dead to herself, and dead
In Him to all beside.

6 Thus would I live; yet now
Not I, but He,
In all His power and love
Henceforth alive in me.

7 One sacred Trinity,
One Lord Divine;
May I be ever His,
And He for ever mine!

Latin Hymn, Eighteenth Century; tr. 1858.

964

Luke xxii. 32. "*I have prayed for thee.*"

Tune Bohemia. Or St. Barnabas.
65, 65. D.

1 IN the hour of trial, Jesu, pray for me;
Lest by base denial I depart from Thee:
When Thou seest me waver, With a look recall,
Nor for fear or favour Suffer me to fall.

2 With its witching pleasures Would this vain world charm,
Or its sordid treasures Spread to work me harm?
Bring to my remembrance Sad Gethsemane,
Or, in darker semblance, Cross-crowned Calvary.

3 If with sore affliction Thou in love chastise,
Pour Thy benediction On the sacrifice:
Then, upon Thine altar Freely offered up,
Though the flesh may falter, Faith shall drink the cup.

4 When in dust and ashes To the grave I sink,
While heaven's glory flashes O'er the shelving brink,
On Thy truth relying Through that mortal strife,
Lord, receive me dying To eternal life.

James Montgomery, 1825.

ST. BARNABAS. [H. P. 106.]

URBANE. [H. P. 171a.]

966

John xii. 26. "*Let him follow Me.*"

Tune Urbane. 85, 83. Or Prague.

1 ART thou weary, art thou languid,
Art thou sore distressed?
"Come to Me," saith One, "and coming,
Be at rest."

2 Hath He marks to lead me to Him,
If He be my Guide?
"In His feet and hands are wound prints,
And His side."

3 Is there diadem, as Monarch,
That His brow adorns?
"Yea, a crown, in very surety,
But of thorns."

See Hymn 1079.

4 If I find Him, if I follow,
What His guerdon here?
"Many a sorrow, many a labour,
Many a tear."

5 If I still hold closely to Him,
What hath He at last?
"Sorrow vanquished, labour ended,
Jordan passed."

6 If I ask Him to receive me,
Will He say me nay?
"Not till earth and not till heaven
Pass away."

7 Finding, following, keeping, struggling,
Is He sure to bless?
"Saints, apostles, prophets, martyrs,
Answer, Yes."

Greek Hymn, Eighth Century; J. M. Neale, D.D. (tr.), 1862.

URBANE. (PART II.) [H. P. 292.]

1048 Isa. xii. 2. *"I will trust, and not be afraid."* Tune, URBANE, Part II. 7 5, 8 3.

1 I AM trusting Thee, Lord Jesus,
Trusting only Thee!
Trusting Thee for full salvation,
Great and free!

2 I am trusting Thee for pardon,
At Thy feet I bow;
For Thy grace and tender mercy
Trusting now.

3 I am trusting Thee for cleansing.
In the crimson flood;
Trusting Thee to make me holy,
By Thy blood.

4 I am trusting Thee to guide me;
Thou alone shalt lead,
Every day and hour supplying
All my need.

5 I am trusting Thee for power;
Thine can never fail:
Words which Thou Thyself shalt give me
Must prevail.

6 I am trusting Thee, Lord Jesus!
Never let me fall!
I am trusting Thee for ever,
And for all!

Frances Ridley Havergal, 1874.

EPAPHRODITUS. [H. P. 318.]

982 1 Thess. iv. 13. *"Ye sorrow not even as others which have no hope."*

Tune EPAPHRODITUS. 13 11, 12 12.

1 THOU art gone to the grave! but we will not deplore thee,
Though sorrows and darkness encompass the tomb:
Thy Saviour has passed through its portal before thee,
And the lamp of His love is thy guide through the gloom!

2 Thou art gone to the grave! we no longer behold thee,
Nor tread the rough paths of the world by thy side;
But the wide arms of mercy are spread to enfold thee,
And sinners may die, for the Sinless has died!

3 Thou art gone to the grave! and, its mansion forsaking,
Perchance thy weak spirit in fear lingered long;

But the mild rays of paradise beamed on thy waking,
And the sound which thou heard'st was the seraphim's song!

4 Thou art gone to the grave! but we will not deplore thee,
Whose God was thy Ransom, thy Guardian, and Guide;
He gave thee, He took thee, and He will restore thee,
And death has no sting, for the Saviour has died!

Bishop Heber, 1827.

994

2 Tim. i. 18. "*The Lord grant unto him that he may find mercy of the Lord in that day.*"

Tune Dies Iræ. 888.

DIES IRÆ. Part I. [H. P. 218.]

1 Day of wrath, O day of mourning!
See the Crucified returning,
Heaven and earth in ashes burning!
Oh, what fear man's bosom rendeth,
When from heaven the Judge descendeth
On whose sentence all dependeth!

2 Wondrous sound the trumpet flingeth;
Through earth's sepulchres it ringeth;
All before the throne it bringeth.
Death is struck, and nature quaking:
All creation is awaking,
To its Judge an answer making.

3 Lo, the book exactly worded,
Wherein all hath been recorded:
Thence shall judgment be awarded.
When the Judge His seat attaineth,
And each hidden deed arraigneth,
Nothing unavenged remaineth.

4 What shall I, frail man, be pleading;
Who for me be interceding,
When the just are mercy needing?
King of Majesty tremendous,
Who dost free salvation send us,
Fount of pity, then befriend us.

Part II.

Part II.

5 Think, kind Jesu, my salvation
Caused Thy wondrous incarnation:
Leave me not to desolation:
Faint and weary, Thou hast sought me,
On the cross of suffering bought me;
Shall such grace be vainly brought me?

6 Righteous Judge, for sin's pollution
Grant Thy gift of absolution,
Ere that day of retribution.
Guilty, now I pour my moaning,
All my shame with anguish owning:
Spare, O God, Thy suppliant groaning.

7 Thou the sinful woman savedst;
Thou the dying thief forgavest;
And to me a hope vouchsafest.
Worthless are my prayers and sighing;
Yet, good Lord, in grace complying,
Rescue me from fires undying.

8 With Thy favoured sheep oh place me;
Nor among the goats abase me;
But to Thy right hand upraise me.
Low I kneel with heart submission:
See, like ashes, my contrition:
Save, oh! save me from perdition.

Part III.

Part III.

9 Ah, that day of tears and mourning!
From the dust of earth returning,
Man for judgment must prepare him;
Spare, O God, in mercy spare him,
Lord, all pitying, Jesu blest,
Grant us Thine eternal rest.
Amen.

Thomas of Celano, 1230; *William J. Irons, D.D.* (*tr.*), 1848.

PATROBAS. [H. P. 354.]

Gospel Echoes.

1026 2 Cor. x. 5. "*Casting down imaginations.*" Tune PATROBAS. 77, 77. D. Or SEIR.

1 CAST thyself on Jesus *now*,
Self relinquish wholly;
Low before His footstool bow,
Trust in Jesus solely:
Look away from all to Him,
Nothing here can aid thee:
Jesus is the Good Supreme—
Go! He'll not upbraid thee.

2 Cast thyself on Jesus *now*,
Self relinquish wholly;
Peace and joy thou then shalt know,
Saved in Jesus fully:
He is waiting now to bless,
Waiting now to save thee;
To His loving bosom press,
Gladly He'll receive thee.

Albert Midlane, 1865.

LUCIUS. [H. P. 293.]

1041 Matt. xi. 28. "*Come unto Me.*"
Tune LUCIUS. 86, 889, 8869.

1 WILL ye not come to Him for *life*?
Why will ye die, oh why?
He gave His life for you, for you!
The gift is free, the word is true!
Will ye not come? oh, why will ye die?
Will ye not come? Will ye not come?
Will ye not come to Him, to Him?
Oh, come, come, come to Him!
Come unto Jesus, oh, come for *life*.

2 Will ye not come to Him for *peace*,
Peace through His cross alone?
He shed His precious blood for you;
The gift is free, the word is true!
He is our Peace, oh is He your own?
Will ye not come, etc. . . . for *peace*?

3 Will ye not come to Him for *rest*?
All that are weary, come:
The rest He gives is deep and true,
'Tis offered now, 'tis offered you;
Rest in His love, and rest in His home.
Will ye not come, etc. . . . for *rest*?

PART II.

4 Will ye not come to Him for *joy*?
Will ye not come for this?
He laid His joys aside for you,
To give you joy, so sweet, so true!
Sorrowing heart, oh drink of the bliss!
Will ye not come, etc. . . . for *joy*?

5 Will ye not come to Him for *love*,
Love that can fill the heart?
Exceeding great, exceeding free!
He loveth you, He loveth me!
Will you not come? why stand ye apart?
Will ye not come, etc. . . . for *love*?

6 Will ye not come to Him for ALL?
Will ye not "taste and see"?
He waits to give it all to you,
The gifts are free, the words are true!
Jesus hath said it, "Come unto Me."
Will ye not come, etc. . . . to HIM.

Frances Ridley Havergal, 1873.

PHEBE. [H. P. 282.]

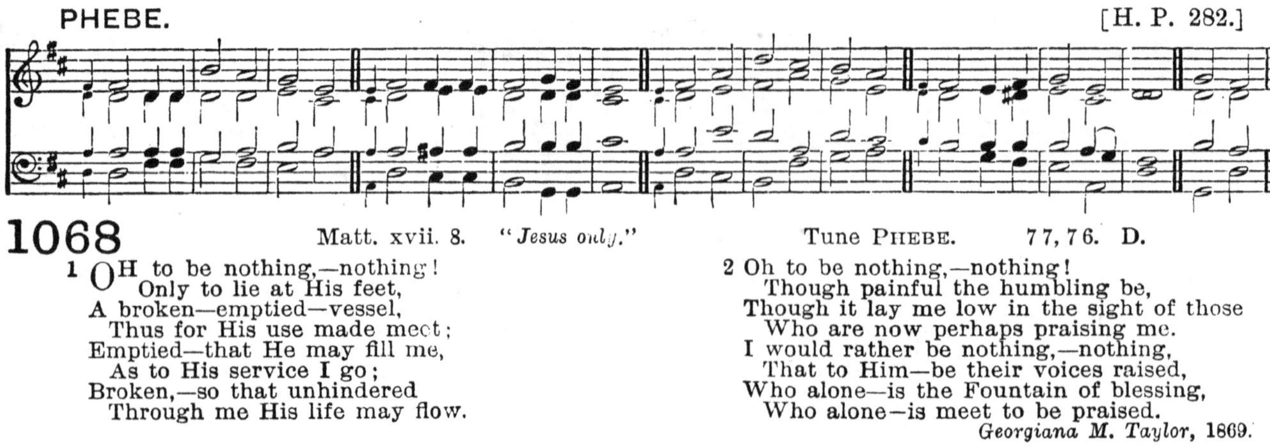

1068 Matt. xvii. 8. *"Jesus only."* Tune PHEBE. 77, 76. D.

1 OH to be nothing,—nothing!
Only to lie at His feet,
A broken—emptied—vessel,
Thus for His use made meet;
Emptied—that He may fill me,
As to His service I go;
Broken,—so that unhindered
Through me His life may flow.

2 Oh to be nothing,—nothing!
Though painful the humbling be,
Though it lay me low in the sight of those
Who are now perhaps praising me.
I would rather be nothing,—nothing,
That to Him—be their voices raised,
Who alone—is the Fountain of blessing,
Who alone—is meet to be praised.

Georgiana M. Taylor, 1869.

These next four hymn scores (numbered 54, 87, 116, and 131) were published in *Songs of Grace and Glory for the Young*. See page 984 of Volume V of the Havergal edition.

EUNICE. [H. P. 333.]

54 Heb. xiii. 5. *"He hath said, I will never leave thee, nor forsake thee."*
Tune EUNICE. 10 10, 10 10.

1 "WHO will take care of me?" darling, you say!
Lovingly, tenderly, watched as you are!
Listen! I give you the answer to-day,
ONE who is never forgetful or far!

2 He will take care of you! All through the day
Jesus is near you, to keep you from ill;
Walking or resting, at lessons or play,
Jesus is with you and watching you still.

3 He will take care of you! All through the night
Jesus, the Shepherd, His little one keeps;
Darkness to Him is the same as the light;
He never slumbers, and He never sleeps.

4 He will take care of you! All through the year
Crowning each day with His kindness and love,
Sending you blessings, and shielding from fear,
Leading you on to the bright home above.

5 He will take care of you! Yes, to the end!
Nothing can alter His love to His own.
Darling, be glad that you have such a Friend;
He will not leave you one moment alone!

Frances Ridley Havergal, 1873.

87 Acts ix. 6. *"Lord, what wilt Thou have me to do?"*

Tune Apphia. 9 8, 9 8. D.

1 OH what can I do for Friend so true,
Oh what can I do for Jesus?
I'll give Him all, and myself give too,
Oh, that will I give to Jesus.

Chorus—Oh what can I do for Friend so true,
Oh what can I do for Jesus?
I'll give Him all, and myself give too,
Oh, that will I do for Jesus.

2 Through the long dark night I have slumbered sweet,
'Neath His loving smile so tender;
Never will I fear, for I know He's near,
Ever near, my great Defender.
Oh what can I do, etc.

3 The meadow and grove rejoice in love,
Resounding the praise of Jesus.
Shall we not join in that song Divine,
"Hosanna to Him—to Jesus!"
Oh what can I do, etc.

APPHIA. [H. P. 332.]

4 Far above we hear voices sweet and clear,
'Tis the angels' song ascending:
And with them we'll sing of our Saviour King,
Of His love, His love unending.
Oh what can I do, etc.

George S. Weeks, 1870.

FORTUNATUS. [H. P. 331.]

116 Isa. lviii. 13. *"Call the Sabbath a delight."*

Tune Fortunatus. 8888, 68, 88, 68.

1 I LOVE the blessèd Sabbath-day,
"The first and best of all the seven,"
I love to sing, to read, and pray,
To hear of God, and Christ, and heaven.
Happy day! happy day!
I love the holy Sabbath-day,
The day my God in love has given,
That I might find the path to heaven.
Happy day! happy day!
I love the holy Sabbath-day.

2 'Tis sweet from earthly toils to rest,
To worship at our Father's throne;
To welcome Christ, the heavenly Guest,
And thank Him for His mercy shown.
Happy day! etc.

3 'Tis sweet the Spirit's power to prove,
With lowly heart His grace to seek;
'Tis sweet to think of joys above,
And thus with God commence the week.
Happy day! etc.

J. Lees, "Sacred Songs," 1858.

131 Matt. xxv. 22. *"Behold I have gained two other talents."* Tune JUNIA. 5 6, 5 6.

1 GOD entrusts to all
  Talents few or many;
None so young or small
  That they have not any.

2 Though the great and wise
  Have a greater number,
Yet my one I prize,
  And it must not slumber.

3 God will surely ask,
  Ere I enter heaven,
Have I done the task
  Which to me was given?

4 Little drops of rain
  Bring the springing flowers;
And I may attain
  Much by little powers.

5 Every little mite,
  Every little measure,
Helps to spread the light,
  Helps to swell the treasure.

6 God entrusts to all
  Talents few or many;
None so young or small
  That they have not any.

James Edmeston, 1846.

This is a list of other hymn scores composed by F.R.H. and not found in *Songs of Grace and Glory*, and their locations in Volume V of the Havergal edition:

1. The score "Enon" was not found in S.G.G. but was published as Number 124 in *Havergal's Psalmody and Century of Chants*, given on page 246 of Volume V of the Havergal edition.

2. The score "Apollos" is given on pages 1466–1467.

3. The score "White Robes" is given on page 1458.

4. The score for "I'm a little pilgrim" is given on page 1472. We do not know with certainty who composed this music, very possibly F.R.H.

5. The un-named score for "The Angel's Song" is given on page 1460. This same score was used for "The Good Old Church of England," given on pages 1412–1413. See also pages 1208 and 1338, and Alberto Randegger's setting of the same words on pages 1079–1082 of Volume V of the Havergal edition.

Please see also on pages 2401–2403 the table list of all of the hymns in *Songs of Grace and Glory* that have words by Frances Ridley Havergal. This list has all the S.G.G. hymns with words by her, both those set to music composed by her and those set to music composed by others.

In the free space here, this is a quotation that gives a glimpse of how musical F.R.H. was. There are several other quotations by or about F.R.H. on music on pages xlvii–lxxii of Volume V of the Havergal edition. F.R.H. wrote this in a letter, in Switzerland, July 9, 1869:[1]

> M. and I both heard the curious *latent music* of the water when our ear was pressed on the pillow, "just like a piano," she said, and truly! It really was like a distant piano playing a monotonous yet sweet melody, always nearly but never quite the same key of G, and harmony merely tonic and dominant in turn, a move of the head occasionally producing the subdominant!

[1] *Swiss and Alpine Poems* by Frances Ridley Havergal, edited by her sister Jane Miriam Crane (London: James Nisbet & Co., 1881), original book pages 77–78, page 298 of Volume IV of the Havergal edition.

FORMS AND PRICES
OF
HAVERGAL'S PSALMODY & CHANTS.
Companion Volume to Songs of Grace & Glory.

		s.	D.
A.	Havergal's Psalmody and Century of Chants, bound in cloth, gilt lettered, with full Prefaces, Indices, and Photographic Portrait	5	0
B.	Ditto, ditto, without Chants	3	6
C.	Chants and Preface alone	1	6

CHEAPER EDITIONS.

D.	Havergal's Psalmody and Chants, without Prefaces and Portrait	1	6
E.	Ditto, Ditto, without Chants	1	0
F.	Chants alone, without Preface	0	9

London:

ROBERT COCKS & CO., NEW BURLINGTON STREET, W.

By Special Appointment

Music Publishers to Her Majesty the Queen, H.R.H. the Prince of Wales, and H.I.M. Napoleon III.,

AND THROUGH ALL MUSICSELLERS.

FORMS AND PRICES
OF
SONGS OF GRACE AND GLORY.

A.	Extra large paper, very superior binding	10	0
B.	Large type, leather gilt	5	0
C.	Large type, cloth gilt and lettered	4	0
D.	Large type, cloth limp	3	6
E.	Small type, leather gilt	2	6
F.	Small type, cloth gilt and lettered...	1	6
G.	Small type, cloth limp	1	0

For reduced terms on Editions A. to E., apply to Rev. C. B. Snepp, LL.M., Vicar of Perry Barr, near Birmingham.

"SONGS OF GRACE AND GLORY." A Hymnal, containing 1,025 Hymns for Private, Family, and Public Worship, Edited by the Rev. C. B. Snepp, LLM., Vicar of Perry Barr. With copious Indices of Authors and Dates, Subjects, Texts, and Tunes; also a Table of Hymns for the Sundays and Holy Days of the Ecclesiastical Year.

London:

WILLIAM HUNT & CO., HOLLES ST., CAVENDISH SQUARE.

This is an advertisement page (after page xx) in the original Robert Cocks edition of Havergal's Psalmody and Century of Chants. *Cocks' publication of H.P.C.C. had the music for the hymns in S.G.G., and William Hunt's publication of* Songs of Grace and Glory *had the words only, without music. Later the words and music were printed together in a "Musical Edition" of S.G.G. This 1880 Nisbet edition of* Songs of Grace and Glory *is the definitive version, published approximately six months after F.R.H. died (June 3, 1879) and approximately six months before Charles Busbridge Snepp died (June 23, 1880).*

Seulement pour Toi.

[Written for and sung by some Swiss peasants at a Sunday afternoon Bible reading, July 23rd, 1876.]

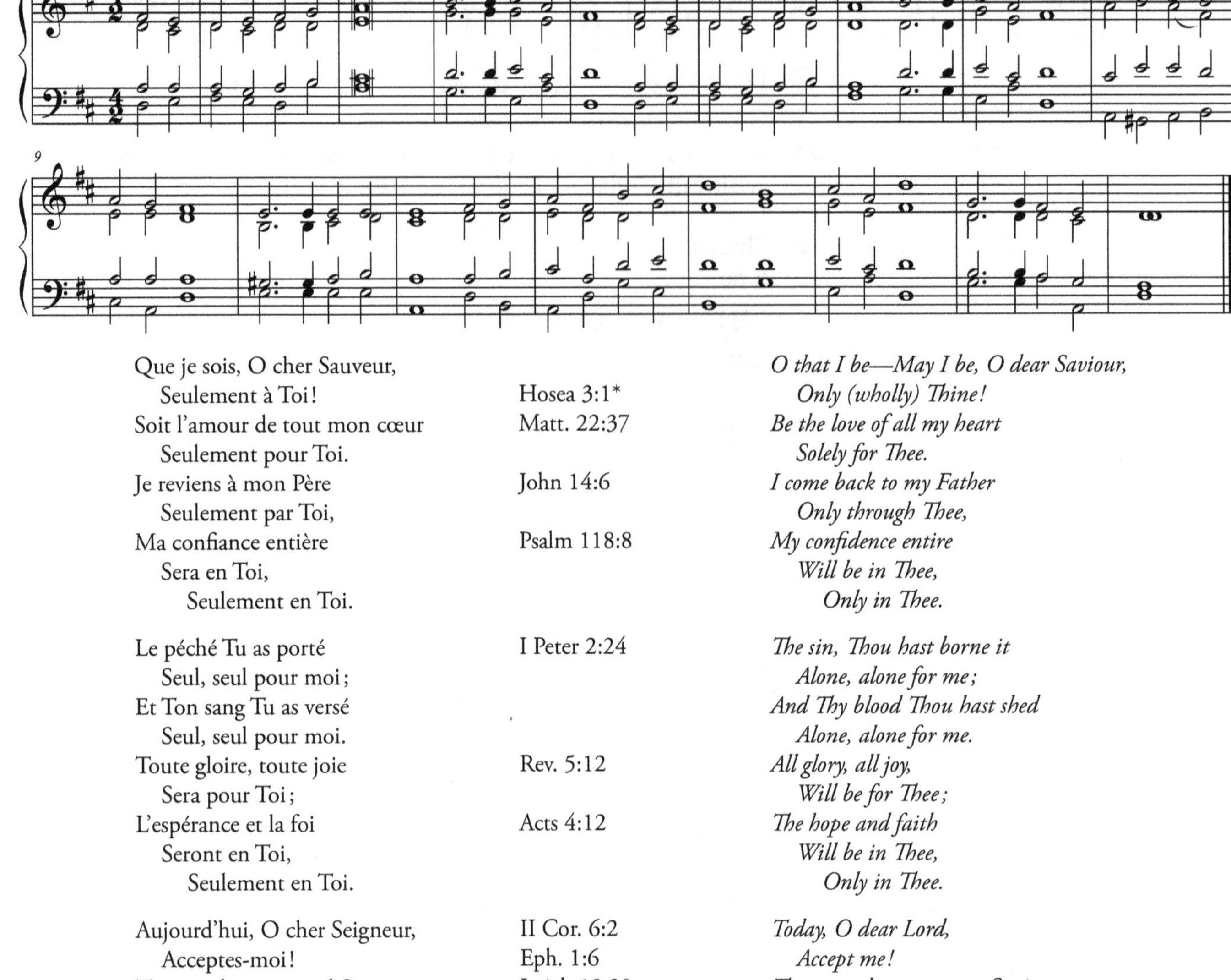

Que je sois, O cher Sauveur,		*O that I be—May I be, O dear Saviour,*
Seulement à Toi!	Hosea 3:1*	*Only (wholly) Thine!*
Soit l'amour de tout mon cœur	Matt. 22:37	*Be the love of all my heart*
Seulement pour Toi.		*Solely for Thee.*
Je reviens à mon Père	John 14:6	*I come back to my Father*
Seulement par Toi,		*Only through Thee,*
Ma confiance entière	Psalm 118:8	*My confidence entire*
Sera en Toi,		*Will be in Thee,*
Seulement en Toi.		*Only in Thee.*
Le péché Tu as porté	I Peter 2:24	*The sin, Thou hast borne it*
Seul, seul pour moi;		*Alone, alone for me;*
Et Ton sang Tu as versé		*And Thy blood Thou hast shed*
Seul, seul pour moi.		*Alone, alone for me.*
Toute gloire, toute joie	Rev. 5:12	*All glory, all joy,*
Sera pour Toi;		*Will be for Thee;*
L'espérance et la foi	Acts 4:12	*The hope and faith*
Seront en Toi,		*Will be in Thee,*
Seulement en Toi.		*Only in Thee.*
Aujourd'hui, O cher Seigneur,	II Cor. 6:2	*Today, O dear Lord,*
Acceptes-moi!	Eph. 1:6	*Accept me!*
Tu es seul mon grand Sauveur,	Isaiah 19:20	*Thou art alone my great Saviour,*
Tu es mon Roi.	Psalm 44:4	*Thou art my King.*
Tous mes moments, tous mes jours	II Cor. 5:15	*All my moments, all my days*
Seront pour Toi!		*Will be for Thee!*
Jésus, gardes-moi toujours	Isaiah 27:3	*Jesus, keep me always*
Seulement pour Toi,		*Only for Thee,*
Seulement pour Toi.		*Only for Thee.*
Que je chante et que je pleure	Psalm 21:13	*O that I sing and that I weep*
Seulement pour Toi!		*Only for Thee!*
Que je vive et que je meure	Romans 14:8	*Let me live and let me die*
Seulement pour Toi!		*Only for Thee!*
Jésus, que m'as tant aimé,	Gal. 2:20	*Jesus, how Thou hast loved me,*
Mourant pour moi,		*Dying for me,*
Toute mon éternité	I Thess. 4:17	*All my eternity*
Sera pour Toi,		*Will be for Thee,*
Seulement pour Toi.		*Only for Thee.*

July 23, 1876

*Note: In F.R.H.'s posthumously published *Under His Shadow,* these Scripture references were given on these lines.

[hymn in French by Frances Ridley Havergal, set to her tune "Onesimus," English translation by David Chalkley]

www.ingramcontent.com/pod-product-compliance
Lightning Source LLC
Chambersburg PA
CBHW062031090426
42740CB00016B/2880

9781937236564